Western Jurisprudence

TIM MURPHY

EDITOR

THOMSON ROUND HALL
2004

Published in 2004 by
Round Hall Ltd
43 Fitzwilliam Place
Dublin 2
Ireland

Typeset by
Gough Typesetting Services
Dublin

Printed by
ColourBooks, Dublin

ISBN 1-85800-378-4

A catalogue record for this book
is available from the British Library

CONTRIBUTORS

Garrett Barden was born in Dublin in 1939. Following undergraduate studies there he studied in Louvain, in Oxford and, after a spell of teaching in New York, in Western Australia where he undertook fieldwork among the Ngatatjara people in the Simpson Desert. Returning to Ireland in 1970, he taught first at the Milltown Institute in Dublin until 1972, and then at the Department of Philosophy at University College Cork until his retirement in 1999. He has held visiting professorships in France, Iceland, Slovakia and the United States. His books include *Towards Self-Meaning* (with P.J. McShane; Gill and Macmillan, Dublin, 1969); *After Principles* (University of Notre Dame Press, Notre Dame, 1990) and *Essays on a Philosophical Interpretation of Justice: The Virtue of Justice* (Mellen, Lampeter, 1999).

Paula D. Baron is Associate Professor of Law at the University of Western Australia where she teaches contract law and intellectual property law. She has published in the areas of legal education, intellectual property, contract law and gender and the law. Her work in psychoanalytic jurisprudence was originally sparked by an interest in the work of Jacques Lacan, and since 2001, she has studied psychoanalytic psychotherapy at the Churchill Clinic in Subiaco, Western Australia.

Patrick Hannon is Professor of Moral Theology at Maynooth. He holds doctorates in Divinity (Maynooth) and Law (Cambridge) and is a member of the Irish Bar. He is the author of *Church, State, Morality and Law* (Gill and Macmillan, Dublin, 1992/Christian Classics, Maryland, 1993). Some of the material in Patrick Hannon's chapter in this volume is adapted from *Church, State, Morality and Law* and from his "Morality and Law" in *Christian Ethics: An Introduction* (B. Hoose ed., Cassell, London, 1998].

Colin Harvey is Professor of Constitutional and Human Rights Law at the School of Law, University of Leeds. His books include *Seeking Asylum in the UK* (Butterworths, London, 2000), *Human Rights, Equality and Democratic Renewal in Northern Ireland* (as editor; Hart, Oxford, 2001); *Sanctuary in Ireland: Perspectives on Asylum Law and Policy* (as co-editor; Institute of Public Administration, Dublin, 2004); and, forthcoming in 2005, *Human Rights in the Community: Rights as Agents for Change* (as editor; Hart, Oxford).

Alan Haugh is a barrister who currently works in-house with the Irish Business and Employers' Confederation (IBEC) and advises principally on employment law matters. He has lectured at the Dublin Institute of Technology, the National College of Ireland, and at University College Cork, and he has also acted as examiner in jurisprudence on behalf of the Honourable Society of King's Inns, Dublin. He has published in a number of journals principally in the area of employment law.

Liam Herrick is Senior Legislation and Policy Review Officer with the Irish Human Rights Commission. He studied law at University College Cork and University College Dublin and he was formerly Research and Parliamentary Officer with the Irish Council of Civil Liberties and Legal Research Assistant with the Law Reform Commission of Ireland. He has also worked for the Irish Department of Foreign Affairs, both at its Permanent Mission to the Council of Europe and in the Human Rights Unit of the Department.

Shane Kilcommins is a graduate of the University of Limerick and the University of Wales, Aberystwyth. He lectured in Aberystwyth and at the Waterford Institute of Technology before coming to lecture at University College Cork in 2001. His books include *The Introduction of Community Service Orders* (Barry Rose Law Publishers, Chichester, 2002); *Alcohol, Society and Law* (as co-editor; Barry Rose Law Publishers, Chichester, 2003); and, as a co-author, *Crime, Punishment and the Search for Order in Ireland* (Institute of Public Administration, Dublin, 2004).

C.L. Lim taught for many years in the United Kingdom before leaving London University's Queen Mary and Westfield College for the United Nations Secretariat in Geneva. He subsequently joined the staff of the Attorney General of Singapore and he now teaches at the National University of Singapore.

J. Paul McCutcheon studied law at University College Dublin and is now Associate Professor of Law and Head of the School of Law at the University of Limerick. His research interests include criminal law, criminal procedure, legal systems, and sports law. He is the author of *The Larceny Act 1916* (Round Hall Press, Dublin, 1988); co-author of *The Irish Legal System* (with R. Byrne; 4th ed., Butterworths, Dublin, 2001) and *Criminal Liability* (with F. McAuley; Round Hall Sweet and Maxwell, Dublin, 2000); and co-editor of *The Confiscation of Criminal Assets: Law and Procedure*

(Round Hall, Dublin, 1999). He has published extensively in journals in Ireland, the United Kingdom, the Netherlands, France, Australia and North America, and he is currently co-editor of *The Irish Jurist*. In 1996 he was a Visiting Fellow at the Australian National University.

Emmanuel Melissaris is a Lecturer in Law at Keele University in the UK. He was previously a Lecturer in Law at the University of Manchester. His research interests lie in philosophy and sociology of law and, in particular, theories of legal discourse; linguistic pragmatics; law and time; and legal pluralism.

Siobhán Mullally is a Senior Lecturer in Law at University College Cork, where she has been lecturing since 1995. She is a graduate of UCC, the London School of Economics and the European University Institute, Florence. From 1990-1995, she was a lecturer in international law at the University of Hull in the UK. From 1992-1993, and again in 1995, she was a visiting lecturer at the Faculty of Law, University of Peshawar, Pakistan. In 1999, she was a visiting research fellow at the Harvard Human Rights Program, Harvard Law School.

Tim Murphy was educated at Cork, Warwick and Maynooth. He has lectured in jurisprudence and constitutional law at University College Cork since 1992. He has also lectured in the UK, France and India. He is the author of *Rethinking the War on Drugs in Ireland* (Cork University Press, Cork, 1996) and co-editor of *Ireland's Evolving Constitution 1937-1997: Collected Essays* (Hart, Oxford, 1998).

George Pavlakos is the City Solicitors' Educational Trust Lecturer in Jurisprudence at the Queen's University of Belfast. His main research interests include the discourse theory of law, legal epistemology and metaphysics. He has co-edited a volume on legal theory—*Jurisprudence or Legal Science?*—that will be published by Hart Publishing of Oxford in 2005.

Gerard Quinn is Professor of Law and Dean of the Law Faculty at the National University of Ireland, Galway where he is also Director of its Disability Law and Policy Research Unit. A graduate of Harvard Law School, he is the co-ordinator for the EU Article 13 Network of Disability Discrimination Legal Experts. He is currently a member of the Human Rights Commission of Ireland and the European Social Rights Committee (Council of Europe). He has acted as head of the Rehabilitation International (RI) delegation to the United Nations Working Group to draft a UN treaty on the rights of persons with disabilities. He has published extensively on international,

European and comparative disability discrimination law. His most recent publication in the field (with Theresia Degener) was *Human Rights and Disability: An Examination of the Current Use and Future Potential of the UN Human Rights Treaties in the Context of Disability* (Office of the UN High Commissioner for Human Rights, Geneva, 2002). [Gerard Quinn's chapter in this volume is a revised version of his article, "The Nature and Significance of Critical Legal Studies", *Irish Law Times*, November 1989, 282].

John Ringrose originally trained as a teacher and has experience of teaching at primary school level for a number of years. After further study he completed undergraduate and postgraduate degrees in law. In recent years he has tutored and lectured on the jurisprudence course at University College Cork. He currently practices as a solicitor in Cork.

Gerard Staunton is an artist and psychotherapist living in Cork. He is a graduate of University College Cork and a member of the Munster Writers' Centre. He is presently at work on a long poem based on Dante's *Commedia*.

Michael Staunton lectures in medieval history at University College Dublin. He was educated at University College Cork and Cambridge University and previously taught at the University of St Andrews in Scotland. Among his books is *The Lives of Thomas Becket* (Manchester University Press, Manchester, 2001).

Judy Walsh is a Lecturer in Law at the Equality Studies Centre, University College Dublin. She is co-author, with her colleagues John Baker, Sara Cantillon and Kathleen Lynch, of *Equality: From Theory to Action* (Palgrave-Macmillan, London, 2004). Since 2003 she is Co-chair of the Irish Council for Civil Liberties (ICCL), a non-governmental organisation that works to defend and promote human rights.

TABLE OF CONTENTS

EDITOR'S NOTE

It is not possible to thank everyone who has contributed to this collective project but first thanks must go to Catherine Dolan at Thomson Round Hall for her brave commissioning of the book. For their chapters and their insights, and for their patience and understanding during the editing of the collection, I thank all of the contributors. For support and encouragement during the editing process, I am particularly grateful to Paula Baron and Shane Kilcommins, and also to Eric Foley, Martin Hazell, Anne Larrabure, Asif and Jabbar Manai, Hilary and Billy Scrivens, John McInerney and Harry Murphy. Thanks also to Orla Fee for her editing of the collection at Thomon Round Hall, and to everyone else there who contributed to the publication.

The late Tommy Larkin and the late Stephen Livingstone also provided support and encouragement for this book. *Ar dheis Dé go raibh a n-anamacha.*

Finally, for their invaluable assistance and support, special thanks to Garrett Barden, Patrick Hannon, Vincent O'Connell and Gerard Staunton.

Tim Murphy
Cork
September 21, 2004

CHAPTER 1

INTRODUCTION: THE NATURE AND SCOPE OF JURISPRUDENCE

TIM MURPHY

Questions concerning law and justice have traditionally been central to humankind's philosophical reflection on its place and roles in the universe. At the beginning of the twenty-first century, as laws and legal regulations expand steadily in volume, scope and influence, these questions are growing in importance. It is often remarked that it is not now possible to recount, much less understand, the major political, social and economic developments in Western societies without attention to legal norms, legal processes, courts and judges. The twentieth century witnessed an incredible mushrooming of national and transnational bodies of law and, particularly in the latter half of that century, the political and socio-economic significance of courts and judges was acknowledged:

> "The number of countries with judicial review of legislation jumped sharply in the aftermath of the Second World War and again following the end of communist rule in Eastern Europe and the Soviet Union. Judicial review of administrative acts is also being significantly strengthened in many countries that long rejected or restricted it. Especially in Western Europe, transnational courts add another dimension of legal norms that can influence social life. Increasingly, scholars are coming to view courts as political actors and to argue that judges, their modes of arguing, the type of evidence they require, even their partisan policy preferences, influence lawmakers and administrative agencies."[1]

This unprecedented expansion of the legal sphere has focused attention on the ideas, theories and philosophies underlying law. Jurisprudence is the

---

[1] S.J. Kenney, W.M. Reisinger and J.C. Reitz, "Introduction: Constitutional Dialogues in Comparative Perspective" in *Constitutional Dialogues in Comparative Perspective* (S.J. Kenney, W.M. Reisinger and J.C. Reitz eds., St Martin's Press, New York, 1999), p.1.

philosophical pursuit of wisdom about law, legal systems and justice. It is also known as "legal theory" or "legal philosophy", or sometimes as the "science of law". Interest in philosophy of law, according to Christopher Gray,

> "thrives today around the world. New developments in law in both age-old and more recently established nations call for a good deal of philosophical reflection. New institutional and disciplinary contexts encourage that reflection and have further increased its range."[2]

This book is an introduction to Western jurisprudence, the tradition in legal theory that stretches from ancient Greek philosophy to contemporary postmodern thought. The volume is designed primarily to serve the needs of law students encountering the subject for the first time, but it will also be of interest to any reader who seeks to remain informed regarding the present state of legal theory. In this introductory chapter we will discuss the nature and scope of Western jurisprudence with reference to the other chapters that make up the book.

Although the question of whether "jurisprudence", "legal theory" and "legal philosophy" should be considered as in some sense distinct has provoked some debate, there is no agreed demarcation and they are usually considered to constitute one more or less coherent body of knowledge.[3] At any rate, a grasp of the interdisciplinary and historical character of jurisprudence is far more significant than demarcation issues for an initial understanding of what the subject involves. Theorizing about law necessarily involves substantial engagement with other disciplines—Julius Stone famously described jurisprudence as the lawyer's "extraversion,"[4] but this characterisation of jurisprudence may mislead slightly in that it suggests perhaps that jurisprudence is the preserve of lawyers only, which is certainly not the case. Another writer has suggested that jurisprudence could be defined as "critical external reflection on law", where "external" means *not* from the internal point of view of the doctrinal analysis of the law within one specific legal system.[5] This critical external reflection on law is undertaken by many non-lawyers and non-legal

---

[2] C.B. Gray, "Introduction" in *The Philosophy of Law: An Encyclopedia* (C.B. Gray ed., Garland, New York, 1999), p.vii.

[3] See J.W. Harris, *Legal Philosophies* (2nd ed., Butterworths, London, 1997), p.5; M. Van Hoeke, "Jurisprudence" in *The Philosophy of Law: An Encyclopedia*, pp.459–461; and J. Penner, D. Schiff and R. Nobles, "Approaches to Jurisprudence, Legal Theory, and the Philosophy of Law" in *Jurisprudence and Legal Theory: Commentary and Materials* (J. Penner, D. Schiff and R. Nobles eds., Butterworths, London, 2002), pp.3–5.

[4] J. Stone, *Legal System and Lawyers' Reasoning* (Maitland, Sydney, 1968), p.16.

[5] M. Van Hoecke, *op. cit.*, p.459.

materials and methodologies are frequently invoked in jurisprudential debate. In addition to encountering philosophy, theology, sociology, economics and several other modes of thought, the student of legal theory is faced with a historical canvas that begins in approximately the fifth century B.C. with the Greek philosophical tradition.[6] Indeed, if there is a case for any demarcation in the subject it is perhaps strongest in relation to the distinction between historical and contemporary jurisprudence. John Kelly, for example, while acknowledging the "astonishing flowering" of Anglo-American jurisprudence during the latter part of the twentieth century, considered that this growth was "so luxuriant that in the modern jurisprudence course it seems to blot out everything else"; perhaps, he suggested, "there is too much sailing under the flag 'jurisprudence' and it might more rationally be divided into two teaching subjects: *(a)* history of legal theory; *(b)* modern philosophy of law".[7]

However one defines or delineates the subject, the study of the *philosophy* of law, or legal *theory*, is not generally easy for a student who has little or no grounding in philosophy itself, a student whose usual expectation of legal education generally precludes the prospect of sustained theoretical reflection. Although there are some who would still deny it, there is a particular perspective on law that has achieved an ideological hegemony in Western legal education, namely the traditional idea of "legal formalism" or "mechanical jurisprudence". This ideology is mentioned and discussed in several chapters of this book and it is worth quoting in full a comprehensive definition of legal formalism that has been proposed recently by Brian Lieter:

> "Let us call 'the class of legal reasons' the class of reasons that may be legitimately offered in support of a legal conclusion, and that is such that, when it supports the conclusion, the conclusion is *required* 'as a matter of law.' The class of legal reasons then will include not only (a) the valid sources of law (e.g., statutes, precedents, etc.), but also (b) the

---

[6] "The reason why Greece has a special place in the history of civilization is not merely that most departments of literature and the visual arts were there raised to levels which later ages agreed to regard as classical, that is, as permanent standards of excellence. It is also because the Greeks were the first people—at any rate, the first of whom Europe retains any consciousness—among whom reflective thought and argument became a habit of educated men; a training for some, and a profession and vocation for others, not confined to observation of the physical world and universe—in which the Egyptians and Babylonians had long preceded them—but extending to man himself, his nature, and his place in the order of things, the character of human society, and the best way of governing it." J.M. Kelly, *A Short History of Western Legal Theory* (Clarendon Press, Oxford, 1992), p.1. For another history of jurisprudence, see S. Strömholm, *A Short History of Legal Thinking in the West* (Norstedts, Stockholm, 1985).

[7] See the note by Tony Honoré in J.M. Kelly, *op. cit.*, p.xvi.

interpretive principles through which such sources yield legal rules, as well as (c) the principles of reasoning (e.g., deductive, analogical) by which legal rules and facts are made to yield legal conclusions. Let us say that the law is 'rationally determinate' if the class of legal rules *justifies* one and only one outcome to a legal dispute. Finally, let us say that judging is 'mechanical' insofar as judges, in reaching conclusions about legal disputes, have no discretion. Judges exercise 'discretion' if they either (a) reach conclusions about legal disputes by reasoning in ways not sanctioned by the class of legal reasons; or (b) render judgments not justified by the class of legal reasons. Given these definitions, we may characterize formalism as the descriptive theory of adjudication according to which (1) the law is rationally determinate, and (2) judging is mechanical. It follows, moreover, from (1), that (3) legal reasoning is *autonomous*, since the class of *legal* reasons suffices to justify a unique outcome; no recourse to non-legal reasons is demanded or required."[8]

The dominance of this ideology in Western legal education makes it perfectly understandable why jurisprudence often appears daunting to students: they are suddenly confronted with a course in legal theory that might contain very little reference—or even no reference at all—to principles, statutes, case-law, or legal doctrine of any kind. Instead of being required to engage in doctrinal analysis students are challenged directly by legal philosophy to identify and analyse their own ethical and political stances. The difficulties for many students in approaching jurisprudence are compounded by the facts that the literature on the subject is vast and its very contents are disputed, or at least variable. On this latter point, for example, R.W.M. Dias wrote that the province of jurisprudence

" has been determined and re-determined because the nature and scope of the subject is such that no delineation of its scope can be regarded as final. On torts or contracts, for example, a student may be recommended to read any of the standard textbooks with the assurance that, whichever

---

[8] B. Leiter, "Positivism, Formalism, Realism" (1999) 99 *Columbia Law Review* 1138 at 1145 (emphases in original). Formalist ideology is also hegemonic in legal scholarship: "Since the late nineteenth century, legal scholarship has overwhelmingly meant the production and publication of articles engaged in doctrinal problem-solving. The assumption of this form of scholarship is that doctrinal problems admit of doctrinal solutions: There is no need to go beyond or outside legal doctrine. Classical doctrinal scholarship represents in this sense an 'internal' perspective—internal to (case) law, that is." C. Collier, "The Use and Abuse of Humanistic Theory in Law: Reexamining the Assumptions of Interdisciplinary Legal Scholarship" (1991) 41 *Duke Law Journal* 191 at 199.

book he does read, he will derive much the same idea as to what the subject is about. With jurisprudence this is not so. Books called 'jurisprudence' vary so widely in subject matter and treatment that the answer to the question, what is 'jurisprudence'?, is that it means pretty much whatever anyone wants it to mean—a depressing start indeed."[9]

But Dias later states, more optimistically, that writings on jurisprudence "are not concerned with expositions *of* law, but with disquisitions *about* law".[10] And this is indeed what jurisprudence amounts to: disquisitions or discussions about law, or about legal systems or justice. Generally speaking, jurisprudence examines the many alternative responses to questions such as: "What is law?"; "What is justice?"; "What is the relation between law and justice?"; "What constitutes a legal system?"; "What roles do law and legal systems play in society?"; "What do courts actually do when they adjudicate?"; and "Whose interests are served by the law?"

In more specific terms, there is a sense in which we can identify what some of the main jurisprudential perspectives on these questions are (or at least a mainstream view of what they are). Hilaire Barnett's research identifies the aspects of general jurisprudential thought that the vast majority of jurisprudence teachers in the UK, Australia and Canada identify as comprising "the heart of Jurisprudence", namely: legal positivism, natural law, law and morals, Marxist legal theory, American legal realism, critical legal studies, law and economics, and feminist legal theory.[11] All but one of these perspectives on legal theory are usually described as "schools" or "movements" because they represent more or less coherent approaches, although the diversity within these broad churches is a recurring theme in jurisprudential literature. "Law and morals", on the other hand, refers to an ongoing jurisprudential debate regarding the relationship between law and morality. All of these perspectives are discussed in this volume but so too are a range of others. We may begin to set out in summary form the themes of the various chapters, in order to begin to develop an understanding of some of the main phases and questions in the history of jurisprudence.

The next three chapters of this collection (Chapters 2–4) deal in different ways with aspects of jurisprudence and legal history during the classical and medieval periods. Jurisprudential study of classical and medieval developments requires us to engage in particular with the disciplines of history, philosophy, and theology.[12] Before the nineteenth century, as Wolfgang Friedmann wrote,

---

[9] R.W.M. Dias, *Jurisprudence* (5th ed., Butterworths, London, 1985), p.3.

[10] *ibid.*, p.7.

[11] H. Barnett, "The Province of Jurisprudence Determined—Again!" (1995) 15 *Legal Studies* 88.

[12] All the branches of philosophy, for example, were developed in ancient Greece and

"legal theory is essentially a by-product of philosophy, religion, ethics or politics. The great legal thinkers are primarily philosophers, churchmen, politicians."[13]

In Chapter 2 Garrett Barden contributes to a tradition established by Aristotle, developed by the Roman jurists and St Thomas Aquinas, and maintained in the twentieth century by Michel Villey. The chapter addresses the general question of whether it is illuminating to distinguish between the naturally and the conventionally just. The distinction between the two is discussed in the context of the definition of justice found in *The Institutes of Justinian*—that justice is the giving to each what is their due, or what they are entitled to. Sophocles' fifth century B.C. play, *Antigone*, and the Ten Commandments form the basis for an introductory discussion of the meanings of "law" and "the just". The theory that is developed in this chapter is that what is naturally just is discovered through an intelligent and reasonable examination of an actual situation. The discovery of the just, therefore, is a method not a doctrine. The chapter examines the different types of justice— distributive, rectificatory and reciprocal—and the author then brings together many of the chapter's themes in a discussion of the question that is addressed by courts. Garrett Barden suggests that this question is *always* of the form: "in the case now being considered, what is due to whom?" In dealing in detail with the tradition of natural *justice*, and by drawing out its significance for some of the central concerns of jurisprudence (*e.g.* the nature of justice, the form of adjudication, the idea of equity), the chapter challenges the conventional portrayal in jurisprudence of an essentially uniform natural *law* tradition as the primary contribution of legal philosophy before the modern era.

Chapter 3 discusses the foundations of Western jurisprudence that were laid during the early and high Middle Ages (from around the fifth century A.D. until around 1250). As Michael Staunton observes in his overview of a broad range of developments, the majority of our written records from the Middle Ages are legal ones, and of all its bequests to Western civilisation, the medieval legacy of law is arguably the greatest. The chapter begins with an account of the Germanic law that predominated throughout Europe after the fall of the Roman Empire, and it then explores the revival of Roman law following the rediscovery in Italy of Justinian's *Institutes* towards the end of

---

all have relevance to the philosophy of law: epistemology (the theory of knowledge); metaphysics (the theory of being and knowing, or the philosophy of mind); logic (the theory of reasoning, proof, thinking and inference); ethics (the theory of how one ought to live); political theory ("quite simply, man's attempts to consciously understand and solve the problems of his group life and organization", G.H. Sabine and T.L. Thorson, *A History of Political Thought* (4th ed., Harcourt Brace, New York, 1973), p.3); and even aesthetics (the theory of beauty).

[13] W. Friedmann, *Legal Theory* (2nd ed., Stevens and Sons, London, 1949), p.4.

the eleventh century. This influenced both the development of canon law and the later emergence of the Continental civil law tradition. The author also looks at the origins of the English common law tradition in the late twelfth century, with particular reference to the dispute between Henry II and Thomas Becket; and to the influence of Magna Carta on the subsequent creation of checks upon state control of law.

Another important part of jurisprudential history is the later medieval contribution of St Thomas Aquinas. The theology advanced by St Thomas in the thirteenth century, and in particular the political theory and the natural law and natural justice theories in his *Summa Theologiae* ("Summary of Theology"), have been extremely influential in the history of political and legal thought. Chapter 4 assesses St Thomas's place in the natural law tradition. His natural law theory is widely regarded as an important landmark in the development of the modern idea of natural law, which is generally understood as involving extra-legal norms that form a basic and universal containing context for human law, and with which human law should be compatible. The theme of Chapter 4 is that St Thomas's natural law theory is primarily an ethical theory and that its portrayal in legal philosophy as a form of standard supervening human law is inaccurate.

Although the development of law and legal theory in the West has been influenced in important ways by the Christian tradition, theology is now widely attacked by modern philosophers and scientists. For example, Roger Scruton suggests that the nature of philosophy can be grasped through contrasts with science and theology. He observes that modern science is the realm of empirical investigation, stemming "from the attempt to understand the world as we perceive it, to predict and explain observable events and to formulate the 'laws of nature' (if there be any) according to which the course of human experience is to be explained"; science's presupposition of the existence of things sets it apart from the concerns of the various branches of philosophy because these arise when thought is "pushed to levels of abstraction where no empirical enquiry can provide a satisfactory answer".[14] By way of contrasting philosophy with theology, Scruton notes that in considering metaphysical issues people might have recourse to an authoritative system of theology; however, if God, "as the first cause and final aim of everything", is invoked purely on a foundation of faith, "then it claims no rational authority beyond that which can be attributed to revelation".[15]

The differences between philosophy, theology and science feature throughout the history of jurisprudence, but the advent of modernity heralded, above all else, the age of science. New debates in legal theory that were

---

[14] R. Scruton, *A Short History of Modern Philosophy* (2nd ed., Routledge, London, 1995), pp.4–5.

[15] *ibid.*, p.5.

engendered by law's subsequent encounters with several new disciplines and modes of thinking and some of these debates are surveyed in Chapters 5–8.

In Chapter 5 Liam Herrick offers an account of the classical legal positivism developed by Jeremy Bentham and John Austin during the late eighteenth and nineteenth centuries. The idea that law was essentially command—the product of the sovereign's will—and that it should be understood and analysed in and of itself and not with reference to political or ethical morality was a huge departure in the new world of quasi-scientific jurisprudence. Bentham was the first significant modern English-speaking legal philosopher and the chapter also provides an overview of Bentham's highly influential utilitarian political philosophy.

While utilitarianism continues to exert considerable influence as a political and ethical theory, the command or imperative theory of law has been superseded by other versions of positivism. One legal theorist, Roger Cotterrell, has nonetheless emphasised the importance of Bentham and Austin in initiating the development of what he terms jurisprudence's "constructive subversion— its challenge to legal professional accepted wisdom"; Cotterrell suggests that their challenge to common law empircism and pragmatism opened up

> "a recognised space for legal theory—for explicitly developed general theory of the nature of law. Jurisprudence taught, for example, the importance of considering theoretically law's systematic and formal character, its bases of authority and its doctrinal unity or autonomy. In this way it facilitated comparison of legal styles and systems, and a more reflexive view of the nature of legal reasoning."[16]

Cotterell also suggests that the next significant phase in the development of jurisprudence's "constructive subversion" was the successful challenge to the idea of law as a self-contained discipline or mode of understanding or reasoning, a phase in which jurisprudence ultimately became the "flagship of interdisciplinarity and multidisciplinarity in legal education".[17] Some of the early phases of this development are discussed in Chapters 6 and 7, which provide overviews of the fields of historical and sociological jurisprudence respectively.

In Chapter 6 Shane Kilcommins assesses the two leading figures in the nineteenth-century historical school of jurisprudence, namely Ferdinand Von Savigny and Henry Maine. Both thinkers adhered to the view that law is a product of evolutionary logic, but they engaged in different forms of historical analysis to discover the organic connections between laws and various societies.

---

[16] R. Cotterrell, "Pandora's Box: Jurisprudence in Legal Education" (2000) 7 *International Journal of the Legal Profession* 179 at 184.
[17] *ibid.*

This chapter outlines and assesses Savigny's "Romantic historicism" and Maine's "evolutionary scientism".

In Chapter 7 Judy Walsh provides an account of the vast field of sociological jurisprudence. Sociology can be defined as the study of human social behaviour. This chapter surveys the the nineteenth and early-twentieth century origins of sociological jurisprudence in the thought of Karl Marx, Emile Durkheim, Max Weber, Eugen Ehrlich, Roscoe Pound and Talcott Parsons. There is also a discussion of contemporary directions in sociological jurisprudence, in particular the ideas of Niklas Luhmann and Pierre Bourdieu, and also "critical empirical" methodology.

While several of the writers who are associated with sociological jurisprudence have had an enormous impact on social and political thought more generally, this is especially so in the case of Karl Marx (who also employed a historical lens in his social and economic theory). We have already mentioned that Marxist legal theory is widely considered to be one of central schools of thought in jurisprudence. The Marxist-socialist tradition emerged as a reaction to liberal capitalism and grew into a powerful international political force during the nineteenth century. It is a tradition that continues to exert considerable influence at the beginning of the twenty-first century; it remains, in Jacques Derrida's words, "complex, evolving, [and] heterogenous".[18] Marx's subsequent impact on jurisprudence is evidenced in several later chapters of this volume; his ideas have impacted, to a greater or lesser extent, on critical legal studies, feminist jurisprudence, critical race theory and many aspects of postmodern thought.

Chapter 8 introduces the key figures and ideas of American legal realism, the movement that dominated American legal thought for the first half of the twentieth century. J. Paul McCutcheon outlines the contributions of Oliver Wendell Holmes, John Chipman Gray, Herman Oliphant, Underhill Moore, Karl Llewellyn and Jerome Frank, and the chapter examines the manner in which they challenged the claim that law constrains judges' decisions in ways that eliminate the influence of their own or others' policy preferences. The realists, in other words, attacked and undermined the traditional idea of "legal formalism" or "mechanical jurisprudence". The validity and correctness of the realist challenge to thinking about adjudication has been accepted by all of the main jurisprudential movements that emerged in the US in the latter half of the twentieth century—although orthodox legal thought, as has been said, remains strongly under the influence of formalist ideology.

Before this volume turns to consider these contemporary American jurisprudential movements, Chapters 9–12 examine other aspects of twentieth-century legal philosophy: the emergence of two new versions of legal positivism

---

[18] J. Derrida, *Spectres of Marx* (Routledge, London, 1994), p.84.

are discussed in Chapters 9 and 10; the ongoing debate about the relationship between law and morality is assessed in Chapter 11; and the modern ethic of human rights, which has grown steadily in prominence since the end of the Second World War, is the subject of Chapter 12.

Whereas both Bentham and Austin had developed a version of positivism that considers that immoral law is still law, both H.L.A. Hart and Hans Kelsen, as George Pavlakos explains in Chapter 9, advanced different versions of positivism that shared nonetheless the premise that law can be determined in a context-independent way, by reference to a set of purely legal criteria. Hart's concept of law superseded the command theory of law in the English-speaking world, and Chapter 9 explores the workings of conceptual analysis in Hart's theory of a legal system as comprising various types of rules.

Chapter 10 offers an overview of the "pure theory of law" proposed by Kelsen, a positivist who has had more influence outside the English-speaking world. Whereas Hart described his concept of law as "descriptive sociology", Kelsen's analytical positivism was founded on a more "scientific" epistemology and outlook. Kelsen viewed legal systems as systems of norms rather than of commands or rules, and he proposed that all norms were validated ultimately by a *Grundnorm* or "basic norm".

The relationship between law and morality is the subject of Chapter 11, in which Patrick Hannon identifies a persistent theme in natural law theory through the ages: that the demands of the moral law are available to a reasoned reflection on what it is to be a human being in the world which we inhabit. The chapter offers a description of morality—in the broadly classical natural law tradition— as the art of right relationship with each other and the world around us. The chapter compares and contrasts law and morality, and also evaluates the well-known jurisprudential debate about the enforcement of morality between H.L.A. Hart and Patrick Devlin.

Chapter 12 introduces the concept of human rights in two stages. Colin Harvey's analysis begins with an account of the historical development of arguments about rights, with particular reference to the arguments on rights advanced by Thomas Hobbes, John Locke, Edmund Burke and Jeremy Bentham. The second stages focuses on a modern debate on rights between Ronald Dworkin and Jeremy Waldron regarding how disagreements over the meaning of rights that are reflected in positive law or legal principles might be resolved.

The next five chapters (Chapters 13–17) deal with the main schools of American jurisprudential thought that have emerged over the past 30 years or so: critical legal studies; law and economics; feminist jurisprudence; critical race theory; and postmodern jurisprudence. These movements represent in very different ways the continuation of the realist project of undermining formalist ideology, and all of them—with the notable exception of postmodern jurisprudence—are forms of normative, political jurisprudence, that is, they include strands that ultimately propose visions of substantive justice to which they argue society and law should conform.

The leftist critical legal studies (CLS) movement is discussed in Chapter 13. Gerard Quinn sets out an account of the liberal edifice, including constitutionalism and the rule of law, that CLS scholarship sought to destabilise. The chapter then analyses four main themes in CLS scholarship—a radical indeterminacy thesis; a concern for the mystification function of law; a concern for the role of ideology in law; and the transformative possibilities of law.

In Chapter 14, Alan Haugh discusses the neo-liberal economic analysis of law associated with figures such as Ronald Coase, Gary Becker, Frank Easterbrook and Richard Posner. The Chicago school of economics' central ideas are discussed, including the notion of efficiency as justice and the human subject as a rational utility maximiser. Posner's views on the specific role of the judge are also examined in this chapter.

For many, the traditional "left-right" opposition of CLS and law and economics may seem outdated, as left-right divisions are often portrayed as increasingly redundant in the contemporary postmodern landscape. The key idea represented by the designation "postmodernity" is that we are now— after the classical, medieval, and modern periods—experiencing a fourth epoch in the history of Western civilization. Specifically, it is suggested that due to political developments and the rapid changes induced by technology, de-industrialization, globalisation and mediaization, there have been crucial social shifts during the latter part of the twentieth century. Jack Balkin has commented that in this sense postmodernity is "neither necessarily a good thing nor a bad thing"; rather it is, he says, "a cultural moment that needs to be interpreted and understood".[19] Many have interpreted the postmodern historical moment as one in which "neo-liberalism", both political and economic, has surpassed its achievement of a certain hegemony and definitively triumphed over opposing ideologies. This triumph was seen as the central aspect of a "new world order" that emerged after the collapse of communism in Eastern Europe and the Soviet Union. Neo-liberalism was thus said to be the ideology that survived the postmodern idea of the "end of history", the most widely-known version of which is associated with Francis Fukuyama. Fukuyama argued that history had ended in the elimination of the great ideological and political battlefields of modernity, of left versus right, capital versus labour, etc. No conflict of dialectical dimensions was left, and as a consequence liberal capitalism and the principles of human rights could not be transcended.[20]

Fukuyama's position has been predictably undermined in several ways in

---

[19] J. M. Balkin, "What is a Postmodern Constitutionalism?" (1992) 90 *Michigan Law Review* 1966 at 1968.

[20] See F. Fukuyama, *The End of History and the Last Man* (Hamish Hamilton, London, 1992).

the short time since he published his "end of history" thesis. On the ideological level, for example, Norberto Bobbio has argued convincingly that the distinction between left and right remains valid, and it rests on differing attitudes towards equality. Acknowledging that human beings are in different respects equal and unequal, Bobbio argues that "on the one side are those who think men more equal than unequal, while on the other are those who think them more unequal than equal".[21] According to Bobbio, the other major permanent, underlying contrast between left and right is that the left believes that most inequalities are social and eliminable; the right that most are natural and unalterable. For the first, equality is an ideal; for the second it is not. For Bobbio, the inequalities of this world—both within rich Western societies and throughout the rest of the world—remain staggering. It is enough, he writes, to look out at "the social question on an international scale, to realize that the Left, far from coming to the end of its road, has only just started out on it".[22]

While ideas of "left" and "right" continue to be contested, the struggle for cultural recognition of difference is usually considered to be the paradigmatic form of postmodern political conflict. Activist groups have been mobilised under the banners of nationality, ethnicity, race, gender and sexuality, and such recognition has to some degree displaced socio-economic redistribution as the principal remedy for injustice. Nancy Fraser suggests that many of the collectivities which are active in this "post-socialist" sense can be described as "bivalent": they are "differentiated as collectivities by virtue of *both* the political-economic structure *and* the cultural-valuational structure of society ... [and therefore] implicated simultaneously in both the politics of redistribution and the politics of recognition".[23]

Chapter 15 explores the shift in contemporary feminist jurisprudence away from liberal political theory, and away in particular from liberal ideas regarding human rights. Siobhán Mullally discusses ethic of care feminism, radical feminism, critical race feminism, and postmodern feminism, and explores the possibility of realising a global feminism that seeks an equality that is of equivalent worth to differently situated individuals and groups.

The critical race theory (CRT) movement emerged out of anti-discrimination law scholarship in the US. In Chapter 16 C.L. Lim provides an account of how CRT grew as North American minority scholars such as Derrick Bell, Alan Freeman, Richard Delgado, Kimberlé Crenshaw and Mari Matsuda developed a race conscious form of legal theory. The chapter also outlines and assesses liberal and other critiques of CRT and suggests that CRT scholarship could and should continue its expansion outside the US.

---

[21] N. Bobbio, *Left and Right* (Polity, Cambridge, 1996), p.66.

[22] *ibid.*, pp.128–132.

[23] See N. Fraser, "From Redistribution to Recognition? Dilemmas of Justice in a 'Post-socialist' Age" (1995) 212 *New Left Review* 69 at 78–82.

Chapter 17 provides an overview of postmodern and poststructuralist jurisprudence. We have already referred to postmodernity; postmodern*ism*, on the other hand, can best be understood from the point of view of epistemology. Postmodernism is said to call the rationalism of modernity into question, particularly as a means of "knowing reality". This postmodern perspective is known as epistemic or cognitive *relativism*. The basic claim of relativism, as put by Harvey Siegel, is that "truth and rational justifiability of knowledge-claims are relative to the standards used in evaluating such claims".[24] In Chapter 17 Emmanuel Melissaris discusses how the postmodern work of Michel Foucault and Jacques Derrida has challenged and undermined two pillars of modern law, the rational and autonomous subject and the objectivity of meaning of the legal text. This chapter also includes a case study in order to explore the potential relevance of postmodern jurisprudence.

Chapters 18 and 19 deal with what are often termed "minor jurisprudences": the mode of psychoanalytic jurisprudence and law-literature jurisprudence. In Chapter 18 Paula D. Baron discusses the influence of psychoanalysis on jurisprudence and in particular the influence of the post-Freudian psychoanalyst, Jacques Lacan. Psychoanalysis is explored as both a theory of subjectivity and a therapeutic practice and the chapter considers the primary ways in which the tradition has impacted on jurisprudence, including surveys of how the psychoanalytic mode of jurisprudence reads legal speech for unconscious meaning; how it addresses legal representations such as the rites and rituals of the law; and how it addresses "legal subjectivity", that is, both the place of the subject in law and of law within the subject.

Chapter 19 deals with law and literature. The authors offer accounts of the two branches of law-literature scholarship: law-*in*-literature, which looks to literary works and theory with a view to illuminating legal and jurisprudential questions or issues; and law-*as*-literature, which applies various literary theories to legal texts or considers legal discourse as a form of rhetoric that might benefit from exposure to literary expression. A selection of texts and commentaries are surveyed with a view to highlighting the possibilities, including the educational possibilities, offered by law-literature scholarship.

The final chapter of this volume does not deal with any jurisprudential "school" or "movement". Instead, against a background discussion of the place of formalist ideology in legal adjudication and legal education, John Ringrose argues in favour of the revival of the idea of a liberal legal education and in

---

[24] See H. Siegel, "Relativism" in *A Companion to Epistemology* (J. Dancy and E. Sosa eds., Blackwell, Oxford, 1992), pp.429–30. In Siegel's account, relativism is demonstratedly incoherent, "because, if it is right, the very notion of rightness is undermined, in which case relativism itself cannot be right"; he argues, however, that the difficulties of formulating a defensible conception of non-relativism have left a vacuum in which there has recently been a resurgence of relativist thought.

particular for an enhanced role for jurisprudence. Chapter 20 emphasises the importance of jurisprudence understood in a broad sense as the development of critical, analytical and reflective thought about law and its place in the wider scheme of things. Charles Collier has referred to what he perceives as "the divergence of legal theory and practice as equally untenable gravitations toward the worst possible extremes of an opposition, with legal theorists taking an impossibly high road and judicial practice firmly in control of the low ground,"[25] but this chapter argues convincingly for the significance of jurisprudence in the ethical practice of law.

What of the future for legal theory? Jurisprudence is obviously not static in any sense, and it continues to face new challenges to which it must adapt and which it must ultimately address. This is not something that jurisprudence has always done with enough alacrity. William Twining remarked that by the mid-1990s, "the discipline of law ... was becoming increasingly cosmopolitan, but its theoretical branch, jurisprudence, seemed to have lagged behind".[26] Now at least, some leading jurisprudential scholars appear to concur about the nature of the main challenge now facing the philosophy of law. Twining himself suggests that globalisation—"those processes which tend to create and consolidate a unified world economy, a single ecological system, and a complex network of communications that covers the whole globe, even if it does not penetrate to every part of it"—raises a pressing need for a revival of "general jurisprudence".[27] This general jurisprudence is not only about considering law from a global perspective; it may be much more restricted in its geographical scope, but it should constitute "a pluralistic vision of legal theory which includes a variety of perspectives and a multiplicity of levels of generality".[28]

In a similar vein, Roger Cotterrell's view that jurisprudence should be constructively subversive—that it should question assumptions that underlie received wisdom about the nature of law in general—leads him to emphasise

---

[25] C. Collier, *op. cit.*, at 270.

[26] W. Twining, *Globalisation and Legal Theory* (Butterworths, London, 2000), p.3.

[27] *ibid.*, p.4.

[28] *ibid.*, p.13. General jurisprudence is contrasted with particular jurisprudence, which focuses on the general aspects of a single legal system or order and its constituent phenomena, for example, American or Irish constitutional theory, or the basic concepts of French or German law. But Twining acknowledges that sharp distinctions between general and particular jurisprudence are of limited value. "General" and "particular" are relative matters: "We need jurisprudence that can transcend jurisdictions and cultures, so far as that is feasible and appropriate, and which can address issues about law from a global and transnational perspective. However, 'thick description' of local particulars set in broad geographical contexts will be as important as ever in the development of a healthy discipline of law in a more integrated world" (p.49).

the importance of "legal pluralism" or "perspectivism" for contemporary jurisprudence. We have mentioned that Cotterrell considered the challenge to common law empiricism and pragmatism by Bentham and Austin, and the challenge by subsequent theorists to the idea of law as a self-contained discipline or mode of understanding, as two earlier phases of this "subversion" of received wisdom. The focus on metropolitan state law in orthodox legal thought is now being challenged, according to Cotterrell, by important changes taking place in the way legal authority is understood and experienced. Transnational law, in its many different forms, demands an adequate legal theory, and "the diversity of legal expectations and traditions within nation-states—reflected in multiculturalism, regionalism and more general demands for recognition of the distinctiveness and diversity of group life—similarly demands legal recognition as a central, not merely peripheral, aspect of legal regulation". [29] According to Cotterrell, jurisprudence needs to examine how extremely diverse forms of legal authority are seeking mutual accommodation in an increasingly complex world; and how new sources of legal authority beyond or apart from those of the nation-state are gradually forming or changing their character:

> "Perhaps jurisprudence must now express the idea that law is to be understood in a variety of ways, its authority is judged from a variety of communal standpoints and its diverse sources increasingly compete with and challenge each other in local, state and transnational jurisdictions."[30]

To undertake properly these and other proposed projects, the established jurisprudential landscape must serve as our starting-point. It is hoped that this collection will provide a relatively comprehensive view of that landscape, and that it will provoke and stimulate thought and debate about a broad range of issues associated with law, legal systems and justice. The volume seeks to heighten awareness of the significance of theory in any effort to comprehend properly the various roles and dilemmas of law. The chapters offer a diversity of perspectives but, as is often said of the array of schools of thought in legal theory, it is not a case of having to choose which perspective is the "correct" one. In formulating one's own perspective on jurisprudence—that is, one's own legal philosophy,—insights can be gleaned from as many accounts of law as one wishes as long as contradiction is avoided. And insights can also of course be gleaned from jurisprudential traditions other than the Western tradition. Yet the field of comparative legal theory—assessing the African, Buddhist, Hindu, Islamic, Western and other jurisprudential traditions in comparative perspective—is probably the most underdeveloped subject in

---

[29] R. Cotterrell, *op. cit.*, at 186.
[30] *ibid.*

academic legal discourse. This will certainly have to change if the challenges to our understandings of law and authority posed by developments such as globalisation, multiculturalism and the growth of transnational law are to be met.

CHAPTER 2

OF THE NATURALLY AND THE CONVENTIONALLY JUST

In memoriam Michel Villey (1914–1988)

GARRETT BARDEN

1. INTRODUCTION

The question addressed in this chapter is this:

"is it illuminating to distinguish between what is naturally just and what is conventionally just?"

How the terms "naturally", "conventionally" and "just" are used here must be made plain, for they are used by different authors, and sometimes by a single author, in very different ways. In the next part of this chapter ("Of 'law' and 'the just'"), when we discuss these different usages more fully, we shall see the importance of the difference—first identified by Aristotle (384–322 B.C.) in the fifth book of the *Nicomachean Ethics*—between "justice" understood as one virtue among many (the virtue of giving to each what is their due, or "particular justice") and justice understood as a synonym of "virtue" or "moral goodness" covering the entire moral life. An understanding of Aristotle's analysis is crucial to an understanding of Western reflection on justice. The distinction between particular justice and goodness as a whole is present in Roman law, from which later European and Western jurisprudence developed and which was for centuries and until comparatively recently the core of legal education in the West.[1] St Thomas Aquinas (c.1225–1274), himself deeply

---

[1] "The loss [of Roman Law in legal education] is all the more noticeable in that in France from the twelfth until the eighteenth century, and in Germany for even longer, legal education was based on the *Corpus Juris Civilis* and the study of the writings of the Roman jurists." M. Villey, *Le Droit et les Droits des Hommes* (PUF, Paris, 1983), p.27. For a succinct account of the Roman invention of law understood as a method of dealing with questions of justice, see pp.33–35.

versed in the writings of the Roman jurists, wrote a commentary on the *Nicomachean Ethics* and in the second part of the second part of his *Summa Theologiae* provides his own, similar analysis of justice and the just corresponding to it.

Aristotle and St Thomas have been and remain influential. It is extremely important to notice at once that both generally use the term "law", rather than "justice", to cover the whole of the moral life. In other words, they understood the moral law to be the commonly accepted moral rules of the community rather than simply a set of statutes enacted by a ruler. They distinguish between "law" understood in this way and "justice" which has to do with giving to each what is due.

"Law" and "justice" are related but not identical and so discussions of "law" and of "justice" will be related but not identical. Furthermore, discussions of "natural law" and of "natural justice", although related, will not be identical. The distinction is sometimes overlooked.[2] Among recent writers who have insisted on this distinction is the great twentieth century French jurist, Michel Villey.[3] The theory of justice and the just put forward here owes much to Aristotle, Cicero, the Roman jurists, Aquinas and Villey.

---

[2] The *Summa Theologiae* is divided into several parts: I, I-II, II-II, and III. Each part is divided into several questions and each question into several articles. Many jurisprudence textbooks, when discussing St Thomas Aquinas, refer exclusively to his discussion of law in Questions 90–97 in the first part of the second part of his *Summa Theologiae* whereas his discussion of justice and what is just is found in Questions 56–71, 120 and 122 of the second part of the second part. In fact, this distinction, which Aristotle and, following him, Cicero, the Roman jurists and Aquinas, thought both clear and important is quite rarely adverted to despite the fact that the Roman formula defining the just as "what is due" is well known and often quoted. See Tim Murphy, "St Thomas Aquinas and the Natural Law Tradition" in this volume.

[3] M. Villey, *Leçons d'Histoire de la Philosophie du Droit* (Dalloz, Paris, 1962), especially Pt II, chap.VII and *Seize Essais de Philosophie du Droit* (Dalloz, Paris, 1969). On the distinction made here, Villey writes: "I began by noticing a feature of the language of Roman law and of the classical philosophers of the naturally just. It seemed remarkable that, in contrast with our usage, they were at pains to distinguish between *the just* and *law*. The jurist must, of course, take note of existing laws; but what is just is not confined within them; the just remains on each occasion and in each case an unknown to be discovered and not a solution that derives entirely from rules given in advance." *Seize Essais*, p.222 ("the just" or "the naturally just" translate Villey's *droit*. There is no easy translation of *droit*. On the European Continent there are not "Faculties of Law" but "Faculties of *Droit* or its equivalent". The German *Recht* is linguistically close to the English "Right" but we do not use it in the same way. That two words are available does not guarantee or impose the distinction made here and, where nothing turns on the distinction, the words *lex* and *jus* in Roman law are sometimes almost interchangeable.

Before moving directly to discuss the naturally just, and in order to clarify by contrast a distinction between "the just" and "law", there is (in the part of the chapter titled "Of laws and authorities") a discussion of Sophocles' tragedy *Antigone* and of the story of the revelation of the Ten Commandments to Moses. This is done for several reasons: first, these texts, which have been very influential in subsequent discussion, treat of law predominantly as command; secondly, neither distinguishes between "law" and "justice"; thirdly, the Ten Commandments include moral rules some of which treat of the moral life, including the religious life, as a whole, and some of which treat specifically of justice. *Antigone* presents a contrast between the authority of the ruler of Thebes and the authority of the laws laid down by the gods; the governing question of the tragedy is this: when there is conflict between them, which is the superior authority? Behind this question is an, as yet, unworked out suspicion that there are, in principle, limits to state power. That suspicion became increasingly acute with the development of Western jurisprudential thought. The suspicion is transformed into a clear question in the *Summa Theologiae* of St Thomas Aquinas, with respect to both "natural law" and to "what is naturally just". The question survives in succeeding centuries: it appears in the eighteenth century in Adam Smith's *Lectures on Jurisprudence* (1766); in the nineteenth century in Wilhelm von Humboldt's *The Limits of State Action* (1840) and in John Stuart Mill's *On Liberty* (1856). It is fundamental to ideas of civil disobedience.[4] Civil disobedience, once accepted, involves two questions, not

---

[4] The question as to whether or not an evil law is a law is obviously related to the issue of civil disobedience. The question is taken up briefly later but, at this juncture, it is worth simply stating that the *jus naturalist*—*i.e.* someone who thinks that there are situations that are naturally just—is not committed to a crude denial that an evil law is a law. But if everything were purely conventional, what would it mean to say that a convention was evil? On the other hand, if a law is a command issued by a sovereign, then something so issued is a law irrespective of its content. Furthermore, from the fact that something is naturally just, it cannot be inferred that it is known to everyone, nor that it should form part of state law. See H.L.A. Hart, "Positivism and the Separation of Law and Morals" (1958) 71 *Harvard Law Review* 593 and N. MacCormick, "Natural Law and the Separation of Law and Morals" in *Natural Law Theory* (R. George ed., Clarendon Press, Oxford, 1992), pp.105–133. There would appear to be no writer, positivist or otherwise, who thinks that no commonly accepted moral norms should be included in metropolitan law—for example, a law forbidding theft—and, equally, no writer who considers that every commonly accepted moral norm or even every correct moral norm should be included in metropolitan law— for example, a law bidding us to be patient and forbidding impatience. For one who accepts that it is perfectly proper to include some, but not necessarily all, moral norms in the metropolitan law, it follows that the simple fact that a moral norm is accepted or correct is not sufficient reason to warrant its inclusion in metropolitan law. See St Thomas Aquinas, *Summa Theologiae*, I-II, q.96, art.2. On civil

one only: the first and more practical question is to determine, in a particular state, what the limits to state power are, and what they might or should be; the second, more theoretical but equally important, question is to discover some principle of limitation.

More influential still in the development of reflection on law in the West is the Biblical story of the revelation of the Decalogue or Ten Words, commonly called the Ten Commandments, to Moses.[5] In the story of the revelation to Moses the imaginative stress is on the fact that the Ten Words are given by Yahweh and form the basis of a covenant between Yahweh and his people. The covenant is not confined to "justice as a part of virtue"—the giving to each what is due—but concerns the moral life as a whole. In the story, "law" is a common term but it is worth remarking that the Hebrew word, *torah*, that is translated as "law" in English and as the equivalent in other European languages, has, according to some scholars, as much the sense of "teaching" than as of "command". In his final discourse in *Deuteronomy*, Moses refers to the law as a teaching.[6] In the story of Moses the authority of the law and the commandments rests not on Yahweh's will only but on truth.

One important, awkward, and at least apparent, exception is the story of the sacrifice of Isaac in *Genesis*. Abraham is commanded by Yahweh to kill his innocent son, Isaac, and to offer him in sacrifice. Abraham agrees. Yahweh intervenes at the last moment, and commands Abraham to spare Isaac and to sacrifice a goat in his place. On this story, William of Occam (1290–1349), the younger contemporary and opponent of St Thomas Aquinas, based his voluntarist theory that actions were good because they were commanded by God. St Thomas's contrary position was that the actions were commanded by God because they were good. Occam's theory is to a great extent the source of the view that the law gets its authority from the Sovereign's will—whether the Sovereign be God or, in Thomas Hobbes, "that great LEVIATHAN ... that *Mortal God* ...", the State.

In the following part of the chapter ("The discovery of what is naturally

---

disobedience, see A. Casado, *La Desobediencia Civil a partir de Thoreau* (Gakoa, Donostia–San Sebastian, 2002).

[5] The Greek "Decalogue" literally translates as "Ten Words". In the translation of *Exodus* 34:28 in *The Jerusalem Bible* (Eyre and Spottiswoode, London, 1968), the Decalogue is referred to as the "Ten Words"; in *Deuteronomy* 4:13 and 10:4 as the "Ten Sayings". In the Authorized King James Version of the Bible (1611) the translation is in each case the "ten commandments".

[6] "Listen, heavens, while I speak: earth, hear the words that I am saying. May my teaching fall like the rain, may my word drop down like the dew." *Deuteronomy*, 32:1–2. In modern Irish, "the ten commandments" are *na deich n-aitheanta*; "command" is given by Patrick Dinneen as the English translation of *aithne* but it is clearly close to many cognate words all of which are associated with "knowledge", "teaching", etc., *Foclóir Gaedhilge agus Béarla* (Irish Texts Society, Dublin, 1927).

just"), three kinds of justice are distinguished—distributive justice, rectificatory justice and reciprocal justice. In each case it is shown that the contrast and possible conflict between the naturally and the conventionally just is not a contrast or conflict between a higher and an inferior command. What by any single person or community is considered to be naturally just can, of course, be formulated in a rule or law but this rule or law derives from an understanding of the social situation and is an expression of that understanding. It is a received teaching. The question governing this part of the chapter, therefore, is this: how can what is naturally just be discovered?

What is "naturally" and what is "conventionally" just will be made clear as the discussion develops but it may be useful to give the preliminary description from Aristotle:

> "What is just in the city is in part natural and in part conventional or legal. What is naturally just ... does not depend on people deciding this or that; what is conventional is that which is originally indifferent but which, when it is established, is no longer indifferent."[7]

It is imperative to recognise that the naturally just is not discovered by discovering higher rules or laws laid down by a sovereign. In Aristotle's phrase, what is just by nature is not originally a matter of indifference that becomes just only following custom, convention, agreement or legal edict. Writing of judgement in the realm of justice—which is, in other words, writing of the jurist's task—St Thomas gives, almost incidentally, an account of the naturally just:

> "[J]udgement is nothing else but a kind of definition or determination of what is just. And something is just in one of two ways: first, *from the nature of the case itself, which is called naturally just*; secondly, from a kind of agreement among men, which is called positively (or conventionally) just."[8]

The phrase in italics is crucial. In Latin it reads: *ex ipsa natura rei, quod dicitur ius naturale*. Literally translated: "from the nature of the thing itself". The "thing" is the case, the situation. *What is naturally just is discovered through an intelligent and reasonable examination of the actual situation. The discovery of the just is a method not a doctrine.* This is the core of the theory of the naturally just.

---

[7] Aristotle, *Nicomachean Ethics*, V.7, 1134b.8–23. In his *Commentary on Aristotle's Nicomachean Ethics* St Thomas Aquinas analyses this passage in Book V, Lectio XII.

[8] St Thomas Aquinas, *Summa Theologiae*, II-II, q.60, art.5 (emphasis added).

The fifth and final part of this chapter is called "The question addressed by the court". It is suggested that the question before a court is *always* of this form: "in the case now being considered, what is due to whom?" The relevant conventional and natural elements involved are not only the case itself, the established rules and precedents, but also the internal features of the enquiry.[9] Is it, for example, simply a matter of conventional rule or is it intrinsic to the nature of investigation that, in a dispute between litigants, the court should hear both sides? Is it simply a matter of conventional rule or is it intrinsic to the nature of investigation that an adjudicator between litigants should be disinterested, impartial, unbiased?

2. OF "LAW" AND "THE JUST"

In A.D. 528, the Roman Emperor Justinian (A.D. 482–565) instructed the jurist Tribonian to make a new code of laws which was to be a compilation or digest of earlier writings including the opinions of the great Roman jurists, Gaius (whose *Institutes*, written about A.D. 170, was the model for the new work),[10] and Papinianus, Paul and Ulpian (all three about A.D. 200). Tribonian and 16 colleagues selected what they considered most valuable in the writings of their predecessors and in A.D. 533 the *Digest* was approved. As well as the immense *Digest*, a shorter and more elementary work, *The Institutes of Justinian*, based upon the *Digest* and compiled by Tribonian, Theophilus and Berythus, was likewise approved.[11] The opening sentence of the first book of the *Institutes* offers a definition of "justice" and "the just" that has survived, through the centuries and through many vicissitudes, in Western jurisprudence. In Latin the sentence reads: *Justitia est constans et perpetua voluntas jus suum cuique tribuens.*[12] And in English: *The virtue of justice is the constant and*

---

[9] The internal features of the enquiry are the focus of most discussions of "natural justice" (sometimes "procedural justice") in the common law tradition. See, for example, P. Jackson, *Natural Justice* (Sweet and Maxwell, London, 1979); see also R.A. MacDonald, "Natural Justice" in *The Philosophy of Law: An Encyclopedia* (C.B. Gray ed., Garland, New York, 1999), Vol.II, pp.573–575.

[10] Gaius' *Institutes* were lost for several centuries and rediscovered by Barthold Georg Niebuhr only in 1816.

[11] So too were the *Codex* and the *Novellae*. Collectively they make up what is known as the *Corpus Iuris Civilis*. An excellent short account of Roman law is P. Ferreira da Cunha, "Roman Philosophy of Law" in *The Philosophy of Law: An Encyclopedia*, Vol.II, pp.760–762.

[12] *The Institutes of Justinian*, Book I, Title I ("Of Justice and the Just"). The *Institutes* contains four Books, each divided into several Titles and each Title into several sections and, from now on in this chapter, will be referred to in this way: *Institutes,*

enduring will (determination) to render to each what is due. The virtue or practice of justice is the habit of being just when the occasion arises and "being just" is "rendering to each what is due". The English phrase "what is due" translates "*jus suum*". A person's *jus* is that to which that person is entitled.[13]

If one is to render to another what is due, one must know what is due and to know this is not always easy. The effort to be just begins with a question that may be expressed in several ways: for example, who is entitled to what?; who owns what?; what belongs to whom?; and what is due to whom? If, say, a cat wanders into your house and you think that it belongs to someone, before you can give the cat to its owner you must discover who is the owner. Your question is: who owns this cat? If you ask the question, you are, in fact, making two very basic, banal and everyday, presuppositions. You presuppose that the cat belongs to someone and that, in most cases,[14] the owner is entitled to get the cat back. If someone persuades you that the cat is feral and belongs to no

---

I.I.1. The first numeral refers to the Book, the second to the Title, and the third to the Section.

[13] The Latin word *jus* in *jus suum* refers linguistically to *justitia* more clearly than does "what is due" refer to "justice". Another translation, then, is: *The virtue of justice is the constant and enduring will to render to each that to which he is entitled.* Yet another: ... *to render to each what belongs to him.* Thomas Hobbes, in the seventeenth century, translates the couple *Jus* and *Lex* as "Right" and "Law" but he does not mean by "Right" quite what is meant by *Jus* in the *Institutes; cf. Leviathan*, Pt I, chap.13. For Hobbes a right is freedom to do or forbear; in Roman law a right (*jus*) is an entitlement. One may, for example, have a *jus* to allow one's neighbour's drain pass through one's yard—that is, a right may be a benefit or a burden; for Hobbes a right is a benefit only. Hobbes' meaning tends to be the modern sense of the term.

[14] The idea that, in order to discover what is just, it may be insufficient to know "what is just for the most part" is very old in Western thought. The clearest early discussion is in Aristotle, *Nicomachean Ethics* (c.330 B.C.), V, 1137a.31—1138a.5. (The page numbers (*viz.* 1137a.31) are common to all modern editions whether in the original Greek or in translation. I have usually used David Ross's translation in *The Works of Aristotle* (Clarendon Press, Oxford, 1928)). The traditional name for the effort to discover what is just when the particular case does not fit easily into the mould of what is just for the most part is *epieikeia* in Greek, *aequitas* in Latin, and, from Latin, in English, "equity". Equity is a procedure or method, not a doctrine or set of laws; the practice or procedure emerges spontaneously before there is any account of it. The translation may mislead for, in the common law, this is no longer how the term is used. St Thomas Aquinas deals with the question of equity in his *Summa Theologiae* in the second part of the second part at Question 120 (II-II, q.120) and in his commentary on Aristotle: *In decem libros Ethicorum Aristotelis ad Nicomachum expositio*, Book V, Lectio. XVI. See G. Barden, "Aristotle's Notion of Epieikeia" in *Creativity and Method* (M. Lamb ed., Marquette University Press, Milwaukee, 1981) and H.G. Gadamer, *Truth and Method* (Sheed and Ward, London, 1975), p.284. There is further discussion of equity later in this chapter.

one, then you accept that the question of ownership doesn't arise. The question, "Who owns this cat?" turns out to be irrelevant if, in fact, the cat belongs to no one.

It may be difficult to discover who owns the cat but the question is hardly complex. In the famous Scottish case of *Donoghue v Stevenson*,[15] Mrs Donoghue, whose friend had bought her a bottle of ginger beer in a stone bottle and in which she found a decomposing snail, looked for redress from Mr Stevenson, the maker of the drink. Mrs Donoghue had no contract with Mr Stevenson; she had not even bought the drink herself. The question before the court was, as always: who, in this instant case, is entitled to what? Another way of phrasing precisely the same question is this: what in this situation is just? In the end the court judged that Mrs Donoghue was entitled to redress. But in coming to this judgement it did not follow an already settled rule or opinion.

The question as to who owns the cat and whether or not the owner is entitled to get the cat back or as to whether Mrs Donoghue is entitled to redress are particular cases of the more general question as to what is just, and can arise only in the context of ownership and entitlement. Where there is literally no ownership and no entitlement, the question as to what is just simply does not arise. If no one owns anything, then a question of the form "Whose is this?" is irrelevant and, if even the notion of ownership is absent, meaningless.

If the question as to who owns the cat does in fact arise, it may well be that to discover the answer to it is not at all easy and may be, in some cases in practice, impossible. It is a very simple question and it arises in particular circumstances about a particular cat; it cannot be asked or answered intelligently in the abstract. Courts deal with particular questions. We are concerned here, not with particular questions but with the form or structure of such questions: who owns what?; what belongs to whom?; and what is due to whom and from whom? This kind of question, and only this kind of question, concerns what is just. The court is, in the end, trying to answer a question of this kind although, in order to reach the answer, prior questions of a different kind may have to be raised and answered. For example, in a criminal trial where Peter is accused of fraud, the prior question is whether or not he is guilty of fraud but the final question is this: what is due to Peter if he has been found guilty of fraud? The final question in a criminal trial where an accused has been found guilty is: what is due to this guilty person? This is the question to which the sentence passed is the answer.

When "justice" and "what is just" are understood in this way, then it is clear that the virtue of justice is one virtue among others. Aristotle, in the fifth book of his *Nicomachean Ethics*, analyses justice and what is just and there

---

[15] *Donoghue v Stevenson* [1932] A.C. 562.

makes it clear that the object of his enquiry is a "justice which is a part of virtue". He refers to this object of enquiry as "particular justice".[16]

However, as Aristotle also makes plain, the word "justice", and associated words, were often used by his predecessors, by his contemporaries and sometimes by himself, as a synonym of "virtue".[17] In that usage, to be "just" is to be "good" or "virtuous".

When writing of the "good" or the "virtuous" Aristotle uses the term "the law":

> "[F]or practically the majority of the acts commanded by the law are those which are prescribed from the point of view of virtue as a whole; for the law bids us practise every virtue and forbids us to practise any vice".[18]

What Aristotle means by "law" is not a set of statutes enacted by a ruler but the commonly accepted moral rules of the community,[19] some of which, but rarely if ever all of which, may be written down.[20] We learn our morals as we learn our language.[21] We speak our language correctly without knowing

---

[16] Aristotle, *Nicomachean Ethics*, V.2, 1130b.6.

[17] *ibid.*, V.1 and 2, 1129a.1–1131a.7.

[18] *ibid.*, V.2, 1130b.23–25.

[19] Aristotle's view of the role of the ruler (the state) in the *maintenance* of the moral law and how precisely "the law has compulsive power" are important but different questions. Modern discussions of "law and morality" are sometimes debates about which moral norms are to be enshrined in and maintained by the metropolitan law and sometimes debates about whether or not a traditionally accepted moral norm is to be accepted. In the well-known debate between H.L.A. Hart and Lord Devlin on whether or not the metropolitan law should continue to make homosexual practices illegal, it is at times difficult to distinguish these quite different questions. Enough here to say that from the assertion that "the law bids us practise every virtue and forbids us to practise any vice" it does not follow that the metropolitan law of a modern state—which is what is commonly meant when people speak of "the law"— should include statutes enjoining citizens to practise every virtue and to refrain from every vice even when there is no disagreement about what are virtues and what vices. It is worth noting, in passing, that St Thomas Aquinas (*Summa Theologiae*, I-II, q.96, art.2) did not think that human positive law should forbid every vice.

[20] Whether or not it would be possible to list all of the accepted moral rules of a community is moot. Furthermore, when a person acts acceptably he is not usually "obeying a rule".

[21] On this idea see J. Gagnepain, *Du Vouloir Dire* (Pergamon, Paris, 1982). Think of speaking your own language correctly; contrast this with writing in a language other than your own that you know reasonably well. It is true that children are also instructed how to speak but more by example than by rule. On the idea of "obeying a rule", see L. Wittgenstein, *Philosophical Investigations* (Blackwell, Oxford, 1963), Pt I, 199 *et seq.*

formulated grammatical and syntactical rules.[22] The rules formulate how we speak but when we speak we only, in a very queer sense, "obey the rules". Similarly, when a person acts well he is rarely "obeying a rule". The important thing about the commonly accepted ideas of what constitutes good behaviour is not that the ideas be written down but that they be known. In many cases, the formulation of these customs in written texts is simply the statement of what is accepted and in that sense prescriptive. So a dictionary tells whomsoever consults it what the correct use and meaning of a word is accepted to be; only in that sense is a dictionary prescriptive.

Dominantly in early Greece, in the Jewish biblical and in the early Christian tradition, little if anything turns on a distinction between "good" and "just".[23] In Aristotle and, many centuries later, in Roman law, they become terms of art. Aristotle initiated the distinction between, on the one hand, "law" (*nomos, lex, loi, ley, gesetz ...*) and, on the other hand, "the just" ["right"] (*to dikaion, jus, droit, derecho, recht*).[24] A distinction often remains in later writers but it is not always the same distinction and different usages have led to considerable ambiguity in the study of jurisprudence.

Particularly in discussions of what is naturally and what is conventionally just, it is vital to determine in which sense an author is using the terms "justice"," what is just" and "the law". Students of jurisprudence will come upon references to the thirteenth century Italian theologian, St Thomas Aquinas, and to his discussion of "natural law"; more rarely will they come upon references to his discussion of the "naturally just". As noted above, his discussion of "natural law" is to be found in the *first* part of the second part of his *Summa Theologiae*; his discussion of the "naturally just" is found in the *second* part of the second part.[25] "The law" for St Thomas (as for Aristotle) treats of the whole of the moral life and, because "particular justice" (*i.e.* the giving to each what is their due) is part of the moral life, the questions are related but they are not the same. *"Natural law"* and *"what is naturally just"* are *not* the same thing.[26]

---

[22] There are no non-grammatical, non-syntactical languages; but there have been, and still are, languages, the grammar and syntax of which have not been analysed and for which, therefore, there are as yet in a sense no rules to follow.

[23] In *Genesis*, Abraham intercedes with Yahweh who intends to destroy the city of Sodom by fire: "Abraham remained standing before Yahweh. Approaching him he said, 'Will you destroy the just man with the sinner?'" *Genesis* 18:22–23. In St Matthew's Gospel, in the King James translation, the Father "maketh his sun to rise on the evil and on the good and sendeth rain on the just and the unjust". *Matthew* 5:45.

[24] See M. Villey: "Torah et to Dikaion" in *La Formation de la Pensée Juridique Moderne* (Montchrestien, Paris, 1968). See also n.3 above.

[25] See n.2 above.

[26] In a recent work, *The Philosophy of Law: An Encyclopedia*, there are articles on

The question of this chapter concerns what is naturally and what conventionally just and the justice that corresponds to each. The virtue of justice is the willingness to bring about what is just, that is, to bring about a situation in which each has what he is entitled to. So much, then, for an initial description of the way in which the term "just" is used here.

A very simple example of what is *naturally* just is that the just situation is restored when the lost cat, in the example, is restored to its owner. If one finds a wallet in a classroom, the just situation is restored when it is returned to whoever owns it. One may or may not be anxious to return the wallet, one may make no effort to discover the owner and, if one does know whose wallet it is, one may or may not return it, but none of this takes away from the simple fact that the just situation is restored when the wallet is returned. Why anyone would be interested in bringing the just situation about is an entirely different question.[27]

A simple example of what is *conventionally* just is a rule that states that a library book must be returned before five o'clock on the day when, as established by a conventional rule, it is to be returned. That the borrowed book is to be returned is natural, that is, it is intrinsic to the practice of lending and borrowing; precisely when it is to be returned is settled conventionally, legally, by agreement.

There are two features worth remembering when contrasting natural and conventional solutions. First, if a naturally just solution is to be effective in a given society it must be discovered, agreed and established in custom or statute. So there is no reason to be surprised when a discovered and agreed naturally just solution is expressed as a rule. It is, of course, obvious that until the naturally just solution is known it cannot be expressed as a rule. Secondly, a conventional solution is normally neither random nor arbitrary but is, rather, an agreed solution to a difficulty to which no "natural" solution can be discovered. Whether inheritance of land is to be according to a rule of primogeniture or of gavelkind or according to some other rule may be conventional but such rules are not arrived at arbitrarily. Some solutions as to how the estate of one who dies intestate will be conventional yet neither random nor foolish.

"Natural Law" and "Natural Rights" that simply do not deal with "what is just by nature" as this is understood here. These articles are well worth reading as a counterbalance to this chapter. As has been said, the article on "Natural Justice" deals for the most part with the just inherent in the court's procedures. Within the account of the just that is given here, "natural justice" so understood is indeed part of what is naturally just. See the final part of this chapter, "The question addressed by the court".

[27] That it would be just to act in a certain way may or may not be, for me, a reason to act in that way. In trivial as well as in important matters, what is a reason for one person may not be a reason for another. See G. Barden, *Essays on a Philosophical Interpretation of Justice: The Virtue of Justice* (Mellon, Lampeter, 1999), chap.9.

Since the virtue of justice is the enduring determination to give to each what each owns and a situation is just when each participant quietly possesses what he owns, it turns out that ownership is fundamental. In a society where, quite literally, no one in any way owns anything, including, for example, clothes or books or pens or bicycles or anything whatsoever,[28] the question as to what is just cannot arise. So we may ask: is ownership just?; is it just that humans own things? The question seems at first sight clear but on reflection turns out to be very strange. If a just situation is one in which each quietly possesses what he owns, a situation in which no one owns anything cannot be just. The question of justice is irrelevant. Neither is such a situation unjust, for an unjust situation is one in which at least one person does not quietly possess what he owns and where no one owns anything, no one lacks the possession of what he owns.

The question as to what is just arises only where people own things. How did ownership arise? Did someone invent the idea of ownership and subsequently try to persuade others of its usefulness or is it part of the spontaneous order of human society.[29] Some have feared that if human society is not an invention it must be "irrational" and, fearing this irrationality, and being unable "to conceive of an effective co-ordination of human activities without the deliberate organization by a commanding intelligence",[30] have attempted to understand society as an organisation established by the agreement of pre-social individuals. This old idea, often called "social contract theory", has been dominant, in one version or another, since the publication in 1651 of *Leviathan* by the English philosopher Thomas Hobbes. Precisely because there are several versions of social contract theory it is better to think of it as an approach rather than as a theory. In the English-speaking world at least, the best-known and most influential recent work in this approach is the American philosopher John Rawls' *A Theory of Justice*.[31] Rawls' question may be put as

---

[28] For a discussion of an attempt to do this, see O. Figes, *Natasha's Dance: A Cultural History of Russia* (Penguin Allen Lane, London, 2002), p.446. Even when a group tries to own literally everything communally, time and use are generally, perhaps necessarily, overlooked. Is the cup of coffee that I have just poured for myself, in no sense whatsoever, mine? Are the clothes that I am now wearing in no sense whatsoever mine for the time being?

[29] That human society and, within it, a trading system, is a spontaneous order and not an organisation is a constant theme in the writings of F.A. Hayek. See, for instance, *The Constitution of Liberty* (University of Chicago Press, Chicago, 1960), esp. chap.10. See also L. Von Mises, *Human Action* (Yale University Press, New Haven, 1946), Pt II, chap.VIII.

[30] F.A. Hayek, *op. cit.*, chap.10 (section 7), p.159.

[31] J. Rawls, *A Theory of Justice* (Cambridge, Mass., Harvard University Press, 1971). James Buchanan and Gordon Tulloch's *The Calculus of Consent* (University of

follows: what organisation of the distribution of income and wealth is fair? He imagines a situation in which the idea of ownership is understood and accepted and in which there is wealth and income to be distributed but in which no one yet owns anything. In this imaginary initial state, the task is to discover a distribution scheme the outcome of which will be just. One is asked to choose a distribution scheme without knowing what one's own place will be in the resultant situation. The rational person, it is supposed, will choose what he thinks best for himself but, since he is choosing blind, he will include in his calculation the chance of his being very badly off were he to choose a very unequal distribution. Rawls' suggestion is that the distribution and criterion of distribution that will be chosen by the rational person when faced with this choice will be what most would accept as just.[32]

Rawls' approach is an outstanding example of a very common way of imagining human society. The wealth, including incomes, of an entire society is imagined as, at all times, commonly owned and the important political question is how to distribute it. Rawls is not the only modern example of this approach to society. It was, in great measure, the approach taken in communist societies, and remains a very influential feature in the approach taken in modern liberal democracies.[33]

This chapter does not adopt the approach of social contract theory.[34] Rather, it supposes that humans live together, and always have lived together, in society. Humans have always owned things although what they own and how they

---

Michigan Press, Ann Arbor, 1965) also adopts a social contract approach but their question—what is the nature of collective choice?—differs from Rawls'.

[32] Later in this chapter, in the discussion of reciprocal justice, it is argued that a trading system or market order has a function but no goal and cannot guarantee a "just" outcome of the kind envisaged by Rawls. On the mirage of the "just" outcome in a market order, see F.A. Hayek, *The Fatal Conceit* (Routledge, London, 1988). See also A. de Jasay, *Against Politics* (Routledge, London, 1997).

[33] It is worth remembering that the communist economies are, for that precise reason, deliberately not market orders but, ideally and as far as practicable, centrally controlled organisations. The general question of distribution is discussed later in this chapter.

[34] The theory of contract as in any way whatsoever the origin of society is the prime and influential example of the attempt to understand society as a rational construction. Hobbes' story is that of an original contract between individuals. For earlier versions of this story of origins, see R. Tuck, *Natural Rights Theories* (Cambridge University Press, Cambridge, 1976). As stated in the text this story has dominated the modern imagination since the seventeenth century. As an account of the historical origin of human society it is in fact utterly mistaken and misleading. See G. Barden, *Essays on a Philosophical Interpretation of Justice: The Virtue of Justice*, pp.1–15. See also G. Barden, "Discovering a Constitution" in *Ireland's Evolving Constitution 1937–1997: Collected Essays* (T. Murphy and P. Twomey eds., Hart, Oxford, 1998).

own them changes over time. As they interact with one another and deal with one another in different ways, as their mode of livelihood changes, the character of their societies changes; new practices arise to replace older ones, new questions come up, new solutions are offered, accepted more or less happily by some, acquiesced in by others, transmitted from generation to generation, questioned, retained or eventually rejected. Human society is a dialectical order.

It is assumed here that ownership is present in all societies but it is not assumed that, at any one moment, what is generally accepted as owned by whomsoever, was originally justly acquired by their ancestors from whom they have inherited it. For much of the mediaeval and modern history of Europe, it was generally accepted or acquiesced in that the Prince, when powerful enough to do so, was entitled to dispossess his opponents and grant the land to his supporters. In modern liberal democracies, it is generally agreed or acquiesced in that the state is entitled to raise taxes, to acquire land through compulsory purchase and so on. In the communist states it is agreed or acquiesced in that the state, representing the people, owns everything and so becomes a vast organisation that arranges for the creation and distribution of the wealth that is common to all.

Different kinds of society exist. Within each there is ownership but the precise character of ownership differs greatly from society to society. In a hunting and gathering society discrete plots of land are not owned by individuals or individual families in the same way as they are owned in a settled agricultural society but this does not mean that land is not owned. Where discrete plots of land are not individually owned, even the idea of this kind of ownership is absent. For ideas of ownership arise as different practices emerge. In a hunting and gathering society, therefore, questions of justice arise that do not arise in an agricultural society and vice versa. A hunting and gathering or nomadic pastoral society does not become a purely or dominantly agricultural society overnight. The development is slow and as different practices of ownership emerge, ownership is understood differently and different questions as to what is just arise; for questions as to what is just arise in response to real situations that are seen as problems and have given rise to disputes. In a society within which parcels of land are not individually owned, bought and sold, obviously no question would arise as to what is to be done if someone "in good faith purchased land from another, whom he believed to be the true owner, when in fact he was not".[35] Equally, obviously, this question is very likely to arise when land is individually owned, bought and sold. We shall consider the Roman solution in more detail later in this chapter, for it is with the nature or character of these questions and with whether or not it is illuminating to distinguish the naturally and the conventionally just in the attempt to answer them that this chapter is concerned.

---

[35] *The Institutes of Justinian*, II.I.35.

3. OF LAWS AND AUTHORITIES

The object of our enquiry in this chapter is particular justice and the just that corresponds to it. But in this part, by way of contrast and precisely because of the fluidity of the term "justice" and of a tradition of natural law—and take note of the term "law" as distinct from the term "just",—in this part we shall consider Sophocles' (497–406 B.C.) tragedy *Antigone* and the Biblical story of the revelation to Moses of the Ten Commandments or Decalogue. Both, but more particularly the story of Moses, have influenced the discussion of law and justice in Europe. Both take "law" to cover the entire moral life. Both take the fundamental and accepted moral ideas of the community to be revealed and authoritative commands.

Sophocles' *Antigone*

The dramatic tension in the tragedy is the irreconcilable conflict between two ideals and its theme is the limit and legitimacy of power. Antigone's two brothers, Eteocles and Polynices, have killed one another. The ruler, Creon has buried Eteocles: he has "used him justly and with lawful rites has hid him in the earth".[36] He has forbidden any citizen to bury Polynices who "died destroying the city the other (Eteocles) defended". The play opens with a discussion between Antigone and her sister, Ismene. Ismene decides to obey Creon's edict. Antigone decides to disobey because she holds to another and higher law that commands her to bury her brother. She buries Polynices and Creon learns of her disobedience. Antigone and Creon meet and in their conversation express an idea of enormous and enduring significance in the history of Western legal and political thought:

> "CREON: ... Now, Antigone, tell me shortly and to the point, did you know the proclamation against your action?
>
> ANTIGONE: I knew it; of course I did. For it was public.
>
> CREON: And did you dare to disobey that law?
>
> ANTIGONE: Yes, it was not Zeus that made the proclamation; nor did Justice, which lives with those below, enact such laws as that, for humankind. I did not believe your proclamation had such power to enable one who will someday die to override God's ordinances, unwritten and

---

[36] The term "justly" here, although it has, in fact, to do with what is due to the dead, is not based on the distinction that Aristotle made somewhat later. Quotations from the play, unless otherwise stated, are from Sophocles, *Antigone* in *The Theban Plays* (D. Grene trans., Everyman, London, 1994). *Antigone* was written about 442 B.C.

secure. *They* are not of today and yesterday; they live forever; none knows when they first were. These are the laws, whose penalties I would not incur from the gods, through fear of any man's temper."

Sophocles makes it very clear that Antigone knew well that, in burying Polynices, she was disobeying Creon's law. The impact of the play depends upon the onlooker recognising both the general virtue of civil obedience and the importance of the supervening laws that, in another translation, " ... are not of yesterday or today, but everlasting. Though where they come from, none of us can tell."[37] There is no suggestion that Creon is an illegitimate tyrant; no suggestion that rulers may not make laws that command obedience; and no suggestion that there is some formal flaw in this edict of Creon's. According to the rule of recognition then at work in Thebes, the edict is recognisable and, to that extent, legitimate.[38] The suggestion in the play is simple: there are laws, "unwritten and secure", that set limits to the ruler's authority.

To us, who are used to statutes and who, even within the common law tradition, are the inheritors of a tradition that, dominantly since the seventeenth century, tends to equate law with the edicts of the state,[39] the couple "unwritten and secure" may be somewhat startling. We tend to think of "unwritten" as almost "unknown" or "controversial" or, perhaps, underhand. For the ancients, on the other hand, the "unwritten" was so clear, so well known, so well established and, sometimes, so important, that it did not need to be written down. The unwritten was, sometimes and in some respects, more secure than the written. And, sometimes, as we shall see below (in our discussion of the Ten Commandments or Decalogue), the written is simply the writing down of the already well-known and accepted unwritten.

Unwritten laws did not necessarily supervene upon written laws. In the *Rhetoric* Aristotle writes of "particular laws by which I mean those established by each people in reference to themselves, which again are divided into written

---

[37] This translation is from *Antigone* in *The Theban Plays* (E.F. Watling trans., Penguin, Harmondsworth, 1947).

[38] On the rule of recognition, see H.L.A. Hart, *The Concept of Law* (Clarendon Press, Oxford, 1961). Hans Kelsen's "basic norm" in his "pure theory of law" is an acknowledgement of the importance of such a rule. For a legitimate command to exist, those to whom it is addressed must be able to recognise it as a command addressed to them that emanates from a source that they already accept as the legitimate source of commands relating to them. See G. Barden, "Legality" in *The Philosophy of Law: An Encyclopedia*, Vol.II, pp.489–491.

[39] *cf.* Thomas Hobbes, *Leviathan*, Pt II, chap.26: "And first it is manifest that Law in generall is not Counsell, but Command ...".

and unwritten".[40] Written and unwritten laws may be of equal status;[41] and, obviously, for peoples without writing, all laws are, necessarily, unwritten. In the *Rhetoric* particular laws are distinguished from general laws: "by general laws I mean those based upon nature". The translation "general laws" can easily mislead; Aristotle does not mean "laws of a very general character" but rather "laws that are found generally prevailing among different peoples". And by "laws" is not meant commands or edicts but rather "usages", "customs", "traditions". These are common to different peoples because these customs or usages are intelligent answers to very ordinary and recurrent problems that are common to different peoples. [42] It is easy to overlook the very obvious point that these customs and traditions, no matter what their source, to be effective must be known, promulgated, and accepted.[43]

In Sophocles' play, Antigone pits the unwritten, secure, eternal, divine, law against Creon's edict. The laws to which Antigone appeals are from the gods and no edicts of the ruler may, rightly, override them. The conflict in *Antigone* is a conflict of laws: which of two conflicting laws is to prevail? In dispute with Haemon, his son and Antigone's fiancé, Creon makes the claim that what he, the ruler, determines to be right for the security of the city is right:

> "HAEMON: No city is the possession of one man.
>
> CREON: Does not the city belong to the ruler?"[44]

The play rests on the contrast between the state and the laws of the gods that govern humans and human society more profoundly than can the laws of the sovereign.

In the *Rhetoric*, Aristotle, referring to the passage in *Antigone* where the

---

[40] Aristotle, *The Art of Rhetoric*, I.xiii.1373b.9–13.

[41] *cf. The Institutes of Justinian*, I.II.3.

[42] This is close to the definition of *jus gentium* in the *Institutes*, I.II.2: "The law of nations (*jus gentium*) is common to all mankind, for all peoples have established certain laws, as occasion and the necessities of human life required".

[43] There are several strands in positivism—a theory of law that is often presented as antagonistic to "natural" law; one of these strands is that positive law is the law actually in place and it is perfectly clear in *Antigone* that both Creon's command and the laws of the gods are in place; in that sense, both are positive laws. The idea that positive law is the law actually in place is akin to the idea that for a law to be effective it must be promulgated. See St Thomas Aquinas, *Summa Theolgiae*, I-II, q.91, art.1.

[44] Earlier in the play Creon claims that "the man the city sets up in authority must be obeyed in all things—just and unjust".

heroine is confronted by Creon, writes: "In fact, there is a general idea of just and unjust in accordance with nature, as all in a manner discern, even if there is neither communication nor agreement between them. This is what Antigone in Sophocles evidently means, when she declares that it is just, though forbidden, to bury Polynices, as being naturally just".[45] Antigone has appealed to divine and eternal laws but the content of the laws is family piety within the accepted religion of the time. Aristotle interprets her appeal as an appeal to what is naturally just. His meaning seems to be that these laws are "general" or "common", that is, commonly found in human society, not laws peculiar to a particular people or a particular state.

Family piety, the content of the eternal law to which Antigone appeals, is in fact a commonly discovered value. It is found in *Deuteronomy* as one of the teachings of the Decalogue; it is found in the *Analects* of Confucius: "When proper respect towards the dead is shown at the end and continued after they are far away, the moral force of a people has reached its highest point".[46] Similar teachings are found in ancient Hindu teaching,[47] and in *The Koran*.[48] The suggestion is that what is morally good is both discovered and common to humans. Against this is the opinion that the morally good is simply an imposition on a morally neutral situation. As the seventeenth century English jurist, John Selden, has it: "I cannot fancy to myself what the Law of Nature means, but the Law of God. How should I know I ought not to steal, I ought not to commit Adultery, unless somebody had told me so?"[49] The contrast between these divergent opinions is present from the beginning of moral, political and legal thinking in Greek thought and thence in Jewish, Christian and Islamic reflection. Plato (c.429–347 B.C.), Aristotle's teacher, argues the case with Protagoras in the dialogue of that name. For Protagoras, the human good is simply what

---

[45] Aristotle, *The Art of Rhetoric*, I.xiii.1373b.9–13. Aristotle does not here use the term "naturally just" with the same precision as he does in the *Nicomachean Ethics*. See G. Barden, "Two Versions of Natural Justice" in *Justice and Legal Theory in Ireland* (G. Quinn, A. Ingram and S. Livingstone eds., Oak Tree Press, Dublin, 1995), pp.37–44.

[46] *Deuteronomy* 5:16; *Analects*, I.9 (see also II.6.7 and 8).

[47] "Your Father is an image of the Lord of Creation, your Mother an image of the Earth. For whomsoever fails to honour them, every work of piety is vain. This is the first duty." *Janet*, i.9. Quoted in C.S. Lewis, *The Abolition of Man* (Fount, London, 1978), in the Appendix, where other examples from many sources are to be found.

[48] "Your Lord has enjoined you to worship none but Him and to show kindness to your parents. If either or both of them attain old age in your dwelling, show them no sign of impatience, nor rebuke them; but speak to them kind words." *The Koran*, "The Night Journey", 17:23.

[49] J. Selden, *Table-Talk: Being the Discourses of John Selden* (1689), chap.78.

each one decides for himself or, in the state, what the ruler decides.[50] For Plato, as for Aristotle, the human good is to be discovered, not simply decided.[51]

The Decalogue

How is the good to be discovered and agreed? In *Antigone* the laws that Antigone claims overcome the edicts of the ruler are, as a matter of social fact, known, agreed and almost beyond question.[52] In the other great story of fundamental laws that has greatly influenced European moral, legal and political thought, the Hebraic story of Moses, the divine origin of the laws is equally crucial.

Stories of the divine origin of basic laws are found in most cultures. *Antigone* and the story of Moses are discussed here because of their considerable influence on later thinking about law. From them come two ideas of great significance: first, that the good is revealed; secondly, that the good is what the lawgiver commands. From the first of these ideas comes the association between the divine law and "natural law" in one of the many, and certainly one of the most influential, meanings of the term; from the second, comes legal positivism.

In the *Torah* the laws defining and governing the people of Israel are set out.[53] Yahweh reveals these laws to Moses who brings them to the people. Of

---

[50] "The ruler" may be a king, a dictator, an elected government, the whole people acting in unison.

[51] Plato and Aristotle differ sharply in their accounts as to precisely how the good is to be discovered; but that it is to be discovered and is not simply the object of one's present desire they agree. Contrast their view with that of Thomas Hobbes in *Leviathan*: "But whatsoever is the object of any man's Appetite or Desire; that is it, which he for his part calleth *Good* ...". And yet in Hobbes, too, the Sovereign's legitimate power is limited and derives from contract, for no one will agree to be ruled by one who seeks the subject's ruin.

[52] Were they utterly and unequivocally beyond question there would be no dramatic tension; the members of the audience would see Creon as simply and unequivocally wrong and Antigone as simply and unequivocally right.

[53] The *Torah* is the Jewish Bible or, from the Christian perspective, the Old Testament. *Torah* is sometimes used to refer to the first five books: *Genesis, Exodus, Leviticus, Numbers and Deuteronomy*. The word *torah* "comes from a Hebrew root meaning 'to point the way, give direction'... It becomes evident that to translate Torah by the word law (as is commonly done) is, while not entirely erroneous, a grave distortion of its full meaning". L.H. Silberman, "Judaism" in *The New Encylopædia Britannica* (15th ed., Micropaedia, Chicago, 1984), Vol.X, p.286. The image of *torah* is found as *tâo* in Confucius and in Lao Tzu: "*Tâo* means literally a road, a path, a way. Hence, the way in which anything is done, the way in which, for example, a kingdom is ruled: a method, a principle, a doctrine". Confucius, *The Analects* (A. Waley trans., Everyman ed., 2000), from the Translator's Preface, pp.23–24.

the very many, sometimes very detailed, laws governing ritual and everyday life, some stand out as of greater importance, namely, the Ten Words of the Covenant, that became known as the Decalogue from the Greek ["ten words"] or, in English, Ten Commandments.

The first thing to notice about these commandments is their divine origin. There are several slightly different versions of this story but crucial to each one is that the law is revealed by Yahweh.[54]

> "Yahweh said to Moses, 'Come up to me on the mountain and stay there while I give you the stone tablets—the law and the commandments— that I have written for your instruction…'. The cloud covered the mountain and the glory of Yahweh settled on the mountain of Sinai; for six days the cloud covered it, and on the seventh day Yahweh called to Moses from inside the cloud. To the eyes of the sons of Israel the glory of Yahweh seemed like a devouring fire on the mountain top. Moses went right into the cloud. He went up the mountain and stayed there for forty days and forty nights."[55]

The laws are revealed by Yahweh, through Moses, to the Israelites who are already a people, who already accept Yahweh as their God and Moses as their leader. The revelation, then, is not only the revelation of the content of the laws but the revelation of their truth and their importance. As in *Antigone*, the security of the laws derives from their divine origin because of which they are both sacred and unquestionable. The question as to how the human good is to be discovered and agreed is settled before it is asked. The Ten Words are beyond question because their source is the revelation by Yahweh to Moses. And what Yahweh teaches is true and trustworthy.[56] It is, however, worth

---

[54] As well as the two slightly different versions of the Ten Words in *Deuteronomy* and *Exodus*, there are other longer compilations that include many or all of the commands, e.g. *Exodus* 34 and throughout *Leviticus*. Very similar teachings are to be found in *The Koran*, e.g. 17:22–17:38.

[55] *Exodus* 24:12–18. The great significance of the revelation is shown by the reference to the six days when the cloud stayed on the mountain and the seventh day when Yahweh called Moses—an image that recalls the creation of the world as recounted in *Genesis*. The 40 days and 40 nights recalls the great flood and prefigures the Israelites 40 years wandering in the desert before reaching the Promised Land. The image of 40 days and 40 nights recurs frequently in the Jewish Bible (Old Testament), for example, in the story of Noah in which the great flood follows 40 days and 40 nights of rain, and it is taken up in the New Testament in the story of Christ's fasting in the desert and in the lapse of time between the Resurrection and the Ascension.

[56] "But, Yahweh, you are close/And all your commandments are true/Long have I known that your decrees were founded to last forever." *Psalm* 119:151–152. C.S. Lewis

examining the content of the Decalogue. The versions in *Exodus* and *Deuteronomy* differ slightly. The version from *Deuteronomy* (5:1–22) is given here:

> "On the mountain from the heart of the fire, Yahweh spoke to you face to face, and I stood all the time between Yahweh and yourselves to tell you of Yahweh's words, for you were afraid of the fire and had not gone up the mountain. He said:
>
> 1. I am Yahweh your God who brought you out of the land of Egypt, out of the house of slavery. You shall have no gods except me.
>
> 2. You shall not make yourself a carved image or any likeness of anything in heaven above or on earth beneath or in the waters under the earth; you shall not bow down to them or serve them. For I, Yahweh your God, am a jealous God and I punish the fathers' fault in the sons, the grandsons and the great-grandsons of those who hate me; but I show kindness to thousands, to those who love me and keep my commandments.
>
> 3. You shall not utter the name of Yahweh your God to misuse it, for Yahweh will not leave unpunished the man who utters his name to misuse it.
>
> 4. Observe the sabbath day and keep it holy, as Yahweh your God has commanded you. For six days you shall labour and do all your work, but the seventh day is a sabbath for Yahweh your God. You shall do no work that day, neither you nor your son nor your daughter nor your servants, men or women, nor your ox nor your donkey nor any of your animals, nor the stranger who lives with you. Thus your servant, man or woman, shall rest as you do. Remember that you were a servant in the land of Egypt, and that Yahweh your God brought you out from there with mighty hand and outstretched arm; because of this, Yahweh your God has commanded you to keep the sabbath day.
>
> 5. Honour your father and your mother, as Yahweh your God has commanded you, so that you may have long life and may prosper in the land that Yahweh your God gives to you.
>
> 6. You shall not kill.
>
> 7. You shall not commit adultery.
>
> 8. You shall not steal.
>
> 9. You shall not bear false witness against your neighbour.

---

remarks in *The Abolition of Man* that "true" here translates *emeth*, a word associated with "trustworthy", "reliable" (p.28).

10. You shall not covet your neighbour's wife, nor set your heart on his house, his field, his servant—man or woman—his ox, his donkey or anything that is his.

These are the words Yahweh spoke to you when you were all assembled on the mountain. With a great voice he spoke to you from the heart of the fire, in cloud and thick darkness. He added nothing, but wrote them on two tablets of stone which he gave to me."[57]

As mentioned above, the version in *Exodus* (20:1–21) is slightly different,[58] but, in both, the Decalogue is divided into two parts. In the first part are four commandments, each concerned with the relation between Yahweh and his people. They are clearly conventional in that, in the story, they set out the terms of a covenant. There is not the least suggestion that they are, in any of the later senses of the term, "natural". This theoretical question arose much later and simply did not occur to the authors of *Deuteronomy* and *Exodus*.

Each of the remaining six commandments concerns the relation of the people among themselves, how they are to act with one another. The startling thing about them is their extreme ordinariness. They are so commonplace, yet so basic, that it is difficult to imagine a human society surviving without these rules being followed by most people most of the time.[59] Every human society

---

[57] *The Jerusalem Bible*, p.103. Some scholars suggest that each commandment was originally as short as are the sixth, seventh, eighth, ninth and tenth and that the enlargements to the first five is the work of later editors. In some Christian traditions, the injunction against graven images is omitted and the tenth divided into two parts. The injunction against images survives in Judaism, is taken up and survives in Sunni Islam, the larger of the two Islamic traditions, but not in the Iranian Shia tradition, and in Christianity, it has been the source of serious dispute in the eight and ninth centuries with the Iconoclasts ("image-breakers") in the Byzantine Empire and in the seventeenth century with the Puritans.

[58] For example, in the commandment concerning the sabbath, the fourth, *Exodus* gives the days of creation as the reason why the people should rest on that day: "For in six days Yahweh made the heavens and the earth and the sea and all that these hold, but on the seventh day he rested; that is why Yahweh has blessed the sabbath day and made it sacred".

[59] Some defenders of natural law—John Finnis is an outstanding example—write of "human flourishing". See J.M. Finnis, *Natural Law and Natural Rights* (Clarendon Press, Oxford, 1980). However "human flourishing" is understood, and it is both difficult and usually unnecessary to make it technically exact, it should be remembered that humans are inescapably—and in that sense "naturally"—social animals and can flourish only in society. The fundamental rules—that are discovered and lived before they are formulated almost as the formulated grammar of a language follows usage—describe the limits outside of which human society would descend into the chaos of "the natural condition" imagined by Hobbes where "the life of man [would be] solitary, poore, nasty, brutish and short". *Leviathan*, Pt I, chap.13.

has developed some idea of the proper relationship between children and their natural or social parents. Societies in which the child's mother's oldest brother is the most important male relative have ideas about the relationship between them. Every human society has a rule against killing. They differ in the precise range of the rule and each society in its own development over time and experience has thought about and refined the basic rule. Adultery occurs in every society but, again, in every society there is found some rule dealing with what is considered to be the proper arrangement of sex and procreation. No society lacks private property—that is, no society lacks the ideas of "mine", "yours", "his", "hers", "ours", "theirs"—although what is privately owned and the detailed rules governing inheritance and other transfer of property differ greatly. A rule against stealing is not added to the idea of ownership; it is, rather, an intrinsic part of the idea. It is impossible to steal what is not owned and if one may take whatever one likes whenever one likes there is no ownership but merely physical possession.[60] There is no society in which disputes do not arise. Witnesses do, of course, lie and bear false witness but the possibility of resolving disputes rests on the, often remote, possibility of discovering what happened. False witness renders the resolution of disputes difficult and, in the limit, impossible. Finally, the desire to have what another owns is common. Jealousy and envy are both common and corrosive. To allow them grow until they overmaster, leads, almost inevitably, to stealing, disregard of ownership, sometimes to murder and towards the collapse of the social order.

The first set of commandments is religious in as much as it tells of the people's relation with Yahweh, their God. The second set is religious only in that it is present in the story as revealed by Yahweh but, in themselves, the commands are entirely secular. Not alone are they secular but it is more than plausible to think of them as basic to any human social order. Humans live and must live in a social order; a social order is not the invention of pre-social individuals and the good of the individual—however this good is understood—cannot be achieved independently of the social order.[61] They are "natural" in that similar rules are commonly found and deal with very basic and commonplace features of any human social order. They express what the Romans were later to call the "law of nations" or *jus gentium* that is "common to all mankind, for all peoples have established certain laws, as occasion and the necessities of human life required".[62]

---

[60] Ownership is an institutional (Neil MacCormick and Ota Weinberger) or jural (Barden) fact; possession is a "physical"—by some called a "natural"—fact. See N. MacCormick and O. Weinberger, *Institutional Theory of Law* (Kluwer, Dordrecht, 1986) and G. Barden, *Essays on a Philosophical Interpretation of Justice*.

[61] *cf.* G. Barden, *Essays on a Philosophical Interpretation of Justice*, pp.6–7.

[62] *The Institutes of Justinian*, I.II.2.

In both the Greek and the Hebrew story, the divine and mysterious origin of basic laws is paramount. In both stories law is, at least to some extent, thought of as command, as an instruction given by a lawgiver to those already bound to obey. In *Antigone* the dramatic question is to discover which of two lawgivers is superior in case of conflict; in *Exodus* and *Deuteronomy* the lawgiver is Yahweh and the opening sentence and the first of the ten commandments of the Decalogue state that he is the lawgiver and that the Israelites are bound to obey. Indeed, from the beginning of the *Torah* and in the other books of what in Christianity is known as the Old Testament, Yahweh is present as lawgiver and the religious history of the Israelites is a history of obedience and disobedience to Yahweh.

It is, therefore, not surprising that in Western moral, political and legal thought, law is often thought of as command. In the surrounding context of the different story of origins associated with social contract theory, the seventeenth-century English philosopher, Thomas Hobbes, defines law thus:

> "By Civill Lawes, I understand the Lawes, that men are therefore bound to observe, because they are members, not of this, or that, Common-wealth in particular, but of a Common-wealth … my designe being not to shew what is Law here, and there; but what is Law; as *Plato*, *Aristotle*, *Cicero*, and divers others have done, without taking upon them the profession of the study of the Law.
>
> And first it is manifest, that Law in generall, is not Counsell, but Command; nor a Command of any man to any man; but only of him, whose Command is addressed to one formerly obliged to obey him. And as for Civill Law, it addeth only the name of the person Commanding, which is *Persona Civitatis*, the Person of the Common-wealth."[63]

This definition of the term "law" is not invented by Hobbes but he states it very clearly and this way of using the term has become so commonplace that any other seems odd, if not perverse. There is, of course, a problem. Law is command but "only of him, whose Command is addressed to one formerly obliged to obey him". Three centuries later, the English jurist, H.L.A. Hart, in *The Concept of Law*, addresses the same problem when he asks how we are to distinguish between a legitimate command—a law—and the bank-robber's command to the teller to hand over the contents of the safe.[64] This problem is not solved in either the Greek or the Hebrew story; it is simply not adverted to.

---

[63] T. Hobbes, *Leviathan*, Pt II, chap.26.

[64] See H.L.A. Hart, *The Concept of Law* (Clarendon Press, Oxford, 1961). See also Hans Kelsen, *Pure Theory of Law* (M. Knight trans., University of California Press, Berkeley, 1967). This is the translation of the 1960 edition of Kelsen's *Reine Rechtslehre*. The first edition was published in Vienna in 1934.

The authority of the lawgiver is taken for granted; Yahweh, Zeus and, in the city, the Ruler are understood to be legitimate Commanders. The Civil Law adds the name of the person Commanding; that is, it identifies the legitimate lawgiver; in Hart's terms, the metropolitan law—the law of a particular jurisdiction; what the Romans called "civil law"—includes a rule of recognition; in Hans Kelsen the "basic norm" legitimates authority.

If the term "law" is understood exclusively in this way, then a "natural law" must be understood as, in some sense, a "natural" command. But if there is a natural command there must be, by definition, a natural commander or lawgiver. Who is the natural Person Commanding? In the Hebrew tradition, the Western Christian tradition and the Islamic tradition the only possible answer is that it is God and now the "natural law" is identified with the "divine law" that can be known only in as much as it is promulgated. There are other possibilities but prominent in many versions of natural law is the idea that the "natural law" is an unwritten but nonetheless somehow formulated and known set of precepts antecedent and superior to any later laws.

Behind all such versions is, however obscurely, the assumption that law is command. I have indicated two sources of this idea and have suggested that "law" need not be understood in this way. However, since the present topic is not "natural law" but "natural justice" I have done no more than suggest this. In the next part of the chapter, on the discovery of what is naturally just, it is utterly crucial to keep in mind that to discover what is naturally just does not involve discovering formulations antecedent and superior to civil law. This has to be insisted upon, so deeply ingrained is the presumption that a contrast between what is just by nature and what is just by convention must be a contrast between superior and inferior laws. *Antigone* is the dramatic presentation of a conflict between laws. The theory of the contrast between the natural and the conventional put forward here is emphatically not a theory of such a conflict.

4. The Discovery of what is Naturally Just

In both the Greek and Hebrew influences on subsequent reflection on morality in the West, the law covered the entire moral life, "for the law", as Aristotle writes in the *Nicomachean Ethics*, "bids us practise every virtue and forbids us to practise any vice", and again, "the majority of the acts commanded by the law are those which are prescribed from the point of view of virtue taken as a whole".[65] This is not a theory of law but a description of what as a matter of fact the law was understood to be.

When Aristotle analyses the moral life as a whole he discusses the distinct

---

[65] Aristotle, *Nicomachean Ethics*, V.2, 1130b.23.

virtues—courage, temperance, liberality, good temper, friendliness and so on—
that make it up. The virtue of justice is one virtue among many, when by
"justice" is meant what Aristotle calls "particular justice"; it is not the whole
of virtue but a particular virtue that has to do with "rendering to each one what
is due". In this part, we turn to an examination of this "particular justice",
keeping in mind the original question as to the distinction between what is
naturally and what is conventionally just.

The virtue of justice is the settled determination to render to each what is
due. The practice of the virtue of justice demands that one knows what is due
and so the question of justice is always of this form: what belongs to whom?
This question is not yet a moral question. Only when one has discovered what
is just, does the personal, practical or properly moral question arise, namely,
will I on this occasion, in these circumstances, be just?[66]

In reflecting on the distinction between the naturally and the conventionally
just it is worth following the traditional distinction between distributive,
rectificatory and reciprocal justice.[67]

Distributive justice

Distributive justice is involved when what is shared is to be distributed among
those who share it. Examples are easy to find. In a raffle or lottery, the ticket
holders are shareholders in the prize which is to be distributed among them

---

[66] By a "moral question" is meant a question as to what one will do. The moral question
arises within the domain of deliberation and choice; morality is not a subcategory of
choice. But the question as to what is just is not a moral question. "Who owns this
cat?", "What is due to those involved when someone buys land in good faith from
someone that he believes to be the owner but who in fact is not?" are not yet moral
questions. "Now that I have discovered who owns this cat, what am I going to do
about it?" "Now that I have determined what is due in case of the mistakenly bought
land, what am I going to do about it?"—these are moral questions. The virtue of
justice is within the moral domain precisely because the question—Will I on this
occasion do what is just?—is a question about what one will do. On the moral or
ethical domain, see G. Barden, *After Principles* (Notre Dame University Press, Notre
Dame, 1990), chap.2.

[67] The distinction stems from Aristotle's *Nicomachean Ethics* although it is commonly
thought that he distinguished, not three, but two kinds of justice—distributive and
rectificatory—and, indeed, he does so explicitly at V, 1131a.30 *et seq.*; and in this
place he considers transactions to be part of rectifcatory justice; but later in the
book (at V, 1133b.30) he introduces reciprocal justice and there analyses transactions.
There is some incoherence in the presentation probably owing to the fact that the
Nicomachean Ethics are more lecture notes than a fully worked out book. Whatever
the better interpretation of Aristotle, it would seem to be more theoretically
illuminating to distinguish justice into three kinds.

according to some agreed method of random selection. In the distribution of political offices, positions are distributed, according to some agreed criterion, among eligible candidates. In cases of separation or divorce, what was jointly owned by the couple is to be divided between husband and wife according to some more or less explicit criterion or set of criteria, either agreed between them or set down by the court. The shareholders in a firm, who jointly own the firm, receive an annual dividend according to a criterion—in this case, according to the number of shares held. In an examination, marks are distributed to a candidate relative to the quality of his paper. In a race, the prize is given according to an agreed criterion, normally, to the runner who finishes first. No question of distributive justice can arise unless it is presupposed that what is to be distributed is jointly owned by those among whom it is to be distributed.[68]

In every human society at any moment in its history there is some pattern of ownership, normally largely accepted or acquiesced in but sometimes in some respects disputed. Some things will be owned by individuals; there is no human society where nothing whatsoever is individually owned. Some things will be jointly owned but precisely what is jointly owned and how it is owned will significantly differ from society to society and, within the one society, from time to time, during the course of its development. So, for example, as a society develops over centuries from hunting and gathering to settled agriculture, the pattern of the ownership of land will change. As patterns of ownership change, the detailed questions within the scope of distributive justice will change.

Precisely how land ownership moved from joint to individual ownership as a society moved from hunting and gathering to settled agriculture is a historical question and there is no reason to suppose that the changes were brought about solely by virtuous transactions. In the history of Europe, for example, changes in the ownership of parcels of land have sometimes come about through agreed sale, sometimes through gift or inheritance, sometimes through force. And what is true of Europe in this regard is also true elsewhere. Some of these changes in ownership have been within the sphere of distributive justice. In the great communist experimental upheaval of ownership in the twentieth century, the ownership of land and other sources of wealth shifted from private individuals or the *mir* to the state.[69] Nonetheless, there were

---

[68] All questions arise upon presuppositions. Thus, the question, "How shall we share this among us?" arises upon the presupposition, however it is arrived at, that "this" belongs jointly to us. On questions and presuppositions, see R.G. Collingwood, *An Essay on Metaphysics* (Clarendon Press, Oxford, 1940).

[69] The *mir* was "originally a self-governing community of peasant households that elected its own officials and controlled local forest, fisheries, hunting grounds and vacant lands. During the seventeenth and eighteenth centuries, as the peasants were enserfed, the scope of peasant self-government was restricted. Nevertheless, to make

questions of distributive justice, for state or publicly-owned positions had to be distributed.

In modern representative democracies, it is, for the most part, taken for granted that the state is entitled to raise taxes from various sources and, from the taxes raised, to pay for its own bureaucracy and a vast array of goods. All this is within the sphere of distributive justice and, evidently, must be largely conventional. Beneath the detailed agreements regarding the distribution of tax revenue, there is the suspicion that the criterion of distribution is not to be simply the will of the parliamentary majority or government. The criterion of distribution is itself open to public discussion and there is a sense, however confused, that the criterion is to be discovered, not simply decided.

The history of the distribution of the franchise among those living in a jurisdiction illustrates this. It is manifestly true that those who are entitled to be electors is settled by statute from time to time. At present, in many representative democracies the extent of the franchise is not, as a matter of fact, much disputed. For example, where citizens of 18 years of age are entitled to be electors, there is little clamour for the age limit to be reduced to 16 or 14 and none that it be raised to 21 or 25. But, as is well known, that every citizen, irrespective of sex or financial situation, should be enfranchised was not always accepted. Why do we accept an age limit? There is clearly something conventional, even somewhat arbitrary, about setting the lower limit at 18 but also clearly something else at work; perhaps the conviction that most people at 18 are capable of coming to a reasonable decision about which candidate to vote for. No doubt 10-year-old children are excluded on the grounds that they are incapable. And here again is something based on an understanding of the nature of the case. But perhaps children are excluded because they are dependent on their parents or guardians and so do not contribute to the community as do adults. One of the reasons against extending the franchise to women was that women were incapable of coming to a reasonable decision; equally based on an understanding, although a mistaken one, of the nature of the case. These examples show that: (1) convention is neither arbitrary nor fanciful; and (2) that what is thought to be the nature of the case, depends, and must depend, on one's fallible understanding of the nature of the case.

---

taxes imposed on its members more equitable, the *mir* assumed communal control of the community's arable land and periodically distributed it among the households according to their sizes (from 1720). ... The system was also favoured by Slavophiles and political conservatives, who regarded it as a guardian of old national values, as well as by revolutionary Narodniki (Populists), who viewed the *mir* as the germ of a future socialist society. The *mir* was effectively destroyed after Prime Minister P.A. Stolypin initiated a series of agricultural reforms, encouraging peasants to leave the commune and assume private ownership of land (1906)." *The New Encyclopaedia Britannica*, 15th ed., Vol.VI, p.927.

The manner of distributing seats in parliament in representative democracies is also largely conventional. Each elector has one vote. How obvious and unquestionable is this? How obviously and unquestionably wrong would it be to suggest that electors between 18 and 30 were to have one vote each; those between 30 and 60, two votes each; those over 60, one vote each? Once one has moved from unanimity to some form of majority rule, the question as to which form of majority election is to be chosen arises and this is largely conventional but within limits set by an understanding of the nature of the situation. Why else would it be obviously and unquestionably correct to refuse a criterion based on height or weight or hair colour? And why is it that a criterion apparently based on skin colour is never that in reality but is always based on some understanding of the nature of the difference between, say, white and black people?[70] The effort to discover who commonly owns that which is to be distributed among the owners is, at least in part, an effort to understand the nature of the situation. When someone, who is not yet considered to be an owner, claims to be, the claim will be based either on the fact that he fulfils the present criterion or that the criterion should be changed. Oddly enough, it can happen that the criterion in force as it is understood, under which the claimant has no present entitlement, is actually based on criteria under which the claimant would qualify. For example, if women are excluded from the franchise, the criterion in force distinguishes between men and women and the female claimant has no present entitlement but, if on examination, it is discovered that the criterion distinguishes between men and women on the mistaken grounds that men are capable of reasonable judgement whereas women are not, then, when it is recognised that the grounds are mistaken, the female claimant qualifies under the deeper understanding of the criterion.

Notice that when it is said that something is commonly owned, there must already be some, at least inchoate, idea of how to identify those who own it, the manner in which they own it and the manner in which ownership is to be shared among them. The members of a hunting and gathering group commonly own their hunting ground; they own it as land over which they hunt; they share it in as much as each knows which part of it is his for the present hunt. How more precisely they do this is part of the common sense of the group and is taught to children as they grow up in the community. The owners know in practice what it is they own, how they own it and how shares in it are to be distributed. How the practice grew up and became commonly accepted is a difficult, often impossible, question to answer. The nearly overwhelming rationalist temptation to resort to a form of social contract theory and suppose that it began with a sovereign doling out shares is to be resisted.

---

[70] It is nonetheless remarkable that colour has never been the reason given for discrimination but always the sign of something else; the same is true of discrimination on grounds of sex.

Distributive justice is not benevolence; nor does it supplant benevolence. A very simple example may illustrate this. If a group of children is given a bar of chocolate, the children in the group commonly own the chocolate and each is entitled to a share when it is distributed among them. If they consider themselves as equals for this purpose—they will not, and cannot, be equals for all purposes—they will conclude that each should receive an equal share. This is an example of distributive justice and each member of the group has a right or entitlement to his share. But if one of a group of children has a bar of chocolate that properly belongs to him, he may or may not decide to share it with the others. If he decides to share it with them, this is an example of benevolence and none of the others has a right or entitlement to a share.

Rectificatory Justice

Rectificatory justice—also known as commutative or corrective justice —comes into play when one person has, wrongly, what belongs to another.[71] Examples are ready to hand and commonplace. Suppose that Peter goes to a restaurant and, after his dinner, leaves, taking with him by mistake, the umbrella that belongs to Paul. Peter now possesses what belongs to Paul. He does not yet know this, having taken the umbrella in error. Paul may not yet have discovered his loss. No one, perhaps, yet knows what is, in fact, the case. It begins to rain and Peter puts up what he thinks is his umbrella only to discover that it is not. He now knows that he has in his possession an umbrella that, justly, belongs to another. He knows, too, that the just situation will be restored if he brings the umbrella back to the restaurant, discovers who owns it and restores it to its owner. The unjust situation would then be rectified. It is important to notice that a situation may be unjust although no one has knowingly acted unjustly. In other words, an unjust situation may be brought about by mistake.

Suppose, now, a situation similar in some respects. After his dinner, Peter goes to the umbrella stand, sees another's umbrella that he prefers to his own, takes it and leaves. Once again, he possesses what belongs to another. The difference, of course, is that he knows this and, having no interest in justice, has no intention of rectifying the unjust situation. Whether or not the situation can be rectified and, if it can, how it is to be rectified, are important but different questions.

In both cases, Peter has, wrongly, what belongs to another; unknowingly and indeliberately in the first case; knowingly and deliberately in the second. In both cases, the situation is unjust. The possibility of there being an unjust situation and so a need for rectificatory justice rests on things being owned.

---

[71] See the interesting discussion, under the title "Corrective Justice", by Richard Ponser in *The Philosophy of Law: An Encyclopedia*, Vol.I, pp.163–165.

Peter can neither take in error nor steal Paul's umbrella unless Paul owns the umbrella. If, quite literally, nothing in any way whatsoever belongs to anyone then to steal is impossible and so no question of what is just or unjust can arise. A rule against stealing would be irrelevant where there was no ownership, where nothing in any sense belonged to anyone at any time. Where there was not even the idea of ownership, stealing and a rule against it would be literally unintelligible.

Stealing is traditionally thought to be naturally unjust. This must mean that where there is ownership stealing is unjust and that, in turn, must mean that the ideas of ownership and of stealing fit together. Just as one cannot understand stealing without understanding ownership, so the understanding of ownership includes an understanding that stealing is unjust, that is, it includes an understanding of the fact that stealing brings about an unjust situation. Someone convinced that it was in no sense unjust that Peter took Paul's umbrella simply does not understand what is meant when the umbrella is said to belong to Paul.[72]

A comparison of two situations can show the distinction between the conventional and the natural. Suppose that Peter and Paul live in a community in which there is a legitimate formulated rule, commandment or law against stealing. If Peter steals Paul's umbrella he has broken the rule. Suppose that they live in a community in which there is a legitimate formulated rule requiring that they make their monthly V.A.T. returns to the Revenue. If Peter fails to make his returns he has broken the rule. The question about the natural and the conventional is this: are the two situations similar in that both may be adequately described by saying that in each case Peter broke a rule?

In the Aristotelian-Roman-Thomist understanding of the difference between the naturally and the conventionally just, the first situation concerns the natural and the second the conventional. The rule governing the making of V.A.T. returns is conventional: "it is originally indifferent but when it has been laid down it is not indifferent" that V.A.T. returns be made monthly.[73] The rule forbidding stealing, on the other hand, is thought to be an understanding and a formulation of what is naturally or intrinsically unjust and that no human decision can make just.[74] And what is naturally or intrinsically just or unjust is

---

[72] It is important to distinguish between: (a) the fact that stealing brings about an unjust situation; and (b) the moral demand and the decision not to steal. A person may well recognise that his action will bring about an unjust situation without agreeing that he should not, or will not, bring it about.

[73] Aristotle, *Nicomachean Ethics*, V.2, 1134b.19. Notice that in making V.A.T. returns the business is not paying tax but acting as tax collector. When it is said that the rule that this be done is legitimate, many assumptions are made. The dispute, discussed above, between Creon and Antigone is a dispute about assumptions.

[74] St Thomas Aquinas, *Summa Theologiae*, II-II, q.57, art.2.

discovered by examining, not human nature, but the nature of the situation. This is what St Thomas means when he writes that the just is "in the thing", that is, it is discovered by an examination of the situation or case.[75]

It is more important to get the question clear than to learn its traditional answer, for an answer cannot properly be understood until the reader knows to what precise question it purports to be the answer. Furthermore, it falls to the student to become personally convinced that a question is genuine before spending time trying to answer it. Let us, therefore, try to formulate the question anew: In a society where people own things, is it entirely a matter of command and convention that stealing is unjust or is stealing unjust because stealing is incompatible with owning?

The question needs some commentary. First, it must be stressed again that the question of stealing arises only in a society in which things are owned. Secondly, to own something means more than merely to possess it. For Robinson Crusoe, living entirely alone on a desert island, "to possess" and "to own" are synonymous or nearly so. Were a man to spend his entire life alone— something in reality impossible—he would have no occasion to distinguish between ownership and possession. The very idea of ownership would not occur to him for ownership is essentially a social thing and there is, in fact, in every human society, a recognised idea of ownership and, generally, a fairly good idea in some detail as to who owns what. What constitutes ownership, what can be and is owned and who owns it, differs from society to society and from time to time. There are societies in which land is not privately owned but to infer from this that land is not owned in any sense at all is mistaken. Street buskers in our own society often agree among themselves which of them owns a particular pitch at a particular time, but they know very well that they do not own their particular pitch as they own their musical instruments. Similarly, holiday-makers at a beach resort develop customs to book their patch for the day. Effectively, for me to own something requires that both I and others accept the practice of ownership that prevails in the society and the fact that I own this particular thing. Thirdly, if I quietly and agreeably possess what I own, neither more nor less, then the situation is just. Fourthly, what constitutes stealing is determined by what constitutes ownership; it is utterly crucial to remember that ownership is a bundle of entitlements and that what constitutes the bundle differs from society to society.[76]

---

[75] *ibid.*, II-II, q.58, art.10. The phrase "in the thing" is a literal translation of *in re*; *res* and *in re* may be translated as "the case" and "in the case".

[76] There are societies, as has been said, where no particular parcel of land is "owned", as ownership is understood in the modern West, by a particular person; but there are none in which the land in which a people lives is in no sense "owned", in no sense "theirs".

We may now recall our question: In a society where people own things is it entirely a matter of command and convention that stealing is unjust or is stealing unjust because stealing is incompatible with owning? Or, to put it another way: Is a rule against stealing—*e.g.* "Thou shalt not steal"—simply added on to ownership or is it intrinsic to it?

For St Thomas Aquinas the rule against stealing is a formulation of an understanding that stealing is intrinsically unjust and for that reason no decision can make it just. For his younger contemporary, the English theologian, William of Occam, the rule against stealing is thought of as a command that could well have been other. John Selden, already referred to above, in the Occamian tradition, writes in the chapter on the "Law of Nature" in his *Table-Talk*: "I cannot fancy to myself what the Law of Nature means but the Law of God. How should I know I ought not to steal ... unless somebody had told me so?"

According to St Thomas one can discover, yet neither easily nor inevitably, the unjust character of stealing from an examination of ownership; according to Occam and Selden one cannot. Although it is not utterly clear from this brief excerpt from Selden, not only can one not know the unjust character of stealing unless one is told but its unjust character is established for the first time by the injunction against it. Before the command, stealing was a matter of indifference; in other words, to steal is unjust because it is forbidden. For St Thomas, to steal is forbidden because it is unjust.[77]

In this excerpt, Selden writes of the "Law of God", that is, the Decalogue. But "Law of God" may be replaced by "Law of the State" without changing the basic structure of the argument. The root of positivism is here; for, in all its versions, the foundation is that law is authoritative command.[78]

The argument for the assertion that to steal is intrinsically unjust is, in essence, very simple:

---

[77] The question is old. It occurs in Plato's *Euthyphro*, 10a: "Is what is holy, holy because the gods approve it, or do the gods approve it because it is holy?" See the brief discussion in B. Bix, "Natural Law: the Modern Tradition" in J. Coleman and S. Shapiro (eds.), *The Oxford Handbook of Jurisprudence and Philosophy of Law* (Oxford University Press, Oxford, 2002), pp.66–68. As has been said, whatever position one adopts there still remains the question: Why be just? That it would be unjust to do something is a reason for not doing it only for someone who decides that it is for him a reason. Until he accepts it as a reason, it is simply a fact that may become a reason; *cf.* G. Barden, *Essays on a Philosophical Interpretation of Justice*, chap.9.

[78] Whether the authoritative source is the secular ruler or God is a dispute within positivism. Some natural law theories turn out to be positivist in that their claim to be natural is based on the theory that the source of law is God. Thus, the Decalogue may be understood as the imposition of divine authoritative command on what was originally indifferent—Occam—or the clarification of what could be discovered—St Thomas.

If Peter now possesses what he owns there is a just situation.
If what he owns is taken from him against his will he remains the owner
of it but no longer possesses it and there is an unjust situation.
An act which brings about an unjust situation is unjust.
Stealing brings about an unjust situation.
Therefore, stealing is unjust.

The argument for the assertion that to steal is not intrinsically unjust is likewise
simple:

If Peter now possesses what he owns there is simply a factual situation.
If what he owns is taken from him against his will he remains the owner
of it and there is simply a different factual situation.
An act which brings about simply a different factual situation is
intrinsically indifferent.
Stealing brings about simply a different factual situation.
Therefore, stealing is intrinsically indifferent.

The argument that to steal is intrinsically unjust may be very simple but, as
happens in human living, there are difficult cases. The recurrent medieval
example of a difficult or special case is that of the enraged owner of a sword
who demands that his sword be returned to him by its borrower in order that
he might do ill with it or that of the enemy who demands the return of his
weapon that he may continue to wage war against the city. St Thomas suggests
that in such cases it is not just to return the weapon. *Epieikeia* or equity is the
effort to discern what is just in cases where the formulated rule or law does not
clearly fit. In the *Summa Theologiae* St Thomas asks whether or not this practice
is virtuous, that is, whether or not it is good to proceed in this manner. His
answer is that it is virtuous and is worth quoting in full.

"As has been said above (I-II, q.96, art.6) when we are dealing with
laws, because human acts, about which laws are concerned, consist in
particular and contingent events that may vary almost infinitely, it is not
possible to frame laws that will in no case fail to fit the case. Legislators
concentrate on what happens for the most part and make laws accordingly;
in some cases to apply these laws runs against the character of justice
and counter to the common good that the laws intend. Thus, the law
states that what is deposited is to be returned because for the most part
this is just. However, it can sometimes happen that to do so would be
harmful, as when someone maddened by anger hands over his sword
and, while still enraged, demands it back; or if someone should look for
the return of what he has deposited in order to damage the state. In these
and similar cases it is bad to follow the established law; it is good in

such cases, having put aside the verbal formula of the law, to follow what is just and for the common utility. This is the function of *epieikeia*—that is, what we call *aequitas* (equity). Hence it is plain that *epieikeia* is a virtue."[79]

In general, the idea of ownership is incoherent and makes no sense if what is owned is not to be returned to its owner—hence, the idea of ownership is incoherent if it does not include the idea that to steal is unjust. And yet sometimes the situation is such that what is owned is not to be returned. So it would seem that the general formulation, which purports to express what is naturally just, is not always applicable. The argument here is that the formulation or law expresses what is just and applicable in most cases but not in all. Where St Thomas writes "in most cases", we might be inclined to write "in principle" or "all things being equal".

A new question now arises: if the borrower refuses to return the sword because its owner is maddened with anger, is he breaking a rule of natural justice? Consider a more modern example: Peter and Paul go to the pub in Peter's car. During the course of the evening Peter drinks heavily and becomes incapable of driving. While he is in the lavatory Paul takes the keys from Peter's overcoat pocket and refuses to give them back. The examples are structurally identical.

No one denies that the keys belong to Peter. No one denies that, in principle, in ordinary circumstances, the just situation would be restored were Paul to give the keys back to their owner. There may well be a formulated law stating that what belongs to someone is to be restored to him. In refusing to give back the keys, in these circumstances, is Paul breaking the rule? Obviously he is. Is he going against what is naturally just? He is, if the formulation expresses what is naturally just in all circumstances. St Thomas' argument is that the formulation does not and cannot do so. What is naturally just in these circumstances is to be discovered in the circumstances but, of course, it cannot be discovered, except by lucky accident, by someone who has no idea whatsoever of what is in principle just.

The difficulty surrounding the application of general rules to individual cases is not confined to rules expressing what is naturally just; it arises just as much in cases of the conventionally just. This shows that what is just in any situation is not discovered and realised simply by the application of a formulated rule; even in the ordinary circumstances where the rule does apply, it must be discovered that the situation under scrutiny is in fact one to which the rule applies. After the theatre, the playgoer who has left his coat in the cloakroom,

---

[79] *Summa Theologiae*, II-II, q.120, art.1. See also G. Barden, "Aristotle's Notion of Epieikeia", pp.353–366.

hands in the ticket and ask for his coat. Both he and the attendant understand the situation to be an instance of the ordinary case where what has been deposited is to be returned. But were the attendant to suspect that the case was in some relevant way out of the ordinary he would ask himself whether or not the general rule applied. What is just in a particular situation is discovered by understanding the particular situation; for which understanding an understanding of the general case is illuminating.[80]

We have been trying to deal with the question as to whether or not stealing was naturally unjust and have suggested that it is intrinsic to the idea of ownership that the situation is just when the owner of something possesses what he owns and unjust when he does not. We have suggested also that what is meant by "naturally just" and "naturally unjust" is "intrinsic to the situation". In most circumstances, in principle, it is just that the owner quietly possesses what he owns. In most cases to deprive him of this quiet possession is to produce an unjust situation. In most cases, to deprive him of this quiet possession is to steal. However, in some cases it is not, as in the case of the drunk, his friend and the car keys.

In may happen, of course, that one person has in his possession—but rightly—what belongs to another. Suppose that Peter borrows a book from Paul. Peter now has the book in his possession and intends to read it before returning it. Paul has agreed to this arrangement. He is still the owner of the book. As long as Peter has the book he has, as a matter of fact, something that belongs to another. There is no injustice here but the situation is, in a way, unstable or anticipatory, for, eventually, the book is to be restored to Paul. Aristotle does think of a case of this kind—its technical name being "a loan for use"—as one involving voluntary rectificatory justice but it is somewhat curiously so since there is no injustice.

The practice of lending and borrowing, where it exists, exists within a context of ownership but when something is borrowed, the borrower not the lender—the original owner—possesses what is borrowed. Is the understanding of the practice of lending and borrowing an understanding of what is naturally or only of what is conventionally just?

The practice itself is conventional in two distinct ways. First, and indisputably, a single case of lending and borrowing is conventional in that it is a convention or contract between lender and borrower. Secondly, that the practice of lending and borrowing exists in a particular society at a particular time is conventional in that it is quite possible to imagine a human society in which the practice simply does not occur; in which, so to speak, it has not been invented. Whether such a society exists or has ever existed is an empirical

---

[80] See G. Barden, "Aristotle's Notion of *Epieikeia*" and M. Villey, *Seize Essais*, chap.12bis.

question in historical social anthropology. But it is worth reflecting on the fact that the practice emerges just as soon as two people decide to engage in it and becomes commonplace as others take it up; it requires no central power or state to establish it. If one wants to say that lending and borrowing is natural to humans, the term "natural" here is used crucially differently from the way it is used when it is claimed that there are elements of the naturally just inherent in, or intrinsic to, the practice of lending and borrowing.[81]

The question raised here is neither whether or not the practice of lending and borrowing is natural to humans, nor whether or not the practice is widespread or universal. The question is this: is there a justice intrinsic to, inherent in, essential to and natural to, the practice of lending and borrowing? The practice of lending and borrowing has a nature where the term "nature" is used as it is in such questions as "what is the nature of the orbit of the earth about the sun?" or "what is the nature of tidal movement?" The idea that there is a justice intrinsic to the practice of lending and borrowing rests on the idea that the practice cannot properly be understood without understanding the relations of justice established between borrower and lender, that is, without understanding that lending and borrowing is essentially, naturally, intrinsically and inherently, a coherent set of such relations.

What, then, is the practice of lending and borrowing? It involves two persons—one or both of which may be legal persons, for example, a library—one of whom lends the thing borrowed by the other. The thing lent passes from the present possession of the owner-lender to the present possession of the borrower. What distinguishes this practice from gift-giving or stealing, both of which involve the passing of possession from one person to another, is precisely the jural relations that are established in the transfer and that both lender and borrower understand and accept. What distinguishes lending and borrowing from gift-giving is that the thing—or an agreed equivalent—is to be returned to the owner-lender. This jural relation, established in the act of lending and borrowing, is not a rule added to the practice but what is naturally just in, or intrinsic to, the practice.[82] It is discovered, as we always make discoveries, by examining carefully and trying to understand the practice.

In referring to the returning of something by a borrower to a lender the phrase "or an agreed equivalent" had to be included because there are, in fact,

---

[81] To claim that lending and borrowing is natural to humans is to use the term differently from the way it is used in the *Institutes* (I.II.preamble), where "natural" is what is common to all animals including humans. If the practice is in fact common to humans, then the justice intrinsic to it forms part of the *jus gentium* or what "is common to all humans" (I.II.2). The term "natural", as was said earlier, is used in many different ways; the writer when writing, the reader when reading should be careful to clarify how it is being used.

[82] *The Institutes of Justinian*, III.XIV.

two kinds of thing lent. First, there is the loan of something that is used without being consumed in the use of it and so the identical thing rather than its equivalent can be returned; for example, if one borrows a book or a car or, to take the common Roman example, a horse, one is expected to return the same book, car or horse. This is a "loan for use", of the kind we have been discussing. Secondly, there is the loan of something that the borrower wants to use and to consume in the use of it. It cannot be returned; for example, if one borrows milk or coffee or the like one expects that these will be consumed and cannot be returned. This loan is a "loan for consumption".

If Paul borrows a bottle of milk from Peter, who now owns the milk? Does Peter still own the bottle of milk that Paul has borrowed from him? Let us suppose, as would normally be the case, that Paul intends to consume the milk. The answer in Roman jurisprudence is that Paul becomes the owner of the milk. In general, in a loan for consumption, what is lent becomes the property of the borrower:

> "An obligation is contracted in the practice, for example, in a loan for consumption. This always consists of things which may be weighed, numbered or measured, as wine, oil, corn, brass, silver or gold. In giving these things by number or measure, we so give them that they become the property of those who receive them. And identical things are not returned, but only others of the same nature and quality."[83]

Peter, when he lends Paul a bottle of milk, no longer owns what he has lent. What does he now own? And Paul, while he does own the bottle of milk, is not simply in the position he would be had he bought it or had he been given a present of it. What else does he now own? Both own a debt; one as creditor, one as debtor. This is what in the situation is naturally just. Again, it is in the nature of a debt that it be paid, that is, it is naturally just that Paul extinguish his debt to Peter. But when? It would be absurd if two minutes after Paul had borrowed the milk, Peter called at his flat to demand that the debt be now repaid. Equally, it would be absurd were Paul to suppose that he could repay the debt in 20 years time. A common expectation develops in a community— normally, if one borrows a bottle of milk the expectation in most places is that the debt be repaid within a few days; or a time may be agreed. Here is the element of the conventionally, yet not arbitrarily, just.

In the "loan for use" the identical thing borrowed is to be returned to the lender. If Paul borrows a book from Peter, it is naturally just that he return the identical book. It is "naturally just" because that is what is meant in the practice. When is the book to be returned? This may be explicitly agreed as when books

---

[83] *ibid.*

are lent and borrowed from a library or it may be generally understood. Peter will normally lend the book so that Paul may read it and so the normal length of time that it takes to read the book is included in the transaction. A clear example of this is when, at a lecture, one student lends a pen to another student who is without one. The assumption, mutually understood, is that the borrower wants to use the pen during the lecture only and not for the entire day, week, year or duration of the whole course. In a "loan for use" the lender remains the owner of the thing lent. The borrower owns, for a time, the use of thing borrowed.

> "A person to whom a thing ... (a) is lent that he may make use of it ... (differs greatly from) the person who has received a loan for consumption; for the thing is not given to him that it may become his property, and he therefore is bound to restore the identical thing he received ... (b) and he is indeed bound to employ the utmost diligence in keeping and preserving it; nor will it suffice that he should take the same care of it, which he was accustomed to take of his own property, if it appears that a more careful person might have preserved it in safety."[84]

The part marked (a) in this quotation from *The Institutes of Justinian* describes the "loan for use". It does not establish the practice for the first time but rather formulates in writing the practice that is already common. Precisely how, when and where the practice arose cannot now be discovered for lack of evidence. But why it arose can be known, because why it arose is why it survived: the practice of lending and borrowing was discovered to be useful in the course of human living where, quite commonly, not everyone at every moment has everything he needs. A person borrows a pen because he now needs, but has not now got, a pen.

Because in the loan for use, the borrower does not own the thing borrowed, a question about how he is to treat it arises. It can happen that the thing borrowed gets accidentally destroyed, for example, in a fire, for which the borrower may be in no way responsible and, again in the nature of the case, the question as to what is then due between owner-lender and borrower arises. It can happen that the thing borrowed deteriorates while it is in the possession of the borrower and, again naturally, the question arises as to what is now due. The Roman jurisprudents suggest that, following an examination of the kind of practice that lending and borrowing is, the borrower is bound to take good care of what is borrowed, precisely because, in a loan for use, he does not own it. This Roman answer remains quite explicitly in the French *Code Civil* (in the part titled *Du Prêt*). In many jurisdictions, one who rents accommodation is bound to return it in good order except for normal "wear and tear". This answer

---

[84] *ibid.*, III.XIV.2.

reflects the expectation of lenders and borrowers for no one would lend his car to someone who, he confidently expected, would drive it so badly that the likelihood of its being returned in good order was minimal.

The purpose of this examination of the practice of lending and borrowing is to show that what is naturally just is what is intrinsic to a practice and not some supervening law imposed upon it. The formulation, the written law, expresses the understanding of the practice, often already known, and deals with some of the problems that have arisen and are likely to arise in the future. For it will happen that the thing borrowed is destroyed or broken; that what is borrowed is badly treated. And when these things happen further questions as to what is due arise; some of these questions will reveal what is naturally just and some what is "originally indifferent" and to be solved by the establishment of some convention or agreement. What is crucial is that what is naturally just is not discovered by consulting some higher statute, nor by consulting human nature but by examining and trying to understand the jural nature of the "thing", the case. [85]

It is time to return to the question as to who owns what in a case where someone buys, or otherwise obtains, land from another whom he believes to be the owner but who, in fact, turns out not to be. An answer to the question, and to some issues which the situation gives rise to, is given in Justinian's *Institutes*. It is worth giving and commenting upon the suggested answer to show clearly that the naturally just here has nothing to do with appeal to some higher law but is discovered through a jurisprudential enquiry into the situation:

> "If anyone has in good faith purchased land from another, whom he believed to be the true owner, when in fact he was not, or has in good faith acquired it from such a person by gift or by any other good title, natural reason demands that the fruits that he has gathered shall be his in return for his care and culture. And, therefore, if the true owner afterwards appears and claims his land, he can have no action for fruits which the possessor has consumed. But the same allowance is not made to him who has knowingly been in possession of another's land; and, therefore, he is compelled to restore, together with the lands, all the fruits although they may have been consumed." [86]

First, it is obvious the question arises only within a society in which land is privately owned, bought, sold, given as a gift or the like. Secondly, private ownership of land, like any other kind of ownership, is jural or institutional. [87]

---

[85] See M. Villey, "La Nature des Choses" in *Seize Essais*, pp.38–59.

[86] *The Institutes of Justinian*, II.I.35.

[87] Humans in their ordinary lives together establish jural relationships between themselves and live within a web of such relationships. This means that human

Ownership is a jural relationship between people, not a physical description of an action or situation; hence, in the quotation above, the distinctions between ownership, possession and usufruct.[88] Thirdly, the specific question to which this is an answer is not whether or not the land should be restored to its owner—that is here taken as settled; the specific question is as to who owns the produce of the land. The possessor, who possesses the land in good faith, who thinks that he owns it but in fact does not, has worked and cultivated the land; the produce or fruits of the land are the fruits of his work. Who owns these? The owner or the possessor in good faith? The suggestion here is that the possessor who has worked the land is entitled to the fruits that he has gathered. The text states that "natural reason demands" it. Natural reason is not an appeal to some higher law or to some hidden axiom; it is simply that it seems to the jurists from an examination of the situation that the possessor in good faith owns those fruits that are the result of his care and culture. But why should this be? The argument seems to be that an owner who works his land is naturally entitled to its fruits; that someone who rents the land that he works is entitled to its fruits once he has paid the rent due to the owner and that in this context the possessor in good faith is sufficiently like an owner or like one who has genuinely rented land to be entitled to the fruits of his labour. The opinion—fallible and tentative—arises from a careful consideration of the case. The possessor in bad faith who has knowingly been in possession of another's land is not entitled to the fruits of his labours because he is insufficiently like an owner or usufructuary. That this solution is "natural" simply means that it appears to the enquirer to be rooted in the nature of the case. But there will also be situations where what is just does not appear from an examination of the case and must be settled by decision or convention. The theory of the naturally and conventionally just as worked out here is not a doctrine but a method, an approach to the discovery of what is just.

---

reality is not adequately described in terms of what the Scandinavian realists like Karl Olivecrona (1897–1980) call "material space-time reality". When Peter hands a book to Paul, we do not know what has happened until we know what jural (or "institutional"; see N. MacCormick and O. Weinberger, *op. cit.*) relationships have been established between them. Has Peter given Paul a gift; has he sold him the book; has he lent it to him? See G. Barden, *Essays on a Philosophical Interpretation of Justice*, *passim* but especially chaps. 4 and 8; and M. La Torre "Institutionalist Philosophy of Law" in *The Philosophy of Law: An Encyclopedia*, Vol.I, pp.420–423.

[88] In Latin "ownership" is "dominium"; the "owner" is the "dominus" or "lord"—from which we get "landlord"; "possession" is "possessio"; the English word "usufruct", no longer in common use, is from the Latin meaning "use of the fruits or produce"; the one who is entitled to usufruct is the "usufructuary"—again no longer in common use—or, more or less equivalent to the modern "tenant".

A moment's reflection on the situation will provoke further questions. What, for instance, is just if the possessor in good faith has ploughed but not yet sown when the true owner claims the land? What if the crops are ripening but not yet harvested? These are questions as to what is just, as to who is entitled to what. They are questions that arise from the nature of the case. Some solutions will discern what is naturally, and some what is conventionally, just. But the method is always intelligent enquiry into the situation, not recourse to some higher law.

Reciprocal Justice

Reciprocal justice is the justice at work in exchange or trading.[89] Although trading is extremely widespread—as Adam Smith remarks, it is "common to all men" and, perhaps, "the consequence of a certain propensity in human nature"[90]—it is nonetheless conventional in that there cannot be a genuine trade except by mutual agreement, contract or convention between the trading partners. When two partners trade with each other they establish themselves in a jural relationship. This is not added on to the trading; trading is essentially a jural fact. Where either partner is compelled, what appears to be trade, in reality is not.

In a trade or exchange there are at least two partners, Peter and Paul, and two goods to be exchanged, x and y, the one belonging to Peter, the other to Paul. Peter offers x to Paul on condition that Paul gives him y in return. The exchange succeeds only if Paul is willing to accept x in return for y. Peter will not offer x in return for y, unless, for whatever reason, he wants y more than he wants x; and Paul will not give y in order to get x, unless, for whatever reason, he wants x more than he wants y.[91] Children swapping marbles or whatsoever know this in practice just as well as do the owners of companies who sell their

---

[89] The discussion of reciprocal justice, which might well be called the justice of the market or the justice involved in contract, owes much to the Irish economist David O Mahony.

[90] Adam Smith, *An Inquiry into the Nature and Causes of the Wealth of Nations* (1776), I, chap.ii, 1. In fact, as anthropological research has shown, exchange of some kind— not by any means always market or commercial exchange—is commonly of great significance in human societies. When Adam Smith suggests that trading is natural to humans, he is not using the term as is it used in the phrase "the naturally just". He is using it to refer to that which is found generally.

[91] The structural analysis of a trade between two partners requires no further account of the partners' reasons than that there is reciprocal demand for the offered goods. Why Peter wants Paul's goods more than he wants his own is irrelevant for this analysis. Notice, however, that in trading both partners profit. There are, of course, other analyses within which Peter's reason for his preference might be of great significance.

companies. No one freely sells his shares who wants to keep them more than he wants to sell them; that is what "economic rationality" means and that is the only coherent way of using this commonly misunderstood term.[92] Without this mutual or reciprocal demand there will be no exchange. Demand, as Aristotle wrote, is the yardstick of exchange:

> "All goods must be measured by some one yardstick or measure. And this yardstick is, in reality, demand, which is the universal bond (for if men were in need of nothing, or if there were no proportion between their needs, there would either be no exchange whatsoever or the exchanges would be other than they are); but money has become, by convention, a sort of representative of demand."[93]

Adam Smith, many centuries later, says much the same:

> "But man has almost constant occasion for the help of his brethren, and it is vain for him to expect it from their benevolence only. He will be more likely to prevail if he can interest their self-love in his favour, and shew them that it is for their own advantage to do for him what he requires of them. Whoever offers to another a bargain of any kind, proposes to do this. Give me that which I want and you shall have this which you want, is the meaning of every such offer; and it is in this manner that we obtain from one another the far greater part of those good offices which we stand in need of."[94]

In this great convention—trade or exchange through mutual demand—is there room for what is naturally just? At first sight, apparently not. Suppose Paul to be a cabinet maker who shows Peter a dining table that he describes as a dining table in walnut. Peter looks at the table and buys it for €1,500. Paul has sold the table and Peter has bought it for €1,500. Each has agreed to the exchange and together they have settled the price. In the transaction €1,500 is the agreed representative of their reciprocal demand. The exchange is reciprocally just and is entirely conventional or by agreement. But notice that what is conventional or by agreement is that they trade with each other and that they agree on the value of the things exchanged. What is natural to an exchange is not what precise value is to be put on the goods to be exchanged but the manner in which the value is to be arrived at.[95] The precise value of the

---

[92] See L. Von Mises, *op. cit.*

[93] Aristotle, *Nicomachean Ethics*, V.5, 1133a.25–30.

[94] Adam Smith, *The Wealth of Nations*, I, chap.ii, 2. See J.M. Buchanan and G. Tullock, *op. cit.*, pp.17–18.

[95] An agreed price establishes the value of the good to be exchanged. Within a *trading*

goods is established by agreement between the trading partners. It is intrinsic or natural to trading that this is how value is established.

There are other issues. Suppose Peter brings his table home, only to be told that it is in beechwood not walnut and that beechwood is cheaper than walnut. He confirms with another expert that this is so. The contract between Peter and Paul is vitiated. Peter was willing to pay €1,500 for a walnut table; what he would have been willing to pay for a dining table of the same dimensions in beechwood is unknown. Paul sold him the table *as a walnut table*. The question that now arises is this: in an exchange is it simply a matter of the conventionally just that the partners do not lie or is it naturally just and intrinsic to the practice? (It is, of course, fully accepted that traders—buyers and sellers—do lie and that it is wise to be on the lookout for sharp practice but this is not the question.)

The question may be formulated differently. In the example of the exchange between Peter and Paul of €1,500 for a dining table, sold as being in walnut but is in fact in beechwood, how is Peter's complaint to be treated? How is the case to be investigated? Are we, without reflection on the situation, by simple convention and decision, to decree a rule of *caveat emptor* or, alternatively, a rule of correct description of goods. The matter is not easy but the theory of the naturally just is not a comprehensive list of *a priori* solutions. It is, rather, a method. The rule of the method is this: investigate and discuss the situation, for in a situation where relations of justice are at play—as they are, for example, in exchange—it sometimes turns out that what is just in cases of difficulty can be discerned by correctly understanding the details of the situation. The solutions are the fruit of understanding and judgement and, since human

---

system or *market order*, price cannot be set in any other way. See L. Von Mises, *op. cit.*, chap.XVI. In an organisation of *mercantilist planning*, "price" may be set otherwise. Aristotle is sometimes credited with the idea that if it takes x hours to make a pair of shoes and 100x hours to make a house, then the "natural" exchange rate between shoes and houses is 100 pairs of shoes = 1 house. See the note by D. Ross, *op. cit.* (1133a.6). That this is in fact Aristotle's position is by no means clear and his repeated reference to demand, as in the passage quoted, makes this interpretation at least doubtful. St Thomas in his commentary on the fifth book of the *Nicomachean Ethics* (Lectio IX) seems clear that price is set by mutual demand: "what in reality measures all things (relative to one another in exchange) is demand". On the other hand, a labour-time theory of value in exchange seems to be present in Adam Smith's *The Wealth of Nations*, I, chap.vi, 1 where, incidentally, he uses the word "naturally" very differently from the way it is used here. But see also chap.vii. The desire for a "just" price dissociated from mutual demand survives and is commonly related to some version of a labour-time theory of value according to which the price should be set not by demand but by the labour-time taken to produce the good or service. See G. Barden, *Essays on a Philosophical Theory of Justice*, chap.6, pp.85–86.

judgement is not infallible, they, too, are not infallible. Traditional solutions are those that have been proposed and accepted; these form the common law of the society.

Ours is a trading society where, as Adam Smith writes,

> "it is but a very small part of a man's wants which the produce of his own labour can supply. He supplies the far greater part of them by exchanging the surplus part of the produce of his own labour, which is over and above his own consumption, for such parts of the produce of other men's labour as he has occasion for. Every man thus lives by exchanging, or becomes in some measure a merchant, and the society itself grows to be what is properly a commercial society."[96]

If such a society is to function, most exchanges must be mutually or reciprocally satisfactory. Commercial law formulates the established practices of the society, some of which practices are naturally and some conventionally just. In a commercial or trading society "every man lives by exchanging" and reciprocal justice is "justice in exchange".

Each exchange shifts the ownership of goods from one partner to another and in a commercial society there is an immense multitude of exchanges hourly, daily, monthly, yearly and so on over time. The pattern of ownership in any society at the beginning of any chosen period will differ from that at the end of that period. In the trading system the pattern will change by means of the many exchanges between the trading partners but what the pattern will be at the end of the selected period cannot be predicted from the pattern at the outset. But although the market order has no aims, it does perform certain social functions. One function is to allow trading partners to gain what each wants by exchanging for it what each values less highly.[97]

---

[96] Adam Smith, *The Wealth of Nations*, I, chap.iv, 1. It is sometimes claimed that the economy in which we live is adequately described as a market order. This is not in fact an adequate description, for the system that prevails is, in considerable part, a system of mercantilist planning, that is, centralist organisation. "Mercantilist planning is the system against which Adam Smith protested, and which now dominates most of the world." D. Ramsay Steele, *From Marx to Mises* (Open Court, Illinois, 1992), p.265. The Common Agricultural Policy (CAP) in the European Union and the General Agreement on Trade and Tariffs (GATT), for example, are mercantilist. Still, the description given by Adam Smith in the passage quoted, which does not pretend to be a complete account of any actual society, fits, to some extent, both the economy in which he lived and our own.

[97] "In an occasional act of barter in which men who ordinarily do not resort to trading with other people exchange goods ordinarily not negotiated, the ratio of exchange is determined only within broad margins. Catallactics, the theory of exchange ratios and prices, cannot determine at what point within these margins the concrete ratio

In the trading system, each participant owns whatever he offers in exchange. When he exchanges a good or service for something else, he now owns what he has accepted in exchange. The exchange is just if it has been free and not vitiated by fraud or the like—in which case the court may be involved in the resolution of a dispute—but there can be no guarantee that he has made what he will later think of as a wise choice. This is crucial to justice in exchange. At the time of the exchange, both partners are satisfied with the exchange; otherwise they would not exchange. But it is perfectly possible that either or both will later regret it. Peter, having come in to some money, may decide to open a dress shop. He does so because he expects to trade sufficiently well to cover his costs, including his living costs, and, perhaps, even to make a profit. He rents a premises and buys clothes that he thinks will sell in sufficiently great numbers at a satisfactory price. If his shop succeeds, he will be retrospectively pleased with the original exchange. If his shop fails, he will consider, again retrospectively, that he chose unwisely. At the end of his first year it is unlikely, although possible, that his situation will be precisely as it was at the outset; he is more likely to be richer or poorer than he was. Not only may he compare his position at the end with his position at the outset, he may compare himself with Paul who, we may imagine, began the year with the same amount of money as Peter and, like him, opened a shop. Suppose that Peter failed and Paul succeeded. Where both at the outset were equally well off, at the end of the year one was better off than the other. That this will sometimes be the outcome is inevitable in a trading system. It has nothing whatsoever to do with reciprocal justice for reciprocal justice has nothing whatsoever to do with outcomes.[98]

5. The Question Addressed by the Court

In cases of uncertainty or dispute about what is just, there is no human society in which it has not been discovered that it is crucial to establish independent and, or so it is hoped, impartial and reliable adjudication.[99] There is not the

---

will be established. *All that it can assert with regard to such exchanges is that they can be effected only if each party values what he receives more highly than what he gives away.*" L. von Mises, *op. cit.*, chap.XVI, p.327 (emphasis added).

[98] In a market order or trading system, the "outcome" changes moment by moment. No particular outcome is envisaged or hoped for. When a single participant speaks of an "outcome" he has in mind a period relevant to him alone as in the example. The single participant does, of course, envisage an outcome as when someone invests money in the hope of gain. The single participants have goals; the system does not. The system's function is to allow participants pursue their goals.

[99] "You must not be guilty of unjust verdicts. You must not be partial to the poor, nor

smallest reason to suppose that impartiality is discovered or implemented easily nor that, once implemented in principle, it governs enquiry peacefully and without pressure. Bribery and other pressures from the powerful, whether their power be from wealth, or numbers, or force or some other of the innumerable forms of human prejudice, tend to distort judgement. The existence and corrupting influence of these have long been known. The corruption of power is great enough sometimes to prevent not alone the practice of impartiality but even the very idea of its value. Nonetheless, the question remains: is the establishment of impartial adjudication merely conventional or is it the establishment of what has been discovered to be the nature of the case?

Reflection on this question reveals two things. First, if one is examining a particular adjudicative system, the question as to whether or not it is impartial is a question of social fact. Suppose a system in which impartial adjudication does not exist. If it is now asked whether or not the people living within that jurisdiction have the right to impartial adjudication, the answer clearly is that as a matter of social fact they have not. That is, impartial adjudication is not an entitlement within the system.

Whether or not they should have that right, whether or not that entitlement should be within the system is a good but different question. If it is intrinsic to adjudication that it should be impartial, then an established adjudicative practice that is not impartial is defective. If, on the other hand, there are simply two "indifferently just" general systems of adjudication—one impartial, the other biased—then an established adjudicative practice that is biased rather than impartial is not defective. The only way in which one can discover whether or not impartiality is intrinsic to adjudication is by examining the practice of adjudication. If impartiality is intrinsic, then the rule "Be impartial" is not simply a precept imposed on the practice; rather, as well as being a precept in the imperative mood, it is also a methodological clarification of the practice. And the only way in which one can intelligently examine the practice of adjudication is by examining one's own spontaneous conscious actions when actually engaged in adjudicating.[100] It is of the utmost importance to recognise

---

overawed by the mighty; but in justice shall you judge your neighbour." *Leviticus*, 19:15. In his illuminating article on "Corrective Justice" in *The Philosophy of Law: An Encyclopedia*, Richard Posner remarks that Aristotle's idea "of judging a dispute without regard to the character, merit, or social status of the disputants ... is a notable milestone on the road to the modern conception of the rule of law". Certainly, Aristotle's influence has been great but the idea appears much earlier in Judaism as the passage shows. *Leviticus* dates from the seventh century B.C. and parts of it— including the nineteenth chapter—are considered older. See also *Exodus* (tenth century B.C.) 23:2–3; and *Deuteronomy* (seventh century B.C.) 16:18–20.

[100] On methodological clarification and prescription, see B. Lonergan, *Method in Theology* (Darton Longman and Todd, London, 1971), chap.1.

that neither the precept nor the proposition that impartiality is intrinsic to adjudication is a logical conclusion from some undeniable, self-justifying axiom.[101] It is equally important to recognise that a willingness to be impartial does not follow logically from the proposition that impartiality is intrinsic to adjudication.

Various kinds of adjudication have been established. In archaic societies, for example, the prince was more a judge than a ruler.[102] In modern societies, influenced as they are by Roman Law, the adjudicative function is fulfilled by the courts, and jurisprudents are, or are hoped to be, what the Romans called the "priests of justice"[103]; and jurisprudence is "... the science of the just and the unjust".[104] Aristotle said much the same: "when people dispute they take refuge in the judge; and to go to the judge is to go to justice; for the nature of the judge is to be a sort of living justice".[105]

The deliberations of the court come to a conclusion, a sentence or decision. The French term *arrêt*, which literally means a "stop", indicates that the jurisprudential conclusion differs from the demonstrative conclusion of a logical argument in which the conclusion follows inexorably from the given premises. The jurisprudential conclusion is fallible, revisable, or, to use an older and nearly defunct term, prudential.[106] The scientific conclusion—which also differs from the logical conclusion although it has been confused with it—is likewise fallible and revisable.[107] But the scientific differs from the prudential in that

---

[101] That there are no first principles in the form of given, unquestionable axioms or propositions is the central theme of G. Barden, *After Principles*. See especially chap.4 in which it is suggested that the common and mistaken paradigm of human knowing and valuing is logical system. And logically to conclude that, for example, "Impartiality is intrinsic to adjudication", one must hold prior proposition(s) from which this conclusion follows. See also P.J. McGrath, *The Objectivity of Morals* (Estragon, Durrus, 2003).

[102] See G. Barden, *After Principles*, chap.5, pp.30–111 (esp. pp.90–98 and nn.43, 44); E.E. Evans-Pritchard, *Witchcraft, Oracles and Magic among the Azande* (Clarendon Press, Oxford, 1976) and P. Winch, *The Idea of a Social Science* (Routledge and Kegan Paul, London, 1970).

[103] *Digest*. I.

[104] *The Institutes of Justinian*, II.1.

[105] Aristotle, *Nicomachean Ethics*, V.4, 1132a.20.

[106] See *ibid.*, V.I.5 and P. Aubenque, *La Prudence Chez Aristote* (PUF, Paris, 1963). "Prudence" nowadays has a somewhat negative ring to it; formerly it meant "intelligent judgement in practical affairs" and was a compliment.

[107] The structure of the logical argument is: [1] If P, then Q. [2] And P. [3] Therefore, Q. Here [3] follows logically and necessarily from [1] and [2] taken together. The structure of the scientific argument is [4] If P, then Q. [5] And Q. [6] Therefore (probably) P. Here [6] does not follow logically or necessarily from [4] and [5] taken together because Q could exist for some reason other than the existence of P.

the prudential conclusion is about particular cases and looks to a practical decision that must be made within a reasonable time. The sentence states what, in the particular case, is due and works within the accepted context that what is judged to be just must be realised within a reasonable time.[108] In principle at least, scientific enquiry is free of such limitation.

The court is faced with a difficulty or a dispute. As stated previously, its question always is of the form: what in this case belongs to whom?; what in this case is due to whom?; who in this case is entitled to what? Difficulties and disputes arise within particular societies at particular times about particular cases and so the court considers them partly in the light of what are thought to be the prevailing local conventions, partly in the light of what is thought common to all mankind, partly in the light of what appears to be the nature of the case:

> "Civil justice and the justice of nations are distinguished in this way: every people ruled by laws and customs uses partly its own justice and partly justice common to all mankind. The justice that a people makes for itself belongs to that city and is called civil justice as being proper to that city. That which is established by natural reason among all men is operative in all peoples and is called the justice of nations since all peoples make use of it."[109]

The *jus gentium* (the justice or law of nations) is not a set of rules automatically known by everyone but is discovered as occasion and the necessities of human living require.[110] It is discovered by intelligent questioning and understanding of situations. The question that gives rise to the investigation is always of the form: what, in this kind of situation, belongs to whom? The rule of justice, which regards types or kinds of situations, is the suggested answer to this question and is, therefore, always of the form: X in this kind of circumstance belongs to Y. The conventional rule of justice is of the same structure; the only difference being that the convention is a decision when the nature of the situation does not yield a unique solution. The elements in an adjudicator's intellectual background or context are, then, in part conventional and peculiar to the particular society and situation and in part natural in as much as they discern the nature of the case and, for that reason, are commonly found in human societies.

What is considered to be natural and universal is not known in some peculiar

---

[108] Time presses upon practice as it does not upon theory; the decision as to whether or not to apply for a particular job has to be made before a given deadline.

[109] *The Institutes of Justinian*, I.II.1.

[110] *ibid.*, I.II.2.

or mysterious way.[111] Suppose that Peter wishes to sell a house that he claims belongs to him whereas Paul, on the contrary, claims that the house is his. It is not simply a matter of convention that Peter cannot sell what does not belong to him; the meaning of ownership and sale includes the idea that one cannot sell what one does not own. A written rule, such as "No one can sell what does not belong to him", simply formulates in writing an understanding of the nature of the situation.[112] If Peter is to sell the house, his ownership of it must be established against Paul's claim.

Why does the idea of ownership include the idea that one cannot sell what one does not own? The answer is clear: if Peter sells a thing to Paul, the ownership of the thing is transferred from Peter to Paul. But the ownership of the thing cannot be transferred from Peter if it is not vested in Peter in the first place. Peter can, of course, physically transfer the thing to Paul without owning it but what is transferred in sale is not only the thing but the ownership of the thing. It is naturally just—that is, it is intrinsic to the practice—that if the ownership of a thing is transferred by one person to another, the person purporting to transfer the ownership must be the owner. What is true of sale is true of gift-giving; for gift-giving is not simply the physical handing over of the gift to the recipient but the handing over of the ownership of what is given. This is formulated in Roman law:

> "Another way of acquiring things according to what is naturally just is by transfer; for nothing is more conformable to natural equity than that the will of an owner who wishes to transfer what is his to another, should be ratified. And, therefore, a material thing of whatever kind can be transferred and, when so transferred by the owner, becomes the property of another."[113]

In this passage no distinction is made between the transfer (or handing over) of ownership by gift or by sale. Notice, however, that there is here an assumption that what is owned may be alienated—that is, that the owner is entitled to transfer the ownership of what he owns to another. In other words, ownership is thought to include that entitlement. That entitlement is not necessarily part of ownership; the ownership of land held in entail, for example, cannot be transferred to whomsoever simply according to the will of the present owner. The practical problem faced by the Bennet sisters in Jane Austen's *Pride and*

---

[111] That something is universal is not proof that it is "natural" in the sense of "intrinsic". It is worth reiterating that the term "natural" is often—and quite correctly—used to mean "universal" or "common".

[112] That no one can sell or otherwise transfer what does not belong to him is taken for granted in Justinian's *Institutes*, II.I.35 discussed above.

[113] *The Institutes of Justinian*, II.I.40.

Prejudice stems from the fact that their father owns his house and land in entail and so cannot transfer these to his daughters—a situation not serenely accepted by Mrs Bennet. Here, then, is a nice conjunction of what is naturally and what is conventionally just. That only the owner of the thing owned can transfer ownership of the thing to another is naturally just in that it is intrinsic to both gift giving and selling. That a particular person owns a particular thing in such a way that he is entitled to transfer ownership in a particular way only is conventional.

The adjudicator must have the subtle intellectual background that is the understanding of what is just both naturally and conventionally. One who totally lacked this background—as a small child might lack it—cannot distinguish between the physical handing over of a thing on the one hand and gift-giving or selling or lending on the other; and if he cannot make that basic distinction, much less can he distinguish more subtly between the latter three.

It is easy to know when a thing has been physically transferred from Peter to Paul (a physical fact); more difficult to discover when ownership of the thing has been transferred (a jural or institutional fact). Customs to enable people to discover this grow up in different societies and, for the most part, the transfer of ownership from seller to buyer is achieved without difficulty. Millions of such transfers occur daily between customers and shopkeepers. It is more difficult still to determine when an agreement between buyer and seller has been reached. What constitutes an agreement and what distinguishes it from a sale? In Roman law it is suggested that the agreement or contract of sale is reached when the negotiating parties agree upon a price and before the price is paid: "The contract of sale is formed as soon as the price is agreed upon, although it has not yet been paid, nor even a deposit given; for what is given as a deposit serves only as proof that the contract has been made."[114]

This sentence is clearly the proposed answer to the question: when is the contract of sale completed? It is an answer that expresses an understanding of the practice. Before the price is agreed upon, it may well be that the buyer would like to buy what the seller would like to sell. The buyer is not willing to buy nor the seller to sell at any price whatsoever; what they are looking for is an agreed price and, once they reach a mutually agreeable price, there is nothing more to be done except to realise what they have agreed. For this reason, it is considered to be of the nature of the contract of sale that it is completed when a mutually agreed price is reached.

In contrast to this is the set of conventional rules in Roman law governing a written contract: "But, where there is a written contract, *we have enacted* that a sale is not to be considered completed unless an instrument of sale has been drawn up, being either written by the contracting parties, or at least signed

---

[114] *ibid.*, III.XXIII.preamble.

by them, if written by others."[115] The clause "we have enacted" indicates that
this rule is a convention or public agreement. It is civil justice: how things are
done in Rome. Notice, however, that the convention is not an arbitrary, random
imposition. It is an answer to a practical problem. Before the contracting parties
begin to write the contract they will normally have verbally agreed the price.
What then is the written contract? Is it simply, like the deposit, no more than
proof that a contract was made? Or is it to be taken both as a detailed description
of what was contracted and as the act of contracting. In other words, is the
contracting act the verbal agreement of price or the signing of the written text?
A choice has to be made and under the Emperor Justinian it was enacted that
the signing of the text was the contracting act: from that time onwards, the
Roman judges would understand contract in the light of this convention.

It can and does happen that either party reneges on the agreement, at which
point the court may be asked to adjudicate. It may be that one of the parties to
the alleged contract denies that there was a contract. The court's first question,
then, is to discover whether or not there was a contract. The discovery of the
existence of a deposit given and accepted is sufficient proof that there was a
contract in which case the second question arises: what now is due to Peter
and what to Paul? The answer, given in the same preamble, is: "If a deposit
has been given, then, whether the contract was written or unwritten, the
purchaser, if he refuses to fulfil it, loses what he has given as deposit, and the
seller, if he refuses, has to restore double; although no agreement on the subject
was expressly made."

This answer is interesting for several reasons. First, it rests upon the implicit
assumption that in such a case something is required to restore a just situation
beyond simply returning the deposit. Why is this assumption made? Because,
or so the jurisprudents thought, the existence of the contract established a new
jural relationship between the parties upon which each was entitled to rely.[116]
This implicit assumption expresses an understanding of the nature of the
situation. Precisely what is to be done is conventional. A rule stating that the
purchaser should lose double the deposit and the purchaser restore treble or,
indeed, that each should lose or restore the same amount would also serve. Or,
as does sometimes happen, the court may insist that the contract be honoured.[117]

---

[115] *ibid.* (emphasis added).

[116] That the contract establishes a new jural relationship between the contracting parties
is intrinsic to the act of contracting; without this the words and the actions would
be vacuous—merely sounds. Hence the tag: *pacta sunt servanda* (contracts are to
be honoured); this is less a command than a statement of the nature of contract.

[117] Notice that the court not only states what is just but works within a context that
requires that what is just be done. The court does not always decide that a contract
be honoured, sometimes for no other reason than that it cannot be, as when someone

The task of the court is to determine who in this case owns what. The rule states, for the kind of situation described, who owns what; but the rule is general and the case before the court is particular. In so far as the particular case is, in the court's judgement, an instance of the kind of case envisaged in the rule, the rule is applied. In so far as the particular situation diverges from the general case, anticipated and envisaged in the rule, the task of the court is not to apply the rule but to determine, in the light of that and other rules, what is just. The effort to judge a case not perfectly covered by statute, traditional rule or precedent is, as we have already seen, the business of what Aristotle calls equity.

What is to be done if no deposit has been given? Peter claims that a price was agreed; Paul claims that no price was agreed. Suppose that to this question there is as yet no agreed answer. A question before the court is, as before, whether or not there was a contract. The preamble states that in the case where a price was agreed there was a contract. Accordingly, in the absence of evidence of a deposit serving as proof of agreement, the court is faced with the prior question: was there an agreed price? It will not always, and may only rarely, be possible to discover the answer. In the absence of the answer, what is just?

If, in a particular case, it is impossible to discover the answer, should the court decide the matter as if there had been no agreement and so no contract or as if there had been an agreement and so a contract? In reality, either there was or there was not. If there was, then, apparently, justice is not done if the court judges that there was not. If there was not, then, apparently, justice is not done if the court decides that there was. There is a dilemma that gives rise to a new question that has to do with how the court is to proceed. Does the burden of proof lie with the person who claims that there was an agreement or with the person who claims that there was not? The effort to answer this question forces us to investigate the nature of judicial enquiry and so to discover whether or not there is a natural justice intrinsic to the procedure.

Suppose that there was, in fact, agreement and so a contract. Peter claims that there was agreement. Paul claims that there was not. In fact, Paul is lying but this, by hypothesis, cannot be discovered in this case. If the court were to conclude that there had been an agreement, it would conclude that Paul was lying and, for this conclusion, it has insufficient evidence. There might arise a general principle that a person is to be believed unless the contrary be shown. In the light of that principle, the court would decide that, in the absence of sufficient evidence of agreement, it must decide the case *as if* there had been no agreement and so no contract and so Peter's claim is dismissed. Has a just solution been reached? In one sense, it has not. In reality there was an agreement

---

who agrees to buy or sell something but goes bankrupt before the sale is complete may be unable to honour the agreement.

and, had that been discovered, Peter's claim would have succeeded. In another sense, justice has been done. The court's decision to dismiss Peter's claim against Paul is made in a situation in which, what in fact happened, cannot be discovered. The court's question is no longer what is to be decided in case there was an agreement but what is to be decided in the situation when what actually happened cannot be discovered.

At first sight, it might seem that to decide *as if* there had been no agreement is to decide that Peter lied but, on reflection, this turns out not to be so. Peter is in fact not lying although this, by hypothesis, cannot be discovered. The court does not conclude that he was in fact lying. The conclusion is that Peter cannot produce sufficient evidence to show that what he says occurred, did in fact occur.

The court dismisses Peter's case against Paul because Peter cannot produce sufficient evidence to show that what he claims is true. Strictly, in this example, the court does not determine that there was no contract, but that there is insufficient evidence to conclude that there was.

The same structure is present in criminal cases. Mary accuses Peter of rape. Peter denies this. Again the first task of the court is to discover whether or not Peter raped Mary. Suppose that Mary is telling the truth and Peter is lying but that Mary is unable to establish this. In the absence of sufficient evidence the court will decide *as if* Peter had not raped Mary because, were it to decide on insufficient evidence that he had done so, it would, on insufficient evidence, decide that Peter was lying. Mary, on the other hand, is not convicted of lying but of failing to establish her version of the event. Mary's case fails. What is due to Mary and to Peter? That Mary's accusation against Peter be dismissed. Will justice have been done? In one sense, it will not. Peter did in fact rape Mary. In another sense it will. The court concluded in the light of the evidence before it. And that is all we can ever reasonably do.

In each of these examples, there was a fact. In the first example, there was a contract. In the second example, there had been a rape. The facts were, in each case, denied. In both examples, there was insufficient evidence to allow the court to conclude on these facts. Unable reasonably to conclude that there was a contract or that there had been a rape, the court had no reasonable choice but to state this. In the first case, the court rejects Peter's action against Paul and, in so doing, acts as if there was no contract. In the second example, the court rejects Mary's accusation that Peter raped her and, in so doing, acts as if there had been no rape. The difference between the civil and the criminal example is that in the civil example the conclusion is that there is insufficient evidence to conclude that there was a contract whereas, in the criminal example, in many jurisdictions, the court hands down a verdict of not guilty which is commonly understood as an assertion that Peter did not rape Mary. In Scotland, the verdict of not proven is allowed which is understood as the assertion that Mary did not have sufficient evidence to prove her case but also that Peter did not have sufficient evidence to refute it. There is a conventional element in the verdict of not guilty since it sometimes is a conclusion based on the evidence that the accused did not do what he was accused of doing and sometimes a conclusion based on the plaintiff's failure to produce sufficient evidence to show that the accused did what he was accused of doing.

The natural rule, that is, the rule that expresses what is intrinsic to enquiry, is that a conclusion is based on sufficient evidence. This intrinsic characteristic is not confined to judicial enquiry but is found in everyday, and in scientific, enquiries.

The enquirer begins with a question about something that he wants to understand but, as yet, does not, for example, "As the radius of a circle increases from r=1 to r= 2 to r= 3 and so on, how does the area increase?" The question looks for an answer. Once a suggested answer has occurred to the enquirer, a further question arises: is there sufficient evidence for me to accept the suggested answer? In the absence of sufficient evidence the enquirer remains unconvinced and cannot reasonably accept the suggested answer. Consider this suggested answer: as the radius increases from r=n to r= n + 1, the area increases by $[\pi (n + 1) - \pi (n)]$. No one can reasonably accept this suggestion in the absence of sufficient evidence to convince him or her personally. When one has insufficient evidence, one can neither reasonably assert nor reasonably deny but must remain unconvinced or agnostic. This is not a rule imposed upon enquiry; it is a rule that expresses an understanding of what is intrinsic to enquiry. It is important to realise that what is sufficient evidence for one person may not be for another; personal responsibility is involved in judgement.[118]

Notice, however, a crucial difference between the geometrical example and a court case. In the absence of convincing evidence the scientific enquirer can neither accept nor reject the hypothesis. The enquirer may rest in the agnostic position until convincing evidence one way or the other emerges. In the court case, one cannot simply rest in the position that the evidence is insufficient to allow one to conclude either that there was or that there was not an agreement or a rape. For the properly judicial question is yet to be asked: in the absence of sufficient evidence, what is due? Unless the court answers this question it has failed to be a judicial—as distinct from a merely factual— enquiry. For this reason, the French *Code Civil* (art.4) states that a court that fails to decide is guilty of a denial of justice.

The court is a court of justice and its question is: "what is due to the protagonists?" In the absence of sufficient evidence no-one is to be declared to be guilty. What is due to someone who has been accused but who cannot

---

[118] On the general structure of enquiry, see B. Lonergan, *Insight: A Study of Human Understanding* (Longmans, London, 1957). See also G. Barden and P. McShane, *Towards Self-Meaning* (Gill and Macmillan, Dublin, 1969), pp.34–41.

reasonably be declared guilty? Perhaps nothing other than the verdict "Not guilty" or "Not proven" and freedom to go. Perhaps more than that. It is not possible to say in general. But what is clear is that one who cannot reasonably be declared guilty is not due what is due only to one who is reasonably declared guilty. This is an intrinsic principle of intelligent and reasonable enquiry, not an extrinsic imposition.

The jury states what, on the evidence, the facts are to be taken to be. Beyond stating that what is due to the accused is that he be taken to be guilty or not guilty, it does not usually further determine what is due.

When the fact is settled, the court asks what is due. If Peter is judged guilty of fraud or embezzlement or rape or theft or tax evasion or drunken driving or murder or manslaughter and so on, the question as to what is now due to him arises. The answer to this question—the sentence—concludes the court's work. In some cases, of course, the question is not of guilt or innocence but of, say, the proper division of property in separation or divorce. Here again, the first question to be settled is what the relevant facts are.[119] Here again, when the relevant facts are settled, the question as to what is due to each partner arises and the court's answer to this question concludes its work.

In cases of separation or divorce, where a settlement is disputed, the court is concerned with distributive justice; it determines what is jointly owned and how this is to be shared. In cases of, for example, embezzlement, the court is concerned with rectificatory justice for the embezzlement has brought about an unjust situation and a just situation is to be restored. In some cases of injury—for example, rape—it is difficult to discover how a just situation is to be restored. Perhaps it is because it is so difficult that it seems to many that the injury to the victim is forgotten and the question as to what is due to the victim simply ignored. The question as to what is due to the victim of rape is emphatically not that she was entitled not to be raped. She has been raped and the question as to what is due to her arises in that horrible circumstance.[120]

What is due to Mary? She cannot be unraped. Is Peter's punishment enough? Is Peter's punishment to be understood as what is due to Peter only or as what is due also to Mary? It seems to be naturally just that both questions—What is due to Peter? What is due to Mary?—be asked. More generally, it seems to be

---

[119] In the effort to discover the facts there are often two questions. If Peter is accused of embezzlement, the question is not alone whether or not he or some other is guilty but also whether or not embezzlement occurred. Similarly, if Mary accuses Peter of rape, the question is not alone whether or not Peter rather than another is guilty but also whether or not Mary was raped.

[120] What is due to the victims of crime has been to some extent—and to a greater or lesser extent in different kinds of situation—lost sight of. Richard Posner writes of what is due to the victim as, perhaps, "a more or less emotionally satisfactory (legal) substitute for vengeance", *op, cit.*, p.163.

naturally, not simply conventionally, just that both questions—What is due to the criminal? and What is due to the victim of the crime?—be asked.

The court asks: what in the circumstances is due? Is what is due sometimes naturally due, sometimes conventionally due? The correctness of the suggestion that what is due is sometimes naturally and sometimes conventionally due is best shown in an example. If Peter has stolen €100,000 from Paul, it is "naturally just" that Peter should restore the money to Paul. In other words: Paul is due from Peter the restoration of €100,000. Is Paul due any more than this? He has borne the loss of the use of his money for some time. Is he due some interest? In an economy in which money can be used in this way it would seem so. Precisely how much? This must be, at least to some extent, conventional. Is he due something beyond this? Something quite different?

6. CONCLUSION

We may sum up very briefly. The question as to what is just is of the form, "Who in the circumstances is entitled to what?" The theory of the naturally just put forward here is that by an examination of the circumstances it is sometimes possible to discover what is intrinsically or naturally just and sometimes impossible to do so. When it is possible to do so, this is not done by appeal to a divine law or to any higher law but through an examination and discussion of the case.[121] The whole effort of this chapter has been to show that what is naturally just in a situation is intrinsic to the situation. When it is impossible to discover a just solution intrinsic to a situation, when several solutions seem equally good or, in Aristotle's terms, equally indifferent, what is just must be established by convention. For, as St Thomas wrote, in a passage already quoted in the introductory part of this chapter but worth repeating, something is just "in one of two ways: first, from the nature of the case itself, which is called naturally just; secondly, from a kind of agreement among men, which is called positively (or conventionally) just".[122] The jurist must, of course, take note of existing laws; but what is just is not confined within them; the just remains on each occasion and in each case an unknowable to be discovered and not a solution that derives from rules given in advance.[123]

---

[121] See M. Villey, "De la Laïcité du Droit selon Saint Thomas" in *Leçons d'histoire de la Philosophie du Droit*, pp.203–219 and "La Nature des Choses" in *Seize Essais*, pp.38–59. See also G. Barden, "Le Juge et L'espèce" in *Revue de la Recherche Juridique* (Aix en Provence), 1983 (1), pp.134–142.

[122] St Thomas Aquinas, *Summa Theologiae*, II-II, q.60, art.5.

[123] M. Villey, *Seize Essais*, p.222. See n.3 above.

CHAPTER 3

THE MEDIEVAL FOUNDATIONS OF WESTERN JURISPRUDENCE

MICHAEL STAUNTON

1. INTRODUCTION

The Middle Ages is often regarded as a particularly lawless time in history, an interlude of backwardness, brutality and irrationality between the classical civilizations of Greece and Rome and the origins of modernity in the Renaissance and Reformation. In fact, there has seldom been a time when law was of such central importance as in the Middle Ages. In a society characterised by relative instability and weak central control, law was a vital instrument in the aversion of violence. Where the primary social bond was a contractual one between a lord and his vassal, and wealth and power was overwhelmingly based on landholding, the settlement of disputes and the establishment of rights was a constant imperative. The medieval period was a dynamic one, in which the competing claims of different authorities—royal, ecclesiastical, aristocratic—and the tensions between communities and authorities, stimulated reflection upon the legal basis of that authority. The majority of our written records from the Middle Ages are legal ones: charters, contracts, registers, court rolls as well as collections of law. And of all of its bequests to Western civilisation, the medieval legacy of law is perhaps the greatest.

The two main Western traditions of law originate in the Middle Ages. The civil law tradition, which forms the basis of the legal systems of continental Europe, derives from the rediscovery and analysis of an early medieval compilation of Roman law, Justinian's *Corpus Iuris Civilis*, which began in eleventh-century Italy. This also stimulated the first scientific expression of canon law, which remains the law of the Roman Catholic Church. The English common law tradition, which is followed in most of the English-speaking world, developed out of the practices of the English royal courts of the twelfth century. Furthermore, it was in the medieval period, and specifically between the eleventh and thirteenth centuries, that a distinctive Western jurisprudence came into being.

The medieval period is usually defined as beginning with the collapse of the Roman Empire in the West around the fifth century A.D. and ending around 1500 when the term was coined. It is often subdivided into the early Middle Ages or "dark ages", c.500–1000 AD, the central or "high" Middle Ages, c.1000–1250, and the later Middle Ages. This chapter will concentrate on the first two phases, when many of the foundations of Western jurisprudence were laid. The early phase sees the formation of a new Western European civilisation among the "barbarian" peoples of the north and west under the influence of Christianity and the legacy of Rome. Their approaches to law were unsophisticated in comparison to what went before and after, but they formed the basis of many features of Western thought. From the eleventh century, Europe begins to take on a more recognisable shape, with a new prosperity, a revival of commerce and urban life and the beginnings of national monarchies. This was matched by a major intellectual revival of which legal thought played an important part. Here we find the development of new and lasting systems of law, the emergence of law as a profession, and as a subject of scientific study.[1]

2. GERMANIC LAW

One might wonder whether jurisprudence existed at all between the collapse of the Roman Empire in the fifth century A.D. and the rediscovery of the corpus of Roman law in the eleventh century. No treatise on the nature of law survives from this period, nor did law exist as a scholarly discipline or as a profession.[2] Law did not hold the autonomous position that it later claimed, but instead was bound up with social, religious, political and cultural norms. The term "dark ages" refers not only to supposed backwardness but the difficulty we have in casting light on this period, due to the limited nature of literary expression. But law did exist, as did ideas about law, and they also developed over time.

The Roman Empire was a centralised state, with a sophisticated legal system and a large body of writing on law. From the fifth century, western Europe

---

[1] A vast literature exists on the medieval period. C.R. Backman, *The Worlds of Medieval Europe* (Oxford University Press, Oxford, 2003) provides an accessible introduction. For a survey of medieval legal thought, see J.M. Kelly, *A Short History of Western Legal Theory* (Oxford University Press, Oxford, 1992), pp.79–158.

[2] It could be argued that the Brehon law of early medieval Ireland is an exception, as it was preserved by a lawyer-poet class, and law-schools existed. Brehon law differs in a number of ways from the Germanic law discussed here, but as its influence on Western jurisprudence was marginal, it lays outside the scope of this discussion. But see F. Kelly, *A Guide to Early Irish Law* (Institute for Advanced Studies, Dublin, 1988) and D.A. Binchy, "Irish History and Irish Law" (I, II), *Studia Hibernica* 15 (1975), 7–36, and 16 (1976), 7–45.

came to be dominated by loose federations of tribal peoples who had similar customs and language. The Germanic peoples—the Visigoths, Ostrogoths, Franks, Lombards, Angles, Saxons and others—were made up of nomadic tribes whose incursions had precipitated the fall of the Roman Empire and who now settled on its ruins. There also remained the Celtic peoples of the Atlantic seaboard who had not experienced Roman rule. These "barbarians", as the Greeks and Romans had called them, had no concept of a state. The main bonds of society were the extended family and the tribe. Their kings were primarily military leaders rather than legislators and they ruled over people rather than territories—there was a king of the Lombards but no king of Lombardy. In these societies law was custom, the traditional practices of the people dating back to their immemorial ancestors. It originated in the people, and was the expression of their will, rather than that of their ruler. It was also the possession of a particular people, so that whereas all citizens of the Roman Empire were subject to the same law, early medieval Europe was a patchwork of different customary laws, often overlapping. So, while the Lombards of northern Italy, a Germanic people, had their own laws, the indigenous Italians dwelling among them continued to live according to Roman law.[3]

As this example suggests, the barbarian peoples were not isolated from other influences. Those in the south, in particular, came into contact with the remnants of Roman culture, and the Christian conversion of Western Europe which was largely complete by around 800 A.D. reinforced the Roman legacy. Its most important legacy was literacy, and we find the earliest written sources of Western law in the Germanic law codes. Crude imitations of late Roman codes, they are not really codifications of law in anything like the modern sense, rather a ragbag of offences and penalties. And as this remained an overwhelmingly illiterate people, with only a small minority of monks and clerks able to read and write, they represent just the tip of the iceberg of a large body of unwritten custom. Nonetheless, they offer a valuable insight into the legal mentality of the age.

Typical are the laws of the Ripuarian Franks, who lived on the right bank of the Rhine near Cologne and composed a code around the 630s. As one might expect in a relatively unstable society, a central function of law, as seen in these codes, is the prevention of violence, and in particular of blood-feud, the endless cycles of conflict between extended families. The code is almost entirely devoted to criminal matters but such offences are not understood as

---

[3] On Germanic society, see J.M. Wallace-Hadrill, *The Barbarian West 400–1000* (revised ed., Blackwell, Oxford, 1996) and *Early German Kingship* (Clarendon Press, Oxford, 1971). On Germanic law, see A.S. Diamond, *Primitive Law Past and Present* (Methuen, London, 1971) and F. Kern, *Kingship and Law in the Middle Ages* (Blackwell, Oxford, 1939).

being committed against an authority but against the family of the victim. The offender is not punished by violence or incarceration, but instead is liable to pay a monetary compensation called *wergeld* to the victim's family. These societies were highly conscious of social rank, and this is reflected in the determination of the penalty by the status of the victim. So killing a slave demanded compensation of 36 solidi, a churchman, 100 solidi, but a member of the king's retinue, 600 solidi. Likewise, the life of a woman of childbearing age is valued at 600 solidi, but that of a girl under 12 or a woman over 40 at only 200 solidi.[4] Furthermore, the consequence of the offence rather than the intention of the offender is the primary consideration. So,

"3. i. If a freeman cuts off the ear of another freeman so that he cannot hear, let him be liable for 100 solidi. If, however, [the victim] does not lose his hearing, let him be compensated with fifty solidi.

   ii. If he cuts off the nose so that he cannot blow it, let him be held liable for 100 solidi. If he is still able to blow it, let him compensate fifty solidi."[5]

The private character of the law is echoed in procedure. It was the plaintiff rather than the court who initiated proceedings by summoning the defendant to trial. Although evidence was often presented in court, more weight was attached to other methods of establishing innocence or guilt, which reflected two central features of society: the importance of honour, and the belief in divine guidance. In trial by compurgation, the plaintiff and the defendant each swore to the truthfulness of their case, and then each was joined by "compurgators" who took an oath to their truthfulness. Decision was then based on the number and rank of the compurgators. Trial by ordeal was an appeal to divine judgement.[6] Boiling water or hot iron was applied to the skin and innocence or guilt was determined by the speed it took to heal. Alternatively, in ordeal of battle, trained warriors would fight on behalf of each side before judges to decide the worthy party. These may be unsophisticated practices, but they nonetheless reflect a legal order, grounded in current belief, society and culture.

The key features of Germanic law are that it is largely unwritten custom; it is envisaged primarily as a means of preventing internecine violence; a multiplicity of laws prevails; and the role of central authority is weak. But this

---

[4] *Laws of the Salian and Ripuarian Franks* (T.J. Rivers trans., AMS Press, New York, 1986), pp.174–5.

[5] *ibid.*, p.172.

[6] See R. Bartlett, *Trial by Fire and Water: The Medieval Judicial Order* (Clarendon Press, Oxford, 1986).

was not a static society, and already before the dramatic developments of the eleventh and twelfth centuries, political, social and ideological developments had brought about significant shifts: in particular in the strengthening—both in practice and in theory—of central power, and the growing importance of bonds of lordship.

The Germanic conception of the source of law has been described as "ascending": the power to create law originated in the people themselves, and was granted upwards to their ruler, who must rule within the law and with the consent of the people. This consent was not expressed through election or parliament, but is present, for example, in the tradition of banging on shields to express approvals of laws announced at assemblies. However, from the eighth century onwards kings, with the support of ecclesiastics, began to claim greater authority. A theocratic notion of kingship may be seen in the growing practice of a monarch being anointed with holy oil, and the increasing invocation of parallels with such Old Testament kings as David and Solomon and the Christian emperors of later Rome. In this "descending" scheme, kingship was seen as divine in its origins, and its powers comprised the issuing of new laws.[7]

Such ideas went hand in hand with the practical extension of monarchical rule, which reached an early high-point in the short-lived empire of Charlemagne, king of the Franks (771–814). In the second half of the eighth century, Charlemagne succeeded in extending his rule over a vast territory ranging from the Atlantic to the eastern frontiers of modern Germany. His coronation as emperor by the Pope on Christmas Day, 800 marks the revival of the tradition of the Roman Empire in the West, but now as a distinctively Western entity, rooted in a combination of Roman, Germanic and Christian traditions.[8] His was not only a military achievement but also an administrative and cultural one, involving the establishment of a centralised system of governance through representatives in the regions, and a fostering of learning. One feature of this was the development of centrally-issued legislation applicable to the whole empire, known as "capitularies". While the various legal practices of the diverse peoples were acknowledged, the capitularies acted to amend and supplement them, and were seen as having overriding authority.[9] From the ninth century, other kings, for example in Anglo-Saxon

---

[7] See W. Ullmann, *Law and Politics in the Middle Ages* (Cambridge University Press, Cambridge, 1975), pp.30 *et seq.*

[8] The "Byzantine" Empire, centered on Constantinople and comprising the modern-day Balkan states and Turkey, also considered itself to be a continuation of the Roman Empire.

[9] See D. Bullough, *The Age of Charlemagne* (2nd ed., Elek, London, 1973); R. Collins, *Charlemagne* (Palgrave, London, 1998); and F.L. Ganshof, *Frankish Institutions under Charlemagne* (Brown University Press, Providence, 1968).

England, increasingly promulgated their own law codes. There developed such notions as the king's peace—the idea that an offence was committed against the ruler's guardianship of the people—and concomitant punishments such as death and mutilation rather than compensation payments. Charlemagne's empire fell apart shortly after his death in the face of attacks on Europe by Viking and Magyar invaders, but the title emperor was revived in the tenth century by the rulers of his eastern, German lands who continued to insist on the law-giving power of the monarchy.[10]

The collapse of Charlemagne's empire also fostered the growth of a key factor in the development of medieval society and law: feudalism.[11] "Feudal", like "medieval", has negative connotations, but the development of this social system was an appropriate response to the needs of the time, and was highly influential in the establishment first of local territorial jurisdictions, and later in the development of royal jurisdiction. It originated as a personal contract between a lord and his vassal. The lord provided physical and legal protection and a fief (*feudum*), usually a grant of land. In return, the vassal offered homage and fidelity to his lord, and regular service, usually in military or labour form. This was a relationship of dependence, but it was respectable dependence, and implied rights and obligations on both sides. By the eleventh century, the feudal relationship had progressed from a private arrangement to being the primary bond of society and the basis of public law. This particularly benefited local regional rulers. For example, the French king nominally ruled over a region roughly contiguous with modern-day France, but only had effective control around Paris, while the duke of Normandy had a strong role in the regulation of his people, because almost all free men were part of a pyramid of allegiances, culminating in the duke. The law, while still based on custom, became increasingly that of a territory, with the duke at its head, and his own feudal court.

Western Europe in the year 1000, then, had a multiplicity of legal systems and jurisdictions, often overlapping. The various peoples had their own customary laws, but royal law, feudal law and ecclesiastical law also existed. As yet no effectively-applied universal legal system existed, but this was soon to change.

---

[10] On the German continuation of empire, see, for example, J. Fleckenstein, *Early Medieval Germany* (North-Holland, Amsterdam and New York, 1978) and K. Hampe, *Germany under the Salian and Hohenstaufen Emperors* (Blackwell, Oxford, 1973).

[11] For varying interpretations of feudalism, see M. Bloch, *Feudal Society* (2nd ed., Routledge, London, 1989); F.L. Ganshof, *Feudalism* (3rd ed., Longman, London, 1970); and S. Reynolds, *Fiefs and Vassals* (Oxford University Press, Oxford, 1994).

3. THE REVIVAL OF ROMAN LAW

Western jurisprudence became a scientific reality in the eleventh century with the rediscovery of a book: Justinian's *Corpus Iuris Civilis*, a compendium of laws and legal opinions based on centuries of Roman legal thought and practice. Although the last Western emperor was deposed in 476, imperial rule, institutions, culture and law continued in the eastern, Greek part of the empire, known as Byzantium. Under Justinian, who was Emperor from 527 to 565, the whole body of Roman law dating back centuries was gathered together as a coherent whole. The *Corpus Iuris Civilis* consists of four books: the *Institutes*, an introductory text-book, setting out basic jurisprudential principles; the *Digest* or *Pandects*, fifty books of commentary on a series of topics, based on excerpts from the writings of Roman jurists and intended for the use of judges and practitioners; the *Code*, a collection of imperial laws and decisions in cases arranged according to topics and individual emperors; and the *Novels*, more recent laws gathered during Justinian's reign. This massive volume continued to be studied in the east, but was only known in the west in fragmentary form. Most importantly, the *Digest*, which contained the richest sources of jurisprudence, seems to have been lost. That is, until two manuscripts containing the full *Corpus* were rediscovered in Italy some time in the eleventh century.

Exactly how Justinian's collection was discovered is unclear, but it is unlikely that it was simply stumbled upon. Rather, it reappeared at a crucial time and place, which was witnessing a renewed interest in law. In the early Middle Ages, law did not exist as an academic subject, although such terms as *lex* (law) and *ius* (right) were discussed as part of the study of grammar and rhetoric. Teaching and learning in the main schools of the time, associated with monasteries and cathedral chapters, was overwhelmingly based on the bible and early Christian writers, but in the eleventh century law schools emerged in Ravenna, Padua, Naples, and most importantly Bologna. This must be seen as an early part of a broader intellectual reawakening which is often termed "the Twelfth-Century Renaissance".[12] Between the eleventh and the thirteenth centuries, a new interest in the Latin classics, and in Greek and Arabic science and philosophy, contributed to the discovery of texts hitherto unknown in the west, which in turn further stimulated study. So, for example, a growing interest in the application of logic to theological matters went hand-in-hand with the discovery of previously unknown works by Aristotle. This was aided by more frequent contact between western Europeans and the Greek

---

[12] The term was popularised by C.H. Haskins, *The Renaissance of the Twelfth Century* (Harvard University Press, Cambridge, Mass., 1927). For more recent studies, see R.N. Swanson, *The Twelfth-Century Renaissance* (Manchester University Press, Manchester, 1999) and *Renaissance and Renewal in the Twelfth Century* (R. Benson and G. Constable eds., Clarendon Press, Oxford, 1982).

and Arab worlds, the growth of trade and the beginnings of urban life. The renewal of interest in the study of law can be seen, then, to predate the reception and study of Justinian's *Corpus* in the Italian law schools, but that volume's influence on the further history of jurisprudence is nonetheless profound.

The *Corpus Iuris Civilis* provided what had not existed before in the west: a systematised body of written law. It also provided a methodology and technical vocabulary by which legal questions could be addressed. The *Institutes* begins by establishing general principles of law:

> "Justice is the constant and perpetual desire to give to each man his due right. Jurisprudence is acquaintance with things human and divine, the knowledge of what is just and what unjust...
>
> These are the precepts of law: to live justly, not to injure another and to render to each his own. There are two aspects of this study, public and private. Public law is that which pertains to the Roman state, private that which concerns the well-being of the individual. One then has to observe of private law that it is threefold; for it consists of natural precepts, those observed generally by nations and those of a given state."[13]

The *Digest*, which includes the views of eminent Roman jurists and which received the greatest attention in the Middle Ages, addresses individual topics in an exhaustive manner. For example, Book 23 deals with marriage by addressing in turn betrothals, formation of marriage and the law of dowry. The first five clauses of the section on betrothals will give an example of the methodology involved:

> "1. FLORENTINUS, *Institutes, book 3*: Betrothal is the announcement and mutual promise of marriage in the future.
>
> 2. ULPIAN, *Betrothal, sole book*: 'Betrothal' was so called from the 'solemn plighting of troth', since it was customary for our ancestors to stipulate and solemnly promise their wives-to-be to each other.
>
> 3. FLORENTINUS, *Institutes, book 3*: This is the derivation of the term 'betrothed' for both sexes.
>
> 4. ULPIAN, *Sabinus, book 35*: Agreement alone is sufficient for betrothal. 1. It is agreed that betrothal can take place in the absence of the parties, and this is quite common,

---

[13] *The Institutes of Justinian* (J.A.C. Thomas, ed., North-Holland, Amsterdam and Oxford, 1975), pp.2–3. For discussion of the understanding of justice in the *Institutes*, see Garrett Barden, "Of the Naturally and the Conventionally Just" in this volume.

5. POMPONIUS, *Sabinus, book 16*: as long as the absent parties know of it or ratify it afterward."[14]

The Italian legal scholars who began to study the *Corpus*, and particularly the *Digest*, towards the end of the eleventh century regarded it as the expression of a universal, ideal system, a set of legal principles that embodied the highest legal reason. They approached in a similar way to how contemporary theologians approached the Bible, as an entirely consistent whole where any apparent contradictions were possible to resolve in the light of reason. The *Corpus Iuris Civilis* was nonetheless a challenging work for its eleventh-century students, with complex terms and concepts and apparent contradictions. The early work of legal scholars involved going through the work word by word explaining terms and resolving problems, after discussion and debate. This resulted in the production of *glosses*, annotated copies of the work with comments written between the lines and then out into the margins until there existed a network of references and cross-references often larger than the original work. The work of the Glossators culminates in the *Glossa Ordinaria* of 1250 by Accursius, regarded as the definitive summation of early glosses.[15]

If this did not amount to a critical assessment of Justinian's collection, it nonetheless represents the first stage in a science of Western jurisprudence, based around formal legal training and the application of analytical methods and a technical vocabulary to legal problems. It also had consequences for the practice of law. Although Roman law was seen as the highest law and as having a universal applicability, older practices of customary law continued, but became increasingly influenced by the study of the law schools. It also influenced the form and substance of new systems of urban and commercial law which had recently grown up. In particular, it stimulated the emergence of a new canon law.

Canons are rules of right behaviour, and canon law is the law of the Roman Catholic Church.[16] It derives from a variety of sources: the bible, the writings of such "Church Fathers" as St Augustine and St Ambrose, decrees of early church councils, papal letters and other materials. It had long existed, and collections were made from the fifth century onwards, but before the twelfth century it was an unwieldy mass, lacking both coherent codification and the

---

[14] *The Digest of Justinian* (T. Mommsen and P. Kreuger eds, A. Watson trans., University of Pennsylvania Press, Philadelphia, 1985), vol.3, p.656.

[15] On the medieval reception of Roman law, see H.F. Jolwicz, *Historical Introduction to the Study of Roman Law* (3rd ed., Cambridge University Press, Cambridge, 1972); J.H. Merryman, *The Civil Law Tradition* (Stanford University Press, Stanford, 1969); and D. Ibbetson and A. Lewis, *The Roman Law Tradition* (Cambridge University Press, Cambridge, 1994), especially pp.1–14.

[16] See in particular J.A. Brundage, *Medieval Canon Law* (Longman, London, 1995).

backing of an effective centralised jurisdictional authority. Both of these were achieved at the same time and were bound up together.[17]

From the beginning, Christianity has been associated with law—it is an important theme in the Old Testament and the letters of St Paul. From the fourth century, when the Roman Empire adopted Christianity, the church became associated with universality. Theoretically, Christian doctrine overrode all boundaries between Christians, and laws were only valid if they conformed with the Christian principles. But, in effect, the legal authority of ecclesiastics was local and limited. As seen in the coronation of Charlemagne, and the development of the idea of sacral kingship, popes supported the claims of emperors and strong monarchs as defenders of ecclesiastical privileges and as agents for stable societies in which Christian principles could grow. Emperors, in turn, tried to boost the status of the papacy by removing it from the control of local Roman nobles. But in the middle of the eleventh century, a momentous movement, usually called the Gregorian Reform after the papacy of Pope Gregory VII (from 1073 to 1085), wrested the papacy from imperial control and asserted its authority over matters not only spiritual but temporal also. Early theologians had considered the relationship between spiritual and temporal power in terms of the biblical two swords given to St Peter:[18] the papacy retained one to use in the form of excommunication of spiritual offenders, while the secular power held the other for the protection of the church and its people. Now the papacy began to claim that spiritual authority was greater than temporal authority, and that the jurisdiction of the Pope should override that of any temporal ruler. It even extended to the claim that a pope could depose an emperor. This conflict resulted not only in conflict between empire and papacy between 1075 and 1115, but outright war.[19] The war was inconclusive, but in the long run the papacy emerged stronger, partly due to its development of canon law.

The assertion of papal claims to primacy stimulated an investigation of the canons, in search of material in support of those claims, and this, in turn,

---

[17] This has been described as a "revolution" by H.J. Berman, *Law and Revolution: The Formation of the Western Legal Tradition* (Harvard University Press, Cambridge, Mass., 1983), who discusses the rise of papal power and the growth of canon law in the context of the revival of Roman law.

[18] *Luke* 22:38.

[19] Historians call this conflict the Investiture Controversy, after one of the issues at dispute: the practice of laymen investing senior ecclesiastics with the symbols of office. See G. Tellenbach, *Church, State and Christian Society at the Time of the Investiture Controversy* (Blackwell, Oxford, 1959); W. Ullmann, *The Growth of Papal Government* (2nd ed., Methuen, London, 1955); and K. Morrison, *Tradition and Authority in the Western Church 300–1140* (Princeton University Press, Princeton, 1969), pp.269–360.

stimulated new attempts to codify the law. This coincided with the revival of Roman law in Bologna, though many of the early scholars there supported imperial claims. Irnerius, doctor of law at Bologna and father of the new Roman jurisprudence, was excommunicated by Gregory VII for his support for the Emperor. These attempts at codification culminated in the production of a corpus which was, if not as sophisticated as Justinian's, at least as influential in the Middle Ages: the *Decretum* of Gratian.

We know little about Gratian, but his compilation of canon law was the most-copied book of the Middle Ages after the Bible. Completed around 1140, and commonly called the *Decretum*, its full title is more expressive of its purpose: *Concordia Discordantium Canonum*—"A Concordance of Discordant Canons".[20] In the same way as the students of the *Corpus Iuris Civilis*, he sought to reconcile apparently contradictory elements in canon law in the belief that it comprised a consistent whole that only required the application of reason to reveal. It is also strongly influenced by the emerging theological method today known as scholasticism, which sought to explain through rational means the entire Christian tradition, a movement that culminated in the work of St Thomas Aquinas in the thirteenth century. The first part, the "Distinctions", begins by dealing with divisions between different types and varieties of law. Gratian identifies natural law with what is right and unchangeable, associated with divine law as expressed in scripture, as against human law which is valid in itself but must conform to the practices of the community and natural law. The main part, the "Cases", consists of a series of legal issues, divided into questions. These are answered by canonical authorities from Christian tradition, and reconciled by Gratian's own comments.

Gratian's *Decretum*, along with the newly-found authority of the papacy, helped to establish the first trans-national jurisdiction in the West. As the papacy built up a bureaucracy of lawyers and administrators in Rome and legates in the regions, there was a steady increase in appeals to judgement by the Roman curia according to canon law. The *Decretum* also became the subject of study in the burgeoning law-schools, alongside Justinian's *Corpus*, and some of the most distinguished popes of the era were legal scholars.[21] From the middle of

---

[20] The *Decretum* was ultimately the basis of the *Corpus Iuris Canonici*. For a short introduction to Gratian's method, see S. Kuttner, *Harmony From Dissonance: An Interpretation of Medieval Canon Law* (Archabbey, Latrobe, 1960), and see also S. Chodorow, *Christian Political Theory and Church Politics in the Mid-Twelfth Century: The Ecclesiology of Gratian's Decretum* (University of California Press, Berkeley, 1972).

[21] Roland Bandinelli, distinguished professor of law at Bologna, reigned as Pope Alexander III from 1159–1181, during which time the greatest amount of papal legislation in the Middle Ages was enacted. Pope Innocent III (who was Pope from

the twelfth century, the first universities, a uniquely medieval creation, developed out of schools of law, theology and medicine.[22] In places such as Bologna, which has a claim to the title of the earliest university, students studied the two great works of Roman and canon law, debated contentious points, and developed glosses. In this way questions of equity, justice and individual rights were elaborated, often with lasting consequences. For example, a mid-twelfth century commentary on the *Decretum* examined Adam's response to God's accusation of wrongdoing in the Garden of Eden with the words, "The woman whom thou gavest to be with me, she gave me the fruit of the tree and I ate"[23]— and considered it to be a defence of entrapment. The commentator concluded that if God must summon litigants to defend themselves, humans must also summon them and presume that every defendant is innocent until proven guilty in court. A later elaboration of this theory provided the equally familiar maxim, "God must even give the devil his day in court".[24]

4. THE ENGLISH COMMON LAW

The English common law is the law of the king's courts that took shape during the reign of King Henry II (1154–1189). It was the first unified territorial law to emerge in the West and today it forms the basis of the national legal systems in Britain, Ireland, the US, Canada, Australia and most other former British colonies. There are evident contrasts with the customary law which continued to dominate continental Europe as the English common law emerged. Rather than being based on nationality, it is the law of the land, generally applicable and available to all subjects, and it involves direct government, as established in royal courts and a professional judicial class. It also differs in approach and substance to Roman and canon law. Though those systems did influence the English law, and some codification exists, it is not based on a code, nor is there an emphasis on abstract theoretical principles. Rather it was formed in the developing practice of the royal courts and decisions in individual cases.[25]

1198–1216) studied at Bologna, and his skills as a canonist influenced the reforming legislation of the Fourth Lateran Council of 1215.

[22] See A. Cobban, *The Medieval Universities* (Methuen, London, 1975).

[23] *Genesis* 3:12.

[24] K. Pennington, "Innocent until Proven Guilty: The Origins of a Legal Maxim" in *A Ennio Cortese* (Il Cigno Galileo Galilei Edizioni, Rome, 2001).

[25] The classic work on the English common law, first published in 1895, is F. Pollock and F.W. Maitland, *The History of English Law before the Time of Edward I* (2 vols, 2nd ed., Cambridge University Press, Cambridge, 1968). For a more recent analysis, see in particular J. Hudson, *The Formation of the English Common Law* (Longman, London, 1996), and also R.C. van Caenegem, *The Birth of the English Common*

The English common law crystallised in the second half of the twelfth century, but it originates in an earlier expansion of royal influence over law: the growing concept of the king's peace, the integration of the feudal contract into the public sphere, and the refinement of central administration. The Norman Conquest of England in 1066 and the assertive advancement of royal rights by a series of kings made the king's law, for the first time in Western Europe, applicable to the whole population.

When William, duke of Normandy, conquered England in 1066 he found a system of royal administration that was advanced for its time. The kingdom was divided into territorial administrative units of shires subdivided into hundreds, and kings issued written instructions to their officers in the regions by means of the royal writ. The concept of offences as being against the king's peace, and punishment by death or outlawry had grown as that of compensation payments declined. Most judicial business was nevertheless carried out in the local courts of the shire or the hundred, and the king's court largely functioned as a court of appeal, being mainly limited to those who could approach the king in person. What the Normans introduced was one of the most developed feudal structures of the time in which virtually all free men were part of a hierarchy of loyalties, not just to their immediate lord but ultimately to the king of England. Therefore, the Norman kings of England were, theoretically at least, lords of all freemen in the territory of England, owing them justice, and expecting their people's subjection to that justice.[26]

Henry II came to the throne after a period of civil war and weak central government between 1135 and 1154, a period known as the Anarchy of King Stephen. Although the legacy of Henry's legal reforms far outlives the issues of the day, they emerged as a response to the challenging situation he faced upon accession, the need to reassert royal authority in the face of encroachment from noble and ecclesiastical interests, and the desire to restore law and order. Henry was not only king of England but ruled extensive territories overseas and travelled around them constantly with his own itinerant court, the *curia regis*. This was part of the stimulus for his establishment of permanent governmental offices at Westminster, staffed by professional administrators. The exchequer (named after the chequered cloth upon which accounts were tallied) looked after the king's finances. The chancery was a writing office in which charters, writs and other administrative documents were composed. A central royal high court sat in regular sessions, eventually being divided into

---

Law (Cambridge University Press, Cambridge, 1973) and T.F.T. Plucknett, *A Concise History of the Common Law* (4th ed., Butterworths, London, 1948).

[26] The Anglo-Saxon influence on the development of Roman law has recently been emphasized by P. Wormald, *The Making of English Law: King Alfred to the Twelfth Century*, Vol. 1 (Blackwell, Oxford 1999), and the reign of Henry I (1100–1135) by J. Hudson, *op. cit*. For a summary of the historiography, see Hudson, pp.19–23.

the King's Bench, which dealt with felonies and offences against the king's person, and the Court of Common Pleas, which heard civil cases. In addition, justice was brought to the localities in the form of regular countrywide visitations by royal justices, known as justices in eyre. In this way, then, royal justice was more readily available to those who wished to access it.

Questions over possession of land constituted one of the main concerns of the royal courts, and they tended towards similarity. During the 1160s routine procedures emerged which have come to be known as possessory assizes. For example, a plaintiff who claimed recent dispossession from land could purchase a writ in standardised form from the royal chancery directing the local sheriff to initiate proceedings.[27] Twelve free men of the neighbourhood would then be assembled before royal justices, the next time they visited, and swear as to whether the plaintiff had been unjustly dispossessed. This system was soon extended to criminal cases, where the 12 men would swear as to the guilt or otherwise of the accused. We have seen how compurgators from an early date attested to the truthfulness of a plaintiff or defendant and there were earlier cases of sworn inquests, but here we have a regular procedure in which twelve men are required to give a truthful answer (*verum dictum* = verdict) to a question put to them by an authority on the basis of their likelihood to know the facts. Such sworn inquests came to replace such forms of trial as ordeal and compurgation. Here we see the origins of the modern jury system, though it was not until the fourteenth century that juries were asked to make judgements on the basis of evidence presented.

Though nowhere near as substantial as that of Roman and canon law, the English common law also produced a literature. The earliest attempt to describe the new legal systems, a treatise written in the late 1180s known as "Glanvil", asserts that,

---

[27] For example: "The king to the sheriff, greeting. N. has complained to me that R. unjustly and without a judgement has disseised [dispossessed] him of his free tenement in such-and-such a vill since my last visit to Normandy. Therefore I command you that, if N. gives you security for prosecuting his claim, you are to see that the chattels which were taken from the tenement are restored to it, and that the tenement and the chattels remain in peace until the Sunday after Easter. And meanwhile you are to see that the tenement is viewed by twelve free and lawful men of the neighbourhood, and their names endorsed on this writ. And summon them by good summoners to be before me or my justices on the Sunday after Easter, ready to make the recognition. And summon R., or his bailiff if he himself cannot be found, on the security of gage and reliable sureties to be there then to hear the recognition. And have there the summoners, and this writ and the names of the sureties": *The Treatise on the Laws and Customs of the Realm of England commonly called Glanvill*, (G.D.G. Hall ed. and trans., Clarendon Press, Oxford, 1965), p.167.

"Although the laws of England are not written, it does not seem absurd to call them laws—those, that is, which are known to have been promulgated about problems settled in council on the advice of the magnates and with the supporting authority of the prince [*i.e.* the king]— for this is also a law, that 'What pleases the prince has the force of law'. For if, merely for lack of writing, they were not deemed to be laws, then surely writing would seem to supply to written laws a force of greater authority than either the justice of him who decrees them or the reason of him who establishes them."[28]

However, the author adds, it is impossible to put in writing all the laws and legal rules because of the ignorance of scribes on the one hand and the confused multiplicity of laws on the other. Instead, he proposes to set down some general rules frequently observed in court, which he does largely by reproducing royal writs such as that cited above.[29]

A more sophisticated work is Henry de Bracton's *On the Laws and Customs of England*, which was completed in the mid-thirteenth century. Influenced by the Roman law and the works of the glossators, he borrowed extensively from the civil law, and addressed such questions as the distinction between law and custom, the nature of justice, jurisprudence, equity, natural law, civil law and the law of nations. This was a remarkable achievement for a lawyer working within the English system, but all the more so because he addressed such questions with constant reference to the English context.[30] Just as important is the fact that from the 1190s onwards, court proceedings were routinely recorded and preserved.

Henry II's legal innovations succeeded because they met a need, just as papal jurisdiction was expanding at the same time in response to what would nowadays be called consumer demand. They gave the king of England an unprecedented degree of jurisdictional influence, and in doing so extended his authority at the expense of the other major forces in political life, the church and the nobility. But the English common law had not abolished customary and feudal law—indeed they provided its basis—nor the range of other courts to which people could have recourse. And although absolutist tendencies are evident among Henry II and his successors, absolute rule was not achieved. One of the significant features of the English common law for later generations is that it not only established an English territorial law, but also led to the

---

[28] *ibid.*, p.2.

[29] See above, n.27.

[30] *Bracton on the Laws and Customs of England* (4 vols, G. Woodbine ed., S.E. Thorne trans., Harvard University Press, Cambridge, Mass., 1968–1977). On the influence of Roman law in England, see P. Vinogradoff, *Roman Law in Medieval Europe* (2nd ed., Oxford University Press, Oxford, 1929), pp.97–118.

creation of checks upon royal, and later state, control of law. We can see part of the origin of these restraints in the Becket dispute, and in Magna Carta.

For contemporaries, the most noteworthy features of Henry II's reign was not the advance of the common law but his conflict with Thomas Becket (c.1118–1170), and it is for this that he remains best known.[31] Thomas was a relatively low-born Londoner whose early life was typical of those who advanced to high office through the opportunities provided by the expansion of ecclesiastical and royal bureaucracies. He first served as a clerk in the court of the Archbishop of Canterbury, and studied law for a time at Bologna and Auxerre, though he never became a legal scholar. When Henry came to the throne he appointed Thomas royal chancellor, an office in which Thomas distinguished himself as a loyal servant and friend. When the see of Canterbury became vacant, Henry made Thomas Archbishop, believing that he would prove a valuable ally in asserting royal rights in respect of the church. In particular, Henry wished to limit ecclesiastical jurisdiction, believing that it had contributed to the main challenges which he had set himself to deal with on becoming king: criminal disorder and diminished royal authority. The Normans had introduced to England ecclesiastical courts, common on the continent, which judged those in holy orders and regulated matters of religious concern and some, such as marriage, which we would consider to belong to civil law. During the reign of Stephen, these courts had, in Henry's eyes, adopted an unduly lenient approach to "criminous clerks", those in holy orders who had committed a serious felony. At the same time, papal jurisdiction had made significant inroads into England, with appeals to the papal curia over the head of the king now commonplace. If the lenient treatment of criminous clerks was largely due to the weakness of King Stephen, the increase in appeals to the Pope had parallels elsewhere in Europe, and was probably unavoidable.

Henry's response was typically radical. In January 1164 he enacted a written statement of the "ancestral customs of the realm" regarding the rights of royal and ecclesiastical jurisdictions. The two most important of these "Constitutions of Clarendon" are Clause 3 which states that a clerk convicted in a church court ought to be handed over to royal jurisdiction and be treated there as a layman, subject to punishment of death or mutilation, and Clause 8, that no appeals ought to be made to the pope without the consent of the king.[32] But perhaps most important was the fact that custom—or at least what the king claimed as custom—was being reduced to writing. If it had succeeded, the

---

[31] For the dispute, see F. Barlow, *Thomas Becket* (Wiedenfeld and Nicolson, London, 1986). On the legal issues at stake, see C. Duggan, *Canon Law in Medieval England: The Becket Dispute and Decretal Collections* (Variorum, London, 1982).

[32] For a translation of the Constitutions, see *The Lives of Thomas Becket* (M. Staunton ed., Manchester University Press, Manchester, 2001), pp.91–96.

Constitutions might have stood as one of the most important landmarks in the development of enacted law in England. But it did not succeed, due to the determined opposition of Henry's former friend.

Soon after his appointment as Archbishop, Thomas had shown an unexpected independence, championing the liberties of the church, and tensions between him and the king developed into outright conflict when he rejected the Constitutions. There are two main arguments attributed to Thomas. The first rejects the double judgement implied in Clause 3 according to the biblical reading "God does not judge twice for the same thing".[33] The second is more wide-ranging:

> "Holy church, mother of all kings and priests, has two kings, two laws, two jurisdictions, and two punishments. Two laws, Christ the king of heaven and the worldly king; two laws, human and divine; two jurisdictions, priestly and legal; two punishments, spiritual and bodily. … [Clerks] are ruled by their own law, not under a secular king, but under their own king, under the king of heaven. And if they transgress, they are punished by their own law, which has its own penalty."[34]

Thomas's position was an extreme one, but it reflects the legacy of the assertion of papal rights in the previous century. Its importance here is as a reminder that other jurisdictions continued to exist, and that the extension of the authority of the king's courts could be opposed by defending the rights of those rival jurisdictions. Later that year Thomas fled into exile and did not return to Canterbury for six years. A month after his return he was murdered in his own cathedral by knights claiming to act on the king's behalf. The subsequent outrage throughout Europe forced Henry to abandon the Constitutions—his one major failure in legal reform.

Just as the English common law emerged as a response to contemporary challenges but left a great legacy, Magna Carta is more important in its consequence than in its design.[35] It was a response to specific grievances against a weak and unpopular king, but in its expression it encapsulated principles about the legal relationship between the community and its sovereign which became very influential. King John, who reigned from 1199 until 1216, was the youngest son of Henry II and the beneficiary of his father's extension of

---

[33] The Old Latin version of *Nahum* 1:9.

[34] My translation from *Materials for the History of Archbishop Thomas Becket* (J.C. Robertson ed., Rolls Series, London, 1877), Vol.3, p.268. *Clericus* means both clerk and cleric, reflecting the fact that those who acted as clerks were in religious orders.

[35] See in particular J.C. Holt, *Magna Carta* (2nd ed., Cambridge University Press, Cambridge, 1992).

royal authority. During his reign, the rights of the king were pushed to their utmost: royal courts became a primary instrument of the king's will, being used for the submission of rivals and the amassing of revenues. It became common, for example, for a noble to buy the king's justice so as to influence a judicial decision, or for a trivial offence to result in a massive financial penalty, and lands confiscated for failure to pay. John's failure in war in France prompted aggrieved barons to rebel against him and force him to grant them a charter of liberties—Magna Carta—in 1215.[36]

Many of the clauses in Magna Carta are only of contemporary relevance, dealing, for example, with the expulsion of certain men who had damaged baronial interests. Nor was its intention the complete reversal of the legal practices which had developed over the previous 50 years. Clause 17 states that one ought not have to approach the king himself in order to receive justice, and Clause 18 acknowledges the practice of possessory assizes and declares that they should be held locally. It is rather the arbitrary use of royal courts that is addressed. Clause 20 states that a financial penalties should only be imposed in accordance with the degree of the offence. Of greatest interest to the later development of legal thought are those clauses which relate to the relationship between the king, the community and the law. Clause 39 states:

> "No free man shall be arrested or imprisoned or disseised [dispossessed] or outlawed or exiled or in any way victimized, neither will we attack him or send anyone to attack him, except by the lawful judgement of his peers or by the law of the land."

The reference to trial by one's peers had a narrow meaning at the time, deriving from the feudal practice of the trial of a vassal by his fellow-vassals in the court of his lord. But it eventually came to influence the principle of a right to trial by jury, and forms the basis, for example, of the "due process" Fifth Amendment to the US Constitution. The relationship of the king to the law is stated starkly in Clause 40: "To no one will we sell, to no one will we refuse or delay right or justice." But its most momentous expression is in Clause 61, the "security clause", which states that 25 barons will be chosen to observe and to hold to be observed those liberties that the king has granted. If a transgression is noted and not amended within a certain number of days, "those twenty-five barons together with the community of the whole land shall distrain and distress us in every way they can, namely by seizing castle, lands, possessions and such other ways as they can". Here the king is explicitly placed below the law.

John had no intention of complying with its terms, and war soon broke out.

---

[36] The translation used here is from *English Historical Documents Volume III, 1189–1327* (H. Rothwell ed., Eyre and Spottiswoode, London, 1975), pp.316–24.

The following year John died unexpectedly, leaving his infant son Henry as heir. It was the response of the child's guardians which gave Magna Carta its long-term significance: they reissued the Charter in 1216, with some modifications, as a royal manifesto. Now, rather than peace terms forced upon a king, it stood as a statement of the relations between the king, the community of the realm—originally meaning the nobility and the church—and the law. Modified versions were frequently reissued, and in 1295, as the English Parliament was developing, it was entered on the statute rolls, where a number of its clauses remain. It was incorporated into the Bill of Rights of 1689 which granted the English throne to King William of Orange in return for the recognition of the liberties of the nation, and played an important role in the composition of the US Constitution.[37]

Here we can see that while Roman and canon law derived their sources from general principles and applied them to current issues, the English common law developed as a response to immediate needs, but resulted in the acceptance of general principles.

5. Conclusion

Medieval approaches to law seem inherently contradictory. They considered law to be based upon universal truth, yet accepted a plurality of legal systems. Law was apparently immutable, but continually changed. But this goes to the heart of the medieval world-view of a perfect order of which human society was an imperfect reflection, groping towards an attainable perfection through the application of reason and divine grace. In reality, for most people the imperfect reflection was of more immediate concern than the perfect ideal. A law dominated by prevention of internecine violence was appropriate to a society where that was the greatest obstacle to stability. The regulation of land-holding was essential where that was the foundation of wealth and influence. People bound by mutual contract needed to elaborate the terms of contractual obligation and rights. But it is also important to realize that this was a world dominated by a small elite of monarchs, aristocrats and ecclesiastics. It was these, in particular the ecclesiastics, who formed the intelligentsia, who held up general principles of law, and, most importantly, accommodated them to

---

[37] On the influence of Magna Carta on constitutionalism in Britain, the Commonwealth and the US, see S.E. Thorne, W.H. Dunham, P.B. Kurland, and I. Jennings, *The Great Charter: Four Essays on Magna Carta and the History of Our Liberty* (Pantheon, New York, 1965) and H.D. Hazeldine, "The Influence of Magna Carta on American Constitutional Development" in *Magna Carta Commemoration Essays* (H.E. Malden ed., Royal Historical Society, London, 1917), pp.180–226.

the realities that they found around them. The caricature of the Middle Ages as an interlude of backwardness and irrationality has some truth to it. But it was through the challenges presented by violence and instability on the one hand, and the desire for rational method and routine on the other, that the medieval institutions that last to this day were born.

CHAPTER 4

ST THOMAS AQUINAS AND THE NATURAL LAW TRADITION

TIM MURPHY

1. INTRODUCTION

The natural law tradition is generally considered to be a central part of
jurisprudence. It is a tradition that has ancient origins and that still exerts a
substantial influence on several aspects of the way legal philosophy is
understood and interpreted. This chapter offers an account of the natural law
theory of the Christian theologian, St Thomas Aquinas (c.1225–1274). The
Thomist version of natural law is found in the *Summa Theologiae*, the most
comprehensive statement of his thought.[1] It is generally regarded as the high
point of natural law theorising during the Middle Ages and it has been described
as "the semi-official philosophy of the Roman Catholic Church to this day".[2]

It should be emphasised that this chapter discusses only the place of natural
law in St Thomas's thought; it does not discuss St Thomas's views on the
subject of natural *justice*. The latter was the subject of Garrett Barden's chapter
in this volume, "Of the Naturally and the Conventionally Just", and indeed it
was argued there that the Aristotelian-Roman-Thomist version of natural
justice—and not natural law—was more pertinent to central concerns of
jurisprudence such as the nature of justice, the process of adjudication and the
idea of equity. In many respects this chapter builds on that argument by showing
that the Thomist understanding of natural law is generally misrepresented—
by both proponents and opponents of natural law theory—in the world of
jurisprudence. As Garrett Barden observed:

---

[1] The *Summa* is divided into four parts: Part I deals with God and creation; Part I-II
deals with human action and the virtues in general; Part II-II considers such actions
and virtues in particular detail; and Part III deals with Christ. In the present volume
the *Summa Theologiae* is cited by Part (I, I-II, II-II, III), Question (q.58), and Article
(art.3). Here, all references are to the Blackfriars translation, Vols 1–61, (Eyre and
Spottiswoode, London, 1964–1981).

[2] P. Singer, "Deciding What is Right: Introduction" in *Ethics* (P. Singer ed., Oxford
University Press, 1994), p.243.

"Many jurisprudence textbooks, when discussing St Thomas Aquinas, refer exclusively to his discussion of law in Questions 90 to 97 in the first part of the second part of his *Summa Theologiae* [I-II] whereas his discussion of justice and what is just is found in Questions 56 to 71, 120 and 122 of the second part of the second part [II-II]. In fact, this distinction, which Aristotle and, following him, Cicero, the Roman jurists and Aquinas, thought both clear and important is quite rarely adverted to despite the fact that the Roman formula defining the just as 'what is due' is well known and often quoted."

Whereas Garrett Barden's chapter discussed St Thomas's account of justice in Part II-II, this chapter will have as its focus Questions 90–97 in Part I-II of the *Summa*, where St Thomas speaks of the varieties of law. As indicated in the quotation above, these questions are indeed adverted to in most accounts of legal philosophy, but these accounts usually suggest—incorrectly—that the version of natural law described by St Thomas constitutes his vision of "justice". It will be suggested that Thomist natural law is not of this kind, although other natural law theories—for example, the Stoic conception of "true law" and modern natural law and natural rights theories—most certainly are. Although much lip-service is paid by jurisprudents to the notion of diversity within the natural law tradition, the problem nonetheless remains one of conflation: the assumption that, in the final analysis, all writers who have used the term "natural law" are basically talking about the same thing, or at least similar things, when in fact they are not.

This chapter will first provide examples of the conventional jurisprudential view of Thomist natural law. We will then explore the outlines of pre-Thomist theology, in particular the neoplatonic and voluntarist thought of St Augustine, and also of the Christian rationalism developed subsequently by St Thomas along Aristotelian lines. This form of rationalism provides the context for our subsequent discussion of the natural law theory in the *Summa Theologiae*. Following that discussion we will explore and assess some of the reasons behind the relatively common misunderstanding of Thomist natural law.

2. Images of Thomist Natural Law

Most jurists appear to subscribe to the view that natural law theory—including Thomist natural law theory—involves some definitive idea of justice, that it invariably comprises an independent and unassailable moral order capable of expression in the form of axioms or principles.[3] This understanding of natural

---

[3] There is one important exception to this: most jurists do acknowledge that the natural law theory of Lon Fuller (1902–1978) is substantially different from the standard

law—which we may term idealist natural law theory—considers that an objective moral law exists and that it has "an authoritative and certain source, in some fashion beyond the vicissitudes and fallibility of human enquiry".[4] Proponents of the idealist version of natural law usually insist that positive law, in order to qualify as valid law, must not contradict the supervening natural law principles. As John Kelly remarked, "A central problem of jurisprudence is whether a law, in order to be recognized as such, need conform only to formal criteria, or whether its validity depends also on its not infringing some permanent, higher, 'natural' standard."[5]

Since this understanding of natural law is tantamount to conceiving of natural law as a system of principles or axioms similar in form—but superior in status—to that of contemporary Western legal systems, it is not surprising that it is perpetuated especially by jurists.[6] J.W. Harris, for example, refers to three characteristics of the classical doctrine of natural law: (i) that it is universal and immutable; (ii) that it is a "higher" law; and (iii) that it is discoverable by reason.[7] As to the substance of these characteristics, Harris suggests that the

---

natural law theories, those that equate "natural law" with "justice". Fuller's natural law theory is often referred to as "procedural natural law" as it sets out certain minimum criteria for law to be recognised as such. These criteria—or principles of legality—are: that there must be rules; that the rules must be promulgated and prospective; that they must be noncontradictory, reasonably clear, and possible of performance; and that there must be congruence between the rules as announced and the rules as applied. See L. Fuller, *The Morality of Law* (revised ed., Yale University Press, New Haven, 1969).

[4] G. Barden, "Two Versions of Natural Justice" in, *Justice and Legal Theory in Ireland* (G. Quinn, A. Ingram and S. Livingstone eds., Oak Tree Press, Dublin, 1995), p.39.

[5] J.M. Kelly, *A Short History of Western Legal Theory* (Clarendon Press, Oxford, 1992), p.19. Philosophical discussion of the idealist version of natural law usually focuses on the epistemological issue of how the unassailability and infallibility of the ideal standard is achieved, that is, on the question of how one arrives at the axioms or principles that are said to make up the higher standard or "law".

[6] It is of course perpetuated by others as well: Ernest Barker wrote that the origin of the idea of natural law "may be ascribed to an old and indefeasible movement of the human mind ... which impels it towards the notion of an eternal and immutable justice; a justice which human authority expresses or ought to express—but does not make; a justice which human authority may fail to express—and must pay the penalty for failing to express by the diminution, or even the forfeiture, of its power to command. This justice is conceived as being the higher or ultimate law, proceeding from the nature of the universe—from the being of God and the reason of man." E. Barker, *Traditions of Civility* (Cambridge University Press, Cambridge, 1948), pp.312–313.

[7] J.W. Harris, *Legal Philosophies* (2nd ed., Butterworths, London, 1997), p.7. Although these are presented by Harris as characteristics of "the classical doctrine", the presentation is such that it is perfectly reasonable for another jurisprudential

first two emphasise the "legal" quality of natural law. The universality and immutability of natural law imply that "it is one conception of 'justice', in the sense in which justice stands for the righting of wrongs and the proper distribution of benefits and burdens within a political community"; that it is a "higher" law means "it has a relationship of superiority towards laws promulgated by political authorities". By way of emphasising this "legality", he writes: "If it were merely a system of private ethics, it would not *eo ipse* ["in and by itself"] be mete for enactment by legislatures and judges and would not set criteria for obedience."[8]

The classic contemporary exposition of idealist natural law theory is John Finnis's *Natural Law and Natural Rights* (1980). Finnis attempted a modern reconstruction of St Thomas's theory but with two critical differences: Finnis's theory is a secular theory, which St Thomas's obviously is not; and Finnis proposed a theory of individual natural *rights*, an idea nowhere to be found in St Thomas's work. Finnis claimed that the "basic forms of human flourishing" are discernible by means of "a simple act of non-inferential understanding [that allows one to grasp] that the object of [an] inclination which one experiences is an instance of a general form of good, for oneself (and others like one)".[9] According to Finnis, these basic forms of human flourishing, or "basic goods", are: life; knowledge; play; aesthetic experience; sociability or friendship; practical reasonableness; and religion. Finnis also argued that there are certain "basic methodological requirements" of practical reasonableness. These include, for example, "a coherent plan of life", "the requirements of the common good", and "following one's conscience".[10] For Finnis, as J.W. Harris puts it, "[t]he 'basic goods' and the 'basic methodological requirements' together constitute the universal and unchanging principles of natural law".[11]

Finnis argues that the maintenance of human rights is a "fundamental component of the common good" and in favour of a range of

> "exceptionless or absolute human claim-rights—most obviously, the right not to have one's life taken directly as a means to any further end; but also the right not to be positively lied to in any situation (e.g. teaching, preaching, research publication, news broadcasting) in which factual communication (as distinct from fiction, jest, or poetry) is reasonably expected; and the related right not to be condemned on knowingly false

---

commentator, Margaret Davies, to regard them as "generalities" common to all natural law theories. See M. Davies, *Asking the Law Question* (Sweet and Maxwell, Sydney, 1994), pp.61–63.

[8] J.W. Harris, *op. cit.*, p.7.

[9] J.M. Finnis, *Natural Law and Natural Rights* (Clarendon Press, Oxford, 1980), p.34.

[10] See *ibid.*, chap.V.

[11] J.W. Harris, *op. cit.*, p.15.

charges; and the right not to be deprived, or required not to deprive oneself, of one's procreative capacity; and the right to be taken into respectful consideration in any assessment of what the common good requires".[12]

Although we will refer to Finnis again, a detailed discussion of the epistemological issues underlying his theory is beyond the scope of the present chapter. We should note, however, that his references to these rights as "absolute" and "exceptionless" emphasise the idea of unassailability that is associated with the idealist view of natural law as an objective supervening standard.

The idealist version of natural law has been discussed and put into operation in several different legal contexts, particularly during the twentieth century, and sometimes it has been assumed that the version employed is Thomist. For example, under the 1922 Constitution of the Irish Free State, against the background of a period when the natural law tradition was very much in decline as an intellectual force on the international scene, "unique in this respect among Western countries, natural law actually attained a certain status in the secular legal system".[13] This is a reference to the dissenting judgment of Kennedy C.J. in *The State (Ryan) v Lennon*, in which he declared invalid an amending act which interpolated a new article into the 1922 Constitution on the basis that the amending power conferred on the parliament by the Constituent Assembly was limited and circumscribed. According to Kennedy C.J., the first, "overall" limitation arose from the declaration in the forefront of the Constitution Act that all lawful authority comes from God to the people. The judge continued:

> "It follows that every act, whether legislative, executive or judicial, in order to be lawful under the Constitution, must be capable of being justified under the authority thereby declared to be derived from God. From this it seems clear that, if any legislation ... were to offend against that acknowledged ultimate Source from which the legislative authority has come through the people to the [parliament], as, for example, if it were repugnant to the Natural Law, such legislation would be necessarily unconstitutional and invalid, and it would be, therefore, absolutely null and void and inoperative."[14]

---

[12] J.M. Finnis, *op. cit.*, p.225.
[13] J.M. Kelly, *op. cit.*, p.374.
[14] [1935] I.R. 170 at 204.

This dissent has been invoked in many natural law interpretations of the subsequent 1937 Constitution of Ireland, the text of which was much more influenced by theocratic natural law theory than the 1922 Constitution and where natural law is usually taken to be "theocratic", "Catholic" or "Thomist".[15] The most forthright interpretation of theocratic Catholic natural law as a version of idealist natural law in Ireland was that proposed by a judge, Roderick O'Hanlon (1923–2002). This interpretation is sometimes referred to as "the O'Hanlon thesis":

> "Article 6 and the Preamble [of the Irish Constitution] unambiguously identify 'the most Holy Trinity' as the ultimate source of this higher law. … The State is founded on a Constitution which acknowledges that all authority comes from the Most Holy Trinity to Whom, as our final end, all actions both of men and States must be referred, and which states that all powers of government derive under God from the people. It would appear to follow … that no law could be enacted and no judicial decision could lawfully be given, which conflicted with the Natural Law (which we recognize as being of divine origin)."[16]

The idealist version of natural law is almost unquestioned in academic commentary in the field of Irish constitutional law. For example, one writer argues that interpreting the Irish Constitution in light of natural law is very different from other interpretive strategies because natural law theory is not a methodological stance: natural law, she writes,

> "is a body of principles which can determine the substantive outcome of a case … [N]atural law is a normative account of what rights are. … A consequence of this is that … the standard of constitutionality is supplanted by the standards of natural law rather than the Constitution being interpreted in light of it."[17]

---

[15] For an overview of the theocratic natural law aspects of the 1937 Constitution, see R.J. O'Hanlon, "Natural Rights and the Irish Constitution" (1993) 11 *Irish Law Times* 8. See also B. Walsh, "The Judicial Power, Justice and the Constitution of Ireland" in *Constitutional Adjudication in European Community and National Law* (D. Curtin and D. O'Keeffe eds., Butterworths, Dublin, 1992): "St Thomas Aquinas … saw eternal law, divine law and natural law as unalterable, all based on divine reason and as setting the standards for human law and justice … The [Irish] Constitution appears to reflect an acceptance of the philosophy of St Thomas Aquinas" (pp.147, 149).

[16] R.J. O'Hanlon, *op. cit.*, at 9–10.

[17] A. Kavanagh, "The Quest for Legitimacy in Constitutional Interpretation" (1997) 32 *Irish Jurist* 195 at 213. The present writer, in replying to Judge O'Hanlon's article cited in n.15 above, also presumed the conventional jurisprudential

There is, however, an alternative version of Thomist natural law. Unlike in the case of understanding natural law as a set of norms, principles, or standards, this alternative version—which we may refer to as the virtue understanding of natural law—is a non-absolutist, *ethical* idea of natural law. The natural law, on this view, is operating to its proper effect in human beings when they are acting in accordance with the divine or cosmic intelligence; it is then "showing them the way". The ethical task is to follow "the way" through virtuous reflection and action. Proponents of this version of natural law argue that the moral life is essentially a matter of practical reasonableness and the virtuous pursuit of the good of the community. This chapter will suggest that the natural law theory of St Thomas Aquinas is categorically of the virtue kind. This means that its potential role in relation to positive law is limited: it can be employed *only* as a form of interpretive methodology, and not as a supervening set of unassailable principles to which appeal can be made.

While these claims may appear novel in the jurisprudential context, it is worth remarking that the status of "law" in the work of St Thomas is hugely controversial in several other disciplines. As Cristina Traina has noted, contemporary scholars of St Thomas

> "disagree vehemently over the proper status of law in his theology generally and over the proper role of law in his ethics in particular. In the language of theological anthropology, this is the question, whether human conformity to divinely established ends involves adherence to principle or development of habits or character. Virtue theorists insist that reducing Thomas's ethics to law ignores his emphasis upon growth in the virtues and upon the flexibility of practical reason in pursuit of the good; others counter that it is impossible to ignore the treatise on law or the important role law plays in the extensive ethical discussions in part II-II of the *Summa Theologiae*."[18]

In brief, the remainder of this chapter seeks to demonstrate why the natural law theory of St Thomas should not be thought of as similar to any natural law theory that, in the final analysis, considers "natural law" to be a form of supervening positive law. The use of the term "positive law" should be emphasised here since this is precisely what modern natural law theorists and critics assume natural law to be: a "higher" form of positive law. The reader might also notice something of a paradox regarding the general argument of

---

understanding of natural law, the idealist version. See T. Murphy, "Democracy, Natural Law and the Irish Constitution" (1993) 11 *Irish Law Times* 81.

[18] C.L.H. Traina, *Feminist Ethics and Natural Law* (Georgetown University Press, Washington, D.C., 1999), p.58.

this chapter: in effect it suggests that Thomist natural law theory is not related directly to the central concerns of jurisprudence and that its relation to positive human laws is secondary to its primary, ethical roles. Finally, we should also note that the context of Thomist natural law is essentially theological. One of the unfortunate but unavoidable consequences of this is that many of the concepts and terminology will not be familiar to all students of law and jurisprudence. While St Thomas's writing is, as we shall see, eminently readable and accessible, the theological context highlights the need to set out the main features of Christian thought that formed the background to his work.

3. CHRISTIAN THOUGHT BEFORE ST THOMAS

Christian theology emerged during what is usually known as the patristic period, a term roughly denoting the time from the closing of the New Testament writings (c. A.D. 100) to the Council of Chalcedon in 451.[19] Christianity had been adopted as the official religion of the Roman Empire in 312 and Christian theology had already developed before the conquest of the Western Roman Empire by the German peoples and the subsequent rise of Christianity.[20] Early Christian theology was principally concerned with matters such as the relationship between Christianity and Judaism, and the reasoned defence and justifications of the faith against its critics (*apologetics*). The later patristic period (from about 310–451) may be regarded, according to Alister McGrath, as "a high water mark in the history of Christian theology", and includes the work of the North African theologian, St Augustine (354–430), whom McGrath describes as "probably the greatest and most influential mind of the Christian Church throughout its long history".[21] St Augustine's apologetic work, *De Civitate Dei* ("The City of God") was the first systematic exposition of Christian theology, and incorporates St Augustine's main contributions to Christian thought.

The key influence on St Augustine, apart from the Bible, was the Greek philosopher, Plato (c.429–347 B.C.). The bifurcation of the world into the mundane world perceived by the senses and the transcendent, "ideal" world revealed by thinking had become, by the sixth century B.C., "so firmly a part

---

[19] This periodisation is taken from A. McGrath, *Historical Theology* (Blackwell, Oxford, 1998), p.17.

[20] Pope John Paul II has remarked that the Christian proclamation was engaged from the very first with the philosophical currents of the time, and he instances the discussions of St Paul in Athens with "certain Epicurean and Stoic philosophers". *Acts* 17:18. See John Paul II, *Fides et Ratio* ("Faith and Reason"), Encyclical Letter, para.39, (Veritas, Dublin, 1998), p.59.

[21] A. McGrath, *op. cit.*, pp.24, 26.

of human consciousness that even Kung Fu-tse, the very model of the secular prophet, assumes it, and the Buddha in India, Zarathustra in Persia and Isaiah in Palestine preach it constantly".[22] This "bifurcation" found its greatest Western exposition in the thought of Plato. In Plato's middle period, which included works such as *Phaedo* and *Republic*, he developed an epistemology around the idea that the "transcendent world" is made up of objects, often called "Forms" (*eide*), that we do not sense but about which we can have knowledge. The Forms—such as the Form of justice and the Form of beauty—are the perfect or ideal forms of everything that we know of in this world. Moreover, they are part of an idealist theory of knowledge; in the words of Nicholas White, Plato believed it crucial "that knowledge be thought of as concerning objective facts that hold non-relatively to a particular observer or circumstance of observation".[23]

Plato's realm of pure ideas or "Forms" was the basis for *neo*platonic philosophy, which emerged during the third century and which perceived the transcendent as an emanation giving rise to descending levels or realms such as the realms of the intellect, soul and body. Plotinus (c.205–270) and Porphyry (c.232–305) were among the most significant neoplatonic philosophers. Although neoplatonism was frequently used as a philosophical foundation for paganism, and as a means of defending paganism against Christianity, many Christians—including St Augustine—were also influenced by neoplatonism. The Christian neoplatonists generally viewed the visible world, the realm of flux and flow, as a symbol of the divine reality that remained hidden within:

> "Everything in the visible world appeared to them to be related to God, just as objects of the visible world, in some interpretations of Plato's philosophy, were related to ideal forms of these objects. For the Neo-Platonists, the everyday world, the material world, was largely symbolic; only the immaterial (for the Neo-Platonists: God, the Ideas) was real."[24]

It was St Augustine who more than any other thinker Platonised the Christian structure; indeed he made them virtually coextensive. St Augustine wholly accepted Plato's theory of ideas or Forms: "Ideas are the primary forms, or the permanent and immutable reasons of real things, and they are not themselves formed; so that they are, as a consequence, eternal and ever the same in

---

[22] R.J. Hollingdale, "Introduction" in A. Schopenhauer, *Essays and Aphorisms* (Penguin, Harmondsworth, 1970), p.14.

[23] N. White, "Plato" in *A Companion to Epistemology* (J. Dancy and E. Sosa eds., Blackwell, Oxford, 1992), p.346.

[24] W.P. Baumgarth and R.J. Regan, "Introduction" in *Saint Thomas Aquinas: On Law, Morality, and Politics* (W.P. Baumgarth and R.J. Regan eds., Hackett, Indianapolis, 1988), p.xiv.

themselves and they are contained in the divine intelligence".[25] For St Augustine, then, Plato's realm of pure ideas becomes God's mind; the ideas are eternal and immutable because they are in the mind of God. There was an enormous difference, according to St Augustine, between the real, earthly world and the "ideal", heavenly world (the two worlds—or "cities"—in the *City of God*):

> "The two cities then were created by two kinds of love: the earthly city by a love of self carried even to the point of contempt for God, the heavenly city by a love of God carried even to the point of contempt for self. Consequently, the earthly city glories in itself while the other glories in the Lord. For the former seeks glory from men, but the latter finds its greatest glory in God, the witness of our conscience."[26]

This neoplatonic bifurcation of the world was the general framework within which St Augustine addressed other issues. His negative perspective on earthly existence was based on the view that, although humans possessed free will, this was corrupted by sin. In keeping with this pessimistic view of "the earthly city" and his understanding of human nature as irrevocably fallen, St Augustine stressed the fallibility of human reason.

St Augustine held that there were two varieties of law—the eternal law and the human law. In this particular context the main influence on Christian theology was not Platonism, but rather another Greek philosophy, Stoicism. Stoic philosophy proposed that everything in nature is to be explained by a cosmic reason, *Logos*, and that the wise person should nurture a sense of sovereignty and inner independence and live in harmony with this reason that explains nature. Stoic philosophy also proposed that the law and political organisation be structured around the cosmic reason. Cicero (106–143 B.C.), for example, wrote of a *vis innata*, an innate force in humans through which they could discern the law of nature that they were required to observe. Since human nature is part of cyclical, cosmic nature, "the law which governs the cosmos, that of the divine Logos, provides the law to which human action ought to be conformed".[27] The classic Stoic statement of natural law is that of Cicero in *De Re Publica* ("The Republic"):

> "True law is right reason in agreement with nature; it is of universal

---

[25] St Augustine, *Eighty-Three Different Questions*, 46, 1–2, quoted in W. Morrison, *Jurisprudence* (Cavendish, London, 1997), p.59.

[26] St Augustine, *The City of God Against the Pagans*, Bk.XIV, chap.28 (P. Levine trans., Harvard University Press, Cambridge, Mass., 1966), p.405.

[27] A. MacIntyre, *A Short History of Ethics* (2nd ed., University of Notre Dame Press, Notre Dame, 1984), p.105.

application, unchanging and everlasting; it summons to duty by its commands, and averts from wrongdoing by its prohibitions. And it does not lay its commands or prohibitions upon good men in vain, though neither have any effect on the wicked. It is a sin to try to alter this law, nor is it allowable to attempt to repeal any part of it, and it is impossible to abolish it entirely. We cannot be freed from its obligations by senate or people, and we need not look outside ourselves for an expounder or interpreter of it. And there will not be different laws at Rome and at Athens, or different laws now and in the future, but one eternal and unchangeable law will be valid for all nations and all times, and there will be one master and ruler, that is, God, over us all, for he is the author of this law, its promulgator, and its enforcing judge. Whoever is disobedient is fleeing from himself and denying his human nature, and by reason of this very fact he will suffer the worst penalties, even if he escapes what is commonly considered punishment."[28]

This was the first major expression of the idealist conception of natural law. It contains the features of finality, universality and unassailability that are the hallmark of that conception. Cicero's conception of the law of nature is of an extrinsic, rationally perceptible universal law—it will not be different depending on whether one is, for example, in Rome or in Athens—and of an unchanging law.[29] As regards the issue of the relationship between Cicero's "true law" and positive law, it is evident that Cicero considers the former as a supervening, ideal standard that transcends the latter; in the words of Hadley Arkes, he is widely regarded as having understood the modern idea that, "behind the power

---

[28] Cicero, "The Republic", Bk.III, chap.22, in *De Re Publica, De Legibus* (C.W. Keyes trans., Harvard University Press, Cambridge, Mass., 1928), p.211.

[29] This established the basic equality of all men in a manner that is the antithesis of Aristotelianism. Whereas a premise of Aristotle's thought was that men are unequal, Cicero held that, because all men are subject to one law and so are fellow-citizens, they must in some sense be equal. This Stoic doctrine was compatible with Christianity and facilitated the early fusion of the two. "For Cicero equality is a moral requirement rather than a fact; in ethical terms it expresses much the same conviction that a Christian might express by saying that God is no respecter of persons." G.H. Sabine and T.L. Thorson, *A History of Political Theory* (4th ed., Harcourt Brace, New York, 1973), p.162. To appreciate the significance of the equality doctrine for contemporary Catholicism, we may note that in the *Catechism*, "the sense that the other is one's equal" is, along with "the desire for God and submission to him", a doctrine on which the natural law is said to "hinge". *Catechism of the Catholic Church* (Veritas, Dublin, 1994), p.426. We will discuss the contemporary Catholic understanding of natural law later in this chapter.

of statutes and edicts, was the natural law, which gave us the measure of things that were right or wrong, just or unjust".[30]

According to John Kelly, most of the early Church Fathers simply took this Stoic idea of "true law" as representing God's law, and referred to St Paul's letter to the Romans where he wrote that the Gentiles, though without the law of Moses, still displayed "the effect of the law, written in their hearts".[31] "True law" was understood as what was commanded by God; it was viewed, in other words, in *voluntarist* terms. Voluntarism is generally a position that views reason and intellect as subservient to will; in theology it is the position that all values are so through being chosen and willed by God. It is the basis of command theory, "a theory of ethics within which the command of sovereign to subject is the central element".[32]

St Augustine's view was not radically different from the other Church Fathers—ultimately, as we shall see, it was also voluntarist—but his position was more complex. He (along with St Ambrose, c.339–397) did not adopt the approach of the other Church Fathers because he recognised that the contrasts between the Judaeo-Christian and Graeco-Roman conceptions of God raised a critical question, a question that was first raised by Plato and which continues to be significant in contemporary Christian thought.

For the Stoics, "God" was equivalent to *Logos*, the all-governing, impersonal world reason; a personal God, such as the Christian God, had no place in their scheme. The concept of a personal God, with its emphasis on God's role as the creator, sustainer and preserver of the natural order, envisages God as separate, to an extent, from that natural order. St Augustine saw that this conflict raised the issue of primacy as between nature and a superior will, an issue that in effect defines the extent of God's power. The root of this conflict was the clash between Greek ideas about the rationality and self-sufficiency of cosmic principles and the Old Testament God, who created the world and rules it freely according to his will.

This issue had already been identified as a critical philosophical dilemma in one of Plato's dialogues, *Euthyphro*, in which Euthyphro, who is about to prosecute his own father, discusses the nature of piety or holiness with Socrates, who has just been indicted. When they tentatively agree that what all the gods

---

[30] H. Arkes, "That 'Nature Herself Has Placed in our Ears a Power of Judging': Some Reflections on the 'Naturalism' of Cicero" in *Natural Law Theory* (R.P. George ed., Clarendon Press, Oxford, 1992), p.248.

[31] *Romans* 2: 14–15. Kelly also remarks: "This image is not to be found in Stoic philosophy, but its (presumably unconscious) conceptual affinity with the Stoic doctrine of rationally perceptible natural law was so striking that it gave the latter an easy entrée into Christian theory"; *op. cit.*, p.103.

[32] G. Barden, *After Principles* (University of Notre Dame Press, Notre Dame, 1990), p.136 (n.12).

agree in approving is the holy or the pious (as opposed to what any one or some of the gods agree in approving), Socrates interjects with a question (known as the *Euthyphro* dilemma): "Is the pious loved by the gods because it is pious, or is it pious because it is loved by the gods?"[33] As Anthony Gottlieb comments:

> "This is an excellent question [that] comes down to this: would absolutely anything that the gods approved of count as holy, just because they approved of it, or are they bound to approve only of certain things, namely those which would count as holy whether they approved of them or not? ... Socrates [seems] to have uncovered a dilemma about the relationship between religion and morality. If we ask the same sort of question about what is morally good instead of about what is holy, we can see that we are faced with a revealing choice: either goodness cannot be explained simply by reference to what the gods want, or else it is an empty tautology to say that the gods are good—in which case the praise of the gods would simply be a matter of power-worship."[34]

Whereas the other Church Fathers—through a direct and intellectually misguided adaptation of Stoic doctrine—had arrived at the voluntarist view that the command of God defined the eternal moral law, St Augustine converted the *Euthyphro* dilemma into a dilemma about moral goodness in relation to the Christian God. The dilemma received a voluntarist response from St Augustine: ultimately, like the other Church Fathers, his overwhelming emphasis was on faith in the injunctions of Christian revelation and the teaching of the church. St Augustine placed God's will, as understood from Scripture and church teachings, in the central position in his ethical thought. Armed with faith and knowledge of Scripture and Church teachings, and in receipt of God's grace, human beings can come to share in the eternal law, the divine reason, through obedience to its commands.[35]

---

[33] Plato, *Euthyphro*, 10a, in *Plato: Five Dialogues* (G.M.A. Grube trans., Hackett, Indianapolis, 1981), p.14.

[34] A. Gottlieb, *Socrates* (Phoenix, London, 1997), p.31. John Kelly expressed the *Euthyphro* dilemma as follows: "Had God so commanded Moses because the order of nature had, all along, already contained the precepts which the Decalogue expressed? Did the Decalogue contain natural, already-established precepts, or was it an expression of God's will? If so, had the Decalogue been necessary? Conversely, if what was perceived as the law of nature was in fact itself only the outcome of God's will, it was open to God to change the rules: in which case nature could not be looked to as an infallible, invariable rule of conduct"; *op. cit.*, p.103.

[35] The positive law is seen in St Augustine's theology as a means for the coercive discouragement of vice, that is, the abuse of freedom of will through bad ethical choices; as J.S. McLelland remarks, "The state is irrelevant to the inner life because it has literally nothing to say about redemption, and it is only relevant to human

During the First Christian millennium, theological ethics were thus dominated by a voluntarist form of neoplatonic idealism. The ideal realm was associated with the divine intelligence and considered to contain an unassailable and injunctive moral order. It fell to the thirteenth century Italian theologian, St Thomas Aquinas, to challenge and substantially revise this edifice. St Thomas offered five physico-theological proofs for the existence of God—the famous "five ways"—at the beginning of his most important work, the *Summa Theologiae,* but it was a very different kind of God from the God envisaged by St Augustine.[36] The shift can be described as a shift from voluntarist or command ethics to a Christian rationalist ethics.

4. CHRISTIAN RATIONALISM

The late eleventh and early twelfth centuries can be regarded as a revolutionary period because there was an interlocking of political, religious, economic, legal, cultural, linguistic, artistic, philosophical, and other basic categories of social change.[37] Generally, the thirteenth century—the historical period in which St Thomas lived—was one in which Christianity was ceasing to be hostile to the world and his theology involves a much more positive outlook on humanity than that found in St Augustine's neoplatonic work. The revival of Greek— and in particular Aristotelian—philosophy that took place from around 1200 onwards is the immediate starting-point for any account of the intellectual contribution of St Thomas.

Aristotle's writings, except for his works on logic, had not been available in the West for about one thousand years. The rediscovery (from around 1200 onwards) of his *Physics, Metaphysics, De Anima, Nicomachean Ethics* and the *Politics* presented the Christian world with a fully-integrated system of

---

behaviour in so far as it can batten down some of the more disruptive effects of original sin"; *A History of Western Political Thought* (Routledge, London, 1996), p.103.

[36] See St Thomas Aquinas, *Summa Theologiae*, I, q.2, art.3. For a discussion of the "five ways", see, for example, A. McGrath, *Historical Theology* (Blackwell, Oxford, 1998), pp.130–33 and M. Henry, *On Not Understanding God* (Columba Press, Dublin, 1997), pp.125–34.

[37] Some commentators have observed that the events of the eleventh and twelfth centuries were so important that they not only marked a major, revolutionary discontinuity in the medieval period, but that they actually constituted the beginning of the modern age. Nevertheless, as Harold Berman comments, "the conventional view remains one of skepticism concerning any fundamental break in the historical continuity of Europe during the so-called Middle Ages". *Law and Revolution: The Formation of the Western Legal Tradition* (Harvard University Press, Cambridge, Mass., 1983), p.578.

thought that was both rationally persuasive and largely uninfluenced by religious themes. It was St Thomas, inspired by his teacher St Albert the Great (c.1206–1280), who met the challenge of synthesising neoplatonic Christianity and Aristotelian philosophy. There were other non-Christian influences on St Thomas's theology, which was also deeply and importantly indebted to Maimonides (1135–1204), the greatest of the medieval Jewish philosophers, and also to Islamic philosophers, particularly Avicenna (980–1037) and, as we shall see presently, Averroës (c.1126–1198).[38] St Thomas's thought also drew elements from the *Institutes* of Justinian that had been discovered in Italy in the eleventh century, and from Stoicism, feudal theory, and the contemporary political practice of the Holy Roman Empire and the Italian city-state.[39]

One of the key issues at stake in the task of reconciling Aristotelianism with Christianity was again the clash between Greek ideas about the rationality and self-sufficiency of cosmic principles and the Old Testament God, who created the world and rules it freely according to his will. As has been said, the Christianity developed by St Augustine and the other Church Fathers favoured the latter and accordingly defined God's power as virtually unlimited. The rediscovered works of Aristotle met with a great deal of intellectual resistance among Christian scholars, and this was largely because of their interpretation by the Muslim philosopher, Averroës. In short, Averroës's position implied a rejection of the free, Old Testament God. Averroës restricted God's free exercise of his will by positing some kind of necessity in the creation itself. In other words, the Averroist position—based on Greek ideas of the eternity and deterministic nature of the physical world—held that God was limited in terms of what he could create at the moment of creation.

St Thomas differed from Averroës on this question, but not to the extent of reverting to an Augustinian perspective. St Thomas formulated the tensions between the classical and biblical ideas in terms of the dialectic between the two ways of understanding divine power, the *potentia absoluta Dei* (literally,

---

[38] On Jewish and Islamic thought in the Middle Ages, see generally C. Sirat, *A History of Jewish Philosophy in the Middle Ages* (Cambridge University Press, Cambridge, 1985) and O. Leaman, *An Introduction to Medieval Islamic Philosophy* (Cambridge University Press, Cambridge, 1985).

[39] To get an initial sense of what Christian rationalism entails we may note Paul Sigmund's remark that St.Thomas's harmonisation of often conflicting theories into a single system was motivated by a fundamental belief in the ultimate possibility of the resolution of conflicting theories, itself the result of Christian faith in a rational God who has created an ordered and purposive universe the nature of which can be understood, if only in a limited fashion, by man's reason. "Thomistic Natural Law and Social Theory" in *St Thomas Aquinas on Politics and Ethics* (P.E. Sigmund ed., Norton, New York, 1984), p.181.

the "absolute power of God") and the *potentia ordinata Dei* (literally, the "or-dained power of God"). God's *potentia absoluta* refers to what is theoretically possible for him to do providing it does not involve a logical contradiction. His *potentia ordinata* refers to divine power as God has actually chosen to exercise it in establishing the present order.

St Thomas's attempt to avoid Averroës's necessitarian interpretation of Aristotle—an interpretation that severely limits God's *potentia absoluta*—led him to adopt the position known as Christian rationalism. The common thread running through the various uses of the term rationalism is that philosophies classified as rationalist rend to give undue weight to reason at the expense of everything else.[40] Generally speaking, Christian rationalism emphasises God's intellect or reason as opposed to his will, and it argues for the apparent intelligibility and stability of the world and for optimism regarding the human capacity to acquire reliable knowledge by rational methods.[41] St Thomas's moderate version of rationalism allowed that while nothing exists that God did not create freely, nevertheless the laws of nature or essences that he did create embody some necessary relations. In other words, certain things in and about the created world—including, as we shall see, human nature—are fixed or "given"; they cannot be changed or altered, even by God.

For St Thomas, God's initial act of creation or willing was an act of *potentia absoluta*: it was absolutely free except for the limitation of the principle of non-contradiction. Beyond this interpretation of God's initial creative act, however, St Thomas's synthesis employed Aristotelian metaphysics—especially its essentialist ontology, that is, the theory of immanent purposes in nature. "Every act and every investigation", wrote Aristotle in the *Nicomachean Ethics*, "and similarly every action and pursuit, is considered to aim at some good. Hence the Good has been rightly defined as 'that at which all things aim'."[42] This is based on the idea that the essence or nature of a thing is to be on a trajectory toward an end that fulfils or completes it. St Thomas considered

---

[40] See E. Curley, "Rationalism" in *A Companion to Epistemology*.

[41] M.B. Foster describes a rationalist theology as one that "involves both a rationalist philosophy of nature and a rationalist theory of knowledge of nature. If God made the world according to reason, the world must embody the ideas of his reason; and our reason, in disclosing to us God's ideas will at the same time reveal to us the essential nature of the created world"; "Christian Theology and Modern Science of Nature (II)" (1936) 45 *Mind* 1 at 10. There is an obvious connection between the idea of Christian rationalism and the doctrine of *imago Dei*, the belief that each person, as evidenced by the twin endowment of rationality and freedom, is made in the image of God: the latter doctrine allows for God's reason to be "disclosed" to human reason.

[42] Aristotle, *Ethics* I, 1 (J.A.K. Thomson trans. and ed., Penguin, Harmondsworth, 1976), p.63.

that the created order, containing as it does this purposiveness, is to some extent binding on God; he accepted, in other words, the existence of some necessity in the created world and thus some limitation on God's other power, the *potentia ordinata*. On the question of the capacity of human reason, as Margaret Osler has observed:

> "[F]or Aquinas, as for Aristotle, science consists of demonstrative knowledge of the real essences of things. ... Aquinas concluded that scientific knowledge is demonstrative knowledge of necessary relations embodied in universals. The rationalist components of his epistemology are directly tied to his essentialist ontology, which, in turn, is closely connected to his understanding of the relationship between the absolute and ordained powers of God. ... God created certain natures by his free will; but once these natures have been created, individuals possessing them must have the properties that flow from these natures. ... Necessity in created things arises from their essences, the natures ... that make them what they are."[43]

It is important to emphasise the way in which St Thomas understood the idea that the essence or nature of a thing is to be on a trajectory towards an end that fulfils or completes it. St Thomas understood that this orientation towards fulfilment was intrinsic to the thing, not something extrinsic added to it. Thus, he did not think of God's commands in the Decalogue as mere conventions that might just as well have been different, but as manifestations of what was truly and intrinsically good. St Thomas thought that basic acts like not stealing and not bearing false witness, for example, were good in accord with the created nature of humans. So, to the question in *Euthyphro* as to whether an act was good because the gods commanded it—the act being, therefore, intrinsically or naturally neutral—or whether the gods commanded an act because it was good, St Thomas's answer is unequivocal: God commanded acts that are naturally or intrinsically good and forbade those that are naturally or intrinsically evil.

It is only against this background, which is rarely considered in jurisprudence, that the natural law theory of St Thomas Aquinas can be appreciated properly. His theory is about the human capacity to *discover* what is intrinsically good and intrinsically evil. In the next part we will begin by

---

[43] M.J. Osler, *Divine Will and the Mechanical Philosophy* (Cambridge University Press, Cambridge, 1994), pp.25–26. For an overview of St Thomas's epistemology, see Scott MacDonald, "Thomas Aquinas" in *A Companion to Epistemology*. MacDonald observes that, for St Thomas, humans cannot grasp God's essence, and therefore our knowledge of divine matters via natural theology is non-paradigmatic Thomist knowledge (p.19). See *Summa Theologiae*, I, q.12, especially art.4.

looking at St Thomas's description of "natural law" and then place it in the context of Christian rationalism.

5. NATURAL LAW IN THE *SUMMA THEOLOGIAE*

The immediate context of what is sometimes called the "Treatise on Law" in the *Summa Theologiae* is the consideration of "the extrinsic principles of acts". St Thomas is using the word "principle" in ontological rather than logical terms:[44] he is referring to the extrinsic principles—the bases from which other things proceed—that govern the existence and the dynamic of human acts. He refers to his argument in Part I of the *Summa* establishing that the extrinsic principle inclining to evil is the devil.[45] The extrinsic principle moving to good, he states at the outset of the Treatise on Law, is God, "who builds us up by law and supports us by grace".[46] St Thomas defines law as "naught else than an ordinance of reason for the common good made by the authority who has care of the community and promulgated",[47] and he writes that "leading its subjects into the virtue appropriate to their condition is a proper function of law. Now since virtue is that which makes its possessor good, the consequence is that the proper effect of law on those to whom it is given is to make them good, either good simply speaking or good in a certain respect."[48]

Unlike St Augustine and other earlier Christian thinkers St Thomas identifies *four* main varieties of law—the eternal law, the divine law, the natural law, and positive, human law.[49] St Thomas's account of divine Providence provides that the whole community of the universe is governed by divine reason; this rational guidance of created things on the part of God has the nature of a law and, since it is not subject to time, it can be called the eternal law.[50] The eternal law, in other words, is the divine intelligence; it has been described by M.D.A. Freeman as "God's plan for the universe".[51] The divine law refers to

---

[44] Ontology is the branch of metaphysics that deals with the nature of being. Metaphysics is the theoretical philosophy of being and knowing, or the philosophy of mind.

[45] St Thomas Aquinas, *Summa Theologiae*, I, q.114.

[46] *ibid.*, I–II, Prologue.

[47] *ibid.*, I–II, q.90, art.4.

[48] *ibid.*, I–II, q.92, art.1.

[49] Another variety of law, the law of concupiscence, is rarely mentioned in contemporary accounts of St Thomas's natural law thought. Although, following this practice, it will not be referred to again in this chapter, it may be noted that the law of concupiscence is "the inclination of sensuality that is a deviation from reason". This law is usually discussed as an effect of original sin. *Ibid.*, I–II, q.91, art.6.

[50] *ibid.*, I–II, q.91, art.1.

[51] M.D.A. Freeman, *Lloyd's Introduction to Jurisprudence* (7th ed., Sweet and Maxwell, London, 2001), p.106.

that part of the eternal law that God chooses to reveal, either through Scripture or supernaturally.

Of "natural law" St Thomas asks the question whether this law is "within us". In replying in the affirmative, he establishes the link between his metaphysics and his ethics, and between the eternal law and the natural law:

> "Since all things are regulated and measured by Eternal Law ... it is evident that all somehow share in it, in that their tendencies to their own proper acts and ends are from its impression.
>
> Among them intelligent creatures are ranked under divine Providence the more nobly because they take part in Providence by their own providing for themselves and others. Thus they join in and make their own the Eternal Reason through which they have their natural aptitudes for their due activity and purpose. Now this sharing in the Eternal Law by intelligent creatures is what we call 'natural law'.
>
> That is why the Psalmist after bidding us, *Offer the sacrifice of justice*, and, as though anticipating those who ask what are the works of justice, and adding, *There be many who say, Who will [show] us any good?* makes reply, *The light of thy countenance, O Lord, is signed upon us*, implying that the light of natural reason by which we discern what is good and what evil, is nothing but the impression of divine light on us.
>
> Accordingly it is clear that natural law is nothing other than the sharing in the Eternal Law by intelligent creatures."[52]

The natural law, in other words, is operating to its proper effect in human beings when they are acting in accordance with the divine intelligence. St Thomas explains the significance of behaviour in the world in terms of the two ultimate aims or "ends" (*fines*) of human life. These ends are part of the world as God created it and, in accordance with St Thomas's rationalism, they cannot be changed. One end is a natural, earthly end; it involves the flourishing of body, mind, and soul in human community. The other is the idea that human beings "are created by—sent out from—God not only to accomplish natural, earthly ends but also to participate posthumously in the beatific vision, which is their true happiness and fulfilment".[53]

In relation to earthly, human flourishing, St Thomas fully accepted the reality of the visible world and sought to understand it as such. The function of philosophy, according to him, is to understand reality in terms of its first principles or causes. St Thomas wrote that human reasoning,

---

[52] St Thomas Aquinas, *Summa Theologiae*, I-II, q.91, art.2.
[53] C.L.H. Traina, *op. cit.*, p.58.

"being a movement, has understanding as its point of departure, the understanding, namely, of some few things known naturally prior to rational analysis, which are its unfailing source. And it also has understanding as its point of arrival, when we judge what we have discovered by analysis in the light of those naturally obvious principles."[54]

Nature, he continues, has bestowed on humans both *speculative* principles and *practical* principles. Speculative reason and knowledge is knowledge of philosophy and science, or theoretical knowledge; practical reason and knowledge is knowledge of how to act well, or practical wisdom.

St Thomas writes that the first speculative principles belong to a special habit called—here he quotes Aristotle's *Nicomachean Ethics*—"the under-standing of principles".[55] The first such "understanding" is of the principle of non-contradiction, that is, "There is no affirming and denying the same simul-taneously". This first indemonstrable principle is a principle of speculative knowledge because, for St Thomas, "[t]hat which first appears is *the real*, and some insight into this is included in whatsoever is apprehended"; the principle of non-contradiction is "based on the very nature of the real and the non-real: on this principle ... all other propositions are based".[56]

In terms of practical knowledge, for Aristotle and St Thomas, to know how to live well, how to direct oneself toward the goal of happiness, "one needed to observe and follow the example of prudent persons rather than to learn scientific truths".[57] After his discussion of speculative reason and the principle of non-contradiction, St Thomas turns to practical reason:

"[A]s to be *real* first enters into human apprehending as such, so to be *good* first enters the practical reason's apprehending when it is bent on doing something. For every agent acts on account of an end, and to be an end carries the meaning of to be good. Consequently the first principle for the practical reason is based on the meaning of good, namely that it is what all things seek after. And so this is the first command of the law, 'that good is to be sought and done, evil to be avoided'; all other commands of natural law are based on this. Accordingly, the natural-law commands extend to all doing or avoiding of things recognized by the practical reason of itself as being human goods."[58]

---

[54] St Thomas Aquinas, *Summa Theolgiae*, I, q.79, art.12.

[55] *ibid.*

[56] *ibid.*, I–II, q.94, art.2.

[57] W.P. Baumgarth and R.J. Regan, "Introduction" in *St Thomas Aquinas: On Law, Morality, and Politics*, p.xv.

[58] St Thomas Aquinas, *Summa Theologiae*, I–II, q.94, art.2.

St Thomas continues by stating that since good has the nature of an end, all those things to which man has a natural inclination are naturally apprehended by human reason as being good and, consequently, as objects of pursuit. In other words (and this is a point to which we shall return), the "ought" of human action—that which one ought to do—is located in the "is" of human existence, in human nature and self-understanding.

For St Thomas, the first practical principles belong to the special habit called *synderesis*.[59] *Synderesis* denotes a form of knowledge—a direct moral intuition—that St Thomas considered to be a part of human nature. In the *Summa Theologiae*, he establishes that *synderesis* is a natural habit of the intellect.[60] For St Thomas, a habit is the characteristic disposition or inclination to act in a certain way. A habit could be of the intellect or of the will, innate or acquired, natural or supernatural, good or bad. The habit of *synderesis* is said by St Thomas "to incite us to good and to deter us from evil in that through first principles we both begin investigation and judge what we find".[61] Possession of the intellectual habit of *synderesis* means that human beings have an innate disposition to understand the first principles of human action, and also that they are disposed by nature to recognise that they should seek the good proper to their nature.[62] To reiterate a point made earlier, in St Thomas's theology the term "principle" is to be understood in ontological rather than logical terms: he is referring to the extrinsic principles—the bases from which other things proceed—that govern the existence and the dynamic of human acts.

For accordance with the natural law to be achieved, the habit of *synderesis* must be accompanied by the moral virtue of prudence (*prudentia*). Moral virtues are expressed in the form of characteristic readiness to act in particular matters as prudence dictates; for St Thomas, the cardinal moral virtues of prudence, fortitude, temperance and justice are acquired by human beings during the moral life. St Thomas provides an account of the integral parts of prudence that suggests it is a broad-ranging, practical wisdom; as Cristina Traina has remarked, it is "an umbrella under which fall many habits and virtues, all of which one must possess and employ to reason well".[63] Pamela Hall's work

---

[59] *ibid.*, I, q.79, art.12.

[60] *ibid.*

[61] *ibid.*

[62] *ibid.*, I, q.79, art.13. The habit of *synderesis* is not the same as "conscience". In his response to the question whether conscience is a power, St Thomas argues that, on the contrary, conscience is the application of knowledge to something, that is, an act. He refers to the tendency to name the first natural habit—*synderesis*—as "conscience" and points out that this is because habit is a principle or cause of act; he adds that it is customary for causes and effects to be called after one another.

[63] C.L.H. Traina, *op. cit.*, p.65. The prudential qualities include: memory of what is

shows that prudence generates as well as attends to principles, so that prudence and *synderesis* are related dialectically rather than deductively; moral reasoning is not practical if it styles itself as deduction from principles.[64]

The critical point is that the Thomist, virtue conception of natural law belongs primarily to the practical or ethical rather than to the speculative realm, and therefore it cannot be formulated as a set of axiomatic or injunctive propositions. Instead, "obedience" to the natural law is in the form of complex, virtuous human thought and activity. Human beings, made in the image of God,[65] possess natural reason which incorporates certain natural dispositions. *Synderesis* is one such disposition and it is fundamental, along with prudence, to practical reasoning and practical knowledge. As free and intelligent humans, we are not called upon to obey God in the sense of simply obeying a set of rules or commands; instead, it is our task to pay proper heed to the inclinations that we have derived from him. The only sense in which St Thomas's theory involves "adherence to principle" (to refer again to Cristina Traina's posing of the general disagreement regarding Thomist ethics that was quoted in the introductory part of this chapter) is the sense of adherence to principles that are generated and developed by humans during the virtuous pursuit of the common good.

There are nevertheless some fundamentals. St Thomas argues that the order of the precepts of the natural law is according to the order of natural inclinations. The order of the precepts of the natural law begins with the inclination shared with all substances, self-preservation; it continues with inclinations shared with other animals, "for instance the coupling of male and female, the bringing up of the young, and so forth"; and then it includes man's inclination to good:

> "[T]here is in man an appetite for the good of his nature as rational, and this is proper to him, for instance, that he should know truths about God and about living in society. Correspondingly whatever this involves is a matter of natural law, for instance that a man should shun ignorance, not offend others with whom he ought to live in civility, and other such related requirements."[66]

---

generally the case; understanding; docility; shrewdness; reason in the narrow sense (good counsel); foresight; circumspection; and caution. See *ibid.*, pp.65–67.

[64] P.M. Hall, *Narrative and the Natural Law* (University of Notre Dame Press, Notre Dame, Ind., 1994), pp.39–40. Taken together, it has been suggested that the parts of prudence present a picture of moral reasoning that is "experiential, embodied, consultative, creative, calculating, inductive, flexible, and principled". C.L.H. Traina, *op. cit.*, p.67.

[65] See n.41 above.

[66] St Thomas Aquinas, *Summa Theolgiae*, I-II, q.94, art.2.

When we speak of Thomist natural law, as Columba Ryan has pointed out, we are in a field of ethics or morality rather than in that of legality in a narrow sense, and the natural law should not be thought of as lying alongside of, and somehow superior to, all other laws; as Ryan states, to speak of both natural law and positive law as "laws" is a "category mistake". He observes that only in man, with his capacity to reflect upon and know himself, can there be any question of natural law, "the recognition for himself of how he is to act"; and only in his case, with his freedom of action, can there be a responsible following or deviation from the "rules" of his nature.[67] It should not be overlooked, however, that Thomist moral theology does not deny that individual or "personal" ethics have contexts and consequences and that these include political and social contexts and consequences, since individuals live in society. The Thomist versions of natural law and natural justice have their origins in the ethical thought of classical Greece, where ethical inquiry was not separate from—or separable from—inquiry into political philosophy or political theory. For example, Plato's morals and Plato's politics, as Alasdair MacIntyre observes, are closely interdependent; each logically requires to be completed by the other.[68] Similarly, Aristotle's *Nicomachean Ethics* shows us what form and style of life are necessary to happiness while his *Politics* shows us what particular form of constitution, what set of institutions, are necessary to make this form of life possible and to safeguard it.

6. THOMISM AFTER ST THOMAS AND MODERN NATURAL LAW THEORY

How, we may ask, has Thomist natural law been so widely misinterpreted as being of the kind that inevitably gives rise—like some other natural law theories undoubtedly do—to "a body of principles which can determine the substantive outcome of a case", or as "one conception of 'justice', in the sense in which justice stands for the righting of wrongs and the proper distribution of benefits and burdens within a political community" and as a "higher" law that "has a relationship of superiority towards laws promulgated by political authorities?"[69] How, in short, has Thomist natural law come to be regarded as an earlier version of modern, idealist natural law theories? The beginning of the answer to these questions lies in the period shortly after St Thomas's death in 1274, when the

---

[67] See C. Ryan, "The Traditional Concept of Natural Law: An Interpretation" in *Light on the Natural Law* (I. Evans ed., Burns and Oates, London, 1965), pp.18–19 *et seq*. In a similar vein, Patrick Hannon's discussion of law and morality in this volume rejects the idea of precepts or "rules" that attempt to voluntaristically govern morality; instead, he observes, their author "is the human mind, reflecting on human experience, discovering what is or is not fit living for a creature with a human nature".

[68] A. MacIntyre, *A Short History of Ethics*, p.51.

Averroistic interpretation of Aristotle (for which there was a number of vocal proponents in Paris during the thirteenth century) was condemned by, most notably, the Bishop of Paris in 1277.[70] Many of the condemned propositions were Averroistic in that they restricted God in the free exercise of his will by positing some kind of necessity in the creation itself, but some seemed to go even further than this, condemning any notion of limitation with respect to God's power. After the condemnations it became more difficult to assert—as St Thomas had asserted—necessity in the created world or in human knowledge of the creation. Instead, assertion of the absolute power of God became the primary focus of theological inquiry. William of Occam (1290–1349) is the paradigm medieval thinker in this alternative theological perspective.

Occam's opposition to St Thomas involved an acceptance of the limits that the principle of non-contradiction imposed on divine freedom, but there was a radical reduction in the domain of absolutely necessary relations in the creation, and of necessity in human knowledge. Occam formulated an understanding of the relationship between divine power and the creation that was essentially similar to St Augustine and the other Church Fathers. In stressing the primacy of God's will over his intellect, Occam's voluntanist account of the *potentia absoluta* and the *potentia ordinata* provides that the created world is absolutely contingent. According to Occam, the only restriction on God's power is the principle of non-contradiction: "Anything is to be attributed to the divine power when it does not contain a contradiction."[71] There is thus no basis for *a priori*, necessary knowledge of the kind that St Thomas developed from the metaphysics of essences and internal relations.[72]

---

[69] These quotations are from descriptions of natural law that were cited in the second part of this chapter, "Images of Thomism Natural Law".

[70] Despite the condemnation at Paris, and a slightly later, less direct condemnation at Oxford, Aquinas was canonised in 1323.

[71] William of Occam, *Ordinatio*, in William of Occam, *Philosophical Writings* (P. Boehner ed. and trans., Nelson, Edinburgh, 1957), p.25, quoted in M.J. Osler, *op. cit.*, pp.29–30.

[72] All knowledge, according to Occam, begins with perception of singular entities, sensory representations, and he denied that it is possible to reason from concepts to material reality. Empirical observation is required to attain knowledge of the world. At the same time, faith in God's covenant provides grounds for believing that we can have fairly reliable, if not certain, knowledge of the creation: "In Occam's theology, the absence of necessary connections in the world does not result in chaos. Although God cannot be bound by any of his creations, he can freely choose to follow a stable pattern in dealing with his creation in general and with man in particular. If God has freely chosen the established order, he *has* so chosen, and while he can dispense with or act apart from the laws he has decreed, he has nonetheless bound himself by his promise and will remain faithful to the covenant that of his kindness and mercy, he has instituted with man"; F. Oakley, *Omnipotence,*

The focus of Occam's doctrine concerning the source of human obligation was God's will. As the expression of his infinite goodness, God's will was said to be binding on human beings not because it was congruent with nature, or indeed for any other objective reason, but simply because it was his will.[73] Occam's solution to the *Euthyphro* dilemma was simpler and more influential than St Thomas's: God's will or command is the criterion of ethical action; so God could, for example, have defined stealing and bearing false witness as good and commanded them. Occam's voluntarism constituted a challenge to St Thomas's claim that the moral law could be discerned by natural reason and opened the way for the development of theories of law, including secular theories, based purely on will or command. As Garrett Barden has observed in *After Principles* (1990), in later thought the ethical tradition established by Occam divides into three streams. The first two are versions of command theory: the religious stream, where *God's command* remains the criterion, and the secular, positivist stream, where *the command of the Sovereign* replaces the command of God. [74] Critically, Barden suggests that the *modern* natural law tradition is the third stream arising out of Occam's thought, in which God's command becomes "the innate moral law, conceived, clearly or confusedly, as a set of propositions" and the stream where ethics "conceived as geometry with unassailable axioms is most at home".[75]

Covenant, and Order (Cornell University Press, Ithaca, 1984), p.62 (emphasis in original). For an analysis of how the patterns of thinking that appeared in natural philosophy during the seventeenth century—and which laid the foundations for modern Western philosophy—mirrored the differences between St Thomas's rationalism and Occam's voluntarism. See M. Osler, *op. cit.*

[73] J.M. Kelly, *op. cit.*, p.145. See also M. Villey, *Le Droit et les Droits de l'Homme* (PUF, Paris, 1983), pp.121–23.

[74] The first stream is substantially that of Protestant religions, associated with thinkers such as Martin Luther (1483–1546) and Karl Barth (1886–1968). The second stream includes Thomas Hobbes, Jeremy Bentham, John Austin, Hans Kelsen and H.L.A. Hart. See, in this volume, Liam Herrick, "Classical Legal Positivism and Utilitarianism: Jeremy Bentham and John Austin"; George Pavlakos, "Law as Recognition: H.L.A. Hart and Analytical Positivism"; and Tim Murphy, "Hans Kelsen's Pure Theory of Law".

[75] G. Barden, *After Principles*, p.24. On this view the radically significant shift from St Thomas to Occam is that "for the former the principle of action is an operation, or a person who is the subject of the operation, whereas for the latter the principle is a formula" (*ibid.*, p.136 (n.9)); moreover, common to all versions of the tradition established by Occam is the question of the criterion of action: "If actions are to be distinguished into good and bad, honourable and dishonourable, and so on, it is taken for granted that there must be some criterion. There are several candidates for the position of criterion—God's will, the will of the Sovereign, innate laws—but common is the idea of criterion. Common, too, is the conception of the criterion as a proposition, usually in the imperative mood"; *ibid.*, p.25.

The modern natural law tradition is characterised by its secular nature; by the notion of natural rights; and by the fact that modern rights theories tend to be idealist versions of natural law theory. The idea of a secular natural law, detached from any theological considerations, was advanced first by Hugo de Groot (1583–1645), usually known as Grotius. Grotius viewed the law of nature as essentially the injunction to preserve peace by way of showing respect for the rights of others; and so "rights [came] to usurp the whole of natural law theory, for the law of nature is simply, respect one another's rights".[76] The other innovative aspect of Grotius's theory was methodological; the seventeenth century could regard it as a rational and scientific method for arriving at a body of propositions underlying political arrangements and the provisions of the positive law because, according to Grotius, the reference to the "authorship" of God added nothing of substance to the definition and implied nothing like a religious sanction. In a famous phrase, he wrote that the law of nature would enjoin exactly the same even were we to say there is no God (*"etiamsi daremus non esse Deum"*).[77]

Although the thought of Thomas Hobbes (1588–1679) also played a role in the development of natural rights theories, the most important of the modern natural rights theorists was John Locke (1632–1704), who has been described by István Mészáros as "the idol of modern Liberalism".[78] In Locke's *Two Treatises of Civil Government* (1690), he sought to underpin intellectually the ending of the Stuart dynasty and its claims to divine right in kingship. He did so by offering an account of the basis of the state and of government in terms of a rights-based social contract that was different to that of Hobbes' *Leviathan* and that offered support for emerging capitalist economic principles. As Louis Dupré remarks, the equation of a doctrine of natural law with one of natural rights "developed out of a more radically individualistic questioning of the social pretenses of the contractual theory. Though the theory of rights may be

---

[76] R. Tuck, *Natural Rights Theories* (Cambridge University Press, Cambridge, 1979), p.67. Grotius defined the law of nature as "a dictate of right reason, which points out that an act, according as it is or is not in conformity with rational nature, has in it a quality of moral baseness or moral necessity; and that, in consequence, such an act is either forbidden or enjoined by the author of nature, God". Grotius, *De Jure Belli ac Pacis Libri Tres [On the Law of War and Peace]* (F.W. Kelsey trans., Clarendon Press, Oxford, 1925), Bk. I, chap.I, sect.X.1, pp.38–99.

[77] "What we have been saying would have a degree of validity even if we should concede that which cannot be conceded without the utmost wickedness, that there is no God, or that the affairs of men are of no concern to Him." *De Jure Belli ac Pacis Libri Tres*, Prolegomena, sect.11, p.13.

[78] I. Mészáros, "Marxism and Human Rights" in *Understanding Human Rights and Inter-Disciplinary and Interfaith Study* (A.D. Falconer ed., Irish School of Economics and Ecumenics, Dublin, 1980), p.49.

reinterpreted within the general context of natural law ... its original individualism was far removed from the natural law's fundamental assumption of the essentially social nature of the person."[79]

As has been said, the idea of individual or subjective "rights" does not appear at all in the *Summa Theologiae*, even though the origins of natural rights theories are in the work of Gratian and other canon lawyers during the eleventh and twelfth century and thus pre-date St Thomas.[80] St Thomas's writings emphasise individuals' duties towards the common good rather than individual rights. His implicit view of rights was that they were discoverable objectives of justice. The Roman law definition of justice holds that justice is the constant and enduring will to give to each what is due. The *Summa Theologiae* offers the following reformulation of the Roman definition: "justice is the habit whereby a person with a lasting and constant will renders to each his due."[81] The objective interest of justice, says St Thomas, is called "*the just thing*, and this indeed is a right. Clearly, then, right is the objective interest of justice."[82] Thus, in this conception of justice, a "right" comes into existence in real terms when something is recognised as being due to someone.[83]

Also of significance for modern natural law theory was the challenge posed by the empiricism of David Hume (1711–1776). In his *Treatise of Human Nature* (1739/1740), Hume claimed that natural law, or indeed any "system of morality", was flawed in that it could not support its derivation of values from facts, or of an "ought" from an "is".[84] Natural law theory does require moral

---

[79] L. Dupré, "The Common Good and the Open Society" in *Catholicism and Liberalism* (R. Bruce Douglass and D. Hollenbach eds., Cambridge University Press, Cambridge, 1994), p.180 (emphasis in original). In *The Origin of Capitalism* (Monthly Review Press, New York, 1999), Ellen Meiksins Wood shows how Locke's work is emblematic of a rising agrarian capitalism. She observes that Locke's labour-theory of property—whereby property rights are acquired by "mixing" one's labour with property—conflates labour with the production of profit, and so "Locke becomes perhaps the first thinker to construct a systematic theory of property based on something like ... capitalist principles" (p.87).

[80] See generally B. Tierney, *The Idea of Natural Rights* (Scholars Press, Atlanta, Ga., 1997). See also C.J. Reid, "The Canonistic Contribution to the Western Rights Tradition: An Historical Inquiry" (1991) 33 *Boston College Law Review* 37.

[81] St Thomas Aquinas, *Summa Theologiae*, II-II, q.58, art.1.

[82] *ibid.,* q.57, art.1.

[83] For discussion of the Roman and Thomist understanding of justice, see Garrett Barden, "Of the Naturally and the Conventionally Just" in this volume.

[84] "In every system of morality, which I have hitherto met with, I have always remark'd, that the author proceeds for some time in the ordinary way of reasoning, and establishes the being of a God, or makes observations concerning human affairs; when of a sudden I am surpriz'd to find that instead of the usual copulations of propositions, *is*, and *is not*, I meet with no proposition that is not connected with an

recourse, but it is not necessarily the case, as Hume maintained, that it is derivative of described facts. We may reiterate a point made earlier: when St Thomas states that since good has the nature of an end, all those things to which man has a natural inclination are naturally apprehended by human reason as being good and, consequently, as objects of pursuit. In other words, the "ought" of human action—that which one ought to do—is located in the "is" of human existence, in the fact of human nature and understanding that nature.[85] Hume's attack on natural law theory was nonetheless a major factor in its decline during the eighteenth century.

What of the contemporary Roman Catholic interpretation of Thomist natural law? According to the *Catechism of the Catholic Church*, the "divine and natural" law

> "shows man the way to follow so as to practise the good and attain his end. The natural law states the first and essential precepts which govern the moral life. It hinges upon the desire for God and submission to him, who is the source and judge of all that is good, as well as upon the sense that the other is one's equal. Its principal precepts are expressed in the Decalogue. This law is called 'natural', not in reference to the nature of irrational beings, but because reason which decrees it properly belongs to human nature."[86]

The primary addressee in this understanding, following St Thomas's theory, is evidently the individual human being and not those who frame, adjudicate on, or are subject to, positive, human law. This emphasises the understanding of Thomist natural law as primarily ethical. But in the official Catholic

---

ought, or an *ought not*. This change is imperceptible; but is, however, of the last consequence. For as this *ought*, or *ought not*, expresses some new relation or affirmation, 'tis necessary that it shou'd be observ'd and explain'd; and at the same time that a reason should be given, for what seems altogether inconceivable, how this new relation can be a deduction from others, which are entirely different from it"; D. Hume, *A Treatise of Human Nature*, Bk.III, Part I.I (E.C. Mossner ed., Penguin, Harmondsworth, 1969), p.521 (emphases in original).

[85] The version of the practical syllogism presented by Aristotle and by St Thomas has, according to Garrett Barden, "'ought', or some logical equivalent, in the premises—[The] 'ought' is contained, ... in 'the first principle of morality: the power to ask questions of responsibility'." On this view, the "ought" is the sign, in the practical syllogism, "of our grasp of ourselves as beings responsible for our own future and for the future of our world. It is the sign of our grasp of the present situation as a field of possibility, ordered toward a future for which we are, in part, responsible"; *After Principles*, pp.53–55, 142, quoting an (unpublished) analysis by another Irish philosopher, John Dowling.

[86] *Catechism of the Catholic Church*, p.426.

understanding of natural law, in addition to providing the foundation for the structure of rules to guide ethical action and for "building the human community", the natural law also provides "the necessary basis for the civil law with which it is connected, whether by a reflection that draws conclusions from its principles, or by additions of a positive and juridical nature".[87] On this view, then, the operation of natural law in relation to human law ultimately involves the fallible activities of human reflection or juridical "addition".

The *Catechism's* account of natural law also contains the idea that the "principal precepts" of the natural law are "expressed in the Decalogue". This formulation is an extremely subtle one, originally conceived by the canon lawyer Gratian in his eleventh century *Decretum*. The words have a double meaning, as A.P. d'Entrèves has noted: "They mean that the law of nature is embodied in the Scriptures. But they also mean that the Scriptures do not contradict the law of nature. ... Reason and faith are not incompatible." The formulation marked the beginning of the end for the pessimism and hostility towards the world that underlay the theology of St Augustine. It was expressed by virtually all subsequent Christian thinkers, including St Thomas, and it continues to provide the basis for the complementary roles of faith and reason in Catholic moral thought.[88] Yet there remains some confusion here. For if the principal precepts of the natural law are expressed in the Decalogue, then we appear, on the face of it, to be back to the voluntarism of the Decalogue's commands. However this is not necessarily the case. St Thomas's Christian rationalism holds that the Decalogue was commanded by God because what it commanded was already good, that is, good according to the way in which the world has been created. The voluntarist view is that the Decalogue's commands are good simply because they are the commands of God.

Although Thomism has been enormously influential in the history of Catholicism, there have been several other important influences on the Catholic tradition that have not been Thomist in nature. For example, in the nineteenth century natural law theory was eclipsed by a range of other perspectives and was maintained only in the teaching of the institutional Catholic Church in the form of neo-scholastic theology. Neo-scholasticism, which is sometimes dated from the appearance of Pope Leo XIII's 1879 encyclical *Aeterni Patris*, taught that the existence of God can be known with certainty from the created world through the "natural light of human reason". Neo-scholasticism interpreted faith as "the assent of mind and will to a body of true propositions revealed by God, for which objective supporting reasons—e.g. miracles, especially the resurrection, the fulfilment of prophecies, the continuity of the witness itself of the church—could ... be adduced".[89] John Finnis has suggested that while

---

[87] *ibid.*, p.247.
[88] See A.P. d'Entrèves, *Natural Law* (2nd ed., Hutchinson, London, 1970), pp.40–42.
[89] M. Henry, *On Not Understanding God*, p.222.

the very frequent misreading of St Thomas—that which "treats the deliverances of *synderesis* (i.e. the first principles of practical reasoning) as already crystallized moral principles (in the form of, e.g. the last six of the Ten Commandments)"[90]—finds some support in the wording of occasional passages in the *Summa Theologiae*, it nonetheless makes nonsense of Aquinas's notion of prudence or *prudentia*,

> "reducing it to a mere ability to judge when such a crystallized moral rule is applicable, working with such banal 'arguments' as 'murder is wrong; this is an act of murder; therefore this act is wrong and must not be done'. The capacity to make such arguments could never earn the paramount dignity of status accorded to *prudentia* by Aquinas. Above all, this neo-scholastic theory discards Aquinas's repeated teaching that the first principles of human action are ends ..., so that a man cannot reason rightly in matters of practice, i.e. cannot have *prudentia*, unless he is well disposed towards those ultimate ends."[91]

Indeed another perspective on natural law that has been proposed by Finnis is that the guiding purpose of the natural law tradition is to focus on the individual act of choice. This is in line with the Thomist version of natural law and proposes that natural law be employed as an interpretive methodology in cases of deliberation and choice. This is not to say that such natural law theory does not have application to the broader political context. Its purpose, as Finnis has put it, is

> "to answer the parallel questions of a conscientious individual or a group or a group's responsible officer (e.g. a judge): 'What should I do?' 'What should we decide, enact, require, promote?'. ... The dominant concern is with *judging for oneself* what reasons are good reasons for adopting or rejecting specific kinds of option. Societies and their laws and institutions are therefore to be understood as they would be understood by a participant in deliberations about whether or not to make the choices (of actions, dispositions, institutions, practices, etc.) which shape and largely constitute that society's reality and determine its worth or worthlessness."[92]

---

[90] J.M. Finnis, *Natural Law and Natural Rights*, p.51.

[91] *ibid.*

[92] J.M. Finnis, "Natural Law: The Classical Tradition" in *The Oxford Handbook of Jurisprudence and Philosophy of Law* (J. Coleman and S. Shapiro eds., Oxford University Press, Oxford, 2002) pp.3–4.

This does not appear, on the face of it, to accord with Finnis's earlier view that there are "exceptionless or absolute human claim-rights", but even Finnis has acknowledged that such rights are impossible to interpret, in given situations, in anything like a formalistic fashion.

The modern ethic of human rights was embraced by the Catholic Church only after Pope John XXIII's 1963 encyclical, *Pacem in Terris* ("Peace on Earth"). *Pacem in Terris* contains arguments in favour of a series of specific human rights and since 1963 human rights have become one of the primary ways in which the papacy addresses global social issues. The shift in Catholic thought from hostility to acceptance of the modern ethic of human rights has been greeted with disapproval from some Thomist quarters. Although there are major differences among the thinkers who have shaped the liberal tradition, and these differences include varying degrees of commitment to the common good, modern, liberal Western culture indisputably values autonomous freedom far more highly. In the Catholic perspective, on the other hand, human self-understanding or identity is grounded in the idea of *imago Dei*, an idea that suggests true individual freedom can only be achieved in relation to the practices of society.[93] Although both liberal and Catholic philosophy hold that man is older than the state and the domestic household is antecedent, logically as well as in fact, to the state or civil community, there are many who argue that there is a fundamental incompatibility between the Catholic common good tradition and the liberal individualistic cultural framework implied in the human rights ethic. A clash is perceived, in other words, between the atomism of liberalism and the social nature of Catholic thought, and this clash is said to preclude a coherent Catholic account of human rights.[94]

---

[93] See generally P. Hannon, "Rights: Theological Perspectives" (1998) 42 *Milltown Studies* 90.

[94] Perhaps the strongest objection to human rights theory on Aristotelian-Thomistic grounds is that of Alasdair MacIntyre. See *After Virtue* (2nd ed., University of Notre Dame Press, Notre Dame, 1984). For MacIntyre morality is a practice, and the idea of rights—by maintaining that all persons are entitled to certain forms of treatment independent of their communal bonds, social roles, historical period, and cultural traditions—rests on a concept of the person as individuated or, to use Michael Sandel's term, "unencumbered". See M. Sandel, *Liberalism and the Limits of Justice* (Cambridge University Press, Cambridge, 1982), pp.59–65. MacIntyre holds that for the Catholic tradition to embrace a liberal human rights ethic would be subversive of its own insights into the importance of community and the common good. David Hollenbach argues, however, that there is no *necessary* link between human rights and the liberal individualistic cultural framework. He has proposed a way of construing the Catholic tradition's recent adoption of rights language that is "in deep continuity with its ancient stress on virtuous commitment to the good of community"; in his view, the vision of community that generates the idea of human rights "is the community of all human beings as such". D. Hollenbach, "A

7. Conclusion

There is little doubt but that the theology and natural law theory of St Thomas Aquinas are complex in many respects. The *Summa Theologiae* stretches to 61 volumes in the standard (Blackfriars) edition and there are some who argue that you cannot know or understand any of it unless you know and understand all of it. This does serve to highlight the inter-connections within the lengthy text, but it is nonetheless something of an exaggeration. For many observers, however, the complexity of the theology is not at issue: in a culture that has been secularised, St Thomas's thought is to be rejected simply on the basis that it is "theocratic", "religious", "faith-based".

As we have mentioned, St Thomas explains the significance of behaviour in the world in terms of the two ultimate aims or "ends" of human life. One end is a natural, earthly end, it involves the flourishing of body, mind, and soul in human community; and the other is supernatural, it involves posthumous participation in the beatific vision. Thomist ethics are therefore only apparently detachable from systematic theology: they cannot function without at least implicit reference to criteria that fall outside both unaided human reason and the observable features of nature. So there is indeed an element of religious faith involved in Thomist natural law theory, but perhaps two points are worth raising in this regard, at least insofar as Catholicism overlaps with Thomism. Both points have been emphasised in the work of Patrick Hannon. Firstly, the Catholic theological tradition has always argued its normative or substantive ethical claims on grounds of "reason"—"even when a norm is said to be part of revelation, it is also based on arguments which do not appeal to a purely religious authority".[95] Secondly, the word "faith" is not bound to religious faith: it implies "a trusting or entrusting of ourselves to some vision of reality. ... [I]t is essentially a movement of the spirit in the encounter with reality."[96] Seen in the latter light particularly, the "faith" objection to St Thomas's natural law theory is unconvincing when taken in isolation, based invariably as it is on some other faith, whether theocratic or secular.

Communitarian Reconstruction of Human Rights: Contributions from Catholic Tradition" in *Catholicism and Liberalism*, p.138.

[95] P. Hannon, "On Using Religious Arguments in Public Policy Debates" in *Religion, Morality and Public Policy* (B. Treacy and G. Whyte eds., Dominican Publications, Dublin, 1995), p.69. See also P. Hannon, *Church, State, Morality and Law* (Gill and Macmillan, Dublin, 1992) and G. Whyte, "Some Reflections on the Role of Religion in the Constitutional Order" in *Ireland's Evolving Constitution 1937–1997: Collected Essays* (T. Murphy and P. Twomey eds., Hart, Oxford, 1998).

[96] P. Hannon, *Rights: Theological Resources*, at 93.

CHAPTER 5

CLASSICAL LEGAL POSITIVISM AND UTILITARIANISM

LIAM HERRICK

1. INTRODUCTION

Brian Leiter has observed that positivist theories of law are distinguished by their commitment to two broad theses: a "social thesis"—that what counts as law in any particular society is fundamentally a matter of social fact—and a "separability thesis"—that what the law *is* and what the law *ought to be* are separate questions.[1] As was outlined in Chapter 4 of this volume, "St Thomas Aquinas And The Natural Law Tradition", one of the intellectual roots of legal positivist thought is the implication from William of Occam's fourteenth century voluntarism that law is pure will, with no foundation in the nature of things. Although for Occam the will in question was the will of God, Thomas Hobbes (1588–1679) followed this tradition in *Leviathan* (1651) when he explicitly defined civil law as the commands of the sovereign.[2] The Scottish Enlightenment thinker David Hume (1711–1776) also contributed to the development of legal positivist thought, in particular to its opposition to natural

---

[1] B. Leiter, "Positivism, Formalism, Realism" (1999) 99 *Columbia Law Review* 1138 (reviewing A. Sebok, *Legal Positivism in American Jurisprudence* (Cambridge University Press, Cambridge, 1998)), at 1141–1142.

[2] "[I]t is manifest that Law in generall, is not Counsell, but Command; but only of him whose Command is addressed to one formerly obliged to obey him". T. Hobbes, *Leviathan* (K.R. Minogue ed., Dent, London, 1973), Pt II, chap.26, p.140. Hobbes's definition was a consequence of his explanation of the character of political society (a commonwealth) in terms of the idea of a social contract or covenant. Hobbes argued that the life of primeval man was "solitary, poore, nasty, brutish, and short", and his social contract theory was a theory of subjection to an all-powerful and protective sovereign or "Leviathan". For the contrasts between Hobbes' "contract of subjection" and the "contract of union" found in the later social contract theory of John Locke (1632–1704), see J.M. Kelly, *A Short History of Western Legal Theory* (Clarendon Press, Oxford, 1992), pp.212–219. See also Colin Harvey, "Talking about Human Rights" in this volume.

law theory and its insistence that law and morality are separate domains. In his *Treatise on Human Nature* (1740), Hume claimed that natural law theory, or indeed any "system of morality", was flawed in that it made an illogical jump from fact to value, from the descriptive "is" to the prescriptive "ought".

This chapter sets out the main features of the classical legal positivism developed by Jeremy Bentham (1748–1832) and John Austin (1790–1859). Legal positivism can be characterised generally as the application of positivist philosophy—which emphasises the value of descriptive knowledge of sensory phenomena—to law and legal theory. Of the two figures it is Bentham who was the earlier and the more significant. As Charles Covell has remarked, the contribution of Bentham marked the beginning of the modern tradition in jurisprudence in the English-speaking world.[3] Bentham made two major contributions to Western thought: his development of the idea of legal positivism and his ethical and political philosophy of utilitarianism. Bentham's positivism is usually described as the "command theory of law", and although elements of this theory appeared in 1776 (in *A Fragment on Government*) and 1789 (in *An Introduction to the Principles of Morals and Legislation*), most of what Bentham wrote about the nature of law was not published until 1945, and not definitively until 1970.[4] The works published in Bentham's lifetime were principally concerned with utilitarian philosophy and its prescriptions regarding "the greatest happiness of the greatest number". The command theory of law developed by Bentham became well known only after it was restated by John Austin in the nineteenth century.

In this chapter we will first examine the command theory of law (also sometimes known as the imperative theory) and then give an account of utilitarianism. But before we do so we should remark on Covell's claim that Bentham was the first *modern* English-speaking jurisprudent. In general terms, as Martin Henry has remarked, the modern world stood in opposition to the medieval period, which was perceived as "other-worldly, religion-dominated, feudal and communitarian", and was instead "this-worldly, rationalist, increasingly democratic, individualist, and profoundly marked by the growth of capitalism".[5] Bertrand Russell suggested that almost everything that

---

[3] C. Covell, *The Defence of the Natural Law* (St Martin's Press, New York, 1992), p.1.

[4] J. Bentham, *The Limits of Jurisprudence Defined* (C.W. Everett ed., Columbia University Press, New York, 1945) and *Of Laws in General* (H.L.A. Hart ed., Athlone Press, London, 1970). These writings were discovered in manuscript form by Charles Everett more than a century after Bentham's death. See J.W. Harris, *Legal Philosophies* (2nd ed., Butterworths, London, 1997), p.29.

[5] M. Henry, "God in Postmodernity" (1998) 63 *Irish Theological Quarterly* 3 at 4. The broader "project of modernity" included the scientific revolution, the "Enlightenment" of the eighteenth century, the industrial revolution, the growth of

distinguishes the modern world from earlier centuries is attributable to the "spectacular triumphs" of the early scientific revolution, in particular the developments in physics and astronomy brought about by Nicolaus Copernicus (1473–1543), Johannes Kepler (1571–1630), Galileo Galielei (1564–1642) and Isaac Newton (1642–1727).[6] The rise of modern science was associated with the emergence of modern *empiricism*, an epistemology that emphasises the importance of observation and experience in verifying claims to knowledge. By presenting a picture of objectivity and certainty that no system of metaphysics could rival, the scientific revolution laid the basis for the Enlightenment of the eighteenth century. The dominant note of the Enlightenment attitude was, in John Kelly's words, "one of profound scepticism towards traditional systems of authority or orthodoxy (especially those of religion), and a strong faith in the power of the human reason and intelligence to make unlimited advances in the sciences and techniques conducive to human welfare".[7] This confidence in the power of human reason was the basis for the other major epistemology of modernity, namely *rationalism*, which prioritises reason over experience in verifying claims to knowledge.

These features of modernity are reflected in the thought of Bentham and Austin. The dominant feature of intellectual and social discourse during their lifetimes was one of idealism and unswerving optimism in the potential of science and the capacity of human reason. Above all else the age was dominated by an intense enthusiasm for "progress". The development of the theory of legal positivism during this time can be viewed as part of a wider philosophical and sociological movement founded on confidence in the capacity of man to successfully govern his own affairs using the tools of rationalism and scientific method. Within this wider philosophical and cultural movement Lord Macaulay ranked Bentham with Galileo and John Locke, describing him as "the man who found jurisprudence a gibberish and left it a science".[8]

---

historical consciousness during the nineteenth century, the Romantic movement, and the emergence of contemporary, "technological" civilisation during the twentieth century.

[6] B. Russell, *History of Western Philosophy* (2nd ed., George Allen and Unwin, London, 1961), p.542. Different writers emphasise other aspects of the transformation to modernity: for example, the definitive emergence of the figure of "the individual" in the history of ideas may be situated in the political philosophy of Niccolo Machiavelli (1469–1527) and the Protestant theology of Martin Luther (1483–1546); Alisdair MacIntyre offers the view that these two thinkers "mark in their different ways the break with the hierarchical, synthesizing society of the Middle Ages, and the distinctive moves into the modern world". *A Short History of Ethics* (2nd ed., Routledge, London, 1998), p.121.

[7] J.M. Kelly, *op. cit.*, p.249.

[8] Lord Macaulay's *Works* (G. Trevelyan ed., Longmans, London, 1866), Vol.V, p.613,

At the core of Bentham and Austin's work is a focus on the place of law within human political society. By this we mean a concentration on law as being created, or posited, by political figures, as distinct from a view of law as being dependant on a particular moral code or other abstract or metaphysical standard. The starting point for their legal positivism was the belief that law is a human political phenomenon susceptible to rational analytical examination, and that such analysis contributed to society's efforts to understand and ultimately improve its own governance. In this sense the descriptive command theory of law is preliminary to, and provides a platform for the separate, prescriptive philosophy of utilitarianism.

2. THE COMMAND THEORY OF LAW

As a student, Jeremy Bentham attended the Oxford lectures of William Blackstone (1723–1780) that were to form Blackstone's *Commentaries on the Laws of England* (1769). The lectures inspired in Bentham a deep-seated disillusionment with the confusion and complexity of the English law. As the first university lecturer to teach English law (as opposed to Roman law), Blackstone made an important contribution to the establishment of law as a subject of study, but his essentially uncritical work presented a view of English law as a comprehensive and organic system that was largely beyond improvement in either form or substance. The common law as characterised by Blackstone was a discrete rational system not governed by general principles aimed at particular outcomes—such as those relating to a conception of the common good—but rather a system in which individual rights were to be protected and reconciled by a combination of intuitive judgment and analogy. The common law had been described by Chief Justice Coke in the early seventeenth century as being governed by an "artificial reason".[9] Alan Brudner discusses the influence of Coke and Blackstone in his study of the nature of the common law tradition and describes their shared view of common law reasoning:

> "It was not everyday prudence concerning ends and their most suitable means, but a special form of reasoning from principles to their endless specification in particular cases—a reasoning dependent on analogy and

---

quoted by H.L.A. Hart in his essay, "Bentham's Principle of Utility and Theory of Penal Law" in J. Bentham, *An Introduction to the Principles of Morals and Legislation* (J.H. Burns and H.L.A Hart eds., Clarendon Press, Oxford, 1996).

[9] See *The Reports of Sir Edward Coke in Thirteen Parts* (Moore, Dublin, 1879), 12th Report, p.65.

intuitive judgment, committed to an internal coherence as its chief virtue, and needing a special intellectual training and experience."[10]

This system with its specialised intellectual training was separated from the "natural" reasoning of the general populace and indeed from other political actors by a veil of mystification.

Blackstone's celebration of the English common law tradition presented a target for Bentham's project and was the main focus of his initial venture into legal theory, *A Fragment on Government*, first published in 1776.[11] In Bentham's view, the uncritical acceptance of the common law—and of its supposed "natural law" components—demanded an overhaul of jurisprudence.[12] The mystification of "artificial reason" and the separation of the common law from questions of social policy was particularly problematic for Bentham. Moreover, he rejected the perceived role of precedent in the common law:

> "It is the judges ... that make the common law. Do you know how they make it? Just as a man makes laws for his dog. When your dog does anything you want to break him of, you wait till he does it and then you beat him for it. That is the way you make laws for your dog and that is the way the judges make laws for you and me."[13]

---

[10] A. Brudner, *The Unity of the Common Law: Studies in Hegelian Philosophy* (University of California Press, Berkeley, 1995), p.2. See also John Ringrose, "Jurisprudence and Legal Education" in this volume.

[11] J. Bentham *A Fragment on Government*, (Payne, Elmsly and Brooke, London, 1776). The *Fragment* was part of a broader critique of Blackstone and set out the foundations of Bentham's political theory of utilitarianism, which was not published fully until 1928: J. Bentham, *A Comment on the Commentaries: A Criticism of William Blackstone's Commentaries on the Laws of England* (C.W. Everett ed., Clarendon Press, Oxford, 1928). References to the *Fragment* in this chapter are to the 1977 edition, edited by J.H Burns and H.L.A. Hart (Athlone Press, London).

[12] Blackstone argued that the English common law was based on certain immutable principles of natural law, which, although willed by God, were also capable of being grasped by human reason; the common law was discovered by judges "in accordance with procedures of adjudication in which legal rules and precedents were established through an application to individual cases of the principles of morality and reasonableness that ran through the whole structure of English law". C. Covell, *op. cit.*, p.3.

[13] The passage is from an article entitled *Truth versus Ashhurst; or, law as it is, contrasted with what it is said to be* (Moses, London, 1823). The essay was included in *The Works of Jeremy Bentham* (Simpkin Marshall, London, 1843), Vol.V, published under the supervision of Bentham's executor, John Bowring.

Bentham's objections to the common law tradition went further: it was a tradition with its philosophical origins in the protection of individual autonomy, rather than in advancing any conception of the common good; from Bentham's utilitarian viewpoint, the irrationality of such a crude system was beyond mere reform and he championed the replacement of the common law with a codified system of law based on his proposal for a *pannomion* (from the Greek term signifying a comprehensive code of laws).[14]

Bentham advanced the idea that jurisprudence has two aspects: an expositorial aspect ("the science of law as a system") and a censorial one ("the science of legislation"). The former was Bentham's positivism, concerned with explaining what the law *is*, while the latter was his utilitarianism, concerned with what the law *ought to be*. The former is concerned with understanding the "mechanics" of law and of a particular legal system, whereas the latter is concerned with the substance of laws and operates at the normative level:

> "There are two characters, one or other of which every man who finds any thing to say on the subject of Law, may be said to take upon him; that of the *Expositor*, and that of the *Censor*. To the province of the *Expositor* it belongs to explain to us what, as he supposes, the Law is: to that of the *Censor*, to observe to us what he thinks it ought to be. The former, therefore, is principally occupied in stating, or in enquiring after facts: the latter, in discussing reasons."[15]

By establishing this distinction Bentham wished to allow for rational debate about the ends of law based on a proper understanding of what law actually constitutes. Charles Covell has remarked how the distinction between expositorial and censorial jurisprudence signalled a crucial turning-point in the history of legal philosophy, marking the point at which the study of law came to be regarded as an autonomous discipline of intellectual enquiry, and one to be clearly differentiated from the disciplines of ethics and political

---

[14] The nature of the relationship between positivism and the common law continues to be a subject of some dispute. The main thesis of Alan Brudner's text on the common law (*op. cit.*) is that the conflict between the traditions of positivism and that of the common law is interconnected with the conflict between the political theories of communitarianism, where individual rights are subservient to common good determinations and liberalism, which places individual rights at the centre of the process of legal determination. Others, most notably Lon Fuller, have claimed that the common law tradition, based on politically neutral principles rather than policy, provides a bulwark against political extremism, and that positivism is linked with the rise of totalitarianism in Spain and Germany during the twentieth century. See L. Fuller, *The Law in Quest of Itself* (Chicago, Foundation Press, 1940), p.122.

[15] J. Bentham, *A Fragment on Government*, Preface, para.13.

philosophy, which traditionally had engaged in critical reflection on normative concepts of justice and political morality. The foundation stone of positivist theory is that the "ought" cannot be logically dependent on the "is". The study of law through the lens of legal positivism was the pure, analytical study of law, without any normative dimension:

> "The distinction between expository and censorial jurisprudence ... represented a direct challenge on Bentham's part to the philosophical tradition of natural law, in which the analytical study of law had been inseparable from consideration of the normative concerns of moral and political philosophy. At the same time, the imperative theory—which served as the methodological basis of expository jurisprudence—enabled Bentham to demonstrate that there existed no necessary or conceptually guaranteed connection between law and morality."[16]

Although the separation of expositorial jurisprudence from censorial jurisprudence was the idea at the core of Bentham's thinking about law, his view of the relationship between the two areas of jurisprudence is often misunderstood. As a radical reformist, Bentham viewed the study of expositorial jurisprudence as a necessary precursor to the more important work of the censor. As William Twining puts it, "Bentham distinguished the is and the ought for the sake of the ought".[17] Bentham's view was that the role of the expositor, the jurist who studies the components and concepts that constitute a particular legal system, was inferior and subservient to that of the censor, the law reformer who is guided by the universal laws of utility to recommend change: "[T]he *Expositor* ... is always a citizen of this or that particular country: the *Censor* is, or ought to be the citizen of the world."[18]

Bentham's expository jurisprudence defines law as

> "an assemblage of signs declarative of a volition conceived or adopted by the *sovereign* in a state, concerning the conduct to be observed in a certain *case* by a certain person or class of persons, who in the case in question are supposed to be subject to his power: such volition trusting for its accomplishment to the expectation of certain events which it is intended such declaration should upon occasion be a means of bringing to pass, and prospect of which it is intended should act as a motive upon those whose conduct is in question."[19]

---

[16] C. Covell, *op. cit.*, p.2.
[17] W. Twining, *Globalisation and Legal Theory* (Butterworths, London, 2000), p.17.
[18] J. Bentham, *A Fragment on Government*, p.398.
[19] J. Bentham, *Of Laws in General*, p.1. Bentham devoted a great deal of time and energy to developing his ideas on logic and the science of definition and his work

Covell explains Bentham's definition as meaning that a law always specified a *duty* created through an express *command* or *prohibition* willed by its author. From this basic idea Bentham proceeded to define the law of a political community "as comprising a set of commands and prohibitions, issued by the recognized *sovereign* law-making body or institution of that community, and supported by *sanctions* to be imposed by the sovereign power in the event of any failure by its subjects to comply with the requirements laid down in these commands and prohibitions".[20] This is a definition of law that makes no reference to any moral criterion or standard; immoral law can therefore qualify as "law".

The restatement of the command theory by John Austin was published in 1832 as *The Province of Jurisprudence Determined.*[21] For Austin as for Bentham, the formal structure of legal systems could be analysed without any reference to substantive principles of justice or morality—the "science of jurisprudence" (the description of positive law as it is) was distinct from the "science of legislation" (the determination of positive law as it ought to be). Austin's jurisprudence concentrated almost exclusively on expositorial jurisprudence and his teachings in this area dominated English analytical theory until the time of Hart. The following definition of law, from the first lecture in the series that would comprise *The Province of Jurisprudence Determined,* provides the starting point for Austin's positivism:

> "A law, in the most general and comprehensive acceptation in which the term, in its literal meaning, is employed, may be said to be a rule laid down for the guidance of an intelligent being by an intelligent being having power over him."[21]

In Austin's theory positive human law, as distinct from the law of God, can be identified by a number of verifiable characteristics; "law properly so called" involves a *command*, issued by a *sovereign* supported by a *sanction*. Covell refers to the three central elements of Austin's theory as follows:

> "1) a rule of positive law was to be understood as a general command,

---

exhibits a concentration on clearly defined concepts. Ross Harrison has claimed that Bentham's writings in this area were significant influences for many of the key philosophers of the twentieth century, including Bertrand Russell, particularly in the explanation of terms and the associated development of conceptual epistemology. R. Harrison, *Bentham* (Routledge and Kegan Paul, London, 1983), p.65, quoted in F. Rosen, "Introduction" to *An Introduction to the Principles of Morals and Legislation* (J.H. Burns and H.L.A. Hart eds.), p.xxxiv.

[20] See C. Covell, *op. cit.*, p.1.

[21] References in this chapter are to *The Province of Jurisprudence Determined* (Hackett, Indianapolis, 1998).

which required its subjects to perform or forbear from actions belonging to a certain designated class; 2) the duty or obligation created by a rule of positive law was to be explained in terms of the power of its author to inflict a sanction or punishment in the event of any refusal to obey the command expressed in the rule; and 3) rules of positive law were distinguished from other types of rule, like the laws of God or the rules contained in what he called positive morality, in being the laws set by a superior acknowledged to be sovereign within an independent political society."[23]

For Austin, a society existed as an independent political society when the bulk of its members were in a habit of obedience to a determinate political superior, where this superior was not itself in habitual obedience to the commands issuing from a higher law-making authority. He insisted that it was necessary to the character of an independent political society that its sovereign should be considered incapable of legal limitation. Austin's emphasis on the description of positive law—the principles, notions and distinctions that he believed were common to all advanced systems of positive law—laid the foundation for twentieth century analytical-positivist jurisprudence.

Most aspects of Austin's theory have been subjected to severe criticism, and generally his positivism has been compared unfavourably with Bentham's version, particularly his conception of the sovereign, which is at the same time a more absolute and narrow conception than that of Bentham. In his first lecture, Austin defines sovereignty as "persons exercising supreme and subordinate government, in independent nations, or independent political societies".[24] This idea of supremacy or superiority was central to the vertical view of legal power found in Austin's theory: he defined superiority as signifying "might, the power of affecting others with evil or pain, and of forcing them, through fear of that evil, to fashion their conduct to one's wishes".[25] This vertical conception of power is part of a rejection of any natural or moral supremacy over the law:

"Now to say that human laws which conflict with the Divine are not binding, that is to say, are not laws, is to talk stark nonsense. The most pernicious laws and therefore those which most opposed the will of God, have been and are continually enforced as laws by judicial tribunals."[26]

In his *Concept of a Legal System*, Joseph Raz focuses on the limitations of

---

[22] *ibid.*, p.10.
[23] C. Covell, *op. cit.*, p.4.
[24] J. Austin, *The Province of Jurisprudence Determined*, p.11.
[25] *ibid.*, p.24.
[26] *ibid.*, p185.

Austin's conception of the sovereign, building on the criticisms of earlier writers to offer new insights regarding the difficulties presented by Austin's definition.[27] Raz examines how Austin's doctrine of the illimitability of the sovereign, the view that the sovereign could not be subject to legal duty or be the holder of legal rights necessarily excludes certain constitutional laws from his understanding of a legal system. He also demonstrates that Austin's idea of personal obedience to a sovereign is unnecessarily crude, implying that every change of sovereign involves a change of legal system. Theoretically at least, the restrictive concept of a legal system founded on the will of a particular sovereign raises fundamental questions about the validity of any such system.

Austin's understanding of the term "command" also seems unnecessarily narrow. At the outset, he explicitly excludes from his definition of command all directions that are not backed by a real and practical threat of sanction. For Austin a command does not simply indicate an imperative, it is a binding order from which the object may not escape save by incurring the likelihood of suffering a sanction to be applied. A law is a command that enjoys the general forbearance of a class of people, as distinct from the occasional command of a sovereign. Austin believed that a command should be seen as an expression of the "sovereign will" (an idea that appears also in Bentham's work).

For Karl Olivecrona (1879–1980), however, one of the Scandinavian legal realists, this definition of command represents a basic misconception: it fails to recognise that a declaration of will is descriptive while a command is of its essence an imperative aimed at influencing the actions of others.[28] Olivecrona's distinction might appear somewhat metaphysical and J.W. Harris has argued that the presentation of the command as a declaration of sovereign will in the theories of Bentham and Austin is better understood as a "constructive metaphor"; Harris contends that both writers were simply making use of "convenient and familiar metaphysical language" to explain a more complex conceit.[29] Harris's view is that Bentham thought of the concept of sovereign will, "as a concept, not of political, but of legal theory. As such it would not

---

[27] J. Raz, *A Concept of the Legal System* (Clarendon Press, Oxford, 1980), pp.27–43. The key attack on Austin's representation of positivism has come from H.L.A. Hart and the focus of his attack has been on the trinity of constructs at the centre of that theory: command, sovereign and sanction. By demonstrating that the complexity of the English legal system can be explained more convincingly in terms of rules that can facilitate and regulate as well as simply command, he succeeds most impressively in exposing the naïveté of Austin's model. See Hart, *The Concept of Law* (Clarendon Press, Oxford, 1961).

[28] See K. Olivecrona, *Law as Fact* (Einar Munksgaard, Copenhagen, 1939).

[29] J.W. Harris, *Law and Legal Science* (Oxford University Press, Oxford, 1979), pp.28–33.

purport to point up anything about political society as a whole, but only about the discipline of legal science". Harris suggests that, as a concept of political theory, "sovereign will" is of little value; "but as a conception of legal theory intended simply to explain the logical basis of descriptive legal science, it has much in its favour".[30] But while this explanation may be valid for Bentham's positivism, Harris concedes that the evidence for a metaphorical intention cannot be easily found in Austin's writings.

Another significant departure from Bentham's theory can be found in Austin's view of the sanction, which he restricts to a negative sense of conditional evil, thus excluding Bentham's idea of the absence of rewards as a form of sanction. Austin believed that it is "only by conditional evil that duties or sanctions are enforced. It is the power and the purpose of inflicting eventual evil, and not the power and the purpose of imparting eventual good, which gives to the expression of a wish the name of a command".[31] This passage suggests Austin had in mind a narrower use of the term "sanction" than appears in Bentham's writing, though other passages from Austin's *Lectures on Jurisprudence and the Philosophy on Positive Law* revert to Bentham's conception of sanction.[32] M.D.A. Freeman describes how Bentham's exposition of this component of the command theory again displays greater subtlety than Austin:

> "Sanctions generally play a less prominent part in Bentham's theory than they do in Austin's. And Bentham, perhaps for this reason, is prepared to undertake a more detailed, less crude, taxonomy of motivating forces than Austin was. Thus Bentham thought a sovereign's commands would be law even if supported only by religious or moral sanctions. Further, Bentham's account admits 'alluring motives', the concept of rewards."[33]

Bentham's wide definition of the sanction might be regarded as one of the less appealing aspects of his theory, yet Austin's definition leaves us with a theory that is wholly inadequate in explaining large areas of law. Austin himself ran into some difficulty in explaining precisely why the sanction played such a pivotal role in his theory, as can be seen from the following passage:

> "The truth is, that the magnitude of the eventual evil, and the magnitude

---

[30] *ibid.*, pp.32, 34.

[31] J. Austin, *The Province of Jurisprudence Determined*, p.17.

[32] See J. Austin *The Lectures on Jurisprudence or the Philosophy of Positive Law* (Murray, London, 1873), pp.505–506, quoted in H. Davies and D. Holdcroft, *Jurisprudence: Texts and Commentary* (Butterworths, London, 1991), p.20.

[33] M.D.A. Freeman, *Lloyd's Introduction to Jurisprudence* (7th ed., Butterworths, London, 2001), p 204.

of the chance of incurring it, are foreign to the matter in question. The greater the eventual evil, and the greater the chance of incurring it, the greater is the efficacy of the command, and the greater is the strength of the obligation. ... But where there is the smallest chance of incurring the smallest evil, the expression of a wish amounts to a command, and therefore imposes a duty."[34]

Another difference between Austin and Bentham is that with Bentham a distinction is relatively clear between censorial principles of universal nature and expositorial jurisprudence that is particular to each legal system; however, Austin makes such a distinction *within* his expositorial theory. In attempting to develop a theory for use within legal education he sought to put in place a general conceptual framework which would equip law students, or more specifically the lawyer in training, with the tools to engage in the more particular study of the instant legal system. In his lecture on the *Uses of the Study of Jurisprudence* (1863) Austin attempts to put forward a theory of General or Universal Jurisprudence as a separate area of study from that of English law.

"I mean, then, by General Jurisprudence, the science concerned with the exposition of principles, notions, and distinctions which are common to systems of law: understanding by systems of law, the ampler and maturer systems which, by reason of their amplitude and maturity, are pre-eminently pregnant with instruction."[35]

Austin's proposal of this concept of General Jurisprudence presents many difficulties. For example, how might one define "ampler and maturer" systems of law? Is it indeed possible to find a closed list of items common to each of these legal systems? And, if it is possible to find common elements to all such legal systems, does such a theory run the risk of becoming conflated with theories of what is natural within a legal system?[36]

An important distinction between Bentham and Austin's theory can also be seen in their approaches to the common law. Austin excludes customary law from the category of laws properly so called, but states "custom is transmuted into positive law, when it is adopted as such by the courts of justice and when the judicial decisions fashioned upon it are enforced by the State".[37]

---

[34] J. Austin, *The Province of Jurisprudence Determined*, p.16.

[35] J. Austin, *Uses of the Study of Jurisprudence*, p.367. Page references to Austin's *Uses* in this chapter are from the edition of *The Province of Jurisprudence Determined* cited above (at n.22), which includes *Uses* as an Appendix.

[36] For a detailed criticism of Austin's ideas on General Jurisprudence, see W. Twining, *op. cit.*, pp.15–49.

[37] J. Austin, *The Province of Jurisprudence Determined*, p.31.

As with his sanction-focussed definition of command, Austin's view of the category of "laws properly so called" is narrowly drawn. It also excludes international law entirely; along with custom, to be another example of mere "positive morality". On the other hand, Austin's desire to tailor his theory to the practical reality of the English common law lies in contrast to Bentham's bold proposal to completely replace the common law with a codified system.

3. UTILITARIANISM

One of Bentham's main arguments with the common law was that its structures and traditions often obscured the political content and bias of the system. While legal positivism is theoretically neutral as to the political content of any particular legal system, Bentham believed that a more rational and transparent system and structure of law would demystify its content and create a suitable climate for progressive reform. Law reform was the focus of increasing political and social attention during the early years of the nineteenth century. H.L.A. Hart observed that, by the middle part of the century, there was a growing concern throughout Europe at the state of the criminal law in particular.[38] Sharing the concern of his European contemporaries, Bentham strove for a scientific theory of moral and political philosophy that could provide a coherent and systematic means of addressing the challenges of contemporary social and political issues. This he found in his censorial jurisprudence: the theory of utilitarianism.

The rationalist theory of Joseph Priestley (1733–1804), and in particular his *Essay on Government* (1768), presented Bentham with the idea of "the greatest happiness of the greatest number".[39] Utilitarianism is an ethical theory based on the inherent value of "pleasure" and "happiness", not just of the actor or subject but encompassing also the happiness of a wider group, or even of all citizens or persons. Utilitarian philosophy claims that moral relationships between individuals within a society and, more significantly in a legal sense, between the individual and the state, could and should be governed

---

[38] H.L.A. Hart, "Bentham's Principle of Utility and Theory of Penal Law", p.lxxxii. Bentham was particularly influenced by the writings of the Italian, Cesare Beccaria (1738–1794) on criminal law reform, and by the work of the French philosopher, Claude-Adrien Helvétius (1715–1771) with regard to epistemology. Helvétius's *De L'Esprit [Of the Mind]* (1758) developed the empirical theory that knowledge stems from experience rather than from nature.

[39] See F. Rosen, "Introduction" and R. Shackleton, "The Greatest Happiness of the Greatest Number: The History of Bentham's Phrase" in R. Shackleton, *Essays in Montesquieu and on the Enlightenment* (D. Gilson and M. Smith eds., Voltaire Foundation, Oxford, 1988).

by a unifying scientific law; in other words, that actions could and should be morally and legally distinguished and measured against the standard of the happiness that results.

The basis for his censorial jurisprudence—the principle of utility—is set out by Bentham in *An Introduction to the Principles of Morals and Legislation*; it is the principle

> "which approves or disapproves of every action whatsoever, according to the tendency which it appears to have to augment or diminish the happiness of the party whose interest is in question. ... An action ... [conforms] to the principle of utility ... when the tendency it has to augment the happiness of the community is greater than any it has to diminish it."[40]

Bentham presents a detailed and arithmetic expression of this broad theory by introducing the idea of a "felicific calculus", by which all actions could be measured by predicting what "pleasures" and "pains" would be likely to ensue from particular actions and assessing those consequences in terms of their intensity, duration, likelihood and other factors.

In his writings on penal reform, for example, Bentham advocated the gathering of accurate statistics and the introduction of a comprehensive system of inspection of prisons. In social and political terms Bentham's utilitarianism was synonymous with liberal reformism, and he was an early opponent of the death penalty and passionately critical of the criminalisation of acts which did not create a public mischief: "But all punishment is mischief: all punishment in itself is evil. Upon the principle of utility, if it ought at all to be admitted, it ought only to be admitted in as far as it promises to exclude some greater evil."[41]

One of the main criticisms of utilitarianism as a philosophical doctrine is that reliance on the greatest good of the greatest number may have the potential to lead to oppression of the minority in society by the majority. However, Bentham's own writings emphasise the place of individual security as a component of the common good. Frederick Rosen discusses how an emphasis on security of expectation, particularly in civil law matters, is found in Bentham's writings as a significant nuance to his utilitarianism.[42] He applied

---

[40] J. Bentham, *An Introduction to the Principles of Morals and Legislation*, chap.1, paras. 2 and 6.

[41] *ibid.*, p.158. Bentham's proposals for prison design were highly influential during the nineteenth century, but they have been subjected to acute criticism in more recent times, most notably by Michel Foucault. See *Discipline and Punish: The Birth of the Prison* (A.M. Sheridan trans., Pantheon, New York, 1977).

[42] F. Rosen, "Introduction", pp.xxxv–xxxvii.

this principle of security to private property rights and in this context he qualifies as an economic liberal, albeit a reformist liberal who supported the taxation of inheritance. Similarly, Bentham's keen awareness of the inherent dangers of an over reliance on the principle of utility led him to consider the importance of equality as an important objective of legislation. While Bentham regarded equality as less important than security, he did develop the idea of "diminishing marginal utility", whereby an increase in the wealth of a rich man would bring less happiness than the same increase in wealth of a poorer man.[43]

Bentham famously rejected the idea of natural rights as nonsensical in that they referred to fictitious entities. Utility, in his view, stood in contrast to such fictions as a tangible and calculable barometer for law and social policy. However, as Rosen points out, "This is not to say that Bentham was opposed to rights which were legally established and enforced, as these were real entities to be guaranteed by the sanctions of the state".[44]

Bentham was also an early internationalist. For Bentham, while legal systems may differ in style and form, the substance of the legislation of all nations should be broadly the same. Indeed his work in this area provided a starting point for the comparative law theorising that only developed a century later. A study of the ideas and beliefs that inspired the organisers of the International Congress for Comparative Law in Paris in 1900 shows that they were greatly indebted to Bentham.[45] Like Bentham, the founding fathers of comparative law were also inspired by an optimistic belief in the potential for human progress and harmony and viewed divergences in legal systems as being the creatures of historical accident rather than being based on any significant moral or social differences between nation states. Although the intervening century may have dulled expectations of global harmony and cooperation, the benefits that have accrued to national or "particular" jurisprudence from the tools of comparison are difficult to overstate. The comparative method can be seen as being firmly rooted in the distinction between the expositor and the censor. In Bentham's view an expositorial understanding of the differences and similarities between different national legal systems would inform and assist the process of national law reform.

Bentham wrote extensively on the legal systems of other states and was what Twining somewhat dismissively calls "an early example of the constitution

---

[43] F. Rosen, *Jeremy Bentham and Representative Democracy: A Study of the Constitutional Code* (Oxford, Clarendon Press 1983), pp.211–220.

[44] F. Rosen, "Introduction", p.xxxv. Rosen develops his analysis of Bentham's view of rights in *Jeremy Bentham and Representative Democracy*, pp.55–75.

[45] For a history of the comparative law movement, see K. Zweigert and H. Kotz, *Introduction to International Comparative Law* (Oxford University Press, Oxford, 1998). In his introduction to *An Introduction to the Principles of Morals and Legislation*, Rosen claims that Bentham coined the term "international".

monger and legal 'expert' who offer their services to foreign Governments".[46]
Twining suggests that anyone who is in the business of constitution building
has a vested interest in claiming that his or her legislative skills are transferable;
though a more generous interpretation of Bentham's work in this area might
be that it displayed his strong commitment to testing his theory in the practice
of other legal systems. Twining also shows how Bentham acknowledged the
importance of non-disappointment of local expectations, and that while he
believed that the universality of the principle of utility means that the content
of all national legislations should be broadly the same, Bentham realised that
reform must be based on a careful and sensitive understanding of local custom.
Twining's overall assessment of Bentham's view on the universal applicability
of his theory suggests that experience refined his understanding of the
relationship between utility and laws of individual states: "[T]he principle of
utility and the form of laws in the pannomion are of universal application; but
caution needs to be exercised in legislating for a particular country in case
expectations based on local customs and circumstances should be
disappointed—for the non-disappointment theory is an important principle
subordinate to utility".[47]

4. CONCLUSION

When one comes to evaluate the contribution of both writers to the development
of legal theory, it is obvious that Austin's jurisprudence has a narrower focus
than that of Bentham. Whereas Bentham sought to develop a radical science
of legislation, Austin was concerned primarily with developing only a discrete
science of expositorial jurisprudence. The limited nature of Austin's
jurisprudence has been highlighted, as we have seen, by many commentators.
Austin is regarded as one of the founders of modern legal education, and his
view of the educational value of jurisprudence is purely in the context of
professional legal education. Indeed, his *Uses of the Study of Jurisprudence*
shows how limited the project that Austin saw himself as being engaged in.
He describes how a preliminary study of the necessary concepts of any legal
system, *i.e.* general expositorial jurisprudence, and "the mental habits which
the study of them engenders", would assist the student of English law to acquire
the principles of English legal reasoning more easily.[48] In attempting to tailor
his theory for practical use in the context of English common law education,
Austin ran into the difficulty of reconciling a rationalist approach with an
empirical common law tradition.

---

[46] W. Twining, *op. cit.*, p18.

[47] *ibid.*, p.20.

[48] J. Austin, *Uses on the Study of Jurisprudence*, pp.379–380.

Austin's thinking on the value of studying other legal systems also appears at times to have been somewhat confused. In *Uses of the Study of Jurisprudence* he champions the Prussian model of legal education, which was based heavily on Canon Law and Roman law and characterised by a rejection of particularist study of the national systems.[49] However, elsewhere, Austin justified the study of other legal systems almost purely on practical grounds, such as the practical need for lawyers in British dependencies.[50] In his defence, however, it should be remembered that the study of law as a separate discipline had few advocates at the time and proposals to establish law faculties were only beginning to be entertained. It seems likely that Austin's writings helped greatly in the effort to have law recognised as a discrete discipline in England.

Bentham's jurisprudential system, though relying on the same key constructs, is far subtler and much more flexible than Austin's. Hart was strongly of the view that if Bentham's *Of Laws in General* had been published in his lifetime, it, rather than John Austin's later and obviously derivative work, would have dominated English jurisprudence.[51] The political or "censorial" differences between Bentham and Austin have been examined by Erie Ruben, who has traced the shift in Austin's politics from the optimism and radicalism of his youth to a reactionary standpoint in his later life.[52] Ruben uses Austin's less known pamphlets to show how the advocate of the abolition of English hereditary property doctrines and the admirer of the French Revolution became the champion of the propertied classes and the opponent of the extension of the franchise.[53] Ruben quotes the following passage from the *Plea for the Constitution* (1859) as a demonstration of the older Austin's political conservatism:

> "By my reverence for Mr. B. as a writer on law and legislation, I was naturally led [being then young] to accept his political opinions without sufficient examination. I have since dissented from many of his views of law and of the various subjects immediately connected with it. Even before the Reform of 1832, I had rejected his radical politics and returned to the opinion (Whiggism, liberal Conservatism, or whatever it may be called) which is held, with shades of difference, by the generality of instructed Englishmen."[54]

---

[49] *ibid.*, pp.373, 381–382.

[50] *ibid.*, pp.382–385.

[51] See generally H.L.A. Hart, *Essays on Bentham* (Clarendon Press, Oxford, 1982).

[52] E. Ruben, "John Austin's Political Pamphlets (1824–1859)" in *Perspectives on Jurisprudence* (E. Attwoll ed., Glasgow University Press, Glasgow, 1977), p.20.

[53] See, for example, J. Austin, *Primogeniture* (published in the *Westminster Review* in 1824).

[54] J. Austin, *The Plea for the Constitution* (London, 1859), p.vi. This pamphlet was

The association of positivism with Austin—and also with the formalist theory of adjudication—has created the unfortunate impression that positivism is inherently a conservative legal philosophy.[55] Bentham's writings give a quite different view. His was a radical theory aimed at paving the way for wide-ranging reform of legal systems on rationalist principles and for the substitution of existing legislation and legal norms with laws based on empirical sociological evidence guided by the principle of utility. In many respects Bentham's view of the roles of censor and expositor was prophetic of the model of progressive government that has evolved since the early twentieth century. The Progressive movement that came to prominence in the US in the early years of the twentieth century viewed the legislative function as being properly vested in a body of experts with empirical expertise in the social sciences. This model has evolved in the intervening years into the expert legal and sociological bodies that service and advise political government today. In a contemporary context it is possible to place the role of the technical lawyer, such as the parliamentary draftsman, in the position of Bentham's expositor; such a role would be viewed by Bentham as an institution charged with addressing the technical challenges of implementing legislative policy. On the other hand, agencies such as Law Commissions and Law Reform Commissions, as well as specialist advisory bodies, academics and non-governmental organisations contribute to the legislative process at the censorial level. Bodies such as Law Reform Commissions perform a function that may be described as partially expositorial and partially censorial. In any event, the development of legislative and technical expertise as an aid to government certainly owes a debt to Bentham.

Bentham's writings on expositorial jurisprudence have only become well known in recent years and contemporary analysis of these works has revealed the full breadth and sophistication of his thought. As for Bentham's utilitarian theory, there are persistent advocates of this creed in both the legal and philosophical spheres who have attempted to salvage more sophisticated versions from the persistent attacks of jurists and ethicists throughout the twentieth century, but it has largely been overshadowed by other moral theories, particularly theories based on the concept of rights.

---

deemed too extreme for publication in the *Edinburgh Review*, referring as it did to the natural superiority of the "aristocracy of independent gentlemen" in whom were properly vested the legislative control over society.

[55] For discussion of the perceived relationships between positivism and formalism, see B. Leiter, *op. cit.*

CHAPTER 6

THE HISTORICAL SCHOOL OF JURISPRUDENCE

SHANE KILCOMMINS

1. INTRODUCTION

History offers many perspectives on law, legal systems and legal theory. Leaving aside that much jurisprudence was developed in specific historical circumstances, and leaving aside too the obvious insights offered by legal history to questions of contemporary jurisprudence, there are many contemporary jurisprudential schools that emphasise a historical approach—albeit to differing degrees—in developing their themes and arguments. Indeed, traces of a historical approach to law and legal systems can be found in the analysis of numerous contemporary schools, including critical legal studies, critical race theory, feminist jurisprudence and law and economics, to name but a few.

This chapter deals with another form of historical jurisprudence. The historical school that we shall discuss developed during the nineteenth century. Its central tenet is that law is a product of an evolutionary logic. For advocates of this jurisprudence, laws do not have universal application that can be intentionally applied by law-makers. Rather they are grounded in the character and consciousness of particular peoples and have to be found rather than abstractly made. History plays a pivotal role in this process of discovery. By employing a historical lens, jurists should be able to map out the organic connection between laws and various societies. They should also be able to locate where in the evolutionary schema particular societies were at specific points in time.

There are many figures associated with this form of historical jurisprudence, but its most famous and dominant advocates—though they differ greatly in their respective approaches—include the "Romantic" Friedrich Carl Von Savigny (1779–1861), who wrote in Germany in the early nineteenth century, and the more "scientific" Sir Henry Sumner Maine (1822–1888), who wrote in England in the mid to late nineteenth century. In this chapter each of these jurists will be considered in turn.

2. SAVIGNY'S ROMANTIC HISTORICISM

The emergence of the historical school of jurisprudence, particularly in Germany, must be seen as a reaction against the prevailing natural law doctrines as espoused by jurists such as Christian Thomasius (1655–1728) and Christian Wolff (1679–1754). Their concept of law was premised on a rational system of natural principles which were discoverable as general deductions—without having regard to historical, cultural or social determinants—by law-makers anywhere who employed sufficient prowess. This reason-based natural law spirit facilitated early legislative attempts at codifying legal systems: the Prussian *Allgemeines Landrecht* (General Law of the Land) of 1794, the French *Code Napoléon* of 1804 and the *Allgemeines Bürgerliches Gesetzbuch* (General Civil Code) in Austria in 1811 were all inspired in part by a rationalist enthusiasm for a system of law premised on human nature.[1] Gradually however the belief emerged that such natural law reasoning was ahistorical, especially given its penchant for dismissing the organic development of particular societies. This awakening of a "historical spirit" pointed in the opposite direction to calls for codified laws premised on universal and rational laws of nature. Edmund Burke (1723–1795), for example, concerned by the events of the French Revolution and its legitimation in terms of natural rights and reason, dismissed any attempt to jettison the organic development of societies in favour of arbitrarily produced and rationally discoverable natural law principles. In keeping with this historical awakening, he cautioned against the fashion of pulling down long-standing edifices in favour of new structures that were grounded in nothing more substantial than abstract principles of reason. As he noted in his *Reflections on the Revolution in France* (1790): "When ancient opinions and rules of life are taken away, the loss cannot possibly be estimated. From that moment we have no compass to govern us; nor can we know distinctly to what port we steer."[2]

On a more specific and immediate level, the galvanising event behind the emergence of the historical school was the proposal in 1814 by a Heidelberg professor, Anton Thibaut (1772–1840), for a general unifying code of law—

---

[1] See J.M. Kelly, *A Short History of Western Legal Theory* (Clarendon, Oxford, 1992), pp.258–277. Savigny himself observed: "Since the middle of the eighteenth century the whole of Europe was actuated with a blind rage for improvement. ... Men longed for new codes, which, by their completeness, should insure [*sic*] a mechanically precise administration of justice; ... at the same time they were to be divested of all historical associations and, in pure abstraction, be equally adapted to all nations and all times." *Of the Vocation of our Age for Legislation and Jurisprudence* (Arno Press, New York, 1975), pp.20–21.

[2] E. Burke, *Reflections on the Revolution in France* (P.F. Collier and Son, New York, 1909), para.132.

to be modelled along the lines of those already in existence in Prussia, France and Austria—for all of Germany. The proposal itself was greatly influenced by the growing movement for German national unification during the period and concerns about the fragmented and anomalous state of law in various German states.[3] Savigny responded in the same year with *Of the Vocation of our Age for Legislation and Jurisprudence*. Savigny argued that codification was not the appropriate panacea for Germany's ills. First, the linear lines of descent of the contemporary corpus of legal rules had to be traced before any legal reform along the lines of codification could commence. The material of law, for Savigny, was derived from its entire past; jurists had to be cognisant at all times of the "indissoluble organic connection of generations and ages".[4] Any code that was undertaken too quickly and without proper historical reflection would obscure the "moral energies of the nation".[5] Accordingly a deep knowledge of the history of legal rules was required. This knowledge would facilitate the attainment of a proper organic consistency between popular consciousness and the expression of legal rules in any nation state. Secondly, and because the framers of such codes were not engaged in proper historical enquiries, it followed that the legal principles they selected and promulgated were often technically defective. In addition, a code was static and could not exhaustively provide for the variety of legal conundrums that would be posed as a society evolved. Finally, the craft of codification required excellent expositional and logical skills. Only those nations at the "summit of civilisation" were qualified to undertake the task—in 1814, Germany was not so qualified.[6]

All legal principles, for Savigny, have a long past. It was accordingly only by appropriating the "whole of the intellectual wealth of preceding generations" that jurists could begin to obtain mastery over the internal workings, complexities and nuances of contemporary legal rules.[7] History was therefore a "noble instructress", an anchoring point from which to initiate reform of the law. His legal historicism also had a scientific bent. The object of this science was to trace legal rules, concepts and principles to their roots so as to locate

---

[3] H. Kantorowicz, "Savigny and the Historical School of Law" (1937) 53 *Law Quarterly Review* 326 at 332.

[4] F.C. Von Savigny, *Of the Vocation of our Age for Legislation and Jurisprudence*, p.132.

[5] *ibid.*, p.39.

[6] *ibid.*, p.183. See also J.G. de Montmorency, "Frierderich Carl Von Savigny" in *Great Jurists of the World* (J. McDonell and E. Manson eds., Augustus M. Kelly, New York, 1968), pp.568–589 and R. Zimmerman, "Savigny's Legacy: Legal History, Comparative Law and the Emergence of a European Legal Science" (1996) 112 *Law Quarterly Review* 576.

[7] F.C. Von Savigny, *Of the Vocation of our Age for Legislation and Jurisprudence*, pp.132–133.

their "leading axioms".[8] Savigny believed that the German people would be particularly amenable to such an approach given their natural proclivity towards scientific reasoning.[9] This native tendency could be sustained and buttressed by studying the organic, scientific development of Roman law. He foresaw that Roman law, together with old German law, would be the touchstones for the development of a new legal science in Germany. The former, however, was particularly appealing in that it had the advantage of being able "by reason of its high state of cultivation to serve as a pattern and model for our scientific labours".[10]

His work also placed great emphasis on demonstrating that law was not the product of vacillating or haphazard forces. Rather, as he viewed it, law was closely tethered with the organic development of each society: like the language or the political or moral order of a society, it was shaped by the nation's peculiar soul. It was a manifestation of a self-contained common consciousness. The mystical, romantic and unifying qualities inherent in this concept—which was later termed the *Volksgeist*—are apparent in the early pages of *Vocation of Our Age*:

"In the earliest times to which authentic history extends, the law will be

---

[8] He noted, for example: "In every triangle, namely, there are certain data, from the relations of which all the rest are necessarily deducible: thus, given two sides and the included angle, the whole triangle is given. In like manner, every part of our law has points by which the rest may be given: these may be termed the leading axioms. To distinguish these, and deduce from them the internal connection, and the precise degree of affinity which subsist between all juridical notions and rules, is amongst the most difficult of the problems of jurisprudence. Indeed it is peculiarly this which gives our labour the scientific character." *ibid.*, pp.38–39.

[9] *ibid.*, p.170.

[10] *ibid.*, p.137. Savigny also noted: "[T]he history of the Roman law, down to the classical age, exhibits everywhere a gradual, wholly organic development. If a new form is framed, it is immediately bound up with an old established one, and thus participates in the maturity and fixedness of the latter." *ibid.*, p.49. See also F.C. Von Savigny, *System of the Modern Roman Law* (Hyperion Books, Connecticut, 1867), pp.67–80. This favouring of Roman law over German law resulted in a divisive split in the historical school. Romanists, such as Savigny and Georg Friedrich Puchta (1798–1846), were primarily concerned with purifying Roman law concepts and principles. Once purified they could then be systematically applied to German civil law. Their belief, however, in the fundamental nature of some concepts inherent in Roman law tended towards a form of universalism which was not that far removed from the reason-based natural law that the historical school sought to undermine. Germanists such as Otto Von Gierke (1841–1921), on the other hand, accused Romanists of under-emphasising the nature, traditions and character of old German law. They argued that German national consciousness, rather than Roman orthodoxy, should be the guiding hand in shaping civil law in Germany.

found to have already attained a fixed character, peculiar to the people, like their language, manners and constitution. ... [T]hese phenomena have no separate existence, they are but the peculiar faculties and tendencies of an individual people, inseparably united in nature, and only wearing the semblance of distinct attributes to our view. That which binds them into one whole is the common conviction of the people, the kindred consciousness of an inward necessity, excluding all notion of an accidental and arbitrary origin."[11]

This organic connection of law to people also had cyclical qualities. Savigny suggested that law "grows with the growth, and strengthens with the strength of the people, and finally dies away as the nation loses its nationality".[12] In early times law existed in nondescript form, expressed through the common practices of the people. In this low cultural phase there was no means of giving technical expression to these practices; nor was there any means by which they could be logically defined and applied. Nonetheless, and despite these shortcomings, this was also the period in which the mass of the people had a sharp awareness of the signification of their laws. This awareness was brought about through law's symbolic, customary and non-specialised circuits of operation.[13]

As a society grows increasingly complex, "national tendencies" become more distinct and the social order fragments into different interest groups or "classes".[14] The making of law in this phase becomes a more explicit, specialised concern. The task of giving expression to the prevailing *Geist* is, at this point in a nation's cultural development, passed over to the jurists. These jurists, however, simply act as a conduit for the expression of popular consciousness. As Savigny noted: "Law perfects its language, takes a scientific direction, and, as formerly it existed in the consciousness of the community, it now devolves upon the jurists, who thus, in this department, represent the community."[15] Law in this middle phase has become more "artificial and complex" and has a "twofold life".[16] First, it remains intrinsically connected with the mass of the people. This is what Savigny referred to as the *political*

---

[11] F.C. Von Savigny, *Of the Vocation of our Age for Legislation and Jurisprudence*, pp.24–25. On Romanticism more generally, see, for example, M. Henry, "The Enlightenment and Romanticism from a Theological Perspective" (1998) 63 *Irish Theological Quarterly* 250.

[12] *ibid.*, p.27.

[13] See F.C. Von Savigny, *System of the Modern Roman Law*, p.28.

[14] F.C. Von Savigny, *Of the Vocation of our Age for Legislation and Jurisprudence*, p.28.

[15] *ibid.*

[16] *ibid.*, p.29.

element of law's existence. Second, it has a *technical existence* as a distinct scientific corpus of knowledge that is analysed and applied by jurists. The lines of demarcation between both elements are relatively fluid. The political element, for example, will tend to be more instrumental under a republican order than under a monarchical order. This potent mix of popular participation and juristic craftsmanship marks the high point of a nation's cultural development. It is also the phase that is most receptive to the practice and art of codification. Paradoxically, though this phase is the one most favourable to codification, it is also the one, as Savigny informs us, in which it is superfluous: "But such a phase has no need for a code itself: it would merely compose one for a succeeding and less fortunate age, as we lay up provisions for winter."[17] The crucial point to be derived from organic growth in this middle phase is that the "common consciousness of the people" remains the "peculiar seat of law": the nation's laws continue to be formulated everywhere by "internal silently operating powers" and not by "the arbitrary will of the lawgiver".[18]

In contrast, in the final evolutionary phase of a nation's development, when the rot of cultural decline has set in and a nation begins to lose its identity, law becomes disconnected from the political element. It is in this cultural wilderness that the role of legislation becomes central.[19] But in this regressive stage even the juristic technical element—particularly regarding knowledge of the substantive issues and the art of expression—is in decline.

Savigny's contribution to jurisprudence has been significant, particularly in terms of how law and legal theory developed in the nineteenth century. To begin with, and owing to his protestations about codification, a German Civil Code (*Bürgerliches Gesetzbuch*) was not introduced until 1900. Similarly, in the common law world, his thesis was viewed as a bulwark that could be employed against growing calls for deliberate law making in the form of legislation. Furthermore, his emphasis on Roman law facilitated the emergence of a body of scholars—the Pandectist movement—in Germany who focused attention on the scientific study of Roman law and legal sources.[20] More generally, his belief that law is an expression of a society's social and cultural forms is still considered important.[21] Finally, Savigny's historical approach

---

[17] *ibid.*, p.43.

[18] *ibid*, pp.28–30.

[19] According to Savigny: "[I]nto the history of every people, enter stages of development and conditions which are no longer propitious to the creation of law by the general consciousness of a people. In this case this activity, in all cases indispensable, will in great measure of itself devolve upon legislation." *ibid.*, p.34.

[20] On the Pandectist movement, see J.M. Kelly, *op. cit.*, pp.324–325.

[21] As one commentator noted: "To show that law is itself the expression of a juristic process that runs through the ages was in itself an achievement of the highest order;

has acted, to some extent, as a stimulus for the development of a connection between history and legal scholarship.[22]

Savigny's popularity and significance, however, have not proved to be enduring. There are a number of drawbacks in his historical jurisprudence that have dulled its attractiveness over time. It is, for example, primarily (and ironically) ahistorical in design, compartmentalising huge tracts of history into a neat package of evolution. The creation of this teleological trajectory was greatly facilitated by the romanticism of the *Volksgeist*. Though mystically and patriotically enchanting, this notion of the *Volksgeist* was grounded in blanket generalities rather than historical particulars. Current analyses of how mentalities, values and sensibilities influence law usually adopt a more sophisticated framework than a simple appeal to *Volksgeist*.

Moreover, Savigny's broader thesis was, as one commentator noted, "anodyne in its analysis and conservative in tendency".[23] His response to pressing demands for legal reform was to emphasise dogmatically the continuous nature of evolution and to direct minds back to the distant past of Roman law sources and materials. Though the legal problems posed (and solutions proffered) in contemporary societies are undoubtedly products of the past, they are for the most part answerable to the currents of context and contingency. Their "conditions of possibility", as Michel Foucault would term it,[24] are governed by assumptions, objectives, conventions and intentions that are wholly different from those prevailing under Roman law. The conditions of possibility of such legal problems, accordingly, render it pointless, naïve and anachronistic to harp back to a past beyond the borders of this possibility.[25]

---

but to go on to trace, as Savigny traced, what we might call, the natural history of law, to trace its organic growth as a living thing, evolving with the evolutions of races and kingdoms and tongues, was a still greater triumph." J.G. de Montmorency, *op. cit.*, p.586. See also H. Kantorowicz, *op. cit.*, at 326–343.

[22] See K.J. Smith and J.P.S. McLaren, "History's Living Legacy: An Outline of the 'Modern' Historiography of the Common Law" (2001) 21 *Legal Studies* 251.

[23] D. Hay, "The Criminal Prosecution in England and its Historians" (1984) 47 *Modern Law Review* 1 at 26.

[24] See M. Foucault, *The Order of Things: An Archaeology of the Human Sciences* (Tavistock, London, 1970), p.xxii. On relativism more generally, see C. Becker, "Everyman his own Historian" (1932) XXXVII *The American Historical Review* 221 and C. Beard, "Written History as An Act of Faith" (1934) XXXIX *The American Historical Review* 219.

[25] The task then, of course, becomes one of attempting to highlight discontinuities and write "histories of the present" of particular phenomena. As Foucault noted: "The old questions of the traditional analysis (What link should be made between disparate events? ... What continuity or overall significance do they possess? ...) are now being replaced by questions of another type: Which strata should be isolated from others? What type of series should be established? What criteria of periodisation

Generally, a good deal of the contemporary scholarship on the connection between history and law is of a much more "critical" variety than that espoused by Savigny.[26]

Furthermore, though Savigny viewed law as a cultural and social artefact of the sentiments and values of a nation, he completely ignored the possibility that the law itself could also be shaped and driven by an internal dynamic (through, for example, adherence to precedent, and rules of procedure, fairness and interpretation). As E.P. Thompson has noted: "Law has its own characteristics; its own independent history and logics of evolution."[27] Accordingly, in acknowledging the ways in which cultural and social forces can shape law, one should also remain mindful of its closed and independent qualities.

Finally, Savigny's thesis was premised on the apolitical character of legal rules that could secure freedom for all in equal measure. Whilst romantically comforting and convenient, such neutral assumptions about law and the *Volksgeist* tend on closer inspection to conceal far more than they reveal. What, for example, is the common consciousness of the people today in a (more) multicultural Ireland? How do we determine it? Do our laws reflect the consciousness of the entire population?[28] How do we account for diversity of opinion under Savigny's framework?[29] Can we plausibly suggest today that lawyers in complex societies are the "organs of common consciousness"? Are the values, sensibilities and laws of the Irish society not to some extent shaped by policies of transfer and cultural imitation (for example: internationalism, eurofication, cultural and economic globalisation)?

---

should be adapted for each of them? ... And in what large-scale chronological table may distinct series of events be determined?" M. Foucault, *The Archaeology of Knowledge* (Tavistock, London, 1972), pp.3–4.

[26] See R.W. Gordon, "Critical Legal Histories" (1984) 36 *Stanford Law Review* 57 and R.W. Gordon, "The Arrival of Critical Historicism" (1997) 49 *Stanford Law Review* 1023.

[27] E.P. Thompson, *Whigs and Hunters: The Origin of the Black Act* (Penguin, Harmondsworth, 1975), pp.258–262.

[28] See, for example, I. Bacik and M. O'Connell, *Crime and Poverty in Ireland* (Round Hall, Dublin, 1997).

[29] Consider, for example, the Constitution adopted in a relatively monocultural Ireland in 1937. There were 685,108 votes in favour of its adoption, 526,945 against, and 104,805 spoiled votes. When one adds to these results the fact that the people of Northern Ireland were not entitled to vote on its adoption, the phrase "We the people" in the Preamble of the Constitution appears, as one commentator noted, "quite hollow". See J.A. Murphy, "The 1937 Constitution—Some Historical Reflections" in *Ireland's Evolving Constitution* (T. Murphy and P. Twomey, eds., Hart, Oxford, 1998), p.21.

All of these questions and difficulties combined to undermine the persuasiveness of Savigny's thesis. Though he was significant in that he attempted to introduce a historical element into the study of law in order to demonstrate its organic connection with patterns of behaviour in particular societies, his own version of that history read as surface narrative which, when scratched, revealed a lack of depth and rigour.

3. MAINE'S EVOLUTIONARY SCIENTISM

In England the historical approach to jurisprudence was championed by Sir Henry Maine. Like Savigny, Maine was also concerned with what he perceived to be shortcomings in natural law and utilitarian schools of thought. Both jurists also agreed on the importance of Roman law and the merits of analysing legal change through an evolutionary historical lens. Such comparisons should not however be overplayed. Maine, for example, never acknowledged himself as a disciple of Savigny. The latter's Romanticism, particularly his mystical belief in the *Volksgeist*, would have jarred with Maine's adherence to rigorous scientific history.[30] Similarly Maine's favourable attitude towards codification would not have been well received, as we have seen, by Savigny.

Maine's thinking in particular must be seen as a product of its time. Mid-to late-nineteenth century England was a period in which evolutionary scientific hypothesising, as espoused by thinkers such as Charles Darwin (1809–1882) and Herbert Spencer (1820–1903), was contesting and indeed superseding Creationist accounts of the origins of the complex structures of living organisms.[31] At a time when the Age of Empire was at its highest point, this evolutionary approach proved particularly appealing to an English public for whom "it seemed self-evident that a society organised along the lines of nineteenth century England was evolution's highest creation".[32] Aside from its intonations of self-exaltation, evolutionary metaphors that were premised on progress, development, and adaptation also gave a scientific cloak of legitimacy to the imperial dominance of the period in question. The atavistic, monkey-like caricature of Irish people, for example, as depicted in satiric portraits in *Punch* magazine during the Victorian era, drew upon an evolutionist

---

[30] See S. Humphreys, "Law as Discourse" (1985) 1 *History and Anthropology* 241.

[31] See A.C. Hutchinson and S. Archer, "Of Bulldogs and Soapy Sams: The Common Law and Evolutionary Theory" (2001) 54 *Current Legal Problems* 19. See also W. Coleman, *Biology in the Nineteenth Century: Problems of Form, Function and Transformation* (Cambridge University Press, Cambridge, 1977), p.116.

[32] E. Donald Elliot, "The Evolutionary Tradition in Jurisprudence" (1985) 85 *Columbia Law Review* 38 at 93.

logic that encouraged racism and rationalised the status quo in respect of British rule in Ireland.[33]

Maine fits neatly into this context in his perception of himself as a scientific historian of legal evolutions. Like evolutions in the biological or social arenas, legal developments could also be understood as progressions that could be compartmentalised into a series of incremental stages. For Maine, all legal systems, however dissimilar at particular points in time, followed the same linear trajectory and "would resemble each other in their maturity".[34] It was accordingly necessary to examine legal and social forms in their rudimentary conditions so as to trace the patterns of their developments and to determine possible relationships between the development of societies in different jurisdictions. As he noted in his most famous work, *Ancient Law*, first published in 1861:

> "If by any means we can determine the early forms of jural conceptions, they will be invaluable to us. The rudimentary ideas are to the jurist what the primary crusts of the earth are to the geologist."[35]

The means that Maine would employ to mine such conditions would be scientific history.[36] This scientific history, as envisaged by Maine, could be employed as a stick with which to beat the disciples of natural law and utilitarianism. Maine believed natural law in particular to be the "greatest antagonist of the historical method" given its penchant for substituting "sober" history with abstract "violent controversies".[37] Demonstrating a Burkean disdain for the metaphysical abstractions and *a priori* reasoning inherent in such jurisprudence, he suggested that "we find it easier to convince ourselves of the vastness of its influence than to pronounce confidently whether that influence has been exerted for good or for evil".[38] As regards utilitarians—

---

[33] See L.P. Curtis, *Apes and Angels: The Irishman in Victorian Caricature* (David and Charles, Newton Abbot, 1971). On the evolutionary logic as it related to criminals in the late-nineteenth century, see F. McAuley and J.P. McCutcheon, *Criminal Liability* (Round Hall, Dublin, 2000), pp.106–110.

[34] As quoted in P. Stein, *Legal Evolution: The Story of an Idea* (Cambridge University Press, Cambridge, 1980), p.86.

[35] H. Maine, *Ancient Law* (Dent, London, 1927), p.2.

[36] As he noted: "The truth of history, if it exists, cannot differ from any other form of truth. If it be truth at all it must be a scientific truth." H. Maine, *Village Communities in the East and West* (Murray, London, 1895), pp.265–266.

[37] H. Maine, *Ancient Law*, p.53. See also W. Rumble, "John Austin and his Nineteenth Century Critics: The Case of Sir Henry Maine" (1988) 39 *Northern Ireland Legal Quarterly* 119.

[38] H. Maine, *Ancient Law*, p.47. See also E. Burke, *op. cit.*, para.12.

and though recognising the merits of their rigorous approach and of the aptness in particular of John Austin's vision of law for "civilised" States such as England—Maine believed that they employed conceptions such as *sovereign, obligation, sanction* and *right* which were not discernible in the actual experiences and practices of earlier societies. For example, their conception of sovereignty had very little to say about the process by which power came to be vested in the sovereign. Nor did it reveal the ways in which particular societies curtailed the exercise of that power by the sovereign; according to Maine, the determinants which shape the exercise of this power in any society included "the whole enormous aggregate of opinions, sentiments, beliefs, superstitions and prejudices, of ideas of all kinds, hereditary and acquired, some produced by institutions and some by the constitution of human nature".[39] This failure in utilitarian analyses is therefore "analogous to the error of one who in investigating the laws of the material universe, should commence by contemplating the existing physical world as a whole, instead of beginning with the particulars which are its simplest ingredients".[40]

Central to Maine's theory of jurisprudence was the notion that societies had to pass through a series of transformative stages. In the first and most simple stage, rules were determined by the arbitrary commands of monarchs and patriarchs. Such commands were believed to be the product of divine agency—Maine offered as an example the *Themistes* in the Homeric poems.[41] These commands crystallised into customary laws and habits in the second stage—the "era of oligarchies". The solutions to particular disputes were no longer premised on "extra-human interposition"; rather privileged aristocratic orders or castes monopolised knowledge of the customs and habits by means of oral tradition, thereby exclusively controlling the principles by which disputes were to be settled and order maintained.[42] The third stage was referred to by Maine as the "era of codes". This stage heralded the dissolution of the oligarchic monopolies that had so completely dominated the oral legal tradition. The re-alignment of power relations *vis-à-vis* this legal knowledge base was greatly facilitated by the "discovery and diffusion of writing".[43] New codes—the Twelve Tables of Rome was cited as an example[44]—were viewed as more

---

[39] H. Maine, *Ancient Law*, p.360.

[40] *ibid.*, p.70.

[41] *ibid.*, p.3. The *Themistes* were divine commands which were transmitted by an oral tradition in ancient Greek society. More generally, see H. Orenstein, "The Ethnological Theories of Henry Sumner Maine" (1968) 70 *American Anthropologist* 264.

[42] *ibid.*, pp.6–7.

[43] *ibid.*, p.9. See also J.R. Sutton, *Law/Society: Origins, Interactions and Change* (Pine Forge Press, London, 2001), pp.26–30.

[44] The Twelve Tables, enacted during the fifth century B.C., were the first written laws of the Romans.

coherent and democratic depositaries of law than the oral traditions and patriarchal and monarchical models that preceded them.

It was only after this epoch of codes that the distinction between static and progressive societies became more discernible. Static societies, for Maine, did not progress beyond this point. Progressive societies on the other hand, which were the exception rather than the rule,[45] proceeded to develop and adapt by employing three successive instruments of legal change: legal fictions, equity, and legislation. These mechanisms helped to resolve the tension that existed between the dynamic needs of progressive societies as ranged against the relatively stationary condition of legal rules; "the greater or less happiness of a people depends on the degree of promptitude with which the gulf is narrowed".[46] For Maine, examples of such progressive societies would, unsurprisingly, have included both English and Roman systems.

The first of these mechanisms, the *legal fiction,* was employed by Maine to signify any assumption that concealed the fact that a law had been altered. Such a fiction could be utilised in circumstances where it could not be openly disclosed that a change in the law had taken place. Maine cited the extension of kinship by adoption as an example of a fiction that permitted family ties to be "artificially created". Such fictions however only served their purpose when a progressive society was in its infancy; any remnants in a legal system as it progressed acted as an impediment to "symmetrical classification" and "orderly distribution".[47] *Equity*, operating at a higher state of juristic development than that of fictions, could be used to modify and improve the law in manner that was transparent and avowed. The mechanism of equity comprises a set of principles—from which it derives its authority—that is assumed to have an "intrinsic ethical superiority" over the original law. Like the fictions, it had its time and place and when its "energies" were spent it too was ready to be replaced by the last of the "ameliorating instrumentalities", that of *legislation*. This final legal agency constitutes the most orderly and compendious method of law making. Unlike equity, it derives its authority from the prerogative of

---

[45] According to Maine: "It is only with the progressive that we are concerned and nothing is more remarkable than their extreme fewness." H. Maine, *Ancient Law*, p.13. See also M.O. Evans, *Theories and Criticisms of Sir Henry Maine* (Stevens and Haynes, London, 1896), pp.13–17.

[46] H. Maine, *Ancient Law*, p.15.

[47] *ibid.*, p.16. As Maine noted: "It is not difficult to understand why fictions in all their forms are particularly congenial to the infancy of society. They satisfy the desire for improvement, which is not quite wanting, at the same time that they do not offend the superstitious disrelish for change which is always present. At a particular stage of social progress they are invaluable expedients for overcoming the rigidity of law … ", *ibid.*

an external body and it tends "in all Western societies ... more and more to become the exclusive source of law".[48]

A further central axiom running through Maine's theory of law was the notion of a drift away from the family, as the principal atom of social organisation, and towards the individual as societies progressed. In ancient societies individual identities were determined by respective affiliations with kinship groups. The basic "unit" of society was the family in which individual members were subject to the omniscient power of the *paterfamilias*. Individuality was entirely consumed in a person's attachment to a particular grouping and his or her placement within that grouping (for example as wife, daughter, first son or head of the family). The attachment and placement determined the legal rights and duties of individuals. In contrast to the fixed identities fashioned by such status relationships, modern, progressive societies oscillate more towards contractual relationships that recognise the importance of individualism and individual autonomy. The form of legal reasoning that mirrors this ideology—evident in the shift from "status to contract"[49]—is for Maine a key signifier of progressive societies:

> "The movement of progressive societies has been uniform in one respect. Through all its course it has been distinguished by the gradual dissolution of family dependency and the growth of individual obligation in its place. The Individual is steadily substituted for the Family, as the unit of which civil law takes account. ... The tie between man and man which replaces by degrees those forms of reciprocity in rights and duties which have their origin in the Family ... is contract. ... We seem to have steadily moved towards a phase of social order in which all of these relations arise from the free agreement of Individuals."[50]

The old Irish legal code, the Brehon law, for example, was for Maine, an "authentic monument of a very ancient group of Ayran institutions".[51] These laws could be cited as the useful embodiment of a collection of legal concepts and rules that emphasised kinship as the bedrock of the societal union in early Irish society. Such commitment to notions of kinship greatly restricted rights of succession, private ownership of property and the power to contract. Indeed Maine suggested that this primitive notion of kinship "survived longer among

---

[48] See H. Maine, *Lectures on the Early History of Institutions* (3rd ed., Murray, London, 1880), p.47.

[49] H. Maine, *Ancient Law*, p.100.

[50] *ibid.*, p.99.

[51] H. Maine, *Lectures on the Early History of Institutions*, p.11.

the Celts of Ireland and the Scottish Highlands than in any Western Society".[52] Maine also viewed the Brehon law tracts as being extremely beneficial from a comparative, scientific perspective in that they had been relatively untouched by the influence of the Roman Empire. This enabled him to assert its common basis with other bodies of law that fell under an Ayran social organisation classification.[53] Despite recognising that the tracts possessed great authority, Maine believed, however, that they did not enjoy the force of universal application in Ireland. This led him to speculate about what would have occurred if the tracts had not been replaced by an English legal system:

"If the country had been left to itself, one of the great Irish tribes would almost certainly have conquered the rest. All the legal ideas which, little conscious as we are of their source, come to us from the existence of a strong central government lending its vigour to the arm of justice would have made their way into the Brehon law; and the gap between the alleged civilisation of England and the alleged barbarism of Ireland during much of their history, which was in reality narrower than is commonly supposed, would almost wholly have disappeared."[54]

As we shall see, such speculation tends to reveal a whole lot more about the version of history practiced by Maine, particularly its ethnocentric, imperialist and non-rigorous tendencies, than it does about any pattern of development that Brehon law may have taken but for the invasion and colonisation of Ireland.

Maine's vision of the progress of societies was also founded upon the belief that it should be orchestrated by elites—"the men of intellect and science"— rather than democratic representatives. In *Popular Government,* first published in 1885, Maine argued that elites were a crucial necessity for progress given that the inequalities of wealth and social power which set them apart were the product of the "springs of action called into activity by the strenuous and never ending struggle for existence, the beneficent private war which makes one strive to climb on the shoulders of another, and remain there, through the law of the survival of the fittest".[55] Democracy was simply "monarchy inverted",

---

[52] *ibid.,* p.89. On Brehon law, see M. Daley, *Traditional Irish Laws* (Appletree Press, Belfast, 1997) and F. Kelly, *A Guide to Early Irish Law* (Institute for Advanced Studies, Dublin, 1988).

[53] In particular, it enabled him to "connect the races at the eastern and western extremities of a later Ayran world, the Hindoos and the Irish", H. Maine, *Lectures on the Early History of Institutions*, p.21.

[54] *ibid.,* pp.54–55.

[55] H. Maine, *Popular Government* (Murray, London, 1918), p.22. See also G. Feaver, *From Status to Contract: A Biography of Sir Henry Maine, 1822–1888* (Longmans, London, 1969), pp.230–232 and B. Smith, "Maine's Concept of Progress" (1963) 24 *Journal of the History of Ideas* 407.

offering little more than another form of despotism whatever the rhetoric it
was dressed up in. The fashion of "bowing profoundly" before it was fraught
with the risks of stagnation and the possibility of regression to *status*.[56]

Maine believed that the idea of allowing a progressive society to be steered
by the will of the people was futile because that "will" could not be determined.
Even if it could be determined, it was of doubtful validity given that the masses
of any progressive society were ignorant. For Maine, the natural condition of
the individual was not one of progress and self-development; it was a condition
"not of changeableness but of unchangeableness".[57] The capacity for change
in any such society was limited to the enlightened few. Maine was also sceptical
about vesting too much power in the hands of democratically elected
representatives. He feared that the magnetism of remaining in power would
prove too great a sway with the result that politicians would thus spend their
time "listening nervously at one end of a speaking tube which receives at its
other end the suggestions of lower intelligence".[58] The consequences,
accordingly, of bowing to the democratic impulse would be a tragic mistake
for a progressive society such as England:

> "The true difference between East and West lies merely in this, that in
> Western countries there is a larger minority of exceptional persons who,
> for good reasons or bad, have a real desire for change. All that has made
> England famous, and all that has made England wealthy, has been the
> work of minorities. ... It seems to me quite certain that, if for four centuries
> there had been a very widely extended franchise and a very large electoral
> body in this country ... the threshing machine, the power loom, the
> spinning jenny, and possibly the steam engine, would have been
> prohibited."[59]

And if "average" English men and women—the ones who in no small part
contributed to England's fame and fortune—still had doubts, they should
remember their (scientific) history:

---

[56] H. Maine, *Popular Government*, p.82.

[57] *ibid.*, p.170. The counterproductive tendency that democracy embodies is that "it
comes to pass that an audience of roughs or clowns is boldly told by an educated
man that it has more political information than an equal number of scholars", *ibid.*,
p.78.

[58] *ibid.*, p.38. He also noted: "[E]ach [political] party will probably become more and
more homogeneous, and the opinions it professes and the policy which is the outcome
of these opinions, will less and less reflect the individual mind of any leader, but
only the ideas which seem to be the most likely to win favour with the greatest
number of supporters", *ibid.*, p.33.

[59] *ibid.*, p.98.

"The fact is that, since the century began, we have been victorious and prosperous beyond all example. We have never lost a battle in Europe or a square mile of territory; we have never taken a ruinous step in foreign politics; we have never made an irreparable mistake in legislation. If we compare our history with French history, there is nothing like the disaster at Sedan or the loss of Alsace-Lorraine; nothing like the gratuitous quarrel with Germany about the vacant Crown of Spain. ... Yet, if we multiply occasions for such calamities, it is possible and even probable that they will occur; and it is useless to deny that, with the craving for political excitement which is growing on us every day, the chance of a great false step are growing also."[60]

Maine's comparative approach did have a pioneering resonance in the mid- to late-nineteenth century. Through his work a new emphasis was placed on historical investigation. This historical emphasis, however, was not founded on any sentimentalism or traditionalism. Rather it was premised on its capacity to create a framework for understanding contemporary developments and problems. Through historical enquiry we could trace the "true lines of movement" of the march from the stagnant tribalism of ancient societies to the laissez-faire individualism of modern civilisations.[61] As well as serving as a reference point and a reminder for those operating at the apex of civilisation, this graduated process of development would also serve as a guide for those plotting their way towards enshrining legal and contractual freedom as the driving principles of their societies. His findings, dressed up as scientific propositions, were very well received in England, which is not surprising given that by implication they located his Victorian readership at the very top of the civilised, evolutionary tree.[62] Moreover, his linking of contractual capacity with progress and freedom to some extent confirmed the legitimacy of the use of market conceptions of contract in an expanding industrial age.[63] And, in

---

[60] *ibid.*, pp.150–151.

[61] S. Collini *et al.*, *That Noble Science of Politics: A Study in Nineteenth Century Intellectual History* (Cambridge University Press, Cambridge, 1983), pp.210–218. For subsequent similar evolutionary typologies that have been developed by other social theorists such as Ferdinand Tönnies (*Gemeinschaft* and *Gesellschaft*) and Emile Durkheim (mechanical and organic solidarity), see F. Tönnies, *Community and Society (Gemeinschaft und Gesellschaft)* (Transaction Publishers, New Brunswick, 1996) and E. Durkheim, *The Division of Labor in Society* (Free Press, New York, 1964).

[62] See J.W. Burrow, *Evolution and Society* (Cambridge University Press, Cambridge, 1966), pp.98–99. See also P. Stein, *op. cit.*, p.101.

[63] G. Binder, "Twentieth Century Legal Metaphors for Self and Society" in *Looking Back at Law's Century* (A. Sarat *et al.* eds, Cornell University Press, London, 2002), p.157.

very broad terms, he did capture prevailing ideological currents as they related to the break-up of the fixed status of individuals. The abolition of slavery in the US around the time he wrote, to take but one example, seemed to fit neatly with the status-contract dichotomy that he elucidated.[64]

Maine's findings can be employed as a very loose framework for tracing patterns of any return to ascriptive status—and Maine never denied the possibility of such an occurrence—as the primacy of individual autonomy increasingly gives way to regulated, collective conduct. Provisions that determine that service providers are not free to refuse to provide services to certain categories of people, greater security of tenure for tenants under landlord and tenant agreements, greater protection for employees under employment contracts, the inability of parties on certain occasions to contract out of liability, and the growth of consumer protection—all of these contemporary measures restrain the ability of parties to enter freely into contractual exchanges. Such legal restrictions on the power to contract have acted as *inclusionary* points of reference for those status groupings that suffer from an inequality of bargaining power in the market place. Though Maine's thesis offers little insight into the dynamics of such inclusionary developments—which is not surprising given his failure to capture the genesis of the movement towards collectivism in the late-nineteenth century—he does provide a broad status/contract polarisation that could help shape more discerning, contemporary analyses.

This regression to status line of enquiry can also, however, be flipped over and employed at a more dystopian level to highlight the use of *exclusionary* practices—even where regulated legal protections exist—against particular groupings. The tension between these inclusionary and exclusionary circuits is discernible, for example, in the treatment of Travellers in Ireland. They have acquired legal rights as a grouping in laws as they relate, *inter alia*, to discrimination, incitement to hatred and unfair dismissals, but they still continue to suffer from "caste-like apartheid" in terms of poverty, employment, social exclusion, education, political representation, and access to credit, services, accommodation and living conditions.[65] Maine's thesis can help account for what might be viewed as an emerging "neo-feudalism" that increasingly thinks in terms of "contractual communities" (such as gated residential communities) "which form a complex and expanding archipelago of private governments".[66]

---

[64] See G. Feaver, "The Political Attitudes of Sir Henry Maine" (1965) 27 *The Journal of Politics* 290 at 296.

[65] See M. MacGreil, *Prejudice in Ireland Revisited* (St Patricks College, Maynooth, 1996). See also *Submission by the Irish Traveller Movement on the Irish Government's Second Periodic Report to the UN Committee on Economic, Cultural and Social Rights 2002*, at www.itmtrav.com.

[66] C. Shearing, "Punishment and the Changing Face of Governance" (2001) 3 *Punishment and Society* 203 at 211. Shearing also noted: "In our contemporary

Increasingly the poor and the marginalised find themselves excluded from many "contractual spaces". Their status as unemployed, uneducated, not creditworthy, drug dependent, different or deviant restrict their opportunities to fully participate in social, economic and political life.[67] In this regard, their identities can be seen as fixed through their inability to occupy empowering spaces.

The "status criminalisation" of sex offenders can be cited as another example of such exclusion. In Ireland the Sex Offenders Act 2001 exemplifies the priority currently given to the control of groups of offenders and to the discourse of risk. The legislation introduces a tracking system with notification requirements; provision for the making of sex offender orders where reasonable grounds exist for the protection of the public; mandatory obligations to provide employers with information on previous sexual offence convictions in certain circumstances; and the employment of post-release supervision orders following the release of such offenders from custody.[68] All of these measures facilitate the personal and social control of sex offenders as a status grouping rather than as "individuated" persons.

Moreover, Maine's scepticism about the inefficiencies of democracy at work, in particular the temptation that exists for politicians to pander to the

---

world, we move around this archipelago of governance by moving from one contractual community to another. As we do, we move from one bubble of governance to another. Each of these bubbles of governance has its own rules that set out the conditions of citizenship or, perhaps more accurately, denizenship in these new spaces of governance." *ibid.* See also C. Shearing and P. Stenning, "From the Panopticon to Disney World: The Development of Discipline" in *Perspectives in Criminal Law* (A. Doob and E. Greenspan eds., Canada Law Books, Ontario, 1985), pp.335–349.

[67] As David Garland noted:"[The] dialectic between freedom and control could be said to have characterised the last thirty years. In certain respects, the social liberation of the 1960s and the market freedoms of the 1980s are now being paid for in the way of social control and penal repression. Where the liberating dynamic of late modernity replaced freedom, openness, mobility, and tolerance, the reactionary culture of the end of the century stresses control, confinement, and condemnation. The continued enjoyment of market-based personal freedom has come to depend upon the close control of excluded groups who cannot be trusted to enjoy these freedoms". D. Garland, *The Culture of Control* (Oxford University Press, Oxford, 2001), p.198. See also M. Davis, *The City of Quartz* (Verso, London, 1990); J. Young, *The Exclusive Society* (SAGE, London, 1999); and W. Hutton, *The State We're In* (Abacus, London, 2004).

[68] T. Thomas, "Protecting the Public: Some Observations on the Sex Offenders Bill" (2000) 10 *Irish Criminal Law Journal* 12. See also J. Simon, "Managing the Monstrous: Sex Offenders and New Penology" (1998) 4 *Psychology, Public Policy and Law* 452.

electorate, also has a contemporary appeal. Those interested in crime control, for example, cannot but have noticed its increasing politicisation in recent years. A growing consensus has crystallised among major political parties in countries such as the US, the UK and Ireland about the need for a greater "culture of severity" as regards approaches to criminality.[69] Such a consensus however often takes place at the expense of more enlightened policies that focus on tackling complex issues such as exclusion, social disintegration, poor education and bad housing. Today, very few politicians are willing to adopt policies that run the risk of being perceived as "soft" by a watchful and fearful public. Instead political mantras of more prisons, more police, and more criminalisation are consistently being heard. Penal policymaking, accordingly, increasingly becomes a "form of acting out that downplays the complexities and long-term character of effective crime control in favour of the immediate gratifications of a more expressive alternative".[70]

Despite the possibilities—however unsophisticated—of such insights, Maine is very much confined to distant backwaters in the current jurisprudential landscape. This is so for a number of reasons. First, late-nineteenth century England witnessed a retreat from the laissez-faire individualism that had been signposted by Maine as the key signifier of progressive societies. Slowly the notion emerged that economic and social prosperity could not adequately be attained by the pursuance of such an ideology. From the 1870s onwards, political theorists such as T.H. Green (1836–1882) began to perceive the State as a positive agency that could best guarantee the collective welfare of the population. Similarly the Fabians, adopting a form of liberal socialism, advocated the greater employment of the legislative authority of the State so as to effect greater economic and social order.[71] The events which, in very broad terms, motivated the retreat from the ideology of earlier forms of individualism included: a recognition of the intensity of the problems created

---

[69] See N. Lacey, "Principles, Politics and Criminal Justice" in *The Criminological Foundations of Penal Policy: Essays in Honour of Roger Hood* (L. Zedner and A. Ashworth eds., Oxford University Press, Oxford, 2003); I. O'Donnell and E. O'Sullivan, "The Politics of Intolerance—Irish Style" (2003) 43 *British Journal of Criminology* 41; K. Beckett, *Making Crime Pay: Law and Order in Contemporary American Politics* (Oxford University Press, Oxford, 1997); and D. Downes and R. Morgan, "The Skeletons in the Cupboard: The Politics of Law and Order at the End of the Millennium" in *The Oxford Handbook of Criminology* (M. Maguire *et al.* eds., 3rd ed., Oxford University Press, Oxford, 2002).

[70] D. Garland, *op. cit.*, p.198.

[71] G. Sabine, *A History of Political Theory* (3rd ed., Harrap, London, 1963), pp.676–677. See also M. Loughlin, *Public Law and Political Theory* (Clarendon Press, Oxford, 1992), pp.116–119.

by the industrial revolution;[72] the steady advance of the "professional ideal" which promoted confidence in government administration;[73] the realisation that England's hegemony in world trade no longer prevailed as the US, Germany and Japan caught up and the period of the Great Depression (1873–1896) set in on the domestic front;[74] the growth of Trade Unionism in the late 1880s as employees collectively sought to better their work conditions;[75] a growing awareness of the problems posed by the indirect consequences of free exchange such as disease and pollution; and a deepening consciousness of the need to protect by law the defenceless and the vulnerable.[76]

All of these processes converged in the late nineteenth century to produce one outcome—the extension of the power of the central government to intervene in the regulation of the market and the provision of welfare. Legislation in England and Wales such as such as the Public Health Act 1875; the Education Acts of 1870, 1876, 1880, 1893 and 1899; the Workman's Compensation Act 1897; the Trade Disputes Act 1906; the Old Age Pension Act 1908; and the National Insurance Act 1911, may all be cited as examples of this increased willingness to extend collectivist ideology and the authority of the State. Moreover, from about 1870 onwards, the belief in the unlimited power of freedom of contract began to decline as the judiciary began to restrict the ways in which a contract could be made and performed.[77] Coinciding with such a process was the expansion of tort law. As the values of self-responsibility and self-reliance began to diminish before the demands of social protectionism, tort law and employment law also witnessed, *inter alia*, the development of stricter liability which made individual parties responsible irrespective of fault or implied consent.[78] The more this collectivism advanced, the more it seemed

---

[72] O. MacDonagh, "The Nineteenth Century Revolution in Government: A Reappraisal Reappraised" (1960) III *The Historical Journal* 17.

[73] H. Perkin, *The Rise of Professionalised Society: England since 1880* (Routledge, London, 1989), p.16.

[74] E. Hobsbawm, *Labour's Turning Point: 1880–1900* (Harvester Press, Brighton, 1974), pp.xiii–xiv.

[75] *ibid.*, pp.71–114.

[76] P.S. Atiyah, *The Rise and Fall of Freedom of Contract* (Clarendon Press, Oxford, 1979), pp.22–23. See also R.H. Graveson "The Movement from Status to Contract" (1940–1941) IV *Modern Law Review* 261.

[77] P.S. Atiyah, *op. cit.*, pp.18–30.

[78] P.W.J. Bartrip and S.B. Burman, *The Wounded Soldiers of Industry: Industrial Compensation Policy, 1833–1897* (Oxford University Press, Oxford, 1983), pp.183–184. For similar changes in respect of the image of the criminal, particularly as it related to individual responsibility, see M.J. Wiener, *Reconstructing the Criminal: Culture, Law, and Policy in England, 1830–1914* (Cambridge University Press, Cambridge, 1994).

to deviate from Maine's "status to contract" trajectory. If anything, what appeared to be emerging was a return to status and the socialisation of law. Significantly, this return to status was seen by many as a more important barometer of the progress and civilisation of Western nations than the individualism signposted by Maine.

In such a milieu Maine appeared to lack "any sense of compassion for those who continued to be oppressed by social injustices".[79] His thesis was simply one of an evolutionary march towards the creation of a free market economy. The *raison d'être* of the legal system in progressive societies was merely to facilitate this march, culminating in support for those most capable of expressing themselves freely through contractual relations.[80] As a disciple of the ideology of individualism, Maine appeared to offer academic legitimation for the creation of a free market. His status to contract metaphor was very much part of a determinist teleology "whose elemental parts—'the extension of the market', the 'breakdown of traditional communities and status hierarchies', the 'shift from ascribed to achieved social status', the 'triumph of the middle class' ... [and] the 'revolution of production in the factory system'—are all linked together in a master process of social evolution".[81] By the late nineteenth century, however, sufficient evidence had been produced and diffused which revealed that not everybody was benefiting from the extension of the market and the sanctification of free will. Unemployment, severe poverty, old age, lack of education, ill-health, and the exploitation of the vulnerable demanded greater social intervention and the adoption of a different trajectory to that championed by Maine.

His history of change also increasingly began to read as a "narrative of progress" which concealed far more than it revealed.[82] In short the directions taken by societies cannot be compartmentalised into such a reductionist "unfolding logic". Indeed it was only because of his penchant for broad sweeping generalisations, coupled with his claim that they were scientific in orientation, that he was in a position to create such a neat fit with the evolutionary hypothesis he espoused. His examinations of primitive societies, for example, were often undertaken with one eye on contemporary developments in Western countries such as England. The ease with which he traversed hundreds, sometimes thousands, of years of history to highlight similarities (in the case of the Roman empire) or dissimilarities inevitably led to oversimplification and ahistorical analysis. Plundering history in this manner

---

[79] G.A. Feaver, "The Political Attitudes of Sir Henry Maine: Conscience of a Nineteenth Century Conservative" (1965) 27 *The Journal of Politics* 290 at 315.

[80] See R.W. Gordon "Critical Legal Histories", at 59.

[81] *ibid.*, at 62–63

[82] See R.W. Gordon, "The Arrival of Critical Historicism".

resulted in the distortion of the complexities and intricacies of earlier societies whilst also leading to a "complete misapprehension of the relations between past and present".[83]

Nor should we forget Maine's elitism and ethnocentric imperialism in any discussion of his lack of popularity today. His concerns about the emerging democratic ideology in the late nineteenth century, as already noted, highlighted his preference for hereditary aristocracy over the "average opinion of the entire community".[84] His ethnocentric leanings are evident, for example, in his comments during a lecture to a group of Indian students in which he stated: "[I]if we could search into the hearts of the more refined portions of the Native community, we should find that their highest aspiration was to be placed on a footing of real and genuine equality with their European fellow citizens."[85] Indeed Maine, whilst acting as Law Member for the Council of Governors in India, deplored what he perceived to be the "sentimental equalitarianism" of those who opposed his European-orientated law reforms because they believed they might give rise to oppression or exploitation. As George Feaver has suggested:

> "[I]f the reformed legal system must favour some values over others, Maine, as a good Victorian, entertained no doubt as to the appropriate course. With Europeans coming to India in great numbers, their commercial interests must be protected. If a choice must be made between the adoption of measures designed to satisfy the Europeans' contractual expectations and those that protected the status relationship of the old society, he had no doubt that 'it is the party of the Europeans which must win in the end'."[86]

4. CONCLUSION

Though this school of jurisprudence emphasises the importance of concrete history over abstract reasoning, the very historical nature of the enterprise is

---

[83] H. Butterfield, *The Whig Interpretation of History* (Bell, London, 1963), p.14. See also M. Foucault, *The Archaeology of Knowledge*, p.4.

[84] H. Maine, *Popular Government*, p.35. See also K.E. Bock. "The Moral Philosophy of Sir Henry Sumner Maine" (1976) 37 *Journal of the History of Ideas* 147.

[85] H.S. Maine, *Village Communities in the East and West*, at p.252. See also A. Kuper, "Ancestors: Henry Maine and the Constitution of Primitive Society" (1985) 1 *History and Anthropology* 265.

[86] G. Feaver, *From Status to Contract: A Biography of Sir Henry Maine* (Longmans, London, 1969), p.82. See also R.C.J. Cocks, *Sir Henry Maine: A Study in Victorian Jurisprudence* (Cambridge University Press, Cambridge, 1988), pp.141–195.

questionable. To begin with, both Savigny and Maine employed broad, often abstract, reasoning at the expense of accurate empirical detail. Indeed it was only through reliance on such deliberately vague generalisations that they could manufacture a fit between supposed historical actuality and their evolutionary paradigms. Moreover, both employed "presentist" histories of the past, that is, histories designed simply to explain practices in their own times. For Savigny, this was a codification-free legal system; for Maine, it was a free market economy. These histories were then presented in scientific terms. Yet, under examination, there was nothing rigorous, objective or scientific about the histories that they produced. Indeed any appeal to truth or certainty in historical terms is questionable in itself because it seeks to deny that historical analysis necessarily involves a multiplicity of interpretive choices. As the historian David Lowenthal noted: "[H]istorical narrative is not a portrait of *what happened*, but a story *about* what happened ... [and] ... no process of verification can totally satisfy us that we know the truth about the past."[87]

In addition, both Savigny and Maine viewed the history of law and societies through a continuous lens, naively assuming that all events could follow linear lines of development from status to contract or from primitive to civilised locations. Their histories, as one commentator has observed, must be seen as a product of the nineteenth century when there was a general feeling "of an inexorable ascent to Utopia".[88] More recently, however, there has been a historical backlash against such continuous and progressive narratives. Foucault, for example, has advocated the need to search for discontinuities in history in order to "direct historical analysis away from the search for silent beginnings and the never ending tracing-back to original precursors"; such an historical approach, he argued, was required in order to demonstrate that the "history of a concept is not wholly and entirely that of its progressive refinement".[89] Similarly, CLS scholars argue for the introduction of "critical historicism"—which has been described as "any approach that unsettles the familiar strategies that we use to tame the past in order to normalise the present"[90]—which will employ more structuralist and contexualist techniques

---

[87] D. Lowenthal, *The Past is a Foreign Country* (Cambridge University Press, Cambridge, 1985), p.215. See also E.H. Carr who noted: "The world of the historian ... is not a photographic copy of the real world, but rather a working model which enables him more or less effectively to understand it and to master it. The historian distils from the experience of the past as is accessible to him, that part which he recognises as amenable to rational explanation and interpretation." *What is History?* (2nd ed., Macmillan, Basingstoke, 1986), pp.97–98.

[88] P. Stein, *op. cit.*, p.124.

[89] M. Foucault, *The Archaeology of Knowledge*, p.4.

[90] R.W. Gordon, "The Arrival of Critical Historicism", at 1024. See also M.J. Horowitz,

in the examination of legal rules and principles. These contemporary ways of reviewing the relationship between law and history completely reject the narratives of continuity and progress posited by jurists such as Savigny and Maine. The purpose now is to employ history to "scramble" such narratives—they remain stubbornly persistent in law—by putting forward more contextualised, contested and pluralized interpretations of the past.

CHAPTER 7

SOCIOLOGICAL JURISPRUDENCE

JUDY WALSH

1. INTRODUCTION

As fields of inquiry, law and sociology share similar terrain. Both for example, are concerned with norms that govern human activity and various sets of relationships, such as those between individuals, groups and institutions.[1] Because of this common subject matter and law's regulatory function in modern society it may seem obvious why sociologists ought to be concerned with the legal domain. But what does social theory have to offer lawyers? Sociology can be loosely defined as the study of human social behaviour and, along with allied social sciences such as anthropology, psychology, social work and political science, it has the potential to greatly enhance our understanding of law.[2] In particular, these bodies of knowledge question many of the standard assumptions made by jurists and practitioners about the nature of law and its role in social change.[3] Engagement with sociology allows one to tap into a rich dialogue that has unfolded over the course of centuries.[4] At the same

---

[1] See discussion by S. Vago, *Law and Society* (3rd ed., Prentice-Hall, Englewood Cliffs, 1991), pp.2–6. A useful outline of the interconnections between law and sociology is also drawn in K.L. Scheppele, "Legal Theory and Social Theory" (1994) 20 *Annual Review of Sociology* 383.

[2] For the purposes of this chapter the terms "sociology" and "social science" are used interchangeably as much scholarship in the socio-legal domain crosses traditional disciplinary boundaries.

[3] See further R. Cotterrell, *The Sociology of Law: An Introduction* (2nd ed., Butterworths, London, 1992), pp.1–7. A useful exchange of ideas between two leading socio-legal scholars can be read in R. Cotterrell, "Why Must Legal Ideas be Interpreted Sociologically?" (1998) 25 *Journal of Law and Society* 171, and D. Nelken, "Blinding Insights? The Limits of a Reflexive Sociology of Law" (1998) 25 *Journal of Law and Society* 407.

[4] Sociology emerged as a distinct discipline during the nineteenth century as a result of work carried out by Auguste Comte (1798–1857), Herbert Spencer (1820–1903), Emile Durkheim (1858–1917) and others. Social theory on the other hand, according to Alex Callinicos, is traceable to the Scottish Enlightenment thinkers of the

time it can be a challenging encounter due to the intellectual and methodological differences between law and the social sciences.[5]

Contemporary sociology is awash with explanatory frameworks: systems theory, structuralism, poststructuralism, functionalism, hermeneutics, Marxism in its various versions, critical theory and so on, each with their internal conflicts and sub-divisions. This chapter attempts to sketch the various conceptualisations of law developed by theorists located within some of these frameworks. We will first discuss the ideas of those who laid the theoretical foundations of sociological jurisprudence: Karl Marx, Emile Durkheim, Max Weber, Eugen Ehrlich, Roscoe Pound and Talcott Parsons. We will then look at some contemporary directions in the field, in particular the ideas of Niklas Luhmann and Pierre Bourdieu and the methodological approach known as "critical empiricism". Before examining any particular theory or set of ideas, however, we must first set out some of the central issues in the sociology of law.

2. CENTRAL ISSUES IN THE SOCIOLOGY OF LAW

Given the breadth of perspectives involved in sociological approaches to law it is difficult to isolate common ground. It can generally be said, nonetheless, that scholarship in this field clearly objects to the presentment of law as a bounded, seamless and internally coherent system of rules. Rather it is but one element of social life and so must be studied in this broader context. A further, related insight is that social *control* is not the exclusive preserve of the legal system. Thus while a lawyer might see the legal system as prescribing the rights and duties of various parties, as ultimately providing the locus for resolving disputes and enforcing society's norms, legal sociologists consider that it does not necessarily have a central or definitive role. A variety of normative orders exist in every culture, which do not derive from the state. Examples include the "rules" adhered to by religious and ethnic communities, clubs, business networks, schools and families.

When one accepts that non-state associations are implicated in ordering social life, the terms "law" and "legal system" become open to revision. Sociological conceptions diverge on this point. For some the categories "law"

---

eighteenth century: A. Callinicos, *Social Theory: A Historical Introduction* (Polity, Cambridge, 1999), chap.1. See also P. Strydom, *Discourse and Knowledge: The Making of Enlightenment Sociology* (Liverpool University Press, Liverpool, 2000).

[5] On the methodological difficulties encountered by socio-legal researchers, see R. Banakar, "Reflections on the Methodological Issues of the Sociology of Law" (2000) 27 *Journal of Law and Society* 273.

and "society" imply a separation which cannot be sustained, while others accept the legal professional view that "law" is that body of rules, principles and so on derived from state agencies. The former position has come to predominate and is captured by the elastic phrase, "legal pluralism".[6] According to Patricia Ewick and Susan Silbey, "[b]ecause the term 'law' names assorted social acts, organizations, and persons, including lay as well as professional actors, and encompasses a broad range of values and objectives, it has neither the uniformity, coherence, nor autonomy that is often assumed".[7] However, if "law" exists in a host of social settings the problem arises "of defining legal system so broadly that all social control forms are included".[8] Particular difficulty lies with theorising the parameters and impact of laws applied and enforced by state bodies.[9]

To summarise the discussion so far, socio-legal scholars have not produced a uniform definition of "law", but accept that it is a social phenomenon. The interrelationship between law (however defined), state, and society remains contested. As we shall see in this chapter, of particular concern is the extent to which state law is autonomous from or interdependent with other social forces. Indeed, as Robert Gordon observes, "[t]he classic preoccupation of legal sociology has been to try to pin down what's in this 'autonomous' realm and theorize about its relation to the rest of society".[10]

In epistemological terms, socio-legal research has traditionally been unified by "its dedication to testing ideas empirically rather than relying on logical derivations from premises".[11] Empiricist positions tend to focus on causal and

---

[6] For surveys of the different meanings attached to the term, see S.E. Merry, "Legal Pluralism" (1988) 22 *Law and Society Review* 869 and B. Tamanaha, "A Non-Essentialist Version of Legal Pluralism" (2000) 27 *Journal of Law and Society* 296. Modern polities may be described as legally plural in the sense that several interlocking legal orders co-exist—the state may, for example, act in concert with other political organs to enact bodies of law that have a supra-national or international character (such as the European Union, the Council of Europe and the United Nations)—but this "juristic" version of legal pluralism regards law as a political product derived ultimately from the state. John Griffiths uses the term "juristic" to designate such variants of legal pluralism, as distinct from "social science" forms that focus on normative orders outside the official state apparatus. See J. Griffiths, "What is Legal Pluralism?" (1986) 24 *Journal of Legal Pluralism* 1.

[7] P. Ewick and S. Silbey, *The Common Place of Law: Stories From Everyday Life* (Chicago University Press, Chicago, 1998), p.34.

[8] S.E. Merry, *op. cit.*, at 871.

[9] See, for example, B. Tamanaha, "The Folly of the 'Social Scientific' Conception of Legal Pluralism" (1993) 20 *Journal of Law and Society* 192.

[10] R.W. Gordon, "Critical Legal Histories" (1984) 36 *Stanford Law Review* 57 at 88

[11] F. Munger, "Sociology of Law for a Postliberal Society" (1993) 27 *Loyola of Los Angeles Law Review* 89 at 94.

structural relations that derive from experience or are directly "observable". Roger Cotterrell's distinction between "normative" and "empirical" legal theory may be usefully applied here. Normative legal theory "seeks to explain the character of law solely in terms of the conceptual structure of legal doctrine and the relationships between rules, principles, concepts, and values held to be presupposed or incorporated explicitly or implicitly within it"; advocates of empirical legal theory, on the other hand, believe that law can be best understood through examining its social and historical origins.[12] Legal sociology thus tends to prioritise external perspectives as opposed to the internal understandings of law generated by professional experience, and sociological researchers have brought their analysis of law outside the courtroom to a greater extent than any other jurisprudential tradition. Sometimes described under the rubric "legal consciousness", studies conducted by the law and society movement have explored the deployment of legal concepts by lay people such as trade union officials and employees.[13] Moreover, those studies conducted at traditional legal sites, like courts, tribunals and lawyers' offices, tend to eschew doctrinal analysis in favour of empirical approaches designed to illustrate how law actually affects, is perceived by, and employed by, various social actors including legal professionals. For instance, research on US legal practice indicates a stratified legal profession, with those representing poor clients enjoying a much greater degree of autonomy and decision-making power than their counterparts dealing with businesses and organisations.[14]

---

[12] R. Cotterrell, *Law's Community: Legal Theory in Sociological Perspective* (Clarendon Press, Oxford, 1995), p.24.

[13] See P. Ewick and S. Silbey, "Conformity, Contestation and Resistance: An Account of Legal Consciousness" (1992) 26 *New England Law Review* 731. See also *Law in Everyday Life* (A. Sarat and T. Kearns eds., University of Michigan Press, Ann Arbor, 1993). The American writer Lawrence Friedman describes the law and society movement as "the scholarly enterprise that explains or describes legal phenomena in social terms". It is a deliberately broad grouping and includes researchers from a wide range of disciplinary backgrounds, including sociology, anthropology, political science, history and psychology: L.M. Friedman, "The Law and Society Movement" (1986) 38 *Stanford Law Review* 763. Similar work in Britain is generally termed "socio-legal studies". See further P. Thomas, "Socio-Legal Studies: The Case of Disappearing Fleas and Bustards" in *Socio-Legal Studies* (P. Thomas ed., Dartmouth, Aldershot, 1997). On the French tradition see P. Noreau and A. Arnaud, "The Sociology of Law in France: Trends and Paradigms" (1998) 25 *Journal of Law and Society* 257.

[14] According to Joel Handler: "Strong, rich and confident clients direct their lawyers; on the other hand, lawyers dominate the relationship when clients are poor, or deviant, or unsophisticated." *Social Movements and the Legal System: A Theory of Law Reform and Social Change* (Academic Press, New York, 1978), p.25. See also R. Abel, "Revisioning Lawyers" in *Lawyers in Society: An Overview* (R. Abel and P.

Socio-legal scholars bring the research methods of sociology to bear on their analysis of law.[15] Tools of social inquiry alien to mainstream legal research are utilised in order to generate empirical pictures of the law in action. For example, several researchers have employed ethnographic methods like participant observation in their studies of how "ordinary" people interact with civil, criminal, and administrative law.[16]

Sociological jurisprudents may share the ambition of examining law within a sociological paradigm but there is still no common theoretical framework.[17] Such theoretical pluralism means that socio-legal theory may not have the immediate appeal of, say, critical legal studies (CLS) or feminist legal theory. While the latter are characterised by a commitment not just to explication but also to transformation,[18] many socio-legal scholars show little interest, overtly at least, in political goals. Meanwhile, many of those working in this field challenge the "jurocentrism" attributed to mainstream legal scholarship but also to legal realists and CLS scholars, whose primary method is critique of doctrine.[19] Despite these points of divergence the sociology of law cannot be neatly hived off from the jurisprudential movements discussed elsewhere in this book. Several of the writers included in this chapter are central figures in the critical perspectives developed by CLS, feminist theory and critical race theory (CRT). There is also a degree of overlap with legal realism. Indeed,

---

Lewis eds., University of California Press, Berkeley, 1995), at 15; J.P. Heinz *et al.*, "The Changing Character of Lawyers' Work: Chicago in 1975 and 1995" (1998) 32 *Law and Society Review* 751; and R.L. Nelson, "Ideology, Practice, and Professional Autonomy: Social Values and Client Relationships in the Large Law Firm (1985) 37 *Stanford Law Review* 503.

[15] Methods are essentially the tools of research, the means by which relevant information or data is collected. The choice of method is inevitably informed by the researcher's theoretical stance.

[16] See P. Ewick and S. Silbey, *The Common Place of the Law*; J.M. Conley and W.M. Barr, *Rules Versus Relationships: The Ethnography of Legal Discourse* (University of Chicago Press, Chicago, 1990); S.E. Merry, *Getting Justice, Getting Even: Legal Consciousness Among Working-Class Americans* (University of Chicago Press, Chicago, 1990); and N.K. Denzin, *Interpretive Ethnography: Ethnographic Practices for the Twenty-First Century* (SAGE, Thousand Oaks, 1997).

[17] See further M. Los, "Law from a Phenomenological Perspective" in *Sociological Approaches to Law* (A. Podgorecki and C.J. Whelan eds., Croom Helm, London, 1981) and A. Hunt, *The Sociological Movement in Law* (Macmillan, London, 1978), p.2.

[18] It is true that feminist theory is more associated with a commitment to transformation than CLS but see, for example, R. Unger, "The Critical Legal Studies Movement" (1983) 96 *Harvard Law Review* 561.

[19] See generally D. Trubek, "Critical Legal Studies and Empiricism" (1984) 36 *Stanford Law Review* 575.

many characterise the current law and society movement as an offshoot of realism, whose members share its reformist goals and focus on how the law "actually" works, but are committed to deploying the social sciences in a more rigorous manner than their realist forebears.[20]

Just as critical jurisprudential traditions were inspired by the anti-war, civil rights and feminist movements of the 1960s and 1970s, those who adopt a sociological approach to law are influenced by the socio-political climate of their time.[21] Each theorist will also be constrained by the paradigms of the academic discipline or disciplines with which they are conversant and their personal biographies. The writers canvassed in this chapter are select representatives of general paradigms and inevitably their thoughts on law reflect wider theoretical trends in the social sciences. The conflict/consensus debate and the structure/agency debate are very significant in terms of these wider trends.

A key preoccupation of sociology lies in ascertaining the engines or driving forces of social change. Conflict theory holds that society is fuelled and indeed determined by conflict between individuals and groups who compete with each other for access to social goods.[22] Change is a product of struggle between groups rather than a result of adaptation. Theory in this vein emphasises inequalities in society, particularly unequal power relations such as those between social classes, men and women, and different ethnic groups. Marxist theory remains the quintessential exposition of this approach. Consensus theorists tend to believe in the necessity and inevitability of a transcendent social order based on shared values. Their stance is often associated with "functionalism", a model of explaining social processes that regards societal institutions as evolving and adapting in response to social needs. Although consensus theorists acknowledge the existence of social inequalities, they are inclined to argue that they are inevitable or in some cases functional for society.[23]

---

[20] The legal realist school did forge early alliances between lawyers and social scientists. See J.H. Schlegel, "American Legal Realism and Empirical Social Science: From the Yale Experience" (1979) 28 *Buffalo Law Review* 459.

[21] R.W. Gordon, "Some Critical Theories of Law and Their Critics" in *The Politics of the Law: A Progressive Critique* (D. Kairys ed., 3rd ed., Basic Books, New York, 1998), p.281.

[22] What constitutes these social goods is a contested concept and will not be further elaborated upon here. Examples of work which addresses this question include *The Quality of Life* (M. Nussbaum and A. Sen eds., Oxford University Press, Oxford, 1993) and J. Rawls, *Political Liberalism* (Columbia University Press, New York, 1993).

[23] Rosemary Crompton says that functionalists employ two closely associated arguments to explain and justify material inequalities in a society of political and legal equals:

When law is refracted through these lenses a spectrum of positions emerge as to its role in social change. Marx, for example, regards law as a means of securing and legitimising dominant socio-economic relations. Both Durkheim and Parsons reflect on state law's role as a mechanism of normative integration. Ehrlich locates the engine of change in social norms, the "living law", rather than the formal legal system.

The structure-agency debate in social theory also resonates throughout the sociology of law.[24] At issue is the relationship between the individual actor and the society that she or he inhabits. The term "agency" connotes purposeful action, the understanding that human beings exercise freedom of thought and action and so can change and influence events independently of social constraints. Interpretive approaches to sociology, such as symbolic interactionism, tend to emphasise people's understanding of their own actions, regarding the relationship between the individual and society as a process of symbolic communication between social actors. Structural analysis on the other hand seeks to uncover and explain unconscious forces that determine human behaviour. The term "structure" is defined in various ways but here it reflects the idea that social phenomena do not occur in isolation, instead regularised and fairly entrenched patterns of understanding and behaviour shape the ways in which human beings relate to one other and their environment. On this understanding, examples of social structures would include capitalism (a predominantly market based economy in which the means of production are privately owned and controlled) and racism (social systems that divide people into "races" and privilege some "races" over others).

In turn these social structures are embedded in and reproduced by social systems. The economic, political and cultural systems are amongst the most significant identified by sociologists such as Parsons, due to their core position within social life generally. By analysing societies as systems, theorists purport to explain how various institutions interconnect and evolve over time. Exactly how to configure the legal system, and to reconcile its role in reproducing social structures with the activities of individual actors is a matter of continuing debate. These debates and their methodological implications are rendered more complex by poststructuralism's emphasis on the radical instability of language

---

"[F]irst, that unequal rewards provide a structure of incentives which ensure that talented individuals will work hard and innovate, thus contributing to the improvement of material standards for the society as a whole; and, second, that a broad consensus exists as to the legitimacy of their superior rewards, as such innovators are functionally more important to society". R. Crompton, *Class and Stratification* (2nd ed., Polity, Cambridge, 1998), p.8.

[24] See A. Giddens, *Central Problems in Social Theory: Action, Structure and Contradiction in Social Analysis* (University of California Press, Berkeley, 1979).

and meaning.[25] Advocates of empirical research on the operation of legal systems have reacted to the poststructuralist challenge in a number of ways. According to Cotterrell, scientific method recognises that "all perspectives on experience are necessarily partial and incomplete" but endeavours to overcome these limitations "through systematic collection, analysis and interpretation of the empirical data of experience"; observation then is not an end in itself but is "an essential prerequisite of interpretation".[26] The position is probably best summed-up by Bourdieu: "theory without empirical research is empty, empirical research without theory is blind".[27]

3. THEORETICAL FOUNDATIONS

As M.D.A. Freeman has observed, locating the roots of sociological jurisprudence essentially depends on how far back one goes.[28] We will take as our starting point the responses to modernity contained in the works of Marx, Durkheim and Weber, while Ehrlich is then discussed as an early exponent of legal pluralism.[29] The contributions of Pound and Parsons are also assessed; both these theorists acted as catalysts for the emergence of the sociology of law as a distinct academic subject in the US.

Karl Marx

During Karl Marx's life (1818–1883) the capitalist economic system was in the ascendant. His primary project was to explain its origins, structure and future trajectory.[30] Significantly, Marx considered theoretical writing to be a political practice, in that it does not just describe the world but seeks to change it. To that end he advanced a theory for explaining and understanding societies known as "historical materialism". Key elements of this theory are considered below, followed by an outline of Marxist thought on law. Marx never produced a fully developed position on law; however the allusions to legal concepts and institutions scattered throughout his writings have inspired generations of

---

[25] See Emmanuel Melissaris, "The Other Jurisprudence: Poststructuralism, Postmodernism and the Law" in this volume.

[26] R. Cotterrell, *The Sociology of Law*, pp.4, 14.

[27] P. Bourdieu, *"Vive la crise!* For Heterodoxy in Social Science" (1988) 17 *Theory and Society* 774.

[28] M.D.A Freeman, *Lloyd's Introduction to Jurisprudence* (7th ed., Sweet and Maxwell, London, 2001), p.660.

[29] "Modernity" is a contested concept. Here it refers to the societal changes that accompanied the growth of industrial capitalism throughout the seventeenth, eighteenth and nineteenth centuries.

[30] See generally H. Collins, *Marxism and Law* (Oxford University Press, Oxford, 1982).

jurists. While the Marxist paradigm includes a range of approaches, it is possible
to identify two common strands in this body of work: a focus on the relationship
between law and the economy and an associated concern with law's connection
to class.

Marx and his colleague Friedrich Engels (1820–1895) subscribed to a
conflict model of society, which saw human history as the outcome of economic
rather than political struggles.[31] The primacy of economics flows from Marx's
belief that labour, the active means by which resources are extracted from
nature, constitutes the fundamental essence of human beings. Social change is
fuelled by class struggle between producers (worker-labourers or the proletariat)
and those who derive the benefit of production (employer-owners or the
bourgeoisie). Society is not based on consensus, as Durkheim supposed, but
consists in relations of domination and subordination that stem from the "mode
of production". This expression generally refers to basic socio-economic
systems. Two pertinent examples are the feudal and capitalist modes of
production. These modes are differentiated by the level of development of the
productive forces, in combination with the social relations of production
inhering in each mode. "Productive forces" comprise human labour and the
material means of production (tools, machinery and other forms of technology).
Human beings, acting in concert with one another, innovate and develop new
ways of producing which allows the productive forces to develop. The other
aspect of the mode of production, the "relations of production", represents the
level or degree of control people have over labour power and the other means
of production. Where producers themselves control the means of production
there is little class differentiation. Such would be the case under the communist
system advocated by Marx and Engels.

Classes and the inevitable conflict between them emerge where a minority
controls the productive forces. Under capitalism, class divisions arise because
the direct producers are exploited. Ownership of the means of production lies
in the hands of a few, which allows them to appropriate surplus value, that is,
the labour in excess of what is required to support workers and their dependants.
In legal terms the worker and capitalist are formally equal; the status hierarchies
associated with feudal and ancient (slave) modes of production are not in
evidence. However, in actuality they are unequal because the worker must sell
labour power in order to subsist and the capitalist has exclusive control of the
means of production. Law masks the economic coercion involved in the contract
between employer and worker by developing the universal legal subject
abstracted from his or her actual economic position.[32]

Law's place in the capitalist system is explained with reference to the base/

---

[31] See for example K. Marx and F. Engels, *The Communist Manifesto: A Modern Edition*
(Verso, London, 1998).

[32] Non-communist social relations are not given or fixed; they always involve a

superstructure metaphor employed by Marx. He stressed that all social institutions arise from, and so are secondary to, the relations of production, the material base of society. Law, politics and ideology (systems of ideas) form part of a superstructure that rests upon and is ultimately determined by economic forces. As a reflection of the material base, the form and content of laws are dictated by the dominant mode of production: "[l]egal relations as well as forms of state are to be grasped neither from themselves nor from the so-called development of the human mind, but rather have their roots in the material conditions of life …".[33]

This is not to suggest however, that law is a simple instrument of the dominant class. As an institution, its primary purpose is to maintain the stability of the mode of production. That function is on occasion best served by protecting workers (through for example ensuring minimum working conditions), thereby staving off the possibility of industrial upheaval and the prospect of revolution.[34] Nor is the relationship between law and the economy entirely one-way. According to Marx the superstructure is relatively autonomous, that is, it is not always determined by the material.[35] Marx never fully explained the implications or extent of this interconnection.

For Marx, then, law was essentially a mechanism of state power deployed in order to advance the interests of capital.[36] It serves the function of further

dialectical form of class conflict. Marx derived this idea from Hegel, whose version of the dialectic is often explained using the terms "thesis", "antithesis", and "synthesis". A particular idea at a given juncture might be described as the thesis. All theses contain their own antithesis, or contrary propositions, and the resulting conflict is resolved through formulation of another idea at a "higher level": the synthesis. Synthesis entails negating elements of the original ideas that conflict while preserving other positive elements. Marx appropriated elements of the Hegelian dialectic, but Marx focused on material conditions rather than on ideas. For Marx, capitalism as a thesis contains its own contradiction or antithesis, the proletariat. The proletariat is necessary to create the wealth of the bourgeoisie but their suffering under capitalism would give rise to revolutionary action bringing that system to an end. This socialist synthesis preserves the achievements of capitalism, in particular the collapse of feudalism, but negates exploitation and the concentration of wealth in the ruling class. The downfall of capitalism would be realised upon the development of working class consciousness. For accounts of Hegel's influence on jurisprudence, see *Hegel and Legal Theory* (D. Cornell, M. Rosenfeld and D. Carlson eds., Routledge, New York, 1991).

[33] K. Marx and F. Engels, *Selected Works* (2 vols., Foreign Languages, Moscow, 1962), Vol.I, p.362.

[34] See H. Collins, *op. cit.*, chap.2.

[35] See further K. Marx and F. Engels, *Selected Works*, Vol.II, p.504.

[36] See A. Hunt, "The Problematisation of Law in Classical Social Theory" in *An Introduction to Law and Social Theory* (R. Banakar and M. Travers eds., Hart, Oxford, 2002), p.20.

developing the forces of production through its material orders but also at an ideological level. Conceptions of formal equal rights and duties conceal underlying inequalities of substance. Thus the American and French revolutions of the eighteenth century did not secure a radical break with the pre-existing social order, in fact the "bourgeois freedoms" they established hid the continuing reality of class subordination.[37]

Subsequent theorists have addressed questions left undeveloped by Marx. Divergent views have emerged as to the place of law in a socialist polity.[38] Karl Renner (1870–1950) argues that while the functions of law change, legal forms do not.[39] Since law does not cause injustice as such, it can be used as a functional instrument for change under socialism. The Soviet jurist, Evgeny Pashukanis (1891–1938), took issue with Renner's benign depiction of legal forms.[40] Law instead was a form of regulation specific to capitalism and is based on exchange relations between owners of commodities. Relationships between abstract legal subjects are mediated by rules of contract and property that are facially neutral but reproduce substantive inequalities. Law would "wither away" upon the emergence of communism.[41] A number of problems flow from Pashukanis' conception. One is largely empirical: the objection is that studies of capitalist development reveal that there is no single form of "bourgeois law", rather there is a variety of legal forms which have "co-existed over long periods, complementing and conflicting with one another".[42] The other is ideological: since Pashukanis rejects any positive role for law, his theories may justify the absence of legal constraints associated with oppressive totalitarian regimes. As Hannah Arendt has remarked, "the first essential step on the road to total domination is to kill the legal character in man".[43]

A belief that law *may* act as a check against excesses of power is one shared by many critical writers.[44] An example is found in the work of legal

---

[37] See for example K. Marx, "On the Jewish Question" [1846] in *Nonsense on Stilts: Bentham, Burke and Marx on the Rights of Man* (J.Waldron ed., Methuen, London, 1987).

[38] See, for example, *Legality, Ideology and the State* (D. Sugarman ed., Academic Press, London, 1983).

[39] K. Renner, *The Institutions of Private Law and Their Social Functions* (A. Schwarzschild trans., Routledge and Kegan Paul, London, 1949).

[40] See E. Pashukanis, *Pashukanis: Selected Writings on Marxism and Law* (P. Beirne and R. Sharlet eds., Academic Press, London, 1980).

[41] Marx did not openly speculate on the role law might play in a communist society.

[42] D. Sugarman, "Law, Economy and the State in England, 1750–1914: Some Major Issues" in D. Sugarman ed., *op. cit.*, pp.213–266, at 256.

[43] H. Arendt, *Le Système Totalitaire*, p.211, quoted in A. Supiot, "Ontologies of Law" (2002) 13 *New Left Review* 107 at 117.

[44] See, for example, the observations of feminist legal theorist Robin West in

historian E.P. Thompson who undertook a materialist analysis of a notorious eighteenth century English statute: the Black Act of 1723.[45] This legislation applied the death penalty to actions such as tree felling carried out by agrarian rebels in protest at the extinction of their traditional rights to use common land. He concluded that law usually supports class power by defending rulers' property interests and enforcing criminal law aimed at the working classes. However, law could occasionally act as a site of resistance. Although legal forms evolved in line with capitalist logic these forms also imposed constraints upon the dominant class. He described the rule of law as being a "cultural achievement of universal significance" which by imposing "effective inhibitions upon power and the defence of the citizen from power's all-intrusive claims, seems to me to be an unqualified human good".[46]

Thompson's critical reflection on the legal practices of capital, have been supplemented by numerous analyses of the nature of ideology. There is an intense debate within the academic literature regarding its nature and impact.[47] Marx utilised the concept in various ways, but usually defining it in pejorative terms as a form of false consciousness, which distorts people's understanding of their social condition. Another understanding of ideology—that which is associated with the writings of Antonio Gramsci (1891–1937)—regards it both as the means by which the powerful establish their hegemony *and* as an instrument of social transformation and counter-hegemony.[48] "Hegemony" refers to dominance over both the practices and ideas of a society. Ideologies are certainly affected, but not determined, by economic factors.[49] This relative

---

"Reconstructing the Rule of Law" (2001) 90 *Georgetown Law Journal* 215. Hugh Collins calls the debate amongst Marxists as to whether law can be mobilised to assist subordinate groups "the radical predicament"; *op. cit.*, chap.6.

[45] E.P. Thompson, *Whigs and Hunters: The Origin of the Black Act* (Pantheon, New York, 1975).

[46] *ibid.*, pp.265–266.

[47] For an account of how the concept of "ideology" has been deployed in legal literature, see A. Hunt, *Explorations in Law and Society: Toward a Constitutive Theory of Law* (Routledge, New York, 1993), chap.6.

[48] A. Gramsci, *Selections from the Prison Notebooks of Antonio Gramsci* (Q. Hoare and G. Howell-Smith eds., Lawrence and Wishart, London, 1971).

[49] See also L. Althusser, *Lenin and Philosophy and Other Essays* (B. Brewster trans., Monthly Review Press, New York, 1971). Louis Althusser (1918–1990) distinguished between repressive state apparatuses (RSAs), including agencies such as the police, courts and prisons, and the productive ideological state apparatuses (ISAs). Examples of the latter are institutions like the family, the media and universities which the state influences in a less patent way than the RSAs it controls directly; these sites serve the state by producing and/or transmitting ideology which facilitates the maintenance of the status quo.

autonomy means that the ideological field of any society is likely to contain contradictory ideas and interpretations. Socio-legal scholar Alan Hunt shares this belief that ideas will not always reinforce existing economic relations, and that, on the contrary, they can sometimes serve to mobilise changes and to present counter-hegemonic perspectives and utopias. He demonstrates how legal strategies that result in litigation "failure" may in fact provide the impetus to propel a social movement forward.[50] Bernard Edelman agrees that law is a "site and stake of class struggle".[51] However the relative autonomy formulation is still problematic, as Hunt points out, since it largely circumvents the question of how law and the economic structure interrelate. Indeed Thomas Mathiesen doubts whether "one can ever prove—in a strict sense—the materialist conception of law".[52]

The continued relevance of Marx's ideas is borne out by the prediction of the phenomenon of "globalization" advanced in the *Communist Manifesto*, first published in 1848. As Eric Hobsbawm comments, "what might in 1848 have struck an uncommitted reader as revolutionary rhetoric—or, at best, as plausible prediction—can now be read as a concise characterization of capitalism at the end of the twentieth century".[53] Marx's work has received attention from writers across a range of fields who have extended his concept of class to include non-material forms of class-based oppression.[54] A significant strand of feminist thinking also has its origins in the Marxist tradition and specifically the work of Engels.[55] Focusing on the issue of women's paid and unpaid labour, many socialist feminists attempt to explain the interrelationships between capitalism and patriarchy in the oppression of women, developing the Marxist concept of exploitation and applying it to the family.[56] Feminist

---

[50] A. Hunt, *Explorations in Law and Society*, chap.10.

[51] B. Edelman, *Ownership of the Image: Elements for a Marxist Theory of Law* (Routledge and Kegan Paul, London, 1979), p.134.

[52] T. Mathiesen, *Law, Society and Political Action: Towards a Strategy under Late Capitalism* (Academic Press, London, 1980), quoted in R. Cotterrell, *The Sociology of Law*, p.136.

[53] E.J. Hobsbawn, "Introduction" to K. Marx and F. Engels, *The Communist Manifesto: A Modern Edition*, p.18.

[54] See for example, G.A. Cohen, *Self-Ownership, Freedom and Equality* (Cambridge University Press, Cambridge, 1995). Also relevant here is the work of Pierre Bourdieu, which is considered in the next part of this chapter.

[55] See, in particular, F. Engels, *The Origin of the Family, Private Property and the State* [1845] (Lawrence and Wishart, London, 1940).

[56] See M. Barrett, *Women's Oppression Today: Problems in Marxist Feminist Analysis* (Verso, London, 1980); J. Mitchell, *Women: The Longest Revolution* (Virago, London, 1984); and C. Delphy and D. Leonard, *Familiar Exploitation: A New Analysis of Marriage and Family Life* (Polity, Cambridge, 1992).

legal theorist Catharine MacKinnon uses Marx's conceptual framework in considering the relation between law and gender-based oppression.[57]

Work undertaken by critical legal theorists and socio-legal scholars continues to demonstrate that courts in particular play a significant role in protecting economic power. For example, a primary concern of the US Constitution's framers was how to protect property from potential redistribution by legislative majorities.[58] Constitutionally entrenched rights were the favoured mechanism, a policy that has worked especially well during certain periods.[59] Active judicial promotion of particular economic policies is also apparent—to give just one more example—in the field of European Community law: as Carlos Ball notes, the court's jurisprudence "elevates to the normative status of fundamental rights, capitalist principles that promote free trade and movement across national borders".[60]

Emile Durkheim

When Emile Durkheim (1858–1917) turned his attention to law during the late nineteenth century, sociology was heavily wedded to "positivism".[61] For sociological positivists valid knowledge derives from the methods of the natural sciences, which rely on direct observation of phenomena that can be perceived through the senses. The idea is that society is subject to causal laws, which can be discovered through objective observation of social data. Statistical methods are particularly, though not exclusively, used to interpret this data. A

---

[57] See, for example, C. MacKinnon, "Feminism, Marxism, Method, and the State: An Agenda for Theory" (1982) 7 *Signs* 515 and "Feminism, Marxism, Method, and the State: Toward Feminist Jurisprudence" (1983) 8 *Signs* 635.

[58] See generally J. Nedelsky, *Private Property and the Limits of American Constitutionalism* (University of Chicago Press, Chicago, 1991).

[59] See D. Abraham, "Liberty without Equality: The Property-Rights Connection in a 'Negative Citizenship' Regime" (1996) 21 *Law and Social Inquiry* 1 and C. Sunstein, "Lochner's Legacy" (1987) 87 *Columbia Law Review* 873.

[60] C. Ball, "The Making of a Transnational Capitalist Society: The Court of Justice, Social Policy, and Individual Rights under the European Community's Legal Order" (1996) 37 *Harvard International Law Journal* 307 at 308. See also M. Peebles, "A Very Eden of Innate Rights of Man? A Marxist Look at the European Union Treaties and Case Law" (1997) 22 *Law and Social Inquiry* 581.

[61] This term originated in the work of Auguste Comte who is also credited with coining the term "sociology". See further M.D.A. Freeman, *op. cit.*, pp.660–661. On positivist sociology generally, see N. Blaikie, *Approaches to Social Inquiry* (Polity, Cambridge, 1993), pp.14–15. For detailed discussions of Durkheim's sociology of law, see *Durkheim and the Law* (S. Lukes and A. Scull eds., Blackwell, Oxford, 1984); R. Cotterrell, *Law's Community*, chap.9; and A. Hunt, *The Sociological Movement in Law*, chap.4.

fact-value dichotomy underlies this approach to social inquiry. Scientific study should be apolitical because value judgments lack empirical content.[62] Further, the sociologist is a detached and neutral observer, whose task is to assemble explanations that can be tested under similar conditions by others.

As an adherent of positivism Durkheim believed that researchers should treat "social facts as things".[63] While many social phenomena cannot be measured directly, scientific method can capture their external manifestations and through these indicators arrive at verifiable knowledge about societal processes and events. Law then became a focus for Durkheim in a secondary manner, as the "visible symbol" of social solidarity.[64] Despite his extensive treatment of the subject, Alan Hunt concludes that because Durkheim "used law to advance his more general sociological interests" his writings do not amount to "sociology of law".[65] Nonetheless, his preoccupation with the role of value and beliefs in fostering social stability had a significant impact on other theorists who developed fuller accounts of the legal domain, including Talcott Parsons and Jürgen Habermas. While in agreement with Marxists that "social life must be explained not by the conception of it formed by those who participate in it, but by the profound causes which escape their consciousness", Durkheim argues that the economic factor is "secondary and derived".[66] Instead he identifies the existence of an ideological community as the essence of social life.[67]

Durkheim's abiding interest in social cohesion stemmed from the socio-economic climate of the late nineteenth century. Industrial capitalism had spread from its British base to the rest of Western Europe and North America. Meanwhile laissez-faire economics was coming under attack from the emergent working class movement and key intellectual figures. Durkheim was concerned, as was Adam Smith before him, with the place of morality in industrial society. Uninhibited free market economic policies would lead to *anomie*, a condition that is marked by the relative absence of common regulatory norms, giving rise to social conflict. Moral regulation was thus required to prevent a

---

[62] Michael Freeman attributes the traditional ambivalence towards human rights amongst social scientists largely to the dominance of positivism. Because human rights involve ethical judgments they were considered too subjective and hence unscientific: *Human Rights: An Interdisciplinary Approach* (Polity Press, Cambridge, 2002), chap.5.

[63] E. Durkheim, *The Rules of Sociological Method and Selected Texts on Sociology and its Method* (S. Lukes ed., W.D. Halls trans., Macmillan, London, 1982), p.2.

[64] E. Durkheim, *The Division of Labour in Society* (G. Simpson trans., Free Press, New York, 1966), p.64.

[65] A. Hunt, *The Sociological Movement in Law*, p.65.

[66] E. Durkheim, *The Rules of Sociological Method*, pp.171, 174.

[67] See discussion by A. Hunt, *The Sociological Movement in Law*, pp.63–64.

breakdown in social order and law provided the authoritative framework for expressing and enforcing these moral concerns.[68] In Durkheim's social theory, "law is not *one*, but *the* precondition of the constitution of social life".[69]

Having posited a one-on-one relationship between law and social solidarity, Durkheim proceeded to classify and chart the development of sanctions levied in any given legal system. Sanctions take two principal forms and he terms these "repressive" and "restitutive". Repressive sanctions are imposed by penal laws and predominate in earlier stages of legal development, while the restitutive sanctions associated with civil law, commercial, administrative and constitutional law are linked to the social relations arising from the division of labour in modern societies. It emerges that Durkheim understands the form and substance of sanctions in terms of the function they perform in different societies. Although Durkheim is perhaps best known for applying the methods of the natural sciences to the study of society, he was also the first major exponent of a functional approach to the study of social phenomena including laws. Such analysis would reveal how the particular phenomenon or institution under consideration impacted on the operation of society overall. Clear illustrations of this approach are supplied by his work on legal sanctions and criminality. Restitutive sanctions are aimed at restoring the *status quo ante* and are a means of co-ordinating differentiated elements of society. This integration of diverse needs, interests and values is central to the production of solidarity in modern societies. Repressive sanctions are linked to the strong, shared collective values that underline more "primitive" societies. Durkheim remarked that crime "is not simply the disruption even of serious interests; it is an offence against an authority in some way transcendent".[70] Such insights prompt Durkheim to conclude that the commission of offences is not pathological. Rather, the moral outrage it evinces serves to reinforce social cohesion.

Durkheim's overarching concern with the maintenance of social order

---

[68] Durkheim argued that society produces two forms of social solidarity. The "mechanical" solidarity that characterises regimental earlier societies is based on shared values with only a limited division of labour. Modern society rests on "organic" solidarity, which arises through the functional interdependence of autonomous individuals engaged in differentiated forms of social and economic activity. Generally the division of labour produces social solidarity because individuals are mutually dependent, but because the collective conscience (shared values and ideals) present under mechanical solidarity is weakened, increased regulation is necessary to avoid pathological results. See E. Durkheim, *The Division of Labour in Society*, chaps. 2–3.

[69] W. Schluchter, "The Sociology of Law as an Empirical Theory of Validity" (2003) 19 *European Sociological Review* 537 at 542.

[70] E. Durkheim, *The Division of Labour in Society*, p.85.

coloured his research findings. Each of his primary claims about the nature and function of law has been subjected to rigorous critique.[71] For example, whereas Marx conceived of the state as primarily a coercive entity, Durkheim sees it as a necessary repository of shared values.[72] His account of law is partial in that it neglects to take on board questions of power and conflict, institutional processes and the role of the legal profession. He also seems to assume that law embodies all normative systems.[73] Likewise the evolutionary path he plotted from repressive to restitutive laws has been refuted in numerous studies.[74] Indeed the restorative flavour of Ireland's indigenous Brehon law might be cited as a further example. Nonetheless Durkheim's views on the social function of punishment and its symbolic elements continue to receive attention from criminologists.[75]

Durkheim's positivist methodology finds a contemporary adherent in Donald Black, who insists that law "consists in observable acts, not in rules as the concept of rule or norm is employed in both the literature of jurisprudence and in every-day legal language".[76] Under Black's formulation, the aim of sociology of law is to record changes and discern patterns in the behaviour of law, through for example statistical analyses of criminal court records. Values are external to this scheme and so evaluations of law's "politics" or gendering effects, for example, are not considered legitimate. Thus while Durkheim rendered questions about law's morality central, for Black such issues are irrelevant.

Critiques of positivist approaches to social theory take issue with its assumptions of objectivity, the atomism of the subject, the pursuit of causal laws, and the representation of scientific knowledge as "truth".[77] A particular objection is that, as a member of society, the social scientist cannot in some

---

[71] See in particular S. Lukes and A. Scull, *op. cit.*

[72] Leading Alan Hunt (*The Sociological Movement in Law*, p.63) to conclude that Durkheim's later writings exhibited a tendency to "deify the state. He produces a brand of statism in which the citizen is enjoined to fulfil a duty of obedience to the state as the embodiment of society."

[73] *ibid.*, pp.70–71.

[74] See R. Cotterrell, *Law's Community*, pp.181–183.

[75] See for example D. Garland, *Punishment and Modern Society: A Study in Social Theory* (Oxford University Press, Oxford, 1990)

[76] D. Black, "The Boundaries of Legal Sociology" (1972) 81 *Yale Law Journal* 1086 at 1091. Black's major works include *The Behavior of Law* (New York, Academic Press, New York, 1976) and *Sociological Justice* (Oxford University Press, New York 1989).

[77] See for example M.J. Smith, *Social Science in Question* (SAGE, London, 1998); and J. Baker, K. Lynch, S. Cantillon and J. Walsh, *Equality: From Theory to Action* (Palgrave-Macmillan, London, 2004), chap.9.

way stand outside it as an impartial observer: she necessarily brings her own preconceptions and attitudes to bear on the matter under investigation.

Max Weber

German social theorist Max Weber (1864–1920) developed a systematic sociology of law as part of his overriding ambition to explain the uniqueness of Western society.[78] He identified capitalist development and "rationalism" as the pre-eminent characteristics of modernity and saw law as deeply implicated in these processes. As we shall see, Weber ultimately conceived of modern law in instrumental terms: it facilitates the ordering of increasingly complex economic and social relations and is bound up with the rationalisation of modern life, a process whereby mechanical and impersonal systems come to replace the normative bonds of kin and community.

Given his legal training and background, it is perhaps to be expected that Weber's sociology of law examined the details and techniques of various legal orders.[79] Weber agreed with Eugen Ehrlich's contention that "law" cannot be reduced to coercive measures produced and enforced by the state. However, he did not accept the proposition that state law was the embodiment of other normative orders; rather each type of law has an autonomous existence.[80] Weber defines law in the following terms:

> "An order will be called ... *law* if it is externally guaranteed by the probability that physical or psychological coercion will be applied by a *staff* of people in order to bring about compliance or avenge violation."[81]

This conception of law correlates substantially with conventional sanction-based definitions of law but introduces the element of a "staff", which is "broad and includes non-professional roles and even situations in which individuals merely play a socially recognised 'legal' role".[82]

---

[78] See generally R. Cotterrell, *Law's Community*, chap.7; A. Hunt, *The Sociological Movement in Law*, chap.5; and A. Kronman, *Max Weber* (Stanford University Press, Stanford, 1983).

[79] As K.L. Scheppele notes, Weber "spent seven years being miserable while practicing [law]". "Legal Theory and Social Theory" (1994) 20 *Annual Review of Sociology* 383 at 384.

[80] See A. Hunt, *The Sociological Movement in Law*, p.104

[81] M. Weber, *Economy and Society: An Outline of Interpretive Sociology* (3 vols., G. Roth and C. Wittick eds., Bedminster Press, New York, 1968), p.34 (emphasis in original).

[82] A. Hunt, *The Sociological Movement in Law*, p.104; See also M. Weber, *Economy and Society*, pp.316–319.

Before turning to Weber's account of legal evolution and the relationship
between law, the economy and the political order, it is important to appreciate
that, for Weber, cultures were value systems that could not be equated with
physical processes. Consequently he did not share Durkheim's belief that human
beings and the society they inhabited could be understood by invoking the
methods and concepts of the natural sciences. Instead he sought to explain the
subjective meaning that people attach to their actions and interactions within
specific social contexts and so advocated an interpretive approach to
sociology.[83] Weber's basic unit of analysis is social action, that is, human
behaviour that takes account of, and is oriented towards, others. This
epistemology also differentiates his sociology from that of Marx, who as we
have seen, believed in the primacy of social structures rather than inter-
subjective relations.[84]

The social sciences, according to Weber, must identify the variable interactions between different, yet interrelated, aspects of social life. This project
required a distinct methodology, and one of his more influential tools of sociological analysis was the concept of "ideal types".[85] These are generalized
models of historical situations that can be used as a basis for comparing societies and interpreting social processes. Although the models draw on actual
conditions they do not purport to describe "reality"; rather they are used to put
some "order on experience" so as to gain a greater understanding of infinitely
varied social relations.[86] Weber uses the ideal type to present four major types
of social action engaged in by human beings. Affective action is determined
by emotions and is spontaneous, while traditional action involves forms of
conduct that have become entrenched through "ingrained habituation".[87] He
further identified two forms of rational action. Value-rational action is "determined by a conscious belief in the value for its own sake of some ethical,
aesthetic, religious, or other form of behavior, independently of its prospects
of success".[88] By contrast, purposeful rationality connotes action that is oriented towards the achievement of a consciously chosen goal. Weber believed
that this latter form of social action had come to predominate in Western cultures.

---

[83] M. Weber, *Economy and Society*, p.4.

[84] Both Weber and Marx, however, were centrally concerned with capitalism and saw
conflict and struggle as inherent characteristics of social life.

[85] See generally M. Weber, "'Objectivity' in Social Sciences" in *The Methodology of
the Social Sciences* (E. Shils and H. Finch eds., Free Press, Glencoe, 1949), pp.49–
112.

[86] A. Hunt, *The Sociological Movement in Law*, p.101.

[87] M. Weber, *Economy and Society*, p.25.

[88] *ibid.*, pp.24–25.

Social action takes place within certain frameworks or structures, of which the most significant for Weber are capitalism and bureaucracy. Modern capitalism is characterised by purpose-rational economic action aimed at obtaining profit, it exemplifies the "rationalistic organisation of (formally) free labour".[89] Similarly, modern bureaucracies (systems of administration) exhibit characteristics such as specialised divisions of labour and hierarchical authority structures, which are orientated towards the overarching goal of efficient attainment of the organisation's objectives. The counterpart tendency in legal development, discussed below, is towards formally rational law. According to Hunt, Weber attributes the underlying causes of rationalisation to "the coincidence of two sets of interests, firstly developing bourgeois interest and secondly the interests of absolutist states".[90]

A pervasive theme in Weber's writings is the conditions that sustain the continuance and stability of capitalism. Nonetheless, he took issue with the role played by law and economics in certain Marxian views of history. There is no unidirectional causal link between the material base and superstructure, but a plurality of interlocking social forces.[91] Thus he treated the legal, political and social orders as relatively discrete systems outside the economy.[92] In seeking to explain how various social structures interrelate Weber developed the concept of "elective affinity".[93] It denotes functional compatibility between two or more social forms. When viewed in this light bureaucracy, capitalism, and rational-legality are types of instrumentally rational social organisation that mutually shape and reinforce one another.[94] They are intimately related to—but not determined by—each other. Weber suggests that the development of a political public sphere dominated by the modern bureaucratic state and legal specialists are prominent factors facilitating the emergence of rational law.[95]

---

[89] M. Weber, *The Protestant Ethic and the Spirit of Capitalism* (T. Parsons trans., 2nd ed., Allen & Unwin, London, 1976), p.21.

[90] A. Hunt, *The Sociological Movement in Law*, p.110.

[91] In *The Protestant Ethic*, for example, Weber suggested there was a close connection between the austerity encouraged by Calvinism and the rise of capitalist institutions.

[92] M. Weber, "Class, Status, Party" in *From Max Weber: Essays in Sociology* (H.H. Gerth and C. Wright Mills eds. and trans., Routledge and Kegan Paul, London, 1967), pp.180–195. The idea that there are multiple forms of oppression generated by relatively distinct social systems has been adopted by many egalitarian theorists. See for example J. Baker, K. Lynch, S. Cantillon and J. Walsh, *op. cit.*

[93] See for example Weber's discussion of the elective affinity between economic forms of organisation and structures of social action in *Economy and Society*, p.341.

[94] *ibid.*, pp.224, 654–655.

[95] For example he suggests that only bureaucracy "has established the foundation for the administration of a rational law conceptually systematized on the basis of 'statutes'". *Economy and Society*, p.975.

When Weber considered law's internal operations he noted a tendency for modern Western legal systems to rely heavily on "formal rationality", which basically entails the standardisation of universal rules and uniform procedures.[96] Here law appears as a logically consistent structure of abstract rules, the operative facts and norms applicable to any given case or legal problem are identified by recourse to the system itself. By contrast, when a legal system exhibits "substantive rationality", decisions are influenced by norms derived from extra-legal sources that reflect ethical imperatives, utilitarian goals, or political values.[97]

Formally rational law, although not determined by economic forces, best serves the needs of a capitalist economy, and was found in the actual legal systems of Western capitalist countries apart from that of England. Instead the English system was an admixture of "traditional" law (based on the sanctity of immemorial traditions) and "charismatic" law (rests on the moral character of individuals, including judges and magistrates). Weber saw the exceptional case of England as attributable to other factors specific to that country and in any event, as noted above, the ideal type is simply a heuristic device and makes no claim to historical accuracy.[98]

Weber did not regard the increased rationalisation of social activity as a benign development. In fact he believed that ultimately such a process would trap individuals in an "iron cage" of rule-based, rational control, a theme elaborated on by Jürgen Habermas in recent times.[99] While Weber saw conflict as an inherent component of social life he did not believe that it would fuel any great cleavage in the social order as Marx did. This belief is traceable to his thoughts on legitimation and domination.[100] "Legal domination" is another especially significant ideal type posited by Weber. He uses it to analyse the role of law in securing the political legitimacy that underpins the operation of modern states. Authority or legitimate domination, takes three particular forms. Traditional authority stems from the sanctity of age-old rules and powers: "Obedience is owed not to enacted rules but to the person who occupies a position of authority by tradition or who has been chosen for it by the traditional

---

[96] See M. Weber, *Economy and Society*, pp.655–658. The two forms of rational law are also contrasted with legal irrationality, which typifies legal systems that do not rely on general rules.

[97] *ibid.*

[98] See discussion by A. Kronman, *op. cit.*, pp.120–124.

[99] See n.139 below.

[100] Weber contrasted two types of domination (*Herrschaft*): domination arising from a position of monopoly or quasi-monopoly in economic markets, and domination that stems from the power to command and the correlative duty to obey, namely authority. See generally, *Economy and Society*, pp.941–954.

master."[101] Charismatic authority rests on "devotion to the exceptional sanctity, heroism or exemplary character of an individual person, and of the normative patterns or order revealed or ordained by him".[102] Founders of religions constitute the paradigm case of such individual figures. Rational-legal authority stems from impersonal rules, which have been formulated according to a prescribed legal formula. This latter form of domination gradually supplants the other forms in modern states. It enjoins a populace to obey the "rule of law", not the "rule of men".

Each system of domination in order to be effective must secure legitimacy.[103] In other words, Weber understands domination to be a relational concept. Obedience involves voluntary submission to the will of another and so does not rely primarily on force or repression but on ideological support. Rational-legal authority supplies the basis for its legitimacy by appealing to the merits of bureaucratisation and professionalisation.[104] It rests on the assumption "that norms are made, not discovered, and on the belief that it is this attribute which confers on them their normative status as standards for the evaluative assessment of human conduct".[105] Rational legal rules thus appear to derive legitimacy from the fact that they reflect the human capacity for self-determination. However, Weber "makes only minimal appeal to democratic legitimation".[106] Thus he saw the European projects of codification, not as enhancing the democratic character of law, but as a process of rationalisation, which resulted in the loss of the "metaphysical dignity" he associated with (unwritten) natural law.[107]

The existence of a body of rational legal rules appears therefore to meet the demands of modern political orders for both administrative efficiency and legitimacy based on the exclusion of arbitrariness.[108] These rules specify conditions for the exercise of power and also stipulate the processes by which the rules themselves may be amended. What emerges is a concept of political legitimacy generated by the form rather than the content of law. Once political

---

[101] M. Weber, *Economy and Society*, p.227.

[102] *ibid.*, p.215.

[103] David Trubek notes that Weber "never really explained the legitimation process itself": "Critical Legal Studies and Empiricism", at 597.

[104] See A. Hunt, "The Problematisation of Law in Classical Social Theory", p.23.

[105] A. Kronman, *op. cit.*, p.52.

[106] A. Hunt, "The Problematisation of Law in Classical Social Theory", p.23.

[107] M. Weber, *Economy and Society*, p.875.

[108] See further R. Cotterrell, *Law's Community*, pp.141–143. In his essay *Politics as a Vocation*, Weber advanced a definition of the state that was to become pivotal to Western social theory: States are entities which have a monopoly over the legitimate use of force and law is the primary mechanism which enables the state to secure its authority.

activity adheres to the prescribed legal formula, it is legitimate; consequently the values advanced are irrelevant.

Although the development of rational-legal authority could be regarded as a safeguard against the vagaries and potential biases of human decision-making, Weber envisaged that formalism could override the concern for individual justice that he associated with "substantive rationality". Several writers have critiqued Weber's typology of law on the basis that it is impossible to create a system of rules that do not appeal to political ideologies, religious or other values.[109] Indeed, Hunt suggests that Weber himself makes a value judgment in arguing that rational legality is more advanced that irrational legal thought.[110] Nevertheless current debates, such as those concerning constitutional equality guarantees, illustrate the continuing relevance of the tension Weber identified between formal and substantive justice.[111] When considering the English legal system in particular, Weber also drew attention to the enduring problems of access to justice and the vested interests of legal professionals.[112] Indeed his thoughts on law and domination generally remain central to the sociology of law.

Eugen Ehrlich

Austrian jurist Eugen Ehrlich (1862–1922) contested one of the main tenets of legal positivism by claiming that "law" comprises much more than the norms generated and enforced by state institutions.[113] Central to his notion of legal pluralism is the co-existence of "official law" and "living law".[114] The former essentially consists of "norms for decisions", through which the "state issues

---

[109] See for example R. Cotterrell, *Law's Community*, pp.150–154.

[110] A. Hunt, *The Sociological Movement in Law*, p.100.

[111] See for example S. Mullally, "Equality Guarantees in the Irish Constitution: The Myth of Constitutionalism and the Neutral State" in *Ireland's Evolving Constitution 1937–1997* (T. Murphy and P. Twomey eds., Hart, Oxford, 1998), pp.147–162.

[112] See for example M. Weber, *Economy and Society*, p.892, 976–977.

[113] Ehrlich's ideas were first set out in a text published in 1913, the English language version of which is relied upon here: E. Ehrlich, *Fundamental Principles of the Sociology of Law* (W.L. Moll trans., Harvard University Press, Cambridge, Mass., 1936). For more detailed treatments of Ehrlich's work, see R. Banakar, "Sociological Jurisprudence" in *An Introduction to Law and Social Theory*, pp.33–49; D. Nelken, "Law in Action or Living Law? Back to the Beginning in Sociology of Law" (1984) 4 *Legal Studies* 157; K.A. Ziegert, "The Sociology Behind Eugen Ehrlich's Sociology of Law" (1979) 7 *International Journal of Sociology of Law* 225; and K.A. Ziegert, "A Note on Eugen Ehrlich and the Production of Legal Knowledge" (1998) 20 *Sydney Law Review* 108.

[114] His work was given a hostile reception by Hans Kelsen and others from the analytical jurisprudence tradition; see D. Nelken, *op. cit.*, n.107.

directions to its courts and other tribunals as to manner in which they should decide ... cases" coupled with instructions directed at administrative agencies as to how cases should be processed.[115] Human conduct is, in fact, regulated by the "living law", that is, the norms generated by a host of formal or informal collectivities ("associations"). Occupational organisations, ethnic groups, families, religious communities and other such groupings exist alongside associations that have a formal legal character like trade unions and business entities. Each has an inner ordering which induces respect for norms that are not derivative of state agencies.[116] Ehrlich's theories were no doubt influenced by the ethnic and cultural diversity of Bukowina, the region in south eastern Europe in which he lived and worked.[117]

He also argued that because it is applied in exceptional cases only, the significance of the body of "norms for decisions" is overstated. When disputes occur they are usually resolved without resort to state institutions and laws may not be invoked because people are unaware of their existence, or lack the material or other resources necessary to enforce a claim.[118] Moreover, "official law" will only be effective when in conformity with the "living law", that is, with the social norms that actually guide human behaviour. For Ehrlich, therefore, "the centre of gravity of legal development lies not in legislation, nor in juristic science, nor in judicial decision, but in society itself".[119] Social order is not secured by state compulsion but derives from cultural acceptance of certain "rules" for living. Official legal sanctions affect only a minority of social "outcasts", whose bonds to social associations have been severed because of economic, psychological and other factors.[120]

Given this theoretical orientation, Ehrlich insisted on the importance of mapping the living law through empirical studies. The social practices unearthed should then be compared with the formal content and operation of positive law, so that its workings might be elucidated and ultimately improved.[121] His conception of a plurality of interlocking orders within a given society continues to be strongly influential. The aspect of Ehrlich's work that has proved least palatable concerns the nature of state law. By classifying the state as but one

---

[115] E. Ehrlich, *op. cit.*, p.367.

[116] *ibid.*, chaps II–III.

[117] See K.A. Ziegert, "A Note on Eugen Ehrlich and the Production of Legal Knowledge".

[118] E. Ehrlich, *op. cit.*, pp.368–369.

[119] E. Ehrlich, *op. cit*, p.xv.

[120] *ibid.*, p.68.

[121] R. Banakar, "Sociological Jurisprudence", pp.35–37, points out that Ehrlich's central objective was to develop and improve the science of law, a project which sets him apart from contemporaries like Durkheim and Weber. See further K.A. Ziegert, "A Note on Eugen Ehrlich and the Production of Legal Knowledge".

form of association, he is open to the criticism that he underplays its coercive properties.[122] Further, his and other variants of legal pluralism arguably do not supply adequate criteria for distinguishing non-state law from any other normative order.[123] Several theorists, including Weber and Roscoe Pound, agree that state law is not uniquely productive of social order but take issue with Ehrlich's insistence on the primacy of living law.

Legal pluralism has profound normative and empirical implications. At an empirical level it suggests that official law may have a marginal influence at best on the social order. According to Philip Selznick, this approach to law is based on "the idea that distinctive social fields generate their own modes of self-government, their own rules of right conduct".[124] Contemporary researchers working in the legal pluralist frame have examined the impact of formal law in given settings. In a study of dispute resolution amongst cattle ranchers and their neighbours, Robert Ellickson found that formal rules were of little significance. [125] Likewise Stewart Macaulay concluded that contract law and the use of courts were not central to the conduct of business relationships.[126] The normative dimension is a potentially rich line of inquiry that is less developed in socio-legal research.[127] The inference is essentially that the law of state elites *ought* not to be accorded the weight or priority that it currently enjoys. As Sally Merry observes, "[legal pluralism] ... provides a framework for understanding the dynamics of the imposition of law and of

---

[122] See R. Cotterrell, *The Sociology of Law*, p.31.

[123] See for example B. Tamanaha, "The Folly of the 'Social Scientific' Conception of Legal Pluralism".

[124] P. Selznick, "'Law in Context' Revisited" (2003) 30 *Journal of Law and Society* 177 at 185.

[125] R. Ellickson, *Order Without Law: How Neighbors Settle Disputes* (Harvard University Press, Cambridge, Mass., 1991). Ellickson found that "people frequently resolve their disputes in cooperative fashion without paying any attention to the laws that apply to those disputes" (p.vii). For a critical appraisal of Ellickson's work see D. Litowitz, "A Critical Take on Shasta County and the 'New Chicago School'" (2003) 15 *Yale Journal of Law and the Humanities* 295. For a discussion of how land disputes are resolved in a rural Irish setting, see Chris Curtin, "Social Order, Interpersonal Relations and Disputes in a West of Ireland Community" in *Whose Law and Order: Aspects of Crime and Social Control in Irish Society* (M. Tomlinson, T. Varley and C. McCullagh eds., Sociological Association of Ireland, Dublin, 1988), pp.76–91. Curtin concludes tentatively that litigation "is likely to be resorted to only when all else has failed or when the control of substantial resources are disputed", p.89.

[126] S. Macaulay, "Non-Contractual Relations in Business: A Preliminary Study" (1963) 28 *American Sociological Review* 55.

[127] But see the discussion of the constitutive approach to law in the next part of this chapter.

resistance to law. ... [A]ttention to plural orders examines limits to the ideological power of state law."[128]

Roscoe Pound

Sociological jurisprudence took hold in the American academy through the work of Roscoe Pound (1870–1964). Increased state regulation of all arenas of social life, including the economy as witnessed by the emergence of welfare state institutions, gave rise to the view that law could be deployed to create controlled and orderly social change. Pound's immense body of work aimed to overcome the perceived limitations of two dominant jurisprudential traditions, namely natural law thinking and analytical jurisprudence.[129] Noting a tendency amongst lawyers to apply abstract principles rigorously, irrespective of the underlying policies or the impact of these policies in particular situations, Pound pejoratively labelled the formalism that permeated legal reasoning as "mechanical jurisprudence".[130]

Pound saw law as a dynamic institution designed to manage continually evolving and often conflicting interests.[131] Having mapped the various interests at play in the legal system he attempted to specify the core values (jural postulates), which the law, as mediator of these interests, should maintain.[132]

---

[128] S.E. Merry, "Legal Pluralism", at 890.

[129] N.E.H. Hull observes that Pound's self-description of his approach as "sociological" was motivated by a desire to indicate a break with the traditional schools of legal thought: *Roscoe Pound and Karl Llewellyn: Searching for an American Jurisprudence* (University of Chicago Press, Chicago, 1997), pp.84–85.

[130] R. Pound, "Mechanical Jurisprudence" (1908) 8 *Columbia Law Review* 605.

[131] "The sociological movement in jurisprudence is a movement for pragmatism as a philosophy of law; for adjustment of principles and doctrines to the human conditions they are to govern rather than to assumed first principles ..."; *ibid.*, pp.609–610.

[132] He identified three major types of interest—social, individual and public—through examining the types of claims brought before courts: See further R. Cotterrell, *The Politics of Jurisprudence* (Butterworths, London, 1989), pp.159–162. Jural postulates are "ideas of right to be made effective by legal institutions" and through legal doctrine: R. Pound, *Interpretations of Legal History* (Cambridge University Press, Cambridge, 1923), p.148. Pound stressed however, that these were not the eternal values of natural law but merely those which prevail in a particular time or place. As with "interests" the postulates are to be found by analysing existing law. He listed those applicable to American law as the disapproval of intentional aggressions, the protection of acquired private property, the assurance of good faith in transactions with others, the duty of reasonable care so as to avoid injury to others and a general obligation to control dangerous items in one's possession. See generally R. Pound, *Jurisprudence* (5 Vols., West Publishing, St Paul, 1959), Vol.III, chap.14.

The central task of jurisprudence should therefore be to enhance law's supposed ability to secure or at least manage the attainment of socially desirable ends. Under this vision law is, in effect, an instrument of "social engineering" that can be fine-tuned to operate efficiently and sociology can supply the information needed to guide legal reform.[133] His apparent belief in law's instrumentality can be usefully contrasted with the legal pluralist approach exemplified by Ehrlich. Both writers believed that law was but one of a number of mechanisms of social control but "law" and "society" could be said to occupy an inverse relationship in their respective schemes.[134] And in contrast to Weber's pessimism at the spread of rational legality, Pound saw "in legal history the record of a continually wider recognising and satisfying of human wants or claims or desires through social control; a more embracing and more effective securing of social interests ... in short, a continually more efficacious social engineering".[135] This is not to suggest, however, that Pound regarded law as an appropriate vehicle for enacting radical social programmes, his concern lay instead with improving the internal working of legal institutions so that they adapted to social change; as one commentator has remarked: "his principal objection to bad law was its effect on the legal system rather than on society".[136]

Pound's call for a study of law as it actually is, the "law in action" as opposed to the law in the books still has resonance for socio-legal scholars.[137] The distinction may yield inquiries as to how legal and social norms interrelate, whether court rhetoric matches the realities of adjudicative processes, whether law-making achieves its stated objectives and so on. His own work tended to reflect this latter objective. In a salient essay, "The Limits of Effective Legal Action", he contemplated the relationship between law and social control.[138] A core theme is his recurrent belief in the practical distinction between law and morals. Since law can only deal with observable behaviour, it cannot control

---

[133] See D. Wigdor, *Roscoe Pound: Philosopher of Law* (Greenwood Press, Westport, 1974), pp.189–199, 209.

[134] In particular Pound gave precedence to the law of judicial elites; he regarded judges as people who "see more and know more of life than almost any other class of men" (quoted in D. Wigdor, *op. cit.*, p.220). Hence the "living law" is not the inner order of associations but the "rule which results from judicial treatment of controversies". *ibid.*

[135] R. Pound, *Introduction to the Philosophy of Law* (Yale University Press, New Haven, 1950), p.99.

[136] D. Wigdor, *op. cit.*, p.220.

[137] R. Pound, "Law in Books and Law in Action" (1910) 44 *American Law Review* 12 at 15. This injunction was taken up by the American legal realists, and critical theories that seek to expose law's claims to objectivity and neutrality as masking inequalities of power could be seen as responding to one strand of this project.

[138] R. Pound, *Jurisprudence*, Vol.III, p.353–73.

attitudes and beliefs. Further, certain moral obligations are not amenable to legal enforcement; the duties and obligations arising from family ties constitute one example. On this view, those aspects of family law and social welfare legislation dealing with the care of dependents are misguided. It might be countered that while laws cannot *make* anyone care for another person, and in this sense are not directly enforceable, they can help to establish conditions that support caring relationships. Recent scholarship is less concerned about legal effectiveness in these "private" spheres of life and tends to emphasise law's propensity to impose inappropriate regulatory frameworks.[139]

Another significant limitation identified by Pound, mirroring Ehrlich, pertains to the activation of law.[140] Legal precepts are enforced by state agencies, including courts, various law officers, juries and policing bodies, and generally will only be triggered when individual litigants and complainants come forward. Legal norms therefore lie dormant unless an aggrieved party is in a position to participate in legal proceedings. These observations have an enduring relevance. In states where legal services are essentially privatised, access to courts in civil cases is severely compromised and effectively guaranteed only to those with sufficient resources to meet the extraordinary costs involved.[141] Legal aid schemes are classified as a form of welfare provision and so tend to be subject to qualifying restrictions that exclude large segments of the population.[142] While a wide range of rights is conferred on

---

[139] Jürgen Habermas addresses this problem in his discussion of "juridification", a process whereby increasing areas of life are subject to ever more complex and detailed legal regulation. On this view the welfare state is a double-edged sword because although it cushions people from the effects of market failure, benefits and entitlements are institutionalised in a manner that allows bureaucracies to intrude upon and police the recipients' behaviour. Juridification also has a qualitative dimension in that it stifles communicative action supplanting it with the instrumental rationality Habermas associates with the systems of the market and state. His work posits a revised conception of reason that subsumes but is broader than Weber's instrumental rationality. Whereas instrumental rationality is concerned with "action oriented to success", communicative action arises where "the actions of the agents involved are co-ordinated not through egocentric calculations of success but through acts of reaching understanding": J. Habermas, *The Theory of Communicative Action* (T. MacCarthy trans., Heinemann, London, 1984) pp.285–286; See also J. Tweedy and A. Hunt, "The Future of the Welfare State and Social Rights: Reflections on Habermas" (1994) 21 *Journal of Law and Society* 288.

[140] See discussion by R. Cotterrell, *The Sociology of Law*, pp.50–56.

[141] See further G. Whyte, *Social Inclusion and the Legal System: Public Interest Law in Ireland* (Institute of Public Administration, Dublin, 2002), chap.9.

[142] C. Harlow, "Access to Justice as a Human Right: The European Convention and the European Union" in *The EU and Human Rights* (P. Alston ed., Oxford University Press, Oxford, 1999), p.187.

people, many are excluded from exercising these rights because they lack the resources necessary to do so.[143] Further, as Pound notes, law must provide incentives to ensure that it is invoked.[144] Recent Irish studies of attrition rates in sexual assault cases, which found that the rules of evidence applicable in such trials act as a disincentive to potential complainants, would appear to reinforce this point.[145]

Pound's approach was premised upon an assumption of consensus, and so it maintained and enhanced the legitimacy of the judicial domain. It is, in essence, functional jurisprudence. And as Hunt remarks, Pound "was the propagandist for a sociological jurisprudence, but he cannot be regarded as having given it an adequate theoretical basis".[146]

Talcott Parsons

Talcott Parsons (1902–1979) is one of the key social scientists of the twentieth century. According to his structural-functionalist theory, society is a system with constituent parts that fulfil distinct functions or roles. Parsons' conceptualisation of society as having four major functional goals that it had to realise if it were to survive remains influential. Adaptation to the environment was realised within the economy; the goal attainment objective (achieving collective goals) was the task of the political system; tension management and pattern maintenance (socialisation of people) was the task of the cultural system; while integrative systems played a role in maintaining social cohesion.[147] Integration facilitates adjustments between the subsystems so that they contribute to the effective operation of the system as a whole. The integrative function is therefore central and Parsons attributes this role primarily to the

---

[143] See for example, D. Rhode, "Access to Justice" (2001) 69 *Fordham Law Review* 1785.

[144] "[To] assure enforcement law must largely rely on some immediate and obvious individual advantage which it may use either to bring about obedience to its precept or to furnish a motive to others to vindicate or enforce it": R. Pound, *Jurisprudence*, Vol.III, p.370.

[145] See M. Leane *et al*, *Attrition in Sexual Assault Offence Cases in Ireland: A Qualitative Analysis* (Stationery Office, Dublin, 2001); Dublin Rape Crisis Centre and the School of Law Trinity College Dublin, *The Legal Process and Victims of Rape* (Dublin Rape Crisis Centre, Dublin, 1998).

[146] A. Hunt, *The Sociological Movement in Law*, p.33.

[147] See for example, T. Parsons, *The Social System* (Routledge and Kegan Paul, London, 1951); T. Parsons and N.J. Smelser, *Economy and Society* (Routledge and Kegan Paul, London, 1956).

[148] T. Parsons, "Law as an Intellectual Stepchild" in *Social System and Legal Process* (H. Johnson ed., Jossey-Bass, San Francisco, 1978), pp.11–58.

legal system.[148] Further, as modern society becomes increasingly complex the need for balancing interests and hence law is heightened.[149]

As Cotterrell observes, Parsons' account of law's role in managing changes in the normative structure of society is a substantial contribution to the sociology of law. Although Parsons regarded the various sub-systems as analytically distinct, he illustrates that "what appears in Western societies as the substantial *autonomy* of law and the legal system is a finely balanced and inevitably precarious condition rooted in complex sociological factors touching most important aspects of social life".[150]

In arguing that law regulates social interaction and thereby minimises conflict, Parsons embraces the liberal legal order and its justifications in an unproblematic fashion. This perspective informed much socio-legal research throughout the 1960s and 1970s. Law features throughout Parsons' work, yet he never engaged with debates about the nature of legal doctrine. As a result, his picture of law as a neutral arbiter of social change could be dismissed as partial. Parsons' consensualist view of society and his perceived failure to map historical change have been heavily critiqued by other sociologists, and he is usually depicted as idealizing Western capitalism.[151] However, Parsons' emphasis on the promotion of secular and universal values, as well as his depiction of increasing functional specialisation, influenced both Jürgen Habermas and Niklas Luhmann.[152]

4. CONTEMPORARY DIRECTIONS

This part of the chapter examines two major contributors to contemporary socio-legal theory—Niklas Luhmann and Pierre Bourdieu—and we will also discuss the methodological approach known as "critical empiricism".

Niklas Luhmann

Under systems theory as advanced by Parsons, society is comprised of various sub-systems that fulfil distinct roles and operate independently of one another. The autopoietic (self-reproducing) theory of Niklas Luhmann (1927–1998) holds to that general formula but modifies it in certain important respects.[153]

---

[149] T. Parsons, "The Law and Social Control" in *Law and Sociology* (W.M. Evan ed., The Free Press, New York, 1962), pp.56–72

[150] R. Cotterrell, *The Sociology of Law*, p.85 (emphasis in original).

[151] See for example, N. Elias, *The Civilising Process* (Blackwell, Oxford, 1994).

[152] See M. Deflem, "The Boundaries of Abortion Law: Systems Theory from Parsons to Luhmann and Habermas" (1998) 76 *Social Forces* 775.

[153] Luhmann was introduced to systems theory while a student of Parsons at Harvard

His understanding of social systems is derived from biology; just as biological systems continually reproduce themselves through the ongoing production of cells, the social system self-reproduces its basic elements. Whereas the basic unit of living physical systems is cells, social systems reproduce communications.

The social system comprises several sub-systems that are differentiated from one another in terms of their function or operations. Sub-systems therefore have an internal aspect (the function they carry out) and an environment, which is made up of the other social sub-systems. Systems mark themselves out from their environment through their operations.[154] But operations can only be controlled and observed within the system if it makes a distinction between self-reference and external reference. It does so through following an internal logic driven by a system-specific binary code.[155] For example, science operates according to the code "true/untrue" and law through the code "law/non-law".[156] Information from law's environment, for example from the political system, then is processed solely according to the schema "law/non-law". The doctrine of separation of powers as applied by the Irish judiciary might be considered as an example of this binary code in practice. So-called "political questions", such as decisions as to the distribution of state resources, are classified as non-law and hence not amenable to adjudication.[157]

The legal system's purpose is to stabilise normative expectations; it "acts

---

from 1960 to 1961. See generally N. Luhmann, "Operational Closure and Structural Coupling: The Differentiation of the Legal System" (1992) 12 *Cardozo Law Review* 1419 and N. Luhmann, "The Self-Reproduction of Law and its Limits" in *Dilemmas of Law in the Welfare State* (G. Teubner ed., Walter de Gruyter, Berlin, 1986), pp.111–127. Some useful accounts of Luhmann's work are: M. King and A. Schütz, "The Ambitious Modesty of Niklas Luhmann" (1994) 21 *Journal of Law and Society* 261; H. Baxter, "Autopoiesis and the 'Relative Autonomy' of Law" (1998) 19 *Cardozo Law Review* 1987; M. King, "The Truth About Autopoiesis" (1993) 20 *Journal of Law and Society* 218; and K.A. Ziegert, "The Thick Description of Law: An Introduction to Niklas Luhmann's Theory" in *An Introduction to Law and Social Theory*, pp.55–75.

[154] The legal system is therefore distinguished from other systems, not at an institutional level but in terms of its function. Consequently, "every communication that makes a legal assertion or raises a defense against such an assertion is an internal operation of the legal system, even if it is occasioned by a dispute among neighbors, a traffic accident, a police action, or any other event"; N. Luhmann, "Law as a Social System" (1988/89) 83 *Northwestern University Law Review* 136 at 141.

[155] Luhmann explains that "[w]ithout such closure, the systems would have no way of distinguishing their own operations from those of the environment" (*ibid.*, at 138).

[156] K.A. Ziegert, "The Thick Description of Law", pp.66–70.

[157] See, for example, P. McDermott, "The Separation of Powers and the Doctrine of Non-Justiciability" (2000) 35 *Irish Jurist* 280.

as the immune system of the social system".[158] As with all other systems it is characterized by operative closure and cognitive openness. Operative closure is secured when legal decision-makers ground their decisions solely with reference to law validated by previous legal decisions.[159] Thus Luhmann remarks "only the law can change the law".[160] He shares Hans Kelsen's belief that law regulates its own creation and essentially adheres to a positivist definition of law as a body of rules designed to promote the predictability and calculability of expectations.[161] At the same time, however, law is open to cognitive information generated by other sub-systems. In other words, the legal system does respond to political, economic or cultural phenomena but all feedback from this environment is filtered through the system's binary code.[162] Legislation therefore will not *control* legal operations but it may stimulate them.

The practical implications of Luhmann's theory are developed further by Gunther Teubner.[163] Both writers suggest that all attempts at "social engineering" through law are misguided, because the legal system cannot control the conduct of other systems, but only its own operations. Teubner concludes that law can best promote social reform by providing a broad framework, within which various social systems would self-regulate.[164]

Systems theory and, in particular that of Luhmann, may be critiqued on the basis that it dwells on one side of the structure/agency debate. The behaviours of autopoietic systems are not attributed to the actions of individuals or groups of people and Luhmann neglects to account sufficiently for the possibilities of change via human agency. Legal rules are not self-enforcing but applied and interpreted by a range of participants (with varying degree of authority) in a given legal process. As Cotterrell notes, "even in a formalised, seemingly closed legal system, it is not 'the system' which thinks or communicates, but individual actors (for example, lawyers, judges, lay citizens) whose thinking and communicating creates and sustains the system".[165] Luhmann may also be charged with underplaying the role of power.

---

[158] K.A. Ziegert, "The Thick Description of Law", p.65.

[159] *ibid.*, p.64.

[160] N. Luhmann, "The Self-Reproduction of Law and its Limits", p.113.

[161] See further M. King, "The Truth About Autopoiesis" (1993) 20 *Journal of Law and Society* 218.

[162] Likewise outputs from the legal system to other systems are solely constituted as "law/non-law".

[163] See for example, G. Teubner, "After Legal Instrumentalism?: Strategic Models of Post-Regulatory Law" in *Dilemmas of Law in the Welfare State*.

[164] See further R. Cotterrell, *Law's Community*, pp.67–69.

[165] *ibid.*, pp.107–108.

Pierre Bourdieu

Pierre Bourdieu (1930–2002) was an eclectic scholar and political activist whose writing has transformed sociological understandings of education, culture and class.[166] His social theory seeks to supersede both objectivist positions, as exemplified by functionalism and structuralism, and postmodern subjectivist stances.[167] This theoretical lens leads him to reject formalist and instrumentalist accounts of law.[168] While Bourdieu's model of the juridical field has similar properties to Luhmann's autopoietic legal system, it circumvents some of the difficulties inherent in a systems approach. He too sees law as exhibiting a degree of autonomy or closure, and explores the manner in which knowledge emanating from other sites is translated into a legal code so that it can be processed by the system. However, he pays particular attention to the role of legal actors and explores the division of labour which fuels the competitive dynamics at play *within* the legal field.[169] Legal professionals are actively engaged in the construction of legal meaning, indeed "the juridical field is the site of a competition for monopoly of the right to determine the law".[170]

Bourdieu is keen to highlight the distinct properties of the juridical field. It is closely tied to other forms of power, in particular the political power of the state, but it does not simply reflect other social forces. In practice the juridical field is "relatively independent of external determinations and pressures".[171] This tendency towards closure is not derived from law's inner logic or coherence as analytical jurisprudence supposes but results from practices aimed at ensuring exclusive control of the legal field. Its operation is guided by a set of internal

---

[166] Loïc Wacquant describes the "nexus of antagonistic and competing visions within which and against which Bourdieu developed his own stance": L. Wacquant, "Bourdieu in America: Notes on the Transatlantic Importation of Social Theory" in *Bourdieu: Critical Perspectives* (C. Calhoun, E. LiPuma and M. Postone eds., Polity Press, Cambridge, 1993), p.245.

[167] Following Weber, Bourdieu believes that although there is a clear interaction between the relations of economic production and those of other fields, they are distinct and relatively independent. See P. Bourdieu, "The Forms of Capital" (R. Nice, trans.) in *Handbook of Theory and Research for the Sociology of Education* (J.G. Richardson ed., Greenwood, Westport, 1986), pp.241–258.

[168] Bourdieu's views on law are set out most fully in P. Bourdieu, "The Force of Law: Toward a Sociology of the Juridical Field" (1987) 38 *Hastings Law Journal* 805 (R. Terdiman trans.).

[169] The legal field also protects itself from other institutions in the competition for the right to determine the law.

[170] *ibid.*, at 817.

[171] *ibid.*, at 816.

protocols, assumptions and self-sustaining values that tend to obscure its complicity in sustaining relations of domination and oppression.[172]

As a discourse, law not only reflects power relations; it simultaneously constitutes and legitimises them. In particular through symbolic and linguistic practices the legal field "consecrates the established order by consecrating the vision of that order which is held by the State".[173] Judgments are presented as the inevitable result of principled deliberation and interpretation, thereby distinguishing court decisions from the blatant exercises of power often associated with the political context. Legal language abstracts from "the contingency and historicity of particular situations to establish a general and universal norm which is designed as a model for later decisions".[174] The doctrine of precedent, for example, suggests that judges simply recognise and then apply the relevant rules in a disinterested manner.[175] Following Robert Cover, Bourdieu suggests that law's "truth" is continually constructed from a limited point of view, the normative universe of dominant groups within its interpretive community.[176] Through such processes, law acts as an instrument of symbolic violence, which consists in the imposition of ways of seeing and evaluating the world. Because "the production of representations of the social world ... is a fundamental dimension of political struggles", law is an important site of engagement for oppressed groups.[177]

Critical Empiricism

The contemporary law and society movement's "applied" work seeks to employ theoretical concepts in empirical research. A number of interrelated criticisms have been directed at the ongoing efforts to explicate how law "actually" operates, with many criticisms emerging from within the socio-legal tradition. The primary points of contention appear to stem from tensions between the core disciplines invoked. Traditionally sociology and law have looked at the same subject matter through different lenses and with divergent goals in mind.[178] Friction between these overarching frameworks is manifest in debates

---

[172] R. Terdiman, "Translator's Introduction" to Pierre Bourdieu, "The Force of Law: Toward a Sociology of the Juridical Field" (1987) 38 *Hastings Law Journal* 805 at 806.

[173] P. Bourdieu, "The Force of Law", at 838.

[174] *ibid.*, at 846–847.

[175] For a feminist critique in the same vein, see M.J. Mossman, "Feminism and Legal Method: The Difference It Makes" (1986) 3 *Australian Journal of Law and Society* 30.

[176] R. Cover, "Foreword: Nomos and Narrative" (1983) 97 *Harvard Law Review* 4.

[177] P. Bourdieu, *Sociology in Question* (R. Nice, trans., SAGE, London, 1993), p.37.

[178] See for example F. Munger, *op. cit.*; S. Vago, *op. cit.*, pp.4–6; and D. Nelken,

about the place of legal doctrine within sociology of law, emphases on problem solving and policy reforms as opposed to theory development and radical critique, and so on.

Sociological jurisprudence in the early twentieth century had an instrumentalist policy-oriented focus.[179] Scholarship in this mode was concerned with examining the effectiveness of given legal rules, that is, whether they succeeded in influencing the field of activity at which they are directed. The general idea was that empirical social studies could be used to improve the resolution of legal problems. A shared interest in shattering the closure associated with legal formalism brought some alignment with the social science strain of legal realism. Because sociological jurisprudence sought to enhance law's internal processes, it inspired the introduction of social scientific evidence in court hearings via *Brandeis* and other forms of brief.[180]

As the century progressed, the empirical work carried out by the law and society movement focused on the gap between legal standards and their application, and was increasingly infused with a critical edge.[181] Institutional and policy reform programmes directed at crime and poverty relied heavily on the socio-legal research conducted at American universities and foundations during certain periods.[182] Joel Handler, for example, used social science to critique formal welfare rights and suggested that greater awareness of social factors could enhance the operation of legal institutions in this arena.[183] In a path-breaking study, Marc Galanter described how social and economic advantages are systemically translated into gains for the "haves" as opposed to the "have-nots" in the course of dealings with the legal system.[184] Writing in 1984, Robert Gordon observed that these and other investigations of the

---

"Blinding Insights? The Limits of a Reflexive Sociology of Law" (1998) 25 *Journal of Law and Society* 407; R. Banakar, *Merging Law and Sociology* (2003), chap.2.

[179] L.M. Friedman, *op. cit.*

[180] *Brandeis* briefs stem from a US case—*Muller v Oregon* 208 US 412 (1908); there a lawyer named Louis Brandeis filed a brief (*i.e.* a written document to be produced as evidence in court proceedings), which referred to medical and social science data in support of arguments that legislation limiting the hours worked by women in laundries was constitutionally sound.

[181] F. Munger, *op. cit.*, at 101–105. That is not to suggest that the movement has ever been marked by a reformist or any other consensus; see for example, D. Black, "The Boundaries of Legal Sociology" (1972) 81 *Yale Law Journal* 1086.

[182] See, for example, B. Garth and J. Sterling "From Legal Realism to Law and Society: Reshaping Law for the Last Stages of the Social Activist State" (1998) 32 *Law and Society Review* 409.

[183] J. Handler, "Controlling Official Behavior in Welfare Administration" (1966) 54 *California Law Review* 479.

[184] M. Galanter, "Why The 'Haves' Come Out Ahead: Speculations on the Limits of Legal Change" (1974) 9 *Law and Society Review* 95.

law "in action" have "exploded forever the Formalist fantasy that a universal scheme of neutral, general rules controls equally and impersonally the discretion of every class and faction of civil society".[185]

The liberal reform agendas pursued by many governments during the 1960s and 1970s had, however, given rise to a close functional relationship with socio-legal researchers, and many saw this alliance as stifling more radical scholarship. At this juncture key figures in the law and society movement began to regard analyses of law's efficacy as inherently limiting and as unduly shaped by the policy mandates of public institutions.[186] Richard Abel voiced concerns that "the gap paradigm has been 'exhausted'; that is, critics say it produces repetitive findings that the legal system does not live up to its ideals while it reinforces those ideals by failing to offer a coherent alternative understanding of the role of the legal system".[187] David Trubek drew attention to the problem of funding: "Since there was no agency ready to provide adequate financial support for an autonomous 'discipline' of law and society, their product was often tailored to meet the needs of government agencies and foundations which had policy goals that might be served by law and society knowledge."[188]

There was a sense that socio-legal scholarship was doing little to disrupt conventional accounts of the relationship between law and society and had the unintended effect of feeding law's self-image of universality, objectivity and detachment.[189] It might have revealed oppressive power relations at play but it did not explain how these were generated and sustained. There were also concerns that policy work would pathologise the disadvantaged groups who were frequently the objects of research and justify coercive practices.[190] At the same time, poststructuralist critique corroded faith in the unproblematic use of social scientific methods to arrive at conclusive findings on the "reality"

---

[185] R.W. Gordon, *op. cit.*, at 122.

[186] See R. Abel, "Taking Stock" (1980) 14 *Law and Society Review* 429; A. Sarat and S. Silbey, "The Pull of the Policy Audience" (1988) 10 *Law and Policy* 97; A. Sarat, "Legal Effectiveness and Social Studies of Law" (1985) 9 *Legal Studies Forum* 23; and C.M. Campbell and P. Wiles, "The Study of Law and Society in Britain" (1976) 10 *Law and Society Review* 547.

[187] R. Abel, "Taking Stock", at 438–439.

[188] D. Trubek, "Back to the Future: The Short, Happy Life of the Law and Society Movement" (1990) 18 *Florida State University Law Review* 4 at 29.

[189] Austin Sarat and Susan Silbey argued that the connections to "policy elites of the liberal state" meant "that research apparently critical of aspects of American legal institutions works, paradoxically, to reinforce fundamental assumptions of liberal legalism"; *op. cit.*, p.113.

[190] See for example R. Abel, "Redirecting Social Studies of Law" (1980) 14 *Law and Society Review* 805.

of law. G. Edward White observes that "[o]f all the issues that were to demarcate Critical Legal Studies from the Law and Society movement, the association of objective empiricism with positivism was the most explosive and the most clearly joined. ...[C]ritical theorists came to suggest that by ignoring ideology and autonomy and by not conducting research from an openly normative and critical perspective, reformist scholars were reinforcing the status quo."[191] CLS helped inspire the Amherst Seminar, an intellectual movement in socio-legal work that was to adopt the "critical empirical" approach.[192]

Over the past decades socio-legal scholarship has begun to evince a commitment to a synthesis of normative and empirical concerns. This critical empirical approach purports to takes on board the poststructuralist assault by acknowledging contradiction and contingency, while at the same time positing the existence of relatively durable social structures that unconsciously condition people's actions. [193] A commitment to empirical research is retained and defended through advocacy of a post-positivist stance that does not conceive of social science as generating conclusive knowledge about social reality but one that "continues to keep alive the hope that science can serve as a tool of persuasion, albeit a limited one, in a world with a multitude of values, knowledge perspectives, and criteria".[194] In addition, criticism to the effect that socio-legal research lacked critical "bite" has been met by an open orientation towards progressive scholarship, which tackles social relations of domination and oppression.[195]

A related charge, emanating in particular from adherents of CLS, was that the empirical studies associated with the law and society movement did not adequately deploy or develop theory.[196] A considerable tranche of critical-

---

[191] G.E. White, "From Realism to Critical Legal Studies: A Truncated Intellectual History" (1986) 40 *Southwestern Law Journal* 819 at 835.

[192] See D. Trubek, "Critical Legal Studies and Empiricism" and A. Sarat and S. Silbey, "Critical Traditions in Law and Society Research" (1987) 21 *Law and Society Review* 165.

[193] While the label "critical empirical" has been attached to the most recent wave of socio-legal work, John Brigham points out that it does not reflect the "aspiration to transcend the polarities that designation entails": "The Constitution of Interests: Institutionalism, CLS and New Approaches to Sociolegal Studies" (1998) 10 *Yale Journal of Law and the Humanities* 421 at 431.

[194] A. Sarat, "Off to Meet the Wizard: Beyond Validity and Reliability in the Search for a Post-Empiricist Sociology of Law" (1990) 15 *Law and Social Inquiry* 155 at 165.

[195] See for example D. Trubek and J. Esser, "Critical Empiricism in American Legal Studies: Paradox, Program, or Pandora's Box?" (1987) 14 *Law and Social Inquiry* 3. For further discussion see "Review Section Debate" (1990) 15 *Law and Social Inquiry* 135–80.

[196] See discussion by D. Trubek, "Critical Legal Studies and Empiricism". See also M.

empirical work is now informed by a constitutive theory of social action, which holds that law is not just influenced by society nor does society simply passively receive law. The legal and the social are mutually constituted.[197] Patricia Ewick and Susan Silbey, for example, suggest that "[l]egality is an emergent feature of social relations rather than an external apparatus acting upon social life. As a constituent of social interaction, the law—or what we will call legality—embodies the diversity of the situations out of which it emerges and that it helps structure."[198]

There is clear rejection of functional perspectives, which depending on the underlying politics, tend to conceive of law as either managing evolving social needs or as an instrument that serves the interests of powerful elites.[199] Instead, what emerges is theory aimed at illustrating "law's effects" as opposed to its "effectiveness", taking research beyond instrumental "law and social change" type studies or the judicial behavioural work associated with legal realism.[200]

Constitutive theory draws on a range of socio-legal and critical legal scholarship. The perception that law's subjects are constituted and not just recognised is traceable to the work on legal forms carried out by Pashukanis, Edelman and other writers in the Marxist tradition. These writers believed that law can have a robust impact not only through the material effects of its official orders but also through the ideological or symbolic effects of its language and form. Frank Munger attributes the re-emergence of constitutive theory to Michel Foucault's insight that power is diffuse.[201] A related commitment to legal

---

Galanter and M. Edwards, "Introduction: The Path of the Law Ands" (1997) *Wisconsin Law Review* 375 at 383: "At the risk of overgeneralizing, we would say that law and society scholars tend to be less enthralled by comprehensive theory, more willing to muddle through with partial theories, and less persuaded that theory can yield up unambiguous prescriptions for policy."

[197] "Constitutive work in sociolegal scholarship looks at the way relations among people are formed by or with reference to law." J. Brigham, *op. cit.*, at 422. See also M. McCann, *Rights at Work: Pay Equity Reform and the Politics of Legal Mobilization* (University of Chicago Press, Chicago, 1994); C. Harrington and B. Yngvesson, "Interpretative Sociolegal Research" (1990) 15 *Law and Social Inquiry* 135; J. Nice, "Equal Protection's Antinomies and the Promise of a Co-Constitutive Approach" (2000) 85 *Cornell Law Review* 1392; and P. Ewick and S. Silbey, *The Common Place of Law*.

[198] P. Ewick, and S. Silbey, *The Common Place of Law*, p.17.

[199] See generally R.W. Gordon, *op. cit.*

[200] For a discussion of the difference between law's effects as opposed to law's effectiveness, see A. Sarat, "Pain, Powerlessness and the Promises of Interdisciplinary Legal Scholarship: An Idiosyncratic, Autobiographical Account of Conflict and Continuity" (2000) 18 *Windsor Yearbook of Access to Justice* 187.

[201] F. Munger, *op. cit.*, at 101–105 (describing the initial turn to constitutive theory and the more recent emphasis on the mutual interaction between legal and non-legal spheres).

pluralism is also in evidence. For example, Alan Hunt notes how constitutive theory focuses "on the way in which law is implicated in social practices, as an always potentially present dimension of social relations, while at the same time reminding us that law is itself the product of the play and struggle of social relations".[202]

Because law is not an institutional apparatus that stands outside society but is part of the fabric of social relations much empirical research is committed to exploring the use of law in everyday concrete social practices outside the courtroom. Following Bourdieu, emphasis is placed on the routine instead of the exceptional. For example, in his studies of how citizens mobilise the law, Michael McCann demonstrates that legal norms are given new meanings in contexts outside official state forums. Rights discourse is not the exclusive preserve of lawyers but also provides a "compelling normative language" for union officials and activists in negotiations of improved working conditions.[203] Ewick and Silbey explored the meaning of law by analysing open-ended interviews with adults who discussed their home, work, and community problems.[204] William Felstiner and Austin Sarat sat in on consultations between divorce lawyers and their clients in order to discover how attorneys explained the law and the legal system to lay people.[205] Law was typically described as arbitrary and judges as motivated by many factors other than a concern with "doing" justice. These observations led Sarat and Felstiner to speculate that through expressing "cynicism and pessimism about legal actors and processes" lawyers sought to "control clients and maintain professional authority".[206] By presenting themselves as experts not on the law, but "on local knowledge, insider access, connections, and reputation, lawyers often suggest that their most important contribution is knowledge of the ropes, not knowledge of the rules. They describe a system that is not bureaucratically rational but is, nonetheless, accessible to its 'priests'."[207]

Meanwhile the operation of courts is generally looked at from the perspective of participants. As McCann explains this stance inverts the top-down approach associated with studies of legal doctrine by focusing on

---

[202] A. Hunt, *Explorations in Law and Society*, p.3.

[203] M. McCann, *op. cit.*, pp.60–61. There are clear parallels here with the work on rights conducted by some critical race and feminist theorists; see for example P. Williams, "Alchemical Notes: Reconstructing Ideals from Deconstructed Rights" (1987) 22 *Harvard Civil Rights-Civil Liberties Law Review* 401.

[204] P. Ewick and S. Silbey, *The Common Place of Law*.

[205] A. Sarat and W. Felstiner, "Lawyers and Legal Consciousness: Law Talk in the Divorce Lawyer's Office" (1989) 98 *Yale Law Journal* 1663.

[206] *ibid.*, at 1665.

[207] *ibid.*, at 1685.

"bottom-up jurisprudence".[208] It has been used to illustrate how legal concepts and processes often "reframe" disputes in narrow and confining ways and may sometime force particular understandings of problems or problematic identities on claimants.[209] Such an approach could be seen as exploring the ideological implications of legal pluralism, which was somewhat underplayed in previous law and society work. It potentially disrupts the conventional account of a source-based hierarchy of laws, thereby giving credence to silenced or repressed normative discourse.[210]

Constitutive social theory aims to overcome the structure/agency dichotomy and, in so doing, draws on Bourdieu's work. However, a potential problem is that, by focusing on the legal consciousness and practices of various parties, the social structures at play, so central to Bourdieu's social theory, recede into the background.[211] As with all positions derived from legal pluralism the de-centering of state apparatus can minimise the effects of state power as expressed through law. John Brigham cautions that "[w]hile we should include the margins of society to understand the full effects of state law, they should not constrain research into the constitutive dimension of law".[212] He is keen to stress that the constitutive approach does not endorse a slide into cultural relativism that ignores law's "material" dimensions. Likewise, Merry argues that a Weberian emphasis on how social phenomena are created and imbued with meaning through human interaction is compatible with investigations of the mechanisms that shape these phenomena. The key is to foreground power relations that continually imbue some actors with an ability to influence and control various social institutions.[213]

It is submitted that a constitutive approach mandates that attention be also paid to legal doctrine for only then can we examine "the way 'society' is produced *within* 'law'".[214] While CLS engages largely in critical doctrinal work, socio-legal researchers remain committed to empirical work, which may encompass legal doctrine but refuses to accord it prominence. Robert Gordon, an advocate of constitutive approaches, underscores the importance of doctrinal

---

[208] M. McCann, *op. cit.*, p.21.

[209] See for example L. Mather and B. Yngvesson, "Language, Audience and the Transformation of Disputes" (1980–81) 15 *Law and Society Review* 775.

[210] "Legal pluralism rediscovers the subversive power of suppressed discourses." G. Teubner, "The Two Faces of Janus: Rethinking Legal Pluralism" (1992) 13 *Cardozo Law Review* 1443 at 1443.

[211] See J. Handler, "Postmodernism, Protest and the New Social Movements" (1992) 26 *Law and Society Review* 697.

[212] J. Brigham, *op. cit.*, at 452.

[213] S.E. Merry, *Legal Consciousness*, pp.110–111.

[214] *Per* D. Nelken, "Beyond the Study of 'Law and Society'" (1986) *American Bar Foundation Journal* 323 at 325.

work because these "mandarin materials", as he terms them, are "an exceptionally refined and concentrated version of legal consciousness".[215] One of the most prolific writers in the field, Roger Cotterrell, has also persistently argued that socio-legal research should be directed at legal doctrine and reasoning.[216]

A useful subject for any such engagement might be the manner in which courts prove "social facts".[217] Whereas adjudicative facts concern the parties to a case, social or "legislative" facts relate to the general social and economic climate.[218] Evidence of such contextual matters finds its way into adjudicative processes through a variety of routes.[219] From a constitutive perspective the reception of *amicus curaie* briefs[220] produced by various interest groups might merit especial attention because they frequently draw upon experiential knowledge as opposed to that of professional "experts".[221] There are immediate apparent differences between the extent to which various legal systems are

---

[215] R.W. Gordon, *op. cit.*, at 120.

[216] Cotterrell argues that by making such a move "sociolegal studies would not merely be juxtaposed with traditional legal scholarship but would invade it and begin to reshape it in ways that renewed its vital engagement with the currents of change in society that social scientists studied". "Subverting Orthodoxy, Making Law Central: A View of Sociolegal Studies" (2002) 29 *Journal of Law and Society* 632 at 634.

[217] As David Nelken observes, much socio-legal work has tended to either "transform legal definitions into sociological categories" or "translate sociological insights into legal categories": "Blinding Insights?" at 408. The suggestion here is that constitutive scholars seek to transcend these approaches.

[218] On the distinction between adjudicative and legislative facts, see K. Davis, "Judicial Notice" (1955) 55 *Columbia Law Review* 945.

[219] See C. Boyle and M. MacCrimmon, "To Serve the Cause of Justice: Disciplining Fact Determination" (2001) 20 *Windsor Yearbook of Access to Justice* 55.

[220] Traditionally an *amicus curiae* ("friend of the court") was a supposedly impartial bystander whose expertise was called upon to assist courts in their deliberations, a position which continues to represent third party participation in Irish litigation. But courts in other countries now admit briefs that advocate particular interests; see G. Whyte, *Social Inclusion and the Legal System: Public Interest Law in Ireland* (Institute of Public Administration, Dublin, 2002), pp.97–99. With respect to the US, see J. Kearney and T. Merrill, "The Influence of Amicus Curiae Briefs on the Supreme Court" (2000) 148 *University of Pennsylvania Law Review* 743. For the UK position and comparative material, see Justice/Public Law Project, *A Matter of Public Interest: Reforming the Law and Practice on Interventions in Public Interest Cases* (Justice, London, 1996). On the Australian position, see G. Williams, "The Amicus Curiae and Intervener in the High Court of Australia: A Comparative Analysis" (2000) 28 *Federal Law Review* 365.

[221] As discussed in the conclusion to this chapter sociology of law ought to be sufficiently reflexive to question the place of experiential knowledge in academic scholarship.

prepared to admit and employ the arguments advanced in such briefs. Comparative studies of these practices may be a window onto the legal culture prevalent in any given jurisdiction and in particular on the phenomenon of legal closure.[222] Thus, the dearth of third party intervention in Irish public interest litigation might help explain the formalism that continues to permeate judicial decision-making in that sphere.[223] While legal decision-making in Ireland may appear to exhibit a high degree of closure towards experiential knowledge, courts in other jurisdictions are moving increasingly in directions which accept that social context should be the pre-eminent approach to legal interpretation and, in so doing, place considerable emphasis on the insights generated by social groups.[224] Such a focus might help narrow the gap Edward Rubin identifies between social movement literature and legal scholarship.[225]

Moreover, unless doctrine is "brought back in" socio-legal research will confine its audience to social scientists and policy-makers.[226] Lawyers will tend to regard such scholarship as irrelevant or at best marginal to their understandings of law. More recently, academic journals contain examples of critical doctrinal work informed by a constitutive approach. Julie Nice's examination of US equal protection jurisprudence is an interesting example.[227]

5. CONCLUSION

Authors of key texts in the field disagree as to most fruitful institutional path for the sociology of law. Cotterrell, for example, draws attention to the dangers

---

[222] David Feldman undertakes a comparative study of public interest litigation in order to shed light on the various political theories prevalent in any given polity: "Public Interest Litigation and Constitutional Theory in Comparative Perspective" (1992) 55 *Modern Law Review* 1.

[223] See J. Baker, K. Lynch, S. Cantillon and J. Walsh, *op. cit.*, chap.7. On the nature of public interest litigation, see A. Chayes, "The Role of the Judge in Public Law Litigation" (1976) 89 *Harvard Law Review* 1281.

[224] On the Canadian courts, for example, see S. Sugunasiri, "Contextualism: The Supreme Court's New Standard of Judicial Analysis and Accountability" (1999) 22 *Dalhousie Law Journal* 126.

[225] E.L. Rubin, "Passing Through the Door: Social Movement Literature and Legal Scholarship" (2001) 150 *University of Pennsylvania Law Review* 1. For an account of the different forms of law utilised by US social movements, see J. Brigham, "Rights, Rage and Remedy: Forms of Law in Movement Practice" (1987) 2 *Studies in American Political Development* 30.

[226] As we have seen, many central figures in early sociology of law engaged in doctrinal work.

[227] J. Nice, "Equal Protection's Antinomies and the Promise of a Co-Constitutive Approach" (2000) 85 *Cornell Law Review* 1392.

of "compartmentalisation" which might flow from attempts to establish it as a distinct sub-discipline within academia.[228] Reza Banakar and Max Travers, in contrast, conclude their recent volume by arguing that the sociology of law will best develop as a sub-field of mainstream sociology, thereby facilitating necessary engagement with mainstream theoretical and methodological debates.[229]

For a variety of reasons, including law's institutional strength and the imperative of legal professional training, law and sociology "remain frustratingly apart" within the academy.[230] Perhaps because the construction of a field is not simply a matter of cooperation but a process that is fuelled by conflict and competition,[231] the tendency has been for one or another discipline (usually the law) to take precedence. Establishment of *interdisciplinary* research centres along with undergraduate and postgraduate courses, which provide training in law, sociology and their respective methodologies, are essential to further development of any meaningful synthesis between the disciplines. The promise of interdisciplinary scholarship is that it can supply "tools of understanding" from several different traditions and so transcend the inevitable partiality of particular fields.[232] Interdisciplinarity involves the *integration* of methods and theories from various disciplines as opposed to multi-disciplinary approaches, which tend to simply *juxtapose* traditions.

Debates on the prospects for sociology of law have tended to pivot on the relationships between disciplines within the academy. However, for those who believe—as Marx did—that theoretical writing can, and should, contribute to progressive social change, discussions must also address the relationship

---

[228] R. Cotterrell, *The Sociology of Law*, pp.7–8.

[229] R. Banakar and M. Travers, "Conclusion: Law and Sociology" in *An Introduction to Law and Social Theory*, p.349.

[230] *Per* R. Banakar and M. Travers, "Introduction" in *An Introduction to Law and Social Theory*, p.1. On unsuccessful efforts to integrate social sciences into the law school curricula at several US universities during the early twentieth century, see C. Tomlins, "Framing the Field of Law's Disciplinary Encounters: A Historical Narrative" (2000) 34 *Law and Society Review* 911 and B. Garth and J. Sterling, *op. cit.*

[231] See P. Bourdieu and J. Passeron, *Reproduction in Education, Society and Culture* (R. Nice trans., SAGE, London, 1977).

[232] According to Jack Balkin academic disciplines equip people with useful but limited tools of understanding: "A tool opens up the world to the person who uses it. Yet, it opens up the world in a particular way. The world begins to resemble and seems to be organized around the intellectual tools that lay to hand. As the saying goes, when all that you have is a hammer, everything starts to look like a nail"; "Interdisciplinarity as Colonization" (1996) 53 *Washington and Lee Law Review* 949 at 955.

between the universities and civil society.[233] The normative implications of pluralist and constitutive socio-legal scholarship, in particular, are immense: law both is and *ought to be* wider than that body of doctrine produced by the legal interpretive community (including academics and practitioners). Universities certainly engage in rigorous boundary maintenance procedures within and between disciplines, but they also control what is defined as academic knowledge and what is not.[234] The role of knowledge production within the academy has been problematised by activists and theorists with links to specific social movements. In particular research about marginalised groups can reproduce unequal power relations.[235] Ownership and control of stories of oppression can further add to that oppression as it means that there are now people who can claim to know and understand you better than you understand yourself; there are experts there to interpret your world and to speak on your behalf. Academic knowledge makes an important contribution to human understanding but the perspective offered is necessarily limited. Experiential knowledge—"knowing a person or thing through sustained acquaintance"—provides quite a different perspective on the world.[236] For example, the meaning of poverty as it is understood and acted upon at policy level is as researchers have defined it, not as poor people see it.[237] According to Bourdieu there is no easy resolution to these difficulties. He proposes a radical, ongoing reflexivity wherein one prepares "the conditions for a critical knowledge of the limits of knowledge which is the precondition for true knowledge".[238] Socio-legal scholarship might strive to meet these aspirations through increased collaboration with the communities it writes about.

---

[233] See generally J. Baker, K. Lynch, S. Cantillon and J. Walsh, *op. cit.*, chap.9.

[234] See for example P. Bourdieu and J. Passeron, *op. cit.*

[235] See for example, M. Oliver, "Changing the Social Relations of Research Production" (1992) 7 *Disability, Handicap and Society* 1011 and K. Lynch, "Equality Studies, the Academy and the Role of Research in Emancipatory Social Change" (1999) 30 *Economic and Social Review* 41.

[236] J. Heron, "Philosophical Basis for a New Paradigm" in *Human Inquiry: A Sourcebook of New Paradigm Research* (P. Reason and J. Rowan eds., John Wiley and Sons, Chichester, 1981), p.27.

[237] C. O'Neill, *Telling It Like It Is* (Combat Poverty Agency, Dublin, 1992).

[238] P. Bourdieu, *Sociology in Question*, p.45.

Chapter 8

AMERICAN LEGAL REALISM

J. PAUL McCUTCHEON

1. Introduction

For the first half of the twentieth century legal realism occupied a commanding position in American legal thought. However, it could not be said that legal realism rested on a coherent philosophical foundation. Instead the body of thought that came to be recognised as legal realism was associated with the writings of a number of legal scholars and jurists, the most prominent contributors being Oliver Wendell Holmes, John Chipman Gray, Herman Oliphant, Underhill Moore, Karl Llewellyn and Jerome Frank.

A principal feature of legal realism was the rejection of the black letter formalism that characterised nineteenth-century legal thinking and that still exercises a considerable influence over legal scholarship and practice. In particular, the realists abandoned the view that authoritative legal materials—in the form of binding judicial decisions, statutes and constitutions—and the established methods of legal reasoning could provide a uniquely correct solution to any legal problem. From the formalist perspective the judge could be seen principally as a form of rule technician whose skill lies in his or her ability to master legal materials and to apply the appropriate methodology. Viewed thus, the judicial function is to identify the legal rules to be applied to the facts of the case, a process that would yield a definitive outcome.

Legal realism was sceptical of the formalist claim, or at least of the foregoing caricatured version. The realists were concerned with law as it operated in reality, which from their standpoint meant how the law was interpreted and applied by courts. Having inherited the common law it was understandable that the judicial role would occupy a central place in American realist theories. Given the federal character of the American system there were as many different versions of the common law as there were jurisdictions. The variety of rules applied across the nation indicated that legal outcomes were not inevitable but resulted from choices made by judges who, in any event, adopted a more flexible attitude to *stare decisis* than their counterparts elsewhere in the common law world. Moreover, the power of the courts to annul statutes on the grounds of incompatibility with the Constitution introduced a more obviously political dimension into judicial decision making: for example, the striking down of

1930s "New Deal" laws by the US Supreme Court raised questions both about the juridical basis for the decisions and their effects. Cumulatively these features prompted realists' scepticism and stimulated the search for new answers.

The central unifying claim of realism was that legal rules were indeterminate and that the law as articulated in so-called authoritative sources (the law in the books) did not determine judges' decisions (the law in action). Instead, a wide range of social, political and economic factors that cannot be accounted for by the traditional formalist perspective shaped decisions. The interest of the realists, therefore, was to identify and evaluate the real factors that shaped judicial decisions. Two consequences would flow from this approach. The first was that it would allow for a more accurate prediction of legal outcomes. Second, it would make explicit the real but hidden factors that lie behind the veneer of conventional judicial reasoning.

The origins of American legal realism lie in the works of Oliver Wendell Holmes (1841–1935), a prominent scholar and judge of the US Supreme Court. Holmes wrote that

> "the life of the law has not been logic, it has been experience. The felt necessities of the time, the prevalent moral and political theories, intuitions of public policy, avowed or unconscious, even the prejudices which judges share with their fellow men, have a good deal more to do than the syllogism in determining the rules by which men should be governed. The law embodies the story of a nation's development through many centuries and it cannot be dealt with as if it contained only the axioms and corollaries of a book of mathematics."[1]

Holmes disavowed the ability of general legal propositions to determine the outcomes of cases. He acknowledged that non-legal factors "are the secret root from which the law draws the juices of life" and argued that "the growth of the law is legislative". Holmes urged that we view law from the perspective of the Bad Man. The Bad Man is a hypothetical amoral individual, untroubled by ideas of right and wrong but who seeks assiduously to avoid the unpleasant consequences associated with breaching the law:

> "[I]f we take the view of our friend the bad man we shall see that he does not care two straws for the axioms or deductions, but that he does want to know what the Massachusetts or English courts are likely to do in fact. I am very much of his mind. The prophesies of what the courts do in fact, and nothing more pretentious, are what I mean by the law."[2]

---

[1] O.W. Holmes, *The Common Law* (Little Brown, Boston, 1881), p.1.
[2] O.W. Holmes, "The Path of the Law" (1897) 10 *Harvard Law Review* 457 at 460–461.

Holmes' point was not that the Bad Man should be adopted as an exemplar: rather it was that law should be evaluated from the perspective of a person who is concerned with predicting the consequences of his or her actions. In other words, his analysis of law was descriptive rather than normative, being concerned with what the law is and not how it ought to be.

Like Holmes, John Chipman Gray (1839–1915) focused on the operation of courts. He wrote that the law "is composed of the rules which the courts ... lay down for the determination of legal rights and duties".[3] In his view the law was what courts decide and anything else is merely a source of law: until a court applies a statute or other source it is not law. This is to give an artificially restrictive meaning to "law" but Gray's purpose was to emphasise the legislative dimension to adjudication by denying a source its existence as law until the judge has spoken. Given the wide range of sources of law available to a judge it is inevitable that he or she is forced to make a choice and in so doing will take account of policy factors. In this respect it can be said that nothing is definitively lawful or unlawful until the judge has decided the case.

In this chapter we will examine the sceptical nature of realism and realist views concerning the predictability of judicial decisions. We will then consider the particularly significant contribution of one realist writer, Karl Llewellyn, and also offer an overview of the impact and legacy of the movement generally.

2. THE SCEPTICAL NATURE OF REALISM

American realism's rejection of legal formalism was based on a general scepticism of the ability of the latter to account for the real operation of the law. In the main, realists' scepticism was directed against the claim that rules could provide definitive solutions to cases. In their view the dominant feature of law was its uncertain and indeterminate nature. This feature was the product of several factors. There was such a vast array of inconsistent and typically conflicting decisions that a precedent could be found for virtually any legal proposition. This was exacerbated by the variety of techniques employed to determine the actual propositions for which a decision is said to be authoritative. Moreover, even apparently definitive legal authorities such as statutes are revealed as being inherently uncertain when read against the different canons of interpretation employed by courts. When viewed in this light it is hardly surprising that legal rules could not be considered to provide definitive right answers.

Jerome Frank (1889–1957), a US federal judge, went further. He identified two forms of scepticism, namely rule scepticism and fact scepticism. Rule

---

[3] J.C. Gray, *The Nature and Sources of the Law* [1909] (Dartmouth, Aldershot, 1997), p.54.

scepticism, he argued, principally focused on rules as formally articulated: the assertion was that the law as represented in judicial decisions and statutes could not properly be relied on in predicting decisions. The challenge for rule sceptics was to identify the real factors that influenced judicial determinations, thus making the law more predictable and, therefore, more certain. However, in their efforts to predict legal outcomes, rule sceptics assumed that the facts of a case were as given.

Fact scepticism rejected the latter assumption and concentrated on the uncertainty of the facts of any case. In the view of fact sceptics, even if the rules were certain, it would still be impossible to predict the outcome of a decision because of factual uncertainty. In particular, the unreliability of witnesses and the prejudices of fact finders were identified as contributing to this state of affairs.

Frank was the principal adherent of fact scepticism. The difference between the two groups of sceptics, Frank observed, lay in the target of their enquiries. In the main, rule sceptics concentrated on appellate decisions where the facts of the case have been already determined by the trial court with the appellate court being charged with the task of making a legal determination. In contrast, fact sceptics by and large concentrated on the activities of trial courts where factual disputes are more likely to arise: indeed it is safe to conclude that most first instance disputes raise factual rather than legal issues. Moreover, Frank contended that it is impossible to disentangle rules from the facts of the case: "no rule can be hermetically sealed against the intrusion of false or inaccurate oral testimony which the trial judge or jury may believe". It followed that efforts to identify patterns in judicial behaviour were doomed to failure.

The consequences of Frank's fact scepticism are stark. He rejected the idea that there could be any certainty in the law. Apart from the fact that it would be virtually impossible to accommodate a full and accurate set of biases that influence judges and juries within a predictive model, he argued that in trials the law and fact become intertwined: both are at the centre of the adversarial struggle. In this environment cases are decided on very different grounds and with possibly sinister implications:

> "Many juries in reaching their verdicts act on their emotional response to lawyers and witnesses; they like or dislike, not any legal rule, but they do like an artful lawyer for the plaintiff, the poor widow, the brunette with soulful eyes, and they do dislike the big corporation, the Italian with a thick foreign accent. We do not have uniform jury-nullification of harsh rules; we have juries avoiding—often in ignorance of what they are so doing—excellent as well as bad rules, and in capricious fashion."[4]

---

[4] J. Frank, *Courts on Trial* (Princeton University Press, Princeton, 1949), p.130. See also J. Frank, *Law and the Modern Mind* (Brentano's, New York, 1930).

Frank's fact scepticism is at the extremes of legal realism and is shared by few theorists. However, his observations, no doubt shaped by his experience as a judge, will strike a chord with legal practitioners. The latter understand how difficult it is to predict the outcome of litigation and the prudent among them will couch any advice to clients with the appropriate qualification. They realise the uncertainties posed by the testimony of witnesses, the conflicts of evidence, the differences in expert opinion and the biases of judges and juries. In their view one of the attributes of successful advocacy is to "set up the case" by displaying a mastery of the facts that will convince the adjudicator. The realities of daily life in first instance courts notwithstanding, it is arguable that fact scepticism embraces the mundane and that its revelations are both obvious and banal.

3. PREDICTING JUDICIAL DECISIONS

The logic of fact scepticism is that it is impossible to predict legal outcomes, a stance bluntly acknowledged by Frank. In his view the personality of the judge is "the pivotal fact in law administration". His fellow fact sceptic Joseph Hutcheson, who coincidentally served as both a trial and appellate judge, declared that the key factor in reaching decisions "is an intuitive sense of what is right or wrong for that cause".[5]

In contrast, rule sceptics accepted that it was possible to identify patterns in judicial decisions. However, unlike formalists they denied that those patterns could be explained by the application of pre-existing rules or the conventions of *stare decisis*. Instead, the answers were to be found in a range of factors that existed beyond the formal rules. The challenge was to identify the crucial extra-legal factors that contributed to judicial uniformity with a view to enhancing predictability. In this enquiry what was significant was what judges did, not what they said they did: the non-vocal behaviour of the judge was of principal significance. The jurist was to adopt the stance of a scientist conducting an experiment, recording the stimuli that produce particular legal results.

By denying the importance of the conventional doctrinal approach, realists chose to ignore judicial reasoning and advocated an analysis of judicial response to certain fact situations. This study would identify patterns of judicial behaviour that could not be explained in terms of adherence of formal rules and would ultimately produce accurate predictive models. Paradoxically, in their concern with predictability and their enthusiasm for creating predictive models, realists

---

[5]   J. Hutcheson, "The Judicial Intuitive: The Function of 'Hunch' in Judicial Decision" (1929) 14 *Cornell Law Quarterly* 274 at 285.

shared an important concern with formalists, namely a yearning for legal certainty. As Neil Duxbury put it:

> "[T]he realist notion of predictivism as a science is founded on the idea that the aspiration is a worthy one. That is, predictivist-inspired realism treats as notionally desirable the facilitation of a formally certain, 'prediction-friendly' system of law. At the same time the general predictivist quest for legal certainty betrays an implicit fear of judicial discretion and incertitude. And it is thus that realism, certainly in its predictivist guise, appears to attempt to discredit one formalist conception of law only to replace it with another …".[6]

A truly comprehensive predictive model would incorporate every factor that might conceivably feature in the shaping of legal decisions. The full catalogue of relevant factors is potentially inexhaustible: it would include the personal characteristics and biographies of judges, prevailing social and economic conditions, policy concerns, political climate, moral perceptions, public opinion, the exigencies of effective government and much more. Given this range it was perhaps inevitable that the elaboration of a comprehensive predictive model would elude the realists. Instead their analyses tended to focus on the contexts in which judicial decisions were reached, from which they sought to derive guidance in predicting legal outcomes. As it happened the realists in the main concentrated on commercial law. Thus Herman Oliphant (1884–1939) examined a series of apparently conflicting decisions on the validity of contractual undertakings not to compete. He concluded that:

> "All the cases holding the promises invalid are found to be cases of employees' promises not to compete with their employers after a term of employment. Contemporary guild [*i.e.* trade union] regulations not noticed in the opinions made their holdings eminently sound. All the cases holding the promises valid were cases of promises made by those selling a business and promising not to compete with the purchasers. Contemporary economic reality made those holdings eminently sound."[7]

To the modern eye that observation seems unexceptional but the significance of Oliphant's analysis lay in the fact that by and large it overlooked the courts' reasoning and concentrated on the background facts, namely the different commercial contexts in which the contracts were made. Moreover, it will be

---

[6] N. Duxbury, *Patterns of American Jurisprudence* (Clarendon Press, Oxford, 1995), p.131.

[7] H. Oliphant, "A Return to *Stare Decisis*" (1928) 14 *American Bar Association Journal* 73 at 159–160.

noted that he observed that the decisions were "sound", coinciding with trade union regulations and good economic sense, respectively.

Other writers identified the significance of the socio-economic context in which decisions were reached. In a study of cases in which a buyer who rejected delivery of goods by formally stating his objections lost his right to make other objections, Karl Llewellyn concluded that the courts were "sensitive to commerce and decency". In some of the cases the application of the rule seemed harsh, especially where the buyer became aware of other defects after having rejected the goods. However, on closer scrutiny it appeared that the market for the particular goods had collapsed and the buyers in those cases were attempting to escape their obligations. Thus, by the apparently unjust application of the particular rule the courts ensured that commercial expectations were met. It was "the background facts, those of mercantile practice, those of the situation type" that determined the decisions.[8]

Underhill Moore saw the significance of decisions as lying in the context of institutional responses. He strove for an analysis that matched individual conduct against an institutional response. He attempted to establish what was normal behaviour for an institution, to demarcate deviations from the norm in quantitative terms and to identify the point at which a court will intervene to correct the deviation. His goal was a model that would allow one to predict accurately that a deviation of a certain amount will cause the courts to act.[9] Moore differed from other realists in that his institutional analysis moved beyond the latter's court-centred theories. In this respect Moore highlighted an important feature of the operation of the law that had hitherto been overlooked, namely that the application of the law is a function performed by a range of institutions and actors whose practices are as important as, and sometimes even more important than, judicial rulings in determining legal outcomes. Thus, in their different spheres the practices of administrative agencies and commercial bodies can be more influential in governing the behaviour of individuals than formal rules.

4. The Contribution of Karl Llewellyn

Karl Llewellyn (1893–1962) was the dominant figure in American legal realism. He began by sharing many of the insights of other realists, especially those who would later be identified as rule sceptics. He considered that legal rules bore little resemblance to the actual operation of the legal process. He distrusted

---

[8] See K. Llewellyn, *The Common Law Tradition* (Little Brown, Boston, 1960), pp.124–126.

[9] See U. Moore, "Rational Basis of Legal Institutions" (1923) 23 *Colombia Law Review* 609.

the view that "traditional prescriptive rule formulations are the heavily operative factor in producing court decisions".[10] Instead, he subscribed to the view that what "officials do about disputes is, to my mind, the law itself".[11]

Llewellyn's interests lay in the reality of judicial decision making and to this end the task would be to excavate the real factors that shape judicial opinions. He took the view that cases should be assembled into narrower categories than had previously been the case: the expression of the law in terms of general rules and principles distorts the true picture since, on close examination, apparent similarities will be revealed not to be so. Llewellyn acknowledged the legislative role of judges and in his view this feature of the judicial process was vital in ensuring that legal development kept pace with social change. He also contended that realists should be concerned with the impact of law on society and that decisions should be evaluated in terms of their effects.

Llewellyn moved beyond the critique of formalism and the consequential efforts to elaborate predictive models to produce an account of the broader functions of law. He argued that law was best viewed as a complex but necessary social institution consisting of rules, methodologies, "a body of pervasive and powerful ideals which are largely unspoken" and "men of law" who operate the legal system not with a free hand but circumscribed "by ideas and ideals somewhat controlled". A purpose lay behind the broad canvas he painted: "the wider view of rules in their setting yield rules both righter, and more effective". Like any other institution law was assigned certain functions, which he termed "law-jobs". He identified five categories of law-job:

"1. The disposition of trouble-cases: a wrong, a grievance, a dispute. This is garage-repair work or the going concern of society, with (as case-law shows) its continuous effect on the remaking of the order of that society.
2. The preventive channelling of conduct and expectations so as to avoid trouble, and together with it, the effective reorientation of conduct and expectations in similar fashion. This does not mean merely, for instance, new legislation; it is instead, what new legislation (among other things) is about, and is for.
3. The allocation of authority and the arrangement of procedures which mark action as being authoritative; which includes all of any constitution, and much more.
4. The positive side of law's work, seen as such, and seen not in detail,

---

[10] K. Llewellyn, "Some Realism about Realism: Responding to Dean Pound" (1931) 44 *Harvard Law Review* 1222 at 1237.

[11] K. Llewellyn, *The Bramble Bush* (Columbia University School of Law, New York, 1930), p.12.

but as a net whole: the net organization of the society as a whole so as to provide integration, direction, and incentive.

5. 'Juristic method', to use a single slogan to sum up the task of so handling and so building up effective traditions of handling, the legal material and tools and people developed for the other jobs—to the end that those materials and tools and people are kept doing their law-jobs, and doing them better, until they become a source of revelation of new possibility and achievement."[12]

Cumulatively the performance of law-jobs serves two purposes. The first is a "bare bones aspect" that involves maintaining societal survival and cohesion, which is performed by the first three law-jobs. Secondly, the fourth and fifth law-jobs strive towards efficient operation and the realisation of "man's aspirations". Llewellyn saw law-jobs as being common to all developed legal systems. He even identified the first law-job, the deciding of trouble cases, as featuring in autochthonous systems.[13] However, in seeking to present law-jobs as being universal Llewellyn was forced to rely on levels of abstraction that border on the metaphysical. Moreover, his analysis lacked an account of how the various law-jobs interacted.

Despite his scepticism, a belief in predictability of judicial decisions was a recurring theme in Llewellyn's work. He argued that there is a high degree of predictability, or "reckonability" as he termed it, in judicial decisions, a phenomenon that he attributed to the traditions of the common law. Llewellyn identified a "cluster of factors" that tend to ensure uniformity in decision making. He enumerated 14 such factors including the existence of "law conditioned officials", trained and experienced lawyers, the presence of legal doctrine and known doctrinal techniques, the tradition of there being a right answer, the existence of written opinions, the adversarial method and judicial professionalism. However, Llewellyn did not assign any relative weight to the different factors nor did he explain how they ensured predictability. In fact, they are observations that might be made by any seasoned student of the common law.

Llewellyn also stressed the importance of the "period styles" that are employed by the courts and identified two such styles. One he called the "Grand Style" and the other the "Formal Style". As he presented it, the Grand Style is characterised by the testing of precedents against three types of reason: the reputation of the judge who delivered the judgment; principle, meaning "a

---

[12] K. Llewellyn, *My Philosophy of Law* (Boston Law Co., Boston, 1941), p.185. See also K. Llewellyn, "The Normative, the Legal and the Law-jobs: The Problems of Juristic Method" (1940) 49 *Yale Law Journal* 1355.

[13] See K. Llewellyn and E. Hoebel, *The Cheyenne Way* (University of Oklahoma Press, Norman, 1941).

broad generalization which must yield patent sense as well as order"; and policy, which involves a consideration of the potential consequences that might be associated with the rule under consideration. Legal development brought about in this manner remains in touch with the past and the Grand Style involves a "constant re-examination and reworking of a heritage". In Llewellyn's opinion the Grand Style maximised predictability: "[it] is the best device ever invented by man for drying up that free-flowing spring of uncertainty, conflict between the seeming commands of the authorities and the felt demands of justice". In contrast, the key features of the Formal Style are the belief that rules of law decide cases and that policy is properly a matter for the legislature not the courts, coupled with a general resistance to change even the common law. Llewellyn contended these styles manifest themselves at different times in legal history but his preference for the Grand Style is clear from the tone in which he presents the two models.[14]

It seems that Llewellyn had abandoned the radicalism associated with the sceptical origins of legal realism. His later work shows a greater respect for the common law tradition than is evident in the sceptical strand of realist opinion. His elucidation of the factors that support predictability and his acceptance of the significance of judicial professionalism seem to reflect little more than lawyers' shared understanding of the operation of a common law system: to an extent, any reasonably experienced common lawyer might have made the same observations. But in a different sense that relating of the ordinary is perhaps Llewellyn's strength: he presents a picture of law that reflects reality as understood by everyday practitioners and judges. In doing so he interred the idea that absolute certainty could be achieved and the diametrically opposed belief that the law is entirely unpredictable. In his final work, *The Common Law Tradition* (1960), he contended that the law displays a high degree of uniformity and that results could be predicted with a reasonable measure of accuracy.[15]

5. REALISM EVALUATED

Legal realism was severely criticised from a variety of theoretical standpoints in the middle decades of the twentieth century. Realist theories were considered to challenge the legitimacy of the law in their abandonment of the belief that the law rested on fundamental principles. Observers of a conservative bent associated the realists' support for the New Deal legislative programme with a preference for unlimited state power. In addition, some critics saw danger

---

[14] See K. Llewellyn, *The Common Law Tradition*, pp.35 *et seq.*
[15] See generally W. Twining, *Karl Llewellyn and the Realist Movement* (Weidenfeld and Nicolson, London, 1973).

lurking in realism's disentanglement of law from moral considerations. The rejection of the formalist conception of immutable principles of justice in favour of an instrumentalist view of law as a means to achieving social goals was seen by some as laying the foundation for the abuse of law that was evident in totalitarian regimes.

H.L.A. Hart articulated the positivist objections to realism, or at least the version of realism that holds that the "law consists simply of the decisions of the courts and the prediction of them". He argued that the realist approach adopts an external perspective, ignoring the internal aspect of rules that was vital to Hart's own theory. He also contended that realism did not provide an adequate explanation of the criterion of legality. If law is what the courts do it must be because there is some secondary rule that stipulates that the action of the courts should be recognised as having that effect. Moreover, he suggested that realism failed to account for the phenomenon of legal error and in this it tended to confuse finality with infallibility. A court might have the ultimate say but it is still possible to observe that its judgment was wrong, a conclusion that can only be made by reference to some pre-exiting rule against which the court's decision is measured.[16]

Ronald Dworkin, adopting a very different perspective to Hart, attacked pragmatic theories of law, into which category he lumped realism and the economic analysis of law advanced by more recent writers such as Guido Calabresi and Richard Posner. According to Dworkin pragmatic theories deny that past rulings can provide any justification for a decision and instead seek authority in some "other contemporary virtue" such as justice or efficiency. This stance contrasts with Dworkin's own view of adjudication, the central tenet of which is that courts act on principles rather than policies, the latter being the preserve of the legislature. He argues that pragmatism fails to account for the actuality of judicial practice, that judges recognise and act on legal rights and principles and seek to fit their rulings within a body of past decisions.[17]

Much of foregoing criticism is directed at a caricature of realism. This is especially evident in Dworkin's cruel remark that realism consisted of "silly semantic claims" and that it presented an "unnecessary exaggeration of facts about legal practice better described in a less heated way". Many of the extreme opinions attributed to realists were not uttered by them: realists did not claim

---

[16] See H.L.A. Hart, *The Concept of Law* (2nd ed., Clarendon Press, Oxford, 1994), pp.136 *et seq*.

[17] See R. Dworkin, *Law's Empire* (Fontana, London, 1986), pp.151 *et seq*. On Dworkin's general theory, see Colin Harvey, "Talking about Human Rights" in this volume; on the economic analysis of law, see Alan Haugh, "Law and Economics" also in this volume.

that cases might be determined by such idiosyncratic factors as what the judge ate for breakfast. More importantly, they did not suggest that the revelation that decisions accounted for by factors outside the formal rules brings the legitimacy of the law into question or that judges usurped legislative power. Dworkin, Hart and others ignored Llewellyn's later work, outlined above, in which he essayed a broader formulation of the operation of law. As indicated, Llewellyn accepted that there is a high measure of predictability in judicial decisions and he acknowledged the role of legal doctrine and doctrinal techniques as contributing factors to that state of affairs. In this, of course, he retreated from the apparently radical origins of legal realism and returned to a position that would not unduly trouble traditional theorists.

The latter perhaps points to a more telling criticism of realism, namely that the movement failed to deliver on its early promise, that it offered a false dawn. From this perspective realism is said to have been intellectually lightweight and to have failed to alter either legal practice or legal education. It is pointed out that the manner in which lawyers and judges function and the way in which law students are educated have not changed to any great extent. In particular, realism did not bring about a marriage of law and the social sciences and it did not deliver on its most significant insight that law is political.[18] However, this criticism expects too much of realism. Unlike their successors in the Critical Legal Studies (CLS) movement, realists were not motivated by revolutionary desires or nihilistic impulses.[19] They did not question the core values of western liberal jurisprudence but were concerned to improve the quality of law and its administration. This feature often transcended their scholarly endeavours: Llewellyn was one of the architects of the Uniform Commercial Code while, in his judicial capacity, Holmes delivered important dissenting judgments supporting freedom of speech[20] and laws prescribing maximum hours of employment.[21]

Although legal realism might now seem to be a spent force, its intellectual contribution should not be denigrated. Its insights might seem commonplace but that can be taken as a measure of its impact on modern legal thought. Realists transformed the understanding of the relationship between law and society and they highlighted the instrumental nature of legal reasoning. Realist writers demonstrated that legal concepts are not determined by pre-existing natural categories but are socially constructed, that considerations of policy

---

[18] See L. Kalman, *Legal Realism at Yale 1927–1960* (University of North Carolina Press, Chapel Hill, 1986).

[19] See Gerard Quinn, "Critical Legal Studies" in this volume.

[20] *Abrams v United States* (1919) 250 U.S. 616.

[21] *Lochner v New York* (1905) 198 U.S. 45, in which Holmes famously declared (at 75) that "[t]he Fourteenth Amendment does not enact Mr Herbert Spencer's Social Statics".

are a prominent feature in legal decision making and that the law may properly be judged in terms of its social effects. Many of these observations are now taken for granted but, by bringing the perspective of practising lawyers and judges, realists liberated legal theory from the constraints of legal formalism.[22] Viewed in its historical context it becomes clear that realism effected a significant shift in the way law was perceived and it served as a stepping-stone to more recent bodies of thought such as critical legal studies, post-modernism and the economic analysis of law. Those very different theories have moved far beyond realism but their foundations were set by realist writers.

6. The Legacy of Realism

Over half a century has passed since the demise of realist theorising but realism has left its mark on the legal landscape. At one level (and notwithstanding the fact that realism did not engender any radical restructuring of legal education), this is evident in the law school curriculum with the range of "law and society" or "law in context" courses now on offer and an accompanying body of scholarly literature. Judges and practitioners are more willing to acknowledge policy arguments and to discuss rules in terms of their social impact. More generally, the modern acknowledgement of the political character of law and the role of judges can be seen as part of the legacy of realism.[23]

Realism has also given birth to distinctively American fields of enquiry, namely jurimetrics and judicial behaviouralism. Jurimetrics, a term coined by Lee Loevinger, seeks to employ data handling techniques perfected by the social sciences in legal analysis.[24] With the aid of computers it is believed that large-scale empirical studies of legal problems will reveal new insights and should improve predictability, the enduring concern of realist thinkers. However, as things currently stand computers cannot provide the methodological skills that are vital in legal reasoning. It might be that future generations of intelligent computers will make good this deficit but at present that is a matter better left to the speculations of science fiction.

Judicial behaviouralism marries the interest of legal realism in predictability

---

[22] See generally W.W. Fisher, M.J. Horowitz and T.A. Reed, *American Legal Realism* (Oxford University Press, Oxford, 1993) and W.E. Rumble, *American Legal Realism: Skepticism, Reform and the Judicial Process* (Cornell University Press, New York, 1968).

[23] In their different ways, a realist flavour can be discerned in works such as J.A.G. Griffith, *The Politics of the Judiciary* (5th ed., Fontana, London, 1997) and Paul Bartholomew, *The Irish Judiciary* (Institute of Public Administration, Dublin, 1971).

[24] L. Loevinger, "Jurimetrics—the Next Step Forward" (1949) 33 *Minnesota Law Review* 455.

with methodological techniques borrowed from the social sciences. Proponents of judicial behaviouralism tend to be political scientists rather than lawyers and they view judges as actors in a policy-making process in which legal rules have little weight: in a sense judges are taken to be no different from politicians, administrators or other formulators of policy. With the proper testing of hypotheses against empirical data it is believed that highly accurate predictive models of judicial behaviour can be constructed. While it may be possible to identify the full range of factors that shape judicial decisions it is quite another thing to conclude that their presence caused the judge to decide a case in a particular way. For example, judges from a particular socio-economic class might consistently deliver judgments in favour, say, of plaintiffs suing large financial institutions but this does not establish that they so rule because they were from that social background. Judicial behaviouralism ignores the normative dimension to law and adjudication: it overlooks the important fact that judges act, and believe they act, on the basis that the law governs their deliberations.

CHAPTER 9

LAW AS RECOGNITION: H.L.A. HART AND ANALYTICAL POSITIVISM

GEORGE PAVLAKOS

In memory of Stephen W. Livingstone (1960–2004)

1. INTRODUCTION

This chapter explores the extremely influential analytical legal positivism of
the English legal theorist, H.L.A. Hart (1907–1992). Before we turn to examine
Hart's ideas about law in depth it will prove helpful to set out the broad
intellectual context of his theory and to make explicit its methodological
assumptions. We will therefore first set out the distinction between two basic
types of legal positivism—namely, the positivism that considers that immoral
law is still law and the positivism that considers that law can be determined in
a context-independent way, by reference to a set of purely legal criteria. Whereas
theorists like Bentham and Austin fall into the first category, the positivism of
Hart, like that of the other great twentieth-century positivist, Hans Kelsen,
falls into the second.[1] We shall note, however, that Hart's positivism is
conventionalist as opposed to, as in Kelsen's case, epistemic.

Despite this difference, both Hart and Kelsen were analytical philosophers,
that is, they approached philosophical questions through an *analysis* of legal
meaning. This chapter will explore analytical jurisprudence and introduce a
further distinction as regards the approaches of Hart and Kelsen: the former
engaged primarily in conceptual analysis—studying the various instances of
the application of "law" and trying to make explicit the rules that guide speakers
in using it—whereas Kelsen's analytic approach employed transcendental
reasoning in order to reveal necessary conditions for something that is
uncontrovertibly the case.

It is against this general background that we will assess Hart's concept of

---

[1] The next chapter in this volume discusses the "pure theory of law" proposed by
Hans Kelsen (1881–1973).

law. His fresh approach to jurisprudence will be discussed with particular reference to his ideas concerning law and obligation, convention and authority, the nature of legal theory and the external and the internal aspects of rules. The chapter will conclude with a brief discussion of some criticisms of Hart's theory.

2. TYPES OF LEGAL POSITIVISM

Legal positivism is a doctrine about law's purity. The idea that lies at its core is that law's existence is independent of its moral quality or, as John Austin famously put it, that "the existence of law is one thing; its merit or demerit is another".[2] Although the separation of law and morality has consistently been a key feature of positivism throughout its intellectual history, it is far from self-evident to talk of one positivism only. Instead, it would be more accurate to talk of many positivisms for there has been a plethora of legal philosophies that have cast the idea of the separation of law and morality in different ways. That said, it is still possible to distinguish between two variants of the separation claim which allow a classification of positivist philosophies into two rough groups: the variant that accepts that *immoral law is still law* and the variant that considers that *law can be determined in a context-independent way, by reference to a set of purely legal criteria.*

The view that immoral law is still law is indeed the crudest expression of the positivist idea in that it advocates a radical separation between law and morality. Legal philosophies that adhere to it are largely reactions to the natural law doctrine that only morally sound rules deserve to be called law.[3] Historically, the reaction to this doctrine resulted from dissatisfaction with the kind of morality natural law theory assumed to be sufficient for law's legitimacy. Until the Enlightenment, natural law built the core of a code of legitimacy that served oligarchic forms of government. It often consisted of a corpus of moral imperatives that emerged from a background of, more or less, well-established theological beliefs. The Enlightenment, and subsequently the civic revolutions in America and France in the eighteenth century, challenged this code of legitimacy in at least two ways. On the political level, the proceduralist ideas of participatory democracy could not anymore be reconciled with the

---

[2] J. Austin, *The Province of Jurisprudence Determined* (Cambridge University Press, Cambridge, 1995), p.157.

[3] Notice that this natural law doctrine conceals two ideas that are prima facie contradictory: the radical, almost anarchist, idea that "whatever does not match my morals cannot be accepted as law", as well as the reverse, rather conservative, idea "that anything that is law can be deemed morally justified". See H.L.A. Hart, *Essays in Jurisprudence and Philosophy* (Clarendon Press, Oxford, 1983), p.53.

theological morality that justified the old regime. On the philosophical level, the Age of Reason decisively shifted the seat of morality from God to human rationality with a double effect: on the one hand, theological morality was divested of its universal character, as it was demonstrated that religious belief did not enjoy universal status; on the other hand, it was demonstrated that participatory institutions (*e.g.* parliament) were much better equipped for realising the demands of a new, secular morality, given that no objective morality of divine origin existed. What is more, legislation, as the outcome of parliamentary deliberation, was taken to embody perfectly the demands of the new, human-centred morality. On the face of it, any judgement of the kind "law X is immoral" is rendered inconsistent because it assumes the existence of an objective, self-standing morality whereas the only credible morality that exists is, in fact, the one embodied by the law.

These ideas are clearly discernible in the work of the nineteenth-century utilitarian jurists and political philosophers, Jeremy Bentham and John Austin. Morality, in this context, consists in the principle that those acts that bring about the "greatest happiness for the greatest number" are moral. This principle is directed at anyone who is making a practical judgement and, *a fortiori*, to the legislators who are expected to make laws that increase the overall amount of happiness. What is more, the discussion in the parliament is understood as the optimal process for maximising utility, through the exchange and scrutiny of argument in the context of parliamentary debate. It should not come as a surprise then that utilitarian jurists took statutory legislation to embody a strong presumption of (moral) correctness that should not be compromised by appeals to any obscure moral standards.

In contrast, twentieth-century analytical positivism seems to be best describable as falling under the second variant of the positivist credo of the separation of law and morals, that is, the variant that holds that law can be determined in a context-independent way, by reference to a set of purely legal criteria. This is the more modest idea that law can be determined independently of moral considerations. Once the belief in an independent objective divine morality weakens, the concern relating to it loses its edge. Morality ceased to be over and above societal institutions and, instead, was located at the same level as law, as resulting from the practices of a community. In fact most twentieth century legal philosophers, and certainly Hart and Kelsen, can happily live with the idea that law has to travel together with morality, for it is not a rare phenomenon in modern legal systems that the law explicitly refers to the moral standards of a society or, even, that it seeks legitimacy through them. This fact notwithstanding, there is a different concern that arises with respect to the relation of law and morality: in contrast to divine commands, secular morality is radically fragmented, indeterminate and dependant upon the contingent practices of a community and as such it cannot serve the purpose of a source of uniform normativity. On the other hand, a central function of law is to guarantee social cohesion by generating uniform standards of conduct for the members of a social group. Thus, unless law was kept distinct from morality, it would not be possible to fulfil that function and the ideal of a uniform normativity would have to be abandoned. On the face of it, legal philosophers in the twentieth century argued that it is possible to clearly identify law in a way that is free of moral considerations. As a result, such philosophers rested content with the belief that law is a more basic source of normativity than morality, for it could be determined on the basis of objective, uniform criteria without any need to refer to the latter. It is possible to distinguish two rough forms in which the positivist argument is cast in modern times.

The first is *conventionalism*. This is the form of positivism that pertains to Hart's thought.[4] Conventionalism says that law is the outcome of a social convention that is constitutive for the existence of law, in a similar way that the rules of a game (*e.g.* chess) are for the existence of the game. Admittedly, morality can equally be interpreted as emanating from conventional rules. However, there is a critical difference between morality and law. Law can be conceived of as emanating from a legal convention that is unique to each society. In contrast, sources of morality are many, even within the same community: different groups abide by different moral codes whose existence can be traced back to different conventions, conventions that derive from each group's values and experiences.[5] This is not the case with law, for part of the purpose of the constitutive convention that identifies it is to regulate behaviour in a uniform way. This purpose raises law over and above contingent forms of morality and renders it the most basic form of normativity within human societies. Along these lines, law can claim priority over other regulatory institutions while those need to adjust their regulatory content to the demands of law. A key concept within conventionalism is that of *authority*: the constitutive rules need to identify a law-making authority. Authority derives its legitimacy from the fact that it fulfils the regulatory purpose of law, by generating clearly identifiable norms that override all other normative (including moral) considerations. It is

---

[4] For a contemporary discussion of conventionalism, see A. Marmor, "Exclusive Legal Positivism" in *The Oxford Handbook of Jurisprudence and Philosophy of Law* (J. Coleman and J. Shapiro eds., Oxford University Press, Oxford, 2002), pp.104–124. Compare this with the discussion of conventionalism in the philosophy of science in Karl Popper, *The Logic of Scientific Discovery* (Routledge, London, 2002), pp.57 *et seq.*

[5] Andrei Marmor discusses the view that law is valid on the grounds of a social convention while morality is valid unconditionally, in virtue of its being grounded on universal principles of reason; *op. cit.* Setting aside the merits of such a view, it should be avoided as an interpretation of Hart's understanding of morality, for Hart explains moral rules as being embedded in concrete social practices.

assumed that in legislating the authority has already considered all other relevant normative reasons and, as a result, the addressees of the law are set free from the burden to deliberate themselves.[6]

The second form of contemporary positivism is *epistemic*, consisting in the belief that law forms an autonomous domain of knowledge that ought to be studied as a special *legal science*. The belief in the purity of legal science is interlaced with the idea that there are distinct legal facts (*e.g.* legal norms) that can be identified and studied in an objective way, akin to the way science studies the natural environment. Philosophically speaking, this idea may be underpinned in, roughly, two ways. The first is to say that law has a solid foot on observable social facts that form the building blocks of those social conventions and practices that are constitutive for law. In this version epistemic positivism dovetails with conventionalism. However, the jurisprudential theory that is most commonly associated with epistemic positivism is the one put forward in Hans Kelsen's *Pure Theory of Law* (*Reine Rechtslehre*) and is certainly incompatible with conventionalism. As will be discussed further in the next chapter of this volume, Kelsen insisted that law belongs irreducibly to the realm of normativity. He emphasised the fact that it is impossible to infer our knowledge about the law from the study of empirical facts, be they natural, social or psychological. Legal norms are intrinsically normative and for that reason legal science, to the extent that it wants to "discover" norms, must look for normative facts all the way through. Along these lines, he suggested that it is possible to switch into something like a "legal point of view" by referring to the most general legal norm (*Grundnorm*), one that cannot be perceived by our senses but merely presupposed logically. By switching into the legal point of view legal scientists activate a special "legal faculty" that enables them to

---

[6] This idea has been further developed by Joseph Raz who argues that legal rules are exclusionary reasons. See the first chapter in J. Raz, *Practical Reason and Norms* (Oxford University Press, Oxford, 1999). An exclusionary reason is a second-order reason in the sense that it refers to other reasons for action rather than being itself a reason for action. With respect to law, legal norms are taken to be reasons that prevent agents from considering other normative considerations. As mentioned in the text, the theory is underpinned by the idea that the relevant legislative authority has already considered all relevant reasons before issuing the norm, therefore citizens have a reason for not performing the deliberative process themselves. A central problem with this theory is that the exclusionary function of legal norms is in need of justification itself. One possibility is to say that the value of a uniform, certain and finite regulation overrides all other normative reasons. However, this justification weakens decisively the idea of exclusionary reasons for it renders it an empty formula: "whatever the authority decides is normatively required". If, on the other hand, additional normative considerations are drawn into the picture, then good reasons will always exist for challenging authoritative decisions.

"perceive" norms instead of scattered volitional facts (pertaining to the will of the legislating officials) or mere collections of movements (in the parliament, the courts, etc.).

If one wanted to pass a judgement regarding the grounds for the difference between conventionalism and epistemic positivism, one would most probably locate them in the disparities of the philosophical traditions they belong to: conventionalism falls within the tradition of British empiricism and utilitarianism, whereas Kelsen's positivism is clearly permeated by Immanuel Kant's transcendental philosophy. Despite differences in origin, however, both positivist trends share a common interest in philosophical analysis. To that extent, they can be classified as species of analytical positivism.

3. ANALYTICAL JURISPRUDENCE

The attribute "analytical" applies to philosophical theories that approach philosophical questions through an *analysis* of linguistic meaning. There is a plethora of such theories and any attempt to classify them would most definitely escape the limits of this chapter. In any event, two key ideas run through the various kinds of analytical philosophy. The first is that an analysis of meaning can reveal the nature of the object of the philosophical enquiry. This idea is coupled with the assumption that language is some kind of interface between minds and the environment (the world), hence, by mastering linguistic meaning one can make contact with the world. The second idea is that the analysis of meaning has to attend to the ways language is actually used by competent speakers. This second thesis is especially associated with a particular stream of analytical philosophy, the so-called ordinary language philosophy. Although ordinary language philosophy is not synonymous with analytical philosophy, for the purposes of the present discussion we will assume so. Two reasons may be given for this simplification: first, ordinary language philosophy is the most influential school within the movement of analytical philosophy; and second, ordinary language philosophy is perhaps the one part of analytical philosophy that had an impact on legal theory throughout the twentieth century.

The focus on usage was a key point of the philosophy of Ludwig Wittgenstein (1889–1951). Through it he attempted to replace those theories that tried to explain meaning independently of language, by alleging a one-to-one correspondence between words and objects. The problem with that explanation of meaning was that it implicitly relied on a prior understanding of the expression in question. Take for instance the word "car". In explaining to someone the meaning of "car" as "the word car designates the object *car*", one is relying on the fact that she or he already understands "car". Instead, a non-circular explanation requires attending to the different ways speakers use the expression in question and to the implicit rules that guide the various instances of its use.[7] Mastering those rules equals grasping the meaning of the relevant expression. What is more, knowledge of the conditions and/or criteria for the use of an expression conveys knowledge about the nature of the objects to which the expression applies. For instance, to know the rules for the correct use of "car", *i.e.* to know when it is appropriate to use "car", amounts to knowing the essential properties of cars, *i.e.* what kind of things cars are.

Applied in the domain of law the idea of analysis comprises the study of legal concepts in general and the concept "law" in particular.[8] As already noted, this study is not just a semantic study directed at an illustration of the meaning of "law" but aims deeper. It aims at shedding light on the nature of law by conveying knowledge with respect to the essential properties of the entities "law" applies to. Two different versions of analysis can be distinguished in this context, the first—conceptual analysis—being a clear instance of meaning analysis while the second—transcendental reasoning—is a less obvious one.

Conceptual analysis is supposed to be the tool of analytical philosophy *par excellence*. In the field of legal philosophy it is mainly employed by conventionalist versions of positivism. In this context the legal philosopher is required to study the various instances of the application of "law" and to make explicit the rules that guide speakers in using it. To that extent, it is assumed that the essential features of law can be revealed through the (semantic) rules that guide the use of legal concepts.

In particular, conceptual analysis comprises two levels: the first is *a priori*, for it purports to state rules for the use of legal expressions that reveal *a priori* features of law.[9] *In concreto*, these rules have the form of *analytic* sentences, namely sentences that we are justified in holding true just by grasping their meaning (*e.g.* the sentence: "legal rules give rise to obligations").[10]

The second instance of conceptual analysis consists in stating rules for the use of legal expressions that are *a posteriori* true.[11] These rules have the form

---

[7] The latter, according to Wittgenstein, cannot be taught but are a matter of "natural uptake", one that substantiates through one's participation in a linguistic community. For a brief, albeit accurate review of the ideas connected to the use theory of meaning, see J. Skorupski, "Meaning, Use, Verification" in *A Companion to the Philosophy of Language* (B. Hale and C. Wright eds., Blackwell, Oxford, 1997), pp.29–59.

[8] For the historical background of analytical jurisprudence, see Hart's lucid exposition in his *Essays in Jurisprudence and Philosophy*, pp.271–277.

[9] *A priori* true sentences are those sentences whose truth can be established independently of any empirical proof.

[10] See Hart's discussion on the relation between legal rules and obligation in *The Concept of Law* (2nd ed., Clarendon Press, Oxford, 1994), pp.79–91. *The Concept of Law* was first published by Clarendon Press in 1961. The posthumous second edition includes a postscript by Hart.

[11] *A posteriori* true sentences are those sentences whose truth can be established only by reference to empirical proof.

of sentences that are *synthetic*, namely true in virtue of our empirical evidence with respect to the use of legal language. In stating these, the legal philosopher has to look into the actual instances of the application of legal expressions by the legal community. Thus, if lawyers use "manslaughter" whenever someone kills intentionally upon having been provoked, then semantic rule (SR) applies: "'manslaughter' applies to any instance of intentional killing following provocation". What is more, given that any semantic rule reveals something about the nature of law, one is justified in holding true that provocation is an essential property of manslaughter.

One final word on the difference between semantic rules that are analytic (*a priori* true) and those that are synthetic (*a posteriori* true): all rules that the legal philosopher arrives at through conceptual analysis are supposed to be revealing necessary or essential features of law. Be that as it may, analytic rules indicate features of law that somehow are more fundamental than those revealed by rules that are merely synthetic. The reason is that the former do not depend on experience and, to that extent, are non-revisable. That law is the source of obligations, for instance, is a necessary feature that is part of the conditions of applying "law" (*i.e.* of its meaning), irrespective of experience. Being what they are, analytic rules guide the practice of a legal community but, at the same time, transcend its boundaries and constitute objective, practice-independent criteria against whose background it is possible to judge the correctness of the practice of any community. In contrast, synthetic semantic rules, like the one quoted earlier for manslaughter (SR), allow for revision in the light of new empirical evidence: If the perpetrator was indeed provoked, yet the killing took place 48 hours after the act of provocation, the condition of provocation may be rendered a necessary, albeit not sufficient, condition for applying "manslaughter" to the facts of the case. Such rules are interlaced with the actual empirical conditions for applying legal terms and depend heavily on both the natural environment and the actual practice of the legal community. (Thus, *different* legal communities apply "manslaughter" in different ways, although *all* legal communities make this pattern of behaviour punishable).

Transcendental reasoning is the second version of analytic philosophy, one that pertains to epistemic positivism and is in particular exemplified by Kelsen's work. In a nutshell, transcendental reasoning is employed in order to reveal necessary conditions for the existence of something that is uncontrovertibly the case. Transcendental reasoning usually takes the form of an argument with three premises: the first premise states something that is trivially true (say, "people make promises"); the second premise proceeds to state under what condition this is the case ("for promises to make sense, it is necessary to presuppose the rule 'promises should be kept'"); finally, the conclusion states the stipulated condition as a proposition that is true independent of experience, *i.e. a priori* ("necessarily, promises should be kept").

Premise I: it is the case that P
Premise II: for P to be the case, necessarily condition C must obtain
Conclusion: necessarily C

Kelsen made use of this form of reasoning in order to prove that unless we presuppose a distinct legal point of view, it is not possible to know anything that is legal (rules, contracts, judgements, etc.). What is more, this form of reasoning succeeds in illustrating in the best manner law's irreducibility to other non-normative categories (as, for instance, sociological or psychological facts). This remained a key point throughout Kelsen's philosophy and one that served him to corroborate his claim about the autonomy of legal science.

The remainder of this chapter focuses on Hart's version of conventionalism. Despite Kelsen's immense importance to twentieth-century jurisprudence it was Hart's theory that has had the most profound impact on the English-speaking legal world. The main reason for this is its high relevance to common-law thinking. The exposition attempts to explore the manner in which Hart employs legal analysis in order to illuminate law's nature.

4. Hart's Concept of Law

In the opening pages of his most celebrated work, *The Concept of Law* (1961), H.L.A. Hart declares his dissatisfaction with most of the earlier attempts to answer the question "what is law", for they had merely amounted to *partial* revelations of the truth about law's nature. Instead, he suggests that a fresh start be made in order to reveal the *whole truth* of the matter. What this fresh start consists of is easy to tell from the opening three chapters of the *Concept of Law*. Hart, in applying the lessons of his contemporary analytical philosophy,[12] attempts to answer the question about the nature of law through an analysis of the meaning of legal expressions, as it manifests itself in the day-to-day use of legal language by a legal community (conceptual analysis).[13] Conceptual analysis leads him to the general conclusion that it is impossible to capture law's nature through definitions that fix necessary and sufficient conditions for "law"—so-called definitions *per genus et differentiam*—because such definitions tend to misrepresent as essential certain features of law that are only contingent. Instead, Hart takes conceptual analysis to point at a new

---

[12] See H.L.A. Hart, "Jhering" in *Essays in Jurisprudence and Philosophy*, pp.274–277.

[13] For a clear exposition of conceptual analysis in law, see N. Stavropoulos, "Hart's Semantics" in *Hart's Postscript: Essays on the Postscript to the "Concept of Law"* (J. Coleman ed., Oxford University Press, Oxford, 2001), pp.58–98. For the role of conceptual analysis in philosophy, see F. Jackson, *From Metaphysics to Ethics* (Clarendon Press, Oxford, 1999), chap.2.

type of criteria that guide users in their applications of legal expressions. Contrary to necessary and sufficient conditions, criteria of the new type cannot generate "final", rigid definitions of legal concepts but are revisable or, in Hart's words, *defeasible* in the light of new circumstances the community runs into.[14]

Hart famously attributes the defeasibility of all (and not just legal) meaning to the ignorance of fact and the indeterminacy of aim: it is impossible for legislators to anticipate in the wording of a statute the complexity of the environment and the concomitant impact it has on agents' aims.[15] Think of the rule "no vehicles are allowed in the park". Suppose that it was enacted in the late nineteenth century with a view to controlling the increasing amount of "urban noise" that came as a result of the rapid industrial development of those days. Now imagine that, more than a century later, an accident occurs in the same park when a remote-control toy car causes the injury of an old lady who is taking her afternoon walk. When the case is brought before the court a determination of the legality of the conduct that caused the injury is required. For that the judge will have to answer the preliminary question whether the toy car falls within the meaning of the concept "vehicle" of the statute. For certain, any definition of "vehicle" which is fixed by facts or aims pertinent to the context of the original legislation would fail, for the simple reason that no Victorian legislator could ever foresee the hundreds of types of vehicles that would have appeared a century or so later, nor the diversity of aim that agents (including legal officials) would connect to them. Instead, the present day judge must arrive at a definition of "vehicle" that reflects the facts and the aims of the case at hand. This will most likely bring about a revision of the criteria for "vehicle" pertinent to earlier definitions, and will amount to a fresh, more precise understanding of its meaning. (Thus, for instance, the existence of self-propelled artefacts that serve play might be deemed irrelevant to the meaning of "vehicle" in a statute regarding parks.)

Hart tells us that the concept "law" behaves in a way not dissimilar to "vehicle". It is not possible to provide for an exhaustive definition of "law" that would account for all legal systems at all times. Instead the criteria such a definition comprises are revisable in the light of new circumstances, the idiosyncrasies of different contexts (that is, different societal formations) and the various aims that agents associate with them. The effort to uncover those various aspects sheds light upon the nature of law and its relation with other forms of normativity (morality, ethics, courtesy and custom, to mention only the most important of them). This endeavour unfolds through the method of

---

[14] These ideas are expressed in H.L.A. Hart, "Jhering" and "Separation of Law and Morals" in *Essays in Jurisprudence and Philosophy*.
[15] *The Concept of Law*, p.128.

conceptual analysis, or the systematic exposition of the (semantic) rules that guide the use of legal expressions.

Semantic rules reach beyond the level of meaning and language in that they make explicit criteria for correct applications of legal expressions ("is X a legal rule?"; "is Y a contract?"; and so on). In being about correct applications of legal expressions, these criteria relate to both the level of *how we talk about law* and the level of *how law actually is (law's reality)*. Given certain constraints with respect to our ability to grasp anything independently of thought and language, there might not be a way to plainly state where the boundaries of the two levels lie. It is important, however, not to obscure either level, but instead, to be aware of their synchronic impact upon any theoretical inquiry into law's nature. Awareness with respect to both levels is perhaps the best way for guaranteeing theoretical open-mindedness in our quest for a correct understanding of the nature of law. On the face of it, correctness does not consist of a final, absolute grasp of "the truth" about law (be it in the form of a theory or a definition) but of an ongoing effort to bring the two levels of language and reality into accordance. In practice, such an effort implies that the theorist remains conscious, at all times, of the fact that the whole truth cannot be inferred only from the way we employ legal language or only from a direct, unmediated grasp of law's reality. Instead, the theorist is asked to realise that proximity to truth requires constant awareness of the fact that thought and language are responsible to reality while, at the same time, any grasp of reality is responsible to, or has to fit with, the way we articulate thoughts in language.

Explicated as above, the valuable exercise of conceptual analysis invites the legal theorist to engage in an ongoing process of refining definitions of legal concepts with a view to achieving a more accurate understanding of the nature of law. Refinement is possible by revising existing criteria or introducing new criteria in the light of new considerations. Although the process of revising old and introducing new criteria is far from being linear, it is appropriate to say that it contributes to an overall increase in *legal knowledge*, or knowledge with respect to law's nature. A pertinent question arising in this context is one about the exact relation between the increase in legal knowledge and the various kinds of considerations the theorist takes into account in bringing about the increase. In other words: in what proportions do considerations about the use of legal language (call them *semantic considerations*) combine with considerations about the reality of law (call them *empirical considerations*) in order to generate legal knowledge? Although Hart advances conceptual analysis as a dynamic theoretical exercise for arriving at case-sensitive definitions of "law", he never specifies in detail which part thereof draws upon semantic and which upon empirical considerations.[16]

---

[16] For an idea of the intense contemporary debate on the nature of conceptual analysis

In the light of our earlier distinction between an *a priori* and an *a posteriori* part of conceptual analysis, it is not difficult to illustrate Hart's expositions as accommodating both levels of inquiry. Semantic considerations are gained through the *a priori* part of conceptual analysis: here the theorist locates semantic rules at a high level of abstraction which guide speakers' understanding of "law" irrespective of particular circumstances (*i.e.* concrete legal systems). The criteria for a definition of "law" introduced by such rules are fixed by reference to characteristics of law that transcend specific contexts: characteristics whose rejection would lead to a loss of the meaning of "law". At this level, law is shown to share essential features with other forms of normativity like morality, custom and etiquette, while all of them are sharply contrasted to non-normative regularities of behaviour (habits). On the other hand, empirical considerations pertain to *a posteriori* conceptual analysis: here the theorist aims to state rules for using legal language in a manner that successfully depicts the empirical features of concrete contexts (for instance, those of a particular legal system or type of legal systems). The level of abstraction for these rules is low and they amount to criteria for "law" that are immediately responsible to (and revisable on the grounds of) empirical features of the context under consideration. In a moment we will see that, in Hart's theory, such criteria play the role of differentiating "law" from other types of normativity (morality, ethics, custom and etiquette) for they refer to features of "law" that were developed through the specific functions that legal institutions came to perform within particular societal formations (German, English, US and so on) or types thereof (depending on the criterion of classification: *e.g.* Western, Muslim, Capitalist, Traditional).

For the following two sections we will be reviewing Hart's conclusions regarding law's nature that derive from the two levels of conceptual analysis he employs. Employment of *a priori* conceptual analysis and the involvement of semantic considerations shall be related to his explanation of the normative character of law as a necessary relation between "law" and "obligation". On the other hand, reliance on empirical considerations by way of *a posteriori* analysis shall be shown to underpin Hart's explication of law as the outcome of a social convention. Lest any misunderstanding occur, it should be made clear that Hart never referred explicitly to the method of conceptual analysis let alone drew any distinction between an *a priori* and an *a posteriori* part thereof. To that extent, the exposition at hand is a reconstruction of Hart's thought in the light of the remarks made earlier in this chapter. Be that as it may, it is a reconstruction that purports to take seriously what in Hart's work is, philosophically speaking, the most valuable and innovative part, namely

---

in law, see N. Stavropoulos, *op. cit.* and V. Rodriguez-Blanco, "A Defence of Hart's Semantics as Nonambitious Conceptual Analysis" (2003) 9 *Legal Theory* 99.

his attempt to apply the theoretical tools of his contemporary analytical philosophy to the analysis of law. This endeavour is what invests Hart's work with an unprecedented depth for Anglo-Saxon legal theory and manifests its intellectual superiority *vis-à-vis* his predecessors. Any serious attempt to evaluate Hart's substantive conclusions about the nature of law ought to make explicit the methodological assumptions of his theory.

The Normative Character of Law: Law and Obligation

Early in *The Concept of Law* Hart arrives at the conclusion that legal rules are a species of social rules on a par with rules of morality, ethics, custom, etiquette and so on. This conclusion rests on a general analysis of normative speech, one that makes explicit the fundamental semantic rules that guide the use of regulative expressions and sentences amongst speakers of a language. Insofar as semantic rules refer to actual properties, it is possible for Hart to argue that the various forms of legal, moral, ethical and other rules share a number of core characteristics and, hence, may be grouped together under the genus "social rules". To that extent, the *a priori* part of Hart's conceptual analysis undertakes the task to illustrate the essential characteristics of normativity generally speaking.

Hart argues that, in using social rules, speakers treat them as shared standards of behaviour, standards that can be employed in order to justify or criticise one's own or others' conduct. To that extent, the language of rules presupposes or is necessarily accompanied by the *critical reflection* that some regular pattern of behaviour is a correct standard of conduct: Hart labels this kind of reflection "the critical reflective attitude".[17] The critical reflective attitude comprises two aspects: one subjective, consisting in the reasons speakers have for treating some pattern of behaviour as a binding standard; and one objective, consisting in speakers' demonstration of doing so (a demonstration that usually consists in the actual ways speakers employ normative language in order to criticise, praise or advise others). The latter aspect constitutes, more or less, an empirical fact that can be located in the environment. It should be pointed out that what is crucial for the existence of any rule are not the *actual* reasons speakers have for treating a pattern of behaviour as a correct standard (subjective aspect) but merely the fact that they do so (the objective aspect). To that extent, the upgrading of a pattern of behaviour to a rule acquires an objective standing and becomes empirically transparent to the theorist. This should not come as a surprise: Hart's preoccupation with a neutral, value-free description of law led him to overemphasise the importance of the objective aspect and even substitute it in

---

[17] See Hart, *The Concept of Law*, pp.55–61.

the place of the subjective one.[18] This gave rise to a number of important problems with respect to his account of normativity because the objective, factual aspect of the critical reflective attitude cannot by itself sustain the required connection between the existence of a normative standard on the one hand and the reasons agents have for acting, on the other. This point will be taken up in more detail shortly.

In an attempt to flesh out the critical reflective attitude Hart takes it to indicate the presence of an *obligation*. On the grounds of the concept of obligation Hart distinguishes social rules from two other related phenomena, habits and acts of brute force.[19] Habits are, as it were, incomplete rules; they comprise a regular pattern of behaviour but there is no element of critical reflection that this pattern is a valuable standard of conduct. On the other hand, acts of brute force may indeed entail a certain amount of regulatory power, even though they fall short of generating obligation. What they generate, instead, is the feeling that one is obliged to act in a certain way. To demonstrate this Hart uses the gunman example: when held up at gunpoint and asked to hand over their money, any reasonable person would be expected to comply with the order.[20] However in doing so he or she would not be treating the gunman's order as giving rise to an *obligation* but would be rather experiencing feelings of *being obliged*.[21]

To sum up: Hart's analysis of the use of legal language leads him to the conclusion that for something to be a legal rule it is necessary that the members of a legal community hold the belief that it is a valuable standard of behaviour.

---

[18] Hart was a relativist with respect to morality. As a result he thought of agents' reasons for treating something as a standard of behaviour as being utterly subjective and incapable of supporting objective scientific judgements about the existence or non-existence of rules. In contrast, agents' behaviour was a much more reliable medium for underpinning such judgements. For Hart's relativism in conjunction with his positivism, see his five theses on positivism in "Separation of Law and Morals", p.57.

[19] Hart reserves the term obligation for moral and legal rules only, for he understands obligation as resulting from the threat of serious social pressure (see *The Concept of Law*, pp.85–87). This is not a very clear distinction given that other kinds of social rules (etiquette or courtesy) may also be accompanied by the threat of social pressure that can be serious enough. Social pressure might have an impact on the intensity of the perceived obligation but not on its existence. The latter rather depends on whether some practice is treated as a standard of behaviour, which is to say as a rule.

[20] Hart, *The Concept of Law*, pp.82 *et seq.*

[21] *ibid.* Hart uses the case of the gunman with a view to rejecting John Austin's definition of law as a set of commands backed by threat. Such a definition, Hart submits, is incapable of distinguishing between a legal rule and the command of a gunman, precisely because it fails to apprehend the element of obligation that is in-built in law.

It is only under this condition that a rule can be seen as giving rise to an obligation rather than amounting to an instance of brute force (being obliged). The necessary link between rule and obligation, however, is not peculiarly confined to law but encapsulates an essential feature of normativity in general. To that extent, Hart concedes that law is a species of normativity and legal rules a species of social rules.

Law in Its Own Right: Convention and Authority

Despite appearances, it would be wrong to assume that Hart confuses legal rules with other kinds of social rules. On the contrary, he is very keen on distinguishing the domain of law from other areas of social normativity and in particular morality. The part of his theory that undertakes this task focuses on the empirical differences between practices of law on the one hand and practices of morality on the other. In a more philosophical vocabulary, this part of the Hartian analysis intends to establish sufficient features for the existence of legal rules as opposed to necessary ones, a task that was undertaken by the general part of his theory.

Hart compares practices that give rise to legal rules and those that give rise to moral rules with a view to illustrating that the former are different in content or rationale from the latter, irrespective of their both sharing the property of being normative (*i.e.* of being considered as valuable standards of conduct that give rise to obligations). Moral rules surface as the result of long-standing practices when at a particular point in time the participants of the practice form the belief that some regular pattern of behaviour is a valuable standard of conduct. Owing to the length of the whole process, there is an assumption that the relevant beliefs give rise to obligations that are firmly grounded on a lengthy process of deliberation. In taking their time, so to speak, the participants have had the opportunity to contemplate the various aspects of the practice, to soberly evaluate its effects and even to review and improve some of its components. As a result, the practice raises a strong claim to correctness with respect to the rules it generates. In short, moral practices are about establishing rules of conduct that lay down obligations that reflect the fundamental evaluations of a community about what is right and wrong. These rules emerge from a lengthy process of deliberation, testing and revision that invests them with an increased amount of practical authority.[22]

Hart points out that such rules of morality would have formed the core of traditional legal systems within small-sized communities. In such groups of limited membership, all law was required to do was to offer a rough indication

---

[22] For such a reading of Hart's theory, see J. Waldron, *The Dignity of Legislation* (Cambridge University Press, Cambridge, 1999), chap.1.

of what kind of conduct is permitted or forbidden with a view to guaranteeing the preservation of the community. In this respect, law is indistinguishable from morality, both systems consisting of basic rules of obligation that evolve through a long process of deliberation. Hart calls these rules *primary rules*.[23] But contemporary legal systems seem to be the result of an entirely different process, embodying a rationale that is radically different from the one underlying primary rules. Apparently, at some point in their history, owing mainly to a considerable increase of their membership, most societies developed patterns for modifying or replacing their primary rules in a *deliberate* way without "taking their time" and without being interested or at least principally interested in the correctness of the amounting rules. Those patterns had a number of other characteristics, most important amongst them being the fact that change or modification of primary rules was entrusted to specific people or bodies of people (judges, state officials, legislative bodies). Those patterns soon rose to the status of standards of conduct *vis-à-vis* those who administered the corpus of primary rules and gave rise to a new type of rule, what Hart calls *secondary rules*.[24]

On the face of it, secondary rules are the expression of a rationale that is radically different from the one underlying primary rules: their purpose is not to create obligations that are valid unconditionally, in virtue of their being the considered outcomes of a long-standing deliberation, but instead to effectively administer the system of primary rules (to that extent *secondary rules are rules about primary rules*). This feature makes secondary rules indifferent *vis-à-vis* the content of the obligations that primary rules incorporate. Instead, secondary rules focus on whether primary rules are being created or modified according to the set of conditions specified by them. What is more, Hart maintains that the rationale of secondary rules is much more than a local phenomenon within modern legal systems: in fact, the whole idea of law as we know it today is permeated by the idea of secondary rules, for every developed legal system is founded upon a special secondary rule, one that is the most general secondary rule of the whole system, the so-called *rule of recognition*.[25]

The rule of recognition contains the criteria of legality (or *validity*), which

---

[23] Hart characterises those rules that impose duties as primary, the most common example being the rules of criminal law. For a detailed discussion see H.L.A. Hart, *The Concept of Law*, pp.26 *et seq.* and chap.V *passim.*

[24] Secondary rules are rules that confer upon officials and/or individuals legal powers to create—subject to certain procedures and conditions—structures of rights and duties within the coercive framework of the law. Examples of such rules are those that enable individuals to shape their legal relations with others by contracts, wills, marriages, and so on; or rules of the public law that distribute legislative competences between the various state organs; *cf. op. cit.*, pp.28 *et seq.* and chap.V *passim.*

[25] *ibid.*, pp.94–117.

is to say the criteria for distinguishing between those rules of obligation that are part of the legal system and those that are not (but, instead, form part of morality, custom, ethics, courtesy and so on).[26] Criteria of validity acquire the status of conditions that are necessary and sufficient for something to be a legal rule. Thus they replace the lengthy process by which non-legal social rules are being established. Criteria of validity are content-independent and focus merely on the formal-factual conditions that must obtain for the valid creation or modification of the rules of the system. To that extent, criteria of legality or validity are necessary not because they can be known independently of experience (*a priori*) but because they can be known only with respect to the actual features of each and every particular legal system (*a posteriori*). This fact implies that there is no unique rule of recognition but a plethora thereof; in fact there are around as many rules of recognition as there are legal systems. Furthermore, it is important to point out that each and every rule of recognition plays the role of a *constitutive convention* with respect to some legal system: it is a convention because it owes its existence to the contingent fact of a decision or agreement, on behalf of a community, to treat some set of conditions as constituting criteria of validity for its legal system; and it is constitutive because the legal system a rule of recognition corresponds to cannot exist outside it. On the face of it, rules of recognition carry a striking resemblance to rules of games for they too are the product of choice and are also essential for the existence of the relevant game (*e.g.* chess is what it is because of its rules and otherwise it does not exist independently of them).

Conceptualism or Empiricism? On the Nature of Legal Theory

It was suggested earlier that Hart's conceptual analysis of legal language comprises two parts. One part is interested in the most abstract conditions for a meaningful use of "law" (what was labelled *semantic considerations*) and therefore is not conditioned upon the empirical features of any concrete legal system (*i.e.* it is *a priori*). And another part that is interested in concrete conditions for the use of "law" (what was labelled *empirical considerations*) and therefore focuses on the empirical features of particular legal systems (*a posteriori*).

We saw that the former type of conceptual analysis led Hart to the conclusion that law gives rise to obligations (in other words, it is normative), while the

---

[26] For Hart this is the actual criterion for distinguishing between law and morality. Often he refers to some other differences between legal and moral rules such as the feeling of shame pertaining only to the latter and the generalised social pressure pertaining exclusively to the former. These however fall short of doing the analytical job of distinguishing between law and morality, as Hart himself seems to believe when talking about primitive legal systems.

latter to the conclusion that law is conventional. Together the two modes of analysis—each on a different level of abstraction—tell us what is necessary to know in order to arrive at a full understanding of the nature of law. Along these lines, if one wanted to refer to legal concepts or use legal language meaningfully, one would have to know at least that law is about obligation.[27] If, however, one wanted to refer meaningfully to a particular legal system, say the English or the German, one would have needed more information: one would have needed to know the constitutive convention of that system (its rule of recognition) and the criteria of validity specified by it. The former type of knowledge is *a priori*, having to do with the way we understand "law" in its most general form, while the latter is *a posteriori*, arising from the empirical study of the facts and events that comprise the constitutive convention of the system under consideration.

At this point it is justified to ask: In our understanding of legal phenomena, which of the two carries more weight for the fullest possible understanding of legal phenomena: empirical considerations or the conceptual connection between law and obligation? Admittedly, empirical considerations can be deemed weightier in a trivial sense: given that there is no such thing as ideal law, existing over and above all actual legal systems, it follows that all theoretical enquiry takes place with reference to one or more concrete legal systems and, hence, relies on empirical observations about the facts that put together the constitutive convention (or the rule of recognition) of each one of them. To that extent, our knowledge of the phenomenon law is inescapably interwoven with our knowledge of particular legal system(s). Be that as it may, our question purports to address a less trivial point: In determining the nature of law, even in relation to concrete legal systems, a *conceptual issue* arises which might not be possible to settle through reference to empirical considerations regarding a constitutive legal convention. This aspect stems from law's conceptual relation to obligation. This relation implies that it is not possible to determine the content of "law" independently of the content of "obligation". However, the latter cannot be determined on the basis of a legal constitutive convention because it comprises a large amount of non-legal components: in assessing the existence of an obligation one often has to consider, apart from legal reasons, reasons of a moral or ethical nature.[28] Think

---

[27] To the extent that conceptual analysis is interested in stating semantic rules for the use of concepts the same point can be made by saying that in order to properly use "law" one needs to know the semantic rule (SR): "legal rules give rise to obligations".

[28] This is the case irrespective of the way we understand morality: if morality is understood as comprising a system of rules that are universally valid, then obviously these rules escape the validity criteria of a legal rule of recognition. On the other hand, even if morality is understood as conventional, then again the rules it comprises

for instance of civil disobedience: in assessing their legal obligations "legal dissidents" often refer to reasons that exceed by far the "space" of legal validity demarcated by the relevant rule of recognition. As a result, the content of "law" can only be partly determined on the basis of a legal convention, for the latter fails to deliver a full account of obligating reasons. Recast in those terms the question about the priority of the empirical or the conceptual becomes a question about the relation between law and the other realms of normativity.

Hart decides, somehow surprisingly considering his conceptual analysis of "law", for an analysis of "obligation" in empirical or value-free terms. When in Hart's theoretical system someone asks—what does it mean to know that "law" is intertwined with "obligation"?—Hart seems to want to avoid an answer that would involve the fullest possible set of reasons giving rise to obligations (obligating reasons), for such an answer would have to include all relevant moral or ethical obligating reasons. Such a consideration of the complete set of reasons, Hart points out, is beset by a number of disadvantages.[29] First, in the light of a vast plethora of value-systems, many of which are mutually incompatible, there is no determinate or objective way to arrive at uniform answers with respect to what gives rise to an obligation in a particular case. Second, in postulating completeness of the relevant obligating reasons, such an account becomes extremely time-consuming and extremely difficult, if not impossible, to ever achieve. Finally, and perhaps more importantly, an analysis of legal obligation premised on the fullest possible account of obligating reasons would eschew what, for Hart, is the most central feature of modern legal systems, namely the existence of a practice giving rise to a secondary rule of recognition. In omitting this important aspect, any analysis of law would be mistaking all legal rules for primary rules, a fact true of traditional legal systems—whenever law and morality were not clearly demarcated—but definitely not true of the highly complex modern legal orders.

For all these reasons, Hart opts for an explication of legal obligation that actually does away with obligating reasons. Hart suggests that a legal obligation obtains if and only if the conditions of legal validity are in place. More importantly, these conditions do not comprise obligating reasons (be they moral, ethical or other) but consist of external facts that can be observed and recorded in an objective way (enactment in Parliament, issuance by the appropriate official and so on) and are recorded by the system's rule of recognition. By way of introducing the concept of legal validity, Hart breaks the continuity between legal and other kinds of obligation. Legal obligation becomes an empirical concept that may be asserted on the basis of a series of descriptive

---

cannot be accounted for through a legal convention but, instead, one would need to locate the appropriate moral convention that specifies criteria of moral validity.

[29] See H.L.A. Hart, "Separation of Law and Morals", pp.82–87.

facts, whereas for asserting moral obligation some reference to actual obligating reasons is required.[30] Thus, the *reduction of legal obligation to legal validity* signifies a tactical trade-off between the alleged *shortcomings* of a "deep" analysis of obligating reasons and the *objectivity* that pertains to the empirical facts to be found on the "surface" of the behaviour of those who comply with legal rules.

The External and the Internal Aspect of Rules: Legal Theory's Split Personality

Hart's reduction is available on one important condition: unless his theory were to count as an incomplete report of legal phenomena, it should be still possible to deem accounts of rules in terms of validity conditions *equivalent* to accounts of rules in terms of obligating reasons (call this the *equivalence condition*). In other words, the description of the facts that lie on the *surface* of the behaviour of those who comply with some legal obligation should carry the same informational value with a *deep* account of the reasons that give rise to the obligation in question. This requires that the legal theorist be able to switch between the two accounts without failing to depict the correct nature of legal phenomena. Hart attempts to meet the equivalence condition by alluding to the existence of two aspects of rules or two standpoints for understanding legal phenomena. The first, the so-called *internal aspect* or point of view, pertains to anyone who has developed *vis-à-vis* a legal system what was earlier referred to as the critical reflective attitude; in other words anyone who treats the rules of the system as valuable standards of behaviour. Hart reserves this role for the participants of a legal system. The second, the so-called *external aspect* or point of view, pertains to someone who is "observing" the members of a legal community from some distance, that is, without necessarily sharing the belief that the rules shared by the members of the community are valuable standards of behaviour. The ability to switch between the two points of view is crucial for Hart's reductionist account of legal obligation.

On any superficial understanding of "obligation" it is reasonable to expect that, in so far as someone believes that some rule is a valuable standard of behaviour, he or she should be in a position to offer reasons for corroborating that belief. As we said earlier, however, Hart considers any attempt to refer to the deep structure of obligation to be wrongheaded. Instead, on the validity-based account he puts forward, one should be able to justify one's belief by

---

[30] We said earlier that it is possible to capture even moral obligation as referring to external features of speakers' behaviour. Such an analysis, however, would be even less convincing than in the case of law for it is impossible to identify a unique set of facts (*i.e.* a constitutive convention) that is responsible for generating moral rules.

saying something like "this is a valuable standard of behaviour because it has been validated according to the conditions set in the rule of recognition". For the latter to count as a faithful depiction of legal obligation, two conditions must be in place. The first condition is that it is possible to replace the notion of obligation with some other notion that is indifferent *vis-à-vis* obligating reasons. This task was carried out by Hart's analysis of the conventional character of law as a practice that gives rise to secondary rules, an analysis that, as we have seen, purported to demarcate law from morality, while substituting obligating reasons with the content-indifferent and formalistic notion of legal validity. The second condition requires that there be an external, empirical aspect to each and every legal obligation which corresponds to the facts of legal validity set down in a constitutive legal convention (rule of recognition). For this Hart turns to the *behaviour* of those who are acting under a legal obligation, *i.e.* those who occupy the internal point of view with respect to a legal rule. Uncontrovertibly, such behaviour can be described in value-free terms, without making reference to obligating reasons of any kind but merely by referring to the external, empirical components thereof. In particular, when the behaviour under consideration is the behaviour of those who regard the practice that gives rise to secondary rules as obligatory,[31] then its external components coincide with the criteria of validity spelled out in a rule of recognition.

It is at this point that the external point of view assumes supremacy in Hart's system: once divested of any reference to substantive (moral, ethical) obligating reasons, legal obligation can be easily asserted from the point of view of someone who does not associate obligating reasons with legal standards, someone whose viewpoint is external to the legal practice of the community under consideration (someone who occupies Hart's external point of view). To that extent, the internal point of view and the existence of legal obligations is conditioned upon the possibility of a description of facts from the external point of view.[32] Critics of Hart have pointed out that such a possibility is to be rejected. It is not just that any description from the external point of view fails to depict (the content of) legal obligations, but also that Hart's notion of legal validity runs out of resources when it is asked to explain the validity of the rule of recognition. We turn now to a brief account of these critiques.

---

[31] Hart believes that in order to locate the rule of recognition of any legal system the theorist must focus on the practice of the legal community; see the discussion in *The Concept of Law*, pp.79–91.

[32] This is despite Hart's insistence that the external point of view is parasitical on the internal point of view. The latter would instead require that the notion of legal validity be dependent on substantive obligating reasons, a thesis that traditionally has been associated with theories of natural law.

5. Criticisms and Assessment

Hart's positivist and value-free account of law stands and falls with the possibility to switch between the external and the internal point of view, in other words, to capture legal obligations in purely descriptive terms, through the notion of legal validity, without referring to the deep structure of obligating reasons. Given the centrality of the notion of validity to such an account it is not surprising that Hart's idea of a rule of recognition has been the focus of much critical discussion since the appearance of *The Concept of Law*. Roughly speaking, there are two lines of criticism that can be distinguished for present purposes. First, it has been argued that the notion of legal validity actually fails to account for the totality of types of legal obligation arising within a legal system (call this the *incompleteness thesis*). The second argument gives rise to a deeper objection: that it is insufficient to understand the practice of law as resting upon a secondary rule of recognition that generates criteria of validity because a full understanding of legal obligation requires association with other types of obligation (call this the *connection thesis*). In what follows we will deal with each of the two types in some more detail with a view to demonstrating that they are interrelated.

The incompleteness thesis says that no rule of recognition can offer a complete account of legal obligation for any legal system X. The *locus classicus* of this argument is Ronald Dworkin's *Taking Rights Seriously*. In it Dworkin argues that Hart's notion of legal validity falls short from giving a complete account of legal obligation.[33] Focussing on the judicial practice of modern legal systems, Dworkin points out that judges, more often than not, consider as authoritative for their cases standards that have not yet passed the test of any rule of recognition. These standards, which Dworkin labels *principles* and *policies*, give rise to legal obligations not in virtue of some test of validity, but because they are justified on moral or ethical grounds. The fact that such standards actually figure in legal justifications shows that, after all, Hart's account of legal phenomena was not that accurate. But accuracy is only a minor concern in this case; the realisation that (some) legal obligations may exist independently of a rule of recognition puts Hart's conception of legal validity into serious doubt and generates the need for a new understanding of legal obligation, one that is capable of accounting for obligations of the principle or policy type. For this need to be met, the incompleteness thesis needs to be supplemented by the connection thesis.

---

[33] R. Dworkin, *Taking Rights Seriously* (Duckworth, London, 1977), chaps.2 and 3. Dworkin's legal theory is set out in Colin Harvey, "Talking about Human Rights" in this volume. A somewhat different argument that arrives to similar conclusions can be found in R. Alexy, *The Argument from Injustice* (Clarendon Press, Oxford, 2002), pp.71–74.

In a nutshell, the *connection thesis* says that legal obligations stand in the same line with moral obligations and, hence, that a full understanding of legal practices requires that certain moral and ethical reasons be drawn into the picture.[34] The reason given is that the practice of law should not be understood as *principally* being about the existence of a secondary obligation of recognition, one about recognising criteria of validity, managing legal material and allowing for deliberate changes of the rules of the system. Instead, the connection thesis argues, legal practice needs to be understood as being directly answerable to primary obligations that exist independently or, perhaps, alongside the secondary obligation of recognition. On this understanding, the obligation of recognition is rendered secondary, albeit in the sense that it is amenable to a number of primary obligations that precede the process of recognition.

The connection thesis can be stated as the upshot of a critical enquiry into the foundation (or the validity) of the rule of recognition. A generic version of this argument might run along the following lines: Hart informs us that the rule of recognition is not valid as a legal rule (*i.e.* the notion of legal validity does not apply to it) but, instead, its existence must be explained in a different way to that of legal rules. However that may be, the rule of recognition is still the source of an obligation, albeit one of the secondary kind: the obligation *vis-à-vis* officials to recognise as legal only those norms that pass the validity test. What are, then, the grounds of this obligation? In the case of legal obligations the answer to this question has been rather unproblematic, for, in their case, validity exhausts obligation and no association to the content of other obligations is *prima facie* necessary. With respect to these, one could simply refer to the facts of validity in order to point out the existence of the

---

[34] There is a plethora of authors that can be interpreted as arguing for the connection thesis. For present purposes, suffice it to include in them Ronald Dworkin—*Taking Rights Seriously*; *Law's Empire* (Fontana, London, 1986) and Robert Alexy—*The Argument from Injustice*. In addition most natural law theorists could be interpreted as endorsing some version of the connection thesis; see, especially, J.M. Finnis, *Natural Law and Natural Rights* (Clarendon Press, Oxford, 1980). Hart himself speaks of a minimum content of natural law that necessarily pertains to every legal system. Far from making any reference to substantive moral reasons, the latter constitutes more of a prudential safeguard against forms of government that would lead to the disintegration of social life altogether. Such forms of government, Hart says, should not qualify as legal systems. To this, however, he adds: "... it seems to me that above this minimum the purposes men have for living in society are too conflicting and varying to make possible much extension of the argument that some fuller overlap of legal rules and moral standards is 'necessary'". See H.L.A. Hart, "Positivism and the Separation of Law and Morals" in *Essays in Jurisprudence and Philosophy*, pp.78–82.

relevant legal obligation. This option is not available as regards the existence of the rule of recognition, given that conditions of validity cannot be conceived of independently of the rule of recognition (in fact, they presuppose it). It follows that one has to look elsewhere for a source of validity. Hart attempts to locate a source of validity by conceiving of rules of recognition as species of social rules and then subjecting them to his account of the genesis of social rules. The problem with this explanation is that it cannot sufficiently distinguish secondary from primary obligations. Hart touches upon this problem when he discusses the difficulty in drawing distinctions between different types of primary obligation (especially legal and moral) in early communities. What we find, instead, in those societal formations are just primary obligations that result from the same process of creation: a complex process of "maturation" where social practices evolve in the light of pre-existing primary obligations that determine the evolution of new rules and the content of the obligations they contain. To that extent, social rules that impose obligations are of a uniform type and form a coherent normative web that grows slowly with time.

But the said inability to distinguish *between different types of primary obligation* might also extend to our inability to *distinguish between primary and secondary obligations in the first place*. More specifically, it might be hard to demarcate the obligation embedded in a rule of recognition from all other (primary) obligations that arise from the social practices of a particular community. Given Hart's model of genesis of social obligations it would be hard to justify a separate, *sui generis* kind of obligation that could come into existence independently of all other (pre-existing) social obligations. For, even if it has been possible to detach *legal validity* from an obligation for justification, Hart would still admit that *social validity* is inherently answerable to reasons that are embedded in primary rules. To claim otherwise would amount to treating rules of recognition as legal, something that certainly flies in the face of his explication of rules of recognition as social. In the light of these remarks, every rule of recognition needs to observe the same reasons that primary rules do, and it can only be exempted from those if there is a good justification, namely one that in turn rests on an obligation-imposing primary rule (at least for as long as one remains within Hart's model of social normativity). To that extent, any rule of recognition is a covert primary rule.

The revolutionary conclusion of the connection thesis is that no single set of criteria of validity can be final but, instead, that criteria are revisable in the light of obligating reasons that are embedded in primary rules. On the face of it, even Hart's own contention that the whole enterprise of law is essentially about validity is a *substantive thesis* that derives from obligating reasons rather than a "cool", value-free description of the facts of a distinct social practice (law). Once, however, it has been exposed as a substantive thesis, Hart's analysis might look far less convincing as an understanding of legal phenomena considering that it has to compete with a plethora of other substantive theses that openly accept the relevance of moral obligations in determining legal validity.

CHAPTER 10

HANS KELSEN'S PURE THEORY OF LAW

TIM MURPHY

1. INTRODUCTION

Hans Kelsen born in Prague in 1881 to Jewish Viennese parents who moved back to Vienna shortly after his birth. Although he was resolutely agnostic, Kelsen converted to Catholicism in 1905 to avoid integration problems but nonetheless faced anti-Semitism at various times throughout his life in Europe. He began teaching at the University of Vienna in 1911 and, following World War I, Kelsen was the main drafter of the 1920 Constitution of the Austrian Republic. He was a judge of the Austrian Constitutional Court until 1930 when he was dismissed by the government due to a constitutional crisis concerning the legality of remarriage. Kelsen left Austria and lectured in Cologne until 1933, when he was removed from his post following the Nazi seizure of power in Germany. He then worked at both Geneva and Prague, but was removed from the latter post due to anti-Semitic sentiments among students. Kelsen left Geneva for the United States in 1940, where he taught first at Harvard Law School and later, until his retirement in 1952, at the Department of Political Science at the University of California, Berkeley. Kelsen continued to write and he was still working on his final book when he died in 1973 aged 92.[1]

Kelsen's "pure theory of law" is a positivist theory that has been extremely influential in the world of jurisprudence. In 1963, for example, H.L.A. Hart described Kelsen as "the most stimulating writer on analytical jurisprudence of our day"; a few years later Graham Hughes suggested that, as the last quarter of the twentieth century approached, "there can no longer be any doubt that

---

[1] To date, the only complete biography published was written by Kelsen's former student and assistant Rudolf Aladár Métall, *Hans Kelsen: Leben und Werk* (Deuticke, Vienna, 1969). For a brief sketch based on this work, see N. Bersier Ladavac, "Hans Kelsen: Biographical Note and Bibliography" (1998) 9 *European Journal of International Law* 391.

the formative jurist of our time is Hans Kelsen".[2] Even now, despite a significant waning in Kelsen's influence during that last quarter century, it is not unusual to hear him described as the most important legal philosopher of the twentieth century. His jurisprudence, as we shall mention again, has been referred to in a number of important cases concerning the legality of revolutions, and his theory's intellectual appeal has also been acknowledged in Latin America and the Far East as well as in Europe.[3]

The aim of this chapter is to outline the methodology and main features of the pure theory, which Kelsen began developing during his Austrian years and which received its first complete exposition in 1934. In that year, at the age of 52, Kelsen published *Reine Rechtslehre: Einleitung in die rechtswissen-schaftliche Problematic*, a book that was translated into English only in 1992, under the title *Introduction to the Problems of Legal Theory*.[4] As Kelsen explained at the beginning of this work:

> "More than twenty years ago I undertook to develop a pure theory of law, that is a legal theory purified of all political ideology and every element of the natural sciences, a theory conscious, so to speak, of the autonomy of the object of its enquiry and thereby conscious of its own unique character. Jurisprudence had almost completely been reduced— openly or covertly—to deliberations of legal policy, and my aim from the very beginning was to raise it to the level of a genuine science, a human science. The idea was to develop those tendencies of jurisprudence that focus solely on cognition of the law rather than on the shaping of it, and to bring the results of this cognition as close as possible to the highest values of all science: objectivity and exactitude."[5]

---

[2] H.L.A. Hart, "Kelsen Visited" (1963) 10 *UCLA Law Review* 709 at 728; G. Hughes, "Validity and the Basic Norm" (1971) 59 *California Law Review* 695 at 695.

[3] "His influence was greatest in German-speaking countries, where he is still widely discussed, in Latin America, where he was hailed as a defender of a nonideological treatment of law against natural law theory, and in Japan and Korea, where he is considered to be the model of European legal theory. He is one of the few continental legal theorists to be widely known in the English-speaking world ...". M. Hartney, "Hans Kelsen" in *The Philosophy of Law: An Encyclopedia* (C.B. Gray ed., Garland, New York, 1999), p.480.

[4] H. Kelsen, *Reine Rechtslehre: Einleitung in die rechtswissenschaftliche Problematic* (Deuticke, Vienna, 1934); *Introduction to the Problems of Legal Theory* (B.L. Paulson and S.L. Paulson trans., Clarendon Press, Oxford, 1992). A substantial part of the 1934 book did appear in English in 1934–35 as "The Pure Theory of Law: Its Method and Fundamental Concepts" (C.H. Wilson trans.): (1934) 50 *Law Quarterly Review* 474 and (1935) 51 *Law Quarterly Review* 517.

[5] H. Kelsen, *Introduction to the Problems of Legal Theory*, p.1.

Kelsen's goal in developing the pure theory was to make possible a value-free jurisprudence or a "science of law". This jurisprudence would focus on nothing other than "cognition" of the law, that is, on exactly how law is perceived and recognised. Michael Hartney has observed that nineteenth-century German legal thought had created a "general theory of law" (*Allgemeine Rechtslehre*) as a field of study separate from the "philosophy of law" (*Rechtsphilosphie*, or moral considerations about law), and that Kelsen saw himself "as continuing the project of a general theory of law, but in a way which would remove some of the errors that still infected this discipline. Hence, the need for a purified theory of law, a 'Pure Theory of Law'."[6]

Before turning to the theory itself, it will be helpful to mention Kelsen's three other main works on the pure theory, a theory that he continued to revise throughout his life: *General Theory of Law and State* was published in the United States in 1945 as a restatement of his views for an English-speaking audience;[7] a revised version of the 1934 book was published in 1960 as *Reine Rechtslehre* and translated into English as *Pure Theory of Law* in 1967;[8] and the final revision of the pure theory was published posthumously in 1979 as *Allgemeine Theorie der Normen*, which appeared in English, as *General Theory of Norms*, in 1991.[9]

Opinions vary as to the extent to which Kelsen's various revisions changed his theory. In this chapter our central focus will be on setting out an account of Kelsen's jurisprudence as it is generally understood. We will first examine the epistemological basis of the pure theory and how it gives rise to Kelsen's idea of a legal system as comprising "norms", including a foundational *Grundnorm* ("basic norm"). We will then look at the place of the state in the pure theory, and also at the issue of judicial and administrative decision-making. Finally,

---

[6] M. Hartney, "Hans Kelsen", p.478. It is important to note, however, that Kelsen did not ignore or reject the idea of the "philosophy of law". Nearly one hundred of the 387 titles in Robert Walter's definitive bibliography of Kelsen's works are on—or relate to – the pure theory, but Kelsen also wrote extensively on subjects such as theories of justice, Austrian constitutional law, public law, international law, political and social theory, and the parliamentary system and democracy. See R. Walter, *Hans Kelsen: Ein Leben im Dientse der Wissenschaft* (Manz, Vienna, 1985).

[7] H. Kelsen, *General Theory of Law and State* (Harvard University Press, Cambridge, Mass., 1945).

[8] H. Kelsen, *Reine Rechtslehre* (Deuticke, Vienna, 1960); *Pure Theory of Law* (M. Knight trans., University of California Press, Berkeley, 1967).

[9] H. Kelsen, *Allgemeine Theorie der Normen* (Manz, Vienna, 1979); *General Theory of Norms* (M. Hartney trans., Clarendon Press, Oxford, 1991). The 1991 volume contains a bibliography of Kelsen's publications in English. Other restatements and summaries of the pure theory by Kelsen include "What is the Pure Theory of Law?" (1960) 34 *Tulane Law Review* 269 and "On the Pure Theory of Law" (1966) 1 *Israel Law Review* 1.

we will outline and assess some of the criticisms that the theory has been subjected to over the years.

2. The "Pure Theory" of Law

As George Pavlakos observed in the preceding chapter in this volume, Kelsen's positivism—like H.L.A. Hart's—was a version of the form of positivism that considers that law can be determined in a context-independent way, by reference to a set of purely legal criteria. But whereas Hart's positivism is conventionalist—viewing law as the outcome of a social convention that is constitutive for the existence of law—Kelsen's positivism is epistemic, consisting in the belief that law forms an autonomous domain of knowledge that ought to be studied as a special legal science, in an objective way, akin to the way science studies the natural environment. To quote again from one of Kelsen's own introductions to his theory:

> "The Pure Theory of Law is a theory of positive law. It is a theory of positive law in general, not of a specific legal order. It is a general theory of law, not an interpretation of specific national or international legal norms; but it offers a theory of interpretation. As a theory, its exclusive purpose is to know and to describe its object. The theory attempts to answer the question what and how the law *is*, not how it ought to be. It is a science of law (jurisprudence), not legal politics. It is called a 'pure' theory of law, because it only describes the law and attempts to eliminate from the object of this description everything that is not strictly law: Its aim is to free the science of law from alien elements. This is the methodological basis of the theory."[10]

The purpose of the pure theory, Kelsen says here, "is to know and to describe its object", that is, to know and to describe law. Whereas Hart engaged primarily in conceptual analysis – studying the various instances of the application of "law" and trying to make explicit the rules that guide speakers in using it—Kelsen's analytic approach employed a form of transcendental reasoning in order to reveal necessary conditions for the cognition of law. In simple terms, an issue or question is transcendental if its resolution is not purely a matter of logic or mathematics, and also lies beyond the scope of sense experience. The transcendental reasoning employed by Kelsen is derived from the German philosopher, Immanuel Kant (1724–1804). Kant is revered by many as the modern philosopher who successfully reconciled the competing claims of the

---

[10] H. Kelsen, *Pure Theory of Law* (1967), p.1 (emphasis in original).

two main epistemologies of modernity—rationalism and empiricism. In Kant's epistemology, instead of prioritising reason or experience, the two ways of knowing are combined: the objective world – that which one perceives—is transmuted by certain formal categories or "laws" of the mind; or to put it another way, the mind's categories provide the conceptual structure of experience.

Kelsen approached law—again, the "object" of his theory—with the aim of identifying the necessary conditions for its cognition. What turns an event, or "a natural phenomenon determined by causality", into a legal or illegal act is not, according to Kelsen, its physical existence; rather it is

> "the objective meaning resulting from its interpretation. ... The qualification of a certain act as the execution of the death penalty rather than as murder – a qualification that cannot be perceived by the senses – results from a thinking process: from the confrontation of this act with the criminal code and the code of criminal procedure. That [an] exchange of letters [of a certain content] between merchants constitutes legally a contract, results exclusively from the fact that such an exchange conforms with conditions defined in the civil code. That a document is objectively *as well* as subjectively a valid testament results from the fact that it conforms to conditions stipulated by this code. That an assembly of people is a parliament, and that the meaning of their act is a statute, results from the conformity of all these facts with the norms laid down in the constitution."[11]

In effect, as Dhananjai Shivakumar has observed, Kelsen's claim for his theory is that it explains how legal phenomena must in fact be interpreted and organized within a jurists's mind in order for the jurist to perform the task of recognising certain norms as binding laws: "This effort broadly parallels Kant's argument that categories, such as causality, must be at work in order for the human mind to have ordinary, ordered perception of sensory data. Kelsen ... tries to prove that his understanding of legal validity is a necessary condition of our ability to recognize valid laws."[12]

---

[11] H. Kelsen, *Pure Theory of Law* (1967), pp.3–4 (emphasis in original).

[12] D. Shivakumar, "The Pure Theory as Ideal Type: Defending Kelsen on the Basis of Weberian Methodology" (1996) 105 *Yale Law Journal* 1383 at 1390. Kelsen also explains his methodological approach as follows: "[A]ccording to Kant's epistemology, the science of law as cognition of the law, like any cognition, has constitutive character—it 'creates' its object insofar as it comprehends the object as a meaningful whole. Just as the chaos of sensual perceptions becomes a cosmos, that is, 'nature' as a unified system, through the cognition of natural science, so the multitude of general and individual legal norms, created by the legal organs, becomes

What, then, in more precise terms, is Kelsen's understanding of "legal validity"? Kelsen follows Bentham and Austin in maintaining that rules of positive law are to be differentiated from all other types of social or moral rules in being supported by coercive sanctions, but he denied that the complexity of legal systems could be explained by the command theory. The elements of legal systems should, according to Kelsen, be understood not as commands but as *norms*. By "norm", Kelsen explains, "we mean that something *ought* to be or *ought* to happen, especially that a human being ought to behave in a specific way ... 'Norm' is the meaning of an act by which a certain behavior is commanded, permitted, or authorized."[13] The pure theory proposes that legal systems should be viewed as systems of norms stipulating that, under certain conditions, a coercive measure ought to be applied. The normative character of law consists for Kelsen in recognising that a fact has legal significance only in so far as it has meaning within a normative system, " a system that says that if such and such happens, then such and such *should* be the consequence".[14]

The validity of legal norms is to be determined by their relation to the acts of norm-creation, including legislation, adjudication, and bureaucratic regulation; acts of norm-creation must in turn be validated by other norms. Michael Hartney explains how the pure theory envisages a *Stufenbau* ("step-structure") where norms become progressively concretised:

> "A legal system is a *Stufenbau,* a hierarchical structure of norms; norms at one level are addressed to officials at the next lower level and regulate the creation of norms by these officials. The norms of the constitution are addressed to legislators and regulate the legislative process; the norms in statutes are addressed to judges and regulate judicial decisions; and the individual norms in judicial decisions are addressed to enforcement officials and order them to use coercion against specific individuals. Higher norms are made more specific by lower ones: law flows down in a series from the most general provisions to issue in specific acts of

---

a unitary system, a legal 'order,' through the science of law. But this 'creation' has a purely epistemological character. It is fundamentally different from the creation of objects by human labor or the creation of law by the legal authority." *Pure Theory of Law* (1967), p.72.

[13] H. Kelsen, *Pure Theory of Law*, pp.4-5 (emphasis in original). There is a broader description at the very outset of Kelsen's final work, the *General Theory of Norms*: "The word 'norm' comes from the Latin *norma*, and has been adopted in German to refer primarily, though not exclusively, to a command, a prescription, an order. Nevertheless commanding is not the only function of norms: norms also empower, permit, and derogate" (p.1).

[14] D. Dyzenhaus, *Legality and Legitimacy: Carl Schmitt, Hans Kelsen and Hermann Heller in Weimar* (Oxford University Press, Oxford, 1997), p.102 (emphasis in original).

coercion against specific individuals. All legal norms (except those at the lowest level) are about the creation of more specific norms and so law has this feature of regulating its own creation."[15]

If one takes a specific norm at a certain level in the hierarchy—a judicial decision, for example, that orders enforcement officials to impose a sanction on someone who has committed a crime, or breached a part of the civil law – one should see, according to the pure theory, that such a norm, such an order to enforce, arises legitimately from legislation that has been enacted in accordance with the constitutional provisions governing how legislation should be enacted. The legislation is validated by the constitution; the judicial decision is validated by the legislation; and the actions of the enforcement officials are validated by the judicial decision.

According to the pure theory, statements about the validity of legal norms presuppose effectiveness in two ways: a legal norm loses its validity if it has been ineffective for a long time; and no norm can be valid unless it is a part of a system of norms which is, by and large, effective. In these two ways, as J.W. Harris remarks, effectiveness conditions validity. But how, Harris asks, do we measure effectiveness? "By two criteria: first, is the norm 'obeyed' (in the sense that conduct conditioning the sanction is not performed); secondly, when disobedience occurs, is the sanction applied?"[16]

A critical question arises with regard to the *Stufenbau* or "step-structure" of a legal system: what validates the constitution? The answer is that, for Kelsen, there is a *Grundnorm,* or "basic norm", in every legal system, and it is this that validates not only the constitution but also the entire system. In *General Theory of Law and State* Kelsen compared the basic norm of a religious norm system with the basic norm of a legal order:

> "The basic norm of a religious norm system says that one ought to behave as God and the authorities instituted by him command. Similarly, the basic norm of a legal order prescribes that one ought to behave as the 'fathers' of the constitution and the individuals—directly or indirectly—authorised by the constitution command. Expressed in the form of a legal

---

[15] M. Hartney, "Hans Kelsen", p.479. John Kelly observes that for Kelsen the entire legal system of any country is "a mass of linked ought-propositions or norms and nothing else; such a depiction of law ought to be called a 'pure' theory of law because of its abstraction from everything else except the naked norm; because it is a theory of law as it is, not as it 'should' be (on some standard perhaps of morals, or economic or social utility, matters whose value Kelsen does not deny, but which are extraneous to the law itself and to legal science properly so-called)". *A Short History of Western Legal Theory* (Clarendon Press, Oxford, 1992), p.385.

[16] J.W. Harris, *Legal Philosophies* (2nd ed., Butterworths, London, 1997), p.69.

norm: coercive acts ought to be carried out only under the conditions and in the way determined by the 'fathers' of the constitution or the organs delegated by them. This is, schematically formulated, the basic norm of a single State, the basic norm of a national legal order."[17]

In the same place Kelsen refers to the specific *function* of the basic norm in a way that again sheds light on his epistemological stance:

> "The whole function of this basic norm is to confer law-creating power on the act of the first legislator and on all the other acts based on the first act ... The basic norm ... is valid because it is presupposed to be valid; and it is presupposed to be valid because without this pre-supposition, no human act could be interpreted as a legal, especially as a norm-creating act ... That the basic norm really exists in the juristic consciousness is the result of a simple analysis of actual juristic statements. The basic norm is the answer to the question: how—and that means under what condition – are all these juristic statements concerning legal norms, legal duties, legal rights, and so on, possible?"[18]

It is important to emphasise that the constitution itself is never the *Grundnorm*; rather the *Grundnorm* is higher in the hierarchy than the constitution, and is not purely "legal". As John Kelly observed, when one arrives at the constitution, one does not stop there: "When this point is reached, and it is asked: on what, in its turn, does the authority of the constitution depend, the answer which must be given is one which crosses the frontier, out of the strictly legal sphere, and enters the sphere, perhaps, of group psychology or sheer physical force (or inertia), namely, some proposition such as 'One should obey the constitution'."[19] As we shall see in the next part of this chapter, the movement out of the purely legal and into another, non-legal sphere has, predictably, been the target for much criticism of the pure theory.

Kelsen famously applied his theory to situations where the basic norm changes radically, namely in revolutionary situations. According to Kelsen, when this occurs—that is, when a revolution becomes a successful *coup d'état*—a new basic norm is generally presupposed, authorising and validating the new constitution:

> "Suppose that a group of individuals attempt to seize power by force, in

---

[17] H. Kelsen, *General Theory of Law and State*, p.116.

[18] *ibid.*, p.117.

[19] J.M. Kelly, *op. cit.*, p.386. Harris offers a description of the *Grundnorm* of the United Kingdom legal order: "Coercive acts ought to be carried out only in the ways provided for in the historically first constitution which custom has established"; *op. cit.*, p.74.

order to remove the legitimate government in a hitherto monarchic state, and to introduce a republican form of government. If they succeed, if the old order ceases, and the new order begins to be efficacious, because the individuals whose behavior the new order regulates actually behave, by and large, in conformity with the new order, then this order is considered as a valid order. It is now according to this new order that the actual behavior of individuals is interpreted as legal or illegal. But this means that a new basic norm is presupposed."[20]

Although Kelsen never expressly authorised judicial use of his theory, it was cited as justifying judicial recognition of new regimes following coups in Pakistan (1958) and in Uganda (1965), and also following the Rhodesian Unilateral Declaration of Independence in 1965.[21] On the other hand the pure theory was rejected by the Supreme Court of Nigeria in 1970 and the Pakistan Supreme Court repudiated its earlier decision in 1972.[22]

The pure theory is also said to reveal the "unity" of a legal system: "All law is about the creation of lower norms and is addressed to officials; so there is no distinction in kind between public and private law. All officials (except those at the lowest level) perform both functions: they create law for the next lower level, and in so doing they apply the law of the next higher level. There is only a difference of degree, and not of kind, then, between the various levels …".[23] John Kelly considered that the dissolution of the traditional frontier between "public" and "private" law was the best possible example given by Kelsen of the pure theory's non-contamination by values:[24] "[S]een in this light, 'private' law is revealed as just as much part of the seamless total system as 'public' law, and as equally an expression of the society's political

---

[20] H. Kelsen, *General Theory of Law and State*, p.118.

[21] *State v Dosso* [1958] 2 Pakistan SCR 180; *Uganda v Commissioner of Prisons Ex p Matovu* [1966] EA 514; *Madzimambuto v Lardner-Burke* [1968] 2 SA 284.

[22] *E.O. Lakami and Kimelomo Ola v Att-Gen (Western State)*; *Asma Jilani v Government of Punjab* (Pakistan Leg. decisions 1972, Supreme Court of Pakistan). J.W. Harris observes that while the Nigerian court held that a military coup of 1966 was not a true revolution, so that the legislative capacity of new institutions was limited by reference to the pre-existing constitution, the court's decision was immediately overturned by new legislation declaring that the 1966 coup had been revolutionary. In 1972, when the Supreme Court of Pakistan rejected Kelsen's theory, it held that it was through judicial recognition alone that a new legislative organ acquired competence and that this should be accorded only if a revolutionary constitution embodied the will of the people. In the latter case, Harris remarks, "the court was in the happy position of adjudicating on the legality of one coup after it had been superseded by another"; *op. cit.*, pp.79–80.

[23] M. Hartney, "Hans Kelsen", p.479.

[24] See for example H. Kelsen, *Pure Theory of Law* (1967), pp.280 *et seq.*

premises."[25] Other conventional legal concepts and distinctions are also "dissolved" by the pure theory: an individual "right", for example, is for Kelsen simply a formulation or representation of the norm or norms that impose obligations on others with respect to the individual; the separation of powers doctrine is rendered almost redundant because both administrative orders and judicial decisions are aimed at realising public policy through the "step-structure" of norms; and the notion of sovereignty ceases to be a constitutive concept and becomes merely an expression for both the systematic nature of a legal order and its autonomy from other normative orders.[26]

In the pure theory the distinction between "the state" and "law" also disappears, because the state can be described only in terms of the norms which set out its structure and mechanisms, and these norms do not differ in kind from the other norms in the legal system. The unity of a legal system explains Kelsen's argument, in presenting his definition of law as a coercive order, that the state is an entity that lays exclusive claim to the legitimate use of forceful coercion. This is an idea that can be traced to the sociologist Max Weber (1864–1920). In his essay, *Politics as a Vocation* Weber defined a state as a human community that successfully claims the monopoly of the legitimate use of physical force within a given territory.[27] Kelsen wrote:

> "The development of the law from primitive beginnings to its present stage in the modern state displays, concerning the legal value to be realized, a tendency that is common to all legal orders. It is the tendency gradually and increasingly to prohibit the use of physical force from man to man. Use of force is prohibited by making it the condition for a sanction. But the sanction itself is a use of force…. It is permitted as a reaction against a socially undesirable fact, especially against a socially detrimental human behavior, as a sanction, that is, as an authorized use of force attributable to the legal community … [W]e are confronted with a monopoly of force of the legal community."[28]

It was also proposed by Kelsen that, by defining law as a system of norms and defining the state as simply another name for a centralised legal system, one could see that international law is indeed law (which much traditional

---

[25] J.M. Kelly, *op. cit.*, p.387.

[26] "In short, to say that a legal order is sovereign was for Kelsen to say no more than that it has a basic norm, which it must in any case be presupposed to have in virtue of its being an (existing) legal order." D. Dyzenhaus, *op. cit.*, p.153.

[27] Self-defence in criminal law is generally considered to be the main exception to the rule, although any such forceful coercion (*i.e.* if this defence is accepted in a given case) could also be viewed as authorised indirectly by criminal law norms.

[28] H. Kelsen, *Pure Theory of Law* (1967), p.36.

jurisprudence, defining law as the will of the state, was unable to do). Kelsen viewed international law as a system of norms which make use of coercive sanctions such as reprisals and war. However, as Michael Hartney emphasises, "international law is a decentralized legal system, as law is in primitive societies; its norms arise through custom and treaties, and its sanctions are matters of self-help, decided on and enforced by the subjects of the system, namely individual states".[29]

As one descends the hierarchy of norms in a national legal system, legal content tends to be determined more narrowly. Constitutions, for example, limit the power of legislators, but generally in less specific terms than the wording of statutes that limit the power of administrative agencies and judges. The pure theory acknowledges the roles of discretion and power within the formal bounds of legal authorisation:

> "The constraint exercised by the constitution upon the legislator, as far as the content of the statutes is concerned which he is authorized to issue, is not as strong as the constraint exercised by a statute upon the judge who has to apply this statute. ... But the judge too creates law, and he too is relatively free in this function."[30]

While each layer of the hierarchy restricts the freedom of the layer below it to apply coercive force as it desires, Kelsen does agree with those who argue that even at the level of the judge, legal content is being determined. Kelsen does not, however, claim that judges are completely free:

> "The courts do create law ... [but the] judicial decision is the continuation, not the beginning of the law-creating process ... In the application of law by a legal organ, the cognitive interpretation of the law to be applied is combined with an act of will by which the law-applying organ chooses between the possibilities shown by cognitive interpretation." [31]

But where norms are "defective"—ambiguous, say, or inconsistent—it would seem that the consequence of the systematic unity of law is to leave the judge free to decide as he wishes. As Hartney observes

> "There is no way internal to the law of resolving these difficulties. The standard rules of interpretation are of no use, and there is no scientific way of weighing interests or finding the 'just' solution. While these cases

---

[29] M. Hartney, "Hans Kelsen", p.479.
[30] H. Kelsen, *Pure Theory of Law* (1967), p.353.
[31] *ibid.*, pp.255, 354.

are not covered by any specific legal norm, nevertheless there are no gaps in the law, that is, no cases for which the law does not provide a solution, since the law requires the judge to dismiss a case which cannot be brought under any existing norm."[32]

On the specific issue of political power Kelsen's view was that while the law cannot exist without power, neither is it identical with power: "The law is, in terms of the theory developed here, a certain system (or organization) of power."[33]

3. Criticisms and Assessment

While the pure theory has been extremely influential in terms of legal theory generally, it has also been subjected to a great deal of criticism. Much of this criticism has focused on the idea of the *Grundnorm*, the "impure" aspect of the theory. John Kelly, for example, observed how it is often remarked that Kelsen's model is forced, "at the point of its initial hypothesis, into the sphere of those very elements—psychology, ethics, social behaviour, and so on – which lower down the hierarchy of norms are so rigorously excluded".[34] Margaret Davies has undertaken a deconstruction of the *Grundnorm* with a view to exposing this lack of clarity, Her view is that *Grundnorm* is "a fiction not only because it contradicts reality (that is, it does not exist), but also because it is self-contradictory".[35]

Davies bases her approach on an essay by Jacques Derrida, "The Law of Genre", in which Derrida points out that the definition of a genre, within which we can include areas of knowledge, or any conceptual separation of one intellectual terrain from any other, depends upon there being some "mark" or "trait" which allows us to distinguish or recognise the genre. The "law of genre" determines what falls within the genre, and what falls outside.[36] Davies observes that the *Grundnorm* is a different kind of norm to other norms but, at the same time,

"it is a part of every law: it is in a sense the *most* legal thing, because it is

---

[32] M. Hartney, "Hans Kelsen", p.479. For the argument that Kelsen had more than one position with respect to the question of conflicts between legal norms, see S. Paulson, "On the Status of the *lex posterior* Derogating Rule" in *Essays on Kelsen* (R. Tur and W. Twining eds., Clarendon Press, Oxford, 1986).

[33] H. Kelsen, *Introduction to the Problems of Legal Theory*, p.61.

[34] J.M. Kelly, *op. cit.*, p.388.

[35] M. Davies, *Asking the Law Question* (Sweet and Maxwell, Sydney, 1994), p.268.

[36] See J. Derrida, "The Law of Genre" (1980) *Glyph: Textual Studies* 7, 202.

the essence of law. The basic norm must be at once both internal and external to law, legal and non-legal. And because it is at the heart of what it is to be law, and is reproduced in every law, there is a non-legal dimension of every law… [W]hatever is 'inside' the limit of law is there only because of the mark or 'trace' left there by the 'outside'. In other words, the outside can not be kept entirely out, and nor is the inside ever entirely in."[37]

Davies concludes that the identity of law is reliant on a general principle, the *Grundnorm* or basic norm, which is "itself neither legal nor non-legal, representing a limit or finality which is, however, always requiring that more questions be asked".[38]

J.W. Harris notes that Kelsen's ideas about a change of the basic norm have been criticized for making efficacy the only test for legal recognition of revolutions: "Surely, it has been argued, lawyers take other things into account—such as the justice of the revolutionary cause, or the approval, or disapproval of the populace—not just the fact of enforcement? Whether Kelsen, or his critics, correctly describe what lawyers do in such contexts is a question for historians."[39] While it does seem that at one time Kelsen was thought to hold that lawyers and others *should* recognize a new regime when it is effective, this view cannot be sustained as a correct interpretation of the pure theory. Harris is accurate in remarking that Kelsen's theory is purely descriptive in this regard – Kelsen cites only cases of successful revolution; in other words, Kelsen's theory of a change of the basic norm amounts to "might is Law" rather than "might is right".[40]

Although Kelsen was never able to respond completely and satisfactorily to his theory's critics in relation to all the questions raised about the basic norm, we should remember that he argued that the basic norm is valid because it is "presupposed" to be valid, and that it is presupposed to be valid because without this pre-supposition, no human act could be interpreted as a legal, especially as a norm-creating act. This is not the same as suggesting, as Davies does, that the basic norm is the "most legal thing" or the "essence of law". The key to understanding the basic norm, at least from Kelsen's perspective, is to

---

[37] M. Davies, *op. cit.*, pp.267–268 (emphasis in original).

[38] *ibid.*, p.268. Davies proposes a somewhat similar approach in relation to H.L.A. Hart's "rule of recognition". She notes the conceptual difficulty with a theory that involves officials recognising the rule of recognition, which is itself what recognises them as officials: "There is therefore a problem of what Derrida often calls 'undecideability' precisely at the line of demarcation between law and non-law, where positivist theory ought to be most certain." *ibid.*

[39] J.W. Harris, *op. cit.*, p.79.

[40] *ibid.*

see it primarily in functional terms, that is, functional in relation to knowing and describing law. As we saw earlier, Kelsen views the basic norm as "[existing] in the juristic consciousness" and so the idea is tied to Kelsen's neo-Kantian epistemology, which shapes the pure theory by systematically charting the background assumptions of the jurist's recognition of binding legal norms.

This epistemology, however, has also been questioned. Why, for example, must the validity of a legal norm be derived in the manner described by Kelsen, that is, through the category of imputational links rooted in the basic norm? Stanley Paulson has argued that Kelsen's neo-Kantian argument fails as a methodological grounding in the legal sphere because Kelsen does not demonstrate that this is the *only* way to understand the validity of law. It is possible, for example, that a shared value-system – some notion of justice or morality—underlies the statements of jurists concerning validity, in addition to, or instead of, reasoning by imputational links.[41] In short, as Dhananjai Shivakumar remarks, "Kelsen does not prove that the discovery of the role of imputation leads ineluctably to his account of the chain of validity."[42]

Shivakumar draws on Paulson's arguments in his own defence of Kelsen's theory. According to Shivakumar, the pure theory should be detached from its neo-Kantian basis and instead viewed as an "ideal type", a concept developed by Max Weber. Generally speaking, an ideal type is a conceptual structure that does not depend either on universal applicability or on correctness; instead its success lies in its usefulness as a device with which to analyse particular historical cases. Shivakumar's view is that once Kelsen's "elegant, one-sided model" is freed from its aspiration to provide the one correct reconstruction of legal systems, full purity is possible because what he regards as its "most serious compromise"—its use of a criterion of minimal effectiveness—can be eliminated. We referred earlier to that part of the pure theory which holds that a legal norm, to be valid, must be effectively applied. Shivakumar considers this appeal to "the realm of observable behaviour" as tarnishing the purity of Kelsen's model by introducing the uncertainty that necessarily attaches to any inquiry as to whether a norm has fallen into desuetude. "A pure concept of legal validity need not be compromised by a concern with effectiveness. One

---

[41] See S.L. Paulson, "The Neo-Kantian Dimension of Kelsen's Pure Theory of Law" (1992) 12 *Oxford Journal of Legal Studies* 311. Paulson has written extensively on the pure theory. For other examples of his work, see "Kelsen's Legal Theory: The Final Round" (1992) 12 *Oxford Journal of Legal Studies* 265 and his introductory essay in *Introduction to the Problems of Legal Theory*. An advanced discussion of Kelsen's work can also be found in *Normativity and Norms* (S. Paulson and B. Paulson eds., Clarendon Press, Oxford, 1998).

[42] D. Shivakumar, *op. cit.* at 1395.

can defend [the pure theory] on the basis of our desire to maximise critical insight into the workings of modern bureaucratic justice."[43]

Shivakumar also suggests that Kelsen may himself have recognized the flaw identified by Paulson: there is no trace in the *General Theory of Norms* of the neo-Kantian justification for the pure theory, "and no explanation for this silence."[44] In his defence of the pure theory as an ideal type, Shivakumar refers to the view—again advanced originally by Paulson—that the pure theory is rendered groundless and empty by Kelsen's renunciation of a neo-Kantian method with no other methodological grounding to replace it.[45] Michael Hartney, however, in his introduction to the *General Theory of Norms*, summarises the complex development of Kelsen's theory of norms as a shift from Kantian epistemology to "a Humean view", that is, to the empirical epistemology associated with the Enlightenment thinker, David Hume (1711–1776). In the 1934 version of the *Pure Theory of Law*, says Hartney, the focus is on legal science: "it is legal science which shapes legal norms and creates a legal system free of all contradictions ... [The pure theory] is intended to provide legal science with the correct understanding of what law is and the necessary concepts to allow it to perform its task"; by contrast, in the *General Theory of Norms*,

"the function of normative science is strictly passive: it describes the legal or moral norms created by legal or moral authorities. It plays no part in shaping these norms and it has no power whatsoever to modify them or to eliminate any contradictions in a normative system. The focus is entirely on the authorities who produce the norms. In the close to forty years which separate these two books, there has been a shift from a Kantian view of reason and science to a Humean view: whereas previously reason had an active role, it no longer has any normative function. This explains in part the comment Kelsen made to H.L.A. Hart in the early sixties that Hume was the greatest philosopher of all time."[46]

---

[43] *ibid.*, at 1413. Shivakumar explains that from the perspective of Weberian methodology, "answers to questions regarding the nature of law will suit the investigator's needs depending on which aspects of complex human societies strike her as significant ... Concepts that present a rigorous, one-sided analysis are more effective expository tools than other, more nuanced concepts that offer a more thorough description of law. If one regards concepts of law as tools in the hands of social observers, one can criticize some definitions of law for not being sharp enough to function effectively as ideal types."

[44] *ibid.*, at 1395.

[45] See S. Paulson, "Kelsen's Legal Theory: The Final Round", at 273.

[46] M. Hartney, "Introduction: The Final Form of the Pure Theory of Law" in H. Kelsen, *General Theory of Norms*, p.lii. Hartney reports that Professor Hart confirmed this

Epistemological issues also arise in David Dyzenhaus's investigation of the pure theory in terms of the relationship between legality and legitimacy, in which he seeks to demonstrate the costs of constructing a theory of norms which aims to be purified of all ethical and political considerations. Dyzenhaus argues that Kelsen's relativism is at the root of all the tensions and difficulties in the pure theory, which asks us to accept the highly counterintuitive idea that normativity can be understood scientifically, that is, without reference to politics or ethics. According to Dyzenhaus, Kelsen fails to say properly what the value of such a scientific inquiry is, but nonetheless insists that it is an ethical necessity to accept its value. Even worse, says Dyzenhaus, "the pure theory in some ideal sense dissolves every claimed antinomy between the individual and the community, and thus between the law, seen as the guardian of individual rights, and the state. It thus justifies nothing but at the same time justifies everything."[47]

Although John Kelly acknowledged some impurity in the *Grundnorm* concept, he added that Kelsen's scheme is "coherent and illuminating in spite of it".[48] While the pure theory is generally coherent, the degree to which it is illuminating continues to be hotly debated. One common general criticism of the pure theory is that it is overly logical and divorced from reality. For example, Karl Llewellyn, the American legal realist, described the theory as "utterly sterile".[49] The criticism that the pure theory is too detached from social and political realities is sometimes met with the argument that it was designed in part to allow for attention to moral evaluation of the law to be more rigorously possible.[50] What is being suggested by this argument is that Kelsen wanted to improve (or "purify") the "general theory of law" (*Allgemeine Rechtslehre*) in order to improve the quality of the "philosophy of law" (*Rechtsphilosphie*, or moral considerations about law). And there is surely a sense in which the pure theory *does* offer something of value for those working in the field of what we now generally call jurisprudence: while its orientation appears to be away from the normative concerns of contemporary jurisprudence, the pure theory exposes one of most significant things about law: that each and every law or "norm" is a consequence of a prior political decision.

We referred in the previous part to Kelsen's view of the relationship between

---

anecdote to him, and that it is also recounted in Walter Ott, "Bericht von eimen Besuch bei Prof. H.L.A. Hart in Oxford" (1987) 18 *Rechtstheorie* 534 at 539.

[47] D. Dyzenhaus, *op. cit.*, pp.158–59.

[48] J.M. Kelly, *op. cit.*, p.388.

[49] K. Llewellyn, *Jurisprudence: Realism in Theory and Practice* (University of Chicago Press, Chicago, 1962), p.365 (n.5).

[50] "[T]he theory's object of cognition – the norm – is seen without reference to its content or to such questions as why it is (or is not) obeyed. But Kelsen intends to clarify the field for those who are primarily interested in these questions." M.D.A. Freeman, *op. cit.*, p.258.

law and political power: that law, in terms of the pure theory, is "a certain system (or organization) of political power".[51] This arises from the pure theory's insistence on the element of coercion involved in all legal norms and on the related "unity" of a legal system. This "unity", as has been said, means that traditional concepts—such as the separation of powers, the notion of rights and the idea of sovereignty—and traditional distinctions—such as between public and private law and between the state and law—are exposed as mere ideological constructs. Consider, for example, the way in which the pure theory highlights the public policy dimensions to private law rules of property and contract. These appear to be—and are traditionally perceived as—removed from state action. The pure theory challenges this by suggesting that such constructions and distinctions may in fact be motivated by a desire to encourage deference to administrative actions.[52] Kelsen countered the traditional view that the property relationship—to take one specific example—was primarily about the exclusive power of a person over a thing by arguing that this view was maintained in order to disguise property rights' distinctive social and economic function as "nothing else than a relation of the property-owner to other subjects, who are forbidden access to his property and who are compelled to respect his proprietary powers".[53] There is coercive force behind every legal right and this, as Shivakumar points out, is significant if we value freedom and wish to question the operation of all coercive measures:

> "[Kelsen] wishes to emphasize the procedural system that sanctifies violence and coercion in every society, whether it be democratic or autocratic. ... To claim that the validity of a norm-positing act rests solely on authorization by a higher legal norm separates procedural legitimacy from substantive justification and forces one to consider each layer of the legal bureaucracy as involved in either administering sanctions or shaping their eventual administration."[54]

---

[51] H. Kelsen, *Introduction to the Problems of Legal Theory*, p.61. Consider also the similar description of legal positivism offered by Alfred Verdross (1890–1980): "[Legal positivism] regards law as a mere technique for the realisation of whatever objects men may wish, in other words as a means of organising political power." *Abendländische Rechtsphilosophie* (Vienna, Rechts und Staatswissenschaften (Bd. 16), 1958), p.98, quoted in J.M. Kelly, *op. cit.*, p.223. Verdross was one of many of Kelsen's students at Vienna who went on to become an important legal theorist in his own right. See N. Bersier Ladavac, *op. cit.*

[52] H. Kelsen, *Pure Theory of Law*, pp.281–284.

[53] H. Kelsen, "The Pure Theory of Law: Its Method and Fundamental Concepts" (1934) at 494.

[54] D. Shivakumar, *op. cit.*, at 1408, 1410.

Ultimately, the pure theory calls for special attention to be paid to the idea of the state, a concept discussed to a far greater extent by intellectual communities outside the Anglo-American tradition than within it. The pure theory implies, for example, that the doctrine of separation of powers is an elaborate construct designed in part simply to disguise the fact that when courts adjudicate, and particularly when they adjudicate on actions involving the state, they breach one of the basic rules of procedural natural justice—*nemo iudex in causa sua* ("no person shall be a judge in their own cause"). Adjudication in a state by an "arm of state", is a procedurally unjust element inherent in the idea of statehood. The emphasis on state power and coercion in the pure theory is not "overly logical" or "sterile"; it would seem rather that it raises important questions about the State in a particularly uncompromising way.

CHAPTER 11

LAW AND MORALITY

PATRICK HANNON

1. INTRODUCTION

An account of the relationships between law and morality is a standard feature
of textbooks on jurisprudence, and standard accounts tend to focus on two
questions: whether there is a moral obligation to obey the law and whether it is
the business of the law to enforce morality These questions may arise also for
the discipline of political philosophy and of course for ethics, and the answer
which comes out of any of the disciplines is likely to be influenced by views
concerning the subject matter of the others. So, for example, what legal
philosophers believe about the relationships between morality and law will
depend to some extent on their understanding of politics, and it will certainly
be coloured by what they understand morality to be; and these understandings
need not be at all consciously held or explicitly adverted to.

But it is arguable that of the three disciplines—jurisprudence, political
philosophy and ethics—that of ethics is the basic one, or at any rate that the
experience with which ethics deals, the experience of morality, is as it were
prior to the experience of law and of politics. For moral responsibility would
exist even if there were no laws or no political system, difficult as it may be to
imagine such a state of affairs. Moral responsibility arises directly from the
fact that human beings are able to choose, as we shall shortly see, and though
we are also social beings, so that law and politics follow hard upon, the
originating experience is that of morality.

This is a warrant for taking some time, in a chapter dealing with law and
morality in a jurisprudence textbook, to reflect on morality at some length.
Many authors seem to assume that we all agree on what morality is, or they
leave the reader to infer the theory of morals to which they subscribe, or—
occasionally—they seem unaware that what one makes of the relationships
between morality and law depends at least in part on how one understands
morality. But of course a utilitarian or other consequentialist account of morality
is likely to give rise to conclusions about morality and law (conclusions, indeed,
about law) which differ from those implied in the view of, say, a deontologist.[1]

---

[1] Consequentialist ethics considers that the value of an action derives entirely from

It would be impossible, even if it were desirable, to treat in a chapter every plausible combination of ethical theory and theory of law. Nor would it be especially useful simply to review the main contributions of philosophers and jurisprudents who have written upon the relationship between law and morality. The latter is admirably done elsewhere,[2] and in any case there is no substitute for reading the work of the authors themselves; and if summaries of their thought are required they can be found in standard encyclopaedias of law and of ethics. A better approach may be to enter the discussion by way of one particular viewpoint, and to offer an account that might provide the reader with a starting-point for criticism and debate.

The viewpoint taken here will be readily identified as coming out of the natural law tradition, in its conception both of morality and of law and in its view of the main questions regarding their interrelationships. Not that one is forgetful of the difficulties which natural law theory must contend with. For one thing, its history has shown it to exhibit what H.L.A. Hart has called a "protean" character:[3] it has looked differently at different times and has meant different things to different adherents, as is seen when one examines the various versions propounded by, say, Aristotle, Cicero, Ulpian, St Thomas Aquinas, Grotius, Lon Fuller and John Finnis.[4]

And even when we consider only what is a persistent theme—that the

---

the value of its consequences, whereas deontological ethics holds that there are duties by which one is obliged regardless of consequences. The main ethical theories are explained very well in W.K. Frankena, *Ethics* (2nd ed., Prentice-Hall, Englewood Cliffs, 1973).

[2] A good account, with further references, is in H. McCoubrey and N.D. White, *Textbook on Jurisprudence* (3rd ed., Blackstone, London, 1999). See also M.D.A. Freeman, *Lloyd's Introduction to Jurisprudence* (7th ed., Sweet and Maxwell, London, 2001); B. Bix, *Jurisprudence: Theory and* Context (2nd ed., Sweet and Maxwell, London, 1999); N.E. Simmonds, *Central Issues in Jurisprudence* (Sweet and Maxwell, London, 1986); J.G. Riddall, *Jurisprudence* (Butterworths, London, 1991); J.W. Harris, *Legal Philosophies* (2nd ed., Butterworths, London, 1980); and M.P. Golding, *Philosophy of Law* (Prentice-Hall, Englewood Cliffs, 1975).

[3] H.L.A. Hart, "Positivism and the Separation of Law and Morals" in R. Dworkin (ed.), *The Philosophy of Law* (Oxford University Press, Oxford, 1977), p.36.

[4] Ronald Dworkin has said, somewhat sweepingly, that "the various theories grouped under that title [natural law] are remarkably different from one another, and the name suits none of them", *Law's Empire* (Fontana, London, 1986), p.35. The best short introduction to the history of the concept of natural law is still A.P. D'Entrèves, *Natural Law* (2nd ed., Hutchinson, London, 1970), but there is an excellent summary account in J.M. Kelly, *A Short History of Western Legal Theory* (Clarendon, Oxford, 1992); and *cf.* P.E. Sigmund, *Natural Law in Political Thought* (University Press of America, Lanham, 1971) which provides a selection of key texts, together with commentary and bibliography. M.D.A. Freeman (*op. cit.*) also has a selection of texts.

demands of the moral law are available to a reasoned reflection on what it is to be a human being in the world which we inhabit—cultural and ethnic differences are such as to make one wonder whether any useful general theory of human nature is attainable, or any guidance for right living. Yet the concept of a natural moral order has over centuries proved remarkably resilient in face of the sometimes apparently fatal objections of its critics. The interest in it that was stirred by the need to refute the "positivist" defence of officials and military arraigned at Nürnberg has been replicated more recently in the context of debate about the foundations of human rights.[5]

What follows then is an account of the lineaments of an understanding of morality that is in the broadly classical natural law tradition. An attempt is made to draw attention to aspects of morality that are especially relevant to discussion of its relationship to law. It is hoped that the account will shed light on the response later given to questions about the interrelationships between the two spheres, and in particular to the question whether there is a moral obligation to obey the law, and to that of the legal enforcement of morals.

2. What is Morality?

Morality may be described as the art of right relationship with each other and with the world around us. The use of the word "art" may at first sight be puzzling, and its choice will be explained in due course. But first we must look at other elements in the description.

Relationship is a fundamental feature of being human. We come into the world as the fruit of the relationship of our parents, and if we are to survive we need from the outset to be in some kind of sustaining relationship with another. In normal circumstances a child is in dependent relationship first to the mother, and he or she comes to maturity in a network of relationships which contribute to nurturing and education in a complex variety of ways.

At first our relationships are non-reflective, some even unconscious; spontaneously we just *are*—children or sisters or brothers or pupils or friends, or a doctor's patients or a newsagent's customers. But as we grow in self-awareness we become aware of our relationships, and gradually we become

---

[5] Legal positivism is a theory of law that holds, to speak roughly, that the binding-force of a law is derived by reference to strictly legal (as distinct from moral) criteria. It is the main rival to natural law theory. *Natural Law Theory*, edited by R.P. George (Clarendon, Oxford, 1992), is a collection of essays that shows the diversity of contemporary natural law theories. A highly influential modern treatment is J.M. Finnis, *Natural Law and Natural Rights* (Clarendon, Oxford, 1980). Recent criticism of natural law theory is summarised and evaluated in R.P. George, *In Defence of Natural Law* (Clarendon, Oxford, 1999).

aware of being able to make some choices in their regard. I cannot change the fact that I am the sibling of X and Y, but I find I have some control over the way in which I behave toward them. I cannot avoid being in the relationship of classmate to Z, but I can choose whether or not I want Z to be my friend.

These two characteristics of the human person, awareness and a capacity for choice, are the foundation of morality. For our awareness tells us something about the way the world is, and our capacity for choice allows us to decide how we are going to conduct ourselves in it. A more familiar way of putting this, perhaps, is to say that humans are knowing and free, and that their knowledge and freedom are the basis for morality.

Not that our knowledge is always full and clear, or our freedom absolutely pure. We forget, make mistakes, are sometimes ignorant of truth, and sometimes our judgement is clouded by excess of emotion or by factors deep in our psychology of which we may not even be conscious. Our freedom is always bounded by our knowledge, and it may be trammelled too by compulsions and fears and other stirrings of the psyche, including, again, forces within us of which we may not be aware.

Yet normally we have sufficient knowledge and capacity for choice to be able in some fashion to direct our lives. The recognition that we are always influenced by our make up and our environment has not persuaded people to abandon the language of praise or blame, or to cease to try to change our ways or encourage others to change theirs. Which is to say that people generally hold on to the idea of moral *responsibility*, the idea that we are able to make something of ourselves and of our world, and that we are answerable for what we make of ourselves and how.

So the dimension of our experience which we call morality is founded on our capacity to know and to choose: these characteristics of the human are what enable us to practise the art of relating to other people and to our world. But the description with which we are working mentions "*right* relationship", and the concept of morality includes the notion that there are right and wrong ways of relating.

Right and Wrong, Good and Evil?

Right and wrong in terms of what? For the moment we may think of right as meaning conformity to a standard or rule: of being just, for example, as required by the rule that we ought to be just; or giving food or shelter to a poor person in accordance with a principle that we ought to help people who are in need; or refraining from stealing, according to the precept that we ought not to steal. But why these rules, and where did they come from, and why should we conform to them?

One approach is to say that another way of putting all this is that it is "good" to be just or to help people in need, "evil" or "bad" to steal. Speaking strictly, the terms right and wrong, even in a moral context, are probably mainly descriptive of compliance or otherwise with some standard; though inevitably there is also a suggestion of commendation or disapproval of whatever or whomever is said to be right or wrong. With the expressions good and evil this evaluative ingredient comes into prominence: a good radio is to be prized and praised, as is a good read; and a good person makes, as it were, a demand on our regard.

A good person? It is not hard to judge whether a radio is good or bad, or a book—or indeed a singer or footballer or student. For it is not difficult to find criteria by which these judgements may be made, even if for some of them we may have to allow for "taste", and even if people differ sometimes as to the precise criteria, or how they are to be ranked, or how exactly applied. But a good person? Following a classical philosophical tradition and adapting the OED one might say that we call a thing good when it is what it is called to be. So a person is good when he or she is what he or she is called to be. "Call" is figurative; a religious person may think here of a call of God, but the expression need mean no more than that a particular way of being or acting is according to our nature.

And what is "our nature"? Several answers are possible. If what characterises the human person are reason and freedom, the interlinked powers of understanding and of choice, we are what we are called to be when exercising our freedom rationally. And that indeed is an apt description of what being moral means. But it is abstract and general, and people are more attracted by a somewhat warmer way of putting it; and more than one religious and philosophical tradition would be happy with the proposition that the human person is called to love.

Love is a troublesome word of course, its meaning confused in the variety of its usage. A child loves ice-cream as well as its parents, a whole generation loved the Rolling Stones, Dante loved Beatrice, Hamlet loved Ophelia, and Don Juan loved many women. C.S. Lewis wrote a book called *The Four Loves*, from which it may be seen that even when we use the word aptly we may be talking of different forms of love. But there is at least the residue of a core meaning, and for present purposes we can say that love means wishing people well and doing them good.

So the good person is one who loves. But this is too general, it tells us nothing about how we ought in practice to behave, and we need immediately to give it concrete content. We could say that to love is to appreciate another, to have regard (in more than one sense); and to express this appreciation and regard in our dispositions and attitudes and intentions and actions. We should therefore acknowledge the dignity of others, respect their life and person, aim to do them good, be just and truthful, don't steal from them or take away their good name, refrain from harming them in any way.

Moral Rules

These are some of the "rules" of morality, and they follow from the nature of the enterprise, and the nature of the enterprise is determined by our nature as human beings. Humans are called to love, and the "precepts" or "command-ments" which are a feature of all moral systems are statements of a standard or test of loving. It may be noticed, incidentally, that the rules are of differing kinds. Some are general: respect the dignity of others, respect their life and person, aim to do good. Others are more specific: be just and truthful, don't steal or defame. Of both general and specific kinds some have to do in the first place with states of mind (acknowledgment of dignity, respect, a will to do good, a disposition to justice)—which is why earlier when referring to the content of loving we mentioned, as well as action, an *internal* dimension comprised of factors such as disposition, attitude and intention. This is an important point, for we need to grasp that morality is not just external conformity with rules. T.S. Eliot's Becket expresses a persistent ethical theme in *Murder in the Cathedral* when he reflects that "the greatest treason [is]/ to do the right deed for the wrong reason".

But where do the rules come from? Most immediately they come from the moral tradition of the community into which each of us is born. Tradition refers both to a process of handing on and to *what* is handed on, and a moral tradition in the second sense consists in the values and principles and rules which comprise the "code" of the community. Normally it is handed on through the usual educational processes, formal and informal, at home or in school or in church, or through other educational agencies of society. In our time the media are potent agents of the transmission of moral value and of information relevant to moral assessment: think of the effect of a television documentary about AIDS in Africa or famine in Asia, or the power of a clever advertisement. Think also of the increasing influence of the internet, and the information and value systems to which it gives instant access.

A word on terminology may be in order at this point again. The code just referred to is not necessarily something which is written; the word is used here to designate the ensemble of values and principles and rules in the light of which a community lives or aspires to live its life. A "value" is something that is prized, considered to be important: in a moral context prized and considered important because of its bearing on human flourishing. An older term for the same thing is "good", something which is commendable, prized, thought important, either in itself or instrumentally. Life is a value or a good, as are honour and honesty and the keeping of promises. Societies or families usually rank values—even if not always consciously—in a certain order of priority, and by both teaching and example they try to communicate these to the next generation.

This means, among other things, expressing them in the form of "principles" or "rules" or "norms", which are intended to guide action so that the value is "realised". We saw some examples of these earlier. The value of life, for instance, is recognised in the principle that human life ought to be respected and in the norm or rule that we ought not to kill. The former of these is general, giving a general shape to our thoughts and activities but not on its face saying anything concerning concrete action or behaviour. The second is concrete, referring to a particular kind of act, the kind of act which takes away life. Both kinds are necessary in guiding our lives: the first gives moral meaning to the second, the second helps translate the first into practice.

Notice that the second is also negative in form—it is a prohibition. Now the picture which many people have of morality is of a list of prohibitions; though we sometimes refer colloquially to moral precepts as "do's and don'ts" we seem to find it easier to think of examples of the don'ts. No doubt this is partially explained by the fact that moral education is still often negatively cast: thou shalt not kill, commit adultery, steal, lie, lust, and so on. But perhaps it is in some sense natural to latch on to prohibitions, especially those which are concrete. For one thing they have a relative clarity—each refers to a definite type of action or state of affairs or state of mind. And each helps mark off what is nowadays called the bottom line, beyond which a particular value or good is totally frustrated, so that we are clear at least on morality's minimal demands.

These prohibitions have an irreplaceable function, for it is important to be able to mark off the bottom line; but they are not the whole of morality. There is a great deal more to respect for life than refraining from killing people, and truthfulness is more than not telling lies. Being just and doing justice is more than not stealing, and there are many ways in which a person might fail in faithfulness to his or her spouse or partner apart from adultery or being violently abusive.

In ethical writing the terms "principle" and "rule", together with "norm" and "commandment" and "precept" and "imperative", tend to be used interchangeably. But perhaps one may say that the words commandment, precept and imperative, though used synonymously with the others, possess or at least accentuate an additional nuance. For these words bring out the sense of *obligation* which is a feature of our understanding of morality. We do not think of being just or truthful or fair-minded as merely a good idea; rather we think of these things as somehow *demanded* of us. Demanded by whom and why?

Why be Moral?

Earlier when we asked ourselves where moral rules come from we saw that in the most obvious sense they come from the tradition of the community. Now, again obviously, we can see that the demand that we keep the rules comes from the community, concretely mediated through parents, teachers, peers and society. But where did the community get the rules, and why should it ask us to keep them? It is worth pursuing these questions a little. One of the chief reasons why people—especially the young—resist moral rules is that they reject the authority of whomever they perceive to be imposing them.

Where *do* the rules come from, and why obey them? Their author is the human mind, reflecting on human experience, discovering what is or is not fit living for a creature with a human nature. This discovery is always in process, for there is no end to change in the conditions of our living, and the change forces us to a ceaseless search for the right way for humans to live. There are of course some constants: we are body-spirits, with minds and hearts and will—rational and free, as the philosophers have it. We are sexual beings with an instinct for the reproduction of our kind. We need food, clothing and shelter. We need also to search for the "truth" of things, to comprehend ourselves and our world. There is in us also a "dark side", imperilling our ability to grasp our true good, or our ability to carry through what we recognise to be for our good. And these constants generate certain general requirements of human flourishing, which is another way of saying that the general requirements of morality do not change. But their concrete application varies, and we are never freed from the quest for the right way.

I have used the expression "human flourishing" in reference to the point of being moral; an older expression is "fulfilment", older still (but perhaps misleading) the word "happiness". What is in question is the idea that the point of anything is that it should *be* in the way which best suits the kind of thing it is: that things always aim at the "perfection" of whatever their nature is. And the perfection of a human nature is in the direction of rational choice—or of loving, if you prefer that way of putting it. Humans flourish inasmuch as they exercise their freedom according to the claims of reality, the claims of their own nature and the nature of things generally, or again, more warmly, when they truly love.

Of course some will say that the point of being moral is simply survival: that the demands of morality originated and have their justification in the concrete conditions of the persistence of individuals and of the species. But does this accord with our experience? It may well be that historically the first perceptions of, say, the value of life were self-interested, or that what came to be called the Golden Rule—positively formulated as that you should do unto others as you would have others do unto you—was at first no more than the insight that it is expedient to live and let live. And no doubt in practice we often do what is right from self-interest rather than from nobler motives.

But we are never content for long with this version of things. We are not content with mere survival but are drawn to a certain "quality" in our living. In the context of our relationships that quality includes attitudes such as gentleness and compassion and unselfishness. It calls on us sometimes to turn the other cheek or go the second mile; and it asks some to lay down their life for their friend. Such manifestations of the flourishing of humanity are not explicable in terms of survival merely.

Moral rules come to us out of the tradition of the community, but their ultimate origin is in the race's attempt to make sense of its experience; or, if you like, in human reason reflecting on human nature. And we ought, therefore, to obey the rules not just, as it were, on the say-so of the community or its authorities but because, and to the extent that, they indicate the way of human flourishing. The answer to the question, why be moral? is not that society or a church or even God requires it, but that it is through being moral that we become truly human.

An Art?

The description with which we began spoke of morality as an art, and now it is time to explain why. The word seems apposite at several levels. Its most basic sense is of a skill which comes from knowledge and practice, and we have seen enough to appreciate how morality might be described as an art in this sense. Plainly it requires a knowledge, an ensemble of notions and values and principles which express in the concrete the requirements of the good life. But the good life is to be *lived*, not just known or appreciated in the abstract. Moral knowledge is for putting into *practice*, and the practice both expresses and reinforces our ideas about how we are meant to live.

The word art is suggestive in a second way, for it also intimates a performance or achievement which is more than the simple application of a rule. There are principles of musical composition, for example, but the art of Beethoven is more than his observance of these rules. One could say that among the things which make us regard him as a great composer is the way in which he "works with" the rules, fashioning in music his vision. Vision in this context is not (if it ever is) something of the mind only; music too is, as Wordsworth in *Tintern Abbey* said of poetry, felt in the blood and felt along the heart. And, as in poetry or music, moral sensibility includes an engagement of the feelings and of the imagination which allows us to "see into the life of things".

Justice, as Aristotle said, is not merely the doing of just actions but the doing of them in the way of the just person.[6] That means behaving out of a right intention and motive and attitude, and a general disposition to justice. And a disposition to justice or any other form of goodness, translated into practice, leads to a certain ease of performance. Someone who possesses the appropriate "art" will be observed to play golf or to sing or paint with a kind of fluency. And so it is with morals: disposition translates into habit, and habit tends toward facility, and we develop a "style". In this third sense too, therefore, we might speak of an art of good living.

---

[6] Aristotle, *Nichomachean Ethics*, II.4.

There is a fourth reason for conceiving of good living as an art. It is that the best achievements of the artist are sometimes experienced by him or her (and perceived by others) as somehow "given", as it were from outside. People speak of being "taken over", "possessed", "inspired", so that their performance—as painter, actor, footballer—exceeds in excellence what they had thought to be their potential. This too may happen in the moral life when we appear to transcend ourselves, to be more courageous or loving or truthful than is "natural" for us; and we may aptly speak of having been "gifted". The religious person will think of the concept of grace, which imports the notion of gift from God, as well as empowering and enhancement, but the experience may be recognised and named without recourse to religious perspectives.

3. Morality and Law

We may now turn to compare and contrast morality and law. For the two are interrelated and interdependent, and we live our lives under the influence of each, and sometimes we may confuse the one with the other. Of course morality itself is often called the moral law, but the law now in question is that made as it were additionally by those who have the care of a community—positive law, as it is sometimes called, from a Latin word which means to lay down.

Positive law is there because it was enacted by a lawmaker in some sense of that expression, or perhaps because it grew out of custom. In modern experience it is usually written, and its precepts are to be found in constitutions and charters and statute books and, in some systems, in the decisions of judges. There are understandable reasons for referring to morality as the moral law but the expression may also be misleading, and for clarity we may continue to prefer the term morality in reference to those demands imposed on us not in the first place by decision of a lawmaker or by custom but by our nature as rational and free beings.

Morality and law resemble each other: each has to do with the regulation of behaviour, each deals in rules which enjoin or forbid certain acts or omissions or states of affairs. Morality requires that we respect human life, the law that we drive on a particular side of the road. It is morally wrong to drive in a way that endangers life, it is illegal to exceed the speed limit in a built-up area. And both morality and law *oblige* us in a way that we recognise as more cogent than the force of convention or etiquette or taste. Only in an attenuated sense is anyone obliged to use a fish-knife, and no-one is compelled to read Shakespeare, unless by way of having to comply with, say, the requirements of a course in English literature.[7]

---

[7] In which case, a moral obligation to read Shakespeare might indirectly arise, for the usual case involves the payment of fees by parents or the taxpayer, and there is a

In some matters the scopes of law and morality overlap. They both forbid murder, perjury, rape and theft, to mention but a few of the items which come within the purview of each. They intersect in another sense too, for law requires the support of morality, and aspects of morality may be expressed in law; and morality normally requires that we obey the law. To fail to pay one's taxes is as morally wrong as it is against the law, as is a misrepresentation in the sale of goods or services.

But morality and law differ too, and the differences are profoundly important. For one thing—a point which we have glimpsed already—they differ in their origins: the one has its roots in reasoned reflection on our nature, the other in a lawmaker's *fiat*. Relatedly, the source of obligation of each is different: reason's understanding of the exigencies of human flourishing, and the will of the ruler or of whomever is the bearer of authority in the *polis*.

Another difference between law and morality is that the latter always pays attention to internal factors such as one's disposition or attitude or intention, whereas a good deal of law does not. From the law's point of view it doesn't matter with what degree of resentment I pay my taxes: if I pay them I comply with the law. But from a moral point of view resentment may mar what is ostensibly correct, as when I do a good deed with bad grace. If I wrong someone inadvertently I cannot be blamed morally, since I didn't mean to do so. But if inadvertently I exceed the speed limit or fail to pay my TV licence I can only hope for the indulgence of a police officer or judge; I stand liable to punishment, for I have broken, unquestionably, the law. An incidental implication is that compliance with the law is no guarantee of moral worth; and indeed morality may require that we disobey a law, a proposition that we must look at more closely later.

So although law and morality are in some ways alike and are interrelated and interdependent, the differences between them are radical. The one is not the other, nor can either take the other's place. It is wrong to expect too much of the law: to think that it can make us morally good is to confuse legality with virtue. A propensity to legislate instead of to educate inhibits moral growth. That is not to say, as we shall also shortly see, that law has no role in assisting the promotion of moral value.

Four Questions

H.L.A. Hart (1907–1992) has listed the main questions that may be put about the relationships between morality and law. The first is whether the development of law has been influenced by morality (and vice versa); the second, whether

---

responsibility to live up to the trust and opportunity thereby offered. Similarly one might imagine an indirect obligation to use a fish-knife, as when a refusal to do so amounted to failure to acknowledge the trouble taken by a hostess to provide one.

some reference to morality must enter into an adequate definition of law; a third asks whether the law is open to moral criticism; and the fourth is whether it is the business of the law to enforce morality—more exactly, to make immorality a crime.[8]

The second and third questions have often been debated by moralists and jurisprudents, notably in discussion of the relative merits of legal positivism and natural law theory. We shall shortly meet a practical illustration of their significance, and of course they bear upon the question of whether there is a moral obligation to obey the law. The fourth question has long been associated with the name of John Stuart Mill, though nowadays it is more likely to evoke the names of Hart and Lord Devlin and the famous debate engendered by their exchanges.

Hart's first question is reasonably briefly dealt with. It seems clear that the development of law is influenced by morality, even if morality is not the sole influence. An easy example is that of legislation aimed at ending discrimination on the basis of race or gender; for the impulse toward this sort of legislation comes from the moral insight that people are equal and should be treated equally. Similarly, legislation concerning conditions in the workplace is founded ultimately on such considerations as the dignity of the person, the right to fair remuneration for one's labours, and the need to preclude exploitation—all of which are issues of morality.

That law may influence the development of morality seems equally clear. Legislation concerning drink driving was greeted with reluctance by many drivers, and no doubt is not wholeheartedly accepted by all yet. And it may be complied with reluctantly, and only for fear of punishment, so that the moral value of compliance in an individual case is slight if it exists at all. Yet there are many drivers who, though they complied at first reluctantly, do so now more freely, because they recognise that this law concerns the protection of life and the elimination of a threat to life and bodily integrity. Free choice of an action which is perceived to be for good is, of course, what we mean by moral choice.[9]

---

[8] H.L.A. Hart, *Law, Liberty and Morality* (Oxford University Press, Oxford, 1963), pp.1 *et seq.*

[9] In the medieval tradition, St Thomas Aquinas had a high idea of positive law's place: he included it among the ways in which God "educates" people in goodness. His account of how this happens is nuanced, and his expectations of law were modest. Yet he is clear that it has a role. "From becoming accustomed to shun what is evil and discharge what is good on account of threat of punishment a man sometimes comes to continue on that course from his own taste and choice. Hence law even as punitive brings men to good." *Summa Theologiae*, I-II, q.92, art.2. We should no doubt in any case acknowledge that human motivation is rarely pure. The notion of law as educative is expressed in the trend in modern jurisprudence known as "perfectionism", which includes the view that government has a legitimate interest

Law and Moral Obligation

It has been remarked that Hart's second and third questions are related: whether a reference to morality must enter into any adequate definition of law, and whether the law is open to moral criticism. These are, of course, the questions at the centre of the debate between natural law theorists and positivists, and they bear directly upon the question of whether there is a moral obligation to obey the law. For if it is necessary for the validity of a law that it be not immoral, immorality is a basis for disobedience; and the failure of a law to meet criticism from a moral standpoint is also a reason why someone might decide that he or she was justified in disobeying it.

Normally we are obliged to keep the law of the land, and it is morally wrong to do what is illegal. Laws are laid down in aid of community welfare, and compliance with them is usually a precondition of human flourishing.[10] But a law may be immoral, as when it discriminates unfairly on the basis of race or religion or sex. A law may enjoin an immorality, as in Hitler's Germany in relation to Jews. From a moral standpoint it will not do to seek to justify ourselves by saying "I obeyed the law", or to defend a wrong done under the law by saying "I was only obeying orders". For all that we are normally obliged to keep the law there may be times when we are morally obliged to disobey.

This last theme is as old as *Antigone*, yet as fresh in the memory as the Nürnberg trials after the Second World War. Antigone buried her brother Polynices, defying an order made by Creon, king of Thebes, who had forbidden him honourable burial. In Sophocles' play she defends herself by appeal to a higher law.

> "That order did not come from God. Justice
> That dwells with the gods below, knows no such law.
> I did not think your edicts strong enough
> To overrule the unwritten unalterable laws
> Of God and heaven, you being only a man.
> They are not of yesterday or today, but everlasting,
> Though where they came from, none of us can tell."[11]

---

in promoting ideas as to what the good life is: see B. Bix, *op. cit.* pp.150–153; see also M.D.A. Freeman, *op. cit.*, pp.365–367.

[10] Other explanations of the basis for a moral obligation to obey the law are that we ought to do so out of gratitude, or because we ought to keep the promise to do so which is implied in our "social contract", or because "fairness" demands that we reciprocate the benefits conferred by society by keeping society's laws, or that obedience to law is required by the public good. See J.W. Harris, *op. cit.*, pp.210–217, and M.D.A. Freeman, *op. cit.*, pp.360–361.

[11] Sophocles, *The Theban Plays: Antigone* (E.F. Watling trans., Penguin, Harmondsworth, 1947), p.138.

The notion of a higher law to which all, even rulers, are answerable has persisted in Western thinking in the form of some version of the doctrine of a "Natural Law". Not that all versions of the doctrine have come to the same thing, as was mentioned earlier, and no version has escaped criticism. Yet commentators have seen some such notion at work even in the ostensibly positivist climate of the Nürnberg tribunal for the trial of war crimes. "An order is an order", the accused officials and officers pleaded, meaning that they were obliged to do what was commanded by political and military superiors and were thus justified in what they had done. But the plea did not succeed, and A.P. d'Entrèves has written: "The rejection of the defence of superior orders ... is nothing less than the old doctrine that the validity of laws does not depend on their 'positiveness', and that it is the duty of the individual to pass judgement on laws before he obeys them."[12]

It was remarked earlier that Hart's second and third questions—whether an adequate definition of law must include a reference to morality and whether the law is open to moral criticism—are related. But they are nevertheless separate questions, and one might answer the former negatively whilst giving an affirmative answer to the latter. Positivists characteristically deny a connection between legal validity and morality, but that doesn't mean that they consider that the law is beyond moral criticism; nor do they think that one is always morally obliged to obey the law. John Austin thought that to say that a law was invalid because immoral was "stark nonsense",[13] but H.L.A. Hart recalls that for Austin as for Jeremy Bentham, a positivist stance regarding legal validity went along with the conviction that "if laws reached a certain degree of iniquity then there would be a plain moral obligation to resist them and to withhold obedience".[14]

A non-lawyer might regard these questions as merely technical and perhaps

---

[12] At Nürnberg, d'Entrèves also notes, "the provisions for the ... Tribunal were based, or purported to be based, on existing or 'positive' international law". Nevertheless d'Entrèves believes that "the boundaries of legal positivism were overstepped ... the moment it was stated that the trials were 'a question of justice'", *op. cit.*, p.106.

[13] J. Austin, *The Province of Jurisprudence Determined* (Library of Ideas ed., 1954), p.185, quoted in H.L.A. Hart, "Positivism and the Separation of Law and Morals", p.30.

[14] H.L.A. Hart, "Positivism and the Separation of Law and Morals", p.30. It is interesting to notice a difference between the way in which Hart's second question is handled in the Christian tradition as represented by, respectively, St Augustine whose philosophical antecedent was Plato, and St Thomas Aquinas, shaped as his thought was by Aristotelian doctrine. For Augustine an unjust law is no law, for Aquinas it is law but law deformed. These views derive ultimately not just from the philosophical legacy of each but also from their theological positions concerning the place of law in the divine scheme of things.

fussy, for if on either view one is morally entitled and sometimes obliged to resist unjust law, it seems that what is feared about positivist doctrine—the tyranny of law and of the lawmaker—is in reality a bogey. One author who was not so sanguine was Gustav Radbruch (1878–1949), a German jurisprudent who dramatically repudiated positivism when he saw the way in which Nazi leaders exploited the disjunction between law and morality which positivism espoused. He came to take the view that "the fundamental principles of humanitarian morality were part of the very concept of *Recht* or Legality and that no positive enactment or statute, however clearly it was expressed and however clearly it conformed with the formal criteria of validity of a given legal system, could be valid if it contravened basic principles of morality".[15]

Hart notes that this doctrine can be appreciated fully only if the nuances imported by the German term *Recht* are appreciated. "But it is clear that the doctrine meant that every lawyer and judge should denounce statutes that transgressed the fundamental principles not as merely immoral or wrong but as having no legal character, and enactments which on this ground lack the quality of law should not be taken into account in working out the legal position of any given individual in particular circumstances."[16]

The Enforcement of Morals

Hart's fourth question, whether it is the business of the law to enforce morality "as such", or to proscribe immorality just because it is immoral, was the subject of a debate between himself and Sir Patrick (later Lord) Devlin, following publication of the latter's 1959 Maccabaean lecture on morals and the criminal law.[17] Devlin's lecture was a critique of the Report of a Committee which, under the chairmanship of Lord Wolfenden, had been charged with the task of making proposals for the reform of the law concerning prostitution and

---

[15] H.L.A. Hart, "Positivism and the Separation of Law and Morals", *op. cit.*, p.31. The importance of the point at issue is demonstrated also in the so-called "grudge" cases following the ending of the Second World War. These were the subject of a famous— some think misconceived—debate between Hart and Lon Fuller: see H. McCoubrey and N.D. White, *op. cit.*, pp.50–52 and J.G. Riddall, *op. cit.*, pp.72–78.

[16] H.L.A. Hart, "Positivism and the Separation of Law and Morals", p.31.

[17] Devlin's lecture was first published as the Maccabaean Lecture in Jurisprudence by the British Academy. It later appeared as the first chapter in P. Devlin, *The Enforcement of Morals* (Oxford University Press, Oxford, 1965). There is truth in Brian Bix's comment that discussion of the enforcement of morality has been too strongly influenced by the Hart-Devlin exchanges; the debate's main lines are nevertheless reproduced here both because of this influence and because they offer a convenient framework for a preliminary treatment of the issues.

concerning homosexual activity. Wolfenden's Committee sought a principle
that would allow it to address both sets of concerns—indeed any matter which
involved the criminal law and was regarded as immoral—in a consistent way.
The Committee found their principle in a version of one first enunciated by
John Stuart Mill (1806–1873).

In *On Liberty* (1859) Mill wrote that the only purpose for which the criminal
law can rightfully be used is to prevent harm to others.[18] The version espoused
by the Wolfenden Committee is that the function of the criminal law is "to
preserve public order and decency, to protect the citizen from what is offensive
or injurious, and to provide sufficient safeguards against exploitation and
corruption of others, particularly the young, weak in body and mind,
inexperienced, or in a state of special physical, official or economic
dependence".[19] Devlin interpreted this to mean that "no act of immorality should
be made a criminal offence unless it is accompanied by some other feature
such as indecency, corruption or exploitation",[20] or, of course, if it injures
someone's person or property. It is features such as these that, according to
Wolfenden, bring what is immoral into the public domain. And only when
there is this kind of public dimension is it permissible for the law to take an
interest.

Devlin rejected this on the ground that it was inconsistent with English
law and, more fundamentally, because it did not take account of the fact that
there is a public morality which is necessary for the integrity of society and
which it is the business of the law to enforce. His position may be put summarily
as follows. People who form a civil society do so on the basis of certain shared
ideas, including ideas about right and wrong. A society's existence is threatened
by deviance from the morality so shared, and it is as entitled to protect itself
from moral subversion as it is from political subversion. It is for society to say
how much deviance it will tolerate, and society is entitled to use the criminal
law to enforce its morality when deviance exceeds toleration's bounds. A
legislator will know when this point has been reached by reference to the
standard of the reasonable man (*sic*), "the man on the Clapham omnibus".

On this view there is no private immorality in the sense envisaged by the
Wolfenden Committee. The most private of acts has a social resonance, however
indirectly produced: *any* immorality is of its nature capable of threatening a
society's existence. In theory therefore, there is no immoral act that might not
be proscribed by law. But in practice a line must be drawn, for the individual
"cannot be expected to surrender to the judgement of society the whole conduct
of his life". And in deciding what to forbid, a lawmaker may be helped by
some general principles.

---

[18] J.S. Mill, *On Liberty* (G. Himmelfarb ed., Penguin, Harmondsworth, 1974), p.68.
[19] Quoted in P. Devlin, *The Enforcement of Morals* (1965), p.2
[20] P. Devlin, *The Enforcement of Morals* (1965), p.3.

Private and Public Morality

Before reviewing these general principles it might be useful to look at a core question upon which Devlin and Hart were at odds—whether there is a "private morality" which is, as Wolfenden put it, not the law's business. The expression "private morality" was to prove troublesome, and it may be as well at this point to be clear at least about what it does *not* mean. For a start it doesn't make sense to think of it as referring to the morality of acts done in private; most murders are done in private, and privacy is virtually essential to the thief; and it would be ludicrous to suggest that the law should never intervene in cases of domestic violence.

Nor is it helpful to think of the term "private morality" as referring to what is a matter of private (in the sense of personal) moral judgement. For the question whether something is properly left to the individual's conscience, or whether it is a claim of the moral order, is usually only the starting-point of a debate. So, for example, the claim that women have a moral right to choose abortion comes up against the claim that the unborn have a moral right to life from conception. The first claim says that it is a matter for the personal conscience of a woman whether to have an abortion or not, the second—in a familiar version—maintains that the moral order precludes the directly intended taking of any innocent life. The argument cannot be settled by *asserting* the one right or the other, and there remains for the legislator the question whether either of these moral beliefs is to be "enforced".

Such questions are complicated nowadays by the pluralism of moral belief and practice that is a feature of so many modern societies. For it is a fact of modern life that societies are composed of people of a variety of religious traditions and of none, and the religions have generally been bearers also of a moral tradition, as has agnostic or atheistic humanism. If the law is to reflect and promote moral values—and it must, in some sense, as we have seen— then the question is: whose values? The values of the majority religious (or other) moral tradition? What then of minorities in the community; are they to be coerced into following patterns of behaviour which are contrary to conscience as they experience it, or prevented from acting according to their consciences simply because the majority subscribes to a different world-view?

One of the reasons why it is difficult to think clearly about these questions is that it is difficult to find a starting-point that has the prospect of common acceptance. But perhaps a starting-point is to be found in the general principle that no one should be forced to act against conscience, nor should anyone be restrained from acting according to conscience within the limits of the common good. This principle is founded on the dignity of the human person, based in turn on the twin gifts of reason and the power of choice, and human dignity is possessed equally by all human beings. As already seen, we are at our most human when we act freely, so we ought not to be coerced or restrained beyond what is necessary in terms of a "common good". And this is especially true in the human search for truth, including moral truth.

But what of the proviso? What is meant by the common good? This concept has its roots in classical thought and, as developed by classical and Christian thinkers, is rich and complex. For present purposes it will suffice to adopt a description taken from relatively modern social thought in the Christian tradition, that it is the totality of conditions of social living which enable people to achieve a fuller measure of fulfilment with relative ease. The core idea is that the law should be such as to facilitate the flourishing *of each person,* but in such a way that the flourishing of any person or group is not at the expense of the flourishing of others.

A mistake sometimes made in debates about law and morals is to counterpose the common good and the individual's good. This happens when it is identified with the moral beliefs of a majority of citizens, so that in the Republic of Ireland, for example, it might be identified with the moral values of Christianity. On that premise people could argue that the right of someone from another religious tradition (say Islam) to believe and practise according to his or her faith need not be upheld by law. But this is not so. The common good is the ensemble of conditions of social living enabling *each person* to flourish to maximum potential. It *includes* individual freedoms, including freedom of religious and moral belief and practice.[21]

Of course the exercise of anyone's freedom cannot be at the expense of the rightful freedom of others. A right to freedom of expression cannot mean a right to say what one likes, true or untrue, about someone else in the community, and so we have defamation laws. A right to privacy against trespass cannot be invoked by someone who wishes to conceal the fact that he has bomb-making equipment in the garden shed. A right to the truth does not entail entitlement to pry into the personal business of one's next-door neighbour. The exercise of rights and freedoms of the individuals who make up a society must be harmonized, and in some matters this bespeaks regulation by law. This is often put by saying that the exercise of individual freedom is limited by the requirements of peace, justice and public morality.

---

[21] John Finnis has remarked that the modern "manifesto" conception of human rights is "a way of sketching *the outlines of the common good*, the various aspects of well-being in community": J.M. Finnis, *op. cit.*, p.214 (emphasis in original). Finnis observes also that "human rights can only be securely enjoyed in certain sorts of milieu—a context or framework of mutual respect and trust and common understanding, an environment which is physically healthy and in which the weak can go about without fear of the whims of the strong"; and on this basis he argues for the necessity to retain such concepts as public order and public morality: *ibid.*, pp.216–218.

The Devlin-Hart Debate

And so we return to the question at the core of the debate between Devlin and Hart: whether or in what sense there is a "public morality" which it is the law's business to enforce. Devlin, as was seen, contended that there is, and that it is discerned by reference to the standard of the man in the Clapham omnibus; and he also offered some principles—Devlin calls them "elastic" principles—which might guide the legislator when it comes to the question of which items of this public morality ought to be enforced by law.

The first of these principles is that there should be the maximum freedom consistent with the integrity of society. The law should not attempt to enforce all of a society's moral code, but only those items without the observance of which society would disintegrate. Second, Devlin says, the law should move slowly, for the limits of society's tolerance are apt to shift from time to time. Third, as far as possible privacy should be respected: he sees a value in allowing people what would nowadays be called their personal space. And the fourth elastic principle is that the law is concerned with minimum and not maximum standards of behaviour, and it should not try to do too much.

Lord Devlin's thesis was challenged in *Law, Liberty and Morality* by H.L.A. Hart, then Professor of Jurisprudence at Oxford, whose position was essentially that of John Stuart Mill and the Wolfenden Committee. That is, Hart reaffirmed the view that there is a realm of private morality which is not the law's business, and unless conduct involves an identifiable public harm it ought not to be proscribed by law. On this view the law should confine itself to the prohibition of conduct which would injure others in their person or property, or corrupt or exploit, or violate public sensibility or public order.

In making his case Hart counters Devlin's arguments, and in particular he rejects the latter's concept of a public morality. The detail of their exchanges (for the debate did not end with Hart's rejoinder to the Maccabaean lecture) is beyond the scope of a short chapter such as this. But it is worth drawing attention to Hart's starting-point, for it sets the tone of his contribution as a whole. His starting-point is the contention that the question whether morals should be enforced is itself a moral question. For enforcement involves the curtailment of freedom, and the curtailment of freedom requires moral justification.

In support of this way of looking at the matter Hart points out that legal enforcement has two aspects. The first is that it involves the punishment of offenders, and this is typically done by depriving them of freedom of movement or of property or of association with family or friends, or the infliction of physical pain or even death. But all of these are normally regarded as evil, and normally their infliction is considered wrong. If, therefore, it is to escape moral censure, their infliction requires special justification.

The second aspect of enforcement is no less pertinent to the need for justification. It is that law restricts freedom also in coercing conformity through threat of punishment. One's freedom is just as surely, even if differently, inhibited when one refrains from some act for fear of being put in jail as it is when one is jailed for doing the forbidden deed. And this kind of restriction also needs to be justified, for freedom is valuable both in itself and because it enables people to experiment with various ways of living.

But there is a further reason, according to Hart, why restriction of freedom requires to be justified from the standpoint of morality: "interference with individual liberty ... is itself the infliction of a special form of suffering— often very acute—on those whose desires are frustrated by the fear of punishment".[22] He observes that this is especially true of laws that impose a sexual morality.

For all that there are differences, of vantage point and of perspective, between Lord Devlin's view and that of Hart, they are not without common ground. There is this much at least: that both envisage the main issue as one of reconciling personal freedom and the public interest, in some sense of that expression. Each requires advertence to a social dimension in human conduct, and to a public interest in preventing social harm; and each is prepared to recognise a role for the criminal law in that process.

Indeed one commentator has said that "both are recognizably liberal",[23] meaning no doubt that each puts a premium on freedom. In Hart's case this is clear even in the way he frames the main question, but it is intimated also in Devlin's assertion that "the individual has a *locus standi* too; he cannot be expected to surrender to the judgement of society the whole conduct of his life".[24] And this insight is made concrete in the "elastic principles" to which Devlin would have the legislator advert, and especially in the requirements that there should be toleration of maximum freedom consistent with the integrity of society, and that privacy must as far as possible be respected.

It may be, as is sometimes suggested, that the principal difference between them is one of emphasis; but the difference in emphasis is critical. Devlin's overriding interest is in the "integrity of society", and in that sense he is "conservative". Hart's concern, first and last, is with the protection of individual freedom. Devlin's way of looking at the issues will probably recommend itself to someone whose instinct is to preserve societal values, Hart's will be the more congenial for someone who is inclined to a more "liberal" political view.

Of course, strictly speaking the term "enforcement of morals" is a misnomer. For the law can at best ensure only external compliance, whereas to be moral it is not enough to behave in a way which is merely externally correct.[25] From

---

[22] H.L.A. Hart, *Law, Liberty and Morality*, p.23.

[23] B. Mitchell, *Law, Morality and Religion in a Secular Society* (Oxford University Press, Oxford, 1967), p.18.

[24] P. Devlin, *The Enforcement of Morals*, p.15.

[25] In this connection it is interesting to read what Aquinas has to say about the law's

a legal point of view, as we saw, it does not matter with what degree of resentment I pay my taxes; all the law requires is that I pay them. But from the viewpoint of morality a bad attitude or unworthy motive or perverse intention may mar what, on the face of it, is a good act, as when I give money with bad grace to someone in need. Hence it seems better to say that what the law enforces is a moral code, or at least that part of a code which commands or prohibits observable conduct: that it cannot enforce morality "as such". Indeed if someone refrains from misconduct wholly out of fear of punishment it is hardly correct to speak of morality at all.

And this provides a clue, as James Mackey has suggested, to the truth that emerges from the Devlin-Hart debate, and it shows that each was partly right. "Law does, and must always, make its business what would be morally right for people to do or refrain from doing. That is always true of law, in any form of human society which proposes to be essential to human living … This is the part of the truth that Devlin protected so well on his side of the debate."[26] But it is the merit of Hart's contribution that "he has pointed unerringly to the quite literally demoralising tendency of the apparatus of extraneous punishment and of its ever-present threat".[27]

The truth of such observations as these is underscored if one accepts the description of morality with which this chapter began, that it is the "art" of right relationship with each other and with the world around us. And it is confirmed if one considers that "love" is an apt characterisation of the most fundamental moral imperative. One of the reasons for the choice of the word art was that it suggests a skill which comes from knowledge and practice, and it can be seen that a community's laws offer an intimation of what the community values, and so can aid the process of moral education. And insofar as laws ensure the practice of, say, road safety or fair trade or just industrial relations, they may contribute to the acquisition of skills important for moral development. There is, as we have seen, a pedagogical dimension.

But we saw too that morality is as much a matter of the "heart" as it is of external performance, that it is a matter of being as well as of doing, a matter of attitude and motivation and intention as well as of doing "the right thing", which is one of the reasons why the word love is an appropriate characterisation. And art also involves performance or achievement which is more than the simple application of a rule, and the art of right relationship with others and with our world bespeaks a sensibility which is not ensured by the mere existence of a law. Law's reach does not extend to these dimensions and indeed, as

---

role in regard to virtue: *Summa Theologiae,* I-II, q.96, art.3. Notice also his realism concerning the use of the law in restraining vice: I-II, q.96, art.2.

[26] James P. Mackey, *Power and Christian Ethics* (Cambridge University Press, Cambridge, 1994), p.52.

[27] *ibid.*

Mackey's remark on Hart's contribution indicates, there is always a risk that the coercive element in the apparatus of law may breed a fear which demoralises.

For reasons such as these, and leaving aside the difficulties inherent in ascertaining the value system operative in any society and the problems presented by today's pluralism and multiculturalism, the notion of the law as pedagogue must be viewed with caution. Law does reflect a community's values, and there is a "rhetoric of law"[28] which signals something of the importance which a society attaches to the values which its members profess to hold. And modern practice as regards, for example, equality or health legislation, or such legislation as there is concerning the environment, acknowledges a right and responsibility on the part of government to promote behaviour called for by a moral responsibility. But we need not expect law to make people good, and there is no substitute for moral education.

---

[28] The term is Mary Ann Glendon's, and it is explored in her *Abortion and Divorce in Western Law* (Harvard University Press, Cambridge, Mass., 1987).

CHAPTER 12

TALKING ABOUT HUMAN RIGHTS

COLIN HARVEY

1. INTRODUCTION

Let's start by offering some examples. A foreign terrorist suspect is detained indefinitely without charge or trial and claims that his detention is discriminatory as the law which authorises it does not apply to nationals. An asylum seeker fears persecution if she is sent back to her country of origin and argues that she has a right not to be returned. A radical preacher is denied entry to the UK on public order grounds. He insists that his right to freedom of expression has been violated. A community is disturbed by noise from the nearby airport and claims that its right to privacy is being violated. A young man is placed in a prison cell with a violent and racist prisoner; he is seriously assaulted and later dies. His family claim his right to life was violated. All these scenarios, borrowed from real cases, highlight the types of claims made in the name of rights. In these instances individuals may well mean moral rights, but they tend to be talking about their legal rights. We can also see that not all the people mentioned are citizens. How should we decide these claims and who should have the last word?

Increasingly, people appeal not only to a moral conception of their entitlements, but to the legal provisions which reflect a political commitment to the moral principles. Rights-talk features prominently in political and legal debates. Rights are now well established in national and international law. They have become such a fundamental part of law and politics that the question of whether they are a "good thing" seems irrelevant. The interesting arguments today are over the scope of human rights, their contested meaning, the relationship with other values, and their institutional protection. Can we distinguish the rights of citizens from the rights of all persons? Why do we not agree over the meaning of, for example, the right to privacy? How should we resolve disagreements over the meaning of specific rights?

The aim of this chapter is to introduce the concept of rights in two stages. First, we will note the historical development of arguments about rights. Second, we will focus on modern conversations on rights, with particular reference to the work of Ronald Dworkin and Jeremy Waldron.

2. ARGUING ABOUT HUMAN RIGHTS

In this part the focus is on historical arguments on rights advanced by some of the major figures of political philosophy. We will note the contributions of: Thomas Hobbes; John Locke; Edmund Burke; and Jeremy Bentham. Disagreements over the nature and meaning of rights have a long history. The concept rose to prominence during the period known as the Enlightenment.[1] This was a period when old ideas of authority were being questioned and abandoned. Enlightenment thinkers attacked religious superstition and placed considerable faith in scientific method. Science, it was optimistically believed, might be used to promote a rational and humane social order which would encourage individual freedom. The modern state was steadily evolving and theories of political and constitutional legitimacy were being advanced to justify the new order.

Thomas Hobbes (1588–1679) sought to develop a comprehensive science of man and society and was influenced by his encounter with Euclidean geometry. His work was dominated by the overriding fear of civil war and the search for order. In 1646, he became a tutor to the Prince of Wales at the exiled English court in Paris. In 1652, the year after the publication of his most important work, *Leviathan*, he returned to England and settled in London. He will always be associated in the popular imagination with his famous description of life in the absence of government as "solitary, poore, nasty, brutish, and short".[2] However, Hobbes had an understanding of rights and he located this within a comprehensive political theory. In the state of nature everyone has a right to everything judged to be necessary to their survival. The natural condition of humanity is a "Warre of every one against every one … It followeth, that in such a condition, every man has a Right to every thing, even to one another's body."[3] Conflict over rights is unavoidable unless rights are surrendered to the sovereign. In the state of nature people are able to relinquish their rights to the sovereign in order to provide for their own security. They therefore establish a sovereign "Leviathan". People do not give up all their rights, but what they retain is limited to a right to resist being killed or confined (the right to self-preservation).[4] The sovereign decides on which rights to grant to persons, and these can be withdrawn at any time.

Hobbes thus argued for a concept of natural rights, but these were rights which were given up in order to obtain security under the protection of a

---

[1] W.A. Edmundson, *An Introduction to Rights* (Cambridge University Press, Cambridge, 2004), p.15.

[2] T. Hobbes, *Leviathan* [1651] (R. Tuck ed., Cambridge University Press, Cambridge, 1996), p.89.

[3] *ibid.*, p.91.

[4] W.A. Edmundson, *op. cit.*, p.23.

sovereign. What must be stressed is that Hobbes was writing during a period of religious conflict, civil war and insecurity in England. His arguments in *Leviathan* are anchored in his concern to secure peace and thus he defends the importance of security and order within a political community. The approach displays distrust and fear of individualism and the notion that the person might have rights against the state (it was this sort of thinking which was the problem in England, in his view).[5] Hobbes discounts any idea of civil disobedience. Once the majority opts for a sovereign, a dissenter must consent "or be left in the condition of warre he was in before; wherein he might without injustice be destroyed by any man whatsoever".[6] Hobbes does not present these arguments out of an inherent antipathy to the idea of rights; his overriding objective was to discover how civil war could be avoided. And, in order to secure that, Hobbes was prepared to envisage sovereignty without constraint.[7]

John Locke (1632–1704), after studying at Oxford, joined the household of Anthony Ashley Cooper (later first Earl of Shaftesbury) in 1667 and gained through him numerous official appointments and met many of the leading intellectual figures of his time. In 1672, he became Secretary of the Board of Trade, lived in France for a time and then moved to Holland. In 1689, he returned to England and became Commissioner of Appeals, retiring in 1691. His work reflected the scientific spirit of the times and was the starting point for the British empiricist tradition in philosophy. He is now generally recognised more widely for his arguments in support of natural rights and the possibility this opened up for rebellion against established government. As with Hobbes,

---

[5] An attitude reflected also in the work of Carl Schmitt (1888–1985). See D. Dyzenhaus, *Legality and Legitimacy: Carl Schmitt, Hans Kelsen and Hermann Heller in Weimar* (Oxford University Press, Oxford, 1997), p.95.

[6] T. Hobbes, *op. cit.*, p.232.

[7] *ibid.*: "And because the End of this Institution, is the Peace and Defence of them all; and whosoever has right to the End, has right to the Means; it belongeth of Right, to whatsoever Man, or Assembly, that hath the Sovereignty, to be Judge both of the meanes of Peace and Defence; and also of the hindrances, and disturbances of the same; and to do whatsoever he shall think necessary to be done, both before hand, for the preserving of Peace and Security, by prevention of Discord at home and Hostility from abroad; and, when Peace and Security are lost, for the recovery of the same."; *cf.* C. Schmitt, *Political Theology: Four Chapters on the Concept of Sovereignty* [1922] (MIT, Cambridge, Mass., 1985), p.5: "Sovereign is he who decides on the exception." See also A.V. Dicey, *Introduction to the Study of the Law of the Constitution* (8th ed., Macmillan, London, 1915), p.272: "There are times of tumult or invasion when for the sake of legality itself the rules of law must be broken. The course which the government must then take is clear. The Ministry must break the law and trust for protection to an Act of Indemnity. A statute of this kind is … the last and supreme exercise of Parliamentary sovereignty. It legalises illegality …".

he lived through a period of instability in England. His argument was, however, directed against the idea of absolute monarchy. His *Second Treatise of Government* (1690) can also be seen as a response to Hobbes.[8] Locke used the state of nature idea, but in his conception it is a more complex place. He argued for a range of natural rights, including an understanding of property rights that has generated extensive debate. The state of nature, for Locke, is not a state of war. However, there were problems related to the application and enforcement of natural rights in the state of nature. As a result it is rational for people to seek security in a commonwealth. Individuals retain certain natural rights and these rights are intended to act as a control on government. A crucial factor for Locke was that government requires the consent of the people. Locke recognised the right to install a new government (even by revolutionary means), but only as a last resort and he was aware that rights presented potential problems for government and order.[9] It is this threat of rebellion which would, for Locke, assist in preventing government from abusing its power.[10] Although Locke is regarded as a leading figure in liberal constitutionalist thought, he did not argue for the separation of powers, or judicial review, as we might understand these terms.

Locke's arguments had a practical impact. For example, the American Declaration of Independence (1776) reflected much of his thinking. Thomas Jefferson was influenced by Locke's work and he played the major role in drafting the Declaration. In justifying their break with the Crown, rights were used extensively.[11] It is worth citing the Declaration:

> "We hold these truths to be self-evident, that all men are created equal, that they are endowed by their Creator with certain inalienable Rights, that among these are Life, Liberty and the pursuit of Happiness—That to secure these rights, Governments are instituted among Men, deriving their just powers from the consent of the governed,—That whenever any Form of Government becomes destructive of these ends, it is the Right of the people to alter or abolish it, and to institute new Government, laying its foundation on such principles and organizing its powers in such form, as to them shall seem most likely to effect their Safety and Happiness ...".

---

[8] See J. Locke, *Two Treatises of Government* (P. Laslett ed., Cambridge University Press, Cambridge, 1988).

[9] W.A. Edmundson, *op. cit.*, p.30.

[10] As Martin Loughlin notes, Locke had little to say about the judiciary. See M. Loughlin, *Sword and Scales: An Examination of the Relationship between Law and Politics* (Hart, Oxford, 2000), p.167.

[11] W.A. Edmundson, *op. cit.*, p.31.

The American Revolution generated extensive interest in other states. The revolution in France took place in a different social context; however, the ideas which emerged were remarkably similar. This was, of course, no accident. Thomas Jefferson also played a part in drafting the Declaration of the Rights of Man and of the Citizen (1789). Again, it is worth citing the first three numbered provisions:

"1. Men are born, and always continue, free, and equal in respect of their rights. Civil distinctions, therefore, can be founded only on public utility.

2. The end of all political associations is the preservation of the natural and imprescriptible rights of man; and these are liberty, property, security, and resistance of oppression.

3. The nation is essentially the source of all Sovereignty; nor can any individual, or any body of men, be entitled to any authority which is not expressly derived from it."

The other provisions list selected rights on, for example, freedom of religion and speech, with limitations attached. The Declaration contained the following firm statement on the importance of rights:

"16. Every society in which the guarantee of rights is not assured or the separation of powers not determined has no constitution at all."

Many of the rights were to be routinely violated in the Reign of Terror (1793–1794) when opponents of the Jacobins, and alleged sympathisers with the Counter-Revolution, were executed. However, the provisions of the Declaration reflected the view that national government was there to preserve the pre-political rights of citizens.

It would be a mistake to attribute events in American and France exclusively to the rise of natural rights thought. The ideas, however, were significant in the justifications that emerged and were to find expression in the official documentation. Thus natural rights, in these contexts, were linked with revolution and reform.[12] Intriguingly, although natural rights had an intellectual home in England it was in France and America that the doctrine had a major practical impact (notwithstanding the 1689 English Bill of Rights). Locke's reservations were to return: how can the idea of pre-political natural rights be reconciled with order, security and government? And was there a danger of rights being used to undermine the existing legal, political and moral order?

The stress placed on the rhetoric of rights was to be questioned by even

---

[12] See also T. Paine, *The Rights of Man* [1791–1792] (H. Collins ed., Penguin, Harmondsworth, 1969).

those who were friendly to the aims of the American colonists. In particular, Edmund Burke and Jeremy Bentham objected to talk of natural rights, although both had different ideas about politics and law.[13] Edmund Burke (1729–1797) was distressed by the events in France (though he was a firm supporter of the American colonists' struggle for independence). His *Reflections on the Revolution in France* (1790) is a classic statement of a conservative perspective on rights, although this ascribes more overall coherence to a text which in fact advances a range of views.[14] This work was widely read in Europe. Burke did believe in what he termed "real rights", but disagreed with the French Declaration on the nature and status of rights.[15] For Burke rights were the offspring of convention and could only be understood within a specific social context. He professed to understand what was meant by the rights of Englishmen, but not by the notion of the rights of man. Burke was not persuaded by Locke's social contract, but even if it was correct he followed Hobbes in the view that individuals surrendered their natural rights to government and expressed scepticism about abstract rules removed from context.[16] Burke advanced a number of arguments against the French Declaration, all of which were embedded in his scepticism of abstract reason and its ability to prescribe rights which could be used in all contexts. Rights emerged, in this understanding, from specific political communities, and declarations of rights,

---

[13] W.A. Edmundson, *op. cit.*, pp.41–42.

[14] E. Burke, *Reflections on the Revolution in France* (C. Cruise O'Brien ed., Penguin, Harmondsworth, 1968). Burke was, of course, born in Ireland, where the ideas from America and France were also spreading.

[15] *ibid.*, p.149: "Far am I from denying in theory; full as far is my heart from withholding in practice … the *real* rights of men. In denying their false claims of right, I do not mean to injure those which are real, and are such as their pretended rights would totally destroy. If civil society is made for the advantage of man, all the advantages for which it is made become his right." See also pp.151–152: "What is the use of discussing a man's abstract right to food or to medicine? The question is upon the method of procuring and administering them. In that deliberation I shall always advise to call in the aid of a farmer and the physician, rather than the professor of metaphysics."

[16] *ibid.*, p.151: "Society requires not only that the passions of individuals should be subjected, but that even in the mass and body as well as in individuals, the inclinations of men should frequently be thwarted, their will controlled, and their passions brought into subjection. This can only be done *by a power out of themselves*; and not, in the exercise of its function, subject to that will and to those passions which it is its office to bridle and subdue. In this sense the restraints on men, as well as their liberties, are to be reckoned among their rights. But as the liberties and the restrictions vary with times and circumstances, and admit of infinite modifications, they cannot be settled upon any abstract rule; and nothing is so foolish as to discuss them upon that principle" (emphasis in original).

through their abstraction, could not deal in an easy way with the complexities of social life.[17]

Jeremy Bentham (1748–1832) is well-known as an advocate of utilitarianism and he was certainly not convinced about natural rights. This rejection of natural rights did not impact on his commitment to extensive legal and political reform. William Hazlitt stated:

> "His reputation lies at the circumference; and the lights of his understanding are reflected, with increasing lustre, on the other side of the globe. His name is little known in England, better in Europe, best of all in the plains of Chile and the mines of Mexico. He has offered constitutions for the New World, and legislated for future times."[18]

Bentham advocated legal reform based on his principle of utility. This utilitarian approach to law and politics has retained its significance and several modern schools of thought owe an intellectual debt to Bentham. His hostility to natural rights was reflected in his claim that they were "nonsense upon stilts". But again we must tread carefully here. Bentham did not reject rights; he simply saw no sense in the notion of natural rights. He had no problem with legal rights, particularly if utility recommended their creation. But there was no such thing as pre-political rights. Bentham did believe in legal rights ("from real laws come real rights") and he advanced what we would now term an "interest or benefit theory". Legal rights, for Bentham, only existed by virtue of the existence of corresponding legal duties. Rights relate to duties which benefit the person. While this is significant, we should remember that Bentham's view was that utility was the best guide to legal, political and moral action. We should also note that both Bentham and Burke viewed natural rights arguments as mischievous and not simply flawed logic. Bentham believed that the resulting declarations of rights stood in the way of effective reform and ignored the

---

[17] *ibid.*, p.152: "The metaphysic rights entering into common life, like rays of light which pierce into a dense medium, are, by the laws of nature, refracted from their straight line. Indeed in the gross and complicated mass of human passions and concerns, the primitive rights of men undergo such a variety of refractions and reflections, that it becomes absurd to talk of them as if they continued in the simplicity of their original direction."

[18] W. Hazlitt, *The Fight and Other Writings* (T. Paulin and D. Chandler eds., Penguin, Harmondsworth, 2000), p.265. See generally, J. Bentham, *An Introduction to the Principles of Morals and Legislation* (J.H. Burns and H.L.A. Hart eds., Methuen, London, 1970); J. Bentham, *A Comment on the Commentaries and a Fragment on Government* (J.H. Burns and H.L.A. Hart eds., Athlone Press, London, 1977); and J. Waldron, *Nonsense Upon Stilts: Bentham, Burke and Marx on the Rights of Man* (Methuen, London, 1987).

importance of substantive legislation. Burke objected to the revolutionary feelings they provoked and the false expectations raised. Both therefore believed that natural rights had a practical political impact.

Anyone who now argues that we need not be distracted by debates about moral rights (because of the creation of legal rights) owes something to Bentham's scepticism. And Bentham's arguments surface regularly in, for example, debates in English public law. This is evident in what has been termed the "neo-Benthamite" revival in public law.[19]

3. MODERN CONVERSATIONS ON RIGHTS

The aim in this part is to explore modern understandings of rights by examining the work of two legal theorists: Ronald Dworkin and Jeremy Waldron. This is, of course, a narrow focus. It avoids, deliberately, Wesley Hohfeld's classification of the concept of legal rights and side-steps the ongoing debate about "choice theory" and "interest theory".[20] There are also many other positions, supportive and critical, which have been advanced on rights.[21]

This approach is adopted for two reasons. First, because the focus here is not on how moral rights should be conceptualised, but how disagreements over the meaning of rights that are reflected in positive law (or rights/principles embedded in law) might be resolved. As noted in the previous part, the idea that such things as "natural or inalienable rights" exist has been questioned.

---

[19] See D. Dyzenhaus, "The Left and the Question of Law" (2004) 17 *Canadian Journal of Law and Jurisprudence* 7.

[20] On these issues, see *Theories of Rights* (J. Waldron ed., Oxford University Press, Oxford, 1984). Hohfeld's attempt to bring conceptual clarity to this area remains significant and his insistence on defining what we mean when we use the word "right" in law is important. More recent accounts can be divided into two camps. First, the "choice theory" focuses on the right-bearer and the power she exercises over the corresponding duty. A person has a right when there is a duty over which the right-bearer has control. Second, the "benefit or interest theory" focuses on the existence of a duty to perform an act that is in the interests of another. Will an individual benefit from the performance of the duty? Is the protection of her interests a sound reason to impose a duty on others?

[21] For sceptical perspectives on rights, see *Sceptical Essays on Human Rights* (T. Campbell, K.D. Ewing and A. Tomkins eds., Oxford University Press, Oxford, 2001); M.A. Glendon, *Rights Talk: The Impoverishment of Political Discourse* (Free Press, New York, 1991); C. Douzinas, *The End of Human Rights: Critical Legal Thought at the Turn of the Century* (Hart, Oxford, 2000); and O. O'Neill, *A Question of Trust* (Cambridge University Press, Cambridge, 2002). For an argument in defence of rights see P. Williams, *The Alchemy of Race and Rights* (Virago, London, 1993).

For the purpose of this chapter, however, nothing hinges on whether one views moral rights as "objective" or "subjective".[22]

Second, because the focus here is on modern approaches which take rights seriously, but which reach different institutional conclusions as a result, we therefore want to explore what legal theory has to say about the constitutional protection of rights. The debate between Dworkin and Waldron has significant implications for a modern approach to constitutional and human rights law. Martin Loughlin presents the issue as follows:

> "In Locke's seventeenth-century scheme, the judiciary hardly figured; in Montesquieu's eighteenth-century analysis they performed a significant role as guardians of the citizen's basic liberties. But due to the rights revolution of the twentieth century, their power has increased dramatically and concern has been expressed about the emergence of a system of government by judiciary."[23]

It is to the questions posed by this trend that we next turn.

Taking Rights Seriously I: Ronald Dworkin

Ronald Dworkin is the leading modern advocate of rights within legal and political theory.[24] Loughlin argues that Dworkin is the key figure in the "liberal normativist project" in public law.[25] Central to this approach is the concept of rights. Dworkin does not simply advance an argument in support of rights. His work is an attempt to construct a principled defence of law and its moral core. He makes the following claim:

---

[22] The present writer's view is that moral rights exist beyond the context of their legal recognition.

[23] M. Loughlin, *Swords and Scales*, p.212.

[24] See generally, R. Dworkin, "Hart's Postscript and the Character of Political Philosophy" (2004) 24 *Oxford Journal of Legal Studies* 1; R. Dworkin, "The Threat to Patriotism", *New York Review of Books* (October 23, 2003); R. Dworkin, *Sovereign Virtue: The Theory and Practice of Equality* (Harvard University Press, Cambridge, Mass., 2000); R. Dworkin, *Freedom's Law: The Moral Reading of the American Constitution* (Harvard University Press, Cambridge, Mass., 1996); R. Dworkin, *Law's Empire* (Fontana Press, London, 1986); R. Dworkin, *A Matter of Principle* (Harvard University Press, Cambridge, Mass., 1985); and R. Dworkin, *Taking Rights Seriously* (Harvard University Press, Cambridge, Mass., 1977).

[25] M. Loughlin, *Public Law and Political Theory* (Clarendon Press, Oxford, 1992), p.239. On this approach see p.206: "The emergence of the liberal variant of normativism is linked to the analysis of rights within the British constitution. The movement has been closely bound to attempts to provide for the entrenchment of individual rights in British law."

"If the Government does not take rights seriously, then it does not take law seriously either."[26]

So the idea of rights is tied to the concept of law or the principle of legality as Dworkin might now say.[27] But what is Dworkin's approach to law? He has constructed an anti-positivist legal theory which focuses on its interpretive nature. H.L.A. Hart's legal positivism is flawed, according to Dworkin, as a result of the failure to acknowledge the role of principles in legal order.[28] Arguments of principle are, for Dworkin, propositions of political morality which demonstrate the existence of rights.[29] He has consistently criticised the positivist idea that there are gaps in the law which judges fill with the exercise of discretion. His claim that there is always a right answer has attracted criticism, but it suggests only that judges behave as if there is always a correct legal answer in the cases they deal with. Dworkin also wants to know what exactly it is lawyers, who know all the facts and the law, are disagreeing about in hard cases. They must, for Dworkin, be engaged in an argument about the point of law. Therefore anyone advancing a legal argument functions with a theory about law, whether acknowledged or not.

Adjudication is accorded primacy in Dworkin's work; and he gives particular significance to the role of the judiciary and the courtroom as the forum of principle in constitutional democracies. The super-human judge— "Hercules"—emerges in Dworkin's work in order to provide an ideal example of how his preferred model of law as integrity might function in practice.[30] He is seeking a theory which shows law in its best light. But what has Dworkin to say about rights? He does not believe that rights exist only in law:

"Bentham thought that the idea of moral rights was 'nonsense upon stilts'. But that view has never been part of our [US] orthodox political theory, and politicians of both parties appeal to the rights of the people to justify a great part of what they do."[31]

Dworkin argues that our intuitions about justice are based on the assumption

---

[26] R. Dworkin, *Taking Rights Seriously*, p.205.
[27] On the principle of legality, see Lon L. Fuller, *The Morality of Law* (revised ed., Yale University Press, New Haven, 1969). See also C. Gearty, *Principles of Human Rights Adjudication* (Oxford University Press, Oxford, 2004).
[28] See generally, R. Dworkin, *Taking Rights Seriously*. For an account of Hart's positivism, see George Pavlakos, "Law as Recognition: H.L.A. Hart and Analytical Positivism" in this volume.
[29] See J.W. Harris, *Legal Philosophies* (2nd ed., Butterworths, London, 1997), p.189.
[30] R. Dworkin, *Law's Empire*.
[31] R. Dworkin, *Taking Rights Seriously*, p.184.

that people do have rights and that one right is fundamental. This is a version of the right to equality which he terms the right to equal concern and respect.[32]

> "We may therefore say that justice as fairness rests on the assumption of a natural right of all men and women to equality of concern and respect, a right they possess not by virtue of birth or characteristic or merit or excellence but simply as human beings with the capacity to make plans and give justice."[33]

Dworkin talks freely of the existence of moral rights against government. The result is that a constitutional system may not protect all these rights or interpret them in the correct way. The moral rights may also survive legislation which conflicts with them, thus legitimising civil disobedience. He argues that government should, nevertheless, try to reach the correct answer about the rights of citizens and follow a coherent theory of what these rights are. He accepts the fact that this recognition of individual rights will mean "the majority cannot travel as fast or as far as it would like".[34] If rights are to be meaningful they therefore must have the legal and/or moral capacity to trump the ambitions of the majority.

> "Rights are best understood as trumps over some background justification for political decisions that states a goal for the community as a whole. If someone has a right to publish pornography, this means that it is for some reason wrong for officials to act in violation of that right, even if they (correctly) believe that the community as a whole would be better off if they did."[35]

And it is on this matter that Dworkin believes judges are particularly well placed to act. The argument that judges should engage in debates over moral and political principles, and apply them in concrete cases, raises an obvious objection. Is it really the role of a judge in a constitutional democracy to decide matters of political principle (as opposed to political policy)? Governments are elected for precisely this purpose. How then can judicial activism based on Dworkin's arguments ever be legitimate? Dworkin constructs a response to this criticism. First, he suggests the objection from democracy is as follows: the decision of a legislature elected by a majority of the people is the best way of deciding what rights people have against each other and the community as

---

[32] *ibid.*, chap.6.
[33] *ibid.*, p.182.
[34] *ibid.*, p.204.
[35] R. Dworkin, "Is There a Right to Pornography?" (1981) 1 *Oxford Journal of Legal Studies* 177 at 177.

a whole. Second, and in response, he argues that the legislature is not in any better position to make an accurate decision on rights than the judiciary. He notes the importance of speculative consistency to decisions on rights and suggests that judges have developed this technique well. He lists also the fact that the legislature is subject to pressures that judges are not. Third, he asks whether there are any reasons of fairness why legislation should be the only way of deciding what rights people have.

> "[T]here is no reason to think, in the abstract, that the transfer of decisions about rights from the legislature to courts will retard the democratic ideal of equality of political power. It may well advance that ideal."[36]

Dworkin rejects what he terms the "majoritarian premise" and replaces it with a constitutional conception of democracy.[37] The aim of democracy is to ensure:

> "that collective decisions be made by political institutions whose structure, composition, and practices treat all members of the community, as individuals, with equal concern and respect".[38]

His constitutional conception of democracy has a similar result in practice to the majoritarian conception he criticises because it will often result in the same processes and decisions will tend to be made by elected representatives. However, the crucial difference is that it does not rule out the use of non-majoritarian procedures that would better protect the equal status conditions. This is government subject to conditions. Indeed this is the way we tend to understand the notion of constitutional democracy. When we live in a constitutional democracy we understand that this means the majority will not always get its way. There are some things even a democratically elected government should not be allowed to do. Argument will continue over the interpretation and application of the "democratic conditions", but we believe intuitively that the idea of such conditions is acceptable.

The suggestion in Dworkin's work is that the interpretation of individual rights should be the special responsibility of the judiciary. This springs in part from his pessimism (Dworkin is known rather more for his optimism)[39] about

---

[36] R. Dworkin, *A Matter of Principle*, p.28.

[37] R. Dworkin, *Freedom's Law*.

[38] *ibid.*, p.17.

[39] *ibid.*, p.38: "It is in the nature of legal interpretation ... to aim at happy endings ... The Constitution is America's moral sail, and we must hold to the courage of the conviction that fills it, the conviction that we can all be equal citizens of a moral republic. That is a noble faith, and only optimism can redeem it."

the "defects in the egalitarian character of democracy" and his view that they may be "irremedial".[40]

> "We must also remember that some individuals gain in political power by that transfer of institutional assignment. For individuals have powers under the rights conception of the rule of law that they do not have under the rule-book conception. They have the power to demand, as individuals, a fresh adjudication of their rights. If their rights are recognized by a court, these rights will be enforced in spite of the fact that no Parliament had the time or the will to enforce them."[41]

While this all sounds like a plea for extensive judicial activism, it must take place within the constraints of the "law as integrity" model Dworkin advances. This is a model which includes notions of "fit". However, Dworkin is asking us all to give, for example, the US Constitution a moral reading, on the understanding that the abstract clauses of the Constitution invoke moral principles. Those who argue that law is inherently political are in line with Dworkin, although people mean different things when they make this claim. Because political morality is uncertain, and people disagree, democracies require an authoritative institution to decide. It is evident that Dworkin wants the courts to fulfil this vital role.[42] Not everyone agrees, and some think we pay a heavy democratic price.

Taking Rights Seriously II: Jeremy Waldron

We will now turn to the arguments recently advanced by Jeremy Waldron.[43] David Dyzenhaus views Waldron's work as part of a neo-Benthamite revival in legal and constitutional theory.[44]

> "The revival claims that parliaments in vigorous democracies protect

---

[40] R. Dworkin, *A Matter of Principle*, p.27.
[41] *ibid.*
[42] See R. Dworkin, "Response to Overseas Commentators" (2003) 1 *International Journal of Constitutional Law* 651.
[43] See, in particular, J. Waldron, *Law and Disagreement* (Clarendon Press, Oxford, 1999). See also J. Waldron, "A Right-Based Critique of Constitutional Rights" (1993) 13 *Oxford Journal of Legal Studies* 18; J. Waldron, "Taking Group Rights Carefully" in *Litigating Rights: Perspectives from Domestic and International Law* (G. Huscroft and P. Rishworth eds., Hart, Oxford, 2002); and J. Waldron, *Liberal Rights: Collected Papers 1981–1991* (Cambridge University Press, Cambridge, 1993).
[44] D. Dyzenhaus, "The Genealogy of Legal Positivism" (2004) 24 *Oxford Journal of Legal Studies* 39 at 62.

human rights better than courts and that trust in judges to resolve our
political disputes results in the capture of our political processes by elites
and thus in democratic debilitation."[45]

This revival is having an impact on how, for example, commentators think
about the interpretation and application of the Human Rights Act 1998 in the
UK. Waldron challenges us to consider what it means to really take rights
seriously. He questions the assumption that a belief in rights necessarily entails
support for proposals to institutionalise them in a Bill of Rights.[46] He argues
that theorists of rights should have "grave misgivings" about courts becoming
the main forum for decisions on rights.[47] Waldron views the right to participate
as the pre-eminent right (because it seems particularly suited to dealing with
the circumstances of disagreement), and argues that we disrespect it if we
remove decisions about basic principles of political life to the courtroom. He
therefore starts from a rights-friendly perspective and suggests that there is no
necessary link between this belief and any one institutional reflection of it. In
fact, Waldron thinks that arguments in support of entrenchment reflect a
particular attitude of mistrust:

> "To embody a right in an entrenched constitutional document is to adopt
> a certain attitude towards one's fellow citizens. That attitude is best
> summed up as a combination of self-assurance and mistrust: self-assur-
> ance in the proponent's conviction that what he is putting forward really
> *is* a matter of fundamental right and that he has captured it adequately in
> the particular formulation he is propounding; and mistrust, implicit in
> his view that any alternative conception that might be concocted by elected
> legislators next year ... is so likely to be wrong-headed or ill-motivated
> that *his own* formulation is to be elevated immediately beyond the reach
> of ordinary legislative revision."[48]

Waldron views this attitude as odd when contrasted with the belief in the
autonomy of the individual which is so evident in much human rights thinking.[49]
In response to the tyrannical potential of majority rule, Waldron simply notes
that any procedure attempting to solve the problem of social choice in the face
of disagreement risks injustice.[50] Those who fought for the right to vote did

---

[45] *ibid.*

[46] J. Waldron, *Law and Disagreement*, p.212.

[47] *ibid.*, p.213.

[48] *ibid.*, pp.221–222.

[49] A response to this argument is that the historical record, particularly in twentieth
century Europe, provides a sound basis for this mistrust.

[50] J. Waldron, *Law and Disagreement*, p.247.

not, according to Waldron, do so in order to participate in matters of policy only.[51] They were looking for meaningful involvement, on the basis of equality, in deciding matters of principle in the political community. The rights-based solution to disagreement on matters of principle is therefore, for Waldron, democratic participation.[52] As with Dworkin, he does not believe that there is any fundamental opposition between rights and democracy. His objection to American-style judicial review is based on a conception of rights rather than the suggestion that it is incompatible with democracy. He rejects the argument that judicial review results in more informed and extensive discussion of the issues.[53]

> "It is simply a myth that the public requires a moral debate to be, first of all, an interpretive debate before it can be conducted with any dignity or sophistication."[54]

Waldron also questions Dworkin's argument that constitutional theory should focus mainly on results. As noted above, Dworkin suggests we rely on the institution which is most likely to reach the correct result about the meaning of democracy; the issue of the legitimacy of the decision-maker should not be the main concern. Waldron is not persuaded and believes there is a loss to democracy when an unelected and unaccountable person or institution makes a decision on what democracy requires. He highlights something often neglected; when there is disagreement within a court it is frequently resolved by a simple majority vote. In the case of the US, for example, prediction is sometimes possible on the basis of how the votes "stack up" on the Supreme

---

[51] *ibid.*, p.249. See also p.282: "A theorist of rights should not be in the business of portraying the ordinary members of a democratic majority as selfish and irresponsible predators. But equally a theorist of democracy should not affect a pure proceduralist's nonchalance about the fate of individual rights under a system of majority decision...".

[52] Waldron argues that there is little in modern legal theory that does for legislation and legislatures what Dworkin has done for adjudication with his ideal judge "Hercules". Waldron has undertaken a sustained attempt to present legislation as a respectable source of law by drawing on the work of the major figures in political philosophy. See J. Waldron, *The Dignity of Legislation* (Cambridge University Press, Cambridge, 1999). For the argument that the interpretation of the constitution should be "taken away" from the courts, see M. Tushnet, *Taking the Constitution Away from the Courts* (Princeton University Press, Princeton, 1995). For a sceptical view on Bills of Rights from a neo-republican perspective, see R. Bellamy, *Rethinking Liberalism* (Pinter, London, 2000), chap.8.

[53] J. Waldron, *Law and Disagreement*, p.290.

[54] *ibid.*

Court. Waldron wants us to take rights seriously. But to do so he argues that we must look beyond the courts and return to democratic participation as the basis for our understanding of rights.

4. Conclusions

Rights have gained widespread acceptance in national and international law. When we disagree about rights today we usually, but not always, are arguing over the *interpretation of legal rights*. This is not to deny the existence of moral rights. It is simply to state that the interesting arguments are now occurring within substantive areas of law. There is a range of institutions tasked with the protection of human rights. At the national level, there are human rights commissions, parliamentary committees, NGOs and courts. One of the more intriguing recent trends is the attempt to mainstream respect for human rights in public administration. This reflects the belief that rights should count where it matters to individuals. Internationally, there are treaty-monitoring bodies, commissions, courts and other bodies. While human rights lawyers will look to the courts, few now suggest that the courtroom is the only forum where rights should be debated and enforced. Perhaps all the institutions mentioned are (or should be) engaged in a common enterprise of lending appropriate weight to rights? Some of the debates in legal theory have neglected the subtle variations in national practice and there is a tendency to view American-style judicial review as the norm.[55] This can lead to distortion in the debate.

New constitutional democracies tend to opt for the "democratic conditions" and result-oriented model which Dworkin approves of. Rights are now a secure part of most existing constitutional democracies; and this is generally assumed to be a "good thing". Judges will therefore have a role in their interpretation. Supreme Courts decide important matters of principle and policy on a routine basis. Judgments are widely reported and discussed, sometimes on a transnational basis (a trend evident with recent judgments of the US Supreme Court on issues such as the presidential election and the detention of non-national terrorist suspects). Judges must offer public reasons to justify their decisions. If the reasons are unconvincing or fall short of expected standards then criticism will follow. While it is true to say that judges are unelected, in this general context it is difficult to argue that they are entirely unaccountable for the decisions they make on rights. Given this, perhaps there should be rather less focus on institutional legitimacy and more on the substantive content of legal argumentation. What understanding should judges function with when

---

[55] See K. Roach, *The Supreme Court on Trial: Judicial Activism or Democratic Dialogue* (Irwin, Toronto, 2000).

they come to interpret rights in concrete cases? Which legal theory promotes the best approach to the judicial interpretation of individual rights?

We can and should offer our own constructive interpretations in order to promote principled adjudication. The problems posed by Hobbes have not gone away. Discourses of security and order have re-emerged with some force and are posing profound questions for anyone who claims to take rights seriously. In this context, would we really want to take the constitution away from the courts?[56]

---

[56] See M. Tushnet, *op. cit.*

CHAPTER 13

CRITICAL LEGAL STUDIES

GERARD QUINN

1. INTRODUCTION

Among the shared ideals of most Western states is a commitment to the political premises of liberal-democracy. This shared commitment in terms of political ideology is important because one's expectations of the legal order are powerfully influenced by political philosophy. Indeed, expectations of law are not unique in this respect: there are many occasions when we take implicit stands on essentially philosophical issues without ever realising it.[1] In terms of the relation between law and political philosophy, the special role that law is supposed to play within the liberal democratic polities of the West is best encapsulated in the specifically legal ideologies of "constitutionalism" and the "rule of law".

This chapter examines the jurisprudential school of thought known as the Critical Legal Studies (CLS) movement. In one way or another this scholarship questions the very nature or realisability of "constitutionalism" and the "rule of law". CLS is a movement of the political left in jurisprudence, seeking to attack and undermine the foundations of Western liberalism. In terms of antecedents and influences, CLS has strong trace elements of—in particular— American legal realism and neo-Marxist thought in its substantial body of scholarship.[2] It is generally considered that the heyday of the movement was

---

[1] The idea that every practice instantiates an idea and that we cannot function without some implicit theory of the world was best expressed by the economist, John Maynard Keynes, when he wrote that the ideas of economists and philosophers, "both when they are right and when they are wrong, are more powerful than is commonly understood … Practical men who believe themselves to be quite exempt from any intellectual influences, are usually the slaves of some defunct economist. Madmen in authority, who hear voices in the air, are distilling their frenzy from some academic scribbler of a few years back." Quoted by T. Lowi in *The End of Liberalism* (Norton, New York, 1979).

[2] Among the other influences on CLS thought are the following: critical social theory, the Frankfurt School, literary theory (deconstructionism and semiotics), structuralism and the thought of Herbert Marcuse (1898–1979). For an outstanding example of

during the 1970s and 1980s, when it stood trenchantly in opposition to the emerging law and economics movement, but it still continues to exert a considerable influence on legal theory generally.

The next part of this chapter will set out some of the more important tenets of liberalism, constitutionalism and the rule of law in order to understand the issues at stake in the various debates fuelled by CLS analysis. We will then examine the four main themes in CLS scholarship: a radical indeterminacy thesis; a concern for the mystification function of law; a concern for the role of ideologies in law; and an interest in the transformative possibilities offered by law.

2. LIBERALISM, CONSTITUTIONALISM AND THE RULE OF LAW

As mentioned at the outset, one must look carefully to political theory or the implicit philosophical stands of a particular system to understand the underlying stresses of a given legal regime. In truth the Anglo-American legal tradition owes much more to the political philosophy of liberalism that it does to that of democracy. The outstanding features of classical liberal philosophy can be usefully reduced to the following three propositions: first, that the world can be imagined as divided between two mutually exclusive spheres designated the "public" (state) and the "private" (civil society) respectively; second, that the first important point of departure in all meaningful political and legal debate is a sense of the primacy of the individual in the "private" sphere over all sources of "public" (but only "public") power; and, finally, that the public sphere is legitimate only to the point that it represents a consensual delegation of a limited and well-defined amount of private sovereignty.[3] Everything of significance in the structuring of Western legal systems appears to flow from these propositions.

"Constitutionalism" and the "rule of law" are two devices utilised in the legal regimes of liberal-democracies to achieve the ultimate goals of liberal political theory. "Constitutionalism" embraces the liberal idea of delimiting the "public" realm by emasculating its power. Initially this meant the introduction and enforcement of parliamentary controls over the whims of the executive (Crown).[4] These controls, which were the product of the English

---

structuralist analysis of legal doctrine, see D. Kennedy, "The Structure of Blackstone's Commentaries" (1970) 28 *Buffalo Law Review* 205.

[3] On liberalism as a political philosophy, see M. Carnoy, *The State and Political Theory* (Princeton University Press, Princeton, 1984). See also G.H. Sabine and T.L. Thorson, *A History of Political Theory* (4th ed., Harcourt Brace, New York, 1973), chaps. 32 and 33.

[4] See generally M. Knappen, *Constitutional and Legal History of England* (Harcourt

Glorious Revolution of 1688 in the Anglo-American legal system, were historically unique. Today "constitutionalism" is a much broader ideology and entails principled restrictions on all sources of public power (whether legislative, executive or judicial).[5] Public power is thus effectively fenced-in under constitutionalism by two mechanisms: the "separation of powers" doctrine which separates the legislative, executive and judicial arms of state and which is designed to minimise the risk of the abuse of public power; and justiciable individual rights which throw protective shields around individuals.

What then does the "rule of law" ideology add to the "constitutionalist" mission? The rule of law ideology recognises that even within a constitutionalist regime there must still exist some public power and that public power must sometimes be exercised to secure private rights and to advance the common good.[6] Constitutionalism is concerned with the content of formal law. The rule of law ideology is more concerned with the manner by which public power is transmitted through law to the individual. The rule of law ideology basically entails that when a liberal constitutionalist regime rules, it must rule through law (and not through the arbitrary whim of power-holders) and that the law must have certain adjectival attributes before it can be labelled "good" law. These attributes include appropriate generality, equality, clarity and certainty.[7] Once promulgated law conforms to the requirements of "constitution-

---

Brace, New York, 1942). For an historical account of the development of constitutionalism from its English roots right through to judicial review in the US, see C.M. Kenyon, "Constitutionalism in Revolutionary America" (1979) XX *Nomos* 197; C. Taylor, "Origins of the Unwritten Constitution: Fundamental Law in American Revolutionary Thought" (1978) 30 *Stanford Law Review* 843; and C.G. Haines, *The American Doctrine of Judicial Supremacy* (2nd ed., University of California Press, Berkeley, 1932).

[5] On "constitutionalism" as a political and legal idea see generally the series of essays in (1979) XX *Nomos*. See also *Constitutionalism: The Philosophical Dimension* (A. Rosenbaum ed., Greenwood, New York, 1988) and M.J.C. Vile, *Constitutionalism and the Separation of Powers* (Clarendon Press, Oxford, 1967).

[6] For a historical account of the unique development of the "rule of law" ideology in the West, see Roberto Unger's *Law in Modern Society* (Free Press, New York, 1976), chap.2. Unger posits three types of legal system corresponding to three types of society: customary law/non-statist feudal society; bureaucratic law/state-centred society; and rule of law legal order/constitutionalist state and pluralist society. This typology corresponds to most historical accounts of the rise of the state as a jural idea. See, *e.g.*, J. Strayer, *On the Medieval Origins of the Modern State* (Princeton University Press, Princeton, 1973) and H. Kohn, *The Idea of Nationalism* (Macmillan, New York, 1945).

[7] These adjectival attributes of law within the rule of law ideology are, for example, absorbed in the "principle of legality", that is, they are required to be respected by many international human rights treaties before restrictions to rights can be considered legitimate.

alism" and once it exhibits all the expected traits of "good law" within the "rule of law" ideology one bears an absolute political obligation to obey that law. Conversely, the usage of coercive public power against one who fails to conform his or her behaviour to the requirements of such a law is fully justified. This task of justifying political obligation to the law and, in turn, the specific usages of coercive public power against recalcitrant individuals, is of course central to the whole rule of law ideology.[8]

It should be clear that the rule of law ideology is intimately tied to constitutionalism. The animating ideal of both is the maximising of individual liberty against public power. Constitutionalism is valueless if personal rule in the public domain can still be tolerated. The rule of law is unworkable if the separation of powers is violated—for example, if the courts start to *make* law— and is valueless unless certain islands of immunity against public power are set aside (for example, the right to privacy). Some authors hold to the view that constitutionalism and the rule of law can usefully be considered quite apart from each other.[9] From this perspective a Nazi law clearly condemning a particular group is "good law" if it exhibits all the requisite adjectival attributes of law notwithstanding that it violates one or more of the ethical tenets of constitutionalism. But most authors consider the two ideologies to be bound up with each other. So much so that even if constitutionalism were to cease to exist then the rule of law ideology could act as a carrier or vehicle for the values that constitutionalism was originally designed to serve (maximising individual liberty). Criticism of the political philosophy of liberal-democracy entails, to some degree, a criticism of the legal ideologies of constitutionalism and the rule of law and vice versa.

Much jurisprudential writing functions almost exclusively (albeit not self-

---

[8] Reconciling man to the overpowering might of the modern state is one of the main functions of the rule of law ideology. Hence this ideology is intimately linked to the rise of the state and latterly the nation-state. See *The Nation-State: The Foundations of Modern Politics* (L. Tivey ed., Robertson, Oxford, 1981). On the rule of law as a justificatory theory of state power and political obligation, see C. Pateman "The Problem of Political Obligation" and, by the same author, "Self-Assumed Obligations and Abstract Individualism" in A. Kontos, *Powers, Possessions and Freedom* (University of Toronto Press, Toronto, 1979). That the invocation of the phrase "the rule of law" commonly evokes fear rather than a sense of security is no doubt due to the fact that it is most often invoked by someone in authority legitimating the use of coercive power.

[9] For the argument that a non-democratic system, based on the denial of human rights, might, in principle, conform to the requirements of the rule of law better than any of the legal systems of the enlightened Western democracies, but that it would nonetheless be an immeasurably worse legal system, see J. Raz, *The Authority of Law* (Clarendon Press, Oxford, 1979), chap.11.

consciously) within the "constitutionalist/rule of law" paradigm. Jurisprudents derive perverse pleasure by endlessly debating how to draw the line separating the presumptively coercive "public" realm from the presumptively benign "private" realm. Is homosexuality a protectable activity falling squarely on the private side of the divide? How far should public law interfere with private choices? Do judges necessarily legislate in hard cases and if so how can one square this with the separation of powers doctrine under constitutionalism? These and other questions tend to consume much orthodox jurisprudential debate. This genre of jurisprudential writing can be labelled intra-paradigmatic in that it usually leaves unexamined the underlying political premises that structure debate within liberal-democratic legal regimes.[10] While these questions are immensely important in their own right they only make sense within a particular kind of political-legal system. Most intra-paradigmatic analysis is undertaken by those inside the legal world looking inwardly. Only in the twentieth century did legal theoreticians begin to look outward for an enhanced appreciation of the legal system. Both the sociological jurisprudents and the legal realists of the 1920s and 1930s were insiders looking briefly outwards to help throw light on the deficiencies of the legal system and on how they could be resolved. Only rarely did anyone on the outside look in on the legal system. Marx, to whom law was an epiphenomenon, did so in an almost offhand manner. What mattered to Marx was not the question whether constitutionalism and the rule of law could be made to work but in whose interests did they work most.

By contrast CLS is a concerted movement composed of insiders looking outward to other disciplines, ideologies and philosophies in a rigorous fashion and in an effort to understand the law and to enhance practical legal abilities.[11] Unlike many sociological jurisprudents and realists before them, CLS

---

[10] The idea of a field of study as a paradigm that structures thought comes from T. Kuhn, *The Structure of Scientific Revolutions* (University of Chicago Press, Chicago, 1962).

[11] Although the CLS movement shares with Marxism a concern for the Western legal system in light of the blind spots of its underlying political philosophy (liberal-democracy) it would, however, be quite mistaken to assume that the CLS movement is necessarily or always tied to either a Marxist or neo-Marxist analysis of law. For non-Marxist CLS scholarship, see Roberto Unger, "The Critical Legal Studies Movement" (1983) 96 *Harvard Law Review* 320; *Politics: A Work in Constructive Social Theory* (Cambridge University Press, Cambridge, 1986); and *Politics: A Work in Constructive Social Theory (Vol.II): False Necessity: Anti-Necessitarian Social Theory in the Service of Radical Democracy* (Cambridge University Press, Cambridge, 1987). For commentaries on Unger's work, see H. Collins, "Roberto Unger and the Critical Legal Studies Movement" (1987) 14 *Journal of Law and Society* 387 and S. Holmes, "The Professor of Smashing", *New Republic*, October 17, 1987.

scholarship often questions the very divide between "inside" and "outside" the law and argues that the legal system is not even sufficiently autonomous to warrant separate study.[12] How was the CLS movement formed?[13] In 1964 a "Law and Society" movement was started in the University of Wisconsin. Its task was to encourage scholars to conduct empirical research into the gaps between the law in the books and the law in action. The high point of this movement was achieved with the publication of Laurence Friedman's *History of American Law* in 1973.[14] The book was criticised by two younger radical scholars—Mark Tushnet and David Trubek—as paying insufficient attention to ideology in law and as naïve in its faith in the possibility of a value-free social science.[15] In 1977 Tushnet, Trubek and three newly tenured law professors at Harvard Law School (Duncan Kennedy, Roberto Unger and Morton Horwitz), among others, met in the first annual Critical Legal Studies conference. We will now discuss the main themes of the scholarship that followed from these developments.

---

[12] This has implications for legal education. If the law or the legal sphere lacks autonomy then how much and what kind of "other material" ought to be included in the curriculum? Where should it be taught—in a sociology department, in a politics department, in a theology department? Should it be taught at university at all? On this aspect of the legal education debate, see P. Carrington, "Of Law and the River" (1984) 35 *Journal of Legal Education* 222 and S. Levinson, "Professing Law: A Commitment of Faith or Detached Analysis?" from a symposium entitled "Professing Law: A Colloquy on Critical Legal Studies" (1986) 31 *St. Louis University Law Journal* 3. Carrington has this to say about law teachers who preach the CLS brand of legal nihilism: "[T]he nihilist who must profess that legal principle does not matter has an ethical duty to depart the law school, perhaps to seek a place elsewhere in the academy."; at 227.

[13] On the historical roots to CLS, see G. Edward White, "From Realism to Critical Legal Studies: A Truncated Intellectual History" (1986) 40 *Southwestern Law Journal* 819. See also *Critical Legal Studies* (P. Fitzpatrick and A. Hunt eds., Blackwell, Oxford, 1987); M. Kelman, *A Guide to Critical Legal Studies* (Harvard University Press, Cambridge, Mass., 1987); *The Critical Lawyers' Handbook* (I. Grigg-Spall and P. Ireland eds., Pluto, London, 1992); *The Critical Lawyers' Handboook II* (P. Ireland and P. Laleng eds., Pluto, London, 1997); J.C. Williams, "Critical Legal Studies: The Death of Transcendence and the Rise of the New Langdells" (1987) 62 *New York University Law Review* 429; Note, "Round and Round the Bramble Bush: From Legal Realism to Critical Legal Studies" (1982) 95 *Harvard Law Review* 1669; J. Boyle, "The Politics of Reason: Critical Legal Theory and Legal Social Thought" (1985) 133 *University of Pennsylvania Law Review* 685; and G. Peller, "The Metaphysics of American Law" (1985) 73 *California Law Review* 1151.

[14] L. Friedman, *History of American Law* (Simon and Schuster, New York, 1973).

[15] See especially, M.Tushnet, "Perspectives on the Development of American Law: A Critical Review of Friedman's *A History of American Law*" (1977) *Wisconsin Law Review* 81.

3. Main Themes

Apart from a fairly generalised disenchantment with the political tenets of liberal-democracy, four specific themes tend to bind together much CLS scholarship. These themes are as follows: a radical indeterminacy thesis; a concern for the mystification function of law; a concern for the role of ideology in law; and an interest in utopial transformative possibilities in law.

The Radical Indeterminacy Thesis

Many CLS scholars view legal doctrine as riven with vagueness, conflicts and gaps. Not only is doctrine unstable, traditional methods of legal reasoning are unable (unaided by ideology) to inject stability into the law. A CLS analysis of legal reasoning attempts to show it to be circular, vacuous and inconclusive. Legal doctrine and canons of construction do not solve problems; ideology does. In this critique of legal reasoning CLS is most like its legal realist forbears. But while the realists stressed that doctrinal confusion could be remedied by purging formalism from the law the critical scholars emphasise the endemic nature of doctrinal confusion and the effects of ideology even in post-formalist jurisprudence.

Two popular targets for CLS criticism under this head are, first, the manipulability of the "public/private" divide used in theory and as instantiated in legal doctrine and, second, the abstract notion and/or the practical efficacy of rights. The public/private divide is seen by CLS scholars as an ideological construct that can be flipped almost without limit to suit pre-determined outcomes.[16] Traditional methods of legal reasoning, it is claimed, *empower* courts to see one thing on one side of the divide and now on the other.[17] Traditional methods of legal reasoning do not in other words substantially constrain judgement. Such methods merely *enable* courts to rationalise their preferred outcomes. If true, this corrosive insight causes a rupture in the chain between public power and private security. Because courts are relatively unconstrained in the disposition of contentious matters by legal doctrine *simpliciter* this calls into question the whole workability of the rule of law. The thrust of the CLS claim here is not that the "rule of law" does not work

---

[16] See D. Kennedy, "The Stages in the Decline of the Public/Private Divide" (1982) 130 *University of Pennsylvania Law Review* 1358. See also G. Frug, "The City as a Legal Concept" (1980) 93 *Harvard Law Review* 1059.

[17] See generally, P. Gabel, "Reification in Legal Reasoning" (1980) 3 *Research in Law and Sociology* 25 and J.W. Singer, "The Player and the Cards: Nihilism and Legal Theory" (1984) 94 *Yale Law Journal* 1. For a criticism of Singer's views, see J. Stick, "Can Nihilism be Pragmatic?" (1986) 100 *Harvard Law Review* 332.

but that it tends to work according to the strictures of ideology. By plausibly manipulating the "public/private" divide courts are enabled to make selectively available the corrective power of the state. When CLS scholars engage in the above kind of doctrinal analysis they are sometimes said to be "trashing".[18] The most commonly used tools of trashing are taken from contemporary trends in literary theory. One such tool is known as "deconstructionism". Deconstruction entails a showing of the dependency of meaning on relationships and a showing that choice is inevitable and is usually made for ideological purposes.[19]

The CLS critique of rights is not completely new. Marx put forward his own criticism of civil rights in his early writings.[20] But CLS scholarship gives the standard critique of rights a new twist.[21] To understand the significance of the critique recall that the whole object of constitutionalism and the rule of law combined is to insulate and secure the individual against public power. Rights are vital tools in the achievement of that task. Any viable critique of rights goes to the heart of the constitutionalist mission of effectively segregating the public from the private sphere.

What then are the CLS criticisms of rights? One popular CLS tirade against rights is that they are carriers of the ideology of "possessive individualism" which legitimates an exploitative market economy.[22] While it is undoubtedly true that the ethic of individualism inherent in the notion of a right was an

---

[18] See M. Kelman, "Trashing" (1984) 36 *Stanford Law Review* 293.

[19] For examples of CLS-deconstructionist legal analysis, see C. Dalton, "An Essay in the Deconstruction of Contract Doctrine" (1985) 94 *Yale Law Journal* 997 and M. Tushnet, "Critical Legal Studies and Constitutional Law: An Essay in Deconstruction" (1984) 36 *Stanford Law Review* 623. See also J.M. Balkin, "Deconstructive Practice and Legal Theory" (1987) 96 *Yale Law Journal* 743. For a defence of traditional methods of making sense of texts, see R. Dworkin, *A Matter of Principle* (Harvard University Press, Cambridge, Mass., 1985), chap.2; and O. Fiss, "Conventionalism" (1985) 58 *Southern California Law Review* 117 and "Objectivity and Interpretation" (1982) 34 *Stanford Law Review* 937. See also S. Fish, "Denis Martinex and the Use of Theory" (1987) 96 *Yale Law Journal* 1728.

[20] In *On the Jewish Question* (1843), for example, Marx observed that "none of the so-called rights of man goes beyond egoistic man, man as he is civil society, namely an individual withdrawn behind his private interests and whims and separated from the community". See *Karl Marx: Selected Writings* (D. McLellan ed., Oxford University Press, Oxford, 1977), p.54.

[21] See generally, J.W. Singer, "The Legal Rights Debate in Analytical Jurisprudence from Bentham to Hohfield" (1982) *Wisconsin Law Review* 975 and M. Tushnet, "An Essay on Rights" (1984) 62 *Texas Law Review* 1363.

[22] For the most lucid and famous analysis of the liberal theory of "possessive individualism", see C.B. Macpherson, *The Political Theory of Possessive Individualism* (Oxford University Press, Oxford, 1962).

essential building block in the creation of market societies throughout Europe, it is less clear whether one can separate individualism as a philosophy from the doctrine of economic individualism.[23] To believe in individual rights, to use them, is in a certain way to relegitimate an unjust economic order, according to a standard CLS critique.

Another CLS critique is that rights do not even function to insulate the individual effectively from public power. This is allegedly so because the logic of rights-based argumentation is circular. The basic argument is that the internal logic of rights merely restates questions about freedom rather than resolves them. For example a right bounded by respect for the rights of others is open-textured in that we are not told which rights of others count and to what degree. To that extent the logic of a right invites the exercise of unprincipled judicial discretion. In determining the boundaries to rights and the limits to public power, ideology (and emphatically not legal doctrine) predominates.

Lastly, even if rights did function to effectively insulate individuals against public power then they are still open to the charge that they expose individuals to the full brutalities of private power where such is left unregulated by positive law. Whether such positive law is ever promulgated depends on how interest groups line up in the legislature and on the amount of room left to manoeuvre by market conditions.[24] Whether such legislation will have the desired effect depends partly on the ease with which it can be circumvented and also on the attitude of the bench toward it.

The real effects of rights are three-fold, according to standard CLS criticism: first, by turning a blind eye to the abuse of private power they expose the individual to the brutalities of the market; second, they empower as much as they disempower the state (or one arm thereof, the judiciary); and third, they induce a false sense of justice about the economic and social ordering of the polity. Duncan Kennedy has argued that rights are "by their nature 'formal', meaning that they secure to individuals legal protection for as well as from arbitrariness—to speak of rights is precisely not to speak of justice between

---

[23] On the idea that a rights-conscious culture is essential prerequisite to the rise of a market society, see P. Gabel, "The Phenomenology of Rights-Consciousness and the Pact of Withdrawn Selves" (1984) 62 *Texas Law Review* 1363. Although it is often said that an essential prerequisite to the establishment of a stable liberal-democratic regime is the presence and operation of a free-market society, it is in fact a matter of considerable scholarly speculation as to which comes first, a free-market economy or a stable liberal-democratic society. See, for example, M. Friedman and R. Friedman, *Free to Choose* (Penguin, Harmondsworth, 1980), pp.54–64 and K. Mannheim, *Freedom, Power and Democratic Planning* (Routledge and Kegan Paul, London, 1951), pp.7–17, 29–37.

[24] On the economic constraints to legislation, see C. Offe, *Contradictions of the Welfare State* (Hutchinson, London, 1984).

social classes, races, or sexes".[25] In short, an individual rights ideology cripples progressive social movements as much as it galvanises them.[26]

The above critique of rights has not gone unchallenged.[27] Indeed, not all critical scholars are enamoured with the idea of a world without rights. Roberto Unger, for example, expends much thought in trying to imagine a polity where a conception of rights augments and not undermines genuine citizenship and economic justice. Such a polity requires a new approach to rights theory in the context of the transformative possibilities of law.

The Mystification Function of the Law

If legal doctrine alone fails to solve real problems and if rights serve paradoxically to empower the state then why cannot a judge simply announce his or her ideological preference and decide accordingly? Judges could do so if they wanted to but such honesty, according to the CLS view of things, would make a mockery of the rule of law ideal. Instead judges cloak legal decisions in the garb of orthodox legal reasoning and censor their language with a self-forbearing ordinance. They are strongly motivated to do so by a desire to remain within (and to be seen to remain within) the strictures of the rule of law ideology. The deployment of the sonorous language of the law has, in other words, the effect of mystifying the law. If the layman cannot make sense of a particular ruling it is only because he or she has not been admitted to the select priesthood of the law: the legal profession.[28] This is what Chief Justice Coke meant when he spoke of the "artificial reason" of the law being accessible to the select few.[29]

---

[25] D. Kennedy, "Legal Education as Training for Hierarchy" in *The Politics of Law* (2nd ed., Pantheon, New York, 1990), p.46.

[26] Some proponents of the Critical Race Theory (CRT) movement refute this form of criticism of rights. For example, Patricia Williams, in *The Alchemy of Race and Rights* (Harvard University Press, Cambridge, Mass., 1991), suggests that, "For the historically disempowered, the conferring of rights is symbolic of all the denied aspects of their humanity: rights imply a respect that places one in a referential range of self and others, that elevates one's status from human body to social being"; p.53.

[27] For general defences of rights against CLS attack, see F. Michelman, "Justification (And Justifiability) of Law in a Contradictory World" (1986) XXVIII *Nomos* 71; E. Sparer, "Fundamental Human Rights, Legal Entitlements and the Social Struggle: A Friendly Critique of the Critical Legal Studies Movement" (1984) 36 *Stanford Law Review* 508; and M. Minnow, "Interpreting Rights: An Essay for Robert Cover" (1987) 96 *Yale Law Journal* 1860.

[28] The "priesthood" metaphor is illuminating. Can a doubting legal "priest" remain a priest? Does he or she have an obligation to leave the priesthood? See P. Carrington, *op. cit.*

[29] For an insightful discussion of Coke's famous dictum in *Bonham's Case,* see T.

What are the effects of mystification in the law? Mystification, according to CLS, hides the reality of having to make hard choices in many cases; makes the choice actually made appear natural, apolitical or neutral; leads one not to over-scrutinise the language of the law; and leads one to willingly consent to an unjust economic and political system. Much of the inspiration for this thesis comes from the writings of Antonio Gramsci (1891–1937).[30] A central point to remember about this CLS thesis is the claim that not only are laymen taken in by mystification but so too are the lawyers and the judges themselves. The self-appointed task of many CLS scholars is what one might expect it to be if one were to take Gramsci seriously: namely, to heighten popular consciousness of the social context to law; to form a self-aware counter-hegemonic legal culture; and to engage in a "war of position" with dominant culture and legal ideology. A common denominator between much CLS scholarship in this regard would be the exposition of false necessity in the law and in the legal process. An important point to remember is that CLS scholars attempt to demystify the law not because they believe there is a better or more rational way to regularise adjudication but simply in order to expose past undemocratic choices in the law.

A Concern for the Role of Ideologies in Law

If the law is so uncertain and is shot through with the inevitability of choice then what gives it the appearance of stability? That the legal system is stable is no mere perception. This stability is real. But such stability, according to CLS, is not accounted for by legal doctrine as such. Ideology insinuates stability into an otherwise unstable structure.[31] As has been said, the overarching political

---

Plucknett, "Bonham's Case and Judicial Review" (1926) 40 *Harvard Law Review* 30.

[30] Gramsci posed the question why the predictions of revolution raised by orthodox Marxist thought did not materialise in the industrialised West during the depressed 1920s? The problem with orthodox Marxist thought, according to Gramsci, was that it underemphasised the role of ideology at the level of the superstructure, and particularly the ability of bourgeois ideology to become dominant in popular culture and succeed in winning over the willing consent of the masses. See A. Gramsci, *Selections from the Prison Notebooks* (International Publishers, New York, 1971). See also W. L. Adamson, *Hegemony and Revolution: A Study of Antonio Gramsci's Political and Cultural History* (University of California Press, Berkeley, 1980).

[31] For an example of CLS scholarship that looks at the effect of ideology on the bench and how ideology works itself through legal doctrine to purge it of radical anti-market tendencies, see K. Klare, "Judicial Deradicalisation of the Wagner Act and the Origins of Modern Legal Consciousness 1937–1941" (1978) 62 *Minnesota Law Review* 265.

ideology of the legal system is that of liberal-democracy. Much CLS analysis under this head appears unfocused since it vacillates between a generalised philosophical critique of liberal-democracy as a political ideal and very specific critiques of particular legal doctrines. CLS scholars who engage in the latter kind of work tend to posit complex connections between the underlying structure of a legal field and the animating values of liberal-democracy. The deficiencies of the former, it is said, make patently manifest the structural deficiencies of the latter.

It is important to note a significant point of departure between CLS and Ronald Dworkin's theory about principles and legal ideals in law. Dworkin, like most post-formalist theoreticians since the 1930s, recognises that formal law is incomplete and fails to solve many of the more difficult legal problems that courts often face. Dworkin nevertheless asserts that the judging process is regular and stable and that this stability is accounted for by the existence and power of specifically legal ideals. These legal ideals supposedly emanate from legal doctrine. They form "the soundest theory of the settled law". To solve a hard case one must look both to legal doctrine and to the relevant legal ideal. To identify the relevant legal ideal one must see whether it "fits" with, and also whether it justifies and animates, a given piece of legal doctrine. Once correctly identified such a "legal ideal" will be refracted back by the judge on the legal doctrine and, when the legal doctrine and the best-fitted ideal are taken together, they will supply the answer to a hard case.

CLS scholars agree with Dworkin up to a point.[32] Legal doctrine alone does not solve cases. Legal ideals do play a prominent part in the judging process. But, unlike Dworkin, many CLS scholars locate the source of these ideals as lying outside the law altogether. They maintain that the choice of any particular legal ideal to be attributed to a given piece of legal doctrine has relatively little to do with legal doctrine as such, still less with the satisfaction of some kind of "fit test". Instead it has nearly everything to do with ideology. Ideology comes from the realm of politics and remains squarely outside the narrow legal realm as traditionally understood. This explains the oft-quoted CLS maxims that "all law is politics" and "law is politics using different means". By emphasising this, many CLS scholars are not content merely to point to the lack of democratic legitimacy in the legal process but wish also to point to the sheer impossibility of erecting any workable wall between law and politics.[33]

---

[32] For a useful overview of the main CLS criticisms of Dworkin's theories, see A. Altman, "Legal Realism, Critical Legal Studies and Dworkin" (1986) 15 *Philosophy and Public Affairs* 205.

[33] Similarly many CLS scholars interpret the attempts by others at regularising adjudication through the invocation of extra-legal ideals as simple political manoeuvring. See M. Horwitz, "Law and Economics: Science or Politics?" (1981) 8 *Hofstra Law Review* 905.

The usual CLS targets for analysis in relation to their concern for the role of ideology in law are twofold. Firstly, much CLS scholarship is interested in unpacking the essential premises of liberal-democracy. As we mentioned earlier, the Anglo-American legal tradition owes much more to the political philosophy of liberalism that it does to that of democracy. Indeed the liberal-democratic variant of democratic theory turns out to be more liberal than democratic.[34] So much so that one of the self-assigned tasks of some CLS scholars is to investigate the theoretical possibilities for a separation of "democratic" from "liberal" (and "liberal-democratic") theory and to examine its significance to the ordering of the legal system.[35]

Secondly, much CLS scholarship is concerned with forming an understanding of the dynamics of change within the law. The political premises of liberal-democracy structure the overall orientation of the legal system. But what accounts for specific changes in specific fields? How and why do the boundaries between different legal fields (say, tort and contract) ebb and flow? The CLS answer to these and related questions about legal history tends to rely on neo-Marxist analysis.[36] In other words the motor force to the unfolding of legal history must be sought in an examination of the changing symbiotic relationship between law and the structuring of the economic life of a polity. The law has a measure of autonomy from the dynamics of economics but it cannot ignore changes at the material base of society for too long. To get an accurate picture of legal history one must, therefore, first get an accurate picture of the economy, and then look for a positive correlation between the two. Such an understanding of legal history helps one to better understand how premises are re-ordered regularly within legal doctrine, how boundaries vary

---

[34] For the standard "democratic" critique of liberal-democracy, see C.B. Macpherson, *The Life and Times of Liberal-Democracy* (Oxford University Press, Oxford, 1977) and, by the same author, *Democratic Theory: Essays in Retrieval* (Clarendon Press, Oxford, 1973). See also D. Held, *Models of Democracy* (2nd ed., Polity, Cambridge, 1996) and P. Bachrach, *The Theory of Democratic Elitism* (Little Brown, Boston, 1967).

[35] See, for example, R. Parker, "The Past of Constitutional Theory and its Future" (1981) 42 *Ohio State Law Journal* 223 and M. Horwitz, "The Legacy of 1776 in Legal and Economic Thought" (1976) 19 *Journal of Law and Economics* 621. Many CLS scholars take inspiration from Benjamin Barber's book *Strong Democracy: Participatory Politics for a New Age* (University of California Press, Berkeley, 1984).

[36] Understanding or reinterpreting legal history is a major CLS objective. See M. Horwitz, *The Transformation of American Law, 1780–1860* (Harvard University Press, Cambridge, Mass., 1977); *The Transformation of American Law, 1870–1960: The Crisis of Legal Orthodoxy* (Oxford University Press, Oxford, 1992); and "The Historical Foundations of Modern Contract Law" (1974) 87 *Harvard Law Review* 917. See also R.W. Gordon, "Critical Legal Histories" (1984) 36 *Stanford Law Review* 57.

as between legal subjects and how radical legal change can take place despite the illusion of timelessness and certainty. Such an understanding can lead to an enhanced ability to manipulate legal doctrine and ultimately to better lawyering.

Transformative Possibilities in Law

Much CLS scholarship emphasises the paradoxical co-existence of open-endness with stability in the legal system and accounts for the latter by reference to the predominance of a particular political ideology and a sub-set of conforming legal ideologies. Some CLS scholars employ their talents in drawing out the distinctions between the political premises of liberal-democracy and other more congenial political philosophies. A popular alternative ideology has been that of civic-republicanism.[37] Many CLS scholars see trace elements of such alternative ideologies present and ineradicable within extant legal doctrine. The task of the critically-minded lawyer is to identify these countervailing tendencies and to persuade courts using the manipulative language of the law to act out the entailments of these counter ideologies in specific cases. Sometimes this is called doing "deviationist doctrine".

All CLS scholars assert a preference for a more egalitarian political ideology; one that is as concerned with issues of economic morality and distributive justice as it is with other matters. Many CLS scholars do not condemn outright the market as a mechanism or as an idea; indeed some would advocate what we would call a "social market". All CLS scholars are interested in participatory democracy in both private and public life. They characteristi-

---

[37] The tradition of republican political thought includes the political philosophies of Cicero (106–143 B.C.), Niccolo Machiavelli (1469–1527), James Harrington (1611–1677) and Algernon Sidney (c.1622–1683). On the historical roots of civic-republican theory, see J.G.A. Pocock, *The Machiavellian Movement; Florentine Political Thought and the Atlantic Republican Tradition* (Princeton University Press, Princeton, 1975) and G.S. Wood, *The Creation of the American Republic* (University of North Carolina Press, Chapel Hill, 1969). On the debate about the historical nature and present significance of the ideology of civic republicanism, see M. Horwitz, "Republicanism and Liberalism in American Constitutional Thought" (1987) 29 *William and Mary Law Quarterly* 57 and C.R. Sunstein, "Beyond the Republican Revival" (1988) 97 *Yale Law Journal* 1539. The central components of republican legal theory have been described as including the "pursuit of the common good, popular sovereignty, liberty, virtue, mixed government, and the rule of law, linked by a Roman conception of *libertas* that defined justice between free people as subjection to no one's will or interest, but only to general laws approved by the people for the common or 'public' good of the community". M.N.S. Sellers, "Republican Philosophy of Law" in *The Philosophy of Law: An Encyclopedia* (C.B. Gray ed., Garland, New York, 1999), Vol.II, p.741.

cally attempt to uncouple democracy from liberalism and to replace the liberal concern for the "possessive individual" with a democratic concern for distributive justice.

Critical scholars are often accused of trying to do that for which they criticise others most, namely, impose an unwanted ideology on others. To get over this charge CLS scholars must somehow argue for their preferred ideology in terms of its ethical superiority. This task has consumed much of Roberto Unger's work.[38] Unger has proposed a detailed "programme of empowered democracy", involving a new system of rights, a reorganised system of government and a reconstructed economic system.[39]

4. CONCLUSION

One cannot properly assess the significance of CLS without an appreciation of the predicament of constitutionalism and the rule of law in the twentieth century. Most significant legal debate during this period revolved either around the nature and desirability of a system of government animated by these ideals or by their practicability. Roscoe Pound, for example, was chiefly motivated in his jurisprudential writings by a desire to preserve faith in the "rule of law tradition" and he feared the Marxist critique of law most of all. Pound sought to discredit legal formalism once and for all and salvage something of the rule of law at the turn of the century. The realists took Pound's analysis much further than Pound himself was prepared to do but were silenced by the recrudescence of natural law (especially theocratic natural law) in opposition to the totalitarian dictatorships then emerging in Europe, and also by their co-optation into the New Deal administration of President Franklin D. Roosevelt.

The CLS approach, however, was entirely different, and one cannot simply treat CLS as just another school of legal philosophy, in the fashion of sociological jurisprudence or American legal realism. To do so would be tantamount to applying tendentious intra-paradigmatic standards in the appreciation of CLS. If anything, the CLS "philosophy" of law has to be garnered by a close examination of specific CLS critiques of specific substantive areas of law. Indeed, as we mentioned at the outset, the heyday of CLS was during the 1970s and 1980s, and many CLS scholars moved on to work in, and to apply CLS thought to, specific doctrinal areas. Perhaps it might be said that now the only thing that really unites CLS scholars is a certain predilection

---

[38] For an illuminating analysis of Unger's work in this area, see D. Cornell, "Toward a Modern/Post-modern Reconstruction of Ethics" (1985) 133 *University of Pennsylvania Law Review* 291.

[39] See especially R. Unger, "The Critical Legal Studies Movement" and *Politics: A Work in Constructive Social Theory (Vol.II)*.

for left-oriented perspectives opposing the political philosophy of liberal-democracy and for a broadened understanding of the requirements of justice to include issues of economic morality.

The legacy of legal realism still haunts contemporary jurisprudential debate. If realism as a school is dead the questions raised by realism concerning, *inter alia*, the judging process, the public/private divide, the appropriateness of the doctrine of the separation of powers to the contemporary world and the role of values in law have survived largely unanswered to the present day. As we noted above, in the absence of any genuine post-formalist consensus about the judging process there has developed a tendency for the law to "look outwards" to other disciplines. The problem with this is that there is no agreement about which disciplines to look to or indeed to what extent one must look outwards. This problem is compounded by the fact that some judges, particularly in the US, look outwards to other disciplines not merely to enhance their understanding of the law but also in order to identify principles with which to dispose of particular cases. For example, the principle of "allocational efficiency" in positive economics is advocated as a governing principle in law by Richard Posner and many members of the Chicago school of law and economics.[40] CLS, as we have seen, look elsewhere. Perhaps something can be salvaged of the central promises of constitutionalism and the rule of law. Perhaps these ideologies over-extend themselves and cannot possibly deliver even on their own terms. Maybe a revision of these ideologies is in order. Perhaps it is possible to square a legal regime that falls short of the high expectations set by constitutionalism and the rule of law with the philosophy of liberal-democracy. But perhaps it is liberal democracy itself that requires revision. Certainly these legal ideologies would look quite different if the "civic-republican" political ideology favoured by many CLS scholars were to predominate.

---

[40] See, for example, R.A. Posner, "The Ethical and Political Basis of the Efficiency Norm in Common Law Adjudication" (1980) 8 *Hofstra Law Review* 487 and R.A. Arnold, "Efficiency vs. Ethics: Which is the Proper Decision Criterion in Law Cases?" (1982) 6 *Journal of Libertarian Studies* 49.

CHAPTER 14

LAW AND ECONOMICS

ALAN HAUGH

1. INTRODUCTION

The descriptor "Law and Economics" can be applied to a range of schools of jurisprudence, each of which approaches the study of the interaction of economic theory and law from a distinct perspective.[1] This chapter will discuss primarily the scholarship associated with the Chicago (or neo-classical) school of law and economics, widely regarded as the most influential voice within mainstream law and economics.[2] Given the context of this discussion—in a jurisprudence textbook—it will necessarily deal in the most part with the school's influence from a legal rather than from an economic point of view. However, the influence of the school's core economic theorists in the wider realms of economics and politics should not be overlooked. For example, it has been estimated that about 80 per cent of the economists employed by the US administrations of Ronald Reagan had studied under Milton Friedman at the University of Chicago.[3] Friedman's normative economic analysis was also

---

[1] Neil Duxbury describes the great variety of perspectives one encounters within the general field of law and economic scholarship as follows: "Today, law and economics is a subject over which controversy and confusion reign. Defining the subject is like to trying to eat spaghetti with a spoon. Law and economics can be positive, normative, neo-classical, institutional, Austrian—quite simply, the subject is weighed down by a multitude of competing methodologies and perspectives which are not always easily distinguishable"; *Patterns of American Jurisprudence* (Clarendon Press, Oxford, 1995), p.314. For an excellent survey of many of these distinct perspectives, see N. Mercuro and S.G. Medena, *Economics and the Law: From Posner to Post-Modernism* (Princeton University Press, Princeton, 1997).

[2] "[T]he Chicago approach to law and economics ... has attracted a large following and has come to dominate scholarship within the economic analysis of law." N. Mercuro and S.G. Medena, *op. cit.*, p.51.

[3] This estimation is referred to by Neil Duxbury, who observes that Friedman "not only produced a prodigious amount of technical economic research; more importantly still ... he was able to spread the economic faith of the Chicago school ... beyond the American universities ... Friedman, more than anyone else, was responsible for

profoundly influential on the monetary and economic policies adopted by UK Conservative Governments under Margaret Thatcher between 1979 and 1990.[4]

In addition to Milton Friedman, core contributors to the development of the Chicago school's perspective include Ronald Coase, Guido Calabresi, Henry Manne, Gary Becker, Frank Easterbrook, Robert Bork and Richard Posner. Although the school came of age during the 1960s and the 1970s, its origins date back to the appointment of the first professor of economics within the school of law at the University of Chicago, Henry Simons, in the late 1930s.[5] (At that time, the law school at Harvard was associated with Langdellian formalism and those at Yale and Columbia with realism). The intellectual roots of law and economic scholarship are in the laissez faire ideology associated with Adam Smith, the classical utilitarianism of Jeremy Bentham and John Stuart Mill and the American realist movement. According to John Kelly, the school can be regarded, "in crude terms, as the right wing of American Jurisprudence, critical legal studies being its left".[6] As we shall observe, however, the characterisation of the movement as "right wing" is by no means accepted by all the movement's scholars.

The chief intellectual spokesman for Chicago law and economic scholarship over the last 30 or more years has without doubt been Richard Posner. Posner has combined a long and distinguished scholarly career with an equally distinguished career as a federal appeals judge. His list of publications is prodigious to say the least: he has published at least 50 books and several hundred scholarly articles. Two other of the school's most articulate representatives—Robert Bork and Frank Easterbrook—have also been appointed to the federal bench, and economic analysis of legal thought continues to be one of the most dominant trends within American legal culture. Anthony T. Kronman, for example, referring in particular to the influence of the Chicago school in the 1990s, observed that law and economics is "the most powerful

---

ensuring that the normative dimension of Chicago neo-classicism made as profound an impact on American government as did Chicago law and economics on antitrust adjudication"; *op. cit.*, pp.376–377.

[4] On the influence of Friedman's economic thought on Thatcherite monetary policy, see D. Smith, *Free Lunch: Easily Digestible Economics* (Profile, London, 2003), chaps 11 and 12. Incidentally, Friedman is credited with having coined the phrase, "There is no such thing as a free lunch".

[5] N. Mercuro and S.G. Medena, *op. cit.*, p.52. Richard Posner has observed that the emergence of contemporary Chicago law and economic scholarship "began with Guido Calabresi's first article on torts [1961] and Ronald Coase's article on social cost [1960]"; *Economic Analysis of Law* (4th ed., Little Brown, Boston, 1992), p.21.

[6] J.M. Kelly, *A Short History of Western Legal Theory* (Clarendon Press, Oxford, 1992), p.436.

current in American law teaching today. Law and economics now completely dominates some fields and is a significant presence in most others."[7]

In this chapter we will explore some of the main themes of law and economic scholarship: the view of the human subject as a rational utility maximiser; the idea of efficiency as justice; the positive and normative aspects of the scholarship; and the application of law and economic analysis to ostensibly non-market behaviour. We will then examine the legitimate role of the judge from the perspective of, in particular, Richard Posner. The chapter will conclude by discussing some of the most frequent criticisms of this hugely influential school of jurisprudential thought.

2. MAIN THEMES

The Human Subject as Rational Utility Maximiser

Adam Smith (1723–1790), the "father" of modern capitalist economics, advocated a free market, unfettered by anything more than minimal state interference.[8] Left to its own devices, the market, according to Smith, would, for example, work equally against any temporary monopolies that developed and any price-fixing cartels that were established. This was an inevitable consequence of human nature because individuals, according to Smith, naturally seek to pursue their own self-interest. In the context of trade, pursuit of one's own self-interest translates into seeking the most cost-effective solution. Acting in this way, individuals indirectly but effectively promote society's best interest also by facilitating competition in the market.

Building on Smith's understanding of the relationship between individual human nature and the operation of the competitive, market economy, Chicago law and economic analysis advanced its view of the human subject as a rational maximiser of his or her own self-interest, not only in market but also in non-market spheres.

> "The basic assumption of economics that guides the version of economic analysis of law that I shall be presenting is that people are rational maximisers of their own satisfactions—*all* people (with the exception of small children and the profoundly retarded) in *all* of their activities (except

---

[7] A.T. Kronman, *The Lost Lawyer: Failing Ideals of the Legal Profession* (Belknap Press, Cambridge, Mass., 1993), p.226.

[8] Adam Smith's main economic work was *An Inquiry into the Nature and Causes of the Wealth of Nations* (1776). Chapter 4 of David Smith's *Free Lunch* is a very readable introduction to Adam Smith's contribution to the development of economic thought.

when under the influence of psychosis or similarly deranged through drug or alcohol abuse) that involve choice ... [T]his definition embraces the criminal deciding whether to commit another crime, the litigant deciding whether to settle a case, the legislator deciding whether to vote for or against a bill, the judge deciding how to cast a vote in a case, the party to a contract deciding whether to break it ...".[9]

In short, in any given situation, where an individual is confronted with choice and is in a position to process information relating to the alternatives available to him or her, he or she will rank the possible outcomes according to their relative desirability and ultimately choose that course of action which appears to best maximise his or her satisfactions or utility. This is also known as "rational actor theory" and, as indicated in the above quotation, the process of maximising one's utility applies equally to non-monetary and monetary satisfactions. Furthermore, the process does not always require conscious deliberation in order to be rational: Posner observes that "rational denotes suiting means to ends, rather than mulling things over", and he suggests that "much of our knowledge is tacit".[10] In similar vein, Frank Easterbrook has noted that describing people as rational does not mean that we are computers.[11]

Applying law and economics basic assumption about human nature, we can further analyse the motivation behind an individual's decision to continue a particular activity as follows: he or she will engage in additional units of the particular activity in question as long as the additional benefit derived from the activity is greater than the additional cost incurred. In the language of economics: the actor will continue the activity as long as the marginal benefit from that activity is perceived to be greater than the marginal cost of the activity. The marginal cost also includes an estimation of the opportunity costs involved in selecting a particular course, *i.e.* the cost of not pursuing alternative activities.

The comparison of marginal costs with marginal benefit is the paradigm used by the rational maximiser (an individual or a legal entity such as a corporation) when he (or it) is in a situation which requires a choice to be made between complying with relevant legal rules then in force or engaging in unlawful activity. Even a law-breaker's decision to engage in law-breaking derives from the view that it will maximise his net utility, given his current preferences and opportunity costs.

---

[9] R. Posner, *The Problems of Jurisprudence* (Harvard University Press, Cambridge, Mass., 1990), p.353.

[10] *ibid.*, p.354.

[11] F. Easterbrook, "The Inevitability of Law and Economics" (1989) 1 *Legal Education Review* 3 at 5–6.

Efficiency as Justice

The concept of "efficiency as justice" informs the school's understanding of legal method: analysis of legal rules and legal decision-making should be evaluated from the perspective of economic efficiency. One paradigm of efficiency employed by economists is Pareto efficiency.[12] This paradigm views an activity as efficient if, as a result of the activity, at least one person can be made better off without making anyone else worse off. Although, as we shall see, one leading law and economic scholar, Ronald Coase favoured this paradigm of efficiency, it is regarded by most Chicago law and economic theorists, including Richard Posner, as inapplicable in the context of legal analysis generally and legal reform in particular.[13] They favour an alternative paradigm of efficiency known as Kaldor-Hicks efficiency or "wealth maximization".

The Kaldor-Hicks paradigm was developed in the 1930s to explain the economic rationale underpinning the abolition of Britain's nineteenth century protective tariffs known as the Corn Laws.[14] The paradigm (which serves as the theoretical basis of cost benefit analysis) implies that even if an allocation of resources makes some people worse off, it will still be deemed efficient (or "wealth-maximizing") if those made better off by the allocation would be in a position (hypothetically) to compensate those who have suffered from it. The resulting situation is merely a *potential* Pareto improvement: there is no suggestion that those made better off should compensate those made worse off.

Richard Posner, in his *Economic Analysis of Law*, refers to the following example to illustrate the application of the Pareto and of the Kaldor-Hicks paradigms, respectively:

> "Suppose A sells a wood carving to B for $10, both parties have full information, and the transaction has no effect on anyone else. Then the allocation of resources that is brought about by the transaction is said to be Pareto superior to the allocation of resources before the transaction. A Pareto-superior transaction is one that makes at least one person better off and no one worse off. (In our example, it presumably made both A

---

[12] The paradigm of Pareto efficiency is based on the work of the Italian economist and sociologist, Vilfredo Pareto (1848–1923).

[13] "The Pareto criterion is generally recognized to be quite limited as a guide to legal decision making on the grounds that the ubiquity of losses due to legal change, and the impossibility and/or prohibitive cost of compensating all losses, would forever perpetuate the status quo." N. Mercuro and S.G. Medena, *op. cit.*, p.59.

[14] The paradigm was originally developed by Nicholas Kaldor (1908–1986). J.R. Hicks (1904–1989) extended Kaldor's argument to all market impediments.

and B better off, and by assumption it made no one worse off.) ... In the less austere concept of efficiency used in this book—called the Kaldor-Hicks concept or wealth maximization—if A values the wood carving at $5 and B at $12, so that at a sale price of $10 ... the transaction creates a total benefit of $7 (at a price of $10, for example, A considers himself $5 better off and B considers himself $2 better off), then it is an efficient transaction, provided that the harm (if any) done to third parties (minus any benefit to them) does not exceed $7."[15]

In short, Posner and like-minded law and economic scholars favour the use of the Kaldor-Hicks test of efficiency for the evaluation of potentially wealth-maximising transactions because, as a test or paradigm, it is more realistic in that it takes account of the fact that in reality, although the immediate parties to a transaction may both increase their net worth as a result of the transaction, there may be third parties who are negatively affected as a result of that same transaction. The abolition of the protectionist Corn Laws in early twentieth century Britain, mentioned above, is itself a case in point: Kaldor argued that abolishing the Corn Laws was an efficient development on the basis that the gains to the country as a whole from free trade were likely to be sufficiently great to outweigh the loss to some corn farmers. Kaldor believed that the winners (those who benefited in a free-trade regime) could have purchased the right to remove tariffs from the farmers and still have gains left over. As has been said, a transaction will be efficient, according to the Kaldor-Hicks paradigm, when those whom it affects detrimentally are capable, in theory, of being compensated fully by those whose wealth is increased. The criterion, however, only demands hypothetical, not actual, compensation.

Positive and Normative Analysis of the Legal System

Chicago law and economic analysis claims to provide an explanation, from an economic perspective, for why the common law developed as it did. This claim is often termed the positive aspect of law and economic analysis. The argument is essentially that the common law developed in a manner that generally mimicked the workings of the free market: "[T]he common law is best understood ... as a pricing mechanism designed to bring about an efficient allocation of resources, in the Kaldor-Hicks sense."[16] In other words, it is suggested that judges (consciously or otherwise) developed the most efficient solutions to the legal issues that came before them for decision.

---

[15] Richard Posner, *Economic Analysis of Law*, pp.13–14.
[16] R. Posner, "The Law and Economics Movement" (1987) 77 *American Economic Review* 1 at 5.

Chicago law and economic scholars frequently turn to the law of tort to find examples to illustrate their claims about the applicability of their economic views to legal analysis. A frequently cited judicial decision which illustrates the mindset of the rational utility maximiser at work, in the context of deciding whether to take the risk of engaging in potentially tortious activity, is that of Justice Learned Hand in *United States v Carroll Towing Co.*[17] Justice Hand's formula for determining whether or not a defendant is liable in negligence is as follows. If the actual cost of preventing an accident (B) is less than the economically determined "expected cost" of the accident, then the person who caused the accident is liable in negligence. The "expected cost" is the probability (P) of the accident occurring, multiplied by the loss (L) that will eventuate if the accident actually occurs. If B<PL then the defendant who owes a duty of care to the plaintiff is to be liable for a breach of duty. John Kelly offers a simple but instructive example of how the Hand formula operates:

> "If the possibility of an accident, which if it occurs will occasion a cost or loss of $100, can be assessed as one chance in a hundred, while the cost (to a potential defendant) of taking the precautions needed to avoid it will be $3, the court will tend to recognize the diseconomy of taking those precautions by way of holding that they would go beyond what would be required on the standard of reasonable care ... If the figures in this hypothetical example were reversed, i.e. if the chances of the accident were three in a hundred, and the avoidance cost only $1, the liability would be reversed."[18]

Another important example of law and economic analysis of the legal system is Ronald Coase's analysis of causality. Coase's seminal 1960 article, "The Problem of Social Cost", is widely believed to be the most frequently cited article in the field of economics.[19] The importance of the contribution made to the development of law and economic scholarship by Coases's article cannot be overestimated: it offered insights that overturned conventional thinking in both economics and law.[20] In short, Coase's work—which has both positive and normative aspects—challenges the efficiency of the fundamental common law notion of causality as a means of assigning responsibility.

Coase's principal interest as an economist was the issue of the regulation of business. His economic analysis in this area (and his work generally) is

---

[17] 159 F.2d 1022 (7th Circuit 1947).

[18] J.M. Kelly, *op. cit.*, p.438.

[19] R. Coase, "The Problem of Social Cost" (1960) 3 *Journal of Law and Economics* 1.

[20] It was on the basis of this article and an earlier work ("The Nature of the Firm" (1937) *Economica* 1, n.s., 386) that Coase was awarded the Nobel Prize for Economic Sciences in 1991.

heavily indebted to the ideas of Adam Smith. In fact Coase believed that, as far as the development of economic thought was concerned, the two intervening centuries since the publication of Smith's *The Wealth of Nations* had been largely wasted. Coase's starting point in "The Problem of Social Cost" was to expose what he saw as the inadequacies of conventional welfare economics based on the thinking of the English welfare economist, Arthur Pigou (1877–1959). Pigou's work dated back to 1920 and advocated government action as the only reliable means of improving citizens' overall welfare, including economic welfare. Coase on the other hand was sceptical about government intervention: he insisted that the costs of such intervention should not be assumed to be zero and should be taken into account in any estimation of the benefits alleged to result from government regulation.[21]

In the area of nuisance law, the term externalities refers to the by-products of engaging in an activity which adversely affects the well-being of other parties, *e.g.* when smoke from a neighbouring factory has harmful effects on those living nearby or when cricket balls regularly land in the gardens of houses in the vicinity of the cricket ground. Pigou's belief was that such externalities should be dealt with by government action such as taxation or regulation of the parties responsible for them. The state could thereby ensure that the social costs of any externality will be "internalised" by those parties. Coase claims that this line of argument is superficial because it leads to results which are not necessarily or even usually desirable, *i.e.* not efficient. The victim of the pollution, for example, may be able to reduce or eliminate the cost of the pollution at a lower cost than the polluter.

Coase points out that externalities are not simply produced by one party and suffered by the victim. In fact, they emerge out of the circumstances of both. In other words, situations of harm are reciprocal to both parties. In the pollution scenario, the cost of the pollution is attributable not only to the polluter's actions but also to the fact that the victim is in a position to be affected by the polluter. It could be that the victim has less to lose in avoiding the pollution than the polluter has in preventing it. Coase claims that the appropriate question to ask in these situations is not that of how to restrain the polluter, but how to maximise the net social benefit.

Take the example of a situation in which pollution from a factory causes €100,000 worth of pollution per annum to neighbouring land and it is estimated that the elimination of the pollution would cost the factory €80,000, as opposed to a cost of €50,000 to change the use of the land so that it is no longer affected by the pollution. Pigou's solution would have been to impose an emission tax

---

[21] "Hostility to public intervention in markets beyond what is defensible in strict wealth-maximization terms is a leitmotif of Coase's work." R. Posner, *Overcoming Law* (Harvard University Press, Cambridge, Mass., 1995), p.413.

on the factory. Coase, on the other hand, argues that the more efficient solution would be for the neighbouring landowner to change the use of the land. It follows therefore, in a situation such as the above, where both the landowner and the factory owner are clearly aware of their respective rights and duties and are in a position to make and enforce contracts in their mutual interest, no state interference will be necessary to ensure an efficient outcome. The factory will find it costs less to compensate the neighbouring landowner than it does to eliminate pollution and similarly the landowner may benefit more from accepting compensation than enforcing his strict legal rights, for example by way of a tort action.

Coase's preliminary deduction is that market forces, left to their own devices, will internalise externality costs irrespective of rules imposing liability. Coase's economic analysis has obvious implications for basic common law concepts: principally, it appeared to cast doubt on the efficiency of the common law notion of causality as a means of assigning responsibility. Coase was suggesting, in other words, that the better way to approach the question of externalities is to forget about causation and simply ask which party to a harmful interaction should be induced to change his behaviour. (It could of course be the case that both should be so induced).[22]

Although markets are able to find a way around externalities, according to Coase's view of things, there is still another real-life cost which must be accounted for: in bargaining situations, parties inevitably face transaction costs. These are the costs parties incur in effecting a transfer of rights (including, for example, any legal costs, or the opportunity cost of effecting a transfer of rights). In the example of the factory polluting the surrounding land, the transaction costs that could arise would relate to the cost of getting the landowner to agree to change the use for his land. These costs may in fact be so high as to deter the parties from even attempting to negotiate on the basis of their respective initial rights and duties. In other words, transaction costs play a large role in determining how rights will be used because market forces in themselves—if one accepts Coase's argument—will lead to the right being used in the most efficient manner, but only after deducting the costs involved in making the transactions.

Coase's objective in "The Problem of Social Cost" was simply to raise the question of what sort of arrangements would evolve in a world in which there were no costs involved in carrying out market transactions. His conclusion is usually referred to as the "Coase Theorem": if transaction costs are low, the law's assignment of property rights and liabilities to parties involved in negotiation is unlikely to affect the eventual allocation of resources between them. We can usefully refer, once more, to the example of the pollution from

---

[22] R. Posner, *Overcoming Law*, p.413.

the factory to illustrate the application of Coase's theorem. The cost of measures (whether undertaken by the factory or by the landowner) to counteract the pollution is clearly less than the cost of the damage currently caused by the pollution. Without doubt, efficiency therefore dictates that the pollution should be counteracted and the most efficient method by which this can be achieved is to get the landowner to change the use to which his land is put. The theorem implies that, no matter how rights are initially assigned, this is the solution that will obtain. Suppose, for example, that the court were to assign the landowner the right to be free from pollution. The factory owner could prevent the pollution at a cost of €80,000. However, given that the landowner could solve the problem to his satisfaction for €50,000, it follows that the factory owner would have an incentive to pay the landowner a sum greater than €50,000 but less than €80,000 to take appropriate action. The landowner in turn will be willing to accept a sum greater than €50,000, in the circumstances. On the other hand, if the factory owner is given "the right to pollute", the landowner, faced with a choice between the €100,000 per annum in damage and the €50,000 cost of changing the use of his land is going to opt for the latter. Regardless, therefore, of the initial assignment of rights between the parties, in the absence of transaction costs, the efficient result will prevail, *i.e.* change of use by the landowner.

In assuming the absence of transaction costs, Coase was attempting to impress on economists just how significant such costs can actually be. Furthermore, the way in which disputes over rights and entitlements are resolved will depend on the nature and size of the relevant transaction costs. In situations where transaction costs are relatively low, Coase suggests that it may be more efficient to seek to remedy externality costs by means of private bargaining rather than by formal recourse to law.

By identifying a relationship between transaction costs and dispute resolution, Coase's study demonstrates compelling reasons for engaging in the economic analysis of common law rules. Many of the law's doctrines, procedures, and institutions can usefully be viewed as responses to the problem of transaction costs, being designed either to reduce those costs or, if they are unavoidably prohibitive, to bring about the allocation of resources that would exist if they were zero. The law tries to make the market work and, failing that, tries to "mimic the market".[23] In large part, subsequent law and economic scholarship has concerned itself with expanding on and clarifying aspects of Coase's Theorem.

There is also a normative dimension to law and economic analysis that claims to be able to predict how the law should further develop or be reformed. This further claim builds on the positive dimension of the school's analysis of

---

[23] *ibid.*, p.416.

the development of the common law: if the application of neo-classical analysis to an area of public activity, currently subject to regulation, indicates that such regulation undermines rather than facilitates economic efficiency in the area, then there exists a normative rationale for an economic policy of non-interventionism with regard to the activity in question.

The normative dimension of neo-classical law and economic analysis is based, to a large extent, on the ideas developed by Milton Friedman, the Chicago economist, mentioned at the outset of this chapter. Much of Friedman's work was aimed at demonstrating the superiority of laissez-faire over government control in a variety of domains. An illustrative example is Friedman's thesis of the superior economic efficiency of market-based rather than statutory forms of rent control: the absence of regulation facilitates free market pricing, free market pricing engenders competition, and competition generates allocative efficiency. In other words, when landlords are permitted to set their levels of rent according to going-market rates, they will have more incentive to make property available than when rents are determined by legislation. Because more tenancies will be available there will be greater competition between landlords. This, in turn, will work to the benefit of potential tenants with regard to prices and standards. From such arguments, one deduces the normative proposal that rents ought not to be regulated. Normative proposals, as we shall now discuss, are also put forward in the non-market domain.

Application of Law and Economic Analysis to Ostensibly Non-market Behaviour

We have now briefly indicated some of the principal intellectual currents that informed the law and economic scholarship of the Chicago school. The examples cited to illustrate the school's cornerstone viewpoints, such as its confidence in the superior efficiency of self-regulation by the market over statutory regulation, have all related to matter-of-fact, quasi-economic issues such as attributing liability for the costs of externalities such as pollution, rent control, etc. These issues are clearly not totally uncontroversial; they are, in fact, frequently and hotly debated by individuals affected by them. However, if law and economic scholarship were nothing more than a series of arguments—no matter how convincing in themselves—for privatisation and deregulation, then it may not have given rise to nearly the same degree of controversy and debate within the legal academy. At best, it may have had a continuing but limited application in judicial shaping of, for example, antitrust law (competition law). What, therefore, is it about neo-classical law and economic scholarship that accounts for its enduring and widespread flourishing in the period from the early 1960s onwards?

The answer to this question is partly to be found in the work of those writers who applied the insights of neo-classical economic analysis to explain ostensibly non-market behaviour. The pioneer in this field, as far back as the mid-1950s, was the economist Gary S. Becker. His original work was an attempt to explain the dynamics of racial discrimination in economic terms. In subsequent studies, Becker used neo-classical logic to explain the motivation to marry:

> "[S]ince men and women compete as they seek mates, a market in marriages can be presumed to exist. Each person tries to find the best mate, subject to the restrictions imposed by market conditions."[24]

Becker begins by defining the concept of "income" in broad terms to include children, social life, domestic comfort, etc. He moves on then to claim that men and women seek to maximise their income when choosing their marriage partner. In other words, a person's decision to marry implies "the utility expected from marriage exceeds that from remaining single or from additional search for a more suitable mate ...".[25]

On the basis of their understanding of men and women as rational utility maximisers in all aspects of life, Becker and his disciples (including Posner) have applied similar insights as the above to phenomena such as divorce, extra-marital affairs, fertility, adoption, drug-taking and so on. The not-un-controversial implication of Becker's thesis is that neo-classical economic analysis can be usefully applied to areas of law lacking any apparent market dimension.

In an article co-written with Elisabeth Landes, "The Economics of the Baby Shortage", Posner describes the shortage of babies for adoption and the surplus of unwanted children in orphanages as a "market disequilibrium" which results from excessive government regulation of adoption.[26] Posner and Landes put forward an argument for deregulation of adoption in order to permit adoption agencies to charge childless couples a market price for babies; in turn, mothers could charge a market price for their "product", based on its quality: "In a legal and competitive baby market, price would be equated to the marginal costs of producing and selling for adoption babies of a given quality."[27] According to Posner and Landes the effect of deregulating adoption would be to achieve an efficient equilibrium in the baby market.

The arguments advanced by Posner and Landes in favour of replacing the current, bureaucratic and inefficient adoption procedures with a market-driven

---

[24] Gary S. Becker, *The Economic Approach to Human Behaviour* (University of Chicago Press, Chicago, 1976), p.206.

[25] *ibid.*, p.10.

[26] R. Posner and E. Landes, "The Economics of the Baby Shortage" (1978) 7 *Journal of Legal Studies* 323.

[27] *ibid.*, at 339.

allocative mechanism have been comprehensively discussed by J. Robert S. Prichard.[28] Prichard initially concedes that "quite a robust case for the market [in babies] can be made" and such a market mechanism would appear "to be able make most people [affected by the adoption process] better off".[29] Nine separate grounds are identified in support of these two propositions: (i) the financial incentives available would result in more women producing more babies for adoption and thus ensuring demand is met; (ii) supply of newborns would be undertaken by those best able to produce (taking all relevant genetic, economic and financial factors into account); (iii) quality control mechanisms would develop and these would allow prospective adopters to select their desired child; (iv) the promise of financial reward would provide an incentive for mothers-to-be to look after their own health and the health of their unborn child and thus produce healthier babies; (v) the market for babies would result in an extremely competitive market structure;[30] (vi) there would be a reduction in the number of children whose birth resulted from errors in judgement or failures in contraception being fostered—such children would be more likely to be placed for adoption at birth; (vii) the black market that currently exists for newborn children would be eliminated and there would be little or no opportunity for unscrupulous lawyers or doctors to profit from the adoption process; (viii) various efficiency enhancing mechanisms would develop in the market;[31] and (ix) the emergence of the market for babies would result in some redistribution of wealth in favour of the producers who "would be persons with relatively low opportunity costs" who would thereby acquire "a new source of productive activity at a reasonable level of reward".[32]

Having set out the arguments in favour of a market-based approach to the issue of adoption, Prichard proceeds to set out the counter arguments under three headings: (i) objections based on market failure concerns; (ii) objections in principle to the use of market mechanisms; and (iii) objections on the basis

---

[28] J.R.S. Prichard, "A Market for Babies?" (1984) 34 *University of Toronto Law Journal* 341.

[29] *ibid.*, at 345, 347.

[30] "There would be extremely low entry barriers, a very large number of producers, both actual and potential, slight economies of scale, and enormous difficulties in cartelization. While there might be some brand name identification over time, one would not anticipate that this would lead to significant barriers to entry." *ibid.* at 346.

[31] "In particular, one might anticipate that a futures market would develop in which children in utero could be traded, permitting the reallocation of the risks inherent in childbirth so as to better reflect the various tastes for risks of different participants in the market. Furthermore, one might imagine that market intermediaries might form so as to hold portfolios of children in utero, thus diversifying and reducing the non-systematic risk." *ibid.*, at 346.

[32] *ibid.*, at 347.

that the market-based approach arises from a misconception of the problem which the adoption process currently in place seeks to address. Although Prichard claims that his intention is to highlight the "limits of the market rather than promote its use",[33] he is less than convincing in his attempts to use rational argument to undermine the proposed market for babies. For example, in relation to objections based on market failure concerns, Prichard states that his approach was to meet Posner and Landes' proposal "on its own terms, not objecting to the market in principle but stressing that the market would not work well in this particular context".[34] But ultimately, despite exploring various other possible arguments, he offers only one market-focused argument that, in his own words, could be "counted as a substantial negative effect of the market proposal".[35] This argument centres on the possibility that "good" babies might drive out the "bad":

> "At present, given the shortage of babies, childless couples are prepared to adopt children who are available although, in the eyes of the adopting parents, less than perfect. If the market proposal were adopted, the supply of children with highly desired characteristics would increase and the demand for other children would diminish. This would presumably increase the number of unadopted children suffering from retardation, birth defects, and other undesired characteristics who would subsequently become foster-children. This would presumably reduce the level of welfare both of these children and society in general …".[36]

Prichard grapples to give concrete expression to the intuitive opposition to the market for babies proposal he believes most people share. When discussing objections based on principles or values, he admits difficulty in isolating the focus of the concerns raised. Prichard draws an analogy between a market for babies and the concept of increasing the supply of body parts (hearts, livers, kidneys, etc.) by offering financial rewards to the potential donors of such parts. He observes that most people's reaction to the latter proposal is to resist it and to seek alternative solutions to the under-supply of organs. This pattern of resistance, he argues, is indicative of the same type of concerns that most people have in relation to the proposed market for babies. He then observes:

> "At the same time, I believe that these concerns should be understood as to some extent contingent upon cultural and social values that themselves change over time … We may well be in just such a period of transition to

---

[33] *ibid.*, at 341.
[34] *ibid.*, at 347.
[35] *ibid.*, at 348.
[36] *ibid.*

a society in which the objections to the baby market will lose much of their force. Such a transition was experienced in the late nineteenth century with respect to life insurance, which was thought for a time to represent a form of trafficking in and valuing of lives."[37]

All of the themes of law and economic scholarship that we have outlined impact in various ways on the scholarship's perception of the appropriate role of the judge, the topic to which we now turn.

3. THE ROLE OF THE JUDGE

H.L.A. Hart, in an insightful essay contrasting the history of American and British jurisprudence over a period of 80 years, beginning with the late nineteenth and early twentieth century writings of Oliver Wendell Holmes (1841–1935), identified a consistent preoccupation within the American tradition with what courts do and should do, how judges reason and should reason—a preoccupation not found to anywhere the same extent in the British jurisprudential tradition.[38] It comes as no surprise, therefore, that law and economic scholars—especially those who themselves have served on the bench, such as Richard Posner—should also display an interest in exploring the "craft of judging". Posner, indeed, sees himself very much as the spiritual heir of two of the most famous American judges, Holmes and Benjamin Cardozo (1870–1958), both of whose writings exploring the role and responsibilities of the judge he frequently quotes in support of his own ideas.[39]

As an approach to law and the workings of the legal system, law and economic scholarship certainly shares common ground with a number of other jurisprudential trends—such as American legal realism, critical legal studies, feminist jurisprudence and legal postmodernism—insofar as they each represent a rejection of legal formalism. Formalism can be described as the myth of law as an apolitical, autonomous discipline that can yield neutral and determinate answers with the aid of deductive, syllogistic reasoning. It is characterised "by an absolute indifference to social and economic considerations: law and legal decision-making are to be understood as taking place within a hermetic logical universe of clear-cut legal rules and deductive inferences".[40] As Posner has

---

[37] *ibid.*, at 356–357.

[38] H.L.A. Hart, "American Jurisprudence Through English Eyes: The Nightmare and the Noble Dream" (1977) 11 *Georgia Law Review* 969.

[39] Holmes served on the Supreme Court of Massachusetts between 1882 and 1902, and on the US Supreme Court from 1902 to 1932. Cardozo replaced Holmes as a Judge of the US Supreme Court in 1932 in which capacity he served until 1938. He had previously been a judge of the New York Court of Appeals.

remarked, the only prerequisite to being a formalist is having supreme confidence in one's premises and in one's methods of deriving conclusions from them.[41] There are natural lawyers and positivists whose approach to law can be said to be formalistic. The natural law formalist is quite sure he or she knows the fundamental principles of justice and has the utmost faith in the power of logic to apply them to the facts of a specific case to yield right results. On the other hand, the positive law formalist believes that if the legislative commands that make up the law are properly read and interpreted, they will yield demonstrably correct results in all cases.[42]

Crucial to the formalist's conception of law is the propagation of the myth of law's autonomy or self-sufficiency. The formalist would have us believe that law is autonomous in relation to both society and other disciplines. In short, we should accept that it has its own internal logic that accounts adequately for the development of legal doctrine. But part and parcel of law and economics' sustained attack on every kind of formalism is the rejection of all claims for the centrality of logical reasoning in judicial decision-making. Logic, according to law and economics scholars, will not decide the most difficult cases: "Formalism is the domain of the logician, the casuist, the Thomist, the Talmudist."[43]

Posner's General Theory of Adjudication

Posner's epistemology could be summarised as follows. There are two sorts of questions: those that are "scientific" on the one hand; and those that involve "value judgments" on the other hand, where decisions are not scientific and therefore not readily falsifiable or verifiable and therefore not profitably discussible. Human rationality is pushed to its limit when it crosses from the first to the second sort of question. The realm of reason consists either of empirical verification or formalistic ("mechanical") deduction. Judicial decisions quickly exhaust these activities. It follows, therefore, that the method

---

[40] B. Leiter, "Is There an American Jurisprudence?" (1997) 17 *Oxford Journal of Legal Studies* 367 at 374.

[41] R. Posner, *The Problems of Jurisprudence*, p.41.

[42] "I repeat that legal positivists who believe that the sovereign's commands are readily interpretable are formalists, at least in the sense of believers in right answers to all or virtually all legal questions. I am not a formalist." *ibid.*, p.33. Posner also remarks: "There are not only natural law formalists and positive law formalists but also natural law realists and positive law realists. Most natural lawyers are formalists, though; and while most legal positivists are realists, there are plenty of positive law formalists. It is a safe bet that a majority of legal professionals are formalists"; *ibid.*, p.41.

[43] R. Posner, "What has Pragmatism to Offer Law?" (1990) 63 *Southern California Law Review* 1653 at 1663.

of judicial formalism is predicated on a lie, in so far as it denies the inevitability of the influence of personal values in judicial "reasoning":

> "[It is] inevitable that judicial decisions will be based, at least in part, on value judgments, rather than wholly on technical, professional judgments. Decisions so made are by definition not scientific ...".[44]

Within the "open area" of value judgment only two constraints operate. The first is that the judge must be honest in avowing his or her criteria for decision. Honesty is a constraint because it furnishes a link between "scientific" and "value" judgements through the technique of introducing a verifiable issue of fact about values. This is the question of consensus: is the judge's decision based on values that a consensus of society will accept, or on values that will invite widespread condemnation? He points out that everyone would agree that a judge should not take personal or class preference into account. A decision is result-oriented if it rests on "partisan considerations that are generally agreed to be illegitimate", whereas a decision is principled "if and only if the grounds of decision can be stated truthfully in a form the judge could publicly avow without inviting virtually unanimous condemnation by professional opinion".[45]

The second constraint, according to Posner, is that the judge must be consistent: the grounds for decision in the instant case must be consistent with the grounds that he has used to decide other cases. The requirement of consistency begs a question: what are the criteria for identifying like cases? These can only be identified by determining what are relevant and irrelevant factors. Formalism will only be of minimal assistance at this juncture.

Posner's exploration of the judicial role—particularly in *The Federal Courts: Crisis and Reform* (1985) and *The Problems of Jurisprudence* (1990)—lays great emphasis on the judge as a decision maker in a system of government. He advocates an active role for the judge as a public policy maker: "The judge in the difficult case is more a policy maker than a conventional lawyer ... I shall argue ... for a concept of the judge as a responsible agent rather than as a conduit of decisions made elsewhere in the political system."[46] This argument sets out to challenge the "official" theory of judicial decision-making subscribed to—at least publicly—by the majority of his judicial colleagues, including, for example, Frank Easterbrook.[47] Judge Easterbrook, who is also a noted law-and-economics scholar and a colleague judge of Richard Posner on the

---

[44] R. Posner, *The Federal Courts: Crisis and Reform* (Harvard University Press, Cambridge, Mass., 1985), p.203.

[45] *ibid.*, pp.204–205.

[46] R. Posner, *The Problems of Jurisprudence*, p.134.

[47] See F. Easterbrook, "Method, Result, and Authority: A Reply" (1985) 98 *Harvard Law Review* 622. Other works by Easterbrook include: "The Influence of Judicial

Seventh Circuit US Federal Court of Appeals, robustly defends the so-called Pedigree Theory of political legitimacy in support of his understanding of the judicial role. This method proceeds by enquiring what rules and outcomes have a "proper pedigree" in the form of a chain of logical links to an indisputably authoritative source of law, such as the constitution. Those rules and outcomes are correct and the rest incorrect.

Posner rejects the Pedigree Theory as "quintessentially formalistic and hence anti-empirical". In fact, he suggests it appeals to a covert political theory, "one that regards the judge as agent of legislators, of constitutional framers, or of earlier judges and thus insists that every judicial decision be fairly referable to a command by a principal".[48] The prevalence of this approach to the business of judging may be due in part to the continuing hold of formalist thinking on the legal mind which, according to Posner, is itself part and parcel of the desire of public officials to evade responsibility for their decisions: "Shoving off the responsibility on long-dead framers is a convenient dodge."[49]

Central to Posner's theory of adjudication is the expectation that judges must—within the broad limits set by the legislators and by the makers of the constitution—adapt the law to an ever-changing social environment. To this end, judges must be aware not only of the social ends to which particular laws aspire, but of how social change impacts on the existing legal devices which are the means to those ends. Posner notes, for example, how the coming of the telegraph and the telephone altered the conditions for regulating contracts.[50] Too many judges, he claims, obtain much of their knowledge of how the world works from materials that are systematically unreliable sources of information, especially judicial precedents. He refers acerbically to "the lack of scientific curiosity that is so marked a characteristic of legal thought".[51] Judges need more of the ethic of scientific enquiry as they go about their daily business of adjudicating: they need to be "open-minded, forward-looking, respectful of fact, willing to experiment, disrespectful of Sacred cows, anti-metaphysical".[52]

Review on Constitutional Theory" in *A Workable Government? The Constitution after 200 Years* (Burke Marshall ed., Norton, New York, 1987) and "The Role of Original Intent in Statutory Construction" (1988) 11 *Harvard Journal of Law and Public Policy* 59.

[48] R. Posner, *The Problems of Jurisprudence*, p.135.
[49] *ibid.*, p.142.
[50] R. Posner, "What has Pragmatism to Offer Law?", at 1667.
[51] R. Posner, *The Problems of Jurisprudence*, p.213.
[52] R. Posner, "What has Pragmatism to Offer Law?", at 1668.

The Judiciary and the Legislature

The period from Oliver Wendell Holmes to the decline of the American realist movement at the end of World War II was marked by the refocusing of legal scholarship in the US from the common law to the emergent world of statute-dominated law. According to Posner, one implication of Holmes's description of the judge as an "interstitial legislator" could be that judges and legislators are officials of the same stripe, guided and controlled by the same goals, values, incentives and constraints.[53] If this were true, the judicial role would be greatly simplified; it would primarily be a matter of helping the legislature forge sound policy. But such a view is now naïve, according to Posner, considering the extent to which lobbies influence the legislative process:

> "The legislative process is buffeted by interest-group pressure to an extent rare in the judicial process. The result is a body of laws far less informed by sound policy judgments than the realists in the heyday and aftermath of the New Deal believed. It is no longer possible to imagine the good pragmatist judge as one who acts merely as the faithful agent of the legislature."[54]

Posner also rejects the revised purposive approach to statutory interpretation advanced by Henry M. Hart, Jr and Albert Sacks, precisely because it rests on the assumption that judges and legislators share common values and "stand side by side shoulder to wheel".[55] In *The Legal Process: Basic Problems in the Making and Application of Law* (1958), Hart and Sacks discuss the relationship between the judiciary and the legislature.[56] Given the nature and

---

[53] "Everyone professionally involved with law knows that, as Holmes put it, judges legislate 'interstitially', which is to say they make law, only more cautiously, more slowly, and in more principled, less partisan, fashion than legislators." R. Posner, *Overcoming Law*, p.235. Holmes' description was echoed by Benjamin Cardozo in *The Nature of the Judicial Process* (1921): "We must keep within those interstitial limits which precedent and custom and the long and silent and almost indefinable practice of other judges through the centuries of the common law have set to judge-made innovations".

[54] R. Posner, "What has Pragmatism to Offer Law?", at 1658. "The framers may not have had a lively awareness of this danger [of interest group lobbying]. Their main fear was tyranny of the majority rather than of a minority, yet it is the latter sort of tyranny that is the greater danger in an interest group society, such as the United States has become". R. Posner, "Legislation and Its Interpretation: A Primer" (1989) 68 *Nebraska Law Review* 431 at 433.

[55] R. Posner, "Legislation and Its Interpretation: A Primer", at 446.

[56] H.M. Hart and A. Sacks, *The Legal Process: Basic Problems in the Making and Application of Law* [1958] (Foundation Press, Westbury, 1994).

inevitable exercise of judicial discretion, the judge, according to Hart and Sacks, must be regarded as a legislator of sorts—albeit not operating under the same political or democratic constraints as the elected members of the legislature proper. However, they also suggest that the judge's training, the tradition of judicial reasoning and established judicial procedures, work to ensure his probity and competence and consequently ensure the public's confidence in the judicial function. Carried to its logical extreme, argues Posner, the Hart and Sacks approach implies that the judge can imagine himself as the legislator's alter ego, and can rule accordingly. In Posner's world, the legislator, although susceptible to influence from partisan concerns, has an ear to the ground and has democratic legitimacy—all of which factors differentiate him from the members of the judiciary, which he describes as a "mandarinate".[57]

At the same time, however, legislators can have only a limited and imperfect understanding of the range of factual situations to which a proposed statute may, in the future, be thought to apply. This limitation is further aggravated by the structures of representational government, notably frequent elections, which reduce the incentives and scope for legislators to give time and energy to crafting more sophisticated and far-sighted legislation. Enter the judges as the legislators' necessary "agents in application". Posner uses the analogy of a military chain of command from superior to inferior officer to illustrate the legislature-judiciary relationship.[58] He argues that such a command theory provides "an intelligible starting point for the analysis of statutory interpretation".[59] In construing statutes, judges may be implementing a command or communication from the legislature, but in so doing they do not exercise mindless obedience. Even in an obviously hierarchical enterprise such as the military, situations frequently arise in which subordinates are expected to exercise initiative. The point of the analogy is, therefore, to emphasise the relative freedom of judges:

> "The superior officer's command may have become garbled in transmission or may fail to correspond to conditions on the ground, yet the subordinate must still act, in a way that will best carry out the common enterprise ... The position of judges vis-à-vis legislators is much the same. Often the legislative command is inscrutable, yet the judge must decide the case, so he does the best he can to advance the common enterprise ... the peaceable governance of the United States."[60]

---

[57] R. Posner, "Legislation and Its Interpretation: A Primer", at 450.

[58] See, for example, *The Problems of Jurisprudence*, pp.269–271.

[59] *ibid.*, p.265.

[60] R. Posner, "Legislation and Its Interpretation: A Primer" at 448. This common enterprise, Posner believes, is "both widely shared and compatible with disagreement over specific policies": *The Problems of Jurisprudence*, p.272.

As Posner's ideal judge is going about his business, he will be "trying to do the best he can" rather than trying "to carry out the will of the legislature as such", but he will be naturally concerned with the failure to carry out that will when it can be discerned. In other words, the consequences which the pragmatic judge must take account of when making his decision include such "systemic considerations" as to what the decision will do to the ability of the legislature to effectively carry out its task. To deliberately ignore or deny the will of the legislature would impair inter-branch relations and undermine the legislative process. The pragmatist judge is committed to the ideal of the separation of powers and has an interest in "preserving language as a medium of effective communication".[61] He will never advocate ignoring the will of the legislature unless there will be large gains in substantive justice by so doing. On the other hand, Posner accepts that the court has both a power and duty to make civilised interpretations whereby the effects of unjust statutes are mitigated.[62]

Posner insists that any investigation of the meaning of statutory interpretation and the proper role of the judge therein is, at bottom, a political question.

> "The more one thinks about interpretation in general, the farther one is carried away from the important question concerning statutory interpretation, which is political rather than epistemic: how free *should* judges feel themselves to be from the fetters of text and legislative intent in applying statutes and the Constitution?"[63]

Hard Cases and Judicial Intuition

In his discussions of judicial craftsmanship Posner also addresses the issue of the adjudication of difficult cases in which, for example, novel arguments are advanced on the litigant's behalf, arguments which might have influenced the legislators had they been made to them during the law-making process. For Posner, judges have considerable freedom in deciding difficult cases. This

---

[61] R. Posner, "What has Pragmatism to Offer Law?" at 1664.

[62] On this point, Posner clearly parts company with his intellectual hero, Holmes, who rejected the existence of such a power when he said that if the people of the US wanted to go to hell it was his duty as a judge to help them get there. See *The Problems of Jurisprudence*, p.265.

[63] *ibid.*, p.271 (emphasis in original). "The issue of the proper freedom of judges is intractable at the theoretical level; it ought to be recast in empirical, pragmatic terms. Do we want judges to play a bigger or smaller role in the direction and implementation of public policy? … In any event, if the issue is the proper amount of deference by judges to other officials, why not say so straight out rather than cast it as one of legitimacy?" *The Problems of Jurisprudence*, p.139.

freedom arises in part from the high transaction costs involved in framing legislation (especially in large legislatures) and the very nature of representational government, which makes it inevitable that legislatures will frame legislation in general terms. An inevitable consequence of these inherent limitations on the legislative process in liberal democracies is that courts have a large role to play in shaping public policy.

These are very powerful claims that Posner makes on behalf of the judicial branch of government. He bolsters his claims by offering an account—which purports to be both descriptive and normative—of the process whereby judges apply statutory enactments in the resolution of difficult cases. He claims that the "pragmatic method" he advocates is the one successfully practised by the best judges and therefore an attainable ideal. In the pragmatic view of things, a statute is a resource for coping with the problems of the present. The method adopted by the pragmatic judge is to assess the practical consequences of alternative interpretations suggested by the statute under consideration.[64]

"Practical reason" plays a significant role in the adjudication process, not least in the adjudication of difficult cases where "the judge is in the uncomfortable position of having both to act and to offer convincing reasons for acting".[65] The term practical reason lacks a standard meaning but Posner opts for that meaning found in Aristotle, which "denotes the methods by which people who are not credulous form beliefs about matters that cannot be verified by logic or exact observation".[66] Phrased differently, practical reason is a composite of considerations and methods for inducing non-demonstrably true beliefs. The composite includes "anecdote, introspection, authority, metaphor, analogy, precedent, custom, memory, 'experience', intuition", and other devices".[67] Judicial reasoning, then, is simply the application of a combination of these methods to discern standards, assess them in the light of authoritative pronouncements by the other branches of government, apply the standard to the facts under consideration in a given case and reach a decision.

Posner also considers the role of intuition in the judicial process. Posner is particularly concerned to illustrate what he regards as the shortcomings in the "top-down" theories advanced by writers such as Ronald Dworkin in support of their views on theoretically difficult issues such as abortion rights. Posner readily admits that he finds, for example, the pro-abortion arguments advanced by Dworkin unconvincing and question begging.[68] He argues that theory cannot

---

[64] "[T]he best thing to do when a statute is invoked is to examine the consequences of giving the invoker what he wants and then estimate whether these consequences will on the whole be good ones." *The Problems of Jurisprudence*, p.300.

[65] *ibid.*, p.72.

[66] *ibid.*, pp.71–72.

[67] *ibid.*, p.73.

[68] See R. Dworkin, *Life's Dominion* (HarperCollins, London, 1993).

give objective guidance to the judge faced with adjudicating on complex moral issues. Therefore, the only honest way to proceed, he believes, is "by locating a ground for judicial action in instinct rather than analysis".[69] In other words the judge asked to ratify a law he feels to be terribly unjust will ultimately have recourse to his own ethical intuitions and policy preferences when the conventional legal materials are not up to the job of constitutional condemnation. This was, according to Posner, the approach of the most important American judges, including Oliver Wendell Holmes.[70] Knowledge ultimately rests on the foundation of our intuitions, suggests Posner:

> "Intuition is the body of bed-rock beliefs: the beliefs that lie so deep that we do not know how to question them; the propositions that we cannot help believing and that therefore supply the premises for reasoning."[71]

While candidly admitting "that few judges are equipped to create or even evaluate comprehensive political theories ... and are generally not appointed on the basis of their intellectual merit",[72] Posner is nevertheless not advocating a judicial style that would amount to no more than a naked statement of value. The pragmatic judge will, as a matter of course, test the consistency of his values, taking into account contrary views, and will attend to as much fact as possible, especially data about contemporary moral opinion.

4. CRITICISMS AND ASSESSMENT

We began our discussion in this chapter with an analysis of the fundamental assumption of the Chicago school: the assumption that as rational human beings, we are motivated to make choices which we believe will maximise our individual wealth or utility. A much discussed criticism of the Chicago school— first aired by the school's original critics in the 1970s and 1980s, members of the Critical Legal Studies (CLS) movement—and often repeated since, speaks to this fundamental assumption.[73] The general thrust of this criticism suggests that the concept of wealth-maximisation simply ignores issues such as the initial distribution of societal wealth and is merely a justification for right-

---

[69] R. Posner, *Overcoming Law*, p.192.
[70] Posner records how Holmes once told Harold Laski that he would hold a law to be constitutional unless it made him want to "puke". *The Problems of Jurisprudence*, p.192.
[71] R. Posner, *Problems of Jurisprudence*, p.73.
[72] R. Posner, *Overcoming Law*, p.194.
[73] See, for example, D. Kennedy, "Form and Substance in Private Law Adjudication" (1976) 89 *Harvard Law Review* 300.

wing policies that work to enhance and entrench the power of the status quo while ignoring calls for the redistribution of wealth in society:

> "The normative idea of free choice central to economic analysis of law fails to recognize that economic rationality and market incentives may mask an unequal distribution of economic power ... The problem with Posner's concept of economic justice is that it lacks an appreciation that people can be dominated, coerced, and constituted by a market plagued by distributional inequalities based on factors such as race, class, gender, religion, and sexual preference."[74]

Criticism levelled specifically against the Kaldor-Hicks paradigm mirrors the general tenor of criticism directed at the concepts of the "rational actor" and "wealth-maximization". For example, George Fletcher argues that the paradigm can be utilised to make any reallocation of property rights acceptable so long as that reallocation generates more gain to the winners than loss to the losers.[75] Kaldor-Hicks analysis, suggests Fletcher, leads to a theory of legal intervention that permits the periodic redefinition of property rights in the interest of a dominant group's collective vision.

The Coase Theorem has also been criticised on the grounds that it fails to address the issues of the availability and distribution of income and the relative bargaining power of parties. It has been pointed out, for example, that the victims of "interfering" or injury-causing activities may be in no position, either financially or politically, to negotiate with the party who is the source of the harm. The theorem, it is suggested, not only assumes that people are rational utility maximisers, but also that they are equal in terms of their financial, physical, and psychological ability to contend with the world.

Margaret Davies considers Hand J.'s negligence formula in the context of an examination of the Chicago school's assumptions about the human subject as a rational utility maximiser. According to Davies, Justice Hand's formula (and legal economic analysis in general) requires the substitution of the traditional legal notion of reasonableness with an economic notion of rationality: the reasonable man is being replaced by the rational man! Hand's liability rule, she argues, is formulated only to encourage efficiency: "Like the reasonable man, the rational man is, in the end, a man."[76] This is part of a general critique offered by Davies, from a postmodern feminist perspective, of the basic assumptions she believes underpin law and economic scholarship.

---

[74] G. Minda, "Towards a More 'Just' Economics of Justice—A Review Essay" (1989) 10 *Cardozo Law Review* 1855 at 1864–1865.

[75] G. Fletcher, *The Basic Concepts of Legal Thought* (Oxford University Press, Oxford 1996), pp.159–160.

[76] M. Davies, *Asking the Law Question* (Sydney, Sweet and Maxwell, 1994), p.134.

She suggests that law and economic analysis values a certain type of behaviour historically and culturally associated with educated white men and, as a consequence, it fails to take into account the values associated with women and non-European cultures:

> "This has a fairly clear impact on the way that economic thought has traditionally been applied: in constructing a reality of a particular type, activities traditionally undertaken by women are not seen as part of the market place. Housework, for instance, is not 'economically productive' even though it is obvious that it is work and that it contributes in many ways to the material well-being of a society."[77]

A further criticism raised by a number of the school's critics is that law and economic analysis appears to be oblivious to the effect of illegal (tortious or criminal) activity on the victim. Davies observes that the question of whether or not it is fair that the victim of an accident, for example, should have to bear the loss is not considered:

> "This sort of quantification of a legal concept ... totally disregards the human factor, it is quite incapable of taking into account the justice of a particular case, it reduces a dangerous situation to cold calculation and ... encourages those who frequently create potentially dangerous circumstances to weigh the physical well-being of others against profit. It encourages people to take risks with the safety and well-being of others when the profit to be gained from the risk outweighs any costs to victims."[78]

Posner and his jurisprudential colleagues do address some of these criticisms, after a fashion. Posner suggests, for example, that the issue of the initial distribution of wealth is "uninteresting from a practical standpoint" because its effects, regardless of whether it was egalitarian or not, are "likely to dissipate after a few generations".[79] Furthermore, judges can do little to redistribute wealth although they do have a responsibility, in Posner's view, to put resources into the hands of those who value them most. On the other hand, one of the principal tasks the legislature is charged with is the redistribution of wealth by means of taxation and other measures.[80]

With regard to the general view that the practitioners of Chicago law and

---

[77] *ibid.*
[78] *ibid.*, p.137.
[79] R. Posner, *The Problems of Jurisprudence*, p.338.
[80] *ibid.*, p.345.

economic scholarship stand for a right-wing political agenda, Posner responds by suggesting that this

> "is both an error and an affront to its liberal practitioners (Calabresi, Polinsky, Ackerman, Cooter, Kaplow, Kornhauser, Donohue, others). What is true is that the study of economics instills in most students an appreciation of the social benefits of markets. ... But not everyone who appreciates the benefits of markets is a right-winger: most of the Communist world is at the moment pro-market."[81]

To a large extent, the view of law and economics as right wing is based on the pedigree of the school's economic perspective, which is, as has been said, a contemporary re-statement of the basic insights of Adam Smith. However, as we mentioned also at the outset, a second important intellectual influence on the Chicago school can be traced to the less individualist, utilitarian liberalism of Jeremy Bentham and John Stuart Mill. As Posner notes:

> "We modern Millians are apt to be classified as conservatives rather than as liberals because we are not strongly egalitarian—not as strongly as Mill himself was, allowing for the changed political climate—and oppose various features of the welfare state, whose supporters, though they ought to be called socialists or collectivists, have managed to appropriate the term 'liberal' and to retain it even when they advocate restricting liberty of expression in the name of racial or sexual equality."[82]

In terms of judicial craftsmanship, it seems that Posner's approach, no matter how one goes about combining and applying the different elements, will only solve one half of what he perceives to be the dilemma facing the judge. Without question, Posner's methodology will assist the judge in formulating beliefs as to how he should decide issues before him. The approach, however, will not of itself justify those beliefs or provide criteria for their evaluation. In other words they will not provide the judge with the "convincing reasons" Posner believes he is called upon to supply. To be fair to Posner, he appears to recognise this problem, to some extent, when he admits that some of his enumerated methods of practical reason "belong to the logic of discovery rather than of justification".[83] Intuition and custom or precedent, for example, could generate a pair of contradictory beliefs. The difficulty is that practical reason itself provides no criteria for selecting among such potentially conflicting beliefs.

---

[81] *ibid.*, p.435.
[82] R. Posner, *Overcoming Law*, p.264.
[83] R. Posner, *The Problems of Jurisprudence*, p.73.

To simply select one belief over its negation would be to act arbitrarily. Posner's discussion itself does not, unfortunately, provide criteria for establishing priorities.

In conclusion, the sheer volume of scholarly output that has been generated by writers and theorists associated with Chicago law and economic analysis is by any measure impressive. Equally impressive is the frequency with which their scholarly output is met in turn with critical analysis and comment. Whatever one's views may be in relation to the allegedly conservative political views espoused by members of the Chicago school of law and economic analysis, or indeed of the criticisms most commonly levelled at them by their detractors, it can hardly be denied that the work of the school, considered collectively, has developed into a highly influential interdisciplinary project, combining the techniques and methods of two very distinct disciplines to the mutual stimulation and benefit of both.

CHAPTER 15

FEMINIST JURISPRUDENCE

SIOBHÁN MULLALLY

1. INTRODUCTION

In its liberal incarnations, feminism has been closely associated with the pursuit of women's rights. Building a just and equal society, it was argued, required the recognition and enforcement of equal rights for women. Early liberal feminists saw their task as being a relatively straightforward, if daunting one. Liberal legalism ascribed rights to human beings on the basis of their capacity for reason. The task for feminism was to show that women had the same capacity for rationality and moral action as did men and to claim for women the same rights as were ascribed to men.[1] Liberal feminists sought to "add women in" to existing laws, institutions and processes. Liberal feminists appealed to women and men's common humanity and their common capacity for reason as a justificatory basis for their claims to equal rights. In recent years, however, feminism has become increasingly sceptical of such appeals. Feminism has come to be defined in opposition to liberal legalism and the terms of liberal Enlightenment philosophy. The discourse of rights has been a central tenet of that philosophy, an indispensable tool in the pursuit of the liberal cosmopolitan project. It is now, however, accused of being "an active enemy of women's progress".[2]

This chapter explores the shift within feminist jurisprudence away from liberal political theory, and away, in particular, from liberal ideals of human rights. Feminist critiques of rights have centred on three main themes: (a) the disembedded and disembodied subject of rights; (b) the validity of rights claims grounded on a universal legislating reason; and (c) the ability of a universalist, legislative reason to tackle the multiplicity of contexts and life-situations with which practical reason is always confronted.[3] Rights discourse is accused of

---

[1] See M. Wollstonecraft, *A Vindication of the Rights of Woman* (1789).

[2] M. Nussbaum, *Sex and Social Justice* (Oxford University Press, Oxford, 1999), p.56.

[3] S. Benhabib, *Situating the Self: Gender, Community and Postmodernism in Contemporary Ethics* (Polity, Cambridge, 1992), p.3.

pitching the individual against the community, reason against sentiment, the universal against the particular, the public against the private. The subject of rights, feminist critics have argued, is a divided one, "caught between the moral law and the starry heaven above and the earthly body below".[4] Although striving for unity, it is plagued by tensions, between "autonomy and nurturance, independence and bonding, sovereignty of the self and relations to others".[5] These dichotomies are deeply hierarchical and also deeply gendered. The liberal discourse of rights is accused of privileging one side of these dichotomies and marginalising the other. Amongst the marginalised and excluded are those voices associated with the private, the particular, the affective bases of moral judgement. These include women, the poor, the working class, gays, lesbians, people of colour. All, it is argued, are excluded from a polity that prides itself as being cosmopolitan.

In Ireland, for example, much of feminist jurisprudence comes within the traditions of liberal legalism. Feminist lawyers, academics and practitioners, have sought to "add women in", to seek equality and justice for women, using the tools of rights discourse.[6] Much has been achieved by feminist movements in Ireland. Legislative reforms, often prompted by the requirements of EU membership, have eliminated discriminatory legislative provisions that sought to constrain the roles and opportunities provided to women. The limits of liberal legalism, however, are increasingly being recognised. Anti-discrimination law, in Ireland and throughout the EU, has done little to tackle the broader, structural aspects of gender inequality. Legislative measures to promote gender equality have focused primarily on the pursuit of market equality. Yet, despite guarantees of equal pay and equal treatment, gender remains a significant factor in poverty and social exclusion. In Ireland, one in every four women raising children or managing households on their own, experience poverty.[7] If that woman is old or a lone parent, her situation has worsened over the past decade in relative terms. Women who are homeless, seeking recognition of refugee status or members of the Traveller Community may not even have their experiences of poverty recorded in official statistics.

Challenging the limits of liberal legalism has taken feminist theory down many different paths. Feminist jurisprudence has moved away from the liberal ideals of the autonomous self and the commitment to a universal moral reason. It has taken a relational turn, emphasising the location of the human self in

---

[4] *ibid.*, p.86.

[5] *ibid.*

[6] See, for example, *Gender and the Law in Ireland* (A. Connolly ed., Oak Tree Press, Dublin, 1993).

[7] See National Women's Council of Ireland, *The Hidden Poverty of Women* (NWCI, Dublin, 2001); see also B. Nolan and D. Watson, *Women and Poverty in Ireland* (Combat Poverty Agency, Dublin, 1999).

networks of relationships and the importance of communal values. This chapter examines the work of writers from the four main strands within non-liberal feminist jurisprudence: feminist Ethics of Care; radical feminism; critical race feminism; and finally postmodern feminisms, including neo-pragmatist feminism, poststructuralist feminism and deconstructionist ethical feminism.

2. FEMINIST ETHIC OF CARE

The salience of appeals to community in contemporary critiques of liberalism reflects an "ethical turn", a nostalgia for questions of the moral, the good, the virtuous.[8] It is a "turn" that owes much to Carol Gilligan's studies of moral development and her feminist Ethic of Care. Although Gilligan's claim to have discovered a distinctively female mode of moral reasoning is no longer widely accepted, her work continues to raise an important challenge to the theory and practice of human rights. For feminism, the fundamental question raised by Gilligan still remains: can an Ethic of Care better serve the interests of feminism than an Ethic of Justice and rights?

Gilligan puts forward her proposals for an Ethic of Care in her book, *In a Different Voice*.[9] She argues that there are two moral codes, a feminine one based on caring and the maintenance of relationships and networks, the Ethic of Care, and a masculine one based on a more abstract systemisation of rights and rules, the Ethic of Justice. At stake between these two codes are differences in: (a) moral capacities—learning moral principles (justice) versus developing moral dispositions (care); (b) moral reasoning—solving problems by seeking principles that have universal applicability (justice) versus seeking responses that are appropriate to the particular case (care) and; (c) moral concepts—attending to rights and fairness (justice) versus attending to responsibilities and relationships (care).[10] Gilligan also argues that two competing visions of the human self underlie these distinct moral codes. She claims that the prevailing values of justice and autonomy imply a view of the individual as separate and of relationships as either hierarchical or contractual. In contrast, she says, the values of care and connection, salient in women's thinking, imply a view of the self and the other as interdependent and of relationships as networks, created and sustained by attention and responsibility.[11]

---

[8] See generally, N. Lacey, *Unspeakable Subjects: Feminist Essays in Legal and Social Theory* (Hart, Oxford, 1998).

[9] C. Gilligan, *In a Different Voice: Psychological Theory and Women's Development* (Harvard University Press, Cambridge, Mass., 1982).

[10] W. Kymlicka, *Contemporary Political Philosophy: An Introduction* (Clarendon Press, Oxford, 1990), p.265.

[11] C. Gilligan, "Remapping the Moral Domain: New Images of the Self in Relationship"

By recovering "the lost Ethic of Care", Gilligan seeks to change the image of the human self and to correct an individualism within moral theory that has been centred within a "single interpretive framework".[12] Rights discourse is part of that framework—a framework that feminists argue has developed in response to a limited set of questions, namely, "What are the circumstances in which essentially solitary individuals might agree to come together in civil society, what would justify them in doing so and how might conflict be prevented when they do?"[13]

This limited and partial view of human interaction, Gilligan argues, has defined the scope of ethics of justice and rights. Human interdependence is presumed to be optional. The facts of human biology, in particular reproductive biology, are ignored. The role of carers who spend their daily lives not in avoiding conflicts with "strangers", but in caring for dependent others is also ignored. Alison Jaggar points out that the assumption of innate human selfishness and competitiveness "overlooks the fact that millions of people (most of them women) have spent millions of hours for hundreds of years giving their utmost to millions of others".[14] And, of course, the long overlooked "moral proletariat" is mostly women.[15] If theoretical account were taken of these facts, feminists argue that the liberal problematic would be transformed and egoism, competitiveness and conflict would themselves become "puzzling and problematic".[16]

In place of the "isolated, atomistic" self associated with liberal individualism, Gilligan presents a relational view of the self and a dialogic view of identity formation. This different way of describing the self can be arrived at, she argues, by paying closer attention to the experience of women. For women, Gilligan claims, "the self is known through the experience of connection, defined not by reflection but by interaction, the responsiveness of human engagement".[17] She argues that this relational view of the self is reflected in the Ethic of Care. As noted above, the Ethic of Care implies a view of the self and the other as interdependent and of relationships as networks, created

---

in *Reconstructing Individualism: Autonomy, Individuality and the Self in Western Thought* (T.C. Heller, M. Sosna and D.E. Wellbery eds., Stanford University Press, Stanford, 1986), p.242.

[12] *ibid.*, p.239.

[13] A.M. Jaggar, *Feminist Politics and Human Nature* (Rowman and Allanheld, Totawa, 1983), p.40.

[14] *ibid.*, p.45.

[15] A. Baier, "The Need for More than Justice" in *Justice and Care: Essential Readings in Feminist Ethics* (V. Held ed., Westview Press, Boulder, 1995), pp.49–50.

[16] A.M. Jaggar, *op. cit.*, p.41.

[17] C. Gilligan, "Remapping the Moral Domain: New Images of the Self in Relationship", p.241.

and sustained by attention and responsibility. "Different images of the self", Gilligan argues, "give rise to different visions of moral agency which, in turn, are reflected in different ways of defining responsibility".[18]

Gilligan's relational view of the self is an attractive one. Her thesis, linking empirical claims about psychological modes of development to proposals for a feminist Ethic of Care, is a powerful one. However, Gilligan's claim to have discovered a distinctively "feminine" mode of moral reasoning has attracted much criticism. Her thesis repeats many of Western political philosophy's attempts to distinguish the intuitive, emotional dispositions said to be required for women's domestic life from the rational, impartial and dispassionate thought said to be required for men's public life. Feminism has devoted a great deal of energy to repudiating these claims. Many feminists disagree with the claim that different modes of moral reasoning correlate with gender divisions. To the extent that correlations can be found, disagreement has arisen as to why such differences exist. Powerless groups, it is pointed out, often learn empathy because they are dependent on others for protection. As Susan Okin argues, women, "as subordinates in a male-dominated society", have to develop psychological characteristics that please the dominant groups and fulfil its needs.[19] This point was made by John Stuart Mill, in his essay, *On the Subjection of Women* (1869). Women, he argued, are brought up from the very earliest years in the belief that their ideal of character is the very opposite to that of men: "not self-will, and government by self-control, but submission, and yielding to the control of others".[20] Women and oppressed classes or minority groups are often associated with an Ethic of Care precisely because of the constraints imposed upon them by dominant groups.[21] This argument is put strongly by Catharine MacKinnon. She argues that any special ability women may have for caring and connection can be attributed to the negative aspects of subordination. Women value care, she says, "because men have valued us according to the care we give them".[22] Affirming women's differences perpetuates the belief that those attributes traditionally associated with women really are women's—rather than simply those that have been attributed to women.

---

[18] *ibid.*, p.241.

[19] S.M. Okin, "Thinking Like a Woman" in *Theoretical Perspectives on Sexual Difference* (D. Rhode ed., Yale University Press, New Haven, Conn., 1990), p.154.

[20] J.S. Mill, *On the Subjection of Women* (S.M. Okin ed., Hackett, Indianapolis, 1988), pp.15–16.

[21] S. Harding, "The Curious Coincidence of Feminine and African Moralities: Challenges for Feminist Theory" in *Women and Moral Theory* (E. Kittay and D. Meyers eds., Rowman and Littlefield, Savage, 1987), p.307.

[22] C.A. MacKinnon, *Feminism Unmodified: Discourses on Life and Law* (Harvard University Press, Cambridge, 1987), p.39.

Reason versus Sentiment

Other difficulties arise with the feminist Ethic of Care. Care theorists emphasise
the role of sentiment and emotion in moral reasoning. Without a well-developed
moral disposition, they argue, we cannot know what the principles of justice
require of us when faced with concrete moral problems. Moral duties cannot
be fulfilled by "cold unfeeling moral agent[s]".[23] Quoting David Hume, Annette
Baier argues that the "cold jealous virtue of justice" may yet prove to be too
cold.[24] Respect for rights, she says, is quite compatible with a great deal of
human misery and suffering. This argument is taken up by Richard Rorty.
Rorty frequently invokes the work of Care theorists such as Annette Baier to
support his arguments for a "liberalism without foundations". In his essay,
"Human Rights, Rationality and Sentimentality", Rorty argues that we need
to overcome our suspicion that sentiment is too weak a force for moral
reasoning.[25] He points to the emergence of a human rights culture which, he
says, seems to owe nothing to increased moral knowledge and everything to
hearing sad and sentimental stories—to what Annette Baier refers to as a
"progress of sentiments".

But could, or should, this "progress of sentiments" replace appeals to rights-
based moral principles? Sad and sentimental stories are not enough. We have
to move beyond those stories, to attempt an explanation and to identify possible
responses to a problem. This requires an appeal to principles, the recognition
of a duty to respond. Appeals to sentiment and emotion can help to garnish
support for the enforcement of moral principles. However, they cannot deny
the necessity of such principles. As Hannah Arendt has noted, the capacity for
exercising an "enlarged mentality", the ability to take the standpoint of the
other, is not empathy. In fact, an empathetic nature may make it difficult to
draw the boundaries between self and other, such that the standpoint of the
"concrete other" can emerge.[26] Allowing distinct voices to be heard requires
principles, institutions and procedures.

Relying solely on appeals to moral sentiment also ignores the value of
public reason, the need for public standards of justification and for democratic
dialogue. These values have been central to much of feminist theory.
Emphasising moral disposition and the role of sentiment runs the danger of

---

[23] C.H. Sommers, "Filial Morality" in *Women and Moral Theory*, p.78.

[24] A. Baier, *op. cit.*, p.51.

[25] R. Rorty, "Human Rights, Rationality, and Sentimentality" in *On Human Rights: The Oxford Amnesty Lectures* (S. Shute and S. Hurley eds., Basic Books, New York, 1993), pp.112–134.

[26] S. Benhabib, *Situating the Self*, p.168. See H. Arendt, "The Crisis in Culture" in *Between Past and Future: Six Exercises in Political Thought* (Meridian, New York, 1961), pp.220–221.

denying the validity of such values. The view that moral problems should be solved not by appeal to public rules or principles but through the exercise of moral sensitivities by the "morally mature agent" has considerable conservative potential. Without moral principles, we cannot ensure the democratic accountability of moral reasoning. At times, it seems as though care theorists ignore this need.

Ethical Particularism

Allied with the emphasis on sentiment and emotion is a concern with the obligations that arise from special relationships—ethical particularism in other words. Ethic of Care theorists argue that the universalist ethic of rights cannot accommodate ethical particularism. Ethical particularism requires that preferential consideration be given to the interests of those with whom one has a special relationship—members of one's family or local community, for example. Ethical particularism is defined in opposition to ethical universalism, which is presumed to require us to treat all persons with equal impartiality. This presumption, however, is based on a misunderstanding of human rights theory and practice. The ethical universalist principle of human rights can provide for and indeed requires various kinds of partiality and differential treatment.

The moral domain is a complex one. Human values and relations are of diverse sorts and so are the moral principles that apply to them. Loyalties to one's family or community are relevant in determining what moral principles apply and when. Universal human rights principles, however, provide a limit on the pluralistic differentiation permitted. As Alan Gewirth points out, racism and sexism are not justified forms of particularism. Neither are national chauvinism or restrictive asylum and refugee laws.[27] Ethical particularism risks excluding many of those who fall outside family or community networks. This conservative potential can be seen, for example, in Richard Rorty's appeal to a "solidarity" without "common humanity". Our sense of solidarity, Rorty argues, is strongest, "when those with whom solidarity is expressed are thought of as 'one of us', where 'us' means something smaller and more local than the human race". That is why, he argues, "because she is a human being" is "a weak, unconvincing explanation of a generous action".[28] A person's claim to moral consideration depends, therefore, on "being one of us", being of the community. Rorty himself insists that the force of any "we"—any sense of

---

[27] A. Gewirth, "Ethical Universalism and Particularism" (1988) LXXXV *Journal of Philosophy* 283 at 298.

[28] R. Rorty, *Contingency, Irony and Solidarity* (Cambridge University Press, Cambridge, 1989), pp.190–191.

moral community—must depend on the contrast with a human "they". The implications of this line of reasoning can be seen in the following statement:

> "I claim that the force of 'us' is, typically, contrastive in the sense that it contrasts with a 'they' which is also made up of human beings—the wrong sort of human beings."[29]

As Nicola Lacey puts it, the inclusionary surface of the language of community is here masking the exclusion of the "hated Other".[30] Principles of human rights guard against such exclusionary tendencies, distinguishing between justified and unjustified forms of ethical particularism.

The Ethic of Care could, of course, embrace the language of ethical universalism. Gilligan herself avoids the language of universality. However, the "different voices" articulated in her study, seem to indicate that women's care and sense of responsibility for others are frequently universalised.[31] A caring perspective could express as fully universalisable a morality of social concern as does the language of justice and rights. It is only universalisable, however, if one appeals to something like a shared humanity or a universal principle of equal moral worth. Once considerations of this kind are introduced, then the distinctions between a Care perspective and an Ethic of Justice and rights seem even less clear.[32]

Rights versus Responsibilities

Perhaps the most serious challenge raised by Ethic of Care theorists is the claim that rights discourse promotes a kind of "asocial individualism". Gilligan argues that rights are essentially self-protection mechanisms that can be respected simply by "leaving others alone". Rights-based duties, she says, are limited to reciprocal non-interference. In contrast, she argues, accepting responsibility for others requires some positive concern for their welfare.[33] The emphasis on responsibilities rather than rights finds echoes in communitarian and duty-based legal philosophies, both of which are critical of the international human rights movement. Care theorists share with communitarians nos-

---

[29] *ibid.*, p.190 (emphasis added).

[30] N. Lacey, *Unspeakable Subjects*, p.139.

[31] S.M Okin, *op. cit.*, p.158.

[32] George Sher notes that a universalisable care perspective would seem to be at least closely related to that of the familiar impartial and benevolent observer, found in Kantian and other universalist theories. "Other Voices, Other Rooms? Women's Psychology and Moral Theory" in *Women and Moral Theory*, p.184.

[33] C. Gilligan, *In a Different Voice*, pp.22, 136, 147.

talgia for "community" and for communal values, a nostalgia, they argue, that cannot be satisfied by rights discourse.[34]

In 1998, on the fiftieth anniversary of the Universal Declaration of Human Rights, this nostalgia took on a concrete shape, this time in the form of a draft "Declaration of Human Responsibilities".[35] The Declaration was drafted by the InterAction Council, a non-governmental body established in 1983 under the initiative of the late Prime Minister Takeo Fukuda of Japan. The Council's membership includes academics, activists, politicians and religious leaders from all parts of the globe. An initial reading of the Declaration suggests that it owes more to communitarian thinking than to feminism. However, in employing the language of responsibilities rather than rights, it addresses the concerns voiced, in particular, by Ethic of Care theorists. The Council argues that an exclusive insistence on rights results in "conflict, division, and endless dispute"; a declaration of human responsibilities is necessary, they argue, to bring freedom and responsibility "into balance", to move "from the freedom of indifference to the freedom of involvement".[36]

Underlying the move towards an ethics of responsibility, however, is a fundamental misunderstanding of the nature of human rights. It is clear from Gilligan's writings that she presumes a libertarian view of rights, a view of rights as protections against unwanted governmental interference. To use Isiaih Berlin's terms, it is a concern with negative rather than positive liberty.[37] It is a view of rights that is prevalent within the constitutional jurisprudence of the US—rights as freedoms from rather than rights to. International human rights law, however, has begun to move away from this conception of rights. Properly understood a duty or responsibility is the correlative of any rights claim— whatever the justificatory basis offered for that claim. The idea of duties or responsibilities is not antithetical to human rights principles. In fact, it is of the very essence of a human rights claim. For each rights claim, there is a respondent, a duty-bearer. It may be the state. It may be another individual. A commitment to human rights, therefore, ties us into a network of reciprocal obligations.

---

[34] This criticism can be found also in Marxist critiques of rights. In his essay, "On the Jewish Question", Marx argued that the individual subject of rights is "withdrawn behind his private interests and whims and separated from the community". *Early Writings* (R. Livingstone and G. Benton trans., Penguin, Harmondsworth, 1975), p.230.

[35] See "A Universal Declaration of Human Responsibilities" proposed by the InterAction Council, September 1, 1997, reproduced in H. Steiner and P. Alston, *International Human Rights in Context: Law, Politics and Morals* (Oxford University Press, Oxford, 2000), pp.351–353.

[36] See the Introductory Comment and Preamble to the proposed Universal Declaration of Human Responsibilities.

[37] I. Berlin, *Four Essays on Liberty* (Oxford University Press, Oxford, 1969).

Take, for example, Alan Gewirth's fundamental principle of human rights, the "Principle of Generic Consistency": "Act in accord with the generic rights of your recipients as well as of yourself".[38] Gewirth argues that rights claims can be understood as entailing "a communitarian conception of human relations, relations of mutual assistance, social solidarity and important kinds of equality".[39] Understood in this way, the principle of human rights becomes a principle of social solidarity. The opposition between rights and responsibilities, or a rights and duty-based morality begins to collapse. A fundamental distinction remains, however. That distinction concerns the vision of the self underlying human rights based traditions on the one hand and duty-based traditions on the other. A commitment to human rights implies a limit on the bonds of community, to use Will Kymlicka's phrase, a limit on the "internal restrictions" that a community can place on its members.[40] For feminists, this limit is one that cannot be dispensed with. Though feminists can and must recognise the location of the human self within networks of relationships, without a commitment to the overriding priority of individual autonomy, feminism loses its critical potential. It can only claim, therefore, a partial and strategic alliance with communitarianism. To the extent that communitarian or duty-based legal traditions deny the overriding priority accorded to individual autonomy, they cannot be reconciled with the concerns and interests of feminism.

At the root of the problem is the "embedded" or "situated" vision of the human self underlying communitarian philosophies. Communitarians such as Michael Sandel emphasise the constitutive character of social roles and advocate a situated vision of the self. The isolated, atomistic autonomous self, is not, Sandel argues, a free and rational agent, but rather a person wholly without character, "without moral depth".[41] This vision of the self has much in common with the relational self proposed by Gilligan and other Ethic of Care theorists. However, it raises considerable difficulties for the feminist agenda. What, for example, "are the precise moral bearings of the self's being constituted by the communities to which it belongs?"[42] Must the demands or obligations deriving from communities or networks of relationships always be

---

[38] See A. Gewirth, *The Community of Rights* (University of Chicago Press, Chicago, 1996); *Human Rights: Essays on Justification and Applications* (University of Chicago Press, Chicago, 1982); and *Reason and Morality* (University of Chicago Press, Chicago, 1978).

[39] A. Gewirth, *The Community of Rights*, p.6.

[40] W. Kymlicka, *Multicultural Citizenship: A Liberal Theory of Minority Rights* (Clarendon Press, Oxford, 1995).

[41] M.J. Sandel, *Liberalism and the Limits of Justice* (Cambridge University Press, Cambridge, 1982), p.179.

[42] A. Gewirth, "Human Rights and Conceptions of the Self" (1988) 18 *Philosophia* (Israel) 129 at 145.

fulfilled? Is the freedom and autonomy of the self "exhausted" by its membership in communities, by its integration into networks of relationships? The demands of the community have often been problematic for feminism. As Seyla Benhabib and Drucilla Cornell put it, "situated females often find it impossible to recognise their true selves amidst the constitutive roles that attach to their person".[43] Or to quote from Rabindranath Tagore's "Letter from a Wife" (1914): "In your joint family, I am known as the second daughter-in-law. All these years, I have known myself as no more than that". Situated and relational visions of the human self come perilously close to a kind of moral conventionalism that does not distinguish between the self and its roles. Pursuing a feminist agenda involves constantly challenging the dictates of the gendered subject. Ultimately, this requires an overriding commitment to the principle of individual rights and the principle of individual autonomy.

Despite its shortcomings, the feminist Ethic of Care can still offer much to the project of transforming the theory and practice of human rights. Martha Minow has taken on this task. In her work on US family law, she develops a concept of relational rights and responsibilities, which, she argues, best translates the insights of Ethic of Care theorists into law and policy.[44] She identifies three distinct strands within contemporary legal and political theory on the family: contract-based, community-based and rights-based. None, she argues, captures the paradoxical features of family life. Contract-based theories view family relationships solely as contractual relationships, ignoring their affective and emotional bases. Community-based theories look to existing moral standards within the community to determine the appropriate norms and standards for the regulation of family life. In doing so, they risk marginalising the perspectives of non-traditional families who may not have strong political representation within a community. Rights-based theories, Minow argues, pit individuals against each other without adequate attention to the web of relationships within which individuals find themselves.

However, Minow is not rejecting the idea of rights *per se*, but rather the liberal individualism at the heart of legal and political culture in the US. Although she argues that an Ethic of Care cannot be simply injected into existing legal rules and standards, she does not suggest abandoning the prevailing Ethic of Justice. She argues that the principles of justice must be applied to political practice to ensure an equality of participation and a radical democratisation of

---

[43] *Feminism as Critique: On the Politics of Gender* (S. Benhabib and D. Cornell eds., University of Minnesota Press, Minneapolis, 1987), p.12.

[44] M. Minow and M.L. Shanley, "Relational Rights and Responsibilities: Revisioning the Family in Liberal Political Theory and Law" (1996) 11 *Hypatia* 4. See also M. Minow, *Not Only for Myself: Identity, Politics and the Law* (New Press, New York, 1997) and *Making all the Difference: Inclusion, Exclusion and American Law* (Cornell University Press, Ithaca, 1990).

law and policy-making processes. She proposes a view of rights as claims grounded in and arising from human relationships—"intimate associations".[45] A society cannot be "well-ordered", she says, if it is not characterised by an Ethic of Care. We cannot simply presuppose the contribution made by caregivers. Quoting Eva Kittay, she argues that economic and political structures must take upon themselves "the primary responsibility of maintaining structures that will support the principles of care".[46] Minow argues for a more inclusive and trustworthy political process, one in which exclusions and disadvantages based on gender, race, ethnicity and class no longer play a role. She argues for an expanded concept of rights, one that does not presume an isolated atomistic human self, one that recognises the need to support the work of carers and one that pays attention to the process through which law and policy is formed. This does not point to an abandonment of rights-based theories or a return to an Ethic of Care. Rather it points to a transformation of the legal and political spheres and a radical transformation of the prevailing ideas of rights particularly within US legal and political culture. Such transformations have already begun to take place within the theory and practice of international human rights law.[47] The insights of an Ethic of Care and responsibility can assist in the transformation of the Ethic of Justice, but cannot ultimately replace it.

A commitment to the ideal of "separate spheres", premised on the complementarity of gender roles and a presumption of natural sex differences between women and men, is central to much Roman Catholic teaching. In the drafting of the Irish Constitution of 1937, this ethos was to find its way into the constitutional provisions on the family. Article 41.2.1° leaves little room for debate as to the nature of women's citizenship under the Irish Constitution, "… the State recognises that by her life within the home, woman gives to the State a support without which the common good cannot be achieved". The category "woman" that is here invoked does not admit of much difference or diversity. A woman's citizenship was to be defined, first and foremost, by her "life within the home". The conflation of woman and mother is reinforced further by Art.41.2.2°, which provides, "The State shall … endeavour to ensure, that mothers shall not be obliged by economic necessity to engage in labour to the neglect of their duties in the home". If women are to "neglect their duties in the home" and enter into paid employment, Art.45.4.2° of the "Directive

---

[45] M. Minow and M.L. Shanley, *op. cit.*, at 23, quoting K. Karst, "The Freedom of Intimate Association" (1980) 89 *Yale Law Journal* 624.

[46] E. Kittay, "Taking Dependency Seriously: Equality, Social Cooperation, and The Family and Medical Leave Act considered in light of the Social Organization of Dependency Work" (Conference on Feminism and Social Action, University of Pittsburgh, November 1993), quoted in M. Minow and M.L. Shanley, *op. cit.*, at 24.

[47] See generally H. Charlesworth, C. Chinkin and S. Wright, "Feminist Approaches to International Law" (1991) 85 *American Journal of International Law* 613.

Principles of Social Policy" directs the state to ensure that "citizens" are not forced by economic necessity to enter "avocations unsuited to their sex". That the then prime minister and main architect of the 1937 Constitution, Eamon de Valera, presumed a differentiation in gender roles within the family is evident from his contributions on the constitutional provision on equality. Article 40.1 guarantees equality before the law. The corresponding provision in the 1922 Constitution had included the phrase, "without distinction on grounds of sex". De Valera thought this additional phrase was unnecessary. His justification for deleting the phrase, however, refers repeatedly to the realm of "political life", a qualification that went unnoticed by parliamentary colleagues. Clearly, in his view, the domestic sphere was to be subject to different tests of justice.[48]

From a feminist Ethic of Care perspective, Art.41.2 could be welcomed as recognition of the distinct role played by many women within the domestic sphere. Women continue to account for the majority of homemakers and carers working full-time in the home. Article 41.2, however, has failed to provide any support for rights claims arising from this work. De Valera justified the gender-specificity of Art.41.2 by appealing to the need to protect women and to ensure that their "inadequate strength" was not abused. This concern to protect, however, has not translated into a concern to support or empower women within the domestic sphere. In *L v L*, a married woman invoked Art.41.2 to support her claim that a woman working as a full-time homemaker and mother should be entitled to a proprietary interest in the family home.[49] In the High Court, Barr J. concluded that the Court had a positive obligation to interpret Art.41.2 in a way that recognised marriage as an equal partnership. If a woman chose to work full time in the home, she should receive reasonable

---

[48] The gender-differentiated nature of citizenship and the situating of women firmly within the domestic sphere provoked a huge outcry from the women's movement. The Women's Graduates Association led the opposition to the draft Constitution. Hanna Sheehy-Skeffington, a leading feminist activist and a pacifist who had supported DeValera in the Irish civil war at the beginning of the 1920s, was one of the most vocal opponents. The 1916 Proclamation, she argued, had given Irish women "equal citizenship, equal rights and equal opportunities". Subsequent constitutions had "filched these" or "smothered them in mere empty formulae". John A. Costello, a former Attorney-General, expressed concern that the maxim *expressio unis*, as applied to Art.41.2.1, could exclude women's life outside the home from constitutional protection. Opposition to the Constitution was rejected as "anti-Catholic" and as lacking respect for the Church teachings on "the position, the sphere, the duties of women". An editorial in the *Irish Press* described the opposition to the Constitution as a "revolt against the authority and teaching of Pius XI". Reverend John Charles McQuaid (later archbishop of Dublin), commenting on feminist opposition, noted that "nothing would change the law and fact of nature that women's natural sphere is the home".

[49] *L v L* [1989] I.L.R.M. 528 (High Court); [1992] 2 I.R. 77 (Supreme Court).

economic security within the marriage in return for the economic and emotional sacrifice this choice involved. Barr J. held that the wife and mother in this case was entitled to a 50 per cent beneficial ownership in the family home. This finding, however, was reversed on appeal by the Supreme Court. Drawing a clear line between the public and domestic sphere, Chief Justice Finlay concluded that Art.41 did not create any particular rights within the family, nor did it grant individual members rights against other family members. It dealt only with the protection of the family from external forces.

Following on from the *L v L* case, the Irish Government introduced the Matrimonial Home Bill 1993, which sought to guarantee joint ownership of the family home. The Bill was the subject of a Supreme Court referral by the President under Art.26 of the Constitution.[50] Finding the Bill to be unconstitutional, Finlay C.J. concluded that the intervention by the state in the family was not "reasonably proportionate" and constituted a failure by the state to protect the authority of the family. This view was reiterated by Costello J. in *Murray v Ireland*.[51] In his view, the rights in Art.41 attached to the institution of the family itself rather than to any personal rights that an individual might enjoy by virtue of family membership. On this reading, the Constitution protects the family as a unit but does not inquire into relations within the family.

A reluctance to invoke Art.41.2 to support claims arising from women working full-time in the home was seen more recently in Ireland in *Sinnott v Minister for Education*.[52] The case involved a young man, Jamie Sinnott, who suffered from a severe form of autism, and who was suing the state for its failure to defend and vindicate his personal rights and his right to a free primary education under Art.42, appropriate to his needs, for as long as he was capable of benefiting from it. Jamie was joined in the action by his mother, Kathy Sinnott, who claimed *inter alia*, that the failure of the state to provide free education facilities appropriate to the needs of her son, had imposed inordinate burdens on her as a single parent and full-time mother, and had deprived her of constitutional rights pursuant to Arts 40, 41 and 42 of the Constitution. Kathy Sinnott was seeking recognition of her role as a carer within the family, and through an argument that relied on a relational understanding of rights and responsibilities, she argued that the state's failure to protect her son's rights also breached her constitutional rights as the primary carer within the family. Chief Justice Keane, giving judgment on behalf of the majority of the Supreme

---

[50] *Re Article 26 and the Matrimonial Home Bill 1993* [1994] 1 I.R. 305. Article 26 of the Irish Constitution provides for a procedure whereby certain types of proposed legislation can be referred by the President to the Supreme Court, in order to assess the constitutionality of the legislation prior to enactment.

[51] *Murray v Ireland* [1991] I.L.R.M. 465.

[52] *Sinnott v Minister for Education* [2001] 2 I.R. 545.

Court, rejected her arguments, noting that while her position evoked "respect, admiration and compassion", these were not grounds in law for any award of damages. In a dissenting judgment, Denham J. highlighted the relational nature of rights and responsibilities within the family. She noted that Kathy Sinnott had rights and duties as a parent within the family unit. A breach by the state of the rights of one member of the family unit could have a negative impact on the family, and particularly on the person charged with the primary care of the family—in this case, Kathy Sinnott. Denham J. also attempts to rescue Art.41.2, which she argues, does not assign women to a domestic role, but rather seeks to give recognition to the work performed by women in the home. In this case, she concluded, the state had failed to give due recognition to the work performed by Kathy Sinnott, work, Denham J. noted, that was of "immense benefit for society". Denham J.'s arguments stand in marked contrast to the reluctance of the majority of the judiciary to inquire into relations within the family and to give legal recognition to the work of carers within the home. The majority of the Supreme Court acknowledged the work undertaken by Kathy Sinnott, but refused to acknowledge any rights arising from her role as a carer. The transformative potential of rights is blocked by a deeply gendered division between the public and the private spheres and a presumption that the tests of justice that normally apply within the public sphere do not extend to domestic relations.

3. RADICAL FEMINISM

Perhaps the best-known radical feminist in the field of jurisprudence is Catharine MacKinnon, who continues the critique of liberal theories of rights. Rather than focusing on difference, however, she focuses instead on dominance and subordination. For MacKinnon, gender is not only the way in which women are differentiated socially from men; it is also the way in which women are subordinated to men.[53] MacKinnon constructs a "grand theory" of women's oppression, identifying sexuality, specifically heterosexuality, as the principal site of women's oppression. Sexuality, she says, is the linchpin of gender inequality. Women are sexual subordinates. Female sexuality is distorted and manipulated to meet the interests of a class/sex that does not share female interests. The organised expropriation of female sexuality for male use has

---

[53] See C. MacKinnon, "Feminism, Marxism, Method and the State: An Agenda for Theory" (1982) 7 *Signs: Journal of Women in Culture and Society* 515–544; "Feminism, Marxism, Method, and the State: Toward a Feminist Jurisprudence" (1983) 8 *Signs: Journal of Women in Culture and Society* 635; *Feminism Unmodified* (1987) and *Toward a Feminist Theory of the State* (Harvard University Press, Cambridge, Mass., 1989).

material consequences for women in the forms of rape, pornography and sexual harassment. The question then is how to respond to this "organised expropriation"? What strategies should be adopted to correct the distortions of patriarchal ideology?

Appeals to a universal moral theory are rejected by MacKinnon. Claims to objectivity, she claims, are part of the structure of male power. "Abstract rights", she says, "will authorize the male experience of the world."[54] Instead, she suggests paying closer attention to the "standpoint" of the oppressed class—women. This standpoint is not just different; it is also, she argues, epistemologically advantageous. MacKinnon identifies women's status as that of a victim. She then privileges that status by claiming it gives access to an understanding about oppression that others cannot have. Pain and subordination provide the oppressed with a motivation for criticising accepted interpretations of reality and for developing new and less distorted ways of understanding the world. The experience of being a victim reveals truths about reality that non-victims cannot see. For MacKinnon, the strength of feminism "originates" in the experience of "being dominated, not just in thinking about domination".[55] The standpoint of women is discovered through a collective process, a process of consciousness-raising. The process of gaining knowledge is a collective one and is guided by the special interests and values of the participants in the process. The aim of such knowledge is ultimately practical.

This reliance on experiential methodology informs MacKinnon's critique of human rights law and practice. While much of MacKinnon's work targets the "male discourse of rights", it is in her essay "Crimes of War, Crimes of Peace" that MacKinnon specifically turns her attention to international human rights law.[56] At the heart of MacKinnon's criticisms is a concern with the justificatory basis underlying human rights claims. Human rights claims, she argues, rely for support on the workings of a universal legislating reason. For MacKinnon, feminist methodology requires abandoning this idea of reason. MacKinnon traces the origins of international human rights law to the experience of the Holocaust. That experience, she argues, left us with the enduring belief that survival depends on "blending in". So many Polish Jews died, she says, because they only spoke Yiddish. "They could not 'pass' as not Jews."[57] Recognition and survival depended on meeting the dominant standard. MacKinnon draws an analogy with the psychology of battered women, "keeping

---

[54] C. MacKinnon, "Feminism, Marxism, Method, and the State: Toward a Feminist Jurisprudence", at 658.

[55] C. Menkel-Meadow, "Feminist Legal Theory, Critical Legal Studies, and Legal Education" (1988) 38 *Journal of Legal Education* 57 at 61.

[56] C.A. MacKinnon, "Crimes of War, Crimes of Peace" in *On Human Rights: The Oxford Amnesty Lectures*.

[57] *ibid.*, p.104.

your head low keeps you alive". This, she says, is the equality of the Enlightenment, the standard of equality that has been incorporated into international human rights law. It is an equality principle that was constructed under genocidal conditions. By adhering to the same understanding of equality, we continue to live under genocidal conditions.[58]

MacKinnon does not dismiss the idea of rights entirely. However, she is sceptical of the human rights movement, turning instead to domestic, "homegrown" civil rights movements. She gives a number of reasons for this turn. Civil rights movements, she argues, can contribute to social change and to a process of consciousness-raising in a way that the human rights movement cannot. They don't fall prey to the abstract theorising of human rights.[59] They rely on an experiential methodology, beginning from concrete experiences of inequality and discrimination in civil society and in the domestic sphere. They practice a jurisprudence that, in MacKinnon's view, is "social, contextual, relational and anti-hierarchical".[60] By providing direct civil remedies for harms suffered, civil rights can also distribute power from government to people as well as redistributing power among people.[61] MacKinnon also argues that civil rights claims transcend the division between the public and the domestic sphere. Civil rights, she says, "begin at home or close to it"; in contrast, "human rights seem to improve the further one gets from home".[62] In support of her claims, MacKinnon invokes the equality jurisprudence of the Canadian Supreme Court, a jurisprudence, she says, that emerged from concrete social movements and ultimately saw equality rights win out over the claims to freedom of expression of anti-Semites and pornographers.[63]

---

[58] *ibid.*, p.105.

[59] MacKinnon is perhaps best known for her advocacy of a civil-rights approach to pornography. See generally C. MacKinnon, *Only Words* (Harvard University Press, Cambridge, Mass., 1993); *In Harm's Way: The Pornography Civil Rights Hearings* (C. MacKinnon and A. Dworkin eds, Harvard University Press, Cambridge, Mass., 1997); C. MacKinnon, "Pornography, Civil Rights and Speech" (1985) 20 *Harvard Civil Rights—Civil Liberties Law Review* 1.

[60] C. MacKinnon, "Crimes of War, Crimes of Peace", p.103.

[61] In 1982, MacKinnon and Andrea Dworkin drafted an anti-pornography ordinance, defining pornography both as a violation of civil rights and as discrimination. The Ordinance sought to make a civil remedy available to women who had been "harmed" by pornography. It was adopted by the city of Indianapolis but met with opposition both from civil liberties groups and feminists and was ultimately found to in violation of the US Constitution's First Amendment guarantee of "free speech". See *American Booksellers Association, Inc., et al., Plaintiffs /Appellees v William H. Hudnut, III, Mayor, City of Indianapolis, et al., Defendants*, Seventh Circuit (Decided August 27, 1985).

[62] C. MacKinnon, "Crimes of War, Crimes of Peace", p.104.

[63] *R v Keegstra* [1990] 3 SCR 697; [1992] 2 WWR 1: A high school teacher and

It is not always clear whether MacKinnon is confining her criticisms to the "received traditions" of human rights law and practice, to the positive law of human rights and its mechanisms of enforcement—or whether her criticisms are directed against the idea of human rights *per se*. At times she refers to human rights, "as currently defined",[64] suggesting the possibility of redefinition. To the extent that her criticisms concern the "received traditions" of human rights law, they are clearly valid. Failures to recognise harms experienced uniquely by women as human rights violations, hesitation at crossing the public/ private divide to allow for "horizontal applications" of human rights norms or to extend the concept of State responsibility, are all well documented. However, human rights theory and practice have begun to address these failures. The 1979 UN Convention on the Elimination of All Forms of Discrimination Against Women directly addresses issues of inequality and discrimination arising within the domestic sphere (Art.16) and imposes an obligation on all States Parties to eliminate discrimination in all fields, both public and private (Art.2).[65] The evolving international norms on violence against women address violence occurring within the family, the community and the workplace as well as state-sanctioned violence.[66] MacKinnon recognises this. However, she argues that the potential for reform is limited. The public/private divide continues to manifest itself in appeals to the authority of "culture" and "tradition". Referring to the reservations entered by States Parties to the Convention, MacKinnon notes that even where international instruments could be interpreted as prohibiting practices of sexual abuse, their "cultural supports are more likely to provide the basis for exempting states from their reach than

---

mayor were convicted under s.319(2) of the Canadian Criminal Code for incitement to hatred against an "identifiable group"—in this case, the Jewish people. Keegstra had argued unsuccessfully that s.319(2) infringed his rights to freedom of expression under the Canadian Charter of Rights and Freedoms. In *R v Butler* [1992] 2 WWR 577, the Canadian Supreme Court upheld restrictions on the availability of pornography, not because of lack of decency, but because the material in question was incompatible with the promotion of equality.

[64] C. MacKinnon, "Crimes of War, Crimes of Peace", pp.103–104.

[65] *Convention on the Elimination of All Forms of Discrimination Against Women*, adopted December 18, 1979, entered into force September 3, 1981, G.A. Res. 34/ 180, 34 UN GAOR, Supp. (No.46), UN Doc. A/34/46, at 193 (1979), reprinted in 19 ILM 33 (1980).

[66] *Declaration on the Elimination of Violence Against Women*, adopted December 20, 1993, GA Res. 48/104, UN Doc. A/48/29, reprinted in 33 ILM 1049 (1994). Article 1 defines violence against women as "any act of gender-based violence that results in, or is likely to result in, physical, sexual or psychological harm or suffering to women, including threats of such acts, coercion or arbitrary deprivation of liberty, whether occurring in public or in private life".

the foundation for a claim of sex discrimination".[67] The closer to home one gets, as MacKinnon says, the less human rights one appears to have. Women have tended to be closer to home. However, the possibility of widening the domain of human rights law does exist. The difficulty lies not in the concept of human rights *per se*, but rather in the reluctance of political actors to extend the reach of human rights norms.

MacKinnon advocates civil rights in place of human rights. Yet conflicts between cultural rights and gender equality are at least as likely to arise within civil rights movements. MacKinnon herself argues that equality should not be located in the elimination of "irrational differentiation" but rather in the "affirmative claims of cultural particularity".[68] Yet it is those very claims that have often hindered the implementation of women's human rights, as MacKinnon herself points out. Relying on the experiential methodology of consciousness-raising does not overcome this potential for conflict. At times MacKinnon seems to presume that a unitary feminist standpoint will emerge from the process of consciousness-raising, from the concrete practices of civil rights movements. However, given that many women do not perceive themselves as being oppressed and not all those who do agree on its origins or its implications, the question of whose standpoint to credit remains unresolved.[69] How can any one experiential account claim special authority? As Deborah Rhode asks: "How can feminists wed to experiential analysis respond to women who reject feminism's basic premises as contrary to their experience?"[70]

This raises the problem of "false consciousness". For MacKinnon, different modes of moral reasoning are the product of false consciousness.[71] She argues that women have been silenced:

> "When you are powerless, you don't just speak differently. A lot, you don't speak. Your speech is not just differently articulated, it is silenced. Eliminated, gone. You aren't just deprived of a language with which to articulate your distinctiveness, although you are; you are deprived of a life out of which articulation might come."[72]

Yet MacKinnon herself participates in this silencing. She is often brutal in her condemnation of women's so-called complicity.[73] By her condemnation,

---

[67] C. MacKinnon, "Crimes of War, Crimes of Peace", p.87.

[68] *ibid.*, p.104.

[69] D. Rhode, "Feminist Critical Theories" (1990) 42 *Stanford Law Review* 617 at 624.

[70] *ibid.*, at 622.

[71] See D. Cornell, *Beyond Accommodation: Ethical Feminism, Deconstruction, and the Law* (Routledge, London, 1991), pp.133–135.

[72] C. MacKinnon, *Feminism Unmodified*, p.39.

[73] D. Cornell, *Beyond Accommodation*, p.136.

however, she devalues women's voices. She "writes off" those who do not agree with her, dismissing the disagreement as a product of false consciousness.[74] Patricia Cain asks, "Where is MacKinnon's feminist method? To whom does she choose to listen?"[75]

Other difficulties arise with MacKinnon's "feminism unmodified". MacKinnon argues that male power is omnipotent. Few, if any, aspects of life are free of male power. Male hegemony is, she argues, "metaphysically nearly perfect". This raises the question of how feminist consciousness is possible at all: "If we are all the products of a hegemony of inequality, how can any of us be feminists?"[76] The processes of social construction are not as determinate as MacKinnon would have us believe. If it were, then feminism would not be possible. The possibility of reinterpreting our "sexualised" reality, of recognising the reality of gender inequality, would also not be possible. As Drucilla Cornell puts it, "Who are the 'we' that 'see' and why do we, how can we, see differently so as to be able to reinterpret the meaning of our 'sexualised' reality?"[77]

MacKinnon is also accused of essentialism. She is criticised for falsely universalising women's experiences. Her failure is a failure to apply feminist methods, a story of a broken promise. Just as Marxism collapsed gender and race into class, so MacKinnon collapses issues of race and class into gender.[78] MacKinnon denies these accusations. Women, she argues, share a collective social history of "disempowerment, exploitation, and subordination".[79] To speak of social treatment "as a woman" is not, she says, "to invoke any universal essence ... or ideal type". Rather, it refers to a "diverse material reality of social meanings and practices such that to be a woman 'is not yet the name of a way of being human'".[80] This explanation of women's collective experience

---

[74] See W. DuBois, C. Dunlap, C. MacKinnon and C. Menkel-Meadow. "Feminist Discourse: Moral Values and the Law—A Conversation" (1985) 34 *Buffalo Law Review* 11.

[75] P. Cain, "Feminist Jurisprudence: Grounding the Theories" in *Feminist Legal Theory: Readings in Law and Gender* (K. Bartlett and R. Kennedy eds, Westview Press, Boulder, 1991), p.263.

[76] E. Jackson, "Catherine MacKinnon and Feminist Jurisprudence: A Critical Appraisal" (1992) 14 *Journal of Law and Society* 195 at 198.

[77] D. Cornell, *Beyond Accommodation*, p.130.

[78] C. Smart, "Feminist Jurisprudence" in *Dangerous Supplements: Resistance and Renewal in Jurisprudence* (P. Fitzpatrick ed., Pluto, London, 1991), p.142. See also A. Harris, "Race and Essentialism in Feminist Legal Theory" (1990) 42 *Stanford Law Review* 580.

[79] C.A. MacKinnon, "Reflections on Sex Equality under the Law" (1991) 100 *Yale Law Journal* 1281 at 1294.

[80] *ibid.*

of discrimination suggests a denial of some common essence of humanity, or at the very least a set of common interests. Once we abandon the presumption that a unitary feminist consciousness will emerge, it is not at all clear how MacKinnon, within the constraints of her own methodology, can identify those common interests.

4. FEM-CRITS AND CRITICAL RACE FEMINISM

Postmodern feminism shares with Ethic of Care theorists a concern with the significance of difference. This concern, however, is taken further. Postmodern feminism is concerned not only with differences between women and men but also between women themselves. It is because of its championing of the standpoint of the "other(s)" that postmodernism has been identified as a crucial ally by many contemporary feminist thinkers. The concern with difference, with the valuing of the "Other", finds expression in an aversion to universalist moral theory. The "grand narratives" of the Enlightenment—including liberal theories of rights—are contrasted with the *petits récits* of women, children, fools and primitives. As Seyla Benhabib points out, if there is one commitment that unites postmodernists from Michel Foucault to Jacques Derrida to Jean-François Lyotard, it is the critique of Western rationality as seen from the perspective of the margins, "from the standpoint of what and whom it excludes, suppresses, delegitimises, renders mad, imbecilic or childish".[81]

The term postmodernism refers to many things. For the purposes of this chapter, postmodernism can be understood as a movement that radically calls into question the fundamental presuppositions of modern philosophy itself. Certain themes recur in postmodern writings. A central theme is the claim that Western culture is experiencing an interrelated series of deaths: (i) the death of Metaphysics; (ii) the death of the subject; and (iii) the death of History.[82] The first thesis, the "death of Metaphysics", is associated with the end of foundationalism. "Foundationalism" is the view that a justificatory basis can be found for the grand narratives of science or philosophy or law, in empirically observable facts, in self-evident ideas or in *a priori* truths. Claims to "objectivity" and "neutrality" are exposed by anti-foundationalists as representing only sectional interests, partial truths. Postmodern critics argue that the reluctance to admit the partiality of such perspectives arises from the desire to "master the world by enclosing it within an illusory but absolute system ... beyond history, particularity and change".[83] The "death of the

---

[81] S. Benhabib, *Situating the Self*, p.14.

[82] J. Flax, *Thinking Fragments: Psychoanalysis, Feminism and Postmodernism in the Contemporary West* (University of California Press, Berkeley, 1990), p.29.

[83] *ibid.*, p.34.

subject" thesis concerns the conception of the human self. In place of the abstract, autonomous self associated with liberal human rights theories, postmodern thinkers emphasise the "radical situatedness and contextualization" of the human self. The "death of History" thesis expresses a disillusionment with the ideals of progress, an awareness of the atrocities that have been committed in the name of technological and economic progress and a rejection of the claims of any particular group or organisation to be acting in the name of progress.

Some critical legal studies (CLS) scholars have applied the insights of postmodern thinking to law and legal theory. Postmodern legal thought is portrayed as a moment of rapture—a moment which "opens space for the marginal, the different and the 'other'".[84] CLS scholars have challenged the law's claims to objectivity and neutrality, exposing the value-laden nature of legal reasoning. The discourse of rights has been a central target of the CLS movement. Rights consciousness is accused of blocking transformative, counter-hegemonic thought, of oversimplifying complex power relations. The acquisition of a right, it is argued, creates the impression that a power difference has been resolved. An illusory space is created, a space within which illicit domination is supposedly prohibited.[85] For the CLS movement, however, legal rights do not resolve problems. Rights discourse transposes a problem into one that is defined as having a legal solution.[86] These solutions, however, serve only to reinforce the *status quo*. The discourse of rights is accused of being "shot through" with internal contradiction, with "irreducible, irremediable, irresolvable conflict". Attempts to balance "competing concerns" serve only to repress and deny the presence of such contradictions.[87] Fem-crits argue that articulating feminist arguments in terms of abstract rights and neutral rules reduces feminism to "a line-drawing debate". Frances Olsen calls on feminists to stop trying to fit their goals into abstract rights arguments and instead to call for "what we really want".[88]

This critique of rights, however, raises a number of problems. As one critical race theory (CRT) scholar, Patricia Williams, has pointed out, rights discourse has been of central importance to the American black civil rights movement: "It is the magic wand of visibility and invisibility, of inclusion and exclusion,

---

[84] C. Douzinas and R. Warrington, *Postmodern Jurisprudence* (Routledge, London, 1991), p.15.

[85] M. Kelman, *A Guide to Criticial Legal Studies* (Harvard University Press, Cambridge, Mass., 1987), p.290.

[86] C. Smart, *Feminism and the Power of Law* (Routledge, London, 1989), p.144.

[87] M. Kelman, *op. cit.*, p.3. See also Gerard Quinn, "Critical Legal Studies" in this volume.

[88] See F.E. Olsen, "Introduction" in *Feminist Legal Theory* (F.E. Olsen ed., Dartmouth, Aldershot, 1995), Vol.I.

of power and no power ...".[89] Critical race feminists take on the fem-crit suspicion of liberal legalism, but take this further to interrogate the concept of "race" and to expose the racist underpinnings of many liberal political arrangements.[90] Critical race feminists, however, are less likely to abandon the discourse of rights, recognising the power of rights discourse to support a claim to inclusion, for those who wish to be included.

At the heart of critical race feminism is a concern with intersectionality, with recognising the multiple forms of discrimination faced by women. Critical race feminists are concerned, in particular, with the overlapping axes of discrimination faced by women on the basis of "race" and gender. For women in Ireland, the intersectionality of "race" and gender is only recently being recognised and discussed. For women in immigrant communities or minority ethnic groups, such as the Traveller community, multiple forms of discrimination are encountered on a daily basis. At present in Ireland, thousands of citizen children and their parents are facing *de facto* deportation. A second-class category of citizenship has been created through judicial decisions and ultimately, a constitutional amendment in 2004, with children's worth and value defined solely with reference to the legal status of their parents.[91] What reasons are given to deny the full benefits of citizenship to the children of the majority of immigrants to Ireland? There are concerns about losing control of the nation's political destiny, of diluting the nation's cultural heritage. Appeals are made to the integrity of the asylum process and to the need to ensure certainty and predictability in immigration flows. The ability of new communities to assimilate and of the host community to accommodate these communities is questioned. These concerns are not new. They have been heard in many different forms in many jurisdictions. They reflect an assumed commonality within the Irish nation and a denial of the humanity of the stranger. The discourse of immigration control in Ireland is a highly gendered one. As Ronit Lentin has noted, the bodies of immigrant women, their reproductive capacities, have

---

[89] P. Williams, "Alchemical Notes: Reconstructing Ideals From Deconstructed Rights" (1987) 22 *Harvard Civil Right-Civil Liberties Law Review* 401 at 431.

[90] See generally A.K. Wing, *Critical Race Feminism: A Reader* (New York University Press, New York, 1996). See also M. Matsuda, "When the First Quail Calls: Multiple Consciousness as Jurisprudential Method" (1989) 11 *Women's Rights Law Review* 9.

[91] See generally *J.M. Kelly: The Irish Constitution* (G. Hogan and G. Whyte eds., 4th ed., Butterworths, 2003), pp.1635–1638. Included in the text of the 2004 constitutional amendment is the following provision: "Notwithstanding any other provision of this Constitution, a person born in the island of Ireland, which includes its islands and seas, who does not have, at the time of the birth of that person, at least one parent who is an Irish citizen or entitled to be an Irish citizen is not entitled to Irish citizenship or nationality, unless provided for by law."

been subject to detailed scrutiny and comment by government, civil society and media. The hypocrisy underpinning both the discourses of immigration and reproduction are clearly illustrated in the *Baby O* case.[92] The case involved a Nigerian woman, seven months pregnant and subject to a deportation order from the state, following a failed application for asylum. Taking judicial review proceedings challenging the validity of the deportation order, she argued that the duty to defend and vindicate Baby O's right to life prevented the state from deporting her to Nigeria, where infant mortality rates were substantially higher and the standard of living, substantially lower. The Attorney-General, acting on behalf of the Minister for Justice, Equality and Law Reform, appealed to the common good, to the need to defend and vindicate the territorial integrity of the state and to the Minister's right to deport failed asylum seekers. The Court agreed with the submissions of the Attorney-General. The threat posed by higher infant mortality rates could not engage the protection of Art.40.3.3.[93] The state's duty to defend and vindicate the right to life of the unborn did not extend to ensuring the health and well-being of Baby O, or even to ensuring a safe delivery. Article 40.3.3 could not be relied on to invoke unenumerated social and economic rights, which the Court held were not implicit within the constitutionally protected right to life. The Court upheld the deportation order and also refused a final application to stay the order pending an appeal to the European Court of Human Rights. If Baby O was born in Ireland, she could have claimed Irish citizenship, since this case took place before the constitutional amendment of 2004 that limited the claim to birthright citizenship. But the "common good" required a speedy deportation of the mother and foetus. Again, the narrative of nation was to prove exclusionary. The self-styled "pro-life" movement, preoccupied at the time with another referendum on abortion, had little to say in support of Baby O or her mother.

Critical race feminism highlights the intersectionality of discriminatory practices and the many unfulfilled promises of liberal legalism. Exposing the gendered nature of liberal discourse is not sufficient. Nationality, ethnicity, colour, all form overlapping axes of discrimination. The equality agenda in Ireland has expanded to include "race", disability, sexual orientation and other grounds of discrimination. However, at the same time, immigration control has tightened. Ireland has fallen quickly into the folds of "Fortress Europe". Family, reproduction and nation have, as in many other jurisdictions, become, yet again discourses of exclusion and control for immigrant women. For

---

[92] *O v Minister for Justice, Equality and Law Reform* [2002] 2 I.R. 169.
[93] Article 40.3.3 states in part: "The State acknowledges the right to life of the unborn and, with due regard to the life of the mother, guarantees in its laws to respect, and, as far as practicable, by its laws to defend and vindicate that right".

immigrant and minority ethnic women in Ireland, the language of rights is a powerful one, with potential to provide at least a minimal protection from a potentially brutal state.

Martha Minow has also questioned the wisdom of denying rights discourse to historically disadvantaged groups: "I worry about those who have, telling those who do not, 'You do not need it, you should not want it'."[94] Feminists have been concerned at the seemingly endless relativism and fragmentation of CLS and postmodern legal theory. Postmodern feminists have sought to avoid the dangers of such relativism and to maintain an ethical dimension to feminism. We will turn now to examine those attempts and question whether they can offer the resources necessary for a critical and emancipatory feminism.

5. POSTMODERN FEMINISMS

This part will examine three types of postmodern feminism: neo-pragmatist feminism; poststructuralist feminism; and deconstructionist ethical feminism.

Neo-pragmatism

Neo-pragmatist feminists rely on a relational view of the human self and a feminist perspective that is contextual and claims to be non-essentialist in aspiration. This perspective is based on what Margaret Radin claims is a "new mediating way of thinking"—a way of thinking that rejects the rationalism associated with Enlightenment philosophy.[95] Enlightenment philosophy is associated with a drive to establish communication between "local canons of rationality"—an attempt to make them answerable to a single standard.[96] Radin and others argue that this drive is either misguided or sinister in its own right. Criticism centres on the Enlightenment demand that what exists should justify itself before a timeless "tribunal of reason". Neo-pragmatists refuse to yield to this demand. Justification (or legitimation), they argue, is always local and context-relative. In Nancy Fraser and Linda Nicholson's words, feminism must "tailor its method and categories to the specific task at hand, using multiple categories when appropriate and forswearing the metaphysical comfort of a single feminist method or feminist epistemology".[97] Concepts of justice and

---

[94] M. Minow, "Interpreting Rights: An Essay for Robert Cover" (1987) 96 *Yale Law Journal* 1860 at 1910.

[95] M. Radin, "The Pragmatist and the Feminist" (1990) 63 *California Law Review* 1699.

[96] S. Lovibond, "Feminism and Postmodernism" (1989) 178 *New Left Review* 5 at 6.

[97] L. Nicholson, *Feminism/Postmodernism* (Routledge, New York, 1990), p.35.

rights are viewed as additional tools to be employed or not as the situation requires.

Neo-pragmatism leaves many questions unanswered, however. What counts as a more or less useful idea or suggestion? How do we know if one particular tool will bring us closer to or further away from a just society if we cannot even begin to define what justice is? Within the confines of neo-pragmatism, we cannot settle the matter by positing non-contingent ends or goals. Feminist methods, Katharine Bartlett says, are means to feminist ends.[98] But what are those ends? If knowledge of those ends is always contingent, unstable and subject to revision, then how do we know what to keep and what to revise? If we are to make pragmatic judgements as to whether something "works", we need to know to what end we are working and to be able to assess that end in and of itself. Nancy Fraser argues that feminists share the general purpose of opposing male dominance.[99] But not all feminists agree on what counts as dominance or what counts as subordination. The key, Fraser argues, is to avoid "metaphysical entanglements".[100] We might wish to avoid metaphysics, but we cannot avoid entanglements that require us to offer a normative justification for the pursuit of feminist ends. Without such entanglements we cannot even begin to define dominance, subordination or inequality. We need to be able to defend feminist goals in and of themselves, not simply as one amongst a number of equally valid ends or goals. The eclectic neo-pragmatist methods of Fraser and others cannot help us in this.

Neo-pragmatism has been heavily influenced by Richard Rorty's anti-foundationalist liberalism.[101] The limits of this approach can be seen in Rorty's underlying relativism. Rorty, for example, claims that

> "evolution has no purpose and humanity no nature. So the moral world does not divide into the intrinsically decent and the intrinsically abominable, but rather into the goods of different groups and different epochs."[102]

Claims based on the "greater good" of feminism, Rorty argues, are like claims that "mammals are preferable to reptiles, or Aryans to Jews". At another point,

---

[98] See K. Bartlett, "Feminist Legal Methods" (1990) 103 *Harvard Law Review* 829.

[99] N. Fraser, "Pragmatism, Feminism, and the Linguistic Turn" in *Feminist Contentions: A Philosophical Exchange* (S. Benhabib, J. Butler, D. Cornell and N. Fraser eds., Routledge, New York, 1995), pp.166–167.

[100] *ibid.*, p.166.

[101] See R. Rorty, "Human Rights, Rationality, and Sentimentality"; *Contingency, Irony and Solidarity*; and *Philosophy and the Mirror of Nature* (Blackwell, Oxford, 1980).

[102] R. Rorty, "Feminism and Pragmatism" in *The Tanner Lectures on Human Values* (G.B. Peterson ed., University of Utah Press, Salt Lake City, 1990), p.9.

he argues that "the enslavement of one human tribe or race by another, or of the human females by the human males, is not an intrinsic evil."[103] The plasticity of human selves seems to be limitless. Feminism, however, cannot be limitless. Defining those limits requires more than intuitions or situated judgment. Human rights principles, transformed to take account of feminist concerns can assist in defining limits and providing normative justifications for doing so.

Poststructuralist feminism

Poststructuralist feminists take the emphasis on sexual and other differences much further; neo-pragmatism, they argue, compromises too much. In suggesting a way of reasoning through difference, particularity and heterogeneity, neo-pragmatist feminists are accused of seeking to eliminate difference. For poststructuralist feminists, there can be no "middle ground". This argument is made most forcefully by Iris Marion Young.[104] For Young, any attempt to reason through difference is a violent act, an act that fails to respect or to recognise the significance of difference. This violence can be seen most clearly, she argues, in universalist moral and political theories. The appeal to universality is a "totalising movement"; it seeks "to engulf the alterity of things in the unity of thought".[105] Such movements, she argues, are impelled by a "logic of identity". According to this logic, reason is ratio; it involves "the principled reduction of the objects of thought to a common measure, to universal laws". For Young, too much is lost in this "principled reduction". It leads, she argues, not to progress or to increased knowledge but to closure and silencing. The attempt to bring particulars under a universal category creates a distinction between inside and outside. The "totalizing movement" always leaves a remainder—an "excluded domain". Those falling within the "excluded domain" return to disrupt and fragment the unity of the dominant discourse—the discourse of universal human rights or the unity of the feminist "we".[106] So, for example, the discourse of international human rights law is frequently disrupted by appeals to religious difference, to cultural traditions and practices, to the requirements of domestic legal systems. Similarly, claims to a unified

---

[103] *ibid.*, p.10.

[104] See I.M. Young, "The Ideal of Community and the Politics of Difference" (1986) 12 *Social Theory and Practice* 12; "Impartiality and the Civic Public: Some Implications of Feminist Critiques of Moral and Political Theory" in *Feminism as Critique: On the Politics of Gender; and Justice and the Politics of Difference* (Princeton University Press, Princeton, 1990).

[105] I.M. Young, "Impartiality and the Civic Public", p.61.

[106] Butler J. "Contingent Foundations: Feminism and the Question of Postmodernism" in *Feminists Theorize the Political* (J. Butler and J.W. Scott eds., Routledge, New York, 1992), p.14.

feminist "we" are brought into question by the reality of differences between women.

For Young and other poststructuralist feminists, such disruption and fragmentation is inevitable. Potentially fragmenting forces include "the specificity of women's bodies and desire, the difference of race and culture, the variability and heterogeneity of the needs, the goals and desires of each individual, the ambiguity and changeability of feeling".[107] From the poststructuralist perspective, any attempt to impose order or structure on diverse experiences or events will be constantly undermined by the unintended effects of the violence required to impose such an order.[108] That violence, Young argues, shifts difference into dichotomous normative oppositions: essence-accident, good-bad, normal-deviant. In moral and political theories these normative oppositions reappear—between the universal and the particular, justice and care, reason and sentiment, the public and the private. These dichotomies are not symmetrical, they stand in a hierarchy: "the first term designates the positive unity on the inside, the second less-valued term designates the left-over outside".[109] These dichotomies are also deeply gendered. The binary oppositions which reappear in liberal political theory and in legal systems, privilege one presence—male, rationality, objectivity—and marginalise its opposite—female, irrationality, subjectivity.[110]

Poststructuralist feminists also attack the unified subject of universalist moral theory. For Young this presumption of a unified subject is and can only be a fiction. It is a mistake, she says, that is repeated both by liberal and cultural feminists. The "relational" or "connected" view of the self proposed by Gilligan, Minow and others, presupposes a state in which individuals will cease to be "opaque, other, not understood, and instead become fused, mutually sympathetic, understanding one another as they understand themselves". This ideal of "shared subjectivity", Young argues, denies difference in the sense of "the basic asymmetry of subjects". It is, she argues, doomed to failure. Despite our best efforts, difference cannot be eliminated.

If not a relational, connected self, what is to replace the liberal ideal of the autonomous self? Young proposes a "de-centred" view of the human self. Any individual subject is, she says, "a play of differences that cannot be comprehended". The subject is always a "heterogeneous presence", not just "situated" or contextualised but radically de-centred. It can no longer be seen as an origin or source of reason—only as a product of multiple, social and psycho-

---

[107] I.M. Young, "Impartiality and the Civic Public", p.67.

[108] J. Flax, *op. cit.*, p.32.

[109] I.M. Young, "Impartiality and the Civic Public", p.62.

[110] K. Bartlett, *op. cit.*, at 838.

logical forces.[111] Recognising this, she argues, requires us to abandon the liberal ideal of the autonomous freely choosing self. It requires us also to abandon the "connected" vision of the self, favoured both by relational feminists and communitarians.

Difficulties arise with these proposals, however. Young emphasises the direction of agency. She speaks of the need to redefine the public sphere, of the need to promote heterogeneity in public and to remedy the disadvantages of "socially excluded" groups. Yet the possibility of agency itself seems to be put in question. The de-centred subject, lacking in autonomy or in any kind of identity, is unlikely to be an effective agent of social transformation. The "fractured, opaque self" celebrates heterogeneity, opacity and difference, but at the cost of belittling the importance of a coherent core of individual identity. As Seyla Benhabib points out, an emancipatory feminist politics is not even possible without positing the norms of autonomy, choice and self-determination.[112] Contemplating, giving expression to, and working towards a "heterogeneous public" requires that certain democratic procedures are in place—that a degree of autonomy and freedom is protected. Young speaks as though these procedures can be taken for granted. She presupposes a kind of pluralist, tolerant, "super-liberalism", relying on the very norms of autonomy and the rationality of democratic procedures that she seems to so blithely dismiss.

Instead of appealing to a universalist legislating reason or to communal values, Young emphasises the transformative potential of dialogic practices. She appeals to a communicative ethics that seeks neither the unity of a

---

[111] Three different sources seem to have contributed to the emergence of this "de-centred" view of the self. First, from psychoanalysis has come the idea that the "ego" is not in charge of the individual's life but is in various, ultimately unaccountable ways, affected by the subconscious. In Freudian terms, the self is not "transparent" to itself as it is not "master in its own house": it is controlled by desires, needs and forces that shape both the content of its ideas as well as its capacity to organise and comprehend them. Secondly, from the influence of Saussurean linguistics has come the notion that, just as in language each element or sign only makes sense in relation to and differentiated from the other elements or signs in the overall system, so the self, "I", does not make sense in isolation, but only in relation to and differentiated from such terms as "you", "she", "they", etc. Thus, the self does not enjoy any real autonomy or discrete identity as such. Finally, there is the belief that autonomy belongs, if anywhere, to culture as such, or to the networks of cultural practices within which the self is embedded. However, whereas in structuralism the self was de-centred, meaning was at least preserved in a total system of which the self was one element. In poststructuralist thought neither the self nor the system in which the self is embedded can provide a secure foundation for any final meaning or truth about the human condition.

[112] S. Benhabib, *Situating the Self*, p.16.

transcendent impartiality nor the opposition of reason to sentiment. She argues that the communicative ethics of Jürgen Habermas and Seyla Benhabib remain too committed to the ideals of impartiality and universality.[113] An emancipatory politics, Young says, can best ensure the inclusion of all persons and groups not by claiming a "unified universality" but by explicitly promoting "heterogeneity in public".[114] Young's appeal to dialogic practices is echoed in the work of "newstream" international law theorists. Anthony Carty, for example, argues that the role of the critical international lawyer is to facilitate the process of inter-state/inter-cultural dialogue, to allow a coming together, however temporary and fragile.[115] Marti Koskenniemi also speaks of international law as "a conversation about the right thing to do in particular circumstances".[116] He combines this emphasis on "dialogic practices" with the postmodern commitment to instability, uncertainty and a constant questioning. From this perspective, he says, international law has "no given focus or centre from which it may not deviate without ceasing to be itself".[117] Nicola Lacey adopts a similar strategy. Through democratic exchange, she argues, feminists can engage in a process of normative reconstruction of the legal sphere.[118] If dialogic practices are to be transformative, however, then a commitment to democratic procedures cannot be an optional or a contingent element of such practices. Concepts of rights and justice must underpin the ongoing moral conversation. A free-floating conversation, with "no given focus or centre" cannot provide such guarantees. As Hilary Charlesworth and Christine Chinkin point out, it cannot address the complex forms of structural

---

[113] Rather than appealing to an overlapping consensus or to a single comprehensive doctrine, discourse ethics relies on a virtuous circle—a dialectical process of reflecting on the universal and necessary presuppositions of communicative speech. These presuppositions are identified by Benhabib as the core moral principles of universal respect and egalitarian reciprocity. For her, these core moral principles define the limits of reasonable pluralism. They provide a normative framework within which conflicting cultural claims must be negotiated, whether arising in spheres defined as political or domestic. See *Situating the Self*. See also J. Habermas, *Between Facts and Norms: Contribution to a Discourse Theory of Law and Democracy* (W. Rehg trans., Polity, Cambridge, 1996).

[114] I.M. Young, "Impartiality and the Civic Public", p.59.

[115] A. Carty, "Critical International Law: Recent Trends in the Theory of International Law" (1991) 2 *European Journal of International Law* 66.

[116] M. Koskenniemi, "International Law in a Post-Realist Era" (1994) 24 *Australian Yearbook of International Law* 1 at 17.

[117] *ibid.*

[118] See generally E. Frazer and N. Lacey, *The Politics of Community: A Feminist Critique of the Liberal-Communitarian Debate* (Harvester Wheatsheaf, New York, 1993). See also S. Mullally, "Review of N. Lacey, *Unspeakable Subjects: Feminist Essays in Legal and Social Theory*" (1998) 23 *Journal of Applied Philosophy* 89.

disadvantage encountered by women all over the world.[119] Feminism needs something more.

Iris Young argues that the virtues of city life can assist in promoting a "heterogeneous public sphere". Ideally, she says, city virtues represent heterogeneity, social differentiation (without exclusion), variety, eroticism and publicity.[120] Young is concerned to remedy the disadvantages experienced by "socially excluded" groups. Oppression and domination, she argues, should be the primary terms used in conceptualising injustice. Drawing on the discourse of emancipatory social movements, she argues that oppression has five distinct elements: "exploitation, marginalisation, powerlessness, cultural imperialism, and violence".[121] Implicit within Young's call to end oppression and domination is a belief that rights have been violated and justice denied. She seems to invoke universalist concerns. Yet, at the same time she attacks the exclusionary and totalising force of universalist theories, refusing to rely on a rights-based framework to support her claims. Promoting heterogeneity—at least some kinds—and seeking to remedy the effects of past discrimination are concerns that are at the heart of much of human rights theory and practice. Young fails to propose an alternative. She has no answer to the question, "What concept of reason, which vision of autonomy allows us to retain these values and the institutions within which these values flourish?"[122] Within her "free-floating pluralism", we cannot distinguish between social exclusion and social differentiation, between inclusion and assimilation. Like other postmodern thinkers, Young presumes that a free-floating pluralism would not permit racism, homophobia, poverty or sexism. To make this claim, however, clearly requires us to refer to some universally valid norms. This, of course, is anathema to the postmodernist.

Young sets out to tackle the problems of positivism and reductionism in contemporary political theory. It is here that the root of Young's error can be found. Like others of a postmodern orientation, she conflates positivism with liberalism and universalist moral theory with a denial of difference. This is a reductionist view of universalist moral theory. She presumes that universalism requires us to treat all moral problems with the same rules. From her point of view, universalist moral theory is limited to a formal, mechanistic understanding of equality. She fails to recognise that concepts of justice and rights can and indeed must employ a more complex understanding of equality and difference.

---

[119] See generally H. Charlesworth and C. Chinkin, *The Boundaries of International Law: A Feminist Analysis* (Manchester University Press, Manchester, 2000).

[120] I.M. Young, *Justice and the Politics of Difference* (Princeton University Press, Princeton, 1990), p.13.

[121] *ibid.*, p.9.

[122] S. Benhabib, *Situating the Self*, p.8.

Deconstruction and Drucilla Cornell's ethical feminism

The affirmation of difference, in particular sexual difference, can be seen again in the work of Drucilla Cornell.[123] Cornell combines the deconstructionist techniques of Jacques Derrida and a celebration of feminine sexual difference to create her own particular "ethical feminism". Drawing on the writings of French feminist theorists, Luce Irigaray and Hélène Cixous,[124] she imagines a different way of being human, a way of being in which the "feminine" is reinterpreted, sexual difference is affirmed and fundamental concepts such as equality, rights and justice, are redefined. She rejects the accusations of essentialism sometimes targeted at French feminist writers by Catharine MacKinnon and others. Those accusations, she says, are based on a conflation of femininity with femaleness—with a biological essentialist description of gender identity.[125] For Cornell, the affirmation of the feminine is not the affirmation of some pre-given sexual identity. Sexual difference, she says, defies any rigid logic of definitions, any unified compact subjectivity.[126] Quoting Jacques Derrida, she argues that feminism should not be another excuse for passing out "sexual identity cards".[127] Cornell is critical of the essentialising tendencies to be found in the writings of cultural feminist legal theorists such as Robin West.[128] Although recognising the political and ethical power of West's writing, she argues that West maps the feminine onto "femaleness"— onto an essentialist understanding of women's different biology. She is critical also of the "strategic essentialism" of writers such as Gayatri Spivak.[129] Spivak's

---

[123] D. Cornell, *Beyond Accommodation*; "Feminism, Deconstruction and the Law" (1995) 73 *Radical Philosophy* 23; "The Philosophy of the Limit: Systems Theory and Feminist Legal Reform" in *Deconstruction and the Possibility of Justice* (D. Cornell, M. Rosenfeld and D.G. Carlson eds., Routledge, London, 1992); and *The Philosophy of the Limit* (Routledge, London, 1992).

[124] See L. Irigaray, *The Sex Which is Not One* (C. Porter trans., Cornell University Press, Ithaca, 1985); and H. Cixous and C. Clement, *The Newly Born Woman* (B. Wing trans., University of Minnesota Press, Minneapolis, 1986).

[125] D. Cornell, *Beyond Accommodation*, p.130.

[126] *ibid.*, p.16.

[127] *ibid.*, p.216, n.23.

[128] Robin West is best known for her "separation" and "connection" theses regarding the genders. See R. West, "Jurisprudence and Gender" in *Feminist Legal Theory: Readings in Law and Gender*.

[129] In her essay, "Can the Subaltern Speak?", Spivak describes the "crucially strategic" project of the Subaltern Studies group as that of "subject restoration", as the "strategic use of positivist essentialism in a scrupulously visible political interest". Spivak claims that if strategic essentialism is practiced by the dispossessed themselves, then essentialism can be powerfully disruptive. The phrase "strategic essentialism" has emerged from her work and has been deployed, in particular, by

mistake, she says, is to assume that any appeal to the feminine must inevitably involve essentialism. For Cornell the feminine is a role, a performance that can be restyled, replayed, reinvented. Ultimately, however, it is not clear that Cornell avoids the kind of essentialist tendencies of which she is so critical. Her call to re-symbolise "the feminine within sexual difference" is a risky strategy. As Nancy Fraser points out, even in this abstract, indeterminate form, it entrenches "a conceptually and politically dubious gender binarism".[130] Once it acquires any determinate content—as it must, if it is to be in any way meaningful—the risk is even greater. It leads to the sort of homogenising essentialism that has so-often denied differences of race, class, and sexual orientation between women.

Other theoretical and political questions are raised by Cornell's proposed strategies. She argues that the reality of gender inequality is not unshakeable. The language that allows us to see the reality of injustice also allows us to see differently. The affirmation of sexual difference, she argues, requires an appeal to a "utopian female imaginary space", a constant imagining of an undefined and undefinable utopia.[131] It is not clear, however, what is to follow from this process of ethical imagining. Will it simply lead to further appeals to feminist utopian imaginary spaces? Given the differences that exist between women and between feminists, it is likely that conflicting utopian visions will emerge. Cornell does not tell us how we can move beyond these conflicting utopian visions. Are feminist claims to be just one more "exciting feature" or cluster of features in a postmodern social landscape?

The pursuit of equality—of an equality of citizenship—is a recurring theme in Cornell's work. She argues that equality is defined above all by the recognition of the call of the "Other", the call for us to remember those aspects of human life that are marginalised by dominant legal conceptions.[132] The pursuit of equality, Cornell argues, can be assisted by the celebration of feminine *jouissance*.[133] *Jouissance* can be understood as feminine sexual pleasure, but also, Cornell argues, as a desire for connection with the Other. It is this desire

---

North American feminists. See G. Spivak, *In Other Words: Essays in Cultural Politics* (Routledge, New York, 1987).

[130] N. Fraser, "Pragmatism, Feminism, and the Linguistic Turn" in *Feminist Contentions: A Philosophical Exchange*, p.166.

[131] D. Cornell, *The Philosophy of the Limit*, pp.87–88.

[132] J.M. Balkin, "What is Postmodern Constitutionalism?" (1992) 90 *Michigan Law Review* 1966 at 1989.

[133] *Jouissance* is a term used in contemporary philosophical and psychoanalytic discourse to mean feminine sexual pleasure or desire. It is also used to refer to the experience of perfect completion with the Other, the lack of which is the source of desire. J. Lacan, *Feminine Sexuality* (Macmillan, London, 1982), pp.137–148 and pp.116–117.

that can lead us to answer the call of the Other. It also leads us to imagine alternative sexual identities, identities that can undermine established gender hierarchies. Following Derrida, Cornell argues that this concern to answer the call of the Other brings with it a kind of universality. She is careful, however, to distance her ethical concerns from what she perceives as the essentialising tendencies of most "grand narratives". Universality, she argues, should not be defined in terms of a common set of properties defining the human self or a set of procedures to be followed in responding to a call of the "Other".

This understanding of equality or universality raises a number of difficulties, however. How should feminism define its responsibilities to the "Other"? Are there any limits to those responsibilities, any calls of the "Other" that do not give rise to responsibilities? If feminism is to retain its force, its emancipatory potential, there must be some demands with which it is incompatible, some limits to the "plasticity" of the human self. For Cornell, however, to define those limits risks trampling on the particular. It risks closure and silence. Failing to do so, however, does little to promote a flourishing of difference—unless, of course, we simply presume the existence of a democratic process within which such flourishing can take place. Cornell gives us little in the way of concrete steps to be taken towards an equality of citizenship. She argues that appeals to universal principles—understood as appeals to a common human essence—perpetuate gender hierarchies. She presumes that such universalist appeals define the human self with reference to the "masculine" subject and that aspects of human existence usually associated with the "feminine" are ignored, marginalised and rendered invisible.[134] Certainly this has often been the case. However, it need not necessarily be so. The human subject can be defined differently. Universalist moral theory does not have to rely on essentialist definitions of the human subject. Feminists such as Seyla Benhabib and Martha Nussbaum defend the need for universalist moral theory while at the same time denying the validity of essentialist conceptions of the human self.[135]

Cornell's refusal to invoke universally valid norms means that we are ultimately left with little more than hopeful feminine imaginings. Along with other postmodern thinkers, she seems to value uncertainty and instability. If feminists are to engage in practical-critical activity, however, they must be able to defend their claims against alternative, perhaps more harmful utopian imaginings.

---

[134] D. Cornell, *The Philosophy of the Limit*, p.88.

[135] See generally *Democracy and Difference: Contesting the Boundaries of the Political* (S. Benhabib ed., Princeton University Press, Princeton, 1996) and M.C. Nussbaum, "Public Philosophy and International Feminism" (1998) 108 *Ethics* 762.

6. CONCLUSION

Feminism stands to lose too much in abandoning its roots in the Enlightenment commitment to universality, individual autonomy and human rights. The alternatives proposed do not provide the resources necessary to build a truly global feminism—global in the sense of addressing discrimination and inequality in all its complex variety and monotonous similarity. Feminist lawyers in Ireland and elsewhere are increasingly questioning the limits imposed by legal liberalism and seeking, not only to add women in to existing laws and legal processes, but to engage in a normative reconstruction of the legal sphere.[136] This process of reconstruction will require that questions of distributive justice be given a central place in processes of reform. The pursuit of a politics of redistribution, however, will need to be combined with a politics that recognises the diversity within the category "woman" in contemporary Ireland. Recognising this diversity will be necessary if feminist jurisprudence is to address the multiple forms of discrimination that women experience, and realise the full potential of a "difference feminism"—a feminism that seeks an equality that is of equivalent worth to differently situated individuals and groups.

---

[136] On Ireland, see L. Connolly, *The Irish Women's Movement: From Revolution to Devolution* (Palgrave, London, 2002); C. Coulter, "'Hello Divorce, Good-bye Daddy': Women, Gender and the Divorce Debate" in *Gender and Sexuality in Modern Ireland* (A. Bradley and M.G. Valiulis eds., University of Massachusetts Press, Amherst, 1997) and *The Hidden Tradition: Feminism, Women and Nationalism* (Cork University Press, Cork, 1993); R. Fletcher, "Post-colonial Fragments: Representations of Abortion in Irish Law and Politics" (2001) 28 *Journal of Law and Society* 568; S. Mullally, "Promoting Gender Equality: Beyond the Limits of Non-discrimination" in *Equality in Diversity* (C. Costello and E. Barry eds., Irish Centre for European Law and the Equality Authority, Dublin, 2003); S. Mullally, M. Donnelly and O. Smith, "Making Women Count in Ireland" in *Making Women Count: Integrating Gender into Law and Policy Making* (S. Nott and F. Beveridge eds., Ashgate, London, 2000).

CHAPTER 16

CRITICAL RACE THEORY

C.L. LIM

1. INTRODUCTION

Critical Race Theory (CRT) traces its roots in US anti-discrimination law scholarship. From the "separate but equal" doctrine in *Plessy v Ferguson* in the nineteenth century to the twentieth-century integrationist ideals of *Brown v Board of Education*, CRT has, today, led to some very highly-charged debates on the role of affirmative action as the hand-maiden of integration.[1] It has also drawn deep epistemic insights from the inadequacy of traditional analyses of legal doctrine in these areas. Today, CRT is informed by specific, race-based, claims concerning the grounds of legal knowledge and a critical methodological orientation. Its assumptions, knowledge-production methods, and scholarly form have been deployed not only in the treatment of overtly race-bound issues but also in a distinctly race-based treatment of apparently neutral legal issues (indeed, in "racialising" legal issues). What has emerged is "voice of colour" scholarship. Even some of its staunchest opponents admit that it is "the hottest form of legal scholarship today".[2]

Taking the insights of Legal Realism and the Critical Legal Studies (CLS/ Crits) movement for granted, CRT has chosen white male dominance of legal doctrine and discourse as its principal target. In this it shares much in common

---

[1] *Plessy v Fergusón*, 163 US 537 (1896) (upholding statutory segregation of railway coaches); *Brown v Board of Education*, 347 US 483 (1954) (upholding school desegregation). For those who prefer to head straight for the deep-end, see D. Bell, *Faces at the Bottom of the Well: The Permanence of Racism* (Basic Books, New York, 1992), pp.127–146. Two useful collections of the key writings that depict the Critical Race Theory Movement appeared in 1995: *Critical Race Theory: The Key Writings That Formed the Movement* (K. Crenshaw, N. Gotanda, G. Peller, K. Thomas, eds., New Press, New York, 1995); and *Critical Race Theory: The Cutting Edge* (R. Delgado ed., Temple University Press, Philadelphia, 1995). The latter is currently in its second edition, edited by Richard Delgado and Jean Stefancic, *Critical Race Theory: The Cutting Edge* (Temple University Press, Philadelphia, 2000). See also R. Delgado and J. Stefancic, "Critical Race Theory: An Annotated Bibliography" (1993) 79 *Virginia Law Review* 461.

[2] H. MacDonald, "Law School Humbug" (1995) 5 *City Journal* 46.

with critical feminism. CRT does not accept legal doctrinal certainty, and is opposed to the law and economics movement, but unlike CLS, CRT proponents claim a serious practical ambition, and do not aspire merely to apply new insights to our readings of legal doctrine.[3] Critics who accuse CRT of being "anti-law" admit nonetheless that,

> "By shattering the Crits' claim to speak for the oppressed, this minority critique nearly stopped the movement dead in its tracks. The Crits looked in the mirror and saw faces that were white, heterosexual, and, usually, male—badges of shame in the multicultural eighties. Their bravura evaporated."[4]

In brief CRT has three fundamental aspects. *First*, its substantive legal perspective, which is the extent to which anti-discrimination law and law more generally have failed to capture the viewpoint of people of colour. CRT is concerned not with mere formal legal equality but with racism itself and its redress through critical legal practice and the legal campaign for affirmative action. *Secondly*, it has an epistemic aspect that is concerned with the way in which legal knowledge is produced and organised, including the politics of legal academia as a factor of production in such legal knowledge-making. Thus, the redress of the impact of racism in the US is tied to the intellectual and scholarly exercise of deconstructing racism in the law through scholarship in the best law journals and in the elite law schools. *Thirdly*, CRT has, from the beginning, engaged in an inter-disciplinary methodology that seeks to explain the law through insights gleaned from studies in history, philosophy, politics, sociology and cultural studies and this approach has had a formative influence on CRT scholarship. This, in turn, is closely aligned to a contemporary socio-legal orientation towards narrative jurisprudence, which is about telling real law stories to expose the actual, contingent, and particular legal situations in which people of colour have found and continue to find themselves. Hence the colloquial expression "voice scholarship" generally to denote narrative jurisprudence. This last methodological development is not unique to CRT but to all forms of narrative jurisprudence. Proponents of narrative jurisprudence are engaged in the project of telling counter-stories, commonly involving particular examples of perceptions and lives that contradict the usual, generalized, and widely-believed stories about how our experiences, perceptions and lives connect with the law.

---

[3] For the linkages between CRT and the earlier racial diversity movement of 1960s student activism at the University of California, Berkeley, see S. Cho and R. Westley, "Critical Race Coalitions: Key Movements that Performed the Theory" (2000) 33 *UC Davis Law Review* 1377.

[4] H. MacDonald, *op. cit.*

2. MAIN THEMES

We will now explore in detail the main themes in the writings of a range of leading CRT scholars. We may begin with two early proponents of CRT, Derrick Bell and Alan Freeman, who sought to elicit the material and restorative plight of the black civil rights movement.

Derrick Bell and the "Interest-Convergence" Principle

Derrick Bell is commonly known more through the press than for his work in legal scholarship and practice. After a two-year protest, Bell refused to return to the Harvard Law School in 1992 on account of the continued absence of a black female law professor at Harvard.[5] Bell, now teaching at the New York University Law School, is a *New York Times* bestselling author.[6] Such a high-profile masks Bell's seriousness, and his status as one of the most influential and highly regarded law professors in the United States.

A former US Justice Department lawyer and NAACP Legal Defence Fund litigator, Bell's lasting insight was published in 1980 in the *Harvard Law Review*.[7] In that article, Bell sought to explain the animating principle underlying the seminal school desegregation case of *Brown v Board of Education*.[8] *Brown* marked a turnaround from the "separate but equal" principle established earlier in *Plessy v Ferguson*[9] in the course of the swings and roundabouts of civil rights cases stretching through the century preceding *Brown*. *Brown* marked the end, at least in American legal theory, of desegregation. According to *Brown*,

---

[5] Bell had earlier returned to Harvard after a similar incident at the University of Oregon law school where he was then Dean. At Oregon, Bell had resigned in protest at the refusal of the law school to appoint an Asian American candidate who was ranked third after the first two candidates had rejected Oregon. Harvard, from which he had earlier left for Oregon, invited Bell back then. See "Derrick Bell threatens to leave Harvard Law School" (Original Airdate: April 24, 1990) and "Jesse Jackson supports Derrick Bell" (Original Airdate: September 5, 1990), WGBH, The Ten O'Clock News (on file); "Harvard Law Professor Accuses School of Discrimination", *Washington Post*, March 3, 1992. Harvard has since appointed Lani Guinier, but in 2002 race issues resurfaced shortly after black academic icon, Cornel West, also left Harvard for Princeton; "Comments Concerning Race Divide Harvard Law School", *New York Times*, April 20, 2002. For Bell's own account, see, for example, *Faces at the Bottom of the Well*, at pp.142 *et seq.*

[6] His most recent work is D. Bell, *Ethical Ambition: Living a Life of Meaning and Worth* (Bloomsbury, New York and London, 2002).

[7] D. Bell, "Brown v Board of Education and the Interest-Convergence Dilemma" (1980) 93 *Harvard Law Review* 518.

[8] 347 US 483 (1954).

[9] 163 US 537 (1896).

the elusive and abstract legal protection of equality means integration, not desegregation. Bell had sought to address an earlier article by Herbert Wechsler of Columbia University in which Wechsler had urged that *Brown* could not be justified on legal principle alone, as the legal-theoretical bargain struck therein was inherently arbitrary in that "if the freedom of association is denied by segregation, integration forces an association upon those for whom it is unpleasant or repugnant".[10] The associational right of blacks signified the loss of freedom of association on the part of whites. This led Wechsler to propose what Bell terms the "interest-convergence dilemma":

> "Given a situation where the state must practically choose between denying the association to those individuals who wish it or imposing it on those who would avoid it, is there a basis in neutral principles for holding that the Constitution demands that the claims for association should prevail?"[11]

Underlying the apparent solution in the *Brown* decision to that dilemma, there must then lie a further, "higher" principle if *Brown* were not simply arbitrary. According to Bell, the elucidation of that higher principle is as much reliant on the right reading of American political history as precedent. In acontextual terms, *Brown* would appear arbitrary. But it is not, precisely because Wechsler's analysis was ahistorical and acontextual. Bell explains: "To doubt that racial segregation is harmful to blacks, and to suggest that what blacks really sought was the right to associate with whites, is to believe in a world that does not exist now and could not possibly have existed then."[12] Bell's "interest-convergence" principle proposes that:

> "Racial remedies may instead be the outward manifestations of unspoken and perhaps subconscious judicial conclusions that the remedies, if granted, will secure, advance, or at least not harm societal interests deemed important by middle and upper class whites. Racial justice—or its appearance—may, from time to time, be counted among the interests deemed important by the courts and by society's policymakers."[13]

Underlying this articulation of the interest-convergence principle, lies a deeper insight of what the interest-convergence principle means; namely that:

---

[10] H. Wechsler, "Toward Neutral Principles of Constitutional Law" (1959) 73 *Harvard Law Review* 1 at 22.

[11] *ibid.*, at 23.

[12] D. Bell, "Brown v Board of Education and the Interest-Convergence Dilemma", at 522.

[13] *ibid.*, at 523.

> "[R]acial equality is not deemed legitimate by large segments of the
> American people, at least to the extent it threatens to impair the societal
> status of whites. Hence, Wechsler's search for a guiding principle in the
> context of associational rights retains merit in the positivistic sphere,
> because it suggests a deeper truth about the subordination of law to
> interest-group politics with a racial configuration."[14]

The interest-convergence principle therefore suggests that there is nothing
neutral about legal reasoning and doctrine. The equality principle, and anti-
discrimination law more generally, cannot be explained without accounting
for historical fact and contemporary political contestation.

Bell was to further develop his original thesis in later works, most notably
in his *And We Are Not Saved*,[15] which consisted of an expansion of his Foreword
in the 1985 *Harvard Law Review*.[16] The book is about Bell's fictional alter
ego, Geneva Crenshaw, whose imaginative exploits are designed as a means
to probe America's race consciousness. In the "Chronicle of the Devine Gift"
Geneva becomes the first of her race to hold a tenure-track position in America's
leading law school.[17] She has impeccable credentials and is assured that she is
anything but a token hire. Geneva attracts five other high calibre minority
applicants. The school draws a line at the seventh such minority candidate.
The Dean apologetically says to Geneva that the alumni are beginning to say
that the school is beginning to take on the appearance of a professional
basketball team. Bell's message is that mere acceptance of affirmative action
as a policy is not enough:

> "The interest of blacks in achieving racial equality will be accommodated
> only when it converges with the interests of whites. However, the
> fourteenth amendment, standing alone, will not authorize a judicial
> remedy providing effective racial equality for blacks where the remedy
> sought threatens the superior societal status of middle and upper class
> whites."[18]

---

[14] *ibid*.

[15] D. Bell, *And We Are Not Saved: The Elusive Quest for Racial Justice* (Basic Books, New York, 1987).

[16] D. Bell, "The Supreme Court, 1984 Term—Foreword: The Civil Rights Chronicles" (1985) 99 *Harvard Law Review* 4.

[17] D. Bell, *And We Are Not Saved*, pp.140–161. See also R. Delgado, "Derrick Bell and the Ideology of Racial Reform" (1988) 97 *Yale Law Journal* 923, and D. Bell, *Afrolantica Legacies* (Third World Press, Chicago, 1998).

[18] D. Bell, "Brown v Board of Education and the Interest-Convergence Dilemma", at 523.

Alan Freeman and the "Victim" and "Perpetrator" Perspectives

Like Derrick Bell, Alan Freeman was one of the earliest proponents of CLS, and had attended the first Critical Legal Studies Conference in Madison in 1977.[19] Freeman's methodological breakthrough came to the fore in an article published in 1978 in the *Minnesota Law Review*.[20] That article has been described as having "effectively contrasted the 'victim' and the 'perpetrator' perspectives on civil rights, the one emphasizing the hurt that comes from a thousand, nameless cuts and the other emphasizing causation and individual responsibility for individual acts".[21] Alan Freeman's principal argument was that the law as such employs tools that while seemingly neutral in nature and function result in racially weighted outcomes and are, therefore, ideologically potent. In Freeman's eyes, going through the case law, there were two models or "interwoven themes" of anti-discrimination law:

> "I began to see antidiscrimination law as two interwoven themes, which I then called the 'structural' and the 'individualistic' models. The structural model focused on history, institutions, groups and results, concentrating on issues of effect rather than ones of subjective intent. The individualistic model was abstract, personalized, seemingly ahistorical ... and as preoccupied with intent as it was indifferent to results. ... My conclusion was that the two models would necessarily clash over the question of affirmative action."[22]

According to the structural model then, victims of racism live in a world characterized by inequality, in the material conditions of life and opportunities for advancement. This "victim" perspective resides in a different world from that of the individualistic model, which emphasises instead a formal understanding of the principle of anti-discrimination in legal doctrine. The anti-discrimination principle is triggered by particular factual decisions wherein

---

[19] Speaking of that experience, Freeman wrote in 1988: "I went back to Minnesota in such a blaze of excitement that I told the driver of the taxi I took from the airport all about the event. He got so excited that we met for lunch to talk more two weeks later"; "Racism, Rights and the Quest for Equality of Opportunity: A Critical Legal Essay" (1988) 23 *Harvard Civil Rights—Civil Liberties Law Review* 295 at 313–314.

[20] A. Freeman, "Legitimizing Racial Discrimination Through Antidiscrimination Law: A Critical Review of Supreme Court Doctrine" (1978) 62 *Minnesota Law Review* 1049.

[21] J.H. Schlegel, "Alan and I: Of Community, Critical Legal Studies and All That" (1996) 44 *Buffalo Law Review* 636 at 643.

[22] A. Freeman, "Racism, Rights and the Quest for Equality of Opportunity", at 310–311.

harmful race-based decisions are made and which actually lead to intended harm, loss or injury. This formal model, characteristic of formal legal doctrine, is ultimately indifferent to the objective life conditions of an entire "victim" class. For every intended wrong that leads to harm to someone, an entire class of persons is forgotten in the process. According to Freeman, anti-discrimination law promised black plaintiffs redress, but in actually seeking redress plaintiffs will have to face the legal-doctrinal gatekeepers of intent, causation and harm which typify the law's preoccupation with establishing fault or wrongness before proposing a remedy. At this juncture, legal doctrine parts company, according to Freeman, with the larger aspirations of claimants of colour rooted in actual, every day life, the history of racism in America and the fact that the victims belong to an entire class of American citizens. In methodological terms, legal fault is irrelevant to the nature of the plaintiff's case since fault, while capturing the law's formal intentions, fails to encapsulate what the complaint is really (factually and historically) about. The remedies actually sought by plaintiffs of colour resist dissociation with black history. In this way, Freeman unpacks the meaning of legal campaigns against racism and the court cases and case law they produce. According to Freeman, anti-discrimination law, formally understood, legitimises racism. By focusing on the facts of individual cases, the law ignores a broader and older problem than that presented by the particular case involving the particular complaint of the individual plaintiff.

The "victim" perspective became, for Freeman, a normative device, much like a compass, intended to point the way to what *should* be the case from the victim's perspective, not what *is* the case from the "perpetrator's" perspective. It resists unifying monolithic standards of meaning, as if there was only one (true) way of understanding "what is going on" (*i.e.* the formal understanding of anti-discrimination law). In this way Freeman enacts, against the celebration of the unifying tendencies of monotheistic truth, a counter-celebration of a centripetal counter-force. This counter-force is characterised by the multitude of inter-subjective truths that could serve to put the formal understanding of discrimination, based on intent, fault and causation to a higher test. Freeman believes that exploring personally-held subjective beliefs could reveal flaws in dominant social assumptions.

The enormous transformative power of this victim/perpetrator distinction has since come to exercise a strong influence on the developing self-confidence of voice of colour scholarship. A little more needs to be said, at this juncture, of the *original* point of Alan Freeman's critique. Freeman eventually argued against rights to affirmative action, with the result that he has been criticised, almost denied his place, by some in the CRT movement, notably (as will be seen below) by Kimberlé Crenshaw. John Henry Schlegel explains of Freeman:

> "In reasonably short order he concluded that affirmative action had to go. Law needed the victim's perspective; it did not need to institutionalize,

much less expand, victimization. .... For Alan rights were hollow because the indeterminacy of their verbal formulation allowed community understandings of meaning to shape both application and enforcement. *That was the point of his anti-discrimination piece; racial discrimination could be legitimated in the act of enforcing anti-discrimination law.*"[23]

There are three reasons for Freeman's rejection of affirmative action. First, Freeman believes that what you gain by asserting your rights can also be taken away by someone else asserting theirs. Rights are not intrinsically weighted, in other words, in favour of progressive causes. Democrats in the US have since realised this when Election 2000 resulted in a Republican-appointed Supreme Court majority deciding in favour of a Republican Presidency. Second, rights talk is strategically advantageous as a political tool, particularly as political rhetoric to galvanise participants together towards mutual causes, but this is something quite different from the inner logic of rights as legal concepts. Freeman holds, going back to his first point, that this inner logic is—in functional terms—politically unpredictable. Third, from the viewpoint of a materialist analysis, there is no principled reason to distinguish racial affiliation in addressing the social problem of material disadvantage, or to directly identify race with economic status or function.

Thus Crenshaw misses the mark in criticising Freeman for down-playing the importance of rights to blacks. Freeman admitted that real changes have occurred:

"Slavery was abolished, and formal apartheid has been dismantled. These changes are most evident in public accommodations and voting. Repression through terror, in the form of lynchings and the like, has been largely curbed as well. ... *Yet, although these changes were secured by the granting of 'rights', the promise of the changes in law have been contained and undercut by the very same rights rhetoric ...*".[24]

Freeman also argued that the view that rights are a strategic necessity in the black civil rights struggle only emphasises the experience of rights struggles, but not something in the essential nature or logic of legal rights as such:

"I believe that the manipulability of rights, and their consequent ideological character, does matter and may endanger, rather than sustain, the quest for substantive social justice ... There is, however, a discernible

---

[23] J.H. Schlegel, "Alan and I", at 644–645 (emphasis added).

[24] A. Freeman, "Racism, Rights and the Quest for Equality of Opportunity", at 328 (emphasis added).

difference between the felt authenticity of communal struggle for rights, and defensive complacency about the functional utility of rights."[25]

The main difficulty that some CRT proponents have with Freeman's analysis is precisely that he offered a deeper explanation of racism that is not in itself race-based, but is based instead on traditional class or materialist analysis. According to this deeper explanation, talk of equal rights is part of an overarching liberal rights ideology no different from that which preserves the perpetrator perspective in respect of blacks, but which, in the case of disadvantaged whites, preserves instead an impression of equality between whites irrespective of class. According to this analysis, the reason for a perceived white hostility to affirmative action and other remedial policies in favour of blacks is that such policies threaten the impression of legal equality thus created.[26]

Richard Delgado and "White Scholarship"

Richard Delgado's work has been described (by Bell) as "an intellectual hand grenade, tossed over the wall of the establishment as a form of academic protest".[27] The difficulty faced by CRT at the outset was the psychological obstacle created by the very subject in question; namely, rejecting the purported neutrality or objectivity of legal doctrine and scholarship. The notion of a distinct intra-group subjective consciousness as having relevance to the formation and application of legal doctrine and scholarship remains hotly contested. CRT, to this extent, was handicapped at the outset by the same difficulty faced by proponents of a feminist jurisprudence during the 1980s, which was the idea of a uniquely group-based experiential discourse in legal scholarship and criticism. The history of progressive legal thought has been characterised by an iron law requiring consciousness-raising as the first stage to progressive thought and action. For Delgado, the first challenge early on was therefore to overcome the mental obstacle referred to above and to show that the law story-telling enterprise (or "narrative jurisprudence") of subjective

---

[25] *ibid.*, at 335.

[26] See A. Freeman, "Antidiscrimination Law from 1954 to 1989: Uncertainty, Contradiction, Rationalization, Denial" in *The Politics of Law: A Progressive Critique* (D. Kairys ed., 3rd ed., Basic Books, New York, 1998), p.285. Freeman is certainly not alone in this; see for example D. Bell, *Faces at the Bottom of the Well*, p.39, saying that, "The debilitating effects of poverty know no color line."

[27] R. Delgado, "The Imperial Scholar Revisited: How To Marginalize Outsider Writing, Ten Years Later" (1992) 140 *University of Pennsylvania Law Review* 1349 at 1349 (acknowledging how Bell had characterised Delgado's previous article; citing J. Wiener, "Law Profs Fight the Power" (1989) 249 *Nation* 246 at 246).

experiences actually encountered in the societal milieu presents a pertinent form of sociological evidence as to what is really going on with the groups seeking empowerment in the new forms of legal discourse (or more simply, those seeking to change "everyday law-talk").

Delgado's message, published in 1984, rested on a survey of civil rights scholarship and an epistemic universe of an "inner circle" of white "Imperial Scholars" as evinced in the intellectual preoccupations and orientations of their scholarly writings.[28] Delgado sought to show that this inner circle of 26 white civil rights professors in elite schools who published their work in the best law reviews, tended to focus on issues and remedies that failed to account for what black scholars, in their actual historical experiences, would have thought instead to have been more important and which they would want to talk and know about. Delgado characterises this as a kind of latter-day "minstrel show", and observes that the manner in which these inner circle scholars cross-cite each other "is something like an elaborate minuet".[29]

The desire of black Americans, however, is for specific forms of legal knowledge that are subjectively informed by their own historical experiences. There was also no reason to suppose that they were somehow incapable or less competent since black scholars have no difficulty publishing in mainstream legal subjects and on non-race-related issues. For example, concern with reparations for the devastating history of black people would reject the propriety of the kinds of moral-political justifications that these inner circle scholars would seek for addressing the concerns of blacks. The two principal justifications proposed by the inner circle scholars were a utilitarian argument (that addressing black concerns is conducive to the general welfare of all in society) and a distributive justice argument (that there are adequate material benefits that could be distributed to address black concerns).

According to Delgado, neither utilitarianism nor distributive justice is forward-looking by nature in their prescriptions, and neither would therefore address the past. Black people *are* concerned with the past. The sorts of justifications offered by these inner circle scholars obfuscate that simple fact. If black people were, however, to be given their rightful place in the academic hierarchy, their scholarship would be tuned to entirely different concerns. Delgado, revisiting his principal arguments 10 years later, says:

"I argued that the exclusion of minority scholars' writings about key issues of race law caused the literature dealing with race, racism, and American law to be blunted, skewed, and riddled with omissions. Among

---

[28] R. Delgado, "The Imperial Scholar: Reflections on a Review of Civil Rights Literature" (1984) 132 *University of Pennsylvania Law Review* 561.
[29] *ibid.*, at 563.

the reasons for the curious citation practices I discovered were (1) the mistaken belief that minority authors who write about racial issues are not objective, (2) the mainstream writers' need to remain in control, thus ensuring that legal change does not occur too quickly, and (3) the sense of personal satisfaction resulting from being at the forefront of a powerful social movement."[30]

These highlight a lack of objectivity on the part of mainstream scholars, as reflected in the case of inner circle scholars. Delgado sought to establish—after the intervening decade during which minority scholars had gained a firmer foothold in legal academia—that many of his assertions seem commonplace today. What is noteworthy is that mainstream scholars have demonstrated a wide range of reactions to the minority scholarship that had emerged during the intervening period. This, according to Delgado, includes ways of limiting and moderating the impact of CRT, although there are those who may be counted as having been "converted".

Today, many CRT scholars take for granted the fact that the message has been put across, is not only accepted but common-place, and thus that the minstrel show era is over. To some of them, black issues should be addressed by black people, and others should just move along. However, as we will see below, scholars like Randall Kennedy have voiced opposition to the *a priori* exclusion of white scholars from race scholarship on the basis of a perceived lack of racial status.

Decoding (the Ideology of) Racism Beyond Material Poverty: Kimberlé Crenshaw

One of CRT's most influential founding theorists who stood atop the gains made in the early scholarship of Bell and Freeman, and who saw it as high time to push ahead and *beyond* in the post-minstrel show phase is Kimberlé Crenshaw. Her most important article yet was published in 1988 in the *Harvard Law Review*.[31] In it, Crenshaw's principal message, unlike that of Bell and Freeman, is not directed at the material disadvantages of blacks generally, but at racism itself as ideology. Unlike Delgado's famous contribution above, she is also not as much concerned with the academic and scholarly agenda, or the scholarly politics, as she is with the larger picture. Her concern is with "what is believed about Black Americans, not what Black Americans believe".[32]

---

[30] R. Delgado, "The Imperial Scholar Revisited", at 1349–1350.
[31] K. Crenshaw, "Race, Reform, and Retrenchment: Transformation and Legitimation in Antidiscrimination Law" (1988) 101 *Harvard Law Review* 1331.
[32] *ibid.*, at 1358.

The principal task for black Americans is to deconstruct and better understand what black American identity consists of when viewed from without by other (white) Americans. She illustrates this with a sequence of binary oppositions that go towards such an external characterisation of black identity: "industrious/ lazy", "intelligent/unintelligent", "moral/immoral", "knowledgeable/ignorant", "enabling culture/disabling culture", "law-abiding/criminal", "responsible/ shiftless", "virtuous or pious/lascivious". White images are typified by an image of whites as possessing knowledge, an enabling culture, intelligence, moral rectitude, a responsible nature, and virtue or piety as opposed to the image of blacks which is typified by laziness, a lack of intelligence, immorality, ignorance, a disabling culture, criminality, "shiftlessness" and lasciviousness.[33] More importantly, these images are shared both by the dominant majority and the dominated minority, as general subjective beliefs and also in a manner that is backed by the state coercive apparatus. According to Crenshaw, the Reagan Administration's notion of a "formalistic, color-blind view of civil rights that had developed in the neoconservative 'think tanks' during the 1970's",[34] or what Duncan Kennedy has called "colorblind meritocratic fundamentalism",[35] must be debunked as they serve to conceal the more subtle and pervasive influence of racism.

Crenshaw does not believe—as proponents of CLS generally do—that rights and talk of rights are merely part of a liberal corrosive ideology that undermine social solidarity by enacting ring-fences around individuals in society.[36] According to Crenshaw, rights and rights-talk are, on the contrary, tools that have presented a strategic advantage to black Americans in the civil rights struggle, and which explain how blacks have come this far in the first place. As Crenshaw puts it:

> "Because Blacks were challenging their exclusion from political soci-
> ety, the only claims that were likely to achieve recognition were those
> that reflected American society's institutional logic: legal rights ideol-
> ogy. Articulating their formal demands through legal rights ideology,
> civil rights protestors exposed a series of contradictions. … Rather than
> using the contradictions to suggest that American citizenship was itself
> illegitimate or false, civil rights protestors proceeded as if American citi-
> zenship were real, and demanded to exercise the 'rights' that citizenship

---

[33] *ibid.*, at 1373.

[34] *ibid.*, at 1337.

[35] D. Kennedy, "A Cultural Pluralist Case for Affirmative Action in Legal Academia" (1990) *Duke Law Journal* 705 at 705, 726–727.

[36] M. Tushnet, "An Essay on Rights" (1984) 62 *Texas Law Review* 1363 at 1371– 1382.

entailed. ... [M]aterial advancement alone would be insufficient to eliminate racism."[37]

Crenshaw also attacks, in the same vein, Freeman's critique of the ideology of
rights as the reason for hostility amongst whites to affirmative action policies.
According to Crenshaw, "Freeman argues that affirmative action and other
remedial programs conflicted with beliefs in formal equality, vested rights,
and equal opportunity. Thus the preservation of these myths compelled the
rejection of these remedies, lest whites and people of color discover that these
myths were contingent ideas and thus undermine their beliefs in the legitimacy
of American class structure."[38] Crenshaw argues instead that none of this is
able to explain the factor of race itself, and racism, as part of the motivation
for white hostility, for as she says: "This race-specific explanation of affirmative
action retrenchment is exactly what Freeman's legitimation explanation fails
to analyze adequately."[39]

Getting Seriously Epistemic: Mari Matsuda and the Case for Building an Intra-Disciplinary Coalition in Critical Legal Scholarship

Pushing race law forward and setting the agenda for race law is but half the
battle. There remains the basic issue which Delgado had originally grappled
with, which is whether knowledge-production on race law by minority scholars
is in some way epistemically superior. The most powerful and sustained
argument in this respect is Mari Matsuda's 1987 article in the *Harvard Civil
Rights-Civil Liberties Law Review*.[40] Matsuda, the first Asian American female
tenured law professor in the US, teaches at Georgetown University Law Centre.
She argues for what has come to be known as the "racial standing thesis" (*i.e.*
that minorities are in a privileged position to speak about anti-discrimination
and race issues):

> "[T]hose who have experienced discrimination speak with a special voice
> to which we should listen. Looking to the bottom—adopting the
> perspective of those who have seen and felt the falsity of the liberal
> promise—can assist critical scholars in the task of fathoming the
> phenomenology of law and defining the elements of justice."[41]

---

[37] K. Crenshaw, "Race, Reform and Retrenchment", at 1368.
[38] *ibid.*, at 1361.
[39] *ibid.*, at 1362–1363.
[40] M. Matsuda, "Looking to the Bottom: Critical Legal Studies and Reparations" (1987)
22 *Harvard Civil Rights—Civil Liberties Law Review* 323.
[41] *ibid.*, at 324.

Matsuda explains further:

> "The imagination of the academic philosopher cannot recreate the experience of life on the bottom. Instead we must look to what Gramsci called 'organic intellectuals', grass roots philosophers who are uniquely able to relate theory to the concrete experience of oppression. ... When notions of right and wrong, justice and injustice, are examined not from an abstract position but from the position of groups who have suffered through history, moral relativism recedes and identifiable normative priorities emerge."[42]

There is a crucial difference, however, between Matsuda's and Crenshaw's prescriptions. Crenshaw rejects the CLS attack on liberal rights, for as we have seen, she accounts for the importance of rights-talk as a strategic necessity in the civil rights movement. Matsuda, on the other hand, seeks to demonstrate why CRT should also appeal to CLS. This suggests that Matsuda is a "bridge" between CLS and CRT. In this regard, Matsuda is less focused on anti-discrimination law as such, as opposed to more seriously methodological concerns about the epistemic foundations of CRT and the ways in which CRT could contribute to the broad question of understanding law, legal consciousness and the politically-charged preferences of liberal law. But her insights cut both ways. Just as CRT should appeal to proponents of CLS, Matsuda also seeks to explain why the empowering message and intellectual strategies of CLS do, and should, matter also to minorities. She writes of CLS:

> "Like a pack of super-termites, these scholars eat away at the trees of legal doctrine and liberal ideals, leaving sawdust in their paths. That they do it so well, and so single-mindedly, is compelling; it suggests that this is what the smartest are doing. Never mind that no one knows what to do with all the sawdust."[43]

As others in the CRT movement have noticed, what is nice about talking to Crits generally is that you do not have to start from scratch and can actually move on straight to a fight in a shorter time. The point is that the different shades of progressive scholarship share that much in common, or as Ronald Dworkin explains it, you need common ground to have a real argument in the first place.[44]

CRT, on the other hand, could provide that which CLS is looking for, rising

---

[42] *ibid.*
[43] *ibid.*, at 330.
[44] R. Dworkin, *Law's Empire* (Fontana, London, 1986), pp.65–68.

above the ruins of liberal legal scholarship and capturing something beyond that which has normative significance and which points the way forward for legal scholarship. Harlon Dalton at Yale writes:

> "[W]hether out of social concern or self-preservation, we learned from the start to harness our brains to the problems of the day. We felt the freedom to play with mind puzzles only after the practical intellectual work of the day was done. ... CLS patriarchs (again with some notable exceptions) feel no need to articulate a positive program, and in some cases glory in the absence of one, whereas people of color cannot be satisfied unless and until a program emerges. Similarly, the quite distinct social circumstance of white males has led to a 'rights critique' that is oblivious to, and potentially disruptive of, the interests of people of color."[45]

Matsuda's message too connects with Delgado's critique of the inner circle in "The Imperial Scholar", and simply redirects Delgado's original critique towards CLS:

> "Critical scholars condemn racism, support affirmative action, and generally adopt the causes of oppressed people throughout the world. It is time to consider extending those commitments to the practice of critical scholarship and the development of theory. Such an extension requires deliberate efforts to read and cite the work of minority scholars within and without the law, to consider the intellectual history of non-white America ...".[46]

She then proceeds to show how the principal methods and messages that characterise CLS' trashing of liberal legal scholarship connect and become informed by the insights of CRT, and how CRT therefore points the otherwise elusive way forward towards "reconstruction post-deconstruction". CRT puts flesh on the CLS incoherence thesis, wherein legal doctrinal enquiry cannot be made to produce a single, technically correct, legal solution to legal problems.[47]

According to Matsuda, the adaptative, transformative insights of black culture, a paradigm example of the struggle for American equality, in the appropriation of everyday meaning, and through musical and literary expression

---

[45] H. Dalton, "The Clouded Prism" (1987) 22 *Harvard Civil Rights—Civil Liberties Law Review* 435 at 440.

[46] M. Matsuda, "Looking to the Bottom", at 331.

[47] R. Unger, "The Critical Legal Studies Movement" (1983) 96 *Harvard Law Review* 563.

as well as in speech, coupled with the process of turning the mind inwards, so to speak, towards uncovering these appropriations themselves in furthering more music, literature, speech and other forms of cultural and political expression, became a source of social consciousness and activism for blacks. CLS too is familiar with these acts and processes of borrowing and adaptation.[48] As Mari Matsuda puts it, however: "Those who lack material wealth or political power still have access to thought and language, and their development of those tools will differ from that of the more privileged."[49] Music and speech, and even literature or poetry, are near-universally accessible media forms through which people and groups that are class and materially disadvantaged, and disempowered, can have access to socially-transformative radical thought. Progressive transformative social thought, writing and tunes permeate through the grassroots of popular culture through the co-optation of the various means of cultural expression, and the unremitting adaptation and radical transformation of all available communicative forms.[50] Thus co-optation and adaptative transformation occurred also in respect of the co-optation of "legal doctrine, legal ideals and liberal theory in the struggle against racism".[51]

The Exclusionary Thesis

To other CRT proponents, the flip-side is more important. Comparable to Thelonius Monk's invention of be-bop as an intended jazz form that could not be commodified by White America,[52] Harlon Dalton has observed a self-imposed distance of CRT from CLS, emphasising the serious practical reform programme of CRT. Thus Bell's, Delgado's and Matsuda's insights about racial-hierarchical segregation in legal scholarship are no longer mere insights about creatures of inner-circle complacency, but have become a priority for voice of colour scholarship. Speaking of the "black, brown, red, and yellow folks who have circled around CLS' door in fluctuating numbers for the last ten years", Dalton says proponents of CRT are

> "always invited in for tea, but rarely invited to stay for supper, lest we use the wrong intellectual fork. No matter how smart or bookish we were ... [w]e learned about injustice, social cruelty, political hypocrisy and sanctioned terrorism from the mouths of our mothers and fathers and from our very own experiences. Books sometimes confirmed that

---

[48] H. Dalton, "Clouded Prism", at 444–445; P. Gabel and D. Kennedy, "Roll Over Beethoven" (1984) 36 *Stanford Law Review* 1.
[49] M. Matsuda, "Looking to the Bottom", at 335.
[50] *ibid.*, at 337.
[51] *ibid.*, at 338.
[52] *ibid.*, at 336–337.

reality; more often they misrepresented or were indifferent to our reality. … [W]e learned … as a simple fact of life, that … 'the life of the mind' as an overriding and singular commitment was not possible."[53]

In this way, CRT proponents like Dalton see CLS as a purely intellectual, "Ivory Tower" exercise with no serious practical aspirations or coherent programme for reform. His passing remarks of CLS proponents as the kind of people who stick to the slogan "It don't mean a thing if it ain't got that swing" paired with what he calls a "sonata form as an all constraining way [of legal writing]" suggest that he considers that CLS lacks seriousness.[54] Dalton's view is reminiscent of Delgado's famous line about "a dozen white, male writers who comment on, take polite issue with, extol, criticize and expand on each other's ideas".[55] Matsuda too found evidence of what she calls "segregated scholarship".[56] These sentiments amount to what is known as CRT's "exclusionary thesis", which takes the idea of racial standing even further. Not only can those who have experienced oppression speak with insight, but they are also in a *better* position to know what ought to be done. The exclusionary and racial standing theses, as we shall see below, lie at the bottom of the controversy over racial critiques of law or the so-called racial critiques debate.

The idea of a serious practical programme as CRT's ultimate justification also requires special attention as it dovetails with CRT's roots in anti-discrimination law and the legal campaign for affirmative action characteristic of the early writings of Bell and Freeman. They combine to forge CRT not only as either a theory or a distinct form of legal practice, but as a mutually reinforcing combination of theory and practice—so-called critical race *praxis*.

3. CRITICISMS AND ASSESSMENT

The Liberal Retort: Randall Kennedy and the "Racial Critiques" Debate

Harvard Law School professor, Randall Kennedy, takes issue with CRT and particularly its exclusionary and racial standing theses. In "Racial Critiques of Legal Academia", published in the *Harvard Law Review* in 1989,[57] Kennedy

---

[53] H. Dalton, "Clouded Prism", at 440–441.

[54] *ibid.*, at 441.

[55] R. Delgado, "Imperial Scholar", at 563.

[56] M. Matsuda, "Affirmative Action and Legal Knowledge: Planting Seeds in Plowed-Up Ground" (1988) 11 *Harvard Women's Law Journal* 1 at 2–4 (n.12).

[57] R. Kennedy, "Racial Critiques of Legal Academia" (1989) 102 *Harvard Law Review* 1745.

criticises Bell, Delgado and Matsuda. According to Kennedy, Bell, for example, does not go far enough in distinguishing situations where the facts may evince either that there are not enough blacks who could occupy the role of scholars with racial standing through shortage and through actual, deliberate discrimination. Since both are possibilities, it would be insufficient to draw any fast conclusions as to causes since sheer shortage of numbers could equally be suggested by our intuition. He charges that Bell therefore relies on mere conviction. Similar "micro-criticisms" are directed at Matsuda and Delgado.

But Kennedy's more fundamental objection is with the two notions of racial standing and race-based exclusion. At heart, Kennedy's point is that the identification of race with meritorious scholarship is a highly unstable formula. According to Kennedy, Delgado speaks of the *merits* (presumably by some objective measure or standard) of voice of colour scholarship. However, inner circle scholarship is assumed deficient in Delgado's account not because such scholarship is unmeritorious by some objective measure or standard, but because inner circle scholarship *is white* (*i.e.* the criterion itself is race here, not merit). According to Kennedy, Bell, Delgado and Matsuda are all engaging in another version of racial stereotyping, particularly in treating race in essentialist terms:

> "A substantive conception of blackness is better than the tautological conception. It differentiates the status of racial background from the characteristics that define 'blackness' as an idea, sensibility, or point of view. It affirms the possibility of black scholars thinking 'white' and white scholars thinking 'black'. ... Instead of referring to a 'black' perspective, we should articulate the substantive content of the perspectives to which we refer."[58]

In short, Kennedy argues that, for Bell, Delgado, and Matsuda, merit must still count for something, but if race is to become the criterion for scholarship instead, the notion of race itself is equally if not more problematic than a merit-based criterion:

> "There are many types of classification that negate individual identity, achievement, and dignity. But racial classification has come to be viewed as paradigmatically offensive to individuality ... [T]he use of race as a proxy is specially disfavored because, even when relatively accurate as a signifier of the trait sought to be identified, racial proxies are especially prone to misuse."[59]

---

[58] *ibid.*, at 1803.
[59] *ibid.*, at 1794.

According to Kennedy then, contrary to our everyday experiences race cannot separate the wheat from the chaff since race in no way resembles an objective measure:

> "Evaluative judgments linked to the race of authors should be seen as illegitimate if the purpose of evaluation is to reach a judgment about a given piece of work. ... [T]here is no reason to rely on such a proxy because there exists at hand the most probative evidence imaginable— the work itself."[60]

White scholars like Alan Freeman, for example, would not have qualified under the racial standing thesis.[61]

Race Narrative at Jurisprudence's End

Today Anglo-American legal scholarship has, for the most part, accepted that we are not warranted in taking purportedly authoritative, even formal, explanations of the law at face value. Competing explanations of social, artistic, historical, literary and other human phenomena play a role in the overall process of construing truth and meaning, be it in a realm where questions of artistic worth matter, or our realm in which getting to grips with questions about the law matters.

In this context, Randall Kennedy's argument is best understood as a plea that race *should not* matter from the outset, even if it *does*. Legal scholarship should still *aspire* towards objectivity, and principled moral-political reasoning, even if we are given towards scepticism of such claims to objectivity and neutral principle wherever we find them. The principal difficulty in all this is that this is what masks the reality of neutral legal doctrine. As Neil Gotanda has argued, *non-recognition* of racial distinctions as a fundamental tenet of legal-doctrinal faith is hugely different from the *absence* of perception or cognition of such racial differences. Legal colour-blindness is not tantamount to medical colour-blindness. Legal colour-blindness involves two-steps, not one. The first step involves actual cognition of what it is that ought to be discounted (*i.e.* racial distinctiveness), and the second step involves the

---

[60] *ibid.*, at 1797–1798. For Delgado's reply, for example, see R. Delgado, "When a Story is Just a Story: Does Voice Really Matter?" (1990) 76 *Virginia Law Review* 95. For another critical response, see L.G. Espinoza, "Masks and Other Disguises: Exposing Legal Academia" (1990) 103 *Harvard Law Review* 1878, at 1885–86. For support of Kennedy, see L. Cohen, "A Different Black Voice in Legal Scholarship" (1992) 37 *New York Law School Law Review* 322.

[61] See D. Kennedy, "Racial Critiques", at 1801.

suppression of that perception. Proponents of CRT argue that the second step does not extinguish the first, and view the relationship between the two-steps as one of contradiction.[62]

There is a further practical difficulty that should, first, be overcome; namely, that we need a debate on CRT beyond that engendered by Randall Kennedy's focus on CRT's critique of legal academia, but in a similarly rigorous fashion. We need a similarly rigorous debate on CRT's perspectives concerning the impact of race, class and poverty on issues like discrimination, affirmative action, criminal justice, immigration and speech.

Overcoming the Silence of the Racial Critiques Debate

Just like the sensationalism that proponents and practitioners of CRT seem to court—such as Harlon Dalton quoting Martin Luther King as saying that you would still call a black person with a Ph.D a "nigger"—what outsiders and critics see when they look at CRT is equally sensationalised if access is gained through the eyes of a conservative critic. Worse still is if CRT were to continue to suffer from a general lack of rigorous academic discussion on its merits. What CRT has had to say has been met, in comparison with what CLS has had to say, with relative silence.[63] The racial standing and exclusion theses themselves may tend to support such an outcome. This is bad for CRT since silence as a retort is the most powerful critical weapon available in the academic armoury:

> "Unlike Critical Legal Studies, which provoked a firestorm of protest at Harvard and enormous debate in the law reviews, race and feminist theory have achieved their position of dominance with little argument: their practitioners wear the impregnable mantle of victimhood. Few professors are willing to question publicly the worth of the first-person narrative movement ...".[64]

What is even more troubling is that CRT, in also having turned much of its attention to the regulation of hate speech, is itself consciously sensitive to what is perceived to be racist discourse. Its greatest success in practice has been the imposition, in conjunction with feminism, of speech codes in workplaces beyond the academy to combat speech and forms of speech that

---

[62] N. Gotanda, "A Critique of 'Our Constitution is Color-Blind'" (1991) 44 *Stanford Law Review* 1.

[63] See, however, the collection of essays in the Colloquy on "Responses to Randall Kennedy's Racial Critiques of Legal Academia" in the 1990 issue of the *Harvard Law Review*.

[64] H. MacDonald, *op. cit.*

denigrate or otherwise portray racial and sexual minorities in an ill-light. This may have the side-effect of curtailing robust debate on the merits of CRT. Coupled with overt and predominant academic silence in mainstream academic discourse, there is a risk of a certain amount of intellectual inbreeding on the part of CRT. This is not, however, something that we can attribute wholly to CRT itself. An example would be useful here.

According to Derrick Bell's critique, the advancement of the cause of blacks has been accommodation to the extent that this converges with the interests of the American mainstream. Recently, Mary Dudziak produced voluminous primary evidence in support of Bell's thesis, showing that the amelioration of the plight of black Americans had become United States policy during the Cold War because of the adverse reaction of other countries towards the treatment of black Americans, particularly in the face of the egalitarian promises of the erstwhile Soviet Union. However, critics of America's treatment of the black minority also faced an official counter-offensive in the form of counter-intelligence designed to discredit these critics. This is orthodox history, not conspiracy theory.[65] It is perhaps unsurprising then that minorities today are liable to take even well-intentioned but critical academic debate of progressive scholarship as part of a larger hostile conspiracy.

The consequence of this is a dual challenge: for minority scholars who propound the message of CRT on the one hand, and their real or potential critics on the other hand. While such critics should not deny the presence of CRT through their own silence, proponents of CRT cannot deny such critics their reactions either.

From Movement to School?

Does CRT have the potential to become a universally-appealing school of legal thought? Derrick Bell, perhaps more so than any other, remains the prime exemplar of what CRT stands for today. Strong elements of traditional Marxist political-economic analysis are present in Bell's analysis where he argues that slave holders "appealed to working-class whites, urging that because they were both white, they had to stand together against the threat of slave revolts or escapes".[66] There is also the strong presence of analytical interest in the notion

---

[65] M.L. Dudziak, *Cold War Civil Rights – Race and the Image of American Democracy* (Princeton University Press, Princeton, 2000); T. Borstelmann, *The Cold War and the Color Line* (Harvard University Press, Cambridge, Mass., 2001). See also R. Delgado, "Explaining the Rise And Fall of African-American Fortunes—Interest Convergence and Civil Rights Gains" (2002) 37 *Harvard Civil Rights—Civil Liberties Law Review* 369 (reviewing Dudziak).

[66] D. Bell, *Afrolantica Legacies*, p.12.

of "property in race"; namely, "whiteness" as a species of legal property right.[67] In addition to this materialist account, race as a fetter on the imagination of minorities and a weapon for their continued subordination remains at the forefront of Bell's analysis without going so far as to require racial standing, or to impose the exclusionary thesis.[68] Bell discusses, for example, the role of race as a bond between immigrants in the construction of American identity, helping them "acculturate and assimilate by inculcating a nationalism whose common theme was the disparagement of blacks, rather than uniting across racial lines to resist the exploitation and deprivation that do not respect any color line".[69] He has also described his seminal law school text, *Race, Racism and American Law*,[70] for example, as a book that would "treat discrimination as the evil it is rather than a subject that would be examined 'neutrally'",[71] and he describes race in the latest edition as "an indeterminate social construct that is continually reinvented and manipulated to maintain domination and enhance white privilege".[72]

One question is whether such a combination of neo-Marxist analysis coupled with the deconstruction of race as ideology could have a wider significance than that which it has for the American experience. To do so, CRT may have to amount to more than the two-pronged intellectual attack, that is, "a race intervention into Left (CLS) discourse, and ... a left intervention into liberal, civil rights discourse".[73] The clues to this lie in CRT's ability to encompass the unique concerns of American minorities other than blacks beyond the strategic appeal of the practical politics of racial coalition-building.

---

[67] *ibid.*, p.9, citing also Cheryl Harris' formidable article on "Whiteness as Property" (1993) 106 *Harvard Law Review* 1707 at 1713. See further D. Bell, "Getting Beyond Property in Race" (1999) 1 *Washington University Journal of Law and Policy* 27.

[68] His remark of Alan Freeman as an "inverse oreo"—black inside, white outside—as reported by Schlegel was undoubtedly a high compliment; J.H. Schlegel, *op. cit.*, at 643. In any event, I have found no evidence of Bell advocating the racial standing and exclusion theses as such.

[69] D. Bell, *Afrolantica Legacies*, p.12.

[70] D. Bell, *Race, Racism and American Law* (Little, Brown, Boston, 1973). Alan Freeman, in his review of the second edition (of 1981), described the book as taking "serious issue" with the "liberal myth of the civil rights crusade as a long, slow but always upward pull ... that must ... end in full enjoyment by blacks of all rights and privileges of citizenship enjoyed by whites"; A. Freeman, "Race and Class: The Dilemma of Liberal Reform" (1981) 90 *Yale Law Journal* 1880 at 1883.

[71] D. Bell, *Afrolantica Legacies*, p.112.

[72] D. Bell, *Race, Racism and American Law* (4th ed., Aspen, New York, 2000), p.9. See also the review by Professor Harold Mcdougall of Howard University Law School: "For Critical Race Practitioners: Race, Racism and American Law (4th ed.) by Derrick A. Bell, Jr." (2002) 46 *Howard Law Journal* 1.

[73] S. Cho and R. Westley, *op. cit.*, at 1394.

A common thread in the "other non-white" American experience (with the exception of Native Americans) is that the race issue is coupled with an issue concerning their foreignness or status as immigrants or sojourners. According to Neil Gotanda:

> "In the last two decades, the treatment of Other non-Whites has grown from a regional issue to a divisive national issue. Japanese- and Chinese-Americans have played a significant role in the legal clarification of the status of Other non-Whites. ... Most important in this development has been the persistence of the view that even American-born non-Whites were somehow 'foreign'. This undeserved stigma became, and may remain, an unarticulated basis for the legal treatment of these groups, leading to unfair and often shocking consequences."[74]

The situation of such minorities has until recently been explored only by analogy with the black American experience. This is the critique of the "black/white" binary paradigm by other non-white scholars who, instead, pursue a more textured, overlapping and cross-cutting method of "racial differentialisation".[75] Against this, black CRT proponents like Angela Harris have floated a thesis of "black exceptionalism", which argues for the centrality of the African American experience.[76] However, the situation of Latinos and Asian Americans are as distinctive, just as the Irish-American[77] and Native American[78]

---

[74] N. Gotanda, "Other non-Whites in American Legal History: A Review of Justice at War" (1985) 85 *Columbia Law Review* 1186 at 1188.

[75] See J.F. Perea, "The Black/White Binary Paradigm of Race" (1997) 85 *California Law Review* 1213. See also L. Cao, "The Diaspora of Ethnic Economies: Beyond the Pale?" (2003) 44 *William and Mary Law Review* 1521 at 1536.

[76] L. Espinoza and A.P. Harris, "Embracing the Tar-Baby: Lat Crit Theory and the Sticky Mess of Race" (1997) 85 *California Law Review* 1585. To which Espinoza replied politely that minorities should perhaps focus on their shared experience of racism instead (the article took the form of an exchange).

[77] As Emily Field van Tassel puts it: "Vilified, segregated, excluded, and castigated, the 'paddy' was believed to be an inferior race. 'Bestial', 'simian', 'savage' and 'wild' were descriptions repeatedly applied to the Irish immigrant, who was ridiculed as a 'nigger' turned inside out. The connections drawn between blacks and Irish did not always favor the Irish"; "'Only the Law Would Rule Between Us': Antimiscegenation, the Moral Economy of Dependency, and the Debate over Rights after the Civil War" (1995) 70 *Chicago-Kent Law Review* 873.

[78] See R.A. Williams Jr., "Documents of Barbarism: The Contemporary Legacy of European Racism and Colonialism in the Narrative Traditions of Federal Indian Law" (1989) 31 *Arizona Law Review* 237 and R.A. Williams Jr., "Vampires Anonymous and Critical Race Practice" (1997) 95 *Michigan Law Review* 741 (an honest appraisal of the contemporary academic politics of law school tenure, and in any case the most brilliantly entertaining law review article ever written).

experiences are undeniable, and equally distinctive in their own ways, regardless of how distinctive the black experience has also been. The distinctiveness of the immigrant minority experience, for example, has prompted Robert Chang to call for the study of the immigrant identity as a separate analytic category, such that: "The immigrant would operate as a cognizable legal subject whose immigrant status is the relevant unit on which discrimination operates, and which, necessarily, requires legal remediation to act also upon that immigrant identity aspect".[79]

This unique *"other"* non-white, in this case Asian American, experience is illustrated in one of the most unworthy and subsequently well-publicised episodes in the history of the American Supreme Court. The internment of Japanese Americans during the Second World War in the famous cases of *Korematsu v US*,[80] *Hirabayashi v US*[81] and *Yasui v US*[82] was, at the same time, not unique to the Japanese experience, but one involving the persistent association of "foreignness".[83]

Gotanda cites, amongst others, the 1854 Californian case of *People v Hall*, a case that involved the question of whether a Chinese person could testify against a white person where the California statute of 1850 required that "no Black, or Mulatto person, or Indian shall be allowed to give evidence in favor of, or against, a White man". The California Supreme Court construed this provision to include Chinese within the category "Indian", and referred to:

> "The anomalous spectacle of a distinct people, living in our community, recognizing no laws of this State except through necessity, bringing with them their prejudices and national feuds, in which they indulge in open violation of law; whose mendacity is proverbial; a race of people whom nature has marked as inferior, and who are incapable of progress or intellectual development beyond a certain point, as their history has shown; differing in language, opinions, color, and physical conformation; between whom and ourselves nature has placed an impassable difference, is now presented, and for them is claimed, not only the right to swear away the life of a citizen, but the further privilege of participating with us in administering the affairs of our Government."[84]

---

[79] R.S. Chang, "Migrations, Citizens and Latinas/os: The Sojourner's Truth and Other Stories" (2003) 55 *Florida Law Review* 479. See also R.S. Chang and K. Aoki, "Centering the Immigrant in the Inter/National Imagination" (1997) 85 *California Law Review* 1395.

[80] 323 US 214 (1944).

[81] 320 US 81 (1943).

[82] 320 US 115 (1943).

[83] N. Gotanda, "Other non-Whites", at 1188 *et seq.*

[84] 4 Cal 399 (1854), at 404–405, quoted in N. Gotanda, "Other non-Whites", at 1189.

As Gotanda also points out, in the subsequent Supreme Court case of *US v Wong Kim Ark* the court accepted that a Chinese could, however, become an American, but the dissent of Chief Justice Fuller, who was joined by Justice Harlan, is illustrative of a judicial attitude that "a distinct race and religion, remaining strangers in the land, residing apart by themselves, tenaciously adhering to the customs and usages of their own country, unfamiliar with our institutions, and apparently incapable of assimilating with our people, might endanger good order, and be injurious to the public interests".[85]

Such cases have led to questions as to whether there would be an underlying thread connecting "other non-white experiences" at the level of some legal-explanatory principle (*i.e.* in addition to questions about the legal construction of an Asian-American identity). These questions have already led to the emergence of an Asian-American aspect to the CRT movement, drawing its inspiration from the pioneering work of Neil Gotanda.[86] Nonetheless, such scholarship mirrors orthodox (paradigmatically "black") CRT scholarship with its emphasis on materialist ("economic troubles") and race-based ("nativist") explanations of discrimination.[87]

Lat-Crit scholarship on the other hand, while sharing with Asian Crits the same methodological concerns with "foreignness' and the need to transcend a "black/white" paradigm of the race issue in the US, has identified a *further* nagging difficulty. Latinos have to address questions about their qualifications for *becoming* white, and in this way are confronted with the legal and political construction of the racial properties of whiteness. For example, while an Indiana appellate court found that Mexicans are not legally white because the Mexican population was not anthropologically white (in an era during which federal naturalisation laws required the passing of a racial "whiteness" test), a Texas federal court had earlier found otherwise because the legal "whiteness" of Mexicans was (implicitly) contemplated by a US-Mexican treaty that envisaged the naturalisation of Mexicans as US citizens.[88] These racial ("whiteness") prerequisites cases provide a persuasive form of empirical evidence of the

---

[85] 169 US 649, at 731 (1898), citing *Fong Yue Ting v US* 149 US 698, at 717 (1893); quoted by N. Gotanda, "Other non-Whites", *ibid.*

[86] See K. Aoki, "Critical Legal Studies, Asian Americans in US Law and Culture, Neil Gotanda and Me" (1997) 4 *Asian Law Journal* 19 for a history of the Asian Crit Movement.

[87] R.S. Chang, "Toward an Asian American Legal Scholarship: Critical Race Theory, Post-Structuralism, and Narrative Space" (1993) 81 *California Law Review* 1241.

[88] G.A. Martinez, "Mexican Americans and Whiteness" (1997) 2 *Harvard-Latino Law Review* 321; citing *Inland Steel Co v Barcelona* 39 NE2d 800 (Ind 1942), at 801, and *Re Rodriguez* 81 F 337 (WD Tex 1897), at 349.

contention that there has been a long-term and historical investment in whiteness as a species of property.[89]

4. CONCLUSION

Lawyers are traditionally imbued with an abstract ideal of neutral legal guarantees of formal-legal equality—"colour-blindness" if you like—and there is no rational cause to believe that such colour-blindness does not condition legal thought as a whole. In this regard, American CLS and CRT scholars—for whom there is no such thing as a correct reading of precedent or correct applications of established legal doctrine, but who determine the "worth" of a legal decision on whether the decision makes a "correct political choice"—have struck at the basis of law itself. If what they have to say resonates with us, CRT could transform the study and practice of Anglo-American law, and not just how the law looks at race. Things are already moving apace. The University of California, Los Angeles Law School now allows concentration of a law student's studies on race.[90] As UCLA Law Professor, Cheryl Harris, explains "While CRT has often been presented in the curriculum as a discrete course, in fact, the project has always been directed at the entire edifice of American law and legal culture."[91]

Could CRT's influence in the US extend beyond its influence on American law? CRT has had a real influence on American comparative and international law scholarship.[92] For example, CRT's insights have already been applied to correct previous misunderstandings about non-American legal cultures. One early example is perhaps Karen Engle's argument that (American) liberal international human rights scholarship has glossed over (or simply treated as misguided) the actual preferences of the "Exotic Other Female". Engle argues that liberal legal scholars have been too quick in characterising sub-Saharan women who choose female circumcision, for example, as having simply succumbed to female genital mutilation.[93] Another example is Vasuki Nesiah's

---

[89] See further I.F. Hany López, "White by Law", in I.F. Haney López, *The Legal Construction of Race* (New York University Press, New York, 1996).

[90] C.I. Harris, "Critical Race Studies: An Introduction" (2002) 49 *UCLA Law Review* 1215.

[91] *ibid.*, at 1216.

[92] See B.J. Crossman, "Turning the Gaze Back on Itself: Comparative Law, Feminist Legal Studies and the Postcolonial Project" (1997) *Utah Law Review* 525, reprinted in *Global Critical Race Feminism—A Reader* (A.K. Wing ed., New York University Press, New York, 2000), p.27.

[93] K. Engle, "Female Subjects of Public International Law: Human Rights and the Exotic Other Female" (1992) 26 *New England Law Review* 1508.

criticism of American feminist international legal scholarship for having emphasized gender-based insights at the expense of race-based insights. Nesiah argues that female factory jobs in Sri Lanka are in fact highly prized indigenously, and this should be taken into account in contrast with the classic liberal understanding of the lot of such workers as simply evincing a form of gender exploitation. According to Nesiah, the allocation of such jobs evinces, instead, strong employer preferences in favour of the dominant racial group.[94] If these examples are anything to go by, the next wave of scholarship must also rest in the hands of legal and other scholars working outside the US (*i.e.* non-American scholars). What is seemingly important in the face of a discernible globalisation of American law is that non-American scholars should be able to test CRT's principal themes in their own specific legal cultures for what possible insights they might provide, or indeed reject those themes that are based purely on the American experience. Without that, CRT would be confined to being an entirely American pre-occupation.

---

[94] V. Nesiah, "Toward a Feminist Internationality: A Critique of US Feminist Legal Scholarship" (1993) 16 *Harvard Women's Law Journal* 189, also reprinted in *Global Critical Race Feminism*, p.91.

CHAPTER 17

THE OTHER JURISPRUDENCE: POSTSTRUCTURALISM, POSTMODERNISM AND THE LAW

EMMANUEL MELISSARIS

1. INTRODUCTION

Apart from the grand narratives of the classical legal theories, such as positivism, natural law or, indeed, Dworkinian interpretivism, there is another way of telling the story of the law. It is this alternative, which is customarily referred to as poststructuralism or postmodernism, that we shall discuss in this chapter.[1] This alternative reading of the law is "other" in that, on one level, it understands itself in and through its difference to the "jurisprudence of totality" associated with grand narratives of legal theory. As a by-product of the Enlightenment and modernity, the "jurisprudence of totality" claims to be arriving at right and unique answers regarding law and justice with the use of rational and therefore flawless methodology. The other jurisprudence does not treat the law as having a concrete history that can be reconstructed and interpreted as a seamless web, which will in turn form part of the general project of reconstruction of truth and justice. On the contrary, it explores the law as fragments, whether these fragments are texts or practices, and it introduces new methodologies, which turn from the universal to the local, from the construction of self-contained structures to the reasons for the collapse of such edifices. On another level, the other jurisprudence is always other to itself. It is never fulfilled but rather exists and reproduces itself through a constant deferment of the possibility of justice but also the possibility of theory. Suspicious of totalities, it is fearful of becoming a totality itself. What often ensues is its apparent inability to offer concrete answers to concrete problems or to discuss the problem of the relationship between law and justice in a

---

[1] The majority of the works classified under the headings of poststructuralism and postmodernism are not originally written in English. However, for reasons of accessibility, in this chapter we shall be referring to their English translations.

coherent way. Finally, postmodern jurisprudence is a jurisprudence *of* the other: It rejects the fallacy of consensus theories of law and places the emphasis on what remains silenced. It also displaces ethics from the self and its obligation to the relations with the other.

Before we go on to decipher as much of the above as there is time and space for, a few introductory remarks are called for. Firstly, despite the fact that, in this context, various theorists and theories are examined together and the focus is on their common ground, postmodern jurisprudence is not homogeneous. There are as many differences between its strands as there are commonalities. Secondly, this kind of philosophy resists hagiographies. Precisely because it shifts focus from the author to the text and from the subject to the context, there is always something paradoxical about organising its exposition around authors. However, to the extent that some authors have produced seminal, groundbreaking works, this cannot be avoided. Therefore this chapter cannot but try and balance references to authors and ideas hoping to minimise the undermining force of the paradox. Thirdly, it should be emphasised from the outset that poststructuralism and postmodernism were not legal theoretical movements from the outset. They developed in linguistics, art, architecture, philosophy and many other areas before being applied to the area of law. Therefore, this chapter will be structured around some central ideas of postmodern theory and will then explore their relevance to the law. Fourthly, like all texts, this text is an event in itself. There is no delusion that this chapter is able to (re)produce a faithful mimesis of other texts by reconstructing the intentions of their authors. It is in this light that it should be read and judged.

This chapter will be structured as follows: In the next part we will discuss the distinction between the modern and the postmodern conditions or eras with reference to the work of Jean-François Lyotard. In the following part, the discussion moves to two fundamental ideas underpinning modern law and legal theory, namely, the rational and autonomous subject, and the clarity and objectivity of meaning of the legal text. With reference to Michel Foucault and Jacques Derrida we will show how postmodern thought questions these foundations of modernity. Finally, we will bring the discussion to a real context and try and interpret a particular judicial decision in the light of the critique put forth by postmodern thinkers. We will also discuss the general question of whether postmodernism can be constructive or whether it is exhausted in criticism.

2. AFTER AND BEYOND MODERNITY

What is implied by the prefix "post" in poststructuralism and postmodernism is a temporal but, more importantly, a substantive transcendence of systems of thought that are deemed to have lost their explanatory value in view of historical developments towards the end of the twentieth century.

The definition of modernity, and subsequently the clarification of the content of postmodernity, is not merely a chronological question. On the contrary, it is the most central, substantive problem in the debate between postmodern philosophy and those theories that deny that there has been a paradigmatic change and that maintain that we still experience the project of modernity. Therefore, this question will permeate the whole of this chapter and will surface at various stages of the discussion in one way or another. It is useful, however, to give a very general and brief introduction to the problem as a first impression of what postmodernism tries to transcend.

There are many contradictory opinions on the matter but, for the purposes of understanding postmodernism, it is helpful to place the starting point of modernity in or immediately after the Enlightenment of the eighteenth century.[2] That period bears witness to the establishment of the *reign of reason*. As the Western world emerged from what might be termed the "theological terrorism" of the Middle Ages, a new, secular faith emerged, a faith in the unity of the world and the ability of humankind to discover and describe it with the use of reason. This new intellectual endeavour was based on, and revolved around, the formulation of cross-temporal, universal valid principles. Thus a new kind of metaphysics emerged and permeated all forms of human activity from art to politics. This new metaphysics was accompanied by a moral theory that revolved around the idea of the autonomous, timeless, universal rational subject and the existence of transcendental principles of truth and justice.

In the words of Jean-François Lyotard:

> "I will use the term *modern* to designate any science that legitimates itself with reference to a metadiscourse … making an explicit appeal to some grand narrative, such as the dialectics of Spirit, the hermeneutics of meaning, the emancipation of the rational or working subject, or the creation of wealth."[3]

Modern thought turns from the local to the universal, from the particular to the abstract, in order to draw principles from the latter that will explain and/or justify the former. Kantian transcendental moral philosophy, Marxian social and political theory, liberalism, both economic and political, to mention but a

---

[2] For a brief but comprehensive account of modernity, see N. Murphy and J.W. McLendon, "Distinguishing Modern and Postmodern Theology" (1989) 5 *Modern Theology* 3.

[3] J.-F. Lyotard, *The Postmodern Condition: A Report on Knowledge* (G. Bennington and B. Massumi trans., Manchester University Press, Manchester, 1984), p. xxiii.

few obvious examples, attempt to discover and formulate those unique elements that either explain social evolution or set the normative standards against which practical reason should develop.

Law and legal philosophy became integral parts of the project of modernity. A cursory glance at the major legal theories up until the second part of the twentieth century reveals the robust faith in the possibility of the world as a coherent totality governed by a law, which in turn conforms with a normative metadiscourse. Consider, as examples: Austin's jurisprudence of the sovereign as a singular and unique normative source; Kelsen's self-contained and self-legitimising system of norms; Hart's reliance on unequivocal (and univocal) semantics underpinning the law's justice; the legal realist critique of legal practice that reveals a principled faith in the law as such; Finnis' reworking of natural law theory on grounds of the seven "self-evident" goods that are common to all; and Dworkin's moral cognitivism and his theory of law as interpretive integrity, which leads unmistakeably to the one right answer. Although undoubtedly contradictory in their particularities, all these distinct theories are based on the same premise: truth, justice and the law are discoverable in an objective, rationalistic way.

The history of modernity continued uninterrupted until the twentieth century, when several momentous changes took place in all areas of human activity and self-understanding: the rapid technological development and the changes in the mode of production and the new forms of communication it brought about; the emergence of psychoanalysis and the new perspectives it introduced for the understanding of human motivation and action; the shift of scientific focus from the visible—the phenomenon—to the unseen micro-basis of everything that exists (*e.g.* quantum mechanics that reveal the randomness and contingency of reality); the relativisation of the truth about space and time (*e.g.* Einstein's physics); the proliferation of emancipatory movements especially by groups that reclaimed their voice; and in art, the emergence of schools that moved from representation to the abstract visualisation of space, time and human nature. It soon became apparent to many writers that a re-thinking and re-conceptualisation of the conditions of our existence was called for.

Lyotard's Report on the Transition

A seminal work that often serves as a starting point in accounts of poststructural and postmodern theory is Jean-François Lyotard's *The Postmodern Condition,* which gives a philosophical account of the transition from the modern to the postmodern.[4] The book's subtitle *A Report on Knowledge* reveals his main

---

[4] J.-F. Lyotard, *The Postmodern Condition: A Report on Knowledge.*

aim, which is to record and make sense of the passage from the epistemological paradigm of the Enlightenment to the technologisation or computerisation of all forms of knowledge.

Lyotard starts from the premise that computerisation and the miniaturisation and dispersion of technology are bound to radically change the nature of knowledge. The validity of modern scientific knowledge rests on the possibility of referring to normative meta-orders that provide the criteria, against which the scientific nature of statements will be judged. Some of those requirements are that scientific statements must be provable in the sense that the referent— *i.e.* the idea or thing that the statement refers to or symbolises—must exist in the world; the addressee must be able to bring herself in the position of the addressor, that is she must be able to assent and re-produce the statement with the same claim to validity and truth; the statement must have a unique referent, otherwise it would stand defenceless to the critique on grounds of its inconsistency; by the same token, as long as proof can be produced to support the statement, reality is the way the statement describes it. Scientific knowledge is being expressed and transmitted in one specific linguistic form, in a specific "language game", to use the term of Ludwig Wittgenstein (1889–1951) that was borrowed by Lyotard.[5] Language games are forms of communication, "linguistic codes" to put it crudely, bound to specific contexts or, again in Wittgensteinian terms, forms of life. Apart from being bound to the context, an aspect of language games that cannot be overemphasised is that they always abide by rules that are unique to them. The language game of the acquisition and transmission of scientific knowledge relies on constative utterances—that is, denotative statements of fact that raise a claim to truth[6]—to the extent that they are verifiable or falsifiable by reference to a reality external to them.

---

[5] See L. Wittgenstein, *Philosophical Investigations* (G.E.M. Anscombe trans., Blackwell, Oxford, 1953).

[6] The terminology of constative and performative utterances and the turn from semantics to the pragmatics of communication is associated with the theory of speech acts developed by J.L. Austin (1911–1960), which consists in the thesis that every time we say something we also perform an act *in* saying it. See J.L. Austin, *How to do Things with Words* (Clarendon Press, Oxford, 1962). For instance, when one shouts "Watch it!" one does not only produce a sound but also ascribes a meaning to the locution. This meaning is determined by a number of factors, including the speaker's intention, and not only the words used. So, the same phrase could be a warning or a threat. Furthermore, the meaning ascribed to the phrase by the speaker is not necessarily the meaning that the listener will ascribe to it. Lyotard takes Austinian speech acts to a wholly new direction, in order to show how specific forms of (speech-act) communication give rise to whole discourses, epistemological paradigms and models of legitimation. For an introduction to the work of Lyotard, see J. Williams, *Lyotard: Towards a Postmodern Philosophy* (Polity, Cambridge, 1998). Also useful are G. Bennington, *Lyotard: Writing the Event* (Manchester

In contrast to scientific knowledge "narrative knowledge" is not based on authorship and proof but rather on the customary ways of acquiring, testing and reproducing information. This kind of knowledge can be transmitted with a variety of speech acts. Deontic, *i.e.* normative, or interrogative statements sit as comfortably in narratives as constative utterances. Moreover, narratives embody the rules which permeate and regulate them, rendering reference to a normative meta-order unnecessary. Lyotard illustrates his point with the example of the Cashinahua storytellers, who start their narrations by stating that they were once told the story themselves and, when they conclude the story, they give the name they bear to their audience. It is those statements that legitimate them in telling the story and also account for its truth.[7]

Let us leave the difference between scientific and narrative knowledge to one side for a moment and make a short detour to give an account of Lyotard's analysis of language games or genres of discourse and their incommensurability. Although the idea is present in *The Postmodern Condition*, it is in another work, *The Différend*, that he offers a more elaborate analysis.[8] Lyotard starts by promoting *the phrase* as the only indubitable and indivisible object of analysis. Everything can be understood as a phrase. Even the denial of the phrase must be included in a phrase. What is it that makes possible the transition between one phrase to another in the course of a dialogue, debate or any other instance of use of language? A phrase must be followed by, and linked to, another phrase. But the content of the follow-up phrase is contingent in that there is nothing inherent in the phrase that predicts or dictates its extension. For instance, there are an infinite number of phrases that can follow from the phrase: "I'll come over to your house". However, only one of the possible candidates can be actualised and its actualisation will happen by way of exclusion of the other alternatives. This does not mean that the selected alternative is more correct than the excluded ones. Its selection is dictated by some pre-existing rules that are bound to the specific genre of discourse and not by reference to some external reality.

Therefore, genres of discourse determine which links to other phrases are pertinent but they also set the ultimate communicative goals, the *stakes*, in Lyotard's terminology.[9] Each genre sets its own stakes and the latter is achieved again by way of exclusion of the stakes of other genres. It is at this level that the incommensurability of genres of discourse is revealed. Incommensurability

---

University Press, Manchester, 1988) and G.K. Browning, *Lyotard and the End of Grand Narratives* (University of Wales Press, Cardiff, 2000).

[7] The Cashinahua are an indigenous people of south-eastern Peru who speak their own Cashinahua language, which is also spoken in parts of Brazil.

[8] J.-F. Lyotard, *The Différend: Phrases in Dispute* (G. Van Den Abbeele trans., Manchester University Press, Manchester, 1988).

[9] *ibid.*, p.84.

here means that there can be no meaningful communication between different genres of discourse. They do not, and indeed cannot, have a shared way of making sense of referents and, moreover, they cannot be classified under the same metanarrative, which would unify all the rules of legitimation. They are not permeated by the same rules and they cannot be reduced to a common indivisible element, such as the word, precisely because meaning is bound to the context and it is not the product of the synthesis of some inherent and *a priori* content of the words. Lyotard terms this instance of contact and conflict between incommensurable genres of discourse *"différend"*.

Let us now go back to the tension between scientific and narrative knowledge. Science has prevailed as the ultimate and unique metadiscourse, claiming to be able to provide justificatory rules for all language games. Thus, legitimation became conceivable only in terms of reference to principles or universal truths about the world. Therefore, it involves the application of pre-existing, familiar categories in order to judge the truth, validity or rightness of statements. Lyotard refers to the scientific metadiscourse in the following way:

> "Reality is not what is 'given' to this or that 'subject', it is a state of the referent (that about which one speaks) which results from the effectuation of establishment procedures defined by a unanimously agreed-upon protocol, and from the possibility offered to anyone to recommence this effectuation as often as he or she wants."[10]

The legitimation of scientific statements is strongly interconnected with the justification of axiological or prescriptive statements, that is, statements concerning the rightness or justice of actions. Despite the fundamental, essential differences between those two language games and, moreover, despite the fact that prescriptions cannot be deduced from descriptions, in other words what *is* the case can never lead us to conclusions as to what *ought* to be the case, judgements of truth and rightness seem to collapse into each other. In Lyotard's words:

> "The question of the legitimacy of science has been indissociably linked to that of the legitimation of the legislator since the time of Plato. From this point of view, the right to decide what is true is not independent of the right to decide what is just, even if the statements consigned by these two authorities differ in nature. The point is that there is a strict interlinkage between the kinds of language called science and the kind called ethics and politics: they both stem from the same perspective—the choice called the Occident."[12]

---

[10] *ibid.*, p.4.
[11] J.-F. Lyotard, *The Postmodern Condition*, p.31.

In a nutshell, Lyotard reports the postmodern condition as the new situation—still inextricably linked to modernity and, indeed, stemming from it—which witnesses the proliferation of genres of discourse to such an extent that it is impossible for metadiscourses such as science to claim to be able to provide homogeneous justifications for all language games. He defines postmodernism negatively as "incredulity towards metanarratives", the loss of faith in the possibility of regulating all the co-existing language games or genres of discourse in a way that will do justice to all of them.

The discussion of *différends* can now be transposed from the level of language to the realm of the political. In politics, the occurrence of *différends* means that some forms of life, some social groups, which share a language game that does not coincide with the dominant political system of meaning, will be silenced and disenfranchised. Instead of focusing on the fruitless task of imposing normative supra-orders, we are called to try and acknowledge the instances of *différend*, instances of conflict between genres of discourses leading to the violent imposition of one language game and way of life onto others.

The relevance of Lyotard's analysis for the law should be clear by now. Modern law seeks to become an all-regulating metanarrative. It claims to be able to regulate all social discourses with reference to rules and principles, which are objective and, as such, accepted by everyone. A great deal relies on this idea(1) of consensus. All modern legal theories revolve around it to a certain degree. In the postmodern condition the deceit behind consensus is disclosed. It becomes impossible to shake off the suspicion that "consensus" does not mean that all the possible ways of understanding a debate have been taken into account and all the parties have agreed on one desirable and just decision. Instead, the postmodern perspective highlights that the alternatives have been silenced. It is important to understand that this is not a contingent critique of the law, it is not a conspiracy theory *á la* American legal realism. It is a critique that reveals the inherent inability of the law to make sense of, and communicate with, other discursive genres that it comes in contact with.

3. Two Pillars of Modern Law Challenged: The Subject and Meaning

We may now turn to consider—from the postmodern perspective—two fundamental ideas underpinning modern law and legal theory: the rational and autonomous subject, and the clarity and objectivity of meaning of the legal text.

The Subject

The paradigm of modernity is epitomised in the Cartesian dictum *Cogito ergo sum* ("I think therefore I am"). Descartes promotes the human subject and her reason as the most fundamental explanatory tool and normative principle.

The subject is *autonomous* and *free*. Her autonomy consists in her not depending on her environment for her existence. This, of course, is meant in a metaphysical sense. It does not mean that we are self-sufficient in the sense that we do not need our environment for our subsistence but rather that we *interact* with it rather than being *mutually constituted*. *Interaction* presupposes a dichotomy, a radical separation between the two parties or entities that are interacting. The subject is thus severed from her surroundings but also from other subjects, which become autonomous, complete, self-contained units. This isolation accounts for the subject's freedom as well, her freedom to make choices (moral or otherwise) and to act accordingly. Precisely because she is free to decide and act, the subject is accountable for her actions. To be more precise, this accountability is to be seen as a result of the combination of the freedom of the subject and her rationality.

The subject is *rational*. There are two sides to this. One is epistemological: the rational subject pre-dates the world and the existence of the world presupposes the subject. Therefore, the use of reason becomes the only way of experiencing the physical world as well as the only criterion for the truth of propositions about the world. The other is moral: it is only if there are exceptional circumstances impeding the use of reason that we are not held accountable for our actions.

The Cartesian subject is also *universal* and *diachronic*. The abstraction that is the subject knows no spatial or temporal limits. We all experience the world in the same way and every deviation is precisely that: a deviation due to extraordinary circumstances. The cross-temporality of the subject is what makes it possible to reconstruct past histories, reasons, intentions, aims, thoughts. It is also because of this cross-temporality that we can project the way we think to the patterns of others. Our subjectivity enables us to express normative views and judgements regarding the lives of others, irrespective of how different our context is from theirs.

This understanding of the subject underpins the larger part of post-Enlightenment moral and political theory. Social contract theories revolve around the idea of a free, voluntary association of *individuals* that subject themselves to the general will.[12] This is how Jean-Jacques Rousseau puts it:

"Each of us places his person and all his power in common under the

---

[12] Note here the polysemy of "subject" (*i.e* the existence of many meanings of the term): the subject that becomes the subject of our studies subjects itself to something beyond it.

> supreme direction of the general will; and as one we receive each member
> as an indivisible part of the whole."[13]

But the whole does not collapse into its parts; they remain distinctive and it is
always possible to oscillate between the individual and the collective.

The law, as we know it, is nothing but a reflection of isolated subjects and
the ways in which they freely enter and exit associations and communities.
The system of human rights, which constitutes the cornerstone of Western
legal cultures, safeguards and, at the same time, relies on the notion of the
perpetual subject, her inviolable personal sphere and her ability to define the
boundaries of this sphere. Even group rights that seemingly transcend the
individual do not go so far as to cancel the significance of the latter. Groups
are still voluntary unions of free individuals and they are simply granted some
rights of self-determination in order to define themselves in opposition to other
groups or, more importantly, the state as a whole. So, in a way, groups are
subjectified, they are given the same rights as individuals and they are perceived
in isolation from, and in contradistinction to, their environment.[14]

Private law is the apotheosis of the fetishism of the subject. For example, it
presupposes free individuals entering contractual relationships and accepting
responsibility for non-observance of the terms. Criminal law also reserves a
central place for the subject. Personal responsibility, the ascription of guilt or
innocence to individuals or to groups of individuals, the concept as well as the
forms of punishment—these are but a few principles and practices of criminal
law that presuppose and are underpinned by the notion of the universal, rational,
autonomous subject.

But the fact that this perception of the subject has prevailed in theory (and
has therefore determined political and legal practice to a very large extent)
does not mean that it is the only way of understanding ourselves in the world.
One theorist offering an alternative is Michel Foucault (1926–1984).[15] He
questions the Cartesian subject and understands the person as constituted by
the discourses and institutions in which she partakes.

---

[13] J.-J. Rousseau, *On the Social Contract* (D.A. Cress trans., Hackett, Indianapolis,
1987), p.24.

[14] For a postmodern critique of human rights, see C. Douzinas, *The End of Human
Rights* (Hart, Oxford, 2000).

[15] Michel Foucault was one of the most important and influential thinkers of the
twentieth century. His long and distinguished, albeit not ordinary, academic career
culminated with his election in 1970 as Professor of the History of Systems of
Thought at the Collège de France, a title that he chose and already reveals a lot
about the intellectual task he had set himself. For a very accessible introduction to
Foucault, see G. Danaher, T. Schirato, and J. Webb, *Understanding Foucault* (SAGE,
London, 2000). Also very useful is *The Cambridge Companion to Foucault* (G.
Gutting ed., Cambridge University Press, Cambridge, 1994).

It is extremely difficult to pin down Foucault's research programme and describe it in a coherent manner. On one level, it can be said that Foucault departs from the tradition of French structuralism, which was one of the dominant philosophical and social-theoretical paradigms of the twentieth century. Historically structuralism refers to a predominantly French school of thought that partly breaks paths with the modern paradigm by shifting the focus from the phenomenon itself, whether that be the subject (*e.g.* the person), the sound, the word or a social or cultural phenomenon, to the conditions that make the occurrence of these phenomena possible.[16] Structuralism is rooted in the structural linguistics of Ferdinand de Saussure (1857–1913). Saussure's linguistics are based on the premise that signifiers (signs such as words) and signifieds (ideas) do not have a pre-existing and autonomous meaning.[17] On the contrary, their meaning is determined through their differences to other signifiers and signifieds in what is deemed to be the formal system of language. When applied to other epistemic contexts such as political theory and anthropology, this fundamental idea signifies the departure from the idealistic understanding of political, social and cultural phenomena that looks for their essential, inherent meaning. Instead, analysis turns to the contrasts between phenomena and the underlying conditions which make them possible and determine their meaning.[18] In other words, the meaning of the particular, of the atom, is determined by its placement in the general and its differentiation from other atomic units. As will become clear later on, the boundaries between structuralism and poststructuralism are often difficult to discern, not least because many of the theorists considered today as by and large poststructuralist applied structuralist methodologies at an early stage of their writings and some never explicitly rejected structuralism as a research programme. However, one thing that does differentiate the two schools of thought is that structuralism still places too much weight on the subject. In order for the context to be observed, the observing subject must be radically separated from it. But upholding this dichotomy already perpetuates the project of modernity.

---

[16] Despite the association of structuralism with French theorists, the term was originally associated with the Russian literary theorist Roman Jakobson (1896–1982).

[17] See mainly F. De Saussure, *Course in General Linguistics* (R. Harris trans., Duckworth, London, 1983). See also J. Culler, *Structuralist Poetics: Structuralism, Linguistics, and the Study of Literature* (Routledge, London, 1975) and R. Harland, *Superstructuralism: The Philosophy of Structuralism and Post-Structuralism* (Methuen, London, 1987).

[18] For applications in the context of political theory, see, for example, L. Althusser, *Essays on Ideology* (Verso, London, 1984); N. Poulantzas, *State, Power, Socialism* (Verso, London, 2000); and N. Poulantzas, *Political Power and Social Classes* (Secker and Warburg, London, 1973). For anthropology, see C. Lévi-Strauss, *Structural Anthropology* (M. Layton trans., Allen Lane, London, 1977).

It is mainly the treatment of the subject that differentiates Foucault from structuralism. The focus of his work changed so often that it could be said that it is precisely in this elusiveness that its originality and significance consists. Foucault himself allows us to draw such a conclusion:

> "Do not ask who I am and do not ask me to remain the same: leave it to our bureaucrats and our police to see that our papers are in order. At least spare us their morality when we write."[19]

Foucauldian methodology revolves around two central ideas: *archaeology* and *genealogy*.[20] The archaeological method, which Foucault spelt out in his *Archaeology of Knowledge* in an attempt to systematise the methodology he had used in *Madness and Civilisation*,[21] *The Birth of the Clinic*,[22] and *The Order of Things*,[23] consists in shifting the focus from the subject to rules and relations underlying what he terms *epistemes* or discursive formations.[24] Thus archaeology goes beyond the consciousness of individuals (note how we are already moving back to the discussion of the subject), trying to discover the way discourses develop the conditions of their development independently of agents and actors. This displacement makes possible a historiography of the unconscious that highlights the differences between the ways similar phenomena were perceived in different eras. For example, the discourse on madness and the emergence of the Great Incarceration in the seventeenth and eighteenth centuries provided a case study demonstrating the differences between discourses concerning insanity.[25]

---

[19] M. Foucault, *The Archaeology of Knowledge* (A.M. Sheridan Smith trans., Tavistock, London, 1972), p.17.

[20] It should not surprise the reader that in the Foucauldian universe terms, the meaning of which we thought was settled, acquire a whole different meaning. The curious use of "archaeology" and "genealogy" (a term borrowed from the German philosopher, Friedrich Nietzsche, but also radically altered) provide excellent examples!

[21] M. Foucault, *Madness and Civilisation: A History of Insanity in the Age of Reason* (R. Howard trans., Pantheon, New York, 1965).

[22] M. Foucault, *The Birth of the Clinic: An Archaeology of Medical Perception* (Tavistock, London, 1973).

[23] M. Foucault, *The Order of Things: An Archaeology of the Human Sciences* (Tavistock, London, 1970).

[24] Not surprisingly, Foucault uses *episteme* in a very broad sense so as to cover all systems of thought and not in its narrow sense of "science" or "academic discipline". See G. Gutting, *Michel Foucault's Archaeology of Scientific Reason* (Cambridge University Press, Cambridge, 1989).

[25] See M. Foucault, *Madness and Civilisation*. The Great Incarceration refers to the trend of confining people physically: criminals in prisons, lunatics in asylums,

If archaeology accounts for the inner workings of discourses, genealogy accounts for the possibility of transition from one discourse to another. Without forming grand historical narratives or principles of historical development, genealogy shows the essentially contingent origins of historical development. Contrary to Marxian historical analysis, which privileges the material over any other factor in the historical process, but also contrary to all epistemologies that try to formulate principles permeating historical evolution and to single out recurring patterns, genealogy turns to the apparently small and insignificant and to connections between historical phenomena that cannot be accounted for with recourse to principles of universal and diachronic validity.

Apart from these methodological tools, there is also a substantive thread running through much of Foucault's intellectual production. In a nutshell, it could be said that his main aim was to establish and explain the relationship between knowledge and power in terms of the subjectification of human beings:

> "[My goal] has not been to analyze the phenomena of power, nor to elaborate the foundations of such an analysis. ... My objective, instead, has been to create a history of the different modes by which, in our culture, human beings are made subjects."[26]

Foucault understands power very broadly as an unstructured complex of discourses, institutions, structures, systems of rules and so on.[27] Therefore, power refers to more than relations of forceful domination of one party over another. As such its function is not simply destructive but also enabling in the sense that power relations shape subjectivities, *i.e.* they construct subjects. How is this possible? In Foucauldian terms power and knowledge are intertwined to the extent that they constitute one another, thus losing their conceptual independence. To know something is to control it and to control it is to know it. When controlling something, however, one does not get a knowledge and understanding of the hidden, universal essence of what one controls. In other words, controlling does not provide access to the Cartesian subject that exists beyond the instance of exercise of power. The subject is constructed *through* the exercise of power.[28] For instance, the incarceration of

---

conscripts in barracks, and so on. Again, Foucault uses "discourse" in a very broad sense so as to include not only the exchange of utterances but also all the institutions and procedures at play.

[26] Michel Foucault in *Beyond Structuralism and Hermeneutics/With an Afterword by Michel Foucault* (H.L. Dreyfus and P. Rabinow eds., University of Chicago Press, Chicago, 1982), p.208.

[27] J. Simons, *Foucault and the Political* (Routledge, London, 1995), p.30.

[28] Social constructionism has gained currency in most social sciences. A central piece of literature in this field is P.L. Berger and T. Luckmann, *The Social Construction of*

the mad forms a knowledge (a discourse, an *episteme*) of madness and also constructs the category of "the mad", the subject of the insane.

Let us now bring together all of the above and explain them in their combination with reference to one of Foucault's books that is more closely associated with the law than any other of his works, namely *Discipline and Punish*.[29] In this work Foucault examines the evolution of punitive institutions and practices. He employs the genealogical method to explain the transition from the inhumane, vindictive corporal punishment of the Middle Ages to the civility of incarceration, which reveals a move from power as outright violence to power as knowledge and discipline. An idea epitomising this new conception of power as observation is Jeremy Bentham's *Panopticon*. Etymologically, the *Panopticon* suggests the possibility of watching everything at all times and that was Bentham's aim precisely: the creation of a circular prison with a watchtower in the middle, from which guards would have visual access to all the cells, while they would remain invisible to the prisoners. Thus not only would it be possible for the inmates to be watched always but it would also be impossible for them to know whether they are being observed or not. In that way their behaviour would be controlled not forcefully but through the terror of observation. The genealogical method allows us to draw connections between the emergence of prisons with other institutions and discourses. These other institutions and discourse might seem to be basing their operations on completely different principles but it is soon revealed that they too operate as disciplinary mechanisms: schools, factories, offices (think of open-plan workplaces) and so on and so forth.[30] In the later stages of his work Foucault

---

Reality: A Treatise in the Sociology of Knowledge (Doubleday, New York, 1966). Many would argue that this whole discussion has gone a little too far to the extent that it merely reiterates the widely accepted thesis that there are no language-independent categories or that nothing has a self-evident meaning by nature. Indeed, if one runs a simple keyword search in an academic library database entering the phrase "social construction", the search will yield results ranging from the social construction of American realism (A. Kaplan, *The Social Construction of American Realism*, University of Chicago Press, Chicago, 1988) to the Korean War (J. Milliken, *The Social Construction of the Korean War: Conflict and its Possibilities*, Manchester University Press, Manchester, 2001) and dementia (N.H. Harding, *The Social Construction of Dementia: Confused Professionals?*, Jessica Kingsley, London, 1997). A powerful critique of this uncontrollable wave of social constructionism is offered by I. Hacking, *The Social Construction of What?* (Harvard University Press, Cambridge, Mass., 1999).

[29] M. Foucault, *Discipline and Punish: The Birth of the Prison* (A.M. Sheridan trans., Pantheon, New York, 1977).

[30] Also central in Foucauldian thought is the idea of governmentality (again a neologism: govern-mentality). For a clarification of governmentality and its relevance to law, see A. Hunt and G. Wickham, *Foucault and Law: Towards a Sociology of Law as*

focused on the sexual subject, the way sexual identity is constructed, the rules that govern the discourse of sexuality and the (self-) understanding of the person on grounds of his or her sexual orientation.[31]

In the light of the Foucauldian analysis, the modern myth of the free, autonomous, universal subject collapses. The social person is fragmented and the multiplicity of her social roles is determined by the discourses in which she partakes. Thus the law's claim that it treats the subject as unencumbered and transcendental is proven to be false. The law is a discourse of power that constructs the subjects in a way that will serve and perpetuate its own operations. It must settle and delineate the identity of the parties in a meaningful way, which will be translatable and intelligible in the vocabulary of legal rules and the legal institution.

Meaning and Interpretation

Apart from the idea of the Cartesian subject, modern philosophy relies very heavily on the possibility of discovering the one, objective and clear meaning of utterances, whether they be spoken or written. In jurisprudence this confidence is manifested as the belief in the intelligibility of rules. The hugely influential legal theory of H.L.A. Hart, for example, is based by and large on the clarity of the legal text. Hart's central thesis is that words have a semantic core and a penumbra of doubt. Hard cases arise only when facts cannot be subsumed under the semantic core but seem to constitute borderline cases falling under the penumbra. After we have discovered the meaning of the rule and it turns out that deduction is impossible, that is if it is revealed that there are no available rules that would regulate the instant case, then judges must exercise their discretion. Ronald Dworkin might disagree with Hart on the particulars, and especially the problems of judicial activism and gaps in the law, but his theory of law-as-interpretation revolves around the same central axis: the legal text and the unity of its meaning. To be sure, "legal text" is understood in its broadest possible sense, embracing statutes and court rulings as well as other sources of legal principles, but it is still a text, as Dworkin's chain novel analogy suggests.

Postmodern jurisprudence does not share that faith in the legal text. Where traditional, modern legal theories see intelligibility and certainty, postmodern

---

Governance (Pluto, London, 1994); *The Foucault Effect: Studies in Governmentality* (G. Burchell, C. Gordon and P. Miller eds., Harvester Wheatsheaf, London, 1991); and *Rethinking Law, Society and Governance: Foucault's Bequest* (G. Wickham and G. Pavlich eds., Hart, Oxford, 2001).

[31] M. Foucault, *History of Sexuality, Volume I: An Introduction* (Pantheon, New York, 1978); *Use of Pleasure* (Pantheon, New York, 1985); *The Care of the Self* (Pantheon, New York, 1985).

jurisprudence sees openness, inconclusiveness and indeterminacy. Traditional, modern jurisprudence relies on the text as objectively accessible and independent of its context. Thus, the problems that might arise because of the fact that the text must be interpreted by specific people in specific historical instances is addressed and reduced to a contingent problem of application. Postmodern jurisprudence sheds a different light on the legal text and its meaning. Instead of treating the legal text as a safety mechanism that can lead to objective, substantive fairness and justice despite the inevitable constraints that the real context imposes, postmodern legal thought sees the meaning of the text as *always* contingent on and bound to a context; instead of hoping to discover the one, true, right meaning of the law, the famous Dworkinian right answer, or instead of rejoicing or bragging for having indeed discovered it in specific instances, it recognises that meaning is always deferred and so is the question of justice; instead of interpreting, it "deconstructs".

Much of the postmodern critique of the law on grounds of the constant unattainability of the meaning of the text derives from or rests on the idea of deconstruction, as developed by Jacques Derrida. It is notoriously difficult to summarise the theory of deconstruction, not least because of the perplexity of a lot of Derrida's works.[32] Moreover, to the extent that deconstruction is about the deferment of meaning, it would be paradoxical to try and grasp the one definite meaning of deconstructive texts. However, it is possible to single out a few key points.

Derrida questions the diachronic philosophical tendency to understand the spoken word as prior and superior to the written word. Traditional philosophy holds speech to be giving us direct access to the truth about ourselves and the world, because it embodies thought in an unmediated manner. It can therefore represent thought in the present. What follows from this is that alphabetical, phonetic writing, that is writing that corresponds to sounds and their word-forming combinations instead of representing concepts or ideas, is the most precise and therefore best kind of writing. Or at least it is the best one possible. This is so because all writing is inevitably inferior to speech as a means of representation, for it is twice removed from consciousness and reality. Insofar as writing is the representation of speech, which is a representation in itself,

---

[32] In a very interesting anecdote, John Searle reports that he heard Michel Foucault calling Derrida's writing *"obscurantisme terroriste"*, because his writings are completely unintelligible but when one actually dares voice a disagreement, then the answer they receive is that they didn't understand a thing and that they're idiots. Derrida did not take the joke very gracefully. For a report of the incident, see C. Howells, *Derrida: Deconstruction from Phenomenology to Ethics* (Polity, Cambridge, 1998), p.70. Howells' book is an accessible account of, and a defence of, deconstruction.

and given that it also takes place in the absence of the speaker as well as the referent, it is artificial and parasitic and distorts meaning.

Derrida sees this privileging of speech over writing, this *logocentrism* or *phonocentrism*, as indicative of a specific metaphysics, the *metaphysics of the presence*.[33] The metaphysics of presence relies on the possibility and ability of knowing and describing the state of the world at any given time. Deconstruction rejects this hierarchisation of speech and writing. No language can correspond fully and purely to thought, because it will always rely on symbols, signifiers that are iterable, *i.e.* repeatable. So, speech suffers from exactly the same problem as writing. Deconstruction reveals the impossibility of this project and draws our attention to the constant deferment of meaning, which can only be extracted in relation to another, with reference to what is absent and is never immanent in the symbol, whether that be a word or anything else.[34] Derrida refers to this idea that combines difference and deference with the neological term *différance*.

As a text that, by and large, seeks to provide answers as to the truth or falsity of propositions but also as to the rightness or wrongness of actions in the present, the law is an obvious target for the project of deconstruction. However, it was not until 1989 that Derrida spoke explicitly about law and justice in a symposium entitled "Deconstruction and the Possibility of Justice" at the Cardozo Law School. His paper was entitled "Force of Law: The 'Mystical Foundation of Authority'" and has since dominated the discussions on deconstruction, law and justice. As with the rest of Derrida's work, it is an impossible task to give a summary that would do justice to what is a very complex text full of detours, parentheses and subtle or explicit allusions to other texts. But then again, giving a summary is hardly the point.

Following Montaigne and Pascal, Derrida draws a sharp distinction between justice and the law: justice can never be actualised, it is always to come. Justice is the experience of *aporias,* an irresolvable paradox.[35] The law, on the other hand, cannot give in to paradoxes, it cannot forfeit its duty to provide enforceable reasons for action in particular circumstances.

The first *aporia* is what Derrida calls the "*épokhè* of the rule".[36] Justice

---

[33] J. Derrida, *Of Grammatology* (G.C. Spivak trans., Johns Hopkins University Press, Baltimore, 1976). Very useful as a guide to deconstruction is J. Culler, *On Deconstruction: Theory and Criticism after Structuralism* (Routledge and Kegan Paul, London, 1983).

[34] On the question of textual meaning, see J. Derrida, *Positions* (University of Chicago Press, Chicago, 1981).

[35] In its Greek etymology, *aporia* signifies a lack of resources but also the lack of a passageway or path.

[36] The term *épokhè* is borrowed from the phenomenology of Edmund Husserl (1859–1938). Derrida uses it as meaning the suspension of judgement, or more accurately, the suspension of the pre-existing rule.

demands that rules be not merely followed but reconfirmed at each instance of decision. A judge must reinvent the law for each particular case, for each new decision. Passing a just judgement presupposes freedom, independence from any kind of normative constraint. If judging is only an act of rule-following then it can at best be legal, but it will never be just. Although a decision is guided by the pre-existing rule, it calls for an act of re-interpretation. The law must be reset and judicial decisions must

> "conserve the law and also destroy it or suspend it enough to have to reinvent it in any case, rejustify it, at least reinvent it in the reaffirmation and the new and free confirmation of its principle".[37]

Derrida detects a paradox in this need for simultaneous destruction and creation of the law: no decision can be just in the present tense.

> "For in the founding of law in its institution, the same problem of justice will have been posed and violently resolved, that is to say buried, dissimulated, repressed."[38]

The second *aporia* of the law concerns the "undecidable":

> "The undecidable is not merely the oscillation or the tension between two decisions; it is the experience of that which, though heterogeneous, foreign to the order of the calculable and the rule, is still obliged—it is of obligation that we must speak—to give itself up to the impossible decision, while taking account of law and rules." [39]

The law suffers yet another *aporia*: the spatial and temporal constraints, which dictate the need to make a decision, impose the urgency of a judgement. The amount of information that can be brought into legal discourse is and must be finite, because the instance of deciding interrupts the discourse, marks the end of communication. That moment of urgency can be understood in terms of speech acts. Constative utterances—that is, statements of fact—can only be true or false. They can only be correct but never just. Justice remains exclusive to performative speech acts—that is, utterances with which an act is performed—under the condition that they rest on other prior conventions and

---

[37] J. Derrida, "Force of Law: The 'Mystical Foundation of Authority'" in *Deconstruction and the Possibility of Justice* (D. Cornell, M. Rosenfeld, and D.G. Carlson eds., Routledge, London, 1992), p.23.

[38] *ibid.*

[39] *ibid.*, p.24

subsequently performative acts. Because every constative act relies on a performative one, the truth of the former depends on the justice of the latter. Justice can never be achieved by decision in the present. The instant of precipitation will always play its destructive role. Nevertheless justice is immanent in the law as *a-venir*, it is always *yet to come*.

4. THE RELEVANCE OF POSTMODERN JURISPRUDENCE: A CASE STUDY

So far we have discussed some modern themes in a postmodern light. Now that the background is set, however blurred it might still be, let us try and transpose it to a pragmatic context. The aim is to draw on the abstract postmodern critique of the law in order to shed a different light on actual judicial practice.[40]

Our example comes from English jurisdiction. In *Re C (HIV test)*[41] the Court of Appeal was called to decide whether the trial judge was right to issue an order requested by the local authority that a baby born to an HIV positive mother be tested for HIV. The parents were sceptical of the conventional treatment for HIV and AIDS; the mother had refused medication during the pregnancy and she intended to continue breast-feeding until the child was about two years old. Following a long line of precedent,[42] the Court of Appeal decided that the decisive criterion should be the welfare of the child, which should override the interests of the parents. Moreover, it was not a question of giving the child treatment or not but only whether he should have an HIV test. Given that the latter was rather unintrusive and given that both courts were satisfied with the scientific evidence that there was a real danger of the mother passing the virus on to the baby by breast-feeding, the Court of Appeal dismissed the appeal and maintained the court order that the child ought to be tested for HIV.

Unpleasant as the case may be, it is rather straightforward to a lawyer's eyes. All the judge has to do is apply the pre-existing legal principle giving priority to the best interests of the child after having weighed it up against other, seemingly competing, legal principles, then try and discover the best interest of the child in the instant case and decide accordingly. This principle

---

[40] For a deconstructive critique of the major mainstream legal theories, see R. Warrington and C. Douzinas with S. McVeigh, *Postmodern Jurisprudence: The Law of Text in the Texts of Law* (Routledge, London, 1991) and *Critical Legal Studies* (P. Fitzpatrick and A. Hunt eds., Blackwell, Oxford, 1987).

[41] [1999] 2 FLR 1004; [2000] Fam Law 16.

[42] *Re B (A Minor) (Wardship: Medical Treatment)* [1981] 1 WLR 1421; *Re J (A Minor) (Wardship: Medical Treatment)* [1991] Fam. 33; *Re T* EWCA Civ 805.

is to be found in the legal history of each jurisdiction, which includes both statutes and precedent, as well as in international law and it can be extracted interpretively.[43] *Re C (HIV test)* is a simple case. There is a strong chance that the child might have the HIV virus. For his own sake, it should be known. The parents, and especially the mother, are misguided in holding their beliefs concerning HIV and AIDS and their behaviour is therefore irresponsible and puts their child's life at risk.

Is this the only way of understanding and reconstructing things? Let us have a closer look at the rhetoric of the decision. The lengthier judgment, with which the other two judges simply agreed, was given by Butler-Sloss LJ. Early on in the judgment, she already gives us a first impression of what is going to follow, when she comments on the fact that the mother has disappeared with the child and that the father has chosen not to attend the appellate trial.

> "It is an element of irresponsibility which is very sad, since they are otherwise able, intelligent and responsible people, and there is no doubt that they have in all aspects except one been responsible and caring parents. They indicated to the judge that they were going to stay at home pending any further action that might be taken, such as an application for permission to appeal, and as I said to Mr Horowitz, who represents the mother, they ought to examine their consciences as to whether they ought to be going off like this with their child. They are behaving, as I have already said, in a somewhat irresponsible way."

She then sets the agenda:

> "At the end of the day it is the child who matters. Whether or not the child should or should not be tested is a matter for the welfare of the child, and the behaviour of the parents in a matter as important as this ought not to deflect this court from dealing with it."

Then we get a fuller description of the parents:

> "The background to this sad case is that the mother, *who had one or more previous relationships*, found in 1990, from one previous relationship, that she was HIV positive" (emphasis added).

---

[43] What kind of interpretation is called for is immaterial here. For example, whether a judge employs MacCormick's qualified positivism and his tests of coherence and consistency (D.N. MacCormick, *Legal Reasoning and Legal Theory*, Clarendon Press, Oxford, 1978), or Dworkin's theory of law-as-integrity, the result will be the same.

The mother, we are informed, is fine and well, "from her point of view", some eight or nine years later. She met the father, "whom she has not married" and who was tested negative for HIV and they planned the child. She gave birth at home with the help of a midwife.

Butler-Sloss LJ goes on to deal with the scientific evidence. She tells us that the overwhelming majority of doctors had confirmed that there was a 25–30 per cent chance that this child would be HIV positive and that it was necessary to test the child. The only dissenting opinion came from a doctor in Canada, who had conducted his own experiments and had reached different conclusions with regard to HIV and AIDS.

> "The judge in his judgment chose, *as was his right*, to accept the preponderance of medical evidence, from Great Ormond Street and St Mary's, Paddington, supported, as it was, from Edinburgh, and took the view that this was the *orthodox but also responsible* approach of the medical profession to HIV and AIDS" (emphasis added).

How can this narrative be reconstructed in the light of the postmodern critique of the law? A good starting point seems to be the way the court judges the parents: they are irresponsible, for they refuse to trust the court and have found it preferable to disappear. Their disappearance must be due to the fact that they pre-empt the decision of the court. They feel that they do not really have a case. So, they as well as the court and the social services and doctors know that their choices are morally wrong, that they have opted for the wrong course of action, knowing what the right thing to do would be. This incongruity, however, is recorded in their conscience, which will judge them from now on. Thus the court displaces the judgment from the child and the HIV test to the moral conduct of the parents; more importantly, it (re)affirms its exclusivity to access to truth and justice. The parents' flight is unacceptable, not because, had they stayed, they could have made a valuable contribution to the discovery of the best decision. How could that be the case, when the possibility of the parents' becoming the decisive criterion has already been precluded? The parents' moral wrongdoing lies in them disregarding the court, the only body that can deliver the one, right answer. They show contempt for the godly, omniscient, omnipotent law, and its prophet, the court. They have sinned and will therefore be judged by their conscience.

The story does not end there. The judge makes a passing comment on the mother's sexual history. We learn that she has had one or more previous relationships and that it is from one of these relationships that she contracted the HIV virus. This is clearly a fact that has no bearing whatever on the case. However, it gives us a valuable insight into the way the court has constructed the identity of the mother. They single out one aspect of her life and identify her in its light. In a single phrase she is portrayed as sexually promiscuous, solely to blame for her medical condition and so irresponsible as to endanger her baby's life. She is excluded from the community of decent, reasonable, respectable, morally sound, law-abiding people, thus being marginalised and becoming a threat to and a foe of everything a legal system stands for, including the life and safety of the baby. The same legal system that on other occasions would prioritise a different principle and hasten to declare quasi-property rights of parents over children,[44] here decides to reinterpret parenthood, to build a barrier between the mother and her baby. The child is unencumbered and fully autonomous. The court, in its capacity as a representative of the community, is called on to protect this autonomy and guarantee the conditions that will allow it to flourish in the future. The decision is an outcome of these binary oppositions revolving around the subjectification of the parties, despite the fact that it is masked as a just, principled decision that could not possibly be otherwise.

The court disguises the reasons for its judgment with yet another metanarrative, that of science. The issue before the court is read as a scientific one concerning the behaviour of the HIV virus and its relation to AIDS. In the last instance, it is the answer to these questions that dictate the final decision. The prevailing scientific paradigm as represented by the majority of doctors that testified before the court in *Re C (HIV test)* provides the answer to the scientific dilemma. This answer is privileged by the court over other competing solutions and is immediately transposed to the realm of ethics. Thus a judgment as to what the case *is* determines what the case *ought to be* and *normative* statements are reduced into *descriptive* ones. It is precisely this collapse of practical reason into theoretical reason that Lyotard identifies as one of the defining features of modernity. Once the deception underlying this method has been revealed, the rightness of the final decision is put in doubt.

So, what would be the postmodern answer in the case of baby C? Or is postmodernism incapable of offering any positive solutions? The most common critique of postmodern jurisprudence is precisely that it is irrelevant for the law in practice. It is commonly held that, much as the postmodern critique of the law might be reasonable, it remains nothing but a critique and therefore nihilistic. Postmodern jurisprudence offers no positive alternatives, the argument goes, for it is exhausted in the trashing of established models of theorising the law.[45] Since it concentrates on disclosing the fallacies of the

---

[44] In *Re T* EWCA Civ 805, the parents were health professionals and objected to their baby having an operation. In that instance the Court of Appeal, including Butler-Sloss LJ, took on board the wishes of the parents, although it hastened to assure us that that was not the decisive criterion.

[45] See D.E. Litowitz, *Postmodern Philosophy and Law* (University Press of Kansas, Lawrence, 1997), in which the author distinguishes between positive and negative kinds of jurisprudence.

grand narratives of truth and justice, it would be contradicting itself, if it employed any transcendental, abstract criteria to specific cases. Since it has a vision of justice as undeconstructible, as always *a-venir*, yet to come, it must always concede inability to deliver answers to particular problems. Postmodern jurisprudence cannot reconcile itself, in other words, with the violence of trying to solve the undecidable.[46]

A lot of critics see this postmodern impasse as reactionary and conservative and therefore potentially dangerous.[47] If there is no way at our disposal to differentiate between right and wrong courses of action, if none of our arguments can ever be objectively verified, if there are no channels of communication between different language games and conceptualisations of the world and everything is always a mistranslation and misunderstanding of a text, how is it ever possible to critically evaluate phenomena and ideas such as racism, nationalism, imperialism, capitalism, inequality, totalitarianism? How are we supposed to prioritise axiologically between reasons, values and actions? We cannot discard the project of the Enlightenment by lumping everything that it stands for together so light-heartedly.[48] If we go down that road, values that have been obtained through social and political struggles—values such as humanism, equality, freedom and democracy—lose their meaning and cease to be preferable to their opposites.[49] Even if it is accepted that postmodern philosophy does offer an ethical theory,[50] it cannot possibly be argued that

---

[46] For a suggestion as to how deconstruction can be put to good use in statutory interpretation, see J.M. Balkin, "Deconstructive Practice and Legal Theory" (1987) 96 *Yale Law Journal* 743. This topic is also discussed in P.C. Schank, "Understanding Postmodern Thought and its Implications for Statutory Interpretation" (1991–1992) 65 *Southern California Law Review* 2505.

[47] Jürgen Habermas has offered one of the most fervent criticisms of postmodernism: see J. Habermas, "Modernity Versus Postmodernity" (1981) 22 *New German Critique* 3 and *The Philosophical Discourse of Modernity* (Polity, Cambridge, 1987). Lyotard has responded to that critique in *The Postmodern Condition*. For an account of the debate, see M. Poster, *Critical Theory and Poststructuralism: In Search of a Context* (Cornell University Press, Ithaca, 1989).

[48] A. Hunt, "The Big Fear: Law Confronts Postmodernism" (1990) 35 *McGill Law Review* 507 at 515.

[49] "If 'anything goes' it becomes impossible to distinguish between a moral judgement and self-interest. If there is no means to construct an argument, which makes it 'better' or 'stronger' than another then all judgements, whether legal, political or moral, are arbitrary, and arbitrariness is a step along the road to either anarchy or tyranny", *ibid.*, at 524.

[50] The philosophy of Emmanuel Lévinas (1906–1995) is about the priority of ethics over metaphysics, and it explores ethics as the critique of the liberty and spontaneity of the ego upon realisation of the other. See E. Lévinas, *Totality and Infinity: An Essay on Exteriority* (A. Ling trans., Duquesne University Press, Pittsburgh, 1969).

this theory can be accommodated undistorted in a legal system that is based on the centralisation of the delivery of justice and the universalisation of its substantive and procedural rules. As long as postmodern jurisprudence does not offer more convincing support for the counterintuitive claim that justice can only be bound to the particular and the local, it will offer nothing but a nihilistic pessimism that simply refutes the possibility of progress.[51]

This line of critique is not altogether fair but, by the same token, not altogether unjustified either. It is indeed extremely difficult, if not altogether impossible, for postmodern jurisprudence to put forth any positive regulatory alternatives. Any such effort is bound to always stumble on the fundamental thesis that all regulation as rule-application is based on an instance of violence. To bring the discussion back to our case study, any solution to the question of whether the child ought to have an HIV test or not will be wrong, because it will silence some of the infinite possibilities open before the action that will result from the judgment.

On the other hand though, requiring postmodern legal theory to provide such answers is wrong in the first place. The demand for "positive", final solutions reveals the modern anxiety for a controlled, sensible order that is based on the scientification of the ethical, the political and the legal. Making sense of the law from the vantage point of postmodern jurisprudence can make us aware of the constant openness of practical questions. To be sure, this can be (mis)construed to mean that correct action is impossible, since everything is relative and indeterminate. However, this is not necessarily the case. We can still uphold the emancipatory values of the Enlightenment but at the same time see them in the correct perspective and thus not elevate them to the status of messianic dicta that provide the only bedrock for making sense of the world. Postmodern jurisprudence reveals the danger immanent in universal consensus about the law and justice and makes us aware of new normative vocabularies, new questions concerning law and justice, new conflicts.[52] As Derrida also argues in "Force of Law", the realisation that justice is beyond and above the

---

For an attempt to interpret Derridean deconstruction in the light of Levinasian ethics and thus address the critique of deconstruction as ethically irrelevant, see A. Critchley, *The Ethics of Deconstruction* (2nd ed., Edinburgh University Press, Edinburgh, 1999) in which the author tries See also D. Cornell, "Toward a Modern/Postmodern Reconstruction" (1987) 133 *University of Pennsylvania Law Review* 291.

[51] On the issue of deconstruction and the possibility of doing justice in law, see B. Belay, "Justice: The Law of the Law" in *Applying to Derrida* (J. Brannigan, R. Robbins and J. Wolfreys eds., Macmillan, London, 1996).

[52] For an example of putting postmodern critique to good use, see B. De Sousa Santos, *Toward a New Common Sense: Law, Science and Politics in the Paradigmatic Transition* (Routledge, London, 1995). Santos proposes a new, looser understanding of the law as the dispersal of the normative in the light of new subjectivities.

law does not and should not provide one with an alibi for suspending juridico-political struggles. These should go on and indeed be constantly advanced to further stages. Each advance in politicisation obliges one to reconsider, and so to reinterpret the very foundations of law such as they had previously been calculated or delimited.[53]

---

[53] J. Derrida, "Force of Law", p.28.

Chapter 18

THE INFLUENCE OF PSYCHOANALYSIS ON JURISPRUDENCE

PAULA D. BARON

1. Introduction

Psychoanalysis was originally developed as a form of treatment for neuroses by Sigmund Freud (1856–1939). The term "psychoanalysis" encompasses both a theory of subjectivity and a therapeutic practice. At its theoretical and therapeutic core is the idea of the "unconscious", an area of mental activity of which the individual is unaware, but which nonetheless influences her behaviour. The unconscious is formed by repression, the effort to keep certain thoughts out of consciousness. However, the repressed thoughts of the unconscious constantly erupt into conscious life through slips of the tongue, unintentional behaviour, symptoms and dreams.

In the contemporary landscape, psychoanalysis is differentiated from psychology and psychiatry. The word "psychology" refers to the study of the mind. As a discipline, psychology in the contemporary context has many branches,[1] but is increasingly concerned with the science of behaviour.[2] Psychiatry is that branch of medicine which is concerned with treating mental disease. Amongst the repertoire of psychiatric treatments are electroconvulsive therapy and the use of tranquillisers, anti-depressants and sedatives. Many psychiatrists and psychologists are opposed to psychoanalysis and in most countries are rarely trained in psychoanalysis.[3] In turn, psychoanalysis has given rise to a plethora of different psychotherapies.[4]

---

[1] Such as clinical psychology, cognitive psychology, developmental psychology, social psychology, organisational psychology and so on.

[2] C. Rycroft, *A Critical Dictionary of Psychoanalysis* (2nd ed., Penguin, Harmondsworth, 1995), p.144.

[3] *ibid.*, p.142.

[4] See further, J. Kovel, *A Complete Guide to Therapy: From Psychoanalysis to Behaviour Modification* (Penguin, Harmondsworth, 1976).

It has been observed that, although there exists quite a varied history of jurisprudential recourse to psychoanalysis in Anglo-American common law, psychoanalytic jurisprudence tends to be classified as one of the so-called minor jurisprudences of postmodernism. These "minor jurisprudences" compete with conventional notions of a complete and unified legal system.[5] Even as a "minor jurisprudence", however, the possibilities of psychoanalysis have yet to be extensively addressed.[6] Perhaps this unrealised potential can be attributed to the apparent threat psychoanalysis poses to the conventional view of the order, unity and reason of the legal system and the rational nature of its actors. Where law represents itself in terms of order, stability and unity, psychoanalysis sees law as chaotic, in a constant state of flux, and fragmented; where the law sees the "reasonable man", psychoanalysis sees "chaotic and irrational libidinal subjects, sexual beings, bodies and drives".[7] Yet, it is precisely this opposition that promises the potential for psychoanalysis to provide an alternative, and potentially radical, reading of the law.

In order to have some understanding of psychoanalytic jurisprudence, it is first necessary to have some understanding of core psychoanalytic concepts. Accordingly, this chapter begins by outlining the essential features of Freudian psychoanalysis. It then summarises some concepts important to the theory of Jacques Lacan (1901–1981), the post-Freudian theorist who has had the most significant influence upon jurisprudence. The chapter then turns to consider the primary ways in which psychoanalysis has influenced jurisprudence, considering the work of contemporary commentators who have worked in the psychoanalytic jurisprudential mode. It is necessary, however, to offer a caveat upon this discussion: psychoanalysis is an extremely rich, varied, complex and, indeed, a highly politicised discipline. An outline of psychoanalysis and its influence on jurisprudence cannot pretend to be anything other than attenuated.

---

[5] P. Goodrich and D. Carlson, "Introduction" in *Law and the Postmodern Mind: Essays in Psychoanalysis and Jurisprudence* (P. Goodrich and D. Carlson eds., Michigan University Press, Ann Arbor, 1998), p.2. Similarly, David Caudill notes that psychoanalytic jurisprudence, though employed by some critical scholars, is not a "movement" as such. D. Caudill, "Pierre Schlag's 'The Problem of the Subject': Law's Need for an Analyst" (1993) 15 *Cardozo Law Review* 707 at 708.

[6] P. Goodrich and D. Carlson, "Introduction" in *Law and the Postmodern Mind: Essays in Psychoanalysis and Jurisprudence*, p.3.

[7] *ibid.* See also Pierre Legendre, "The Other Dimension of Law" in *Law and the Postmodern Mind: Essays in Psychoanalysis and Jurisprudence*, who argues that the unconscious appears to challenge fundamentally law's ideas of knowledge, reason and choice.

2. THE FOUNDER OF PSYCHOANALYSIS: SIGMUND FRUED

As a theory of subjectivity, Freudian psychoanalysis is characterised by three primary ideas: the unconscious, resistance and transference. As a therapeutic practice, it is characterised by free association, interpretation and transference.[8]

Freudian Psychoanalytic Theory

Freud described the division of psychic life into the conscious and the unconscious as the "fundamental premise of psychoanalysis".[9] As Freud's daughter, Anna Freud, explains in the following passage, it is the key factor that distinguishes psychoanalysis from other psychological theories:

> "[It] was axiomatic that consciousness equalled psychic activity, an assumption that was in full accord with the popular opinion that people knew what went on in their ideational world, were aware of the origins of their emotional attitudes and phantasies, and were informed about the motives of their actions. ... [The findings of psychoanalysis] not only aim at psychic processes occurring outside of the conscious realm; they also change the proportion between awareness and unawareness of one's own self. They teach that our psychic activity proceeds for the most part unconsciously; that only fragments of this activity emerge temporarily into consciousness; that we, far from controlling our inner life, are in many respects subject to domination by it, to use Freud's formulation ... psychologically we are 'not master in [our] own house'."[10]

Thus, as human subjects, we are fundamentally governed by our unconscious: it makes us, although we do not know it. This unconscious reveals itself in what Freud described as the "gaps" in the "data of consciousness":[11] slips of the tongue, unintentional behaviour (parapraxis), symptoms and dreams.[12]

---

[8] C. Rycroft, *op. cit.*, p.143.

[9] S. Freud, "The Ego and the Id" in S. Freud, *The Essentials of Psychoanalysis* (Penguin, Harmondsworth, 1986), p.440.

[10] A. Freud, "Introduction to the Concept of the Unconscious" in S. Freud, *The Essentials of Psychoanalysis*, p.131, quoting S. Freud, "A Difficulty in the Path of Psychoanalysis" in *The Standard Edition of the Complete Works of Sigmund Freud*, (J. Strachey *et al.* eds., The Hogarth Press and the Institute of Psychoanalysis, London, 1953–1974), Vol.17, p.143.

[11] S. Freud, "The Unconscious" in S. Freud, *The Essentials of Psychoanalysis*, p.143.

[12] See, in particular, S. Freud, *The Interpretation of Dreams* (Penguin, Harmondsworth, 1985), *Jokes and their Relation to the Unconscious* (Norton, New York, 1963), and *The Psychopathology of Everyday Life* (Penguin, Harmonsworth, 1991).

In Freud's theory, this unconscious is formed by repression.[13] Repression is the effort to keep certain thoughts out of consciousness, that is, to push something knowable away from knowledge. Repression revolves primarily around the Oedipal complex. The Oedipus complex is a group of largely unconscious ideas and feelings related to incest and murder: the desire to possess the parent of the opposite sex and to eliminate the parent of the same sex:[14]

> "After the stage of *autoeroticism*, the first love-object in the case of both sexes is the mother; and it seems probable that to begin with a child does not distinguish its mother's organ of nutrition from its own body. Later, but still in the first years of infancy, the relation known as the *Oedipus complex* becomes established: boys concentrate their sexual wishes upon their mother and develop hostile impulses against their father as being a rival ...".[15]

In the Freudian schema, the Oedipus complex is universal: every individual must master it, and anyone who fails to do so falls victim to neurosis (or worse, psychosis).[16] As the peak of infantile sexuality, it exercises a decisive influence on adult sexuality.[17] Even for those individuals who successfully renunciate

---

[13] "Thus we obtain our concept of the unconscious from the theory of repression ...". S. Freud, "The Ego and the Id", p.441. Carl Jung (1875–1961) would later argue that repression formed only part of the unconscious. In the Jungian schema, the unconscious is divided into the personal and the collective. The former contains material of a personal nature (not only repressed Oedipal wishes but everything not consciously registered and everything preconscious) while the latter is a deeper level of the unconscious, common to all individuals. This collective unconscious is composed of inherited characteristics or innate predispositions with which we to respond to life's experiences. Jung used the term "archetypes" to describe these characteristics and predispositions.

[14] Freud, however, also refers to a "complete Oedipus complex" which is one that takes into account the inherent bisexuality of all individuals. "The Ego and the Id", p.456.

[15] S. Freud, "An Autobiographical Study", in *The Freud Reader* (P. Gay ed., Norton, New York, 1995), p.22. Although, in this passage, Freud goes on to state that girls adopt an analogous attitude, Freud was later to revise this view, arguing that girls had an Oedipus complex but it was much simpler than that of boys. Girls compensate for the lack of a penis by developing a desire to receive a baby from the father as a gift. "The Dissolution of the Oedipus Complex" in *The Freud Reader*, p.665.

[16] "It has justly been said that the Oedipus complex is the nuclear complex of the neuroses, and constitutes the essential part of their content." S. Freud, *Three Essays On Sexuality* (Avon, New York, 1962), p.130.

[17] *ibid.*

the desired parent and identify with the rival parent, the adult sexual object will always be based to some degree on the parental prototypes.[18] Adult sexuality thus reflects lingering aspects of the Oedipus complex.[19]

The efforts of consciousness to resist the re-emergence of unconscious material into conscious life during psychoanalysis are known as resistance.[20] Resistance is a form of defence.[21] Defences are techniques by which the ego protects itself, and are instigated by anxiety, arising from three potential sources: the unconscious,[22] a sense of guilt,[23] or realistic dangers.[24] Anxiety is thus neurotic, moral or realistic in character and connected to the ego's three dependent relations: to the id, the super-ego and the external world.[25] The "id" is that portion of the mental region that is foreign to the ego.[26] The "super-ego" is the critical and prohibitive agency operating in individuals, manifesting primarily in feelings of guilt. It originates in an internalisation of identification with parental authority figures (that is, introjection).[27]

Transference is the idea that the relationship of the individual to her present objects is unconsciously influenced by her relationships to past objects, particularly her relationship with her parents. The patient tends to re-enact, rather than remember, early experiences in relationship. Freud called this phenomenon the "compulsion to repeat".[28] Transference is, in the Freudian schema, a universal phenomenon which "dominates the whole of each person's relations to his human environment".[29] Thus, our patterns of relationship

---

[18] In psychoanalysis, "object" is generally taken to mean anything or anyone who is not the subject.

[19] S. Freud, *Three Essays on Sexuality*, p.132.

[20] "The state in which the ideas existed before being made conscious is called by us repression, and we assert that the force which instituted repression and maintains it is perceived as resistance during the work of analysis.", "The Ego and the Id", p.441.

[21] Freud, "An Autobiographical Study", p.18.

[22] *ibid.*

[23] Freud claimed that a sense of guilt "reveals itself as the most powerful of all obstacles to recovery". The subject, however, is unaware of this sense of guilt. "This sense of guilt expresses itself only as a resistance to recovery which is extremely difficult to overcome." "The Ego and the Id", p.470.

[24] S. Freud, "Anxiety and Instinctual Life" in *The Freud Reader*, p.774.

[25] *ibid.*, p.777.

[26] S. Freud, *New Introductory Lectures on Psychoanalysis* (Penguin, Harmondsworth, 1973), p.104.

[27] *ibid.*, pp.95–96.

[28] That is, the subject is "obliged to repeat the repressed material as a contemporary experience of it", rather than "remembering it as something belonging to the past". S. Freud, "Beyond the Pleasure Principle" in S. Freud, *The Essentials of Psychoanalysis*, p.228.

[29] S. Freud, "An Autobiographical Study", p.26.

generally tend to echo our first relationships, generally the relationships with the parental others.

Freudian Psychoanalytic Therapy

As a therapeutic practice, Freudian psychoanalysis is characterised by the concepts of free association, interpretation and transference. Free association describes a mode of thinking used in therapy whereby the subject is asked to report her thoughts without reservation and without concentration:[30]

> "We may assume that whatever associations, thoughts and memories the patient is unable to communicate to us without internal struggles are in some way connected with the repressed material or are its derivatives. By encouraging the patient to disregard his resistances to telling us these things, we are educating his ego to overcome its inclination towards attempts at flight and to tolerate an approach to what is repressed."[31]

The purpose of psychoanalysis in Freud's view was to seek out the individual's repressions and bring them into consciousness. As most repressions are formed during early childhood, the early experiences that are repressed are mostly forgotten. They can be found in symptoms, dreams and free associations, but the subject needs the analyst's assistance to understand them: "These must ... first be interpreted—translated—for, under the influence of the psychology of the id, they have assumed forms of expression that are strange to our comprehension."[32] Thus, "interpretation" in psychoanalytic therapy refers to statements made by the analyst to the patient in which the analyst attributes to dreams, symptoms, slips of the tongue and unintended behaviour an unconscious meaning.

Transference in psychoanalytic practice refers to the intense emotional relationship that develops between subject and analyst. It can be either positive or negative in character. In his discussion of the "Dora" case, Freud argued that, although transferences were generally to be regarded as "facsimiles" which "replace some earlier person by the person of the physician," some were found to be "more ingeniously constructed" and "may even become conscious, by

---

[30] Free association replaced hypnosis as the means of contacting the unconscious. Anna Freud described this development as the "real birth" of psychoanalysis. "Free association is, next to the interpretation of dreams, the second *via regia* to insight into the unconscious.", "Introduction to the Concept of the Unconscious", p.131.

[31] S. Freud, "The Question of Lay Analysis" in S. Freud, *Two Short Accounts of Psychoanalysis*, (Penguin, Harmondsworth, 1962), p.116.

[32] *ibid.*

cleverly taking advantage of some real peculiarity in the physician's person or circumstances and attaching themselves to that".[33] Transference is a universal phenomenon (see above) but is uncovered in the analytic process and used by the analyst. Freud considered it to be an "inevitable necessity" in analytic therapy and ultimately the instrument of change.[34]

3. JACQUES LACAN AND POST-FREUDIAN PSYCHOANALYSIS

Freud's ideas have proved to be both pervasive and controversial. It is commonplace to borrow such Freudian terms as "narcissism"[35] and "repression" or resort to the Oedipus complex to explain family behaviour.[36] Freud remains essential to most psychotherapists and many cultural theorists. At the same time, mainstream psychology has rejected Freud in favour of cognitive science and neurophysiology, while mainstream psychiatry has tended to reject psychoanalysis in favour of psychopharmacology and biological reductionism.[37] Freud's ideas have aroused considerable debate from members of a variety of disciplines: in addition to the views of psychologists and psychiatrists, this debate includes perspectives from, for example, neurologists, pedagogues, social scientists, and even theologians.[38]

One reason for the considerable amount of controversy generated by Freud is the confrontational nature of much psychoanalytic theory. Many people

---

[33] S. Freud, "Fragment of an Analysis of a Case of Hysteria ('Dora')" in *The Freud Reader*, pp.234–235. The "Dora" case was the first of Freud's five major case histories; the others were "Little Hans", "The Rat Man", "Shreber" and "The Wolf Man". "Dora" was in reality one Ida Mauer who went to Freud for analysis in 1900 when she was 18 but left treatment only 11 weeks later. Freud considered the analysis a failure, but the case influenced his subsequent work, particularly in relation to transference.

[34] S. Freud, "Fragment of an Analysis of a Case of Hysteria ('Dora')", p.235.

[35] In its widest sense, narcissism refers to any form of self-love. Although it is often viewed disparagingly, "narcissism" is used in Freudian theory to categorise all forms of investment of energy in the self. C. Rycroft, *op. cit.*, p.107.

[36] P. Gay, "Introduction" in *The Freud Reader*, p.xiii.

[37] D. Caudill, "The Anatomy in Property Law: 'It's not about sex', Or is it?" (1999) 20 *Cardozo Law Review* 1695 at 1701. Cognitive science is the study of mind and intelligence. It is interdisciplinary in nature and encompasses psychology, philosophy, artificial intelligence, neuroscience, linguistics and anthropology. Psychopharmacology is the study of prescription and use of medication in the treatment of mental and emotional disturbances. Biological reductionism refers to the assumption that the primary causes of human behaviour can be explained in terms of biological causes.

[38] P. Gay, "Introduction" in *The Freud Reader*, p.xxv.

strenuously resist the idea that their depression, for example, is the result of an unresolved Oedipus complex. Another reason for the debate over psychoanalysis is the diversity of psychoanalytic thought, both within Freud's own writings, and as between Freud and his followers (who chose to emphasise different aspects of his theory).[39]

Jacques Lacan, the post-Freudian psychoanalyst who has most influenced jurisprudence, urged a "return to Freud"[40] and it has been said that it is not possible to understand Lacan without first having a thorough familiarity with the work of Freud.[41] In particular, Lacan set himself in opposition to Anglo-American ego psychology,[42] one of the two primary movements in post-Freudian psychoanalysis.[43] Yet there are very significant features about Lacanian psychoanalysis that distinguish Lacan's work from that of Freud. Lacan takes up Freud's central themes but applies insights derived from semiology,[44] explicitly linking psychoanalysis to issues of textuality, reading and interpretation, rather than to science or medicine.[45] Thus, Lacan's understanding of such notions as sexuality and the unconscious implies that these are the sites for the production and transmission of meaning. These central concerns of psychoanalysis are both derived from and in turn create cultural

---

[39] David Caudill observes that "'psychoanalysis' is a discipline like 'American political theory' or 'Constitutional Law'—very broad and full of disagreements". "The Anatomy in Property Law: 'It's not about sex', Or is it?", at 1702.

[40] "The meaning of a return to Freud is a return to the meaning of Freud. And the meaning of what Freud said may be conveyed to anyone because, addressed as it is to all, it concerns each individual: to make this clear, one has only to remember that Freud's discovery puts truth into question, and there is no one who is not personally concerned by the truth." J. Lacan, "The Freudian Thing" in J. Lacan, *Ecrits: A Selection* (A. Sheridan trans., Norton, New York, 1977), pp.117–118.

[41] E. Grosz, *Jacques Lacan: A Feminist Introduction* (Allen and Unwin, Sydney, 1990), p.3.

[42] American ego psychology is a psychoanalytic movement that derived from Freud's work "The Ego and the Id" and was furthered by Anna Freud, particularly her work *The Ego and the Mechanisms of Defence* (Karnac Books, London, 1992).

[43] The other is object relations, which focused upon the subject's need to relate to objects. Originally confined mainly to Britain, this movement derived originally from the work of Melanie Klein (1882–1960).

[44] Semiology is the study of signs and significations. Semiology originated with Ferdinand de Saussure (1857–1913), and in particular with the publication of his lecture notes, entitled *Course in General Linguistics*, in 1916. Semioticians such as Roland Barthes (1915–1980) and Jean Baudrillard have analysed the ways in which social life is a sign of the struggle for prestige and status. In addition, they have focused upon the ways in which signs signify meaning, not only in conventional literary texts, but in such forms of culture as advertisements, images and gestures.

[45] E. Grosz, *Sexual Subversions* (Allen and Unwin, Sydney, 1989), p.18.

meaning.[46] Moreover, Lacan refused to consider psychoanalysis in terms of normalisation, adjustment or "cure". Rather, it was an interrogation of the unconscious.[47]

Thus, although Lacan's work shares many basic ideas with that of Freud, his work contains significant differences, and, in particular, his use of terminology is highly specialised. It is therefore necessary to outline particular terms used by Lacan in order to properly understand his theory of human subjectivity.

Lacan and the Three Orders of Reality

Lacan proposed three orders of reality: the real, the imaginary and the symbolic. The real is that which cannot be reduced to, or which escapes, the imaginary and the symbolic: that which is beyond the limitations of speech and imagery.[48] The real is a realm of absolute unity, a world lacking in distinctions, consciousness and subjectivity.[49] The infant is born into the world of the real but remains in it for a very short time. The real is soon replaced by the imaginary.

The imaginary is the world of perfect mirror images and simple negations (everything either is or is not).[50] The child moves from the real to the imaginary at the point at which he or she identifies with an image outside the self, Lacan's famous "mirror stage".[51] In this period, which generally begins around six months of age, the child recognises that it is separate to, and is cognisant of, the absence of the (m)other. It is this recognition that creates a sense of self and an ego. But at the same time, this recognition creates a profound alienation within the subject: despite the child's internal feelings of fragmentation during this period, it identifies with the wholeness of its mirror image. The mirror image thus supplies the individual with an *illusion* of identity and of wholeness.

The symbolic refers to the world of language and of law, that is, the social, cultural and linguistic networks into which the child is born. This is the domain Lacan refers to as the Other.[52] Our imperative to invest in the symbolic order

---

[46] E. Grosz, *Jacques Lacan: A Feminist Introduction*, p.4.

[47] E. Grosz, *Sexual Subversions*, p.19.

[48] J.L. Schroeder, "The Stumbling Block: Freedom, Rationality, and Legal Scholarship" (2002) 44 *William and Mary Law Review* 263 at 328.

[49] *ibid.*, at 331–332.

[50] *ibid.*

[51] "This jubilant assumption of his specular image by the child at the *infans* stage, still sunk in his motor incapacity and nursling dependence, would seem to exhibit in an exemplary situation the symbolic matrix in which the *I* is precipitated in a primordial form, before it is objectified in the dialectic of identification with the other, and before language restores to it, in the universal, its function as subject.", J. Lacan, "The Mirror Stage as Formative of the Function of the I" in *Ecrits: A Selection*, p.2.

[52] "[I]t is in the space of the Other that he sees himself and the point for which he

results, in Lacan's view, from the Oedipus complex. On Lacan's reading, the Oedipus myth seeks to explain the necessary logical course by which the individual becomes a separate being, in a psychic as opposed to a physical sense. Lacan stresses the importance of the paternal function (sometimes called the "Nom-du-Pere", the "name" of the father, or simply "the Law")[53] in breaking the dyadic relationship between mother and child.[54] It is by means of the paternal function that the child is brought into the world of the symbolic, and hence, society. Without a sufficient registration of the paternal function, the individual remains in psychic unity with the (m)other and thus tends to psychosis. The neurotic subject, however, believes that he or she has been split (castrated) by the symbolic.[55]

The symbolic order is characterised by the linguistic notion of signification. Signifiers are not equivalent to, nor do they stand for, any reality outside language. Signifiers only stand for other signifiers within a chain of interpretation. Signification is, therefore, endlessly contingent and the symbolic order always incomplete and in a state of flux.[56] The "anchor" of the symbolic order, that is, the master signifier, is the Phallus.[57]

For Lacan, need, demand and desire are expressions of these three types of human reality. Needs are the real, tangible objects required for survival. The infant, for instance, requires food and to be kept clean and warm. Need is rapidly overlaid by structures of meaning and significance and, in the process, need is transformed into demand and desire.

As the child moves from the real to the imaginary, crying or asking for food begins to mean that the food itself is of less importance than whether the (m)other responds or not.[58] Needs are thus alienated, changed into functions

---

looks at himself is also in that space. Now, this is also the point from which he speaks, since in so far as he speaks, it is in the locus of the Other that he begins to constitute that truthful lie by which is initiated that which participates in desire at the level of the unconscious.", J. Lacan, *The Four Fundamental Concepts of Psychoanalysis* (Penguin, Harmondsworth, 1977), p.144.

[53] Lacan played on the fact that "Nom" in "Nom-du-pere" is similar to the sound of "Non" in French. Thus the "name of the father" is also the "no of the father", that is, the father's prohibition.

[54] Originally, the child and mother are enmeshed: the child is dependent upon the mother and the child is the mother's desire. The intervention of the paternal function breaks this bond and allows the child to develop its own identity in the symbolic order independent of the mother.

[55] J.L. Schroeder, "The Stumbling Block: Freedom, Rationality, and Legal Scholarship", at 336.

[56] *ibid.*, at 328.

[57] E. Grosz, *Sexual Subversions*, p.20.

[58] "Demand in itself bears on something other than the satisfactions it calls for. It is demand of a presence or of an absence—which is what is manifested in the primordial

of the social, imaginary and linguistic,[59] yet they form the basis for demand and desire. In this process of alienation, need becomes split so that its articulated element becomes demand ("I want", "give me") and the remainder is repressed to reappear in and as desire.[60] A demand is always for an (imaginary) object and it is always addressed to an (imaginary) other.[61] But the thing demanded only serves as an excuse to maintain a relation with the other. By demanding an object, the child is asking to be loved. Demand's character, then, is inherently social. The individual demands love and for this reason, the demand is insatiable.[62]

Desire, the *difference* or gap between need and demand, exists in the realm of the symbolic. It is the longing of the split subject to attain a fantasised "wholeness" supposedly lost when the subject was formed. In Lacanian theory the *object a* is the object cause of desire, that which will fulfil desire, fill the lack, and make the split subject whole, either by having it (in the case of a desirable object), or ridding oneself of it (in the case of an undesirable object).[63] But this notion is an illusion: attainment of the *object a* cannot fulfil desire.[64] Indeed, desire is always unfulfilled *because* the subject is always split. Wholeness and subjectivity are mutually inconsistent: "The subject only exists insofar as he desires and desire only exists because it is impossible to satisfy."[65] Thus, the *object a* is nothing more than lack: it is the original lost object, and only desired insofar as it is lost.[66]

---

relation to the mother ...". J. Lacan, "The Signification of the Phallus" in *Ecrits: A Selection*, p.286.

[59] E. Grosz, *Jacques Lacan: A Feminist Introduction*, p.60.

[60] J. Lacan, "Direction of Treatment and Principles of Power" in *Ecrits: A Selection*, p.265.

[61] M. Borch-Jacobsen, *Lacan: The Absolute Master* (Stanford University Press, Stanford, 1991), p.208.

[62] A point also taken up by Darian Leader in *Why Do Women Write More Letters Than They Post?* (Faber and Faber, London, 1996). Leader gives the example of a child who demands sweets in a supermarket. Leader observes that "... in making the request, the specificity of the original object ... is lost: what was a demand for a particular product is transformed, via the act of speaking, into a demand for love. Which of course cannot be satisfied by sweets" (p.55).

[63] J.L. Schroeder, "Rationality in Law And Economics Scholarship" (2000) 79 *Oregon Law Review* 147 at 340–341. With specific reference to property, Schroeder argues elsewhere that "[w]e desire the objects of property not for their own sake but derivatively as a means to our true desire—the desire of and for other persons". J.L. Schroeder, *The Vestal and the Fasces: Hegel, Lacan, Property, and the Feminine* (California University Press, Berkeley, 1988), p.20.

[64] J.L. Schroeder, "Rationality in Law And Economics Scholarship", at 342–343.

[65] J.L. Schroeder, "The Four Discourses of Law: A Lacanian Analysis of Legal Practice and Scholarship" (2000) 79 *Texas Law Review* 15 at 36.

[66] *ibid.*, at 38.

Lacan and Otherness

Lacan differentiates between the "Other" and the "other". The "Other" in Lacanian theory represents the symbolic order: language, law and the ideals inculcated by society. In Lacan's re-reading of Freud's Oedipus Complex, the child is launched into the symbolic when he or she must first register that the Mother is a separate being. That registration is bound up with the realisation that the Mother is a desiring being, that is, she does not merely exist as the guarantor of the child's identity.[67] The moment of separation is both the genesis of separate identity for the child and the source of terror, because of the child's dependence upon the mother.[68]

The attempt to navigate this loss and the beginnings of identity relies upon a third party: the one who is the site of the Mother's desire. This is the paternal function: the law of the Father, his name and the symbolic register of his potency (the phallus) is the original means of separation of the child from the mother and thus of individual identity.[69] As Pierre Legendre puts it:

> "What psychoanalysis designates by general formulas such as the original or the law of the Father is nothing other than an original separation that inaugurates subjective life (in the sense of a separation of the infant from the maternal entity), as subject to the law of differentiation through speech."[70]

Thus, in Lacanian theory the individual subject is always "split" by the symbolic. Lacan's belief that the subject is split does not imply only alienation. Rather the split is definitive of subjectivity itself.[71] The subject is located in consciousness (which deems itself master and knower) and "unconsciousness (the true locus of the [absence of] identity)". The subject is not natural, but a legal and linguistic creation.

The "other" represents the specific other encountered by the subject, but it too signifies a profound alienation in the subject. The child identifies with the other, both its mirror image and those who mirror it. The "I", that is, the subject's ego, is the site of imaginary identifications.[72] By identifying with the other,

---

[67] D. Cornell, "Rethinking the Beyond of the Real" in *Law and the Postmodern Mind: Essays in Psychoanalysis and Jurisprudence*, p.243.

[68] The child's fantasy of absolute security is linked to the fantasy of the "Phallic Mother", the all-powerful, unsexed mother.

[69] D. Cornell, "Rethinking the Beyond of the Real", p.245.

[70] P. Legendre, "The Other Dimension of Law", p.181.

[71] E. Grosz, *Sexual Subversions*, p.19.

[72] By the use of the term "imaginary" in this context, Lacan means the domination of self-image.

the individual imagines that the ego is, indeed, itself, but the ego is the self *as seen by* the self. The ego remains in the realm of the imaginary, but the subject functions in the symbolic:[73] it is only by subjecting ourselves to the "Other" that we can "be". In the symbolic order, we are both speaking beings and spoken for. The ego, however, is tied up with imaginary conflicts and identifications.[74] Thus, the individual is fundamentally divided, both by language and by the imaginary identifications of the "self".

4. THE DEVELOPMENT OF PSYCHOANALYTIC JURISPRUDENCE

Lacanian psychoanalysis, with its emphasis upon subjective experience and the centrality of language, is particularly well suited to the postmodern condition.[75] To date, the main influence of psychoanalysis upon law has occurred in the context of postmodern jurisprudence. Peter Goodrich and David Carlson observe that there have been three primary ways in which psychoanalysis has influenced legal theory: first, to provide an alternative way of reading legal speech; second, to offer alternative ways of reading legal representations; and third, to analyse the place of the subject in legal knowledge and the place of legal knowledge within the subject.[76] This schema provides a useful structure in which to outline the work of some leading contemporary writers who write in, or have been influenced by, the mode of psychoanalytic jurisprudence.

Psychoanalytic Jurisprudence and Legal Texts

As a theory of meaning, psychoanalysis offers law a radical hermeneutic. It is concerned with metaphor, symbol, narrative and ideology. This in itself is not particularly unique: jurisprudential analyses of legal language in these terms

---

[73] "For the subject of which I was speaking just now as the legatee of recognized truth is definitely *not* the ego perceptible in the more or less immediate data of conscious pleasure or alienation in labour." J. Lacan, "The Freudian Thing", p.128.

[74] Early on in Lacan's work the goal of analysis was to get past imaginary conflicts so as to confront the problems between the analysand and the Other. B. Fink, *A Clinical Introduction to Lacanian Psychoanalysis: Theory and Technique* (Harvard University Press, Cambridge, Mass., 1997), p.33.

[75] For many writers, postmodernity is characterised by extreme ambivalence to the hopes and structures of the post-Enlightenment era and also by feelings of personal and social failure and loss of direction. W. Morrison, *Jurisprudence: From the Greeks to Post-modernism* (Cavendish, London, 1997), p.513.

[76] P. Goodrich and D. Carlson, "Introduction" in *Law and the Postmodern Mind: Essays in Psychoanalysis and Jurisprudence*.

are not new. They are a commonplace in critiques of law that range in their theoretical perspectives from legal realism to feminism, from pragmatism to semiotics, and from existentialism to systems theory.[77] Where psychoanalysis, differs, however, is in its attention to the "gaps" in law's "consciousness" as revealed in legal texts. Just as psychoanalysis attends to the signs of soul and desire in the individual's speech, where gaps, slips and condensations of speech as well as repetitions of behaviour are taken as expressions of the unconscious,[78] so it reads legal speech for unconscious meaning.

Psychoanalytic jurisprudence is particularly interested in law's historical patterns of denial, prohibition and interdiction (such patterns of precedent are analytically comparable to traumas and signal repression or absence) and concerned to follow the positive representations of desire in legal texts.[79] In *Oedipus Lex*, for instance, Peter Goodrich seeks to explore the ways in which law constantly spills from the court and text into life. To trace this crossing of boundaries from conscious to unconscious law, he claims, requires a jurisprudence that is attentive to the slips, repetitions and compulsions, melancholy and hysteria of law.[80] On his analysis, the law's "consciousness" of order, science, reason and justice conceals an unconsciousness that is characterised by a *lack* of reason, system and justice.[81] Law's unity of reason is thus a defence against the possibility of fracture and fragmentation. It creates, in turn, an "outside space" of the unfaithful, disordered, seditious or satanic, a persuasive argument as to why "alternative jurisprudences" are condemned or denied by mainstream legal thought.[82]

Indeed, in Goodrich's view, a reading of law's unconscious requires a reading of the institution *against* itself; a reading of the institution's incorporation of its failures, exclusions, losses and traumas. In *Oedipus Lex*, Goodrich achieves this through an historical analysis of law and legal texts. In this analysis, he is particularly interested in the repression of image that is inherent in the law. Goodrich argues that the establishment of the word as the

---

[77] P. Goodrich, *Oedipus Lex: Psychoanalysis, History and Law* (University of California Press, Berkeley, 1995), p.184. Systems theory is the study of the abstract organisation of phenomena. It analyses the principles common to complex entities and the models that can be used to describe them. It was originally proposed in the 1940s by biologist Ludwig von Bertalanffy (1901–1972). Since that time systems theory has developed in diverse ways, influencing philosophy and mathematics as well as having practical applications in a range of areas from engineering to family psychotherapy.

[78] P. Goodrich and D. Carlson, "Introduction" in *Law and the Postmodern Mind: Essays in Psychoanalysis and Jurisprudence*, p.5.

[79] *ibid.*

[80] P. Goodrich, *Oedipus Lex*, p.9.

[81] *ibid.*, p.8.

[82] *ibid.*, p.93.

primary legitimate form of knowing became the basic method of science in the age of print. This development involved a fundamental repression, however: text "forgot" that it was an image and a sign.[83] Hence, the tendency developed to literalise the written word, rather than recognising its role as a mere signifier (and thus its inherently ambiguous and indeterminate nature).

Psychoanalytic jurisprudence has also been used to expose the indeterminacy and patriarchal nature of the legal text. Drucilla Cornell's work, for instance, focuses on legal systems and written laws as mere signifiers for the signified reality of law. As signs, laws must be interpreted. Interpretation is, however, an imperfect process, for two main reasons: first, meaning comes from within the subject and is not transcendental to it;[84] secondly, each sign "is always in referential relation to some other sign or interpretant",[85] that is, signs always refer to other signs beyond their designated objects, disappearing into an infinite chain of signifiers. To try to stabilise this process and achieve some sense of meaning, society must rely upon communal norms.[86] However, these norms are already inscribed by existing power structures: law thus takes its meaning from culture, but culture is marked by power structures, particularly patriarchal power structures, that are prior to law.[88]

Another use of psychoanalytic jurisprudence has been in offering an alternative way to analyse the nature of contemporary legal texts and thus to provide an alternative way of reading and speaking the law. Jeanne Schroeder, for instance, has re-examined conventional academic legal discourse, so-called policy science, through the lens of Lacanian psychoanalysis.[88] Schroeder examines the discourse positions identified by Lacan: the discourse of the master, the discourse of the university, the discourse of the analyst and the

---

[83] *ibid.*, pp.103–104.

[84] D. Cornell, *Transformations: Recollective Imagination and Sexual Difference* (Routledge, New York, 1993), p.24.

[85] *ibid.*, p.25.

[86] *ibid.*, p.37.

[87] This is why, in Cornell's view, laws cannot fix problems; they tend only to reify and entrench them.

[88] "Policy science" refers to the discourse of the university academic as "expert"; this discourse addresses law from the position of the governor rather than the governed, and it views the law as a tool to achieve "objective" purposes. The policy science scholar assumes that the individual will behave rationally and predictably. J.L. Schroeder, "The Stumbling Block: Freedom, Rationality, and Legal Scholarship", at 266. The policy science scholar is thus one who engages in a formalist approach, that is, an approach concerned with classification, representation, the delineation of boundaries, "and the reduction of social phenomena to legal concepts in a process which aims to make a (legal) reality which is both intelligible and manageable". W. Morrison, *op. cit.*, p.290.

discourse of the hysteric.[89] The two masculine positions, the discourses of the master and that of the university, claim to have authority based on power and knowledge respectively.[90] However, such discourses do not address the split subject of the law or take into account an understanding of the governed. The nature of traditional academic legal discourse, policy science, for instance, identifies a general societal goal and, by changing the law, seeks to manipulate the behaviour of individuals so as to better achieve such a goal.[91] It does not speak from the position of the governed.

Schroeder argues that the hysteric's discourse, the discourse of the desiring subject who questions the law, can produce knowledge (which she defines in terms of a greater understanding of the relationship between the law and the subject).[92] The hysteric's discourse is that of negotiation and speculative scholarship.[93] Ultimately, Schroeder argues that we should not reject policy science altogether. Rather, we should aim for a middle ground in which the hysteric's discourse, grounded in the understanding of the governed, can criticise and mitigate the societal goals identified by "masculine" discourse.[94]

Francis Mootz relies upon postmodern psychotherapeutic practice, rather than psychoanalytic theory, to suggest a radical hermeneutic of law. Postmodern psychotherapy is "a hermeneutical, rhetorical, and narrative event that takes place within a social context that is hermeneutically, rhetorically and narratively structured".[95] The postmodern therapist engages the client in a dialogue, the purpose of which is to enhance the client's capacity for social interaction and self-awareness.[96]

Applying this analogy to critical legal theory, Mootz argues that theorists should regard the legal tradition as a "presenting client" and the law as a narratively-structured social process.[97] The role of both analyst and critical

---

[89] The analyst's discourse is a "discourse about discourse". In the Lacanian schema, the analyst assumes the role of the *object a* itself, that is, the analyst plays the role of desire. Thus, where the discourses of the master and the university claim authority and positive content, the discourses of the analyst and the hysteric speak from a position of radical negativity. J.L. Schroeder, "The Four Discourses of Law: A Lacanian Analysis of Legal Practice and Scholarship", at 63–65.

[90] J.L. Schroeder, "The Stumbling Block: Freedom, Rationality, and Legal Scholarship", at n.431.

[91] *ibid.*, at 373.

[92] *ibid.*, at 370–371.

[93] *ibid.*, at 370.

[94] J.L. Schroeder, "Rationality in Law And Economics Scholarship", at 373.

[95] F.J. Mootz, "Psychotherapeutic Practice as a Model for Postmodern Legal Theory" (2000) 12 *Yale Journal of Law and the Humanities* 299 at 361–362.

[96] *ibid.*, at 351.

[97] *ibid.*, at 375.

theorist is not to tell the individual or society how to live (that is, like Schroeder, Mootz eschews the role of "expert"), but rather to work to identify and eradicate distortions that prevent that individual or society from exercising the autonomy to make rational, rather than pathological, choices.[98] To achieve this, the legal theorist should not be unduly confined by any particular theoretical stance. Rather, like the postmodern therapist, the critical legal theorist should embrace openness, utilising a hermeneutic and rhetorical approach, underpinned and guided, but not ultimately determined by, theoretical understanding.[99]

Psychoanalytic Jurisprudence and Legal Representations

Psychoanalytic jurisprudence has also been used to address legal representations, in particular, the role of image and fantasy in the creation of the subject's relationship with the law. In this regard, psychoanalysis is interested in the rites and rituals of law, its architecture, art and other representations that combine to present the fantasy of power to which the subject attaches.[100]

Pierre Legendre, for instance, argues that the law does not limit itself merely to translating or reflecting relations between or among individuals or groups. Rather, it reduces the social to discourse, "a textual order organised to speak to any subject". Particular societies thus set themselves up as theatrical constructions to provide an answer to the question, "why are there laws?". That is, they seek to provide a fiction of origin.[101] This "fiction of origin", as Goodrich has pointed out, is all important to law: law's legitimacy is inseparable from the foundation of its authority.[102]

Societies must also introduce institutional procedures to notify the subject of his separation from things and from the fantasy of being whole.[103] In the past, these procedures were institutionalised by religion. The problem for the industrialised era was how to resolve this same question, "to dramatise the category of negativity so essential to the subject's entry into humanity".[104] Legendre traces the correspondences between the mythical/religious conception of the world and the contemporary conception of the state and of law.[105]

---

[98] *ibid.*, at 323.

[99] *ibid.*, at 378–379.

[100] P. Goodrich and D. Carlson, "Introduction" in *Law and the Postmodern Mind: Essays in Psychoanalysis and Jurisprudence*, p.5.

[101] P. Legendre, *op. cit.*, p.180.

[102] P. Goodrich, *Oedipus Lex*, p.97.

[103] Adopting a Lacanian approach, Legendre argues that language is the institution that separates the subject from the fantasy of being whole.

[104] P. Legendre, *op. cit.*, p.183.

[105] *ibid.*

These themes are taken up by Peter Goodrich. In "The Eucharist and English Law",[106] for instance, Goodrich identifies the origins of law in sacrifice, tracing a movement from theology to jurisprudence. Linking law to the Eucharist, he writes:

> "In psychoanalytic terms, the sacrifice and its repetition in sacrificial rituals, in Communion but also in punishment, binds the law to the power of the symbolic. The sacrifice is an original act of force; the community founds itself through the killing of the father, through an act of foundational violence which comes subsequently to be repeated in purely symbolic forms; the original violence lies in wait, its threat founds an order of law, of obedience to rules, of behavioural normality."[107]

In the place of the Last Supper and its repetition in the Eucharist, there is the social contract—"no less of a sacrifice, no less of a constitutional act"—that binds individuals through the law to the social body.[108]

Goodrich also mourns the increasing sterility of the legal image in ultramodernity.[109] The image, he argues, has a fundamental importance in law: where the mythic role of the text was to open the mouth of the subject, the image "opens the eyes", inscribing the law as both a visible and a seeing presence.[110] Image in the art of law thus serves to both represent and to reflect:

> "It represents in a perfect form the face of power; it portrays the absent cause of law, the other time of authority, while equally reflecting back to the subject of law the image of its own otherness, the mask or persona of legal subjectivity."[111]

The discourse of law can function only if its ceremonies, rituals and other enigmas remain objects of subjective attachment. However, increasingly, the "paradox, poetry and mythologising of the early interpreters of law", "the living colour of the law, its emblems and rhetoric, its heraldry and artistic devices", are replaced in ultramodernity by absolutism, "dressed in no more pleasing garb than the jargon of bureaucratic objectivity in its multifarious specialist

---

[106] P. Goodrich, *Languages of Law: From Logics of Memory to Nomadic Masks* (Weidenfeld and Nicolson, London, 1990), p.60.

[107] *ibid.*, p.60.

[108] *ibid.*, p.64.

[109] Goodrich does not define the term "ultramodernity" but it is usually used to describe the new social world order resulting from the ubiquity of new technologies, and particularly the effects of the digital revolution.

[110] P. Goodrich, *Languages of Law*, p.289.

[111] *ibid.*

forms".[112] In the modern world, the art and poetry of law are replaced by the banality of "advertising hoardings, sound-bites and pervasive commercials".[113]

Psychoanalytic Jurisprudence and Legal Subjectivity

Psychoanalytic jurisprudence has been used to address legal subjectivity in two respects: the analysis of both the place of the subject in law and of law within the subject. It has been claimed that there is a gap or void in contemporary jurisprudence in regard to the subject. Accounts of the subject are rare and the problems such accounts might raise generally evaded.[114] For psychoanalysts, however, the problem of the subject is central.

Lacan's notion of the subject as constituted in, and by, symbolic and imaginary relations has been a particularly significant influence in the reconsideration of the subject in law. Unlike positivism which distinguishes and separates the subject and the law,[115] for Lacan, the subject and the law are inseparable: law inaugurates and maintains separation and thus subjective life. In turn, the subject is caught in a web of language, law, identification and desire.[116] Such a view is highly subversive of the presumed or potential "subject-in-control" which characterises much conventional legal and political theory.[117]

Although Lacan does not give an extended analysis of legal processes or legal institutions, the term "law" appears throughout his work, ordinarily as a reference to the dividing or prohibiting function of law represented by the "Name-of-the-Father".[118] Legendre takes up the Lacanian notion that the "law of the Father" is that original separation of the subject from the maternal entity that establishes subjective life. The "Name-of-the-Father" thus signifies that the individual is subject to the law of differentiation through speech.[119] The logical function of society and the essence of the symbolic function is to put into play, in the unconscious representations of the subject, the power to institute

---

[112] *ibid.*, p.295.

[113] *ibid.*, p.294.

[114] D. Caudill, "Pierre Schlag's 'The Problem of the Subject': Law's Need for an Analyst" at 707. Indeed, Caudill argues that "[m]ost legal thought is structured to repress the problem of the subject" (at 716).

[115] *ibid.*, at 712.

[116] *ibid.*, at 720.

[117] *ibid.*, at 723.

[118] *ibid.*, at 721.

[119] P. Legendre, *op. cit.*, p.181. As Caudill rightly points out, however, references to the "Name-of-the-Father" are not references to paternal adequacy or the presence of a real father. These references are to the so-called "paternal function", the place of the "Name-of-the-Father" as a master signifier. "Pierre Schlag's 'The Problem of the Subject': Law's Need for an Analyst", at 722.

separation by words.[120] The law stands in relation to the individual as the "speaking place of the third".[121] As such the law proffers a system of messages to the subject.[122]

Similarly, Goodrich and Carlson focus upon the ways in which external (public) laws can be understood as "a more or less direct projection of the subjective laws of intimate or erotic association". Psychoanalysis thus reveals the active subjectivity and affect hidden within law,[123] and, in turn, the necessary internality of legal rules:

> "There is no legal subject without an obedient soul, no letter of the law without the *anima legis* of its interpreter, no text without its bearer, no exterior court without its predicate in an interior judgment or court of conscience."[124]

The legal construction of subjectivity is thus the key to understanding the Western jurisprudential tradition.[125] The individual comes to recognise the authority of the social order and to identify with images of power through the symbolic order and the social institution of desire.[126]

This acknowledgement of the inherent link between subjectivity and law provides a very different understanding of the nature of law to the traditional, positivist approach. Schroeder, also adopting the Lacanian view of law, observes that, although laws exist empirically, they are not "pre-existent, objective, necessary determinate, closed or permanent"; rather, laws are "artificial, inter-subjective, contingent, indeterminate, open and shifting".[127] Despite this indeterminacy, by living in society and acting as though the law is objective and determinate, one creates and enforces the law.[128] Thus, law and the symbolic realm can function even without bureaucratic control. The implications of this are that, on the one hand, although the "law" does not exist, the subject cannot

---

[120] P. Legendre, *op. cit.*, pp.181–2.

[121] That is, as the father stands in relation to the child as representative of the symbolic order.

[122] P. Legendre, *op. cit.*, p.182.

[123] P. Goodrich and D. Carlson, "Introduction" in *Law and the Postmodern Mind: Essays in Psychoanalysis and Jurisprudence*, p.6. Affect in psychoanalytic theory refers to feelings and emotions that are attached to ideas. C. Rycroft, *op. cit.*, p.4.

[124] P. Goodrich, *Oedipus Lex*, p.243.

[125] P. Goodrich and D. Carlson, "Introduction" in *Law and the Postmodern Mind: Essays in Psychoanalysis and Jurisprudence*, p.9.

[126] *ibid.*

[127] J.L. Schroeder, "The Stumbling Block: Freedom, Rationality, and Legal Scholarship", at 337.

[128] J.L. Schroeder, "Rationality in Law And Economics Scholarship", at 348.

escape the law;[129] and on the other hand, although it is necessary for subjectivity that there be "law", no specific positive laws are necessary. In fact, it is law's failure that enables it to function and subjectivity to exist.[130]

Psychoanalytic jurisprudence challenges the claim of modern liberalism to have eliminated modes of domination over the subject. Rather, it highlights the ways in which modern liberalism produces modes of domination which, because they do not present themselves as modes of domination, are particularly difficult to challenge or oppose. For instance, contemporary liberal societies champion the ethic and ideal of personal freedom, while simultaneously "making the exercise of that freedom conditional upon personal submission to ... mechanisms of constraint".[131]

Psychoanalytic jurisprudence provides particular insight into the special difficulties of the feminine subject in relation to the law. Goodrich, for instance, is particularly concerned to note the way in which the feminine is repressed by law and legal institutions. He claims that the legitimacy of law has been inseparable from the foundation of its authority: as the validity and logic of law is constructed genealogically, it inevitably replicates a model of patristic power and paternal forms of judgment.[132] "[Law's] logic is thus that of inheritance, its order is that of succession, its power and virtue is that of the fathers."[133] In this context, the feminine exists positively as non-being, excised continuously from the public realm and from its texts, its words, its laws.[134]

Some writers in feminist jurisprudence have utilised psychoanalytic thought to provide an alternative reading of the problems of the feminine subject. Lacanian psychoanalysis holds that the question of sex is not a mere biological given, but a complex symbolic, and thus cultural, construction. The sex of the subject is constructed through the subject's relation to the phallus. The masculine *has* the phallus (because the penis is mistakenly conflated with the phallus); while the feminine is positioned as *being* the phallus (because she lacks the penis/phallus). She becomes the object of male desire (the phallus) by becoming desirable for the man. In turn, he has what she lacks and wants (that is, the phallus).[135] This construct of gender hierarchy continues to "hold sway over our political aspirations and our personal dreams".[136]

---

[129] The place of "no law" is the place of psychosis.

[130] J.L. Schroeder, "The Stumbling Block: Freedom, Rationality, and Legal Scholarship", at 337.

[131] D. Caudill, "Identifying Law's Unconscious: Disciplinary and Rhetorical Contexts" (1997) 54 *Washington and Lee Law Review* 1075 at 1080.

[132] P. Goodrich, *Oedipus Lex*, p.97.

[133] *ibid.*, p.79.

[134] *ibid.*, p.99.

[135] E. Grosz, *Sexual Subversions*, p.21.

[136] D. Cornell, *Transformations*, p.9.

The work of Luce Irigaray focuses more directly on women's civil status, their position as a sex before the law, the need for womankind to be recognised as a genre distinct from mankind, and the importance of translating sexual difference into specific social forms.[137] Irigaray points to the dangers for women of embracing postmodernism too hastily or too uncritically. If, as she argues, all Western theory (including postmodernist theory) fails to recognise sexual difference, then we must examine postmodernism for its sexual subtext. She warns against displacing the male/female binary before the female side has developed its own identity and subjectivity.[138]

Relying upon such ideas, feminist psychoanalytic jurisprudence has provided an alternative reading to the problems of the feminine, law, equality and difference. Drucilla Cornell, for instance, challenges conventional feminist approaches which, she claims, tend to fall into the trap of either portraying the feminine in terms of the maternal or repudiating the feminine altogether. In traditional feminist theory, "formal equality" feminism and "difference" feminism, while both purporting to seek a theoretical justification for an improvement of women's status and freedom, have tended to be opposed. Further, both have been accused of reinforcing and reifying culturally constructed gender binaries: under either theory, Cornell claims that the gender hierarchy is enforced: "Where does women's freedom begin? It should begin with the demand that we free ourselves from the use of gender comparison as the ideal of equality."[139] In order to transcend the binary-divide gender comparison and to provide real opportunity for the feminine, Cornell argues that self actualisation of the individual is essential. In ensuring this, the law plays a very circumscribed role. The proper role of the law is not to assume a person nor to establish the conditions and limits of personhood. Rather, its role is simply to ensure that each individual has an equal chance to transform him or herself into a person.

Three conditions must be fulfilled if individuals are to have this opportunity for self-transformation. These are the "minimum conditions of individuation": the preservation of bodily integrity;[140] the preservation of the individual's access to symbolic forms which allow them to differentiate themselves from others;[141] and the preservation of the imaginary domain (where the idealised person

---

[137] M. Whitford , "Introduction" in *The Irigaray Reader* (M. Whitford ed., Blackwell, Oxford, 1991), pp.12–13.

[138] *ibid.*, p.13.

[139] D. Cornell, *At the Heart of Freedom: Feminism, Sex, and Equality* (Princeton University Press, Princeton, 1998), p.3.

[140] "The right to bodily integrity has to be an essential component of our being recognized as persons: bodily integration is composed of a body image and a sexual imago." *ibid.*, p.36.

[141] See, for instance, D. Cornell, *Transformations*, pp.167–169.

exists). This "imaginary domain" is a very important theme in Cornell's work.[142] She considers it to be a psychic and moral space in which individuals can explore their own individuality and sources of happiness: "The imaginary domain is the space of the 'as if' in which we imagine who we might be if we made ourselves our own end and claimed ourselves as our own person."[143]

Cornell argues that the law's primary concern should be to ensure that these three requirements are met and that all people—men or women—have an equal ability to transform themselves. In practical terms, this means Cornell eschews conventional notions of equality through "legal rights": legal rights as we understand them in contemporary society are based on what men need for well being, "as if there were only one genre of the human species".[144] Rather, Cornell advocates choice and freedom:

> "In a profound sense, feminism starts with our demand for freedom be-
> cause only freedom will let us take up our rightful positions as free and
> equal citizens in the conditions of public reciprocity that make agree-
> ment on constitutional essentials a legitimate overlapping consensus."[145]

Thus, traditional sites of contention for the feminist movement, such as pornography and prostitution, are potentially sites for self-actualisation and should not be prohibited.

So, for instance, in the case of pornography, Cornell argues that prohibition is not the answer. Cornell argues that the lure of mainstream pornography lies in men's attempts to abject the terrifying spectre of the phallic mother which lies repressed in the unconscious.[146] Thus, the arousal of pornography is associated with fear.[147] This being the case, censorship is more likely to encourage, rather than to eliminate pornography: "The murkiness of the pornographic world is part of its deep attraction. Push it underground and it becomes even more desirable".[148] Rather women should seek new and different ways in which pornography can be explored.

The challenge of psychoanalytic feminist jurisprudence to conventional feminism can also be seen in the work of Jeanne Schroeder. Schroeder argues that women do not bring a "different voice" (as commentators such as Carol

---

[142] "My defense of the imaginary domain insists that the law protect it as a right ...". D. Cornell, *At the Heart of Freedom*, p.111.

[143] *ibid.*, p.9.

[144] D. Cornell, *Transformations*, p.145.

[145] D. Cornell, *At the Heart of Freedom*, p.17.

[146] D. Cornell, "Pornography's Temptation" in *Feminism and Pornography* (D. Cornell ed., Oxford University Press, Oxford, 2000), p.560.

[147] *ibid.*, p.561.

[148] *ibid.*, p.565.

Gilligan have suggested) to the law. Insofar as they write and speak law they use a masculine voice. Even cultural feminists speak in a masculine voice, adopting a stereotype of femininity that is the negative of that of masculinity, a mirror image and thus "imaginary" in the Lacanian sense of the term.[149] Schroeder argues that feminists must strive to rewrite the feminine or, perhaps, to speak her for the first time. In doing so, there must be a recognition that castration is imaginary, a myth both in the sense of delusion and in the sense of a story we tell to give meaning to our lives.[150]

5. CRITICISMS AND ASSESSMENT

There are a number of problems inherent in the application of psychoanalysis to law. Not least, as David Caudill observes, psychoanalytic theory is a "hard sell": "the discipline of law is always hesitant to yield turf to outsiders, especially if they appear radical or otherwise non-traditional".[151] This is particularly so in the contemporary environment: Lacanian theory has proved very controversial for a number of reasons. It does not fit neatly into any particular classifications, and, indeed, is capable of offending both postmodernists and traditionalists simultaneously, as Caudill points out:

> "For postmodern theorists, Lacan often represents a traditional approach to knowledge—Lacan is a Freudian to the extent that he believes we can identify our place in language, that we can trace the effects of other people and of culture and of law, not simply on our otherwise independent selves, but in constructing or constituting our highly dependent selves. Just when you think that at least the Freudians would appreciate Lacan, however, Lacan's notion of the limits of psychoanalysis is too postmodern. And for traditional theorists, Freudian or not, Lacan represents what is wrong with postmodernism—confusing jargon, the disappearing self, determinative and ideological language, and relativism."[152]

Ths criticisms regarding language are particularly common. The language of psychoanalysis is often accused of being opaque, obscure and of little assistance in addressing "real life" practical problems. Lacan, along with other influential French theorists, presents stylistic, contextual and conceptual difficulties to the reader.[153] Elizabeth Grosz, for instance, observes that, "French

---

[149] J.L. Schroeder, *The Vestal and the Fasces*, p.125.
[150] *ibid.*, p.128.
[151] D. Caudill, "The Anatomy in Property Law: 'It's not about sex', Or is it?", at 1084.
[152] *ibid.*, at 1089.
[153] D. Caudill, "Pierre Schlag's 'The Problem of the Subject': Law's Need for an

theory is considered appealingly or irritatingly—depending on one's taste—intellectualised and abstract; it seems peripheral to those committed to trans-forming women's lives in more concrete or direct ways".[154]

In Caudill's view, however, discomfort with the language of psychoanalysis reflects a failure to come to terms with one of the basic lessons of Lacanian theory: everyday discourse is already jargonistic, its vocabulary specialised and the possibilities of its discourse limited: language is inherently ideological. Although Lacan offers no solution for transcending the ideology of language, he encourages us to "recognize our place in language and how it constructs us, and then to choose carefully the discourses in which we are trapped".[155]

The opposition to psychoanalytic understandings of law is not helped by the markedly political character of psychoanalysis as a discipline. The various schools of psychoanalysis have developed with little or no tolerance for each other.[156] On the one hand, adherence to a particular school may give rise to a sense of ideological dogmatism and a universalism that erases the difference of the Other.[157] On the other hand, a pluralist approach may threaten to dissolve into theoretical incoherence because of the significant differences between different psychoanalytic schools of thought.

The potential for dogmatism is a theme taken up by Mootz in his argument for a jurisprudence based in psychotherapeutic practice, rather than in psychoanalytic theory. As discussed earlier in this chapter, Mootz is critical of rigid adherence to theory. While acknowledging the value of the work of Goodrich, for instance, he argues that Goodrich falls victim to the inflexibilities of the psychoanalytic model.[158] In Mootz's opinion, Goodrich is least successful when he invokes psychoanalytic theory,[159] and most successful when he utilises the principles of postmodern psychotherapeutic practice and an openness to new understandings.[160]

Analyst", at 708. Although, as Caudill notes, the problem is particularly acute in reading Lacan, who used "a complex and elusive style of writing intended to subvert conventional understandings" at 715.

[154] E. Grosz, *Sexual Subversions*, p.1.

[155] D. Caudill, "Identifying Law's Unconscious: Disciplinary and Rhetorical Contexts", at 1088.

[156] For a history of psychoanalysis as a discipline, see J. Schwartz, *Cassandra's Daughter: A History of Psychoanalysis* (Penguin, Harmondsworth, 1999), and J.A.C. Brown, *Freud and the Post-Freudians* (Penguin, Harmondsworth, 1961). Joseph Schwartz argues that the significance of the considerable disputes of psychoanalysis is not that they occurred—this happens in every field—but that they could not be contained within the discipline (p.12).

[157] D. Cornell, *Transformations*, p.10.

[158] F. Mootz, *op. cit.*, at 305.

[159] *ibid.*, at 380–381.

[160] *ibid.*, at 379.

Freudian and Lacanian theory have been criticised, in particular, for their markedly patriarchal character. Irigaray, for instance, argues that Freudian psychoanalysis takes its phallocentric bias as universal truth. It is thus blind to its own assumptions. Freud takes the development of the little boy as norm, and assumes that a similar model of development must apply to the little girl; her difference is assumed by reference to the male. Irigaray is also critical of the way in which the discipline of psychoanalysis is transmitted, that is, from father to son, with a priority placed upon identification with the father and devotion to his law.[161] Irigaray is also critical of Lacan for what she describes as his ahistorical and social conservatism, as well as a number of key elements in his theory: the primacy of the phallus, and his conceptualisation of the imaginary body of the mirror stage as a male body.[162]

Given these criticisms of psychoanalysis, what is the potential for psychoanalytic jurisprudence? Acknowledging the theoretical diversity of contemporary jurisprudence, and its potential to foster incoherence, Wayne Morrison observes that, ultimately, jurisprudence is about desire: the desire for wisdom and the truth of law. This desire is articulated through speech:

> "The language-games of contemporary jurisprudence speak to the multi-focused nature and sources of these desires. Desire becomes mobile, transitory, unfocussed or, put more correctly, moves in a continual state of (re)focusing."[163]

Psychoanalysis, of all interdisciplinary encounters with the law, is the discipline that speaks most directly to and of desire: the desire of the subject and the desire of law. Psychoanalysis recognises the absolute and fundamental essentiality of law. It is law that establishes the limit, the bounds of the possible. It is, in Lacanian terms, the embodiment of the "no" of the father. At the same time, psychoanalysis also speaks of otherness and the possibilities of creating a space of the other within law.[164] To take up an ethic of difference, however,

---

[161] M. Whitford, *op. cit.*, p.6. As an instance of this, see the essay "The Poverty of Psychoanalysis" by Irigaray, where she writes: "All you have to do to be a real psychoanalyst, woman or man, is read Freud or Lacan—and you'd be better off sticking to the latter." She then poses the questions: what authorises someone to say another is or is not an analyst or to say that a practice is or is not analysis? and continues: "What determines this proscription, and this 'foreclosure'? Your foreclosure? In accordance with what law? In the name of what name? The name of a father of psychoanalysis to whose unconscious any unconscious should be made to conform?" (*The Irigaray Reader*, p.81).

[162] *ibid.*

[163] W. Morrison, *op. cit.*, p.524.

[164] P. Goodrich, *Oedipus Lex*, p.241.

is to oppose precedent, unity, establishment and law precisely because of what it represents and precisely because of how it represents. Psychoanalysis calls on law to acknowledge its fragmentations and the ways in which, by establishing sameness as a norm, it negates otherness.[165] In sum, psychoanalysis both reinforces the necessity of law while critiquing its particular identity.[166]

As a "minor jurisprudence", psychoanalysis has much to offer and its potential is yet to be fully explored.[167] Nevertheless, much of what it says is unpalatable, particularly to a discipline that not only represents itself as unified and authoritarian, but relies upon that representation for its authority. Psychoanalysis calls upon law, as it calls upon the individual, to experience a radical "growing up"; to acknowledge often unpalatable truths. Perhaps it is unsurprising that this may evoke resistance and, in consequence, cause psychoanalytic jurisprudence to remain at the margins, rather than at the centre, of jurisprudential thought.

---

[165] *ibid.*

[166] As Goodrich points out, the unconscious of law signifies the divisions and differences that constitute the particular form of law, and the particular order of social being. *ibid.*, p.240.

[167] See, for instance, on the use of psychoanalytic theory in relation to legal education: P. Baron, "Demand and Desire: A Psychoanalytic Contribution to Understanding the Problems of Student Motivation" (2002) 11 *Griffith Law Review* 332, and "Deep and Surface Learning: Can Teachers Really Control Student Approaches to Learning in Law?" (2002) 36 *The Law Teacher* 123.

CHAPTER 19

LAW AND LITERATURE

TIM MURPHY AND GERARD STAUNTON

1. INTRODUCTION

Law and literature are usually perceived as mutually exclusive realms, both as social practices and as academic disciplines. Whereas law tends to suggest restriction, authority and the exercise of power, literature signals the realm of the creative, the imaginative, and very often, the anti-authoritarian. The American legal realist, Jerome Frank, believed that the traditional formalist desire for legal certainty arose from a desire for the stability and safety that is often associated with the image of the family. Frank drew on his experience and knowledge of psychiatry to suggest that legal certainty was an illusion, a concept used by lawyers as a "father-substitute figure".[1] By contrast, Howard Jacobson argued in a lecture delivered in 2003 that while the family has always preoccupied writers, reading and writing are solitary activities and great literature reflects a timeless desire to escape domestic ties:

> "[L]iterature ... celebrates our attempts to flee family, finding its heroes not in the parents who buck you up or fuck you up, and not in the offspring they enrich or damage, but in the solitary or would-be-solitary, the principled vagabond, anxious, in the language of Jung, to remove himself from 'his original participation mystique with the mass of men'. In the end, isn't it imaginings of escape rather than belonging that we seek to stimulate when we read?"[2]

The contrast in perspectives is extremely stark, reinforcing the suggestion that

---

[1] See J. Frank, *Law and the Modern Mind* (Brentano's, New York, 1930). See also G. Quinn, "The Judging Process and the Personality of the Judge—The Contribution of Jerome Frank" (2002) 2 *Judicial Studies Institute Journal* 141 at 158–159.

[2] H. Jacobson, "Strained Relations", *The Guardian Review*, December 20, 2003 (edited version of the 2003 Robin Skynner Memorial Lecture delivered at the Institute of Family Therapy, London).

law and literature occupy domains that do not—and perhaps should not—intersect: they appear to be worlds apart.[3]

But there is common ground between law and literature. Firstly there is the fact that both law and literature "involve complex written texts and address all human beings as their audience".[4] The importance of language, meaning and interpretation to both legal and literary texts means that very similar issues and questions are raised in both domains. As Stanley Fish has remarked, the central question in both disciplines is, "What is the source of interpretative authority?"[5]

Secondly, although, as Richard Posner has written, the themes of law, legal systems, and justice are "dwarfed" by more exciting themes such as love, religion and war, the former themes can claim nevertheless considerable representation in literature.[6] Thus there remains the opportunity of gaining jurisprudential insights through reading literature. Accordingly many lawyers and literary theorists are prepared to accept that various aspects of literature and literary scholarship may be considered additionally as pertaining to jurisprudential scholarship.

Over the last two decades in particular, law-literature scholarship has developed to the extent that there is now a clearly identifiable field of inquiry denoted variously as "law and literature", or the "law and literature movement", or the "law-literature enterprise". The current recognition of an interrelation between the two areas can be traced back to the writings of two early twentieth century legal figures: John Wigmore and Benjamin Cardozo. Wigmore's lists of "legal" novels and Cardozo's 1925 essay entitled "Law and Literature" recognised law and literature as in some sense (albeit different senses)

---

[3] Costas Douzinas, in a review of Ian Ward's *Law and Literature: Possibilities and Perspectives* (Cambridge University Press, Cambridge, 1995), observes that the relationship between law and literature, "two of the most important but radically divergent types of textual interpretation, is not immediately apparent. The separation between the austere legal institution and the beautiful texts of the literary canon has a long history and an honourable philosophical pedigree. From Plato to most contemporary jurisprudence, law is presented as following a principle of textual parsimony. Law is somber, prosaic and authoritative, its style is to suppress stylishness. Literature, on the other hand, involves flourishes of imagination and playfulness, experimentations with form and style which either have no immediate political or moral purpose or are critical of authority and power." (1996) 59 *Modern Law Review* 318 at 318.

[4] D.K. Pacher, "Aesthetics vs. Ideology: The Motives Behind 'Law and Literature'" (1990) 14 *Columbia-VLA Journal of Law and the Arts* 587 at 587.

[5] S. Fish, "Working on the Chain Gang: Interpretation in Law and Literature" (1982) 60 *Texas Law Review* 551 at 551.

[6] See R. Posner, *Law and Literature: A Misunderstood Relation* (Harvard University Press, Cambridge, Mass., 1988), pp.5–8.

connected: Wigmore highlighted representations of law and lawyers in literary works and Cardozo emphasised the literary characteristics of constitutions, statutes and judicial opinions.[7] The publication of James Boyd White's *The Legal Imagination* in 1973, a discussion of literary and legal language and style, provided an important bridge between the work of Wigmore and Cardozo and the present scholarship.[8] The recent concerted discourse became "an identifiable fledgling" by 1980 and has continued to grow ever since.[9]

This is not to say, however, that "law and literature" has been accepted with open arms into the jurisprudential fold. Like the perspectives brought to bear on legal theory by psychoanalysis, law-literature scholarship is regarded with suspicion by many jurisprudents and as a mere "minor jurisprudence" by many others. Moreover, there is no clearly identifiable ideological bond between the scholars engaged in law-literature scholarship, nor is there any thematic commonality in the work considered as a whole. "Law and literature" is therefore not usually considered as a discrete topic in jurisprudence and is only rarely afforded separate treatment in jurisprudence textbooks.

But a significant body of law-literature scholarship does exist, and a clear distinction is now usually made between two branches of this scholarship— the "law-*in*-literature" branch and the "law-*as*-literature" branch. Although there is some overlap between the two branches, this distinction reflects the different concerns of Wigmore and Cardozo. Law-in-literature looks to literary works for assistance in analysing aspects of law and legal systems as well as concepts of justice generally. Law-as-literature has two subdivisions: the application of literary theories to the law and methods of legal reasoning and the study of rhetoric in the context of legal writing. Writing in the law-literature field therefore contains work on very disparate areas of law, legal theory, literature and literary theory. This chapter will proceed with a discussion of the law-in-literature branch of this scholarship, after which the law-as-literature approach will be considered.

2. LAW IN LITERATURE

As has been said, law in literature examines literary works for assistance in analysing aspects of law, legal systems, and legal theory. An extensive variety

---

[7] See J.H. Wigmore, "A List of One Hundred Legal Novels" (1907) 2 *Illinois Law Review* 574 and B. Cardozo, *Law and Literature and Other Essays* (Harcourt Brace, New York, 1931).

[8] J.B. White, *The Legal Imagination: Studies in the Nature of Legal Thought and Expression* (Little Brown, Boston, 1973).

[9] See Richard Weisberg "Coming of Age Some More: 'Law and Literature' Beyond the Cradle" (1988) 13 *Nova Law Review* 107.

of literature has been discussed by law-literature scholars, including works by William Shakespeare, Jane Austen, James Joyce, Franz Kafka, William Faulkner, Albert Camus, Italo Calvino, Umberto Eco, Ivan Klima, Margaret Atwood—the list goes on and on.[10] Many of these discussions are premised on the notion that exposure to the literary conception of language is of direct benefit to law students and lawyers. As James Boyd White, one of the leading law-literature figures, observes:

> "[Literary discourse is] not propositional, but experiential and performative; not language-free, but language-bound and language-centred; ... not bound by the rule of noncontradiction but eager to embrace competing or opposing strains of thought; not purely intellectual, but affective and constitutive, and in this sense integrative, both of the composer and of the audience, indeed in a sense of the culture in which they work."[11]

In a way that is anathema to the technical, formalist-minded lawyer, humanistic texts "confound the very part of us that wants to think in propositions, arguments, and forced conclusions".[12] White argues that "who we are and become in our talking with others" is not only a central question for literature, "it is a central concern of the law as well, for the law is not simply an instrument for achieving a certain distribution of items in the world, but a way of creating and sustaining a political and ethical community".[13]

In terms of the choice of texts in law-in-literature scholarship, there is often an emphasis on the way certain literature can work to expand the

---

[10] The list is indeed extensive but, as we shall see in the conclusion of this chapter, there is a good deal of controversy regarding the law-literature canon. As regards the authors listed here, discussions of work on Joyce and Kafka are included later in this chapter; for the other writers mentioned, see, as examples: I. Ward, "Literature and the Legal Imagination" (1998) 49 *Northern Ireland Legal Quarterly* 167 (Shakespeare); G. Treitel, "Jane Austen and the Law" (1984) 100 *Law Quarterly Review* 549; B.R. Schaller, "Faulkner's Law: An Analysis of the Interaction of Law and Private Codes in William Faulkner's Short Fiction" (1992) 12 *Bridgeport Law Review* 715; Richard Weisberg, *The Failure of the Word: The Lawyer as Protagonist in Modern Fiction* (Yale University Press, New Haven, 1984), pp.114–129 (Camus); W. Twining, *Globalisation and Legal Theory* (Butterworths, London, 2000), chaps. 6 and 7 (Calvino); and I. Ward, *Law and Literature: Possibilities and Perspectives*, chaps 8 ("Umberto Eco's *The Name of the Rose*") and 9 ("Ivan Klima's *Judge on Trial*"), and pp.132–136 ("*The female voice: 'The Handmaid's Tale'*"; Atwood).

[11] J.B. White, "What can a Lawyer Learn from Literature?" (1989) 102 *Harvard Law Review* 2014 (reviewing R. Posner, *Law and Literature: A Misunderstood Relation*) at 2018.

[12] *ibid.*, at 2036–2037.

[13] *ibid.*, at 2047.

sympathies—legal or otherwise—of the reader. On this subject, White observes:

> "The heart of the teaching of literature lies in the stimulation of our capacity to imagine other people, not only as they suffer or enjoy what we do not, but more deeply as they inhabit different universes of meaning, different spheres of language. For this is what is most ineradicably different about us: that we see and construct the world through different languages, so that what seems wholly natural to me is unseen by you, what moves you leaves me cold, and vice versa."[14]

One writer suggests, for example, that after a reading of Dickens' *Bleak House*, with its satire of the legal system and those who work within the system, a lawyer or law student "can never again be completely indifferent or 'objective' towards the client across the desk".[15] Another has gone so far as to remark that literature generally, "as an aid for the 'sentimental education' of future lawyers, … cannot be surpassed in its ability to highlight the petty injustices and the violence of law and the world".[16]

An elaborate example of work that perceives a role for literature in expanding readers' sympathies and perspectives is John Denvir's use of James Joyce's short story *The Dead* in his discussion of "progressive" American constitutional theory, in particular when considering the arguments of Cass Sunstein for "liberal republicanism" or "deliberative democracy" as a viable alternative to "pluralism". Denvir agrees with Sunstein in his condemnation of pluralism since it "legitimises a system under which the powerful can manipulate the democratic process to force their selfish interests on their fellow citizens".[17] Sunstein's alternative gives primacy of place to social "dialogue" or "deliberation" where political actors achieve a measure of critical distance from prevailing desires and practices so that these practices can be subject to scrutiny and review: "political outcomes will be supported by reference to a consensus (or at least broad agreement) among political equals".[18]

---

[14] *ibid.*, at 2036. See also R. West, "Economic Man and Literary Woman: One Contrast" (1988) 39 *Mercer Law Review* 867. West argues that through reading, hearing, and telling stories, we reach an empathic understanding of "the subjectivity, the pain, the pleasure" of others; "[This is] essential to any meaningful quest for justice, legal or otherwise. It is the knowledge that facilitates community … Without it, we would not crave, much less attain justice!" (at 872 and 877).

[15] C. Dunlop, "Literature Studies in Law Schools" (1991) 3 *Cardozo Studies in Law and Literature* 63 at 70.

[16] C. Douzinas, *op. cit.*, at 321.

[17] J. Denvir, "'Deep Dialogue'—James Joyce's Contribution to American Constitutional Theory" (1991) 3 *Cardozo Studies in Law and Literature* 1 at 2.

[18] C. Sunstein, "Beyond the Republican Revival" (1988) 97 *Yale Law Journal* 1539 at 1550.

Denvir claims, however, that Sunstein's theory suffers "from an impoverished conception of human psychology": it fails to take into account that "reason must compete with love and hate" and it focuses "only on the abstract and the rational [and neglects] too much of the basic social reality confronting the law". For Denvir, Joyce's story of a party hosted by three spinsters in Dublin provides "insight about the emotional dynamic of human interaction that Sunstein's theory neglects". Noting the relative heterogeneity of the party community, and also that "small informal groups are more 'rule-oriented' in their behaviour than we might expect", Denvir examines the discursive interaction in *The Dead* to find that it is "seldom rational" and that "controversial issues are studiously ignored, not explored". Ambiguity and ambivalence, as portrayed by Joyce, are "two facets of social life we hear too little of in constitutional discourse".[19]

Turning to Gabriel's final vision or "recognition" in the story—"Gabriel's ultimate reaction to the discovery of his wife's [Gretta's] inaccessibility and hence his own profound isolation sounds not in irony, but in sympathy"[20]—Denvir argues for "deep dialogue" as the appropriate model for constitutional practice:

> "Sunstein's normative dialogue requires a similar 'recognition'. Its emphasis on rationality not only blinds it to the darker passions that undermine dialogue but also allows it to overlook the sense of communal sympathy that provides the only sound psychological base on which to build a republican politics ... Just as Gabriel learns from Gretta's story, we are schooled both in intellect and sentiment by Joyce's. [The story] supports Sunstein's theory only by transforming it; communal sympathy, not rational discourse, is the cement binding a community. We engage in dialogue as equals because of this common bond, not the reverse."[21]

The impact of Denvir's analysis will, like most law-literature discussions that try to use literature to enhance empathy or understanding, vary from reader to reader. The same will apply on those occasions when the insights of literature into law are of a more direct kind, with chapters or passages or even just sentences that challenge us to reflect jurisprudentially. Consider, for example, Paulo Coelho's novel, *Veronika Decides to Die*. The main themes of this book are not related to law, legal systems or justice. It is principally the story of a woman, Veronika, who attempts but fails to commit suicide by taking an overdose of sleeping pills. When she wakes up in Villette, a local hospital,

---

[19] J. Denvir, *op. cit.*, at 3–7.
[20] *ibid.*, at 10.
[21] *ibid.*, at 10–13.

Veronika is told that she has only days to live because of irreparable heart damage. Coelho's narrative follows Veronika through the subsequent days at Villette, and includes her relationship with another patient, Mari. We learn that Mari had spent 40 years working as a lawyer prior to her hospitalisation and we read her reflections on life outside hospital, "which was becoming unbearably difficult for everyone". In Mari's view, writes Coelho,

> "... this difficulty was due not to chaos or disorganization or anarchy, but to an excess of order. Society had more and more rules, and laws that contradicted the rules, and new rules that contradicted the laws. People felt too frightened to take even a step outside the invisible regulations that guided everyone's lives. Mari knew what she was talking about ... She had lost her innocent vision of Justice early on in her career, and had come to understand that the laws had not been created to resolve problems, but in order to prolong quarrels indefinitely."

Mari goes on to consider the expulsion of Adam and Eve from Paradise, how God had devised an arbitrary rule with no foundation in law—"Of the tree of the knowledge of good and evil thou shalt not eat"—and then found a way of persuading someone to break it, merely in order to invent Punishment. Eventually, Mari reasons,

> "God expelled the couple, and their children paid for the crime too (as still happens with the children of criminals) and thus the judiciary system was invented: the law, the transgressions of the law (no matter how illogical or absurd), judgement (in which the more experienced triumphs over the ingenuous) and punishment."

When God "had a change of heart and sent His Son to save the world", the Son fell into the "tangle of clauses, jurisprudence and contradictory texts that no one could quite understand" and was crucified. Mari concludes that, if she were to leave Villette, she would not go back to the law, she would not spend her time "with mad people who think they're normal and important, but whose sole function in life is to make everything more difficult for others". She will, she concludes, be "a seamstress, an embroiderer, I'll sell fruit outside the Municipal Theatre".

Although Mari does acknowledge that "justice" and "law" have one vital function—the protection of the innocent—she also believes that "they did not always work to everyone's liking". Mari's views are radically *anti*-law and *anti*-lawyers; indeed they may even cause offence in some quarters, or draw ridicule from others. Yet this is precisely the kind of writing that fits, in a loose but highly provocative way, with Costas Douzinas' suggestion regarding the reading of literature generally, that it can offer "a wealth of cultural values and understandings which enlarge our vision of the world and creatively expose us to ideas, principles and histories unknown or alien to our community or tradition, but indispensable in developing a culturally pluralistic, morally responsive and personally sensitive view of law and culture".[22] Mari's views may be radically anti-law, and they may not be current in traditional legal education or among legal professionals, but the legal reader of Coelho's narrative may well find him or herself asking whether they are altogether eccentric in terms of the realities often experienced by clients.

Coelho's reference to the Bible might also remind us that several texts that have been influential as Scripture have been regarded also as superlative works of literature. To take an example from the Christian tradition, this is certainly true of the parable of the Good Samaritan. One fine example of literary analysis that seeks to emphasise how literature can work to expand our sympathies and challenge our perspectives is found in Andrew McKenna's discussion of this story.[23] The text of the parable of the Good Samaritan may first be set out:

> "And behold, a lawyer stood up to put him to the test, saying, 'Teacher, what shall I do to inherit eternal life?' He said to him, 'What is written in the law? How do you read?' And he answered, 'You shall love the Lord your God with all your heart, and with all your soul, and with all your strength, and with all your mind; and your neighbour as yourself.' And he said to him, 'You have answered right; do this, and you will live.' But he, desiring to justify himself, said to Jesus, 'And who is my neighbour?' Jesus replied, 'A man was going down from Jerusalem to Jericho and he fell among robbers who stripped him and beat him and departed, leaving him half dead. Now by chance a priest was going down that road; and when he saw him he passed by on the other side. So likewise a Levite, when he came to the place and saw him, passed on the other side. But a Samaritan, as he journeyed, came to where he was; and when he saw him, he had compassion, and went to him and bound up his wounds, pouring on oil and wine, and took care of him. And the next day he took out two denarii and gave them to the innkeeper, saying, "Take care of him and whatever more you spend, I will repay you when I come back." Which of these three, do you think, proved neighbour to the man who fell among the robbers?' He said, 'The one who showed mercy to him.' And Jesus said to him, 'go and do likewise.'"[24]

---

[22] C. Douzinas, *op. cit.*, at 320.

[23] A. McKenna, *Violence and Difference: Girard, Derrida, and Deconstruction* (University of Illinois Press, Urbana, 1991), pp.211–221.

[24] *Luke* 10:25–37.

McKenna first draws our attention to the significance of the fact that it is a lawyer who poses the question at the outset of the story—"The lawyer is a man charged with knowledge of the law, which for Jesus' hearers is knowledge as such, all that is worth knowing, all that passes for knowledge."[25] In the story the lawyer is testing Jesus—he wishes not so much to know how to inherit eternal life as to know whether or what Jesus knows. Jesus realises he is being tested and asks another question, imitating the lawyer. The lawyer answers and Jesus confirms this answer as correct; "You have answered right; do this, and you will live". McKenna notes that Jesus' answer confirms the lawyer in his knowledge of the law (as stated in *Leviticus* 19:18 and *Deuteronomy* 6:5), but in this particular narrative, it is the lawyer, not Jesus, who is made to answer his own question. Then the lawyer, desiring to "justify" himself, seeks clarification; "And who is my neighbour?". McKenna refers us to the conceptualised explanation of the word *justify*:

> "Justification as lawfulness, righteousness, or acceptability to God bears on the limits, the boundaries, the confines of the law—literally on the definition of the law. What is the content of the law, what is its referent; what is the relation of words to things? So the questioning, the testing, the contest goes on, and Jesus ... retorts with a story ... [F]or the second time Jesus does not answer the question put to him ... The structural unity of question, counterquestion, answer, and counteranswer thematizes interpretation as a matter of questions and answers while rendering the difference between question and answer problematic. Jesus answers a question about the law, about its reference, with a story that ends with a question."[26]

Jesus, in other words, refuses resolutely to be propositionally reductive, and insists instead on being discursive.

In the story, the man travelling the notoriously dangerous road between Jerusalem and Jericho was likely to be a Jew, like one of Jesus' hearers.[27] It is

---

[25] "One need not be an archeologist or biblical ethnographer to know that; one need only recall what the Law is from the time of its revelation through Moses, to recall the Law as the foundation of Israel and therefore as representing to the Hebrews, to Jesus' hearers 'the only ethnological encyclopedia available or even conceivable'." A. McKenna, *op. cit.*, p.212, quoting R. Girard, *Things Hidden since the Foundation of the World* (S. Bann and M. Metteer trans., Stanford University Press, Stanford, 1987), p.160.

[26] A. McKenna, *op. cit.*, p.215.

[27] "The man traveling is one of them", writes McKenna, "that is, one of us, one of our own as we listen to the story. He is also one of us as we interrogate the law in its relation to life. The performative dimension of Scripture is essential." *ibid.*

therefore expected by the hearers that the priest and the Levite would help the man, their fellow-countryman; what is not expected is that a Samaritan—who were considered as abject by Jews[28]—would help; but the Samaritan does help, and in so doing he performs a double reversal of expectations. Relying on the insight of the French philosopher, René Girard, that the theoretical voice of Scripture is that of the victim, McKenna argues that the differences between the attitudes of the priest and the Levite on the one hand, and the Samaritan on the other, make the wounded man the centre of the story.

> "The victim, in a word, serves to deconstruct the differences informing the culture of Jesus' hearers ... The good Samaritan, who for contemporary auditors is a cipher for concerned care, mercy and charity, is an oxymoron to Jesus' hearers, who are nonetheless placed by this story in the ditch awaiting succor. That is the governing strategy of the story, to put the hearer in the place of the victim, to interpret the law from the place of the victim, to interpret the law as the perspective of the victim ... Jesus' question closes the narrative, consistent with the strategy of answering a question with another question ... We do not test the law; it tests us."[29]

In sum, McKenna's analysis emphasises that the questioner is made to answer his own question, "made to see and hear the law as what one grasps with eyes and ears that see and hear, not with a mind bent on questions"; the parable can have but one meaning for the hearer-victim: "It asks only that we listen to what we say, that we take that word literally, telling us that to interpret the law, to know the truth, we have to look around, but especially look from under, as from underfoot, from where the downtrodden are."[30]

---

[28] McKenna quotes Robert Funk on this point: "A Jew proud of his bloodline and chauvinist about traditions would not allow a Samaritan to touch him, much less minister to him. In going from Galilee to Judea, he would cross and then recross the Jordan to avoid going through Samaria. To the question of who among you will permit himself to be served by a Samaritan, the answer is only those who have nothing left to lose by so doing can afford to do so." "The Good Samaritan as Metaphor" in *Semeia 2: The Parable of the Good Samaritan* (J.D. Crossan ed., Scholars Press, Missoula, 1974), p.79.

[29] A. McKenna, *op. cit.*, pp.218–219.

[30] *ibid.*, p.221. It is worth remarking that McKenna's interpretation of the parable bears strong resemblances to the epistemological bias toward the poor advocated by "liberation theology", a form of theology that has its origins in Latin American society and politics and that constitutes the major attempt to find some common ground between the traditions of Roman Catholicism and Marxist socialism. The key thinker of this movement is Gustavo Gutièrrez and his work argues that this

Another example of law-in-literature scholarship is the debate initiated by Robin West when she used the fiction of Franz Kafka to criticise Richard Posner's economic analysis of law.[31] The particular subject of West's criticism is Posner's contention that wealth-maximising consensual transactions are morally desirable because they promote well-being and autonomy and that this therefore supports wealth-maximisation as a rule of judicial decision making.[32] West invokes scenarios in Kafka's fiction—from works such as *The Trial*, "A Hunger Artist" and "The Judgement"—to suggest that individuals often consent to transactions for the same reasons some of Kafka's characters do: because of a desire to submit to authority. In *The Trial*, for example, Joseph K. meets a woman who works in the court in which he is being tried. The woman enters into voluntary sexual relations with her husband, with "a student of the Law Court" and with the Examining Magistrate. For West, such depictions of consensual sex provide a stark contrast to Posner's world:

> "In Posner's world, consensual sex, like any other consensual transaction, should strengthen the parties' sense of autonomy, increase well-being, and render the world more moral. Yet in Kafka's fiction, consensual relinquishment of control over one's sexuality rarely promotes autonomy or well-being. Instead, sexual actors are often driven by an urge to obey a person of the opposite sex who is perceived as powerful."[33]

---

epistemological bias, also known as the preferential option for the poor, means that we should imitate God's concern for the poor, meeting immediate needs and transforming the institutions and practices that cause poverty. See G. Gutièrrez, *A Theology of Liberation: History, Politics, and Salvation* [1973] (revised ed., C. Inda and J. Eagleson trans. and eds, Orbis, Maryknoll, 1988).

[31] See R. West, "Authority, Autonomy, and Choice: The Role of Consent in the Moral and Political Visions of Franz Kafka and Richard Posner" (1985) 99 *Harvard Law Review* 384; R. Posner, "The Ethical Significance of Free Choice: A Reply to Professor West" (1986) 99 *Harvard Law Review* 1431; R. West, "Submission, Choice, and Ethics: A Rejoinder to Judge Posner" (1986) 99 *Harvard Law Review* 1449.

[32] For an account of Posner's jurisprudence, see Alan Haugh, "Law and Economics" in this volume. The significance of the role of autonomy to Posner's views and to liberal theory generally is emphasised strongly by West: "Authority, Autonomy, and Choice", at 384.

[33] R. West, "Authority, Autonomy, and Choice", at 397. For example, the woman explains her involvement with the student to K: "The man you saw embracing me has been persecuting me for a long time. I may not be a temptation to most men, but I am to him. There's no way of keeping him off, even my husband has grown reconciled to it now; if he isn't to lose his job he must put up with it, for that man you saw is one of the students and will probably rise to great power yet. He's always after me, he was here today, just before you came."

According to West, then, Kafka's literature helps to demonstrate that Posner's attempt to defend wealth maximisation on principles of consent "rests on a simplistic and false psychological theory of human motivation".[34] This is an example of the use of literature to investigate aspects of human nature and psychology and, in so doing, to undermine one of the leading schools of contemporary Western jurisprudence.[35]

Often in fact literature demonstrates precisely the limitations of any purely economic analysis. Consider the dilemma faced by Jean Valjean at a pivotal moment in the narrative of Victor Hugo's *Les Misérables*. He is a successful and well-respected businessman employing numerous workers who appreciate his genuine concern for their welfare. Nobody knows that he is an escaped convict. His crisis of conscience is provoked by the arrest of another man who is mistaken by the authorities for Valjean. This other man is, unlike Valjean, still pursuing a life of crime. So it might be argued that society will benefit from this man's imprisonment. On the other hand if Valjean intervenes by confessing his identity, a great many men, women and children will suffer, since many of his workers will be unlikely to find alternative employment. So Valjean considers. He ultimately decides to confess because he cannot accept being responsible for another man's wrongful conviction.

During Valjean's vacillations, Hugo skilfully draws the reader into an uneasy identification with the protagonist. The reader therefore finds him or herself forming an opinion as to justice based on economic criteria. But Valjean ultimately concedes that economic considerations are altogether beside the point. What matters is that he cannot allow another man to be held responsible for his crime. This implies that evaluating the likely economic consequences of judgments as a guide to arriving at such judgments may seduce and distract us from essential principles of law.

One might indeed suggest that the practice of subjecting decisions to an economic analysis represents an insidious intrusion of received ideas into the far more complex and intricate domain of human values that the law needs to engage with. If one of the partners in a "palimony" suit submits that they have been given an envelope on their partner's departure which, it transpired,

---

[34] R. West, "Authority, Autonomy and Choice", at 385.

[35] Whereas West reads Kafka as making manifest the meaning of a bureaucratised world in which no one is really free, Posner's counter-argument is based largely on what he considers the misuse of Kafka's writings: "If you do not read Kafka tendentiously, looking for support for one ethical or political position or another— if you abandon yourself to the fiction—you will not, I think, be inclined to draw inferences about the proper organization of society"; "The Ethical Significance of Free Choice", at 1435. West herself recognises that "literature, like politics, may be endlessly contested [and that] the use of literature may have merely shifted the battleground"; "Submission, Choice and Ethics", at 1456.

contained not money but only a love letter, one might be readily inclined to sympathise with the recipient's disappointment. Consider however the situation of the character Tralala in Hubert Selby Jnr's *Last Exit to Brooklyn*. Selby depicts a society without the least intimation of deep or subtle human values where individuals are driven almost invariably by self-interest, the adrenalin of the moment and the most basic kinds of sensation-seeking and self-abandonment, involving exploitation and violence on a frequent and casual basis. In an incident, almost unique in involving some authentic empathic sentiment, Tralala enjoys a relationship with a military man on leave, prior to his returning to duty. His love letter offers therefore an unprecedented opportunity for Tralala to recognise herself as personally valued (whereas she has previously experienced herself only as being sexually desired). She opens an envelope left with her by her former lover on his departure but seeing that there is no money contained in the envelope, Tralala throws the love letter away without reading it. She returns to her habitual way of life with disastrous consequences.

It is not uncommon for those who enjoy positions of wealth, power and influence to be tempted, as Valjean was, to trace an intimate relation between what advantages or disadvantages themselves and what advantages and disadvantages society in general. Nor is it uncommon for those of the disempowered who are without significant access to culture and who are driven largely by desperation to assume, as Tralala does, that only material acquisitions are of value. It might be argued that a legal system directed by essentially economic concerns would mirror back to both such constituencies a confirmation of their assumptions and prejudices. Much of the attraction of economic analyses derives from their relative accessibility. Such analyses speak perhaps to concerns of self-interest or fears regarding security that are familiar to most of us. The economic argument shouts loudly but it is not the only argument. Literature allows the other arguments to be heard.

3. LAW AS LITERATURE

As mentioned at the outset, there are two subdivisions of law-as-literature scholarship: the application of forms of literary theory to studies of the law and jurisprudence, and the study of rhetoric as a means of enhancing various forms of legal writing. In relation to the former, to begin with a notable example, Ronald Dworkin has referred to literature as a kind of model for law. In *Law's Empire* (1986), Dworkin equated the process of judicial decision making with writing chapters in a "chain novel".[36] As Brian Bix explains:

---

[36] R. Dworkin, *Law's Empire* (Fontana, London, 1986), pp.228–232.

"The subsequent authors are constrained by what has been written before, but still retain a significant level of freedom. However, within that freedom the authors have an obligation to make the text the best it can be. Similarly for judges who are constrained—to a point—by precedent, and who are to make the law the best it can be."[37]

Dworkin's approach here might be seen as at odds with his general theory of law and judicial decision making, which considers law as a branch of modern political philosophy. Richard Posner, among others, has dismissed Dworkin's literary allusions, suggesting that the standards that Dworkin would use in interpreting legal enactments are not literary, but philosophical: "[H]e would read the enactment in a way that would make it the best possible statement of political philosophy."[38] Posner also rejects any general similarity between legal and literary interpretation. His view of judicial interpretation and decision making emphasises the significance of the intentions of the legislature, and he juxtaposes this with "the test of a literary interpretation", which "can be purely pragmatic and utilitarian—does it make the work of literature richer, more instructive, more beautiful?"[39]

Notwithstanding views such as Posner's, one particular form of non-legal interpretation—deconstruction—has had a huge impact on jurisprudence. Deconstruction originated in the philosophy of Jacques Derrida as a series of philosophical practices regarding the interpretation of texts, including literary texts, and has been employed in a variety of legal fields. In a highly influential article, Jack Balkin argued that two deconstructive practices in particular— the inversion of hierarchies and the liberation of text from author—have relevance "to what legal thinkers do when they analyse legal texts ... [and] to the study of ideology and the social and political theories underlying our legal system".[40]

Described in its simplest form, the inversion of hierarchies involves the identification of hierarchical oppositions, followed by a temporary reversal of

---

[37] B. Bix, *Jurisprudence: Theory and Context* (2nd ed., Sweet and Maxwell, London, 1999), p.222.

[38] R. Posner, *Law and Literature: A Misunderstood Relation*, p.227. For Dworkin's general theory of law, see Colin Harvey, "Talking about Human Rights" in this volume.

[39] R. Posner, *Law and Literature: A Misunderstood Relation*, p.245.

[40] J. Balkin, "Deconstructive Practice and Legal Theory" (1987) 96 *Yale Law Journal* 743 at 746. Derrida has also addressed questions of law and justice directly. See "Force of Law: The 'Mystical Foundation of Authority'" in *Deconstruction and the Possibility of Justice* (D. Cornell, M. Rosenfeld and D.G. Carson eds., Routledge, London, 1992). Derrida's essay is discussed by Emmanuel Melissaris in "The Other Jurisprudence: Poststructuralism, Postmodernism and the Law" in this volume.

the hierarchy and an investigation of what happens when the given "common sense" arrangement is reversed. This approach was developed by Derrida to expose the bias in Western thought that he calls the "metaphysics of presence", a hidden premise that what is most apparent to our consciousness—what is most basic or immediate—is most true or foundational.[41] For example, Balkin offers a deconstruction of the notion of identity:

> "Philosophers have regarded identity as a basic ground for metaphysical thought: Anything that exists is identical to itself. Difference is a derivative concept based upon identity: Two things are different if they are not identical. The deconstructionist wants to show that the notion of identity, which is so basic, so 'present', actually depends upon the notion of difference. Self-identity depends upon difference because a thing cannot be identical to something unless it can be different from something else. Identity is comprehensible only in terms of difference, just as difference can only be understood in terms of identity ... [We see] that what was thought to be foundational (identity) is itself dependent upon the concept it was privileged over (difference)."[42]

Another important deconstruction of Derrida's involves the distinction drawn by the Swiss linguist, Ferdinand de Saussure (1857–1913), between *langue* (language) and *parole* (everyday speech), where "langue" is used to refer to how a system is formally coded and "parole" to how the system is more informally articulated—generally in a looser, more ambiguous fashion. Saussure argued that it was *langue* that was fundamental to the understanding of language because the system of relations among various signs is what constitutes a language: "Specific examples of *parole*, that is specific speech acts by speakers in a linguistic community are only possible because of the preexisting *langue* that speakers unconsciously rely upon to understand each other."[43] Language, then, is a system of differences, with words given meaning because they carry "traces" of other words from which they are distinguished. But Saussure's privileging of *langue* over *parole* is challenged by Derrida, who suggests that neither of the two concepts can be regarded as foundational in a theory of language because each is mutually dependent upon the existence of the other; again, each carries traces of the other.[44] No matter how far back

---

[41] See J. Derrida, *Of Grammatology* (G. Spivak trans., Johns Hopkins University Press, Baltimore, 1976).

[42] J. Balkin, *op. cit.*, at 748.

[43] *ibid.*, at 750. For example, the word "cat" is possible in English because English speakers can distinguish it from "bat", "cot", and "cad".

[44] See J. Derrida, "Semiology and Grammatology" in J. Derrida, *Positions* (A. Bass trans., Athlone, London, 1981).

we go in history, Balkin observes, "each speech act seems to require a pre-existing linguistic and semantic structure in order to be intelligible, but any such structure could not come into being without a history of pre-existing speech acts by past speakers".[45]

Deconstructionist techniques have been employed in a variety of ways in the legal or jurisprudential context. Balkin highlights the general point that legal doctrines are based upon a group of foundational concepts and principles that involve "a privileging, in disguise, of one concept over another".[46] Balkin inverts hierarchies to demonstrate, for example, the contradictions inherent in the US Supreme Court's jurisprudence on the doctrine of standing. By holding that the Constitution requires a plaintiff to show "actual injury" to sue, the Court privileges plaintiffs who have actual injury over plaintiffs whom the Court classifies as purely "ideological". Balkin shows one way to deconstruct this opposition:

> "The goal would be to examine the standard arguments for the actual injury requirement: Plaintiffs with actual injury are more reliable, more adversarial, and more likely to present a concrete record for decision. We could then use these arguments against themselves to demonstrate that ideological plaintiffs also possess these desired traits. Conversely, we could show how plaintiffs who possess actual injury, but who lack ideological zeal, are less dependable, less adversarial, and less likely to produce a concrete record for decisionmaking than their ideological counterparts."[47]

Derrida's proposal that texts be considered without reference to any particulars of authorship challenges the traditional legal assumption that interpretation should focus on the identification of an inherent meaning placed in the text by the author(s). Balkin considers, as an example, a published opinion of a judge

---

[45] J. Balkin, *op. cit.*, at 751.

[46] *ibid.*, at 754.

[47] *ibid.* Although in this example Balkin refers to the "goal" of the inversion, it is important to note that, strictly speaking, the object of inverting hierarchies is not to establish a new conceptual or doctrinal approach, but rather to investigate what the reversal reveals to us. The investigation may give rise to the view that a new conceptual or doctrinal approach should be established, but not necessarily. For examples in other contexts, see C. Dalton, "An Essay in the Deconstruction of Contract Doctrine" (1985) 94 *Yale Law Journal* 997; M. Tushnet, "Critical Legal Studies and Constitutional Law: An Essay in Deconstruction" (1984) 36 *Stanford Law Review* 623; and (on the criminal law concerning rape) M. Camilleri, "Lessons in Law from Literature: A Look at the Movement and A Peer at Her Jury" (1990) 39 *Catholic University Law Review* 557 at 571–574.

appearing in a case report, and asks what is the legal effect of this opinion on subsequent cases:

> "The simple theory of interpretation would suggest that (if the precedent is binding) what the judge/author intended is the principle that controls succeeding cases. However, this will not do. The intent of the author does not control, but rather the interpretation of the author's intent as derived by subsequent readers of the text controls. It is the text as read, and not the text as written, that becomes the law."[48]

The meaning of texts is dependent on the context in which they are read and interpreted. It is in this sense, as James Boyd White has remarked, that lawyers and judges live "at the edge of languages where they can and do break down and where new formulations must be made"; indeed White goes to the extent of suggesting a sense of the lawyer's life as one of art, an art of invention and imagination, "constrained, as art always is", by one's responsibilities to one's materials and to one's world.[49]

Another example of work by law-as-literature scholars involves the application of Harold Bloom's theory of poetry—the "anxiety of influence"—to law. Like the device of "liberating" the text from the author, Bloom's theory, formulated in a series of books written during the 1970s, has been discussed in terms of its relation to the traditional formalist idea of adherence to precedent in the law.[50] The "anxiety of influence" is a reference to the anxiety that writers undergo in trying to break free from the influence of their predecessors. Bloom claims that it is by subverting the meaning of previous texts through "misreadings" that writers achieve originality and poems achieve meaning. Bloom's work identifies six separate types of relationship that may obtain between a text and its precedents. These "revisionary ratios" are summarised by Kenji Yoshino:

> "*clinamen*, or swerving, where the poet seeks to correct an error in the preceding text; *tessara*, or completion, where the successor fills out lacunae in the predecessor's work; *kenosis*, or emptying out, where the iconoclastic son demystifies the godlike father by showing him to be as fallible as the son; *daemonization*, where the successor adopts the antithesis of the precursor; *askesis*, where the poet curtails his gift to

---

[48] *ibid.*, at 782.
[49] J.B. White, "What can a Lawyer Learn from Literature?", at 2022–2023.
[50] For Bloom's theory, see H. Bloom, *The Anxiety of Influence: A Theory of Poetry* (Oxford University Press, New York, 1973); *A Map of Misreading* (Oxford University Press, Oxford, 1975); and *Poetry and Repression: Revisionism from Blake to Stevens* (Yale University Press, New Haven, 1976).

truncate the precursor's achievement in a milder form of *kenosis*; and *apophrades*, where the successor so overwhelms the predecessor that he reverses the father-son relationship".[51]

David Cole has characterised the struggle that judges face in dealing with legal precedents in terms of Bloom's theory of poetry. Cole argued that judges are more bound by precedent than poets; that great judges must, however, break from precedent in the manner of poets; and finally that great judges cannot *overtly* break from precedent because they must appear to cleave to it.[52] Yoshino's law-literature analysis is somewhat subtler: rather than simply stating that the anxiety of influence applies in both law and literature, Yoshino shows how two of Bloom's ratios—*apophrades* and *clinamen*—are similarly employed in two literary texts and in two legal texts. He suggests that such an analysis demonstrates that the consequences of the use of "Bloomian" strategies in law and literature are different: "Greatness in the law is not necessarily the same as greatness in literature, in that restraint in the face of precedent may have value in the former field that it does not have in the latter one."[53] More generally Yoshino proposes that the taxonomy of rhetorical strategies developed by Bloom can provide a useful way of speaking about legal opinions:

> "Because the law has not developed such a vocabulary on its own, these terms can usefully be employed to identify and discuss rhetorical strategies in the law … While certain convergences between law and literature may be little more than adventitious, the rhetorical and theoretical concerns developed by Bloom can help readers identify how cases subvert precedent to achieve meaning. Through such a process, a text—whether literary *or* legal—conducts and invites strong misreadings."[54]

While it might be harsh to describe Yoshino's discussion as "adventitious", he exaggerates somewhat with the suggestion that law has not developed such a

---

[51] K. Yoshino, "What's Past is Precedent: Precedent in Literature and Law" (1994) 104 *Yale Law Journal* 471 at 474. See also P. Gewirtz, "Remedies and Resistance" (1983) 92 *Yale Law Journal* 585.

[52] D. Cole, "Agon at Agora: Creative Misreadings in the First Amendment Tradition" (1986) 95 *Yale Law Journal* 857.

[53] K. Yoshino, *op. cit.*, at 481. Yoshino's case-study illustrates how Tom Stoppard's *Rosencrantz and Guildenstern Are Dead* exemplifies *apophrades* (in relation to *Hamlet*) whereas Aimé Césaire's *Une Tempête* exemplifies *clinamen* (in relation to *The Tempest*), and how, in the US Supreme Court decision, *Planned Parenthood v Casey,* 112 S.Ct. 2791 (1992), where the relevant precedent was *Roe v Wade,* 410 U.S. 113 (1973), the joint opinion of O'Connor, Kennedy, and Souter JJ. exemplifies *apophrades*, and the opinion of Chief Justice Rehnquist *clinamen*.

[54] K. Yoshino, *op. cit.*, at 509–510.

taxonomy—or "vocabulary"—on its own. One could suggest, for example, that judgments, to the extent that they discuss cases that might be relevant precedent, are replete with such "vocabulary". This may primarily be an attempt—as the critical schools suggest—to mystify the indeterminate workings of the law, but it nonetheless constitutes a particular form of classifying what has gone before. The standard introductory text on law and the legal system in any common law jurisdiction introduces students to a taxonomy comprising terms such as "binding authority" and "persuasive authority", *ratio decidendi* and *obiter dicta*, etc. From another perspective, Karl Llewellyn's *The Common Law Tradition* (1960), although it was written at a time when its author had retreated from his earlier, more radical realist position, contains a taxonomy of approaches to precedent far more extensive than Bloom's or the standard introductions. In a discussion of what he calls the "leeways of precedent" Llewellyn offers an "incomplete" selection of 64 "available impeccable precedent techniques".[55] Llewellyn argues that these techniques are "in current, accepted, unchallenged use" and that the multiplicity "disposes of all questions of 'control' or dictation by precedent". One's view of Llewellyn's account will depend on one's jurisprudential perspective, but his taxonomy does suggest the inadequacy of Bloom's theory for law (and perhaps also hints at its limitations in relation to literature).

Those who entertain doubts as to the relevance of literary criticism to law often assert that any so-inspired analysis can have little effect on legal procedure in practice and provide moreover scant insights towards an understanding of the law as it is applied in the real world. Posner, for example, in his review of Guyora Binder and Robert Weisberg's *Literary Criticism of Law* argues that the authors, "in more than 500 pages of tightly packed print dense with learning", discuss "a set of scholarly literatures that have no practical significance for law", and moreover that modern literary theory has "nothing" to offer law.[56] Given that Posner notes the selectivity of many of the legal cases chosen for discussion by the authors, complaining that such cases are highly atypical of routine legal procedure, it might be useful to attempt an application of the law-as-literature approach with reference to a routine contemporary case—and to outline clearly what hypothesis is being tested.

The hypothesis ventured here is that appropriate literary approaches can assist in revealing to one the *deep structure* of specific legal contests and

---

[55] K. Llewellyn, *The Common Law Tradition* (Little Brown, Boston, 1960). For an account of Llewellyn's jurisprudence, see J. Paul McCutcheon, "American Legal Realism" in this volume.

[56] R. Posner, "What has Modern Literary Theory to Offer Law?" (2000) 53 *Stanford Law Review* 195 (reviewing G. Binder and Robert Weisberg, *Literary Criticisms of Law* (Princeton University Press, Princeton, 2000)) at 195.

resolutions in such a way that correspondences may be discovered to other legal contests that, on the surface, appear altogether distinct. The case selected as an example is that of *Sadek v Medical Protection Society.*[57]

The main purpose of the Medical Protection Society was to provide advice and representation to individual members who had professional problems. The society was open to medical practitioners, dental practitioners and others connected with the medical and dental professions. Dr Sadek, a member of the society, had been provided by the society with advice and representation in relation to disciplinary proceedings brought by his employer, a National Health Service trust. When the disciplinary proceedings were resolved adversely to Dr Sadek, he sought further advice from the society about possible proceedings against the trust in an employment tribunal. Ultimately, when the society decided to dissociate itself from Dr Sadek's situation, Dr Sadek commenced proceedings in an employment tribunal against the society, alleging race discrimination and victimisation.

One of the preliminary matters under consideration for the tribunal was whether it had jurisdiction in respect of Dr Sadek's complaint under s.11 of the Race Relations Act 1976. The tribunal held that it did have jurisdiction, since the society came within both "an organisation of workers" (the first category in s.11(1)) and "any other organisation whose members carry on a particular profession or trade for the purposes of which the organisation exists" (the third category).[58] The society appealed to the Employment Appeal Tribunal who, deeming that the society belonged within the third category, dismissed the appeal—but without expressing an opinion as to whether the society belonged within the first category.

The Medical Protection Society appealed to the Court of Appeal, including in its submissions the claim that most of its members could not adequately be referred to as *workers* since they practised *professions*, and a further issue arose on appeal as to the relationship between the first and third categories in s.11(1).

Lord Justice Kay decided that the words "any other organisation" applying to the third category implied that an organisation could not belong both to the first and to the third category, and that one might not properly assign an organisation to the third category unless one had first excluded it from the first and second categories. He judged that the society did in fact belong to the first category, being consequentially "an organisation of workers" within the meaning of s.11(1). Although both the employment tribunal and the appeal tribunal had erred to some extent, the tribunal of first instance had been correct

---

[57] *Sadek v Medical Protection Society* [2004] EWCA Civ 865.

[58] The only other category in s.11(1)—the second category—refers to "an organisation of employers" and was irrelevant to the *Sadek* case.

in its designation of the society as an organisation of workers. The judge commented that the society's submissions had invested the concept of profession with an aura and exclusivity that, notwithstanding its historical validity, was inconsistent with the language of the Act (in which "profession" was defined in s.78(1) as including "any vocation or occupation").

The case summarised above appears a relatively representative example of the legal process in practice. As has been said, the present intention is to study this case in reference to the hypothesis that a deep structure underlying the deliberations may be revealed, which might prove relevant to a dissimilar and apparently unrelated legal issue.[59] As has been mentioned (in the discussion of deconstruction), literary theory observes a basic distinction between *langue* (language) and *parole* (everyday speech), where "langue" is used to refer to how a system is formally coded and "parole" to how the system is more informally articulated. Analysing the above case in the light of such a distinction might suggest that whereas the Medical Protection Society contended that the paired terms "worker" and "professional" were oppositional elements inherent in the code (*langue*), the Lord Justice determined that such mutual exclusivity as was suggested pertained rather to *parole*. In other words, the distinction between workers and professionals was not a structuring principle in law but a convention of usage lacking in any formal grounding.

Literary theorists also distinguish between *syntagmatic* chains and *paradigmatic* relations. Syntagmatic elements are such as can be permutated variously within a common set comprising them. The terms "goalkeeper", "midfielder", "forward" and "defender", for instance, belong to a syntagmatic chain, as do also the terms "singer", "lead guitarist", "bass guitarist" and "drummer". One might intelligently enquire as to whether someone is playing as a forward or as a defender. Or one might enquire as to whether one is playing lead or bass guitar. But it violates the code to ask whether someone is playing in midfield or on drums. The two separate sets, the former relating to footballers and the latter relating to a group of musicians, are in paradigmatic relation to each other. They occupy alternate universes of discourse.

The Employment Appeal Tribunal expressed more confidence in the society's belonging to the third category in the legislation—"any other organisation whose members carry on a particular profession or trade for the purposes of which the organisation exists"—than they did in the society as representing "an organisation of workers". It would therefore appear that they interpreted the phrase "profession or trade" *paradigmatically*, being of the

---

[59] Such is a fairly standard expectation relating to a mode of analysis. For example in science, one seeks to excavate, from specific instances, formulae of more general application, and in medicine one seeks to apply findings in regard to lower organisms to the investigation of higher organisms.

opinion that the said phrase involved two significantly distinct varieties of occupation: they presume "trade" to refer to non-professional workers. The Lord Justice however viewed the terms profession and trade as *syntagmatically* related—interchangeable as far as the law was concerned. The initial tribunal had regarded the first and third categories as syntagmatic, accepting that an organisation could belong to both categories at the same time. The Lord Justice decreed that the words "any other organisation" rendered the two categories mutually exclusive, so deeming the first and third categories as standing in *paradigmatic* relation to each other. He glossed his decision with the significant suggestion that distinctions based on an aura enjoying historical validity were paradigmatic in relation to more specifically statute or code-centred distinctions. Therefore one could not substitute a perception based on history or tradition for one based on law.

Now, it can be argued that the deep structure delineated above has relevance for child custody cases in family law. Consider the criticism often made (by both women and men) of court procedures in such cases, where it is alleged that parents are frequently not perceived or treated equally under the law but are regarded differently, depending on whether they are male or are female. This criticism is often supplemented by the claim that womanhood can tend to be invested with an exclusivity and aura—a feminine as against a professional mystique—with likewise little beyond historical custom and the relics of traditional prejudice to recommend it. The argument in favour of parents being treated equally implies that the terms "father" and "mother" represent for legal purposes interchangeable elements in a syntagmatic chain, the gender of the parent being considered arbitrary, as long as one's parenting is deemed appropriate. The argument that womanhood (in reference to legal practice) is invested with an aura dependant upon traditional associations often accompanies an appeal that the law demonstrate its more usual preference for *langue* over *parole*.

Consider now a separate criticism frequently made of the family law courts, and frequently by the same persons as propose the criticisms outlined above. It is often argued that the courts do not adequately recognise that the child is likely to suffer through failing to have access to both parents. This criticism is often accompanied by the assertion that access to both parents is important as both parents fulfil contrasting (or even complementary) functions. To claim that both parents fulfil contrasting or complementary functions implies that the terms "father" and "mother" are in paradigmatic relation to each other and thereby lends some potential support towards treating them differently. The valorisation of the two-parent over the single-parent family appears no less dependent on *parole* than the alleged idealisation of womanhood referred to earlier.

Family law tends, due to the particular sensitivity of many of the issues it encounters, to allow *parole* more influence over *langue* than is usual with law.

This *modus operandi* would perhaps benefit from being articulated in a properly systematic fashion so that it may be clarified precisely where the law is making appeal to its code and where it is drawing upon extraneous considerations. The distinction between syntagmatic and paradigmatic associations (the presumption of legal equivalence or difference applying to parents of separate gender) might also be clarified more precisely. Though here again the courts perhaps tend to prefer to pick and mix perspectives, there seems in this instance less obvious justification for so doing. Put plainly, legal equivalence and legal difference appear, even allowing for context, to be mutually exclusive options. One might suspect that, as in the *Sadek* case, much unnecessary confusion might be avoided by an unequivocal declaration as to which supposition is to be upheld.

But the argument ventured here does not depend on the virtue or otherwise of the speculations entered into immediately above. Even assuming the judgment in the *Sadek* case to be sound, it is not hypothesised that a law-as-literature analysis will necessarily guide us towards a similarly correct decision in some other connection (in this instance, in regard to family law). It is hypothesised only that it may reveal a similarity in the way of deep structuring that might not otherwise have become apparent. It may not necessarily help us in making interpretations but perhaps it may help us in understanding more thoroughly what it is that we are interpreting.

To recapitulate: in attempting an exemplification as to how the law-as-literature model might be systematically applied to legal studies, we relied upon the identification of potential parallels linking basic elements of literary theory with basic structures familiar from law. We made comparisons between the *langue/parole* distinction and the legal distinction between inferences that are code or statute-based and those not so based. We compared the distinction between syntagmatic and paradigmatic associations to that between interchangeable and mutually exclusive categories. We might easily have offered alternative correspondences, relating, for example, the *langue/parole* distinction to the distinction obtaining between direct and circumstantial evidence and the syntagmatic/paradigmatic distinction to issues regarding influential or counter-indicative legal precedents. It may be suggested in conclusion that an extensive list of such potential correspondences between the terms, themes and approaches of literary theory and those of law and legal procedure might set out more transparently the arguments in favour of the relevance of the law-as-literature approach, allowing such to be more saliently supported and queried than is perhaps the case when the claims being made on its behalf are more abstract and disparate.

As regards the other subdivision of law as literature, the study of rhetoric as a means of enhancing various forms of legal writing, both legal and literary texts are studied. As Marijane Camilleri observes, skills and model examples in argumentation, advocacy, persuasion, and communication are of value to lawyers and are available in literature:

> "Precision and eloquence in language can help to shed the 'masks' of inaccessible and stilted legal terminology ... Critical probing of judicial opinions, legal arguments, and political debates may be easily handicapped if the lawyer lacks the language sophistication needed to penetrate deceptive language devices ... Literature could provide the law professor with many memorable illustrations of clear and persuasive language and could be an enormously effective teaching tool for developing written and oral legal advocacy skills."[60]

There are also several studies of law as rhetoric. Many of these focus on judgments because "a major contention of some scholars is that the judicial opinion is the law's most literary form".[61] Richard Posner has, in fact, suggested that the *only* way in which lawyers and judges can learn from literature is by studying and developing "craft values" of meticulousness, attention to detail, impartiality and "tricks" of rhetoric.[62] Here James Boyd White again takes issue with Posner:

> "For [Posner] there is no moral or ethical significance to style; one decides what one wants to decide on the merits, then dresses it up as persuasively as possible; the text that persuades the most is the one that is most to be admired, and this is as true of judicial opinions as of other forms of literature. The decision a judge reaches can be criticized on the merits, as right or wrong, just or unjust. But what he says in defense or explanation of his judgment has meaning only insofar as it succeeds or fails to persuade. Except for the very limited 'craft values', one cannot, in Judge Posner's view, criticize a text in ethical or political or moral terms."[64]

This position is completely unacceptable to White, who suggests that what Posner misses is that in our speech, just as in our other conduct, we engage in

---

[60] M. Camilleri, *op. cit.*, at 581.

[61] Simon Petch, "Borderline Judgements: Law or Literature?" (1991) 7 *Australian Journal of Law and Society* 3 at 3. See also S. Levinson, "The Rhetoric of the Judicial Opinion" in *Law's Stories: Narrative and Rhetoric in Law* (P. Brooks and P. Gewirtz eds, Yale University Press, New Haven, 1996) and Richard Weisberg, "How Judges Speak: Some Lessons on Adjudication in *Billy Budd, Sailor* with an Application to Justice Rehnquist" (1982) 57 *New York University Law Review* 1.

[62] See R. Posner, *Law and Literature: A Misunderstood Relation*, chap.6.

[63] J.B. White, "What can a Lawyer Learn from Literature?", at 2037.

[64] *ibid.*

ethically and politically meaningful action. The contribution of rhetoric, from Aristotle onwards, according to White, is to help us see that "in all our talk we define ourselves, our audience, and a relation between us".[62] Rhetoric, then, is constitutive of a social and ethical reality:

> "In judging political figures, including judges, we properly ask ourselves what relation they establish with us: is it at heart manipulative, authoritarian, deceptive? Or is it based upon respect and mutuality? In other words is it a community that seeks to make democracy possible? Rhetoric is a way of pursuing such questions … [I]t is a mode of criticism, in which we can engage only if we recognize that our talk is as real, as substantive, as our other action."[65]

4. CONCLUSION

Perhaps the most outstanding feature of law-literature scholarship in the context of jurisprudence generally is the absence of *any* common ideological bond between the scholars involved. James Boyd White has remarked that "[the movement is not inherently left-wing] unless a general opposition to bureaucratic forms of life and speech be thought to deserve that characterisation",[66] but even such opposition is not shared by all law-literature scholars. Those who choose to study literary rhetoric to enhance legal rhetoric, for example, combine an interest in the law-literature field with some dedication to the bureaucracy of law. Similar ideological divisions are evident elsewhere. For example, while one writer has suggested that there are essentially two kinds of literary texts which are employed by the law-in-literature branch—those that describe the alien nature of the legal process (*e.g.* Dickens' *Bleak House*) and those which use law itself as a metaphor for *anomie* or alienation (*e.g.* Kafka's *The Trial*; Dostoevski's *Crime and Punishment*),[67]—another has written that literature can provide law students with "a vehicle for articulating, and a source for discerning, a public commitment to a shared moral value system".[68] The contrast between these two perspectives is just an indication of the different political agendas with which it is possible to approach "legal" interpretations of literature.

There has also been intense political disagreement over the question of the law-literature canon. Judith Resnik observes that it is a crucial question

---

[65] *ibid.*, at 2038.
[66] J. White, "What Can a Lawyer Learn from Literature?", at 2027 (n.40).
[67] I. Ward, "The Educative Ambition of Law and Literature" (1993) 13 *Legal Studies* 323 at 329–330.
[68] M. Camilleri, *op. cit.*, at 594.

"what (and who) is given voice; who privileged, repeated, and invoked; who silenced, ignored, submerged, and marginalized. Law and literature have shared traditions—of silencing, of pushing certain stories to the margin and of privileging others. An obvious example in literature is the exclusion of certain books from the canon of the 'great books'."[69]

Although the definition of literature in law-literature scholarship has broadened to include both films and television productions,[70] most of the scholarship continues to deal with work from the more conventional literary canon. In a 1990 article Resnik and Caroline Heilburn challenged what they saw as the overwhelmingly masculinist bias of the law and literature movement,[71] and more recently work has emerged that seeks "to engage in the active de-canonization of the field of law and literature, and to show through example how the inclusion of literature emerging from a wide variety of ethnic experiences in America would challenge the settled assumptions of the field".[72]

It is hoped that the account of "law and literature" given here, and the selection of examples, will demonstrate the huge diversity in this field and also highlight some potential roles for this scholarship in legal education. As Ian Ward has suggested, the ambition of law-literature studies is primarily educative.[73] In a broad sense, the scholarship is a battle against what Edward

---

[69] J. Resnik, "Constructing the Canon" (1990) 2 *Yale Journal of Law and the Humanities* 221 at 221. Costas Douzinas also raises this important general issue: "[L]aw and literature treats as authoritative literary and legal texts which are already part of their respective canons. The process through which particular texts are selected and authorized is not examined. Might it be that they are selected because they fit particular patterns of power, property and hierarchy? What about the lost texts, the suppressed texts, the ignored texts?"; *op. cit.*, at 321.

[70] See, for example, P.N. Meyer, "Law Students go to the Movies" (1992) 24 *Connecticut Law Review* 893 and S. Gillers, "Taking 'L.A. Law' More Seriously" (1989) 98 *Yale Law Journal* 1607.

[71] C. Heilburn and J. Resnik, "Convergences: Law, Literature and Feminism" (1990) 99 *Yale Law Journal* 1912.

[72] G. Desai, F. Smith and S. Nair, "Introduction: Law, Literature, and Ethnic Subjects— Critical Essay" (2003) 28 *MELUS* 3 at 3. Milner Ball observes: "Literature was urged upon the law school with creative pluck. After the agenda made room for Homer and Melville, however, the audacity and openness stalled. For the most part, studies in Law and Literature still do not venture outside a narrow range of standard, Harvard-and-its-sisters approved literature. Where are the new, more difficult translations, the equivalents in our practice to the topics [Stanley] Fish refers to in English studies: 'The Trickster Figure in Chicano and Black Literature' or 'Lesbian Feminist Poetry in Texas'?"; "Confessions" (1989) 1 *Cardozo Studies in Law and Literature* 185.

[73] I. Ward, "The Educative Ambition of Law and Literature", at 323. See also A.

Said has identified as one of the main pressures "that challenge the intellectual's ingenuity and will"—specialisation. In his 1993 Reith lectures, Said stated:

> "The higher one goes in the education system today the more one is limited to a relatively narrow area of knowledge. ... In the study of literature, for example, ... specialisation has meant an increasing technical formalism, and less and less of a historical sense of what real experiences actually went into the making of a work of literature. Specialisation loses you sight of the raw effort of constructing either art or knowledge; as a result you cannot view knowledge and art as choices and decisions, commitments and alignments, but only in terms of impersonal theories or methodologies."[74]

The role of law-literature scholarship in this battle against specialisation should not be underestimated. It is important to remember that the sociology of academic law, in the common law world and in many other types of legal system also, has traditionally been dominated by formalist ideology—the view "that law is a self-contained body of rules which operates by means of a distinctive system of conceptual thought".[75] However, the many and varied challenges to formalism are well documented in several places in this volume, and there is little doubt that law has declined as an autonomous discipline, albeit more in the US than, say, in Ireland or the UK.[76] The growth of interdisciplinarity in the American legal academy has encouraged the development of law-literature scholarship and courses are now offered in Law and Literature at several US law schools.[77] The idea behind such developments is not only to expand legal education beyond the intellectualism of legal formalism but also beyond the social sciences in general and towards the humanities.

Bradney, "An Educational Ambition for 'Law and Literature'" (2000) 7 *International Journal of the Legal Profession* 343.

[74] E. Said, *Representations of the Intellectual: The 1993 Reith Lectures* (Vintage, New York, 1996), pp.76–77.

[75] M. Loughlin, *Public Law and Political Theory* (Clarendon Press, Oxford, 1992), p.22. For discussion of formalism in legal education, see John Ringrose, "Jurisprudence and Legal Education" in this volume.

[76] See R. Posner, "The Decline of Law as an Autonomous Discipline: 1962–1987" (1987) 100 *Harvard Law Review* 761.

[77] See, for example, Elizabeth Villiers Gemette's empirical surveys of law and literature courses: "Law and Literature: Joining the Class Action" (1995) 19 *Valparaiso University Law Review* 665 and "Law and Literature: An Unnecessarily Suspect Class in the Liberal Arts Component of Law School Curriculum" (1989) 23 *Valparaiso University Law Review* 267.

In conclusion, the scholars engaged in this field of inquiry have collectively made a powerful case for law-literature discourse and any attempt to entirely dissociate law and literature would now appear ill-considered.[78] The scholarship aims to influence a course of study which is often "complex, inaccessible or downright dull" to become something that the students "might better enjoy and thus, inevitably, better understand".[79] Jack Balkin, in his study of deconstructionosm and legal theory, compares deconstruction to psychoanalysis to answer the charge of "nihilism" advanced against the former, that is, the charge that if the results of a deconstructive reading can themselves be deconstructed, deconstruction threatens to become an endless series of reversals and counter-reversals, without any logical stopping point. Balkin points out that the psychoanalyst reverses the privileging of the conscious over the unconscious as the motivation for human behaviour; and that there is also a focus in psychoanalysis on the marginal, the everyday events and free associations of ideas, the dream material. Furthermore, he says, both deconstruction and psychoanalysis offer critical theories, and part of what this involves is that their goal is not to develop a series of true factual propositions, but to achieve enlightenment and emancipation, and also that they are confirmed not by a process of experimentation and empirical verification, but through a more complicated process of self-reflection: "The critical theorist determines whether she has achieved enlightenment and emancipation in terms of knowledge and beliefs she has developed in the course of applying the critical theory."[80] In response to that old chestnut, *"Quid custodit ipsos custodes?"*, we might like to be able to answer: The guardians will be guarded by the law. But for this to be viable, lawyers and law students must have access to self-reflection. One of law-literature scholarship's great merits is that it emphasises so comprehensively this imperative.

---

[78] Summarising the essential interconnectedness of law and literature, Marijane Camilleri has written: "[T]he law and literature movement has a triangular dimension. Literature offers law its substance, its interpretive devices, and its rhetorical excellence. Each point of congruence between law and literature provides a source of limitless possibilities and alone would justify the reference to literature in legal education. Literature reflects knowledge about true human nature; law governs societal activity upon a formulation of true human nature. Ideally, human action should comport with the fullness of human knowledge. It is natural, therefore, not strange, for lawyers to take lessons from literature"; *op. cit.*, at 594.

[79] I. Ward, *Law and Literature: Possibilities and Perspectives*, p.ix.

[80] J. Balkin, *op. cit.*, at 765.

CHAPTER 20

JURISPRUDENCE AND LEGAL EDUCATION

JOHN RINGROSE

1. INTRODUCTION

An enduring myth, which still survives amongst many within the legal profession, and for that matter within the legal academy itself, is the notion that law is in some sense autonomous. The majority of those directly involved with, or studying, the operations of the law continue—albeit to a greater or lesser extent—to subscribe to the view that law is basically a closed and logical system. This "black-letter" understanding of the law advocates the formal syllogistic application of law to the facts of cases, an approach sometimes known as "formalism" or "mechanical jurisprudence".[1] This approach usually assumes that "law" is intelligible as a coherent phenomenon, that there is consistency, predictability and ultimately "closure": a systematic isolation of the legal system from such things as politics and culture.[2] When law is assumed to be a self-contained social phenomenon, it is presented as a "scientific" enterprise that excludes theoretical and non-legal factors, deeming them to be irrelevant to legal reasoning. The traditional view is that this formalistic approach promotes continuity, objectivity and absence of controversy, attributes which are calculated to induce public confidence in the administration of justice and a general respect for the law.[3]

---

[1] "Black letter" refers to black or gothic type that was often used in formal statements of principles or rules at the start of a section in a piece of legislation, typically followed by a commentary. W. Twining, *Blackstone's Tower: The English Law School* (Sweet and Maxwell, London, 1994), p.151.

[2] See D. McBarnet and C. Whelan, "The Elusive Spirit of the Law: Formalism and the Struggle for Legal Control" (1991) 54 *Modern Law Review* 848 at 848. See also A.C. Hutchinson, "The Role of Judges in Legal Theory and the Role of Legal Theorists in Judging (or 'Don't Let the Bastrararaches Grind You Down')" (2001) 39 *Alberta Law Review* 657 at 660.

[3] On formalism as a theory of the judicial process, see F. Schauer, "Formalism" (1988) 97 *Yale Law Journal* 509. See also M. J. Horwitz, *The Transformation of American Law, 1780–1860* (Harvard University Press, Cambridge, Mass., 1977); T.C. Grey,

As a consequence the contents of law degree syllabi tend largely to be of a utilitarian and practical nature. Many would argue that the standard law degree offers a very narrow form of education for its students. Core substantive law subjects, such as contract, tort and land law, focus largely on legal rules and principles, with little emphasis on the theory behind them. Instead law students are inculcated into a doctrinal legal mindset where law is presented and taught as if it consists purely of rules and regulations, internally coherent and discrete from the other bodies of knowledge taught within the academy. The emphasis is on serving the needs of the legal profession rather than the needs of the student. Indeed some would venture so far as to claim that university law schools often resemble vocational "trade schools" serving the needs of the legal profession rather than a participating member of the wider university community, whose traditional *raison d'être* is to provide its students with a liberal university education and endeavour to participate in the dispassionate search for the truth.[4]

This preference for doctrine over theory has had a profound effect on the nature of legal education.[5] This chapter will explore the place of jurisprudence in legal education, with particular emphasis on common law undergraduate legal education. The rise and fall of legal formalism as a theory of adjudication will first be considered and we will then examine the origins of formalism in legal education and its continued survival in that domain—notwithstanding the fact that the influence of formalism in the legal process has greatly diminished over the last half century. We will then explore the arguments in favour of the revival of the idea of a liberal legal education. These arguments suggest that the narrow, vocational legal education that has predominated in the past is thoroughly inadequate in terms of meeting the needs of law students in the twenty-first century. In the final part, the case will be made that a liberal legal education could and should be achieved by adopting an interdisciplinary jurisprudential approach in legal education generally. Exposure to insights from subjects outside of law will provide a law student with a proper university education and will help to equip them with the skills to operate successfully— as lawyers or otherwise—in a constantly changing world.

"Modern American Legal Thought" (1996) 106 *Yale Law Journal* 493; and P.S. Atiyah, *The Rise and Fall of Freedom of Contract* (Clarendon Press, Oxford, 1979).

[4] See M. Thornton, "Law as a Business in the Corporatised University" (2000) 25 *Alternative Law Journal* 271. See also R. Pring, *Closing the Gap: Liberal Education and Vocational Preparation* (Hodder and Stoughton, London, 1995), pp.184–185.

[5] "Doctrine" refers to the concepts, rules, standards, principles and institutions derived from primary and secondary sources of law. In contrast "theory" is restricted to perspectives derived from outside the body of doctrine, from such disciplines as economics, history, psychology, literary criticism, philosophy, and political science. See B.D. Cooper, "The Integration of Theory, Doctrine, and Practice in Legal Education" (2002) 1 *Journal of the Association of Legal Writing Directors* 50 at 51.

2. THE RISE AND FALL OF FORMALISM AS A THEORY OF ADJUDICATION

What are the reasons for the traditional dominance of the formalist mindset in relation to thought about law? How did this theory of adjudication become so hegemonic in the legal world? The reasons are multifarious and a full account is beyond the scope of this chapter, but we may note nonetheless a range of important historical factors.

English common law judges in the early seventeenth century sought to preserve their status as the sole arbiters of legal disputes by insisting that the legal arena was totally separate and distinguishable from the political arena. Up until the early seventeenth century successive English kings had interfered in the judicial process, sometimes deciding cases themselves or disposing of judges who made decisions with which the monarch disagreed. To assert their independence, judges sought to promote the idea that judicial decisions were based not on politics but on technical and legal criteria as interpreted by a professional legal culture. In the *Prohibitions Del Roy* case (1607), however, the King was denied participation in the adjudication process of his Court on the basis that he lacked professional legal training and the attribute of "artificial reason" which legal professionals acquired after many years of immersion in the practice of law. Sir Edward Coke (1552–1634), the Chief Justice, famously stated that the King

> "was not learned in the laws of his realm of England, and causes which concern the life, or inheritance, or goods, or fortunes of his subjects, are not to be decided by natural reason, but by artificial reason and judgement of law, which law is an act which requires long study and experience, before that a man can attain to the cognizance of it ...".[6]

In *Dr Bonham's* case Coke affirmed that he considered the common law to be superior to Acts of Parliament,[7] but with the elevation of parliament's role in the law-making process in the eighteenth century, it began to become apparent that judge-made law was of an essentially undemocratic nature: legislation was the function of legislatures who were elected by the electorate and therefore accountable to them.[8] In order to avoid the hostility and anger of Parliament

---

[6] Reported in *The Reports of Sir Edward Coke In Thirteen Parts* (Moore, Dublin, 1879), 12th Report, p.65. For an overview of common law history and theory, see M. Davies, *Asking the Law Question* (Sweet and Maxwell, Sydney, 1994), chap.2.

[7] (1610) 8 Co. Rep. 118a.

[8] In many ways judges liked legal formalism as it made their job easier. Society was becoming increasingly complex, throwing up sometimes intractable problems which heretofore were expected to be solved by the courts but which now became the concern of the legislature and government. See P.S. Atiyah, *The Rise and Fall of the*

and the wider society, the judiciary decided it was best to be discreet about their legislative or creative role. Judges began to insist that they merely applied the law and perpetuated the myth that law was something outside of society and politics. If judges were to state more openly what they were doing, society through their legislature in Parliament might respond by severely limiting judicial power.[9]

It was also in the best interests of the emerging legal profession to portray law as a separate domain of knowledge distinct from moral, philosophical or any other type of knowledge. By perpetuating the myth that law could only be interpreted by those who had been trained in the "artificial reason" of the law, an obvious chasm was opened up between the law and the public. It now appeared to the non-lawyer that the chasm was only bridgeable by a fee-charging priesthood initiated in the intricacies of the law:

> "[T]he separation of law from [ordinary, natural] reason provided the greatest assurance of keeping the law out of the hands of the amateur, and therefore, beyond his control. ... By making the law a thing apart, the agreeable gulf between lawyer and lawman might be preserved. Distance would encourage respect."[10]

Moreover the common law lawyer or judge approached law from a very practical and pragmatic viewpoint. The "artificial reason" of the law was a product of reflective practical experience: it sought solutions to concrete problems. As a result it was not a theoretical or systematic turn of mind. Instead artificial reason sought to secure effective practical outcomes through convergence of judgement on common solutions. From this perspective, larger theoretical coherence, when it did not serve the end of convergence of judgement, was at best a luxury, and more typically an obstacle to achieving that end.[11]

A formalistic understanding to law also suited the interests of the emerging mercantile classes and nascent capitalism. As cities and commerce developed, the trading and industrial classes appreciated the benefits of living under rationally comprehensive and relatively predictable rules. For merchants to order their business relations with any degree of certainty they needed a legal

---

Freedom of Contract (Clarendon Press, Oxford, 1979), p.384 and J. Goldsworthy, *The Sovereignty of Parliament: History and Philosophy* (Clarendon Press, Oxford, 1999), pp.111–112.

[9] P.S. Atiyah, "Judges and Policy" (1980) 15 *Israel Law Review* 346 at 362–369.

[10] H. Nenner, *By Colour of Law: Legal Culture and Constitutional Politics in England, 1660–1689* (University of Chicago Press, Chicago, 1977), p.117.

[11] G.J. Postema, "Classical Common Law Jurisprudence (Part II)" (2003) 3 *Oxford University Commonwealth Law Journal* 1 at 3–5.

framework that was public and prospective, with qualities of generality, equality and certainty. The laissez-faire form of capitalism that developed in the emerging liberal European societies of the eighteenth and nineteenth centuries encouraged the distinction between politics on the one hand and adjudication on the other. A formalist approach to law along with a judiciary trained in the classical style of law, ignorant of commercial and social realities and public law approaches to regulation, permitted elites and corporatist groupings to remain dominant.[12] Indeed Max Weber (1864–1920) has argued that formal rationality, that is the impersonal administration of generally knowable pre-existing law, was what allowed capitalism to develop.[13] The rule-boundness of formal rationality operated as a means of pacifying conflicts of interest.[14]

The judiciary retreated from any involvement in policy issues in the nineteenth century and this continued until the mid-twentieth century. During this period the judiciary played a very non-interventionist role and strictly adhered to the notion that law should be insulated from politics. The autonomy of private law was based on this formalism and non-intervention. For example, judges dealt with private law contracts on the basis of a highly complex and artificial formal language that often had little obvious connection to the real-world issues as experienced by the people involved in the dispute, and yet they generally left it to the freedom of the private parties to decide what was actually to be done.[15]

The rise of the welfare state led to the overt intervention of government in areas previously regarded as beyond the proper reach of state action. Now the state was becoming involved in the tasks of overt redistribution, regulation and planning. The welfare state impacted on the law as there was a turn from

---

[12] See J. Singer, "Legal Realism Now" (1988) 76 *California Law Review* 467 at 477–499.

[13] See M. Weber, *Law in Economy and Society* (M.Rheinstein ed., Harvard University Press, Cambridge, Mass., 1954). See also D.M. Trubeck, "Max Weber on Law and the Rise of Capitalism" (1972) 3 *Wisconsin Law Review* 720 and Judy Walsh, "Sociological Jurisprudence" in this volume.

[14] In traditional informal systems of justice it was more difficult to expect impartiality and fairness from the local arbitrator or adjudicator. This was because in many small communities the judge knew everyone, including their families and life histories, and decisions would be made with this background in mind, with a focus less on the strict application of rules than on coming to a resolution satisfactory to all. Under this system justice was essentially *ad hoc*, not based particularly on pre-defined rules and principles. For an interesting study on how the emergence of printing led to a decline in informal local justice, see M.E. Katsh, *The Electronic Media and the Transformation of Law* (Oxford University Press, New York, 1989).

[15] See generally G. Edward White, "From Sociological Jurisprudence to Realism: Jurisprudence and Social Change in Early Twentieth Century America" (1972) 58 *Virginia Law Review* 999.

formalistic to purposive or policy-oriented styles of legal reasoning, and from concerns with formal justice to an interest in procedural and substantive justice. With the rise of the welfare state administrative officials were given broad discretion to achieve policy goals. The decline in rule formalism brought judges' reasoning closer in style and method to the instrumental rationality of the administrative bureaucracy. Courts were now charged to police unconscionable contracts, to void unjust enrichment, to control economic concentrations, and to determine whether a government agency has acted in the public interest. As a consequence courts often resembled administrative, if not at times political, institutions. In short, law's function had changed. It had become an active instrument for economic and social change, perceived by many as a management technique aimed at the promotion of social and economic development. The judge was no longer an agent for the conservation of texts of law but the co-author of legal, economic and social change. Many courts were now willing to exercise their powers of judicial review and were more willing to control and question the use of executive power. In acting as a brake to executive power, the judge could not but give effect to distinctive political values, so a claim that the judiciary was politically neutral would seem somewhat paradoxical.[16]

With the rise of positive social rights, as part of the move from the liberal state to the welfare state, private law also became politicised.[17] Instead of appearing as the formal expression of private intentions it became an inextricable mixture of legal, political, economic and other social elements. For example contract law became more political as judges intervened more directly in contractual affairs and recognised the power conflicts between contractual actors. Judges often corrected and rewrote contracts in order to translate relevant policy goals into contracts; adjudication thus became an opportunity for contracts to be regulated, rather than simply enforced.

The rise of a culture of rights in the aftermath of the atrocities of the Second World War has also contributed to erode formalist hegemony in the adjudicative domain. Most post-1945 constitutions now contain explicit protections of constitutional rights. The typically broad and open-ended drafting style of these and other instruments—such as the European Convention of Human Rights and the treaties established under the European Union—have contributed to a more purposive style of judicial interpretation.[18]

---

[16] J. Bell, *Policy Arguments in Judicial Decisions* (Clarendon Press, Oxford, 1983), p.3.

[17] See R. Unger, *Law in Modern Society* (Free Press, New York, 1976) and J. Bell, *op. cit.*

[18] See, generally, *The Judicial Process in Comparative Perspective* (P.J. Kollmer and J.M. Olson eds., Clarendon Press, Oxford,1989), pp.117–211. This development is seen particularly in the UK where the courts were traditionally noted for their strict

3. FORMALISM AND LEGAL EDUCATION

We now turn to the question of why legal *education* has tended to be of a doctrinal nature, with a very strong emphasis on black-letter law and a tendency to ignore or at best marginalise theoretical issues and the study of non-legal subjects. Early common law lawyers learned through doing; legal education was by way of apprenticeship and was of a very practical nature. Rather than being located in universities, training of lawyers was instead located in articles of clerkship for prospective solicitors and the Inns of Court for barristers. English common law was not to be taught in the universities until the late eighteenth century.[19] In fact up until the mid-twentieth century most legal practitioners had never studied law at university; and if they had attended university it was to study another subject, very often in the humanities.

The apprenticeship system of legal training afforded little opportunity to ponder theoretical issues and did not lend itself to any overarching systemisation of the law.[20] Some criticised the calibre of lawyer the system was producing; it was argued that this model contained a number of pedagogical weaknesses producing narrowly educated "pettifoggers".[21]

To combat these criticisms and elevate the standing of the legal profession in the eyes of the public, William Blackstone (1723–1780) made a determined effort to establish the foundations for university study of the common law system and his lectures at Oxford between 1753 and 1765 (later published as the *Commentaries on the Laws of England*) made a strong plea for the systematic teaching of English law within the universities. Early legal education in the universities constituted a relatively liberal education in the law and sought to provide an alternative to the narrowness of the apprenticeship model. This was evident in Blackstone's law degree in Oxford at the end of the eighteenth century. It represented a move away from the emphasis on practicality that had

---

textual approach to statutory interpretation, reinforced by the exact and detailed style of legislative drafting characteristic of the British Parliament. See L. Levitsky, "The Europeanization of the British Legal Style" (1994) 42 *American Journal of Comparative Law* 347.

[19] In the Middle Ages, Oxford and Cambridge set their face against the study of English law and professional training in law in favour of canon law (until the Reformation) and civil law. For a brief overview of the history of legal education in England, see J.H. Barker, *An Introduction to English Legal History* (Butterworths, London, 1971), pp.68–77.

[20] See generally *Learning the Law: Teaching and the Transmission of English Law, 1150–1900* (J.A. Bush and A. Wijffels eds., Hambledon, London, 1999).

[21] The term "pettifogger" was common throughout England in the sixteenth, seventeenth and eighteenth centuries and referred to those lawyers who specialised in the narrow, technical aspects of the law, such as pleading, and was often a term of derision equating such practitioners with charlatans.

been institutionalised since medieval times. The Blackstonian project was an attempt to reform the common law world in the most fundamental way—by transforming its practitioners into enlightened lawyers able to understand both the historical context and the "artificial reason" of the common law.[22] The liberal education recommended by Blackstone sought to create the ideal "gentleman", a term connoting honesty, integrity, and public service: in the context of the legal profession, a gentleman would not be tempted to "prostitute his Talents and the Honour of his profession, to pervert the Course of natural justice, to oppress the indignant, and beggar the Fatherless, for the sake of a paultry fee".[23] Liberally educated gentlemen "of distinction and learning" would not only raise the status of law as a branch of learning; by steadily pursuing, promoting, and expounding the social purposes of law, they would also improve the public reputation of lawyers and the courts and give legal literature at least a veneer of scholarly respectability.[24]

Early university-based legal education in the US also attempted to produce law graduates who would be more than simply legal technicians. The first university- based law course was provided by the College of William and Mary in the State of Virginia in 1779, when Thomas Jefferson established George Whyte as the first professor of law.[25] Jefferson believed that the new nation needed virtuous leaders who would preserve its republican form of government. He believed that lawyers, by the nature of their work, were well positioned to provide this direction and leadership. Accordingly, he urged not merely that aspiring lawyers be taught the details of legal doctrine and the nuances of proper pleading, but that they also be afforded a broad understanding of political theory, modern and ancient history and moral philosophy.[26]

However, despite these early attempts to transform legal education into a university based "liberal" education, legal education through apprenticeship remained the preferred route for prospective lawyers. As has been said, the common law and its practitioners in the eighteenth and nineteenth centuries operated in a very pragmatic and practical manner. This encouraged and cultivated the learning of law by apprenticeship and as a result a university

---

[22] See generally M.D. Gordon, "The Vinerian Chair: An Atlantic Perspective," in *The Life of the Law* (P. Birks ed., Hambledon, London, 1993), 194–209.

[23] R. Campbell, *The London Tradesman* (Gardner, London, 1747), p.74.

[24] D. Lemmings, "Blackstone and Law Reform by Education: Preparation for the Bar and Lawyerly Culture in Eighteenth-Century England" (1998) 16 *Law and History Review* 211 at 252.

[25] Whyte derived much of the content of his early lectures from Blackstone's *Commentaries*.

[26] M. Davison Douglas, "The Jeffersonian Vision of Legal Education" (2001) 51 *Journal of Legal Education* 185 at 186. See also P.D. Carrington, "The Revolutionary Idea of University Legal Education" (1990) 31 *William and Mary Law Review* 527.

education in law was viewed by many as an expensive and unnecessary luxury. Many early law chairs were unfilled or, if filled, law lectures were very poorly attended. Because most law degrees were taught by part-timers their standard was generally not high and if one was going to the time and expense of a university education many thought it better to study the classics. As a result early law degrees went into decline and the subject did not attract the abler student. Ultimately, the judges, the leading counsel and the solicitors of the day did not regard reading law at the universities as an appropriate way to prepare for the profession. With Blackstone's retirement in the late 1760s, law teaching declined until it was revived in a serious way by John Austin and Andrew Amos at University College, London in 1826. After a brisk start, it rapidly declined. The first graduating LL.B. class in 1839 totalled three; by 1900 the Faculty had produced a mere 135 graduates in law.

University law degrees only really began to re-emerge when compromises were made by the law professors. More practical subjects were introduced to appease the professions. The older universities introduced subjects like land law, tort and contract and even persuaded the professional associations to exempt those who had read law at the universities from certain parts of the professional examinations. Moreover, to placate the profession, such subjects were normally taught within the doctrinal framework, regarded as legitimate by the profession. The broad spirit of inquiry that was growing in other disciplines did not cross over into law. The pioneers of English academic law in the late nineteenth century had to establish their professional legitimacy "in the eyes of the sceptical universities and a largely hostile profession" by claiming a special body of expertise of which they had a monopoly; the academic jurist, therefore, specialised in the systemisation of the (relatively chaotic) common law through scientific exposition and analysis.[27]

This doctrinal approach began attracting prospective law students who now saw the law degree as more practical and useful in preparing them for a career in the law than they had heretofore. Now universities were engaged primarily in coaching undergraduates for their final professional examinations. From a British perspective, changes in the entrance requirements for the legal profession's admitting bodies reinforced an emphasis on a doctrinal approach to legal education. In England and Wales the Solicitors Act 1922 provided those with approved law degrees certain exemptions from Law Society exams. Many articled clerks (the equivalent of modern day trainee solicitors) worked far from Oxbridge or London but wished to avail of these exemptions. Provincial law schools sprang up to meet their needs. In each case it was the

---

[27] D. Sugarman, "Legal Theory, the Common Law Mind and the Making of the Textbook Tradition" in *Legal Theory and Common Law* (W. Twining ed., Basil Blackwell, Oxford, 1986), pp.28–29.

policy of the Law Society to promote an alliance between their local branch
and the institutions of higher education in the area.[28] Inevitably the students
who attended law courses were anxious to acquire no more than the particular
type of knowledge (or information) required for the professional examination.
It was clear that the university law school was now subordinated to the legal
profession, with courses slanted towards the immediate needs of the profession,
and with little or no attempt made to integrate legal education and the broader
educative mission of the universities. In the US, law schools were somewhat
more independent but at the height of the formalist period Christopher
Columbus Langdell (1826–1906) offered a style of legal study which was
scientific, autonomous of the other humanities and social sciences, and able to
serve the demands of laissez-faire economics.[29]

We have already discussed the decline of legal formalism as a theory of
adjudication since the rise of the welfare state in the twentieth century. The
question must now be asked: in light of its decline in the adjudicative domain,
why has legal education persevered with the doctrinal approach? There would
appear to be a number of reasons. From the point of view of legal academics,
for example, doctrinal law is relatively easy to teach, and interpreting and
evaluating legal texts is the cheapest and the quickest way for authors to get
into print. Doctrinal writing requires neither specialised expertise nor time-
consuming acquisition of skills or data. This is no small benefit in an academic
field that, unlike other disciplines, does not train its practitioners to be scholars.
Many law schools offer no education in social science research techniques
and only limited exposure to serious interdisciplinary work. Legal scholars
without other advanced degrees face serious costs and time constraints if they
wish to become more than dabblers in non-legal materials and methodologies.[30]
Interdisciplinary classes take time to design and implement. Law teachers who
lack special training or a background in the social sciences or the humanities
may feel insecure about engaging in non-formalistic legal education and
scholarship without appropriate training.[31] There may be a fear of potential

---

[28] See B. Abel-Smith and R. Stevens, *Lawyers and the Courts: A Sociological Study
of the English Legal System 1750–1965* (Heinemann, London, 1967), pp.181–183.

[29] See generally W.B. Carter, "Reconstructing Langdell" (1997) 32 *Georgia Law Review*
1. See also G. Edward White, *op. cit.*

[30] D.L. Rhode, "Law, Knowledge, and The Academy: Legal Scholarship" (2002) 115
Harvard Law Review 1317 at 1353.

[31] This difficulty is less prevalent in the US today as a significant number of the present
generation of legal academics have postgraduate qualifications in fields other than
law, and since legal education is a postgraduate course of study in the US, all law
students have a minimum of four years university education in a non-legal field of
study. There are also a significant number of legal academics in the US who, after
attaining PhDs in the humanities but failing to secure academic tenure in those

over-stretching, that law professors who write articles relying on non-legal subjects are likely to make claims that are wrong.

The doctrinal approach to legal education is additionally attractive to university and law school administrators as it is a comparatively cheap course to provide. Law schools are encouraged to mass-produce service-orientated professionals by offering technocratic skills-based courses which satisfy the professional admitting authorities.[32]

Another factor in the adherence to formalism in legal education is that non-doctrinal approaches often provoke howls of dissent from students who expect, or have learned to rely on, instruction according to the formalist paradigm. Law professors are in a sense trapped in doctrinal roles because of the expectations of their students:

> "Take any group of middle-class, first year law students and try any other approach than a doctrinal, rule-focused one. They hate the alternatives because the alternatives undercut the notion that law is specialized knowledge available to, and for sale by, the professional lawyer."[33]

The doctrinal approach sets law, as an academic subject, apart from the other social sciences.[34] David Sugarman has suggested that legal academics can be viewed as self-serving in this regard. A majority of academic lawyers, supported by a profession that is anxious to maintain its status in the face of competition from accountants and other professional groups, are still committed—albeit often only implicitly—to a traditional "black-letter" law degree.

---

disciplines, went back to study law and were subsequently successful in acquiring tenure in law schools. See H.T. Edwards, "The Growing Disjunction between Legal Education and the Legal Profession: A Postscript" (1993) 91 *Michigan Law Review* 2191 at 2198.

[32] See M.J. Berger "Perspective: A Comparative Study of British Barristers and American Legal Practice and Education" (1983) 5 *North Western Journal of International Law and Business* 540 at 567.

[33] J. H. Schlegel, "Searching for Archimedes—Legal Education, Legal Scholarship, and Liberal Ideology" (1984) 32 *Journal of Legal Education* 103 at 108.

[34] John Henry Schlegel has suggested that empirical social science threatened the academic "discipline" of law: "It suggested that the words of the law might not be too important, that the special preserve of the law professor might not be too special and that, since law was not just rules, the rule of law might not be just a matter of following rules." *American Legal Realism and Empirical Social Science* (University of North Carolina Press, Chapel Hill, 1995), p.255.

4. THE IDEA OF A LIBERAL LEGAL EDUCATION

Despite the power and influence of formalist practice and ideology, there are some signs of support for a revival of the idea of a liberal legal education. While a vocational education focuses on imparting the necessary skills and knowledge required to practice a particular trade or job, a liberal education has a far broader and more ambitious goal in sight. A liberal education instils in the student the ability to teach him or her self. While the term referred originally to the medieval liberal arts curriculum for the education of "free men", the modern reference to liberal education is to the broad fields of learning across the natural sciences, the social sciences and the humanities, as distinct from professional education. An education such as this is "liberal" because it frees our innate natures and encourages and fosters the realisation of our potential. As a result a liberal education involves the personal development of the individual and attempts to train a person for "life" rather than for "work".[35]

A liberal approach to legal education is even more appropriate when it is considered that more than half of law graduates never go on to practice law.[36] This is a fact that law schools tend to play down considerably, usually preferring the public image of strong associations with the legal profession. But in a complex, unpredictable, and rapidly changing world, pursuit of the best life— both personally and professionally—demands flexibility, resilience, and the capacity to learn adaptively, gaining new skills and abilities in response to changing circumstances. Therefore preparation for any profession or career must include an education that enables the individual to cope with change, to adapt to new environmental conditions, and to flourish by continually learning and employing new strategies. Legal education that accomplishes this will not focus on imparting a particular body of knowledge, or a particular set of techniques and skills. Instead it will foster personal and intellectual agility and resourcefulness.

Insofar as university legal education can contribute to the formation of legal professionals, it is too often overlooked that good lawyers need much more than doctrine. Because law in modern society is so complex and immense in scope and because lawyers are called on to discharge such a diversity of tasks, legal training must equip lawyers to see beyond the narrow confines of

---

[35] See J. Macfarlane *et al.*, "Education for Life or for Work?" (1987) 137 *New Law Journal* 835.

[36] In the UK, for example, a report on legal education noted that less than half of all law graduates go on to become practising lawyers and that "university law degrees will continue to be the foundation for a wide variety of careers, not just the practising legal profession". *The Lord Chancellor's Committee on Legal Education and Conduct—Review of Legal Education: Consultation Paper*. First Report on Legal Education and Training (Lord Chancellor's Office, London, 1996), para.1.21.

doctrine to the ideas underpinning the law, as well as to the real-world effects of that law. To do this intelligently, lawyers must make use of non-legal fields in addition to the law. Because of the complexity of issues confronting lawyers the range of useful scholarship should extend beyond the limitations of traditional scholarship: different approaches and disciplines provide new insight into the law, some of which are likely to be of great use to the legal profession and the justice system generally.[37]

At a certain level, most practitioners know that the functions of lawyers are more than merely doctrinal. Lawyers, as Duncan Kennedy has written,

> "are more than just legal technicians. They shape deals and they make law. They invent new forms of social life, they fill gaps, resolve conflicts and ambiguities. They mold the law, through the process of legal argument, in court, in briefs, in negotiations. ... [The lawyer's activity] is not neutral, and the better your legal skills, the less neutral you become."[38]

In the UK the Ormrod Report (1971) reviewed the desirable mix of university and apprenticeship elements in legal education and considered that the skills needed of modern lawyers required a substantial university component in legal education. The professional lawyer, the report stated,

> "required a sufficiently general and broad based education to enable him to adapt himself to new and different situations as his career develops. ... [H]e must also generate a critical approach to existing law, and appreciation of its social consequences, and an interest in, and a positive attitude to, appropriate developments and change."[39]

In a similar vein, the Pearce Report in Australia (1987) argued that in educating law students it is desirable to cultivate a student's intellect in a spirit of free inquiry and to encourage independent thought and enquiry about the law:

> "[A] good undergraduate [law] course should provide an intellectual base for life long critical reflectiveness about legal institutions, the professions and one's own work, in the actual and changing conditions of social life

---

[37] See M.J. Saks, H. Larsen and J. Carol, "Is there a Growing Gap Among Law, Law Practice, and Legal Scholarship?" (1996) 30 *Suffolk University Law Review* 353 at 357.

[38] D. Kennedy, "The Responsibility of Lawyers for the Justice of their Causes" (1987) 18 *Texas Law Review* 1157.

[39] *Report of the Committee on Legal Education* (Cmnd 4595, HMSO, London, 1971), para.100.

and legal practice ... Law courses should expose students to an understanding of the processes and functions in society of law and legal institutions, to the variety of modes of social control, to the moral and political outlooks embedded in law and conceptions of professional roles, to questions of justice, to the relevance of social, political and moral theories and forces to law, legal institutions and their change and development, and to the information and understanding to be drawn from the social sciences and social science research for the purpose of evaluating law."[40]

More recently in the UK the Lord Chancellor's Advisory Committee on Legal Education and Conduct recommended that the degree course in law "should stand as an independent liberal education in the discipline of law, not tied to any specific vocation".[41]

Some academics have also been vocal in their belief that it is not the role of the university law school to produce practitioners. John Goldring, for example, has argued that a university education should go "beyond mechanical competencies" and "provide an opportunity for people to learn to think and explore ideas for themselves".[42] And David Weisbrot has suggested that law schools should provide "a broad general liberal education freed from the imperatives of producing lawyers for a particular style of practice".[43] A student who has a training in economics or moral philosophy will probably be able to ask more penetrating questions of the law than one who does not:

"The law school ... which sees its role as the training of lawyers ... has lost its way. ... The law school is a place to study, to examine, to criticise and to suggest reform to the body of norms that constitute a given legal system. The legal educator does not have a responsibility to train lawyers

---

[40] D. Pearce *et al.*, *Australian Law Schools: A Discipline Assessment for the Commonwealth Tertiary Education Commission* (Australian Government Publishing Service, Canberra, 1987), Vol.1, p.105.

[41] *The Lord Chancellor's Committee on Legal Education and Conduct—Review of Legal Education: Consultation Paper*. First Report on Legal Education and Training, para.4.6.

[42] J. Goldring, "Networking: Law Schools and Practical Legal Training Institutions" (1993) 11 *Journal of Professional Legal Education* 81.

[43] D. Weisbrot "The Changing Nature of Australian Legal Practice: Some Implications for Education and Practical Training Providers", Paper presented at the Australasian Professional Legal Education Council Conference at the Australian National University, Canberra, November 1993. See also A. Bradney, "Accountability, the University Law School and the Death of Socrates" (2002) 1 *Web Journal of Current Legal Issues* 9.

except in the crucial sense that she must send them off to the profession
with a deep understanding, not only of how the law works, but of how it
may work better."[44]

An educational philosophy that is too definite and closed is a block to proper
enquiry and discussion. A black-letter approach in legal education teaches
students not to think, or at least not to think too much and instead focuses on
the mechanical inculcation of rules and principles. Students who have been
bred intellectually into a closed and hierarchical tradition will bring a narrow,
autocratic approach to situations of advice and decision. They will be limited
in sympathy and argument, and unimaginative in social and professional
progress: "Today we expect the law to serve the whole community and therefore
its practitioners must be bred to an openness of sympathy and understanding
to the whole of human need, value and practice. Reflection offers a logical
basis for that kind of education".[45]

5. THE ROLE OF JURISPRUDENCE

What is the role of jurisprudence in terms of providing a broader, liberal legal
education? Historically there has always been hostility within the legal
profession towards legal theory.[46] The renowned nineteenth-century constitutional theorist, Albert Venn Dicey (1835–1922), asserted that jurisprudence
is a word "which stinks in the nostrils of the practising barrister".[47] According
to another commentator of the period, the legal practitioner of the late-
nineteenth century was "never more than tolerant" of jurisprudence, and even
toleration was exceptional, "the more usual attitude being one of disgust and
scarcely veiled contempt".[48] Today, jurisprudence is a subject that is still
regarded with suspicion by many practising lawyers and it also often elicits a
negative reaction from law students. But of course it has its proponents and
advocates too. As one legal theorist has noted, "[a]s with exercise, there are
people who are passionate about jurisprudence, people who dislike it, and

---

[44] M. Spence, "The Role of the Law Professor in Legal Education", Speech given at
the China University of Political Science and Law, May, 2002.

[45] A. Beck, "Legal Education and Reflection" (1985) 19 *Journal of the Association of
Law Teachers* 193 at 198.

[46] P.S. Atiyah, *Pragmatism and Theory in English Law* (Stevens, London, 1987), p.3.

[47] A.V. Dicey, "The Study of Jurisprudence" (1880) 5 *Law Magazine and Review* 382
at 382.

[48] W.W. Buckland, "Difficulties of Abstract Jurisprudence" (1890) 6 *Law Quarterly
Review* 436 at 436.

people who believe in its value without actually engaging in it".[49] The argument of this chapter is that jurisprudence should be given an enhanced and expanded role in the delivery of university legal education.[50]

The consequence of a legal education that places an overemphasis on doctrine is to instil an intellectual superiority in students in terms of their relationships with the law and with non-lawyers. Jurisprudence offers some form of antidote to this by making the student realise that law is not isolated from the rest of society. It broadens a student's perspectives on law by showing her that there is a plurality of perspectives; Ian Duncanson has described this as "adding some plurality to the homogenising protocols of law as a disciplinary enterprise".[51] It cannot be emphasised enough that the black-letter or doctrinal approach to legal education, although unpopular amongst theorists, is still the fundamental basis for legal education throughout the world. Yet while many lawyers would recognise that there might be a range of legal answers to a particular problem, formalism offers us only right and wrong answers. Students of law are often asked to apply legal rules to a hypothetical set of facts with the implicit assumption that there is one "correct" legal solution. This promotes a closed and narrow view of the law and perpetuates a dismissive attitude to any analysis of the impact of non-legal factors on the law and the insights that may be gained from the fields of, say, economics, sociology, philosophy and political science. Robert Gordon has noted "the fact that many practitioners do not appreciate the practical value of non-doctrinal scholarship—especially theoretical, interdisciplinary, and critical work—does not mean that it has none"; we should "hardly count theory as useless", Gordon observes, "if it helps one understand social reality, even if it does not help one manipulate it".[52] Much

---

[49] N. Duxbury, "Legal History: The Narrowing of English Jurisprudence" (1997) 95 *Michigan Law Review* 1990 at 1990.

[50] There is an ongoing debate whether jurisprudence should be compulsory or simply offered as an option in a law degree curriculum. Others argue over whether legal theory is marginalised by being taught as a separate subject and whether theory should instead permeate throughout the degree from beginning to end. See H. Barnett, "The Province of Jurisprudence Determined—Again!" (1995) 15 *Legal Studies* 88.

[51] I. Duncanson, "The Ends of Legal Studies" (1997) 3 *Web Journal of Current Legal Issues* 12. There is an extensive literature of the role and value of jurisprudence in legal education. See, for example, H. Barnett and D. Yach, "The Teaching of Jurisprudence and Legal Theory in British Universities and Polytechnics" (1985) 5 *Legal Studies* 151; M.C. Nussbaum, "The Use and Abuse of Philosophy in Legal Education" (1993) 45 *Stanford Law Review* 1627; P. Birks, "The Academic and the Practitioner" (1998) 18 *Legal Studies* 397; and A. Hunt, "The Case for Critical Legal Education" (1986) 20 *Journal of the Association of Law Teachers* 10.

[52] R.W. Gordon, "Lawyers, Scholars and the 'Middle Ground'" (1993) 91 *Michigan Law Review* 2075 at 2111.

theoretical and interdisciplinary work that was of little interest to lawyers and judges has in fact reshaped the legal landscape. The impact of economics on antitrust law, game theory on negotiation, cognitive psychology on problem solving, and feminist theory on equal protection issues are amongst the obvious examples, and the list can be readily extended.[53]

Richard Devlin argues that jurisprudence is a multi-dimensional interrogative process in the pursuit of a better understanding of the nature and functions of law. He believes it focuses on seven key questions:

"(1)What is the nature of law? (2) Why, or when, is a law valid? (3) What roles or functions do legal institutions, rules and procedures fulfil in society? (4) How does the law fulfil those functions? (5) How important is law in society? (6) What perspectives overtly or covertly inform legal institutions, rules and procedures? (7) What is the relationship between law and social change?"[54]

One of the most important functions of legal scholarship should be to address these questions and to expose the historical, structural, and the ideological underpinnings of current legal norms and to assess their social value. For many harried practitioners and judges, preoccupied with deadlines and dockets, such assessments may seem beside the point. Scholarship that argues for fundamental changes in doctrinal frameworks, social policy, or rules of professional conduct may be even less welcome to lawyers who benefit from existing practices. But such work can nonetheless contribute to informed policymaking and help shape the views of students who could someday guide reform efforts. Interdisciplinary jurisprudential scholarship represents the influx of voices that have long been denied a place in traditional legal discourse, and if the law is to continue towards the goal of justice for all, those voices have to be heard.

As legal adjudication has become less formalist the importance of jurisprudence is greater than ever before for the law student. Bob Hepple has argued that because the courts now show a greater willingness to construe statutes purposively, students need to know how to ascertain the purposes of a statute. The statute needs to be studied in its social and political context, and the student needs to understand how statutes are adapted to work in

---

[53] *ibid.*, at 2084–2086. The impact of interdisciplinary scholarship on law has been more significant in the US than in Ireland or the UK. See R. Posner, "The Deprofessionalization of Legal Teaching and Scholarship" (1993) 91 *Michigan Law Review* 1921 at 1925–26. See also D. Bell and E. Edmonds, "Students as Teachers, Teachers as Learners" (1993) 91 *Michigan Law Review* 2025 at 2034–2037.

[54] R. F. Devlin, "Jurisprudence for Judges: Why Legal Theory Matters For Social Context Education" (2001) 27 *Queen's Law Journal* 161 at 164–651.

circumstances quite different from those contemplated by the legislator.[55] The role of legal theory in achieving these goals is widely acknowledged; indeed Richard Devlin argues that jurisprudence provides judges with an opportunity for self-reflection that can help them increase their legitimacy as holders and exercisers of social power.[56]

Jurisprudence also has the special task of permanently challenging central and general assumptions of professional thought. It is in the business of broadening legal perspectives, breaking down internal-external distinctions that legal thought creates, letting light into the professional house of law and showing the house from many angles. As Roger Cotterell has observed, legal theory exists to question assumptions that underline received professional wisdom about the nature of law in general, rather than about the nature of particular legal fields. It should require students to understand that the current view is not the only available view of the social world that law inhabits. Broadening perspectives on law involves revealing to students that the dominant professional views of law are partial, a particular view of law that can co–exist with others. What jurisprudence has to offer then, according to Cotterell, is a permanent constructive challenge to existing professional legal thought, a challenge declaring that there is a plurality of perspectives on law, and that any teaching suggesting only a single perspective to be available is false and dangerous.[57] According to Marc Galanter, in the formalist model of law, legal norms are set apart from, and privileged over, social norms, and it is therefore the legal rather than the social norms that are used to determine outcomes where conflict arises.[58] Thus "law" is confined to a particular framework, one that sets it apart from social life and which promotes an image of autonomy that is used to maintain its power and authority over social relations in general, thereby sustaining a sense of hierarchy while at the same time maintaining an image of neutrality and equality within its own domain.[59]

It must also be remembered that it is impossible, in a standard undergraduate degree in law, to teach even a fraction of the law that a student who becomes a professional will need to know in three years. In addition much of the law that students learn while in law school will change several times during a student's subsequent legal career. "The particular laws one learns as a student

---

[55] B. Hepple, "The Renewal of the Liberal Law Degree" (1996) 55 *Cambridge Law Journal* 470 at 481.

[56] R.F. Devlin, *op. cit.,* at 169.

[57] See R. Cotterell, "Pandora's Box: Jurisprudence in Legal Education" (2000) 7 *International Journal of the Legal Profession* 179 at 179–184.

[58] M. Galanter, "Justice in Many Rooms: Courts, Private Ordering and Indigenous Law" (1981) 19 *Journal of Legal Pluralism and Unofficial Law* 1 at 20.

[59] A. Griffiths, "Legal Pluralism" in *An Introduction to Law and Social Theory* (R. Banakar and M. Travers eds, Hart, Oxford, 2002), pp.292–293.

may change and change again at the whim of the legislator. The skill of weighing, evaluating and making arguments, once acquired is never lost and is always at the centre of a lawyer's skills."[60]

As a concluding comment it may be remarked that reforming legal education to give a greater role to interdisciplinary jurisprudential perspectives could be seen as vital for the self-respect of legal academics. After all there still tends to be a negative view of lawyers in the academy.[61] P.S. Atiyah, for example, remarked how, in the English legal system, "the scholar as teacher is a person with a decidedly inferior status".[62] Another writer has suggested that "the predominant notion of academic lawyers is that they are not really academic... their scholarly activities are thought to be unexciting and uncreative, comprising a series of intellectual puzzles scattered among large areas of description".[63] However, the American jurist Mark Tushnet has observed that the existence of "exotica" in legal scholarship connects the legal academy to the university as a whole, "and so applies a patina of high culture to the more mundane orientation of law schools"; jurisprudence, Tushnet notes, connects law to philosophy, to literary studies and to recent trends in scholarship that cross disciplinary bounds such as structuralism and feminism. In doing so, he says, jurisprudence "may legitimate, not so much the law, but the legal academy as a whole as a place properly attached to the university and not just a professional training ground".[64]

---

[60] N. McCormick, "The Democratic Intellect and the Law" (1985) 5 *Legal Studies* 172 at 180.

[61] W. Twining, *op. cit.*, p.123.

[62] P.S. Atiyah, *Pragmatism and Theory in English Law*, p.35.

[63] T. Becher, *Academic Tribes and Territories: Intellectual Enquiry and the Cultures of Disciplines* (Open University Press, Milton Keynes, 1989), p.30.

[64] M. Tushnet, "Legal Scholarship in the United States: An Overview" (1987) 50 *Modern Law Review* 804 at 816–817.

INDEX